ADOBE® COLDFUSION® 8

Advanced Application Development

web application construction kit

VOLUME 3

Ben Forta

with Charlie Arehart, Jeffrey Bouley, Jeff Tapper, Matt Tatum, Raymond Camden, Robi Sen, and Sarge Sargent

Adobe ColdFusion 8 Web Application Construction Kit, Volume 3: Advanced Application Development
Ben Forta
with Charlie Arehart, Jeffrey Bouley, Jeff Tapper, Matt Tatum, Raymond Camden, Robi Sen, and Sarge Sargent

This Adobe Press book is published by Peachpit.

Peachpit Press
1249 Eighth Street
Berkeley, CA 94710
510/524-2178
510/524-2221 (fax)

Find us on the Web at: www.peachpit.com
To report errors, please send a note to errata@peachpit.com

Peachpit is a division of Pearson Education

Editor: Judy Ziajka
Technical Reviewer: Nicholas Tunney
Production Editor: Lupe Edgar
Compositor: Maureen Forys, Happenstance Typo-O-Rama
Proofreader: Liz Welch
Indexer: Ron Strauss
Cover design: Charlene Charles-Will

ISBN 13: 978-0-321-51547-6

ISBN 10: 0-321-51547-3

9 8 7 6 5 4 3 2 1

Printed and bound in the United States of America

Biographies

Ben Forta

Ben Forta is Director of Platform Evangelism at Adobe Systems, Inc., and has more than two decades of experience in the computer software industry in product development, support, training, and marketing. Ben is the author of the best-selling ColdFusion book of all time, *Macromedia ColdFusion MX 7 Web Application Construction Kit*, as well as books on SQL, Java Server Pages, Windows development, Regular Expressions, and more. More than half a million Ben Forta books have been printed in more than a dozen languages worldwide. Ben helped create the official Adobe ColdFusion training material, as well as the certification tests and study guides for those tests. He writes regular columns on ColdFusion and Internet development and spends a considerable amount of time lecturing and speaking on application development worldwide. Ben welcomes your e-mail at `ben@forta.com` and invites you to visit his Web site at `http://forta.com/` and his blog at `http://forta.com/blog`.

Charlie Arehart

A veteran ColdFusion developer since 1997, Charlie Arehart is a longtime contributor to the community and a recognized Adobe Community Expert. He's a certified Advanced ColdFusion Developer and an instructor for ColdFusion 4, 5, 6, and 7 and served as technical editor for the *ColdFusion Developers Journal* until 2003. Now an independent contractor (`carehart.org`) living in Alpharetta, Georgia, Charlie provides high-level troubleshooting and tuning assistance and training and mentoring for ColdFusion teams. He also helps run the Online ColdFusion Meetup (`coldfusionmeetup.com`, an online ColdFusion user group) and is frequently invited at speak to developer conferences and user groups worldwide.

Jeff Bouley

Jeffrey is an accomplished Web systems, component, database, and client application developer, consultant, project manager, and author. He brings more than 14 years of hands-on client, Internet, Web, and back-end integration project experience, providing solutions with and for Universal Mind, Adobe, NASA, Macromedia, Allaire, Int'l Speedway Corp., Accenture, Quest Technologies, Lockheed Martin, and Perot Systems. His knowledge covers ColdFusion, Flex, Flash, Java, C# and VB.Net, ASP, Visual Basic (using COM), and Oracle, Microsoft SQL Server, and MySQL databases; he has also worked with various ESRI GIS products (ArcObjects, ArcSDE, ArcIMS, and ArcGIS). Jeffrey holds a master's degree in management of technology from the University of Miami and a bachelor's degree in information systems from the University of Central Florida.

Jeff Tapper

Jeff Tapper is a founding partner of Tapper, Nimer and Associates, Inc., whose focus is on training, mentoring, designing, and developing of rich Internet applications (RIAs). Jeff has been developing applications with ColdFusion since 1995 and is an Adobe Certified Trainer for all ColdFusion, Flash, and Flex classes. He has worked on eight ColdFusion, Flash, and Flex books and is thrilled to collaborate with Ben on this book, the fourth they have done together.

Matt Tatum

Matt Tatam started developing in ColdFusion in its second version. He has assisted large organizations around the world in implementing ColdFusion solutions. As a trainer, he has taught ColdFusion, JRun, Java, JSP, Spectra, XML, ActionScript, and Flash as well as non-Adobe products and technologies. He has previously authored books and articles on Flash and ColdFusion. Today he enjoys a balance of family, R&D, and ColdFusion.

Ray Camden

Raymond Camden is the owner of Camden Media, Inc., a Web development and training company. A long-time ColdFusion user, Raymond has worked on numerous ColdFusion books, including the *Macromedia ColdFusion MX 7 Web Application Construction Kit*, and has contributed to the *Fusion Authority Quarterly Update* and the *ColdFusion Developers Journal*. He also presents at numerous conferences and contributes to online Webzines. He has founded many community Web sites, including `CFLib.org`, `ColdFusionPortal.org`, and `ColdFusionCookbook.org`, and is the author of open source applications, including the popular BlogCFC (`www.blogcfc.com`) blogging application. Raymond can be reached at his blog (`www.coldfusionjedi.com`) or via email at `ray@camdenfamily.com`. He is the happily married proud father of three kids and is somewhat of a *Star Wars* nut.

Robi Sen

Robi Sen is a managing partner for Twin Technologies, a premiere Web 2.0 software development house specializing in delivering mission-critical Web applications for Fortune 500 companies as well as the defense, intelligence, and healthcare sectors. Robi has also been in executive leadership positions with Department 13 and Vobis Communications over a distinguished 20-year career in the software industry.

Sarge Sargent

Sarge is a former senior product support engineer for ColdFusion and JRun with Adobe's North American Customer Care organization. During his tenure with Allaire, Macromedia, and now Adobe, he has also supported Breeze/Connect, Contribute Publishing Services, and Flex. He is well-known in the ColdFusion community as an expert in configuration, optimization, scalability, security, and LDAP integration. A Certified ColdFusion Developer and MCSE, he has served as contributor and technical editor or reviewer for several ColdFusion books, written several Developer Connection and Knowledgebase articles for the Adobe Web site, and spoken at several conferences and user groups. Sarge is currently Adobe's technical account manager for Flash and Flash Media Server. Although his focus is now on serving the Adobe Flash platform community, ColdFusion will forever remain in his blood. Sarge continues to share his onion on his blog at `www.sarge-way.com`.

Dedications

Charlie Arehart

I'd like to dedicate this book to my wife of seven years and the love of my life, Kim. I couldn't do all I do without your patience, support, and encouragement. Thank you, my love. God truly blessed me when He brought you into my life.

Jeff Bouley

I dedicate this book to my wife Shannon, who is due to deliver our two boys Brennon and Brodie into the world on December 11. It is through her support and the new soon-to-be responsibility of becoming a father that I dig deep every day to better myself on both personal and professional levels.

Jeff Tapper

This book is dedicated to my wife, Lisa, and our children, Kaliope and Kagan.

Matt Tatum

To my wife for all her support. To my children for reminding me what really matters.

Ray Camden

To my wife, Jeanne—you are my best supporter, my best friend, and the absolute best thing in my life. Thank you.

Sarge Sargent

As always, I dedicate my work to my fam.

Acknowledgments

Ben Forta

Thanks to my co-authors, Charlie Arehart, Jeff Bouley, Ray Camden, Sarge, Robi Sen, Matt Tatum, and Jeff Tapper, for their outstanding contributions. Although these books are affectionately known to thousands as "the Ben Forta books," they are, in truth, as much theirs as mine. Thanks to Nancy Ruenzel and the crew at Peachpit for allowing me the creative freedom to build these books as I see fit. Thanks to Wendy Sharp for stepping in as acquisitions editor on this revision and to Judy Ziajka for so ably shepherding this book through the publication process (without her we'd still be struggling through Volume 1). Thanks to Nicholas Tunney for his through and insightful technical editing. Thanks to Damon Cooper, Tom Jordahl, Dean Harmon, and the rest of the ColdFusion team for creating yet another phenomenal edition of an already phenomenal product. Thanks to the thousands of you who write to me with comments, suggestions, and criticism (thankfully not too much of the latter)—I do read each and every message (and even attempt to reply to them all, eventually), and all are appreciated. And last, but by no means least, a loving thank you to my wife, Marcy, and our children for putting up with (and allowing) my often hectic work schedule. Their love and support make all I do possible.

Charlie Arehart

First, I want to thank Ben for having me as a contributor to this series. With so many excellent authors among the current and past contributors, I really feel privileged. I also want to thank him for all his contributions to the community. Again, as with my fellow authors, I follow in the footsteps of giants. In that regard, I want to acknowledge the awesome ColdFusion community. I've so enjoyed being a part of it, as both beneficiary and contributor, since 1997. This book's for you.

Jeff Bouley

I would like to thank Ben for his tireless efforts in getting the truth out about a product that can and has provided many benefits to enterprise IT organizations, and also for once again including me with a stellar team of ColdFusion gurus to write this book.

Ray Camden

I want to thank my wife and kids for understanding while I worked night after night. I want to thank Ben for once again asking me to help out with this monster of a book. Thank you to Adobe for answering my unending stream of questions and also putting up with suggestions. (They were all good ideas, really!)

Sarge Sargent

Thanks to Ben for having me on the project again. Special thanks to my family for being a rock and a refuge for me. Xtra-special thanks to my wife Nicole for granting me permission to work on this project and for being my "Ambassador of Quon." Bob!

CONTENTS AT A GLANCE

CONTENTS

Introduction

In this Introduction

Who Should Use This Book?

Adobe ColdFusion was the first Web application server (created actually before the term existed) and remains the world's leading cross-platform Web development tool. Although ColdFusion remains an easy (and even fun) product to learn, some of its more advanced features and technologies require substantial know-how and experience.

This book was written for ColdFusion programmers. If you have yet to write ColdFusion code, this is not the book you need—at least not yet. Instead, grab copies of *Adobe ColdFusion 8 Web Application Construction Kit, Volume 1: Getting Started* (ISBN 0-321-51548-X) and *Adobe ColdFusion 8 Web Application Construction Kit, Volume 2: Application Development* (ISBN 0-321-51546-3). Those books teach you everything you need to know to get up and running (including extensive coverage of prerequisite technologies such as Internet fundamentals, the basics of application and database design, and the SQL language). They also teach you everything you need to know to write real-world Web-based applications.

ColdFusion 8, the latest version of ColdFusion, introduces and extends many new high-end technologies designed to let you create highly secure, scalable, and extensible applications. This book teaches you how these technologies work, how they are used, and how to incorporate them into your own applications.

How to Use This Book

This is the eighth edition of *ColdFusion Web Application Construction Kit*, and what started off as a single volume a decade ago has had to grow to three volumes to adequately cover ColdFusion 8. The books are organized as follows:

- **Volume 1:** ***Adobe ColdFusion 8 Web Application Construction Kit, Volume 1: Getting Started*** includes Chapters 1–23 and is targeted at beginning ColdFusion developers.

- **Volume 2:** ***Adobe ColdFusion 8 Web Application Construction Kit, Volume 2: Application Development*** includes Chapters 24–40 and covers the ColdFusion features and language elements that are used by most ColdFusion developers most of the time.
- **Volume 3:** ***Adobe ColdFusion 8 Web Application Construction Kit, Volume 3: Advanced Application Development*** includes Chapters 41–81 and covers the more advanced ColdFusion functionality, including extensibility features, as well as security and management features that will be of primary interest to those responsible for larger and more critical applications.

These book are designed to serve two different, but complementary, purposes.

First, as the books used by most ColdFusion developers, they are a complete tutorial of everything you need to know to harness ColdFusion's power. As such, the books are divided into sections, and each section introduces new topics building on what has been discussed in prior sections. Ideally, you will work through these sections in order, starting with ColdFusion basics and then moving on to advanced topics. This is especially true of the first two books.

Second, the books are an invaluable desktop reference tool. The appendixes and accompanying Web site contain reference chapters that will be of use to you while developing ColdFusion applications. Those reference chapters are cross-referenced to the appropriate tutorial sections, so that step-by-step information is always readily available to you.

The following paragraphs describe the contents of *Adobe ColdFusion 8 Web Application Construction Kit, Volume 3: Advanced Application Development.*

Part VIII: Advanced ColdFusion Development

Chapter 41, "More About SQL and Queries" (online), teaches you how to create powerful SQL statements using subqueries, joins, unions, scalar functions, and more. You also learn how to calculate averages, totals, and counts and how to use the `EXISTS`, `NOT EXISTS`, and `DISTINCT` keywords.

Chapter 42, "Working with Stored Procedures" (online), takes advanced SQL one step further by teaching you how to create stored procedures and how to integrate them into your ColdFusion applications.

Chapter 43, "Using Regular Expressions" (online), introduces the powerful and flexible world of regular expression manipulation and processing. Regular expressions allow you to perform incredibly sophisticated and powerful string manipulations with simple one-line statements. ColdFusion supports the use of regular expressions in both find and replace functions.

Chapter 44, "ColdFusion Scripting" (online), introduces the `<CFSCRIPT>` tag and language, which can be used to replace blocks of CFML code with a cleaner and more concise script-based syntax. `<CFSCRIPT>` can also be used to create user-defined functions, which are introduced in this chapter, too.

The Extensible Markup Language (XML) has become the most important way to exchange and share data and services, and your ColdFusion applications can interact with XML data quite easily.

Chapter 45, "Working with XML" (online), explains what XML is and how to use it within your ColdFusion code.

Chapter 46, "Manipulating XML with XSLT and XPath" (online), explains how to apply XSL transformations to XML data, as well as how to extract data from an XML document using XPath expressions.

Chapter 47, "Using WDDX" (online), explains how Web Dynamic Data eXchange (WDDX) can be used to deliver part of the promise of XML quickly and easily. WDDX can be used to dramatically simplify the sharing and exchanging of structured data using an underlying XML format, even between ColdFusion and other technologies and applications.

Chapter 48, "Using JavaScript and ColdFusion Together" (online), builds on the knowledge you gain in Chapter 47 by showing you how to use WDDX to pass data back and forth between ColdFusion on the server and JavaScript on the client.

Chapter 49, "Using XForms," explores one particular XML specification, XForms, which can be used to build sophisticated and highly reusable form interfaces.

The Internet is a global community, and multilingual and localized applications are becoming increasingly important. Chapter 50, "Internationalization and Localization" (online), explains how to build these applications in ColdFusion so as to attract an international audience.

Chapter 51, "Error Handling" (online), teaches you how to create applications that can both report errors and handle error conditions gracefully. You learn how to use the `<cftry>` and `<cfcatch>` tags (and their supporting tags) and how these can be used as part of a complete error-handling strategy.

Chapter 52, "Using the Debugger" (online), explores the ColdFusion Eclipse-based line debugger and offers tips and tricks on how to best use this tool.

In Chapter 53, "Managing Your Code" (online), you learn about coding standards, documentation, version control, and more, as well as why these features are all so important.

Continuing with the topic of coding standards, Chapter 54, "Development Methodologies" (online), introduces several popular independent development methodologies designed specifically for ColdFusion development.

Part IX: Creating High-Availability Applications

Chapter 55, "Understanding High Availability," introduces the basics of high availability, including load balancing, fail-over, Quality of Service (QoS), clusters, and more.

To address scalability and high availability, it is important to understand how to measure and gauge system performance. Chapter 56, "Monitoring System Performance," introduces the monitoring tools provided by the underlying operating system as well as the powerful ColdFusion Server Monitor.

Chapter 57, "Scaling with ColdFusion," analyzes and compares the various hardware- and software-based scalability solutions available to you, emphasizing the differences between them and any special issues that need to be addressed as a result.

Chapter 58, "Scaling with J2EE," explores Java 2 Enterprise Edition–based scalability, as well as the benefits of running ColdFusion on top of this powerful platform.

Because session state information is usually very server specific, creating server clusters (or server farms) requires you to rethink how you manage session information. Chapter 59, "Managing Session State in Clusters," teaches you how to manage sessions and session state across clusters when necessary and how to leverage J2EE-based session-state management.

Chapter 60, "Deploying Applications," rounds out Part IX by teaching application deployment techniques and strategies.

Part X: Ensuring Security

Chapter 61, "Understanding Security," explains the risks and introduces important security fundamentals, such as encryption, authentication, authorization, and access control.

ColdFusion is managed using the ColdFusion Administrator, a Web application written in ColdFusion itself. This application must be carefully secured, and Chapter 62, "Securing the ColdFusion Administrator," discusses strategies to secure the application while still ensuring access to those who need it.

Chapter 63, "ColdFusion Security Options," introduces ColdFusion's security framework and explains how (and why) to leverage the underlying operating system's security features.

Sandboxes allow the creation of virtual security entities to secure files, directories, data sources, and even CFML language elements. Chapter 64, "Creating Server Sandboxes," explains in detail how to use this powerful feature.

Chapter 65, "Security in Shared and Hosted Environments," tackles the security concerns unique to shared and hosted servers. Server sandboxes are also explained, along with databases, remote access, and other important issues.

ColdFusion features an Administrator API, which can be used to build custom ColdFusion Administrative consoles and applications. Chapter 66, "Using the Administrator API," introduces this powerful management tool.

Part XI: Extending ColdFusion

Chapter 67, "Using Server-Side HTTP and FTP," teaches you how to use these Internet protocols from within your own code. With the help of these protocols, you can easily write applications that interact with other servers and services anywhere on the public Internet and private intranets, and even implement syndication services of your own.

ColdFusion can both create and consume Web Services, providing integration with all sorts of systems and services. Chapter 68, "Creating and Consuming Web Services," explains what Web Services are and why they are of so much interest.

Another popular way to share data is via RSS and ATOM data feeds. ColdFusion supports both, allowing easy feed creation and consumption. Chapter 69, "Working with Feeds," explains how to use this functionality in your own applications.

Chapter 70, "Interacting with the Operating System," introduces the powerful and flexible ColdFusion `<cffile>` and `<cfdirectory>` tags. You learn how to create, read, write, and append local files; manipulate directories; and even add file uploading features to your forms. You also learn how to spawn external applications when necessary.

Chapter 71, "Server-Side Printing," introduces the `<cfprint>` tag and explains how it can be used to generate printed output on the ColdFusion server.

Chapter 72, "Interacting with Directory Services," covers directory services and the LDAP protocol and how to use both of them simply and easily via the `<cfldap>` tag.

Microsoft Exchange has become a critical tool for many organizations. ColdFusion features sophisticated Exchange integration, which can be used to provide calendaring, scheduling, and more within your applications. Chapter 73, "Integrating with Microsoft Exchange," explains how to use the ColdFusion Exchange tags to access the power of Exchange programmatically.

Chapter 74, "Integrating with .NET," explains .NET basics and teaches you how to interact with .NET objects and assemblies.

Chapter 75, "Extending ColdFusion with COM," introduces COM and DCOM objects and shows how they can be used with ColdFusion.

Chapter 76, "Integrating with Microsoft Office," continues this discussion with detailed coverage of integration with Microsoft Office applications using COM and other techniques.

Chapter 77, "Extending ColdFusion with CORBA," introduces CORBA technology. You'll learn about CORBA objects, how ORBs work, and how to take advantage of this distributed processing technology.

ColdFusion is built on underlying Java infrastructure. Chapter 78, "Extending ColdFusion with Java," teaches you how to combine the strengths of ColdFusion and its Java foundations to leverage the best of both worlds. Included is coverage of servlets, Enterprise JavaBeans (EJBs), and more.

The CFAPI is used to write ColdFusion add-ons in C/C++ or Java. Chapter 79, "Extending ColdFusion with CFX," explores the CFAPI interface and explains how and when to use this powerful feature.

Although primarily used to power Web applications, ColdFusion can interact with all sorts of systems and services via gateways. The ColdFusion gateway engine provides access to sockets, JMS, asynchronous processing, and more. Chapter 80, "Working with Gateways," introduces gateway technology and explains how to use gateways as well as how to create your own.

Chapter 81, "Integrating with SMS and IM," continues this topic with coverage of three specific gateways: the SMS gateway used to interact with SMS on devices, the Lotus Sametime gateway used to interact with that IM technology, and the XMPP gateway used to interact with IM via the XMPP protocol.

The Web Site

The accompanying Web site contains everything you need to start writing ColdFusion applications, including:

- Links to obtain ColdFusion 8
- Links to obtain Adobe Dreamweaver
- An explanation of how to obtain Eclipse and the ColdFusion Eclipse plug-ins
- Source code and databases for all the examples in this book
- Electronic versions of some chapters
- An errata, should one be required
- An online discussion forum

The book Web page is at `http://www.forta.com/books/0321515473`.

And with that, turn the page and start reading. In no time, you'll be taking advantage of the power of ColdFusion 8.

Online Content

Additional material for this volume is available online at `http://www.forta.com/books/0321515473`. These chapters are published in printable PDF format and include supporting downloadable code listings.

Part VIII: Advanced ColdFusion Development

Chapter 41, "More About SQL and Queries," teaches you how to create powerful SQL statements using subqueries, joins, unions, scalar functions, and more. You also learn how to calculate averages, totals, and counts and how to use the `EXISTS`, `NOT EXISTS`, and `DISTINCT` keywords.

Chapter 42, "Working with Stored Procedures," takes advanced SQL one step further by teaching you how to create stored procedures and how to integrate them into your ColdFusion applications.

Chapter 43, "Using Regular Expressions," introduces the powerful and flexible world of regular expression manipulation and processing. Regular expressions allow you to perform incredibly sophisticated and powerful string manipulations with simple one-line statements. ColdFusion supports the use of regular expressions in both find and replace functions.

Chapter 44, "ColdFusion Scripting," introduces the `<CFSCRIPT>` tag and language, which can be used to replace blocks of CFML code with a cleaner and more concise script-based syntax. `<CFSCRIPT>` can also be used to create user-defined functions, which are introduced in this chapter, too.

The Extensible Markup Language (XML) has become the most important way to exchange and share data and services, and your ColdFusion applications can interact with XML data quite easily. Chapter 45, "Working with XML," explains what XML is and how to use it within your ColdFusion code.

Chapter 46, "Manipulating XML with XSLT and XPath," explains how to apply XSL transformations to XML data, as well as how to extract data from an XML document using XPath expressions.

Chapter 47, "Using WDDX," explains how Web Dynamic Data eXchange (WDDX) can be used to deliver part of the promise of XML quickly and easily. WDDX can be used to dramatically simplify the sharing and exchanging of structured data using an underlying XML format, even between ColdFusion and other technologies and applications.

Chapter 48, "Using JavaScript and ColdFusion Together," builds on the knowledge you gain in Chapter 47 by showing you how to use WDDX to pass data back and forth between ColdFusion on the server and JavaScript on the client.

Chapter 49, "Using XForms," explores one particular XML specification, XForms, which can be used to build sophisticated and highly reusable form interfaces.

The Internet is a global community, and multilingual and localized applications are becoming increasingly important. Chapter 50, "Internationalization and Localization," explains how to build these applications in ColdFusion so as to attract an international audience.

Chapter 51, "Error Handling," teaches you how to create applications that can both report errors and handle error conditions gracefully. You learn how to use the `<cftry>` and `<cfcatch>` tags (and their supporting tags) and how these can be used as part of a complete error-handling strategy.

Chapter 52, "Using the Debugger," explores the ColdFusion Eclipse-based line debugger and offers tips and tricks on how to best use this tool.

In Chapter 53, "Managing Your Code," you learn about coding standards, documentation, version control, and more, as well as why these features are all so important.

Continuing with the topic of coding standards, Chapter 54, "Development Methodologies," introduces several popular independent development methodologies designed specifically for ColdFusion development.

PART IX

Creating High-Availability Applications

CHAPTER 55
Understanding High Availability

IN THIS CHAPTER

If you are reading this book, chances are your goal is not only to build a rock-solid ColdFusion application, but also to keep that application running at full speed through active and less-than-active times. At the beginning of the Internet boom, circa 1996, the Internet consisted of hundreds of pages of information, mostly published by universities and private individuals. Although these informational Web sites were important, if one of them was down for maintenance in the middle of the day, or if a Web server was over utilized on a Friday morning, nobody lost real business because few people were doing business on the Internet.

Those days are over. Businesses, organizations, and even governments are relying more and more on Internet-related revenue-generating activities such as selling products and communicating with business partners. Consequently, CIOs and CTOs alike are demanding better performance and more reliability from their Web sites. They now expect e-commerce sites to be profitable, making it more important than ever to maintain highly available Web sites. In today's terms, downtime means thousands of dollars of lost revenue, and in some cases security and safety risks.

With the advent of broadband Internet connections and faster personal computers, consumers demand more and more from the Web sites they visit. If response times do not meet customer expectations, companies run the risk of damaging their public images. Reliance on the Internet as a tool to conduct business is increasing every day, and so is our ability to create scalable, stable environments for hosting Web sites.

Enter the concept of *high availability*. Because today's Web applications must be available all the time without exception, and because today's servers—though highly advanced—are still mechanical devices, you must put thought and planning into a Web application's design to ensure its success. Fortunately, once you have the key pieces in place, a highly available Web application is often easier to manage than a standard Internet site.

The first few chapters of this book show how to build a highly available ColdFusion site architecture, understand Web site performance, and allow the site to expand into the future. ColdFusion 8 is now more scalable, faster, and more robust than ever and supports architecture based on the latest Java technology standards (Java 1.6). This chapter gives you an idea of how to ascertain your current level of availability from within ColdFusion, and makes suggestions for understanding and improving your Web site's uptime and strengthening its architecture.

High Availability Explained

High availability refers to your Web application's capability to respond 99.99 percent of the time. You'll achieve this figure, which works out to about one hour of downtime per year, by designing network architectures and Web applications that eliminate all single points of failure or that have a high degree of fault tolerance (redundancy at every level within the hosting provider, network, server, and Web-application architecture).

Here's an example: You have a basic Web site that contains a single Web server and a single database server. One day a power surge causes a power supply failure in the Web server, and the site goes down. If that server's running an e-commerce site, you might lose business irreparably. However, if you've built the site on a cluster of two or more Web servers, the end user can navigate the site normally and may never know that any component failure occurred. Ideally, all your servers would remain healthy all the time; however, that uptime percentage I mentioned earlier does not mean each server will maintain individual uptimes of 99.99 percent. Rather, this percentage refers to the Web application's total uptime as seen by the end user. See Table 55.1, which describes uptime percentage and downtime per year for an application running continuously 24 hours a day, 7 days a week, and 365 days a year.

Table 55.1 Uptime Percentage Corresponding to Downtime per Year

UPTIME PERCENTAGE	DOWNTIME PER YEAR ALLOWED
99.999	Approximately 5 minutes
99.99	53 minutes
99.9	8 hours, 45 minutes
99	87 hours, 36 minutes

In the rest of this chapter, I'll give you a conceptual idea of how to consider high availability when you are planning an application.

➜ Chapter 56, "Monitoring System Performance," Chapter 57, "Scaling with ColdFusion," Chapter 58, "Scaling with J2EE," and Chapter 59, "Managing Session State in Clusters," will show you how to apply high availability concepts while performance-tuning and scaling your application.

The largest problem many application developers and network engineers face is knowing precisely when a problem exists. To improve your Web site's uptime and stability, first you must think about how to determine the site's actual availability from a performance perspective. Most sites crash because of too great a load on the server, and improper performance tuning.

How Do I Know My Server Load?

The amount of traffic on a Web server at any given time is called the *load*. The *percentage load* is a measure of that Web server's utilization.

Load and Performance Testing

So, you are ready to launch your Web site. Before launching any Web application that you anticipate will generate moderate to large amounts of traffic, you should perform a structured server-load test. This is basically a calculated simulation of anticipated site traffic during a given period. The load test will assess the optimal performance of your Web site and help you define the maximum load it can handle. Ascertaining the maximum load a Web site or service will handle before crashing is called *stress testing*.

Using a performance-testing package, you can author scripts that generate a given number of requests during a given period (say, 8 hours) or simulate a given number of users or sessions. The performance-testing package generates a load on the server by simulating the click stream of multiple users and then reports the server response times. By gradually increasing the number of users you're simulating and monitoring the server response times, you can project how much traffic will cause your Web server to go down. You can also model complex behavior such as peak times, sudden traffic spikes, and special conditions (such as users leaving), allowing you to create very accurate models of real-world system use.

Selecting a load-testing product can sometimes be difficult since there are a wide number of available tools. These tools range from open source free tools to tools costing tens of thousands of dollars. Some questions to keep in mind as you select a tool are how often will you use the tool, how complex are the tests that you need to run, how important is it that you get accurate performance results, whether you need to accurately simulate network connections, and whether you need to benchmark other parts of your application besides the application layer (such as third-party messaging tools or the database). Use these questions to help narrow your selection; then try a few products before selecting the one that's right for you. Several packages the author has used include the following:

- WebLoad has an excellent free open source edition that is the best open source testing tool around (`http://www.webload.org/`). It also has a commercial version and plug-ins that support things like Flex and AMF test automation.
- Mercury Interactive offers several options, including hosted load testing and software such as LoadRunner (`http://www.mercury.com`).
- Keynote provides hosted, Web-based testing services (`http://www.keynote.com`).
- RadView's WebLoad software is available at `http://www.radview.com`.
- Empirix has a suite of products including e-Load Expert (`http://www.empirix.com`).
- Open STA also offers a free open source testing tool (`http://www.opensta.org`).
- Microsoft offers a free Web application stress tool (`http://www.microsoft.com`).

- Searching the Web with Yahoo or Google found several sites discussing load testing, including Knowledge Storm, `http://www.knowledgestorm.com`, which listed many solutions and information on this subject. Typically, the more expensive solutions provide more functionality and can simulate more simultaneous users.

Here are some tips for preparing to load-test your Web site. First, compile site-usage statistics using your Web server's statistics logs. If your site is new, attempt to estimate usage of your Web site. Estimating these statistics can be difficult. At the very least, try to estimate the peak number of users and/or sessions per hour and the most popular route through your site.

TIP

If you are developing a new application or site for which you want to do realistic testing, ask around on forums or email lists for people to share their applications statistics with you. Often organizations with similar sites will be happy to share at least some general statistics that will help you get an idea of what numbers to use in your testing.

These are some of the most important usage statistics for your Web site:

- Average number of users and/or sessions per hour
- Peak number of users and/or sessions per hour
- Most popular path through site based on analyzed traffic or real-use cases
- Most CPU-intensive Web pages or activities (such as logging in to the Web site, or performing database-intensive activity such as running queries and inputting large amounts of information)
- Most requested page(s) and top entry page(s)
- Average length of stay on site
- Most popular connection speeds used by visitors (56 Kbps, DSL or cable, T1, and so forth)
- Average response time or latency for pages
- CPU usage and other performance-monitoring statistics

After gathering your statistics or estimates, prepare test scripts and parameters. Test scripts simulate traffic patterns and usage throughout the site, and parameters set expectations for site performance.

A typical test script might include an area where users log in to the site and post information. The test script would simulate how users browse, log in, and post information on the site. For an e-commerce site, the test script might simulate users browsing for products, adding items to a shopping cart, and checking out.

NOTE

Users do not always browse your site the way you want them to, so you may need to develop your test scripts to reflect this. One way to do this is simply to record real users or to once again mine your logs for information on what paths and average times users spend on specific pages or actions.

The site's login sequence, shopping cart, and user checkout all query the database server. Including these sections of the site in the performance test is essential to ascertaining the Web server's response time when making requests to the database server.

In general you want to make sure you cover these parameters in your test scripts:

- Maximum number of users and/or sessions to simulate (if your Web site's peak number of users is, say, 500 per hour, you may want to test it for 1,000 users per hour to ensure that your site will not crash during peak usage)
- Length of sessions (each user stays on your site for an average of 5 minutes)
- Length of the test (usually a minimum 1-hour test with at least a 20- to 30-minute "smoke" test before you start your real testing)
- Ramp-up times (adding users and/or sessions gradually and sporadically to simulate real Web traffic)
- Connection speed mix (majority of test users will access the site over a 56 Kbps connection; others will access over DSL or cable connections)

Now it is time to prepare your Web site for the load test. First, deploy a good copy of your application to your testing server, or to the production server if the site is not live. It is best to use a server that exactly reflects your production environment thus accurately reflecting your live Web site's performance. Second, turn on performance-monitoring tools. Third, perform the load test.

TIP

Never load-test your site on your production servers if your application is live. You don't want to crash your own Web site!

Assessing the results of the load test will provide valuable information pertaining to the Web site's performance and bottlenecks. Most load-testing software provides statistics on users and/or sessions attempted per hour, concurrent users and/or sessions per minute, page latency or response time per hour, and errors encountered. The concurrent users and session statistics will indicate your Web site's peak performance capability.

NOTE

Often called response time, latency is the delay experienced between the moment when a request is made to the server and the point at which the user can view the page.

If you run your performance test and notice that you have immediate problems with site response under very little simulated traffic, you have a bottleneck that requires examination. Typical bottlenecks for Web servers include CPU, memory, network, other servers (such as the database server), and code. Identifying and correcting bottlenecks before launching the site will help to avoid frustration and extra expense after launch.

Chapter 56 includes more detail on how to monitor and understand the performance of your Web servers, identify bottlenecks, and tune servers to run efficiently. Inability to handle the load is one of the most common causes for site failure, so knowing what to expect beforehand will put you ahead of the game.

NOTE

When configuring your Web and database servers, pay specific attention to any extra, nonessential software you load on each server. Even software as simple as an enterprise-monitoring agent or an antivirus program can have an impact on your server's performance.

The High-Availability Plan: Seven Must-Haves for Building High-Availability Solutions

You have seen all the monitoring reports, and you have responded to the ColdFusion alarms. You now have the information you need to start building a plan. Start by looking at the failure points.

Once you have a good idea of how much traffic your servers can take, it's time to start building a plan to solidify the availability of your site and achieve that 99.99 percentile. The following action items are the most important considerations to ensure that your site will be up, available, and free of single points of failure that can dead-end site traffic:

- Implement a load-balanced Web server cluster to make server downtime invisible.
- Choose a network host that offers circuit redundancy.
- Install a correctly configured firewall to protect against unwanted visitors.
- Use RAID Level 5 on database servers.
- Implement a backup and recovery strategy and process.
- Calculate a level of risk that is both business-smart and cost-effective.
- Choose fault tolerance systems to reduce failure points.

The following sections describe each of these items in detail.

Implement a Load-Balanced Web-Server Cluster

The easiest and most effective way to make server downtime invisible and increase the availability of any site is to provide load balancing and failover for a Web server cluster. Use of load balancing devices allows the system to distribute traffic load evenly among all systems in your cluster, ensuring that no single server becomes unavailable due to intense load. *Failover* specifically applies when a server in your cluster becomes unresponsive due to a disaster such as software or hardware failure. Having a failover system allows your cluster to switch to backup hardware, seamlessly shifting traffic—for example, from the main database server to a backup database server.

Load balancing and failover accomplish two goals:

- Maximize server efficiency by balancing Web traffic between servers

- Redirect traffic from nonresponsive Web servers, allowing server failures to go unnoticed by the end user (this is the failover)

Load balancing technology comes in three flavors:

- Software-based
- Hardware-based
- Combination software and hardware

Software-Based Load Balancing

Adobe's ColdFusion 8 Enterprise server includes the capability to cluster multiple instances of ColdFusion (described in Chapter 57). This capability allows you to use ColdFusion clustering for failover or as a software-based load balancer. Software-based load balancers communicate on the network level and maintain a heartbeat with other servers in the cluster to identify server health. If a server in the cluster fails to respond to the heartbeat, the server *fails over*—that is, traffic is redirected away from the affected server.

A number of open source and free open source software load balancing solutions are available, especially for Linux (`http://lcic.org/load_balancing.html`). However, software-based load balancing is usually only good for smaller systems, because at some point the software used to load-balance a cluster may begin to affect the cluster's performance. The occurs because each machine has to spend some of its available resources running the clustering software, as well as sending and receiving information over the wire to determine which machines are running and busy, so that the software can decide where to route traffic. Hardware-based solutions are usually faster, much more reliable, and offer a number of features not included in software solutions.

NOTE

Server heartbeat is defined as continual communication of a server's status to all other servers within the cluster and/or the load balancing software or device.

Hardware-Based Load Balancing

Cisco's LocalDirector and F5's BigIP series use a server-based architecture to load-balance in front of the Web server cluster. Each server-based load balancer works differently. Hardware-based load balancers are more efficient (and more costly) than software-based ones because they actively monitor each connection to each server in the cluster (rather than relying on the servers to manage their own connections and balance the load). The hardware load balancer contains the virtual address of the site (usually the `www.domain.com` name) and redirects traffic to each of the servers in the cluster according to a predefined algorithm (such as round robin or least connections). When the load balancer determines that a server is nonresponsive or is displaying bad content, the load balancer removes that server from the cluster.

Hardware load balancers are a better choice for high-traffic sites because they offload the cluster-management overhead onto a dedicated machine. In addition, they are more flexible when it comes to things like managing persistent (sticky) sessions and filtering traffic. It is generally best practice with any load balancing system (hardware or software) to make sure there is some redundancy. By configuring two hardware load balancers in tandem, you can set one to fail over in case the other goes down, thus eliminating the single point of failure inherent in placing a single server in front of your Web cluster. Figure 55.1 demonstrates how a hardware load balancer handles site traffic.

Figure 55.1

A typical hardware load balancing configuration.

NOTE

Hardware load balancers are in general so cheap in relationship to what they offer that it is almost always better to use a hardware load balancer rather than a software load balancer, especially if you are using more than two machines.

Combination Software and Hardware Load Balancing

Using ColdFusion 8's clustering in tandem with a hardware load balancer, you can combine the monitoring and reporting capabilities of ColdFusion 8 with the cluster-management features of a hardware load balancer. ColdFusion can also supply redundancy if the hardware load balancer fails.

Choose a Network Provider with Circuit Redundancy

When most users type a Web address into their browser, they do not realize that data can go through 10 to 15 stops en route to the destination Web server. These stops (called *hops*) can be local routers, switches, or large peering points where multiple network circuits meet. The Internet really is similar to a superhighway, and like any congested highway, it's prone to traffic jams (called *latency*). As far as your users are concerned, your site is down if there are any problems along the route to your site, even if your ColdFusion servers are still alive and ready to deliver content. Imagine that you are driving along the freeway on a Monday morning and it becomes congested. Knowing an alternate route will allow you to move around the congestion and resume your prior course. Hosting your Web applications on a redundant network allows them to skirt traffic problems in a similar fashion.

Always choose a hosting provider that can implement redundant network circuits (preferably two major Tier 1 upstream providers such as WorldCom, Sprint, or AT&T). Many hosting providers have multiple circuits from multiple providers configured with Border Gateway Protocol (BGP). A BGP configuration enables edge routers linked to the Internet to maintain connectivity in the event one of the upstream providers fails. Without some form of network redundancy, you're at the mercy of a single network provider when it comes to fixing the problem.

For sites with truly massive traffic and to guarantee best performance, many organizations (such as eBay) opt for geographic redundancy. This involves creating clusters of duplicate systems that service users within designated regions, to guarantee availability as well as the fastest possible network performance. These configurations are complex and expensive to set up and run, but companies such as Cisco are now making products that midsized businesses can afford for establishing geographically distributed systems. When you need the best performance and availability, you may want to consider geographic redundancy and load balancing which is sometimes also called global load balancing (for a excellent discussion on global load balancing refer to `http://www.foundrynet.com/services/documentation/sichassis/gslb.html`).

NOTE

If you are hosting your Web application in-house, make sure you have a backup circuit to a network provider, in case the primary circuit becomes overutilized or unavailable. Also, make sure you've got a tested action plan in place to reroute traffic if necessary.

Install a Firewall

Every day, Internet hackers attack both popular and unpopular Web sites. In fact, most hackers don't target a particular site intentionally, but rather look for any vulnerable site they can use as a launching point for malicious activity. Web servers deliver information on specific ports (for example, HTTP traffic is delivered on port 80 and SSL on 443), and generally listen for connections on those ports (although you can run Web traffic on a different port if you wish). Hackers examine sites on the Internet using any number of freely available port-scanning utilities. These utilities do exactly what their name suggests: They scan points on the Internet for open ports that hackers can exploit. The best practice is to implement a front-end firewall solution, and then, if possible, place another firewall between the front-end Web servers and the database servers.

Firewalls accomplish two tasks:

- Mitigate downtime risk by examining all incoming packets, allowing only necessary traffic to reach front-end Web servers.
- Protect database and integration servers against unauthorized Internet access by allowing only communication directly from front-end Web servers.

NOTE

Broadband Report.com (`http://www.dslreports.com/scan`) has a free port-scanning utility that runs from the Web, letting you know which open ports are running on your server. Although the site is geared toward DSL and cable users, anyone can use the port scan.

You can build an efficient and inexpensive firewall solution using Linux's ipchains package. Red Hat Linux, for example, uses GNOME Lokkit for constructing basic ipchains networking rules. To configure specific firewall rules, however, use iptables in Red Hat (see `http://www.redhat.com`). For better security, the most commonly implemented front-end firewall solutions include Cisco's PIX Firewall (`http://www.cisco.com`), Netscreen's Firewall (`http://www.netscreen.com`), and Checkpoint's Firewall-1 (`http://www.checkpoint.com`). You must ensure that your firewall is secure as well. This means you should not run any other services on the firewall except those that are absolutely necessary.

Most vendors, including Cisco, sell load balancing switches with built-in firewalls. The best thing to do is create a list of desired capabilities and establish a budget; then contact several vendors for quotes on affordable solutions that will meet your needs and restrictions. Be aware, too, that many modern firewall tools offer features other than port blocking. Many provide intrusion detection, intrusion alerts, blocking denial-of-service attacks, and much more.

NOTE

If you really cannot implement a front-end firewall solution when setting up your system, make sure you know exactly what ports and services are open on your system. Do not install services you won't use, and survey those you do use to make sure they're necessary.

Use RAID Level 5 on Database Servers

Although you can build a database cluster in addition to your Web server cluster, database clusters are more complex to manage and might be impractical, depending on the size of your Web application, for your specific organization. If you have the resources for only a single database server, ensure that it is in a RAID Level 5 configuration. RAID (Redundant Array of Inexpensive Disks) stripes data across a number of disks rather than one, while reserving a separate disk to maintain CRC error checking.

TIP

Always give your transaction logs the best-performing volumes in the disk array. In any busy online transaction processing (OLTP) system, the transaction logs endure the most input/output (IO).

Disks in a RAID array are SCSI hot-swappable. If one disk in an array fails, you can substitute another in its place without affecting the server's availability. Additionally, it is a good idea to replicate your database at regular intervals to another database server.

Another option is to use a storage area network (SAN), which is essentially a series of hard drives, allowing massive amounts of storage. SANs are highly fault tolerant and robust and allow you to not only boot multiple systems from them, but when so configured, they allow you to restore and recover a database from them in the event of a disaster scenario. One effective and relatively cheap way of adding a higher level of availability to your database layer is to use two database servers, where one is a live server that replicates the database to a SAN, and the other is a hot failover server that reads from the SAN if the primary, live server fails. This configuration provides a high level of redundancy as well as simple failover without the cost of expensive hardware, software, and database cluster management. Still, your best option is to have multiple clustered databases if you can afford it.

Calculate Acceptable Risk

There is always a trade-off between cost and fault tolerance. Some organizations utilize two or three Web servers configured in a cluster with a single, "strong" nonclustered database server. The database server has redundant CPUs, power supplies, disk drives, disk and RAID controllers, and network connections. This offers a good degree of availability without the additional cost of a second database server and clustering technology. Implementing a network-based tape backup strategy is another effective, cost-saving alternative and should be part of any disaster recovery plan.

Although these are reasonable risk-management approaches for some, they will be insufficient for those who need 99.999 or even 100 percent uptime. For organizations needing absolute availability, the costs and complexity of creating and managing such systems rapidly increase. If you can afford to lose a few hours or days worth of data, a simple web cluster without a database cluster is more than reasonable.

Only your budget limits the amount of redundancy you can incorporate into your system architecture. In other words, analyze your needs and plan accordingly. Any hardware can fail for virtually any reason. It is always best when arranging high availability to imagine the worst disaster and then plan based on that.

Redundant Server Components vs. Commodity Computing

It is recommended that you implement a fault-tolerant configuration with redundancy at every level, in order to achieve better than 99.9 percent uptime for a Web application. Most server manufacturers offer dual or triple power supplies, cooling fans, and so on in their server configurations. Choose redundant power supplies to keep servers operating in case of power supply failures. In addition, ensure that you have an uninterruptible power supply (UPS) that will power the server for a limited time in case of total power failure. Most major co-location facilities will also have their own backup generators in case of major power outages—another important consideration. In many server lines, the very low-end servers do not offer the capability to add any of these options.

Another popular approach (at Google, for instance) is to have lots of very cheap redundant servers instead of lots of redundant components. Often this arrangement is far less expensive and easier to manage—especially with recent super-low-cost blade computers—than maintaining high-end, massively redundant servers. This approach is gaining in popularity and is a major part of the emerging "grid" computing paradigm being pushed by IBM, Oracle, HP, Dell, Microsoft, and other major vendors.

Figure 55.2 shows a standard, highly available application design, including clustered Web servers, clustered database servers, Network Array Storage (NAS), redundant switches and routers, and redundant firewalls.

Figure 55.2
Basic high-availability site design.

Disaster Planning

Disaster planning and recovery processes are critical when designing and developing a high-availability system, but for some reason these needs are rarely adequately addressed. Unless your data, code, application, and hardware are not important to you, the first thing and last thing to consider is what to do when everything goes wrong. Making your system redundant and having offsite backup to prevent loss of data is not enough. Recovering from a disaster may involve rebuilding servers, applying specific patches, making tuning and configuration changes, preventing sensitive data from being exposed, as well as validating and "scrubbing" data.

Recovering from a disaster, especially one of large magnitude, can be a daunting affair if you have not clearly and systematically addressed the recovery process. Here are some excellent resources for coming to grips with disaster recovery and planning:

- Disaster Recovery Journal (`http://www.drj.com/`)
- Disaster Resources (`http://www.disaster-resource.com/`)
- Simply Googling the Web will reveal a wealth of tutorials, papers, and actual plans from various organizations that you can reuse to suit your specific needs.

NOTE

Recent laws such as Sarbanes-Oxley require organizations of a certain size to have disaster recovery plans.

Some Truths About Web Hosting

Web site performance and availability depend as much on who hosts the site and where it's hosted as on brilliant coding. In the last few years, hundreds of businesses have sprouted up that offer inexpensive Web hosting, but many of them do not guarantee uptime or specific service levels. When you're designing a new Web application, you should consider the hosting question in the early design stages.

For a highly available Web site, the choice of host is important. The host can provide many features, including Internet connectivity, redundant power, backup generators, disaster recovery, on-demand bandwidth, and managed services that guarantee a 99.99 percent or greater uptime. An uptime percentage of 99.99 translates to roughly an hour of downtime per year. Choose a hosting provider that will not only guarantee this uptime but also provide some sort of reparation to you in the event that the provider fails to meet this agreement.

NOTE

Always choose a hosting provider that can implement an explicit service-level agreement (SLA) indicating how responsive they will be in the event of every type of site outage. Without an SLA, it's not clear whether you or the hosting provider is responsible for recovering your application during a site outage.

Active Site Monitoring

ColdFusion 8 provides greatly enhanced information for monitoring site availability. But to get a true idea of how your site looks to the outside world, you should set up an active monitoring tool using another software product to collect information from outside your network. Most good ISPs and hosting providers offer some type of monitoring service, such as DeepMetrix's ipMonitor (`http://www.deepmetrix.com`).

If you are working on your own, however, I recommend using Mercury SiteScope, which provides a graphical dashboard of information enabling you to track and report server and site availability over days, weeks, and months. An evaluation copy of SiteScope is available at `http://www.mercury.com/us/products/application-management/foundation/monitors/sitescope/`.

These types of reporting features are essential when you're analyzing trends to create a high-availability plan for your Web application.

TIP

Just seeing if you can open port 80 isn't enough–you need to implement more sophisticated server monitoring. Test for Web server health by checking specific URLs and looking for validation strings in returned Web pages.

Several other packages operate similarly to SiteScope and run on Windows, Solaris, and Linux platforms. If you are not keen on setting up and managing your own monitoring station, a few services, such as Keynote's Performance Management Solution (`http://www.keynote.com`), will monitor your site from locations around the globe. Information received from your monitoring tool and these services is essential in determining and assessing availability. If your site is down due to network latency or other Internet-related issues, comparing the data produced by multiple monitoring tools or outside sources located in different locations will let you know which users couldn't get to your site. If you notice that one network provider is consistently slow or is not meeting its uptime agreement, you should reevaluate your use of that provider.

The Quality-of-Service Guarantee

For high-bandwidth network transmissions, Quality of Service (QoS) is the idea that a network provider can predetermine and guarantee transmission rates and network quality for a client. Clients can choose a certain QoS bandwidth guarantee from a network provider, and the network will prioritize packet transmissions for that client based on a predetermined service level through the use of the Resource Reservation Protocol. This type of guarantee has become essential with the growing popularity of streaming-video multicasts. A client who plans to broadcast a high-bandwidth event at a specific date and time can contact the service provider and order the appropriate bandwidth reservation to get prioritized delivery of packets during that reservation period.

Another possible QoS guarantee may ensure 99.999 percent availability of the internal local network, individual server uptime of 99.9 percent, and clustered server uptime of 99.99 percent. The QoS guarantee ensures that your site won't be inaccessible at a critical time.

What Next?

So where do we go from here? You now have a good background in understanding high availability and its benefits for your Web site. How do you implement it using ColdFusion, you ask? Chapters 56 through 59 of this book discuss various aspects of monitoring system performance, scaling with ColdFusion, and managing session state in a cluster. Understanding all these topics will aid you in building a highly available Web site running ColdFusion.

CHAPTER 56

Monitoring System Performance

IN THIS CHAPTER

One of the hardest things to do when working with any programming language or application server is to understand why an application is behaving unexpectedly after it has been deployed. Perhaps you are experiencing inexplicable slowdowns in performance, rapid spikes in memory usage, sudden unresponsiveness, or other strange behavior that cannot be specifically tied to your application code. This can be an incredibly frustrating experience trying to understand what's going on with your application but in this chapter you will learn how to use a number tools to help you monitor and understand what is wrong with your system allowing you deal with any problems may arise.

In this chapter we will help you understand the tools and information you have at your disposal for troubleshooting your ColdFusion applications and removing performance bottlenecks.

Monitoring Your ColdFusion 8 Server

Monitoring system performance involves two major approaches: historical analysis and active system monitoring.

You can incorporate many methods into your monitoring activities. Usually you need to implement a combination of monitoring activities into your infrastructure to comprehensively monitor the site. Let's first discuss analysis of past system performance, or historical analysis. Next we will look at active system monitoring of ColdFusion Web servers—which may involve setting up server probes, utilizing performance monitors and third-party utilities, and other techniques.

Developing a Baseline

One of the first things you want to do before you start monitoring a application is have or create a baseline for your system. A baseline is a set of metrics that define how your system and application should behave under normal conditions. Usually you do this by using a load and application testing system such as WebLoad to develop a performance baseline for your application. You should know exactly how much memory your application uses, how many requests a second it can handle, the level of CPU usage during normal operation, and so on (Chapter 55, "Understanding High Availability," describes various testing tools for gathering this information.

Once you have created your system baseline, you'll have a set of metrics against which to compare your system's operation, which will help you in locating problems. Every time you make a significant changes to the system, apply patches, upgrade ColdFusion, or apply new code, run your tests again and compare the system performance with your original baseline data. Do this as soon as you make the changes on your test environment, so you can see before deployment whether the alterations will have a negative impact on the application's overall performance, stability, and viability.

Historical Analysis

One of the most important methods for understanding your application, successfully troubleshooting it, and improving it, is historical analysis. Historical analysis is simply comparing data collected from your system over time to see what patterns, trends, or changes emerge. You can use historical analysis to detect security threats, bugs, problems with performance, bottlenecks, and much more.

ColdFusion 8 offers several features for analyzing historical performance on your application server. By combining this data with other information stored on the server, you can create a clear picture of how your application is performing.

Analyzing ColdFusion Log Files

A consistently small system log file correlates to a healthy Web site. Regular monitoring of the ColdFusion log files is a key component to maintaining and improving your ColdFusion applications. Concentrating on reducing the number of errors that appear in the log will eventually produce a healthier, more responsive site. ColdFusion 8 log files consist of several files representative of functions within the ColdFusion server, shown in Table 56.1.

Table 56.1 ColdFusion Log Files

LOG FILE NAME	DESCRIPTION
`Application.log`	Records every ColdFusion error on your site.
`Customtag.log`	Records errors in custom tags.
`Car.log`	Records errors associated with site archive and restore.
`Eventgateway.log`	New in ColdFusion 8, this log records event gateway events.
`Exception.log`	Records stack traces for exceptions that occur in the server.
`Flash.log`	Records Flash Remoting errors.
`Jrun.log`	When ColdFusion is connected to an external Web server, this log stores Java run-time errors. It is stored in `[cfusionmx]\runtime\lib\wsconfig\1`.
`Mail.log`	Records errors generated when sending mail through a mail server.
`Mailsent.log`	Records email messages sent.

Table 56.1 (continued)

LOG FILE NAME	DESCRIPTION
`rdservice.log`	Records errors that occur in the ColdFusion Remote Development Service (RDS). RDS provides remote HTTP-based access to files and databases.
`Server.log`	Records errors for the ColdFusion server.
`Scheduler.log`	Records scheduled events. Indicates initiated events and whether they succeeded.

The `Application.log` file records every ColdFusion error on your site. Two types of errors in particular clearly indicate a performance problem.

The first is a "Request timed out" message. This error comes up if a ColdFusion page takes longer to process than the `TIMEOUT` value you set in the ColdFusion Administrator. If your server is experiencing performance problems, some pages take so long to process that they trigger this error. If you have set your `TIMEOUT` value to 20 seconds, you have no way of knowing whether the pages that *aren't* timing out are taking 5 seconds or 15 seconds to process. If you're getting "Request timed out" errors for only a few specific ColdFusion pages, odds are those pages are at least one source of your performance problems. If these errors are spread evenly across most or all of the pages on your site, a single bottleneck may be affecting everything.

It's normal for ColdFusion to rely heavily on the processor and to grab memory as necessary to pull a large number of records from a database. Memory usage should climb, plateau, and then release. However, if you find that memory use on your Web server is increasing without ever releasing, look in the application log for database-related activity. If you find many errors (and especially if you see entire queries in the application log with associated errors), examine your database queries and see how you can tighten them up. Other issues can create what appear to be memory leaks, from threads never releasing, to synchronization issues. One of your best resources for solving these sorts of problems is the collection of log files described here.

The `Exception.log` is one of the more useful ColdFusion logs and probably the first place you should look if you are seeing ColdFusion application errors. Many ColdFusion developers are uncomfortable with the exception log because it shows Java stack traces, which are very detailed and full of seemingly undecipherable Java messages. When properly understood, however, the stack traces offer detailed information on exactly what was happening when the system experienced the problem that created the exception. A full discussion of Java stack traces is beyond the scope of this book, but you'll find an excellent introduction to this topic at `http://java.sun.com/developer/technicalArticles/Programming/Stacktrace/`. Once you understand these exception messages, you can quickly determine hung threads, failed requests, memory problems, and much more. Even without a full grasp of the stack traces, you will be able to see which file threw the exception, at what time, and what part of ColdFusion experienced an issue.

Though not as useful at first glance as the exception log, the `Server.log` also provides information related to the stability of your Web servers that might further substantiate your application log findings. Search this log for "ColdFusion started," which indicates how often your Web server has been started and stopped.

NOTE

ColdFusion Administrator allows you to review all your logs, but in general you will want the capability to search for specific events, errors, and time ranges to get useful information from your log files. To do this, you want something like MS Log Parser 2.2 (`http://www.microsoft.com/downloads/details.aspx?FamilyID=890cd06b-abf8-4c25-91b2-f8d975cf8c07&displaylang=en`), which lets you parse log files using SQL-like commands.

Other Logs

ColdFusion 88 provides for tracking long-running requests. In the Debugging & Logging > Logging Settings section of the ColdFusion Administrator, you can set a benchmark (in seconds) and display any requests that take longer than the setting. Additionally, you can log all pages that run longer than a given number of seconds to your `Server.log`. See Figure 56.1 for setting logging of long-running pages.

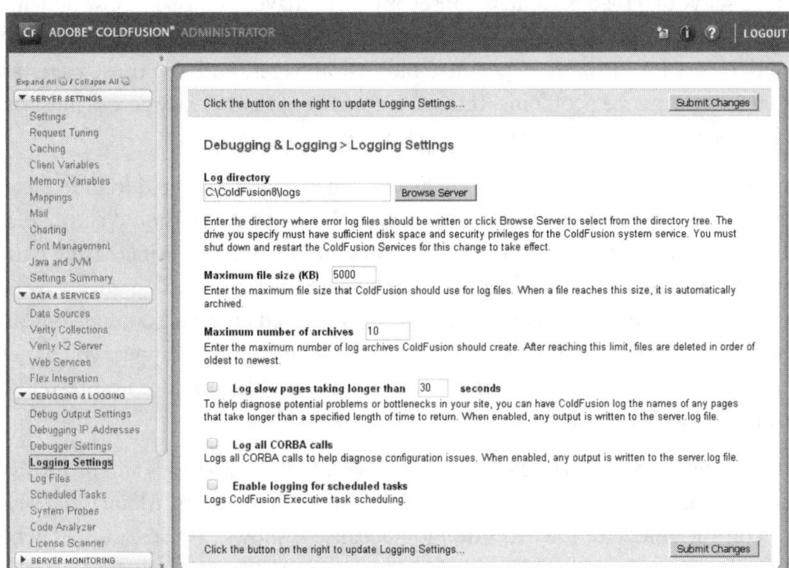

Figure 56.1

Log pages that are running too long.

Periodically reviewing all of your logs will create a clear picture of how your ColdFusion applications are functioning and provide information for resolving issues that may arise during the normal course of operation.

JRun Metrics

If you are using the standard version of ColdFusion, or ColdFusion for J2EE deployed on JRun, you can take advantage of yet another set of log files, as well as the enhanced logging capability in

JRun. Look in the ColdFusion 88 install directory and go to `\runtime\logs`. You will see the logs listed in Table 56.2.

Each of these logs supplies additional information about ColdFusion, although the data is usually not particularly helpful in that much of it is duplicated in the standard ColdFusion logs.

Table 56.2 JRun Logs for ColdFusion

LOG NAME	FUNCTION
`coldfusion-err.log`	ColdFusion stack traces.
`coldfusion-event.log`	ColdFusion event log.
`coldfusion-out.log`	ColdFusion services events, and data from garbage collection.

Enhanced ColdFusion logging is another tool that can provide extremely detailed and specific information about a variety of ColdFusion metrics. These metrics are listed in Table 56.3.

Table 56.3 JRun Metrics

METRIC	DESCRIPTION
`listenTh`	Threads listening for a new connection.
`idleTh`	Threads waiting for a new request.
`delayTh`	Threads waiting to run.
`busyTh`	Threads currently running.
`totalTh`	Total worker thread count.
`delayRq`	Requests delayed due to high concurrency.
`droppedRq`	Requests dropped.
`handledRq`	Requests handled.
`handledMs`	Milliseconds spent servicing requests not including any delay time (`delayMs`).
`delayMs`	Milliseconds spent in delay state.
`bytesIn`	Bytes read from requests.
`bytesOut`	Bytes written to responses.
`freeMemory`	Kilobytes of free memory in the heap.
`totalMemory`	Total kilobytes in the heap (in use and free).
`sessions`	Current number of active J2EE sessions.
`sessionsInMem`	Number of J2EE sessions in memory.

As you can see, this is an extensive list of very detailed information! Using JRun metrics, you can see when threads are hanging, when specific requests are not responding, the amount of free memory, and more. The only disadvantage to using JRun metrics is that when they are turned on, they have an impact on system performance. In addition, this feature creates some very large log files, so it's best to enable it only when you are troubleshooting.

To enable JRun metrics, first find your `JRun.XML` file, usually found in the ColdFusion root. The path will look something like this:

```
C:\CFusion\runtime\servers\coldfusion\SERVER-INF\jrun.xml
```

After you have found this file you should make a back up since we are going to change this file and if you make any mistakes ColdFusion server may not restart. Usually it is easy enough just make a copy of `jrun.xml` and call it `jrun_original.xml` or whatever is easy for you to remember. Now that you have made a backup copy, open `jrun.xml` with any text editor. Look for this entry and uncomment it:

```
<service class="coldfusion.server.jrun4.metrics.MetricsServiceAdapter"
name="MetricsService">
<attribute name="bindToJNDI">true</attribute>
</service>
```

Then find this entry:

```
<service class="jrunx.logger.LoggerService" name="LoggerService">
```

and edit its attributes. You want to change `metricsEnabled` to True, and `metricsLogFrequency` (the interval, in seconds, to log metrics) to somewhere between 5 and 10 seconds. So you should have something that looks like this:

```
<attribute name="metricsEnabled">true</attribute>
<attribute name="metricsLogFrequency">5</attribute>
```

The information that will be recorded to the logs will look something like this:

```
10/14 12:11:23 metrics Web threads (busy/total): 0/2 Sessions: 2 Total Memory=7052
Free=3303
```

Next, split the logged information into its own log file. Do this by editing this line:

```
<attribute name="filename">{jrun.rootdir}/logs/{jrun.server.name}-
event.log</attribute>
```

to this:

```
<attribute name="filename">{jrun.rootdir}/logs/{jrun.server.name}- {log.level}.
log</attribute>
```

Once you have changed the `jrun.xml` file, you will need to save the file and restart ColdFusion for these settings to take effect. Once you restart ColdFusion you will see that all the metrics data you record while troubleshooting will go to a separate log, `coldfusion-metrics.log`.

NOTE

Do not forget that turning on JRun metrics has a performance impact on your server and rapidly creates very large log files. Make sure that once you have resolved your issues or captured all the information you need, turn off the JRun metrics.

Analyzing Web Server Log Files

Sherlock Holmes often said "Eliminate all other factors, and the one which remains must be the truth." Trying to debug and troubleshoot your application can sometimes seem an impossible task when the problem is not apparent or obvious. In these cases you need to look methodically at everything that may be affecting your system. One of the major components in a ColdFusion application is the Web server, and careful monitoring and analysis of its logs are crucial to maintaining system performance. Additionally, the Web server logs often provide clues to other issues, such as gaps that might allow security breaches or attacks, as well as information on how real users are experiencing the application.

For all these reasons, good log-analysis software is essential in analyzing your Web server's log files. Since Web server log analysis isn't specific to ColdFusion we will not delve deeply into it. You should know, however, that without a good log-analysis tool, you'd be severely handicapped in all your other performance-analyzing ventures. If you don't have a log-analysis tool right now, you might like to look at Analog (`http://www.analog.cx/`), which is one of the most popular free Web log parses. Another excellent open source tools is AWstats (`http://awstats.sourceforge.net/`). If you need more-powerful analytic tools, consider WebTrends's Enterprise Suite (`http://www.webtrends.com/`), one of the most popular commercial Web log-analysis tools. It offers ad hoc reporting and graphical representations of logged data.

Analyzing Web server logs will tell you about visits, users dropping off in the middle of a transaction, and general user activity. You can set up your Web server to store valuable statistics about your site. These can be very beneficial for tracking information about your site and then comparing the data to your load testing data. You can find how many users are visiting, peak loads, page-load times, and most-visited site sections, among other information. This analysis can also show where visitors are leaving your site, maybe due to problems such as errors or slow page-load times. Understanding how your users interact with your site can be very beneficial in creating a high-performance Web site.

Active Monitoring

In addition to reviewing the ColdFusion logs and Web server logs, it's helpful to have a good picture of how your Web server looks from outside the network (especially if you think you might have a network bottleneck). If you are managing your own Web server and it is located offsite, a good network-monitoring package will give you some perspective on server uptime, as well as any network latency coming to and going from your Web site. If you don't have a monitoring package yet, take a look at Mercury SiteScope (`http://www.mercury.com/us/products/business-availability-center/sitescope/`). When you run SiteScope on a machine connected to a network other than the one hosting your server, SiteScope will check the health of your site at specific intervals. It provides a graphical dashboard of server activity, viewable through a Web browser. Besides SiteScope, a number of great open-source monitoring tools are available that will run on Linux.

If your server is managed by someone else or hosted at a co-location facility, the management company should have a monitoring tool in place. It's good practice to ask routinely for the server's uptime percentage, as well as time frames and explanations for any outages. Not only will you be checking up on the efficiency of your management company, but you might also get an idea of how traffic and usage affect site downtime.

Server Probes

ColdFusion applications are often used for serious enterprise applications that rely on a variety of things beyond just databases, including LDAP, SMTP, POP, Web Services, ERP systems, and others. Knowing what is happening with all these disparate systems can be crucial to successful troubleshooting in a timely manner. ColdFusion offers a method to do just that—through *server probes*. These not only monitor parts of your application, but recognize failure conditions, send alerts, and even resolve the situation (for example, restarting a service by running a batch file). The results of your probes are also logged to the `Scheduler.log`.

Setting Up a Probe to Verify Content

The first type of server probe you should set up is a simple content match. This probe loads the Web page at an interval you set. ColdFusion Application Server (CFAS) then attempts to match your specified content with the Web page content (provided that CFAS can view the content as part of the source). If your Web server is delivering the content as expected, the System Probes page displays the status as success. However, if the Web server is displaying anything other than the expected content (such as a ColdFusion error page), the System Probes page displays a status of Failed. ColdFusion gives you the option of sending an email notification, executing a program, and logging the error.

For example you could create a simple ColdFusion template called `probe.cfm` and put the word *Alive* in it. Then you would setup a probe that would call this page, for example every hour, and have it look for the word *Alive*. If Alive is not returned it will email you.

To set up a content match probe, follow these steps:

1. Create a file called `Probe.cfm` that just contains the word Alive. Place that file your Web root.
2. In ColdFusion Administrator, select Debugging & Logging and choose System Probes in the Debugging and Logging category. If you haven't set up any probes yet, your System Probes menu will be similar to that in Figure 56.2.
3. Click the Define New Probe button to create a new probe.
4. In the Probe Name box, enter the name of the probe as in Figure 56.3.
5. Enter the frequency with which you want ColdFusion to load the page. Set it to at least 60 seconds. Also make sure to set the start time which is required. Optionally you can setup an end time, which defines when your probe will stop running, much like a scheduled task, but usually you will not use this setting.

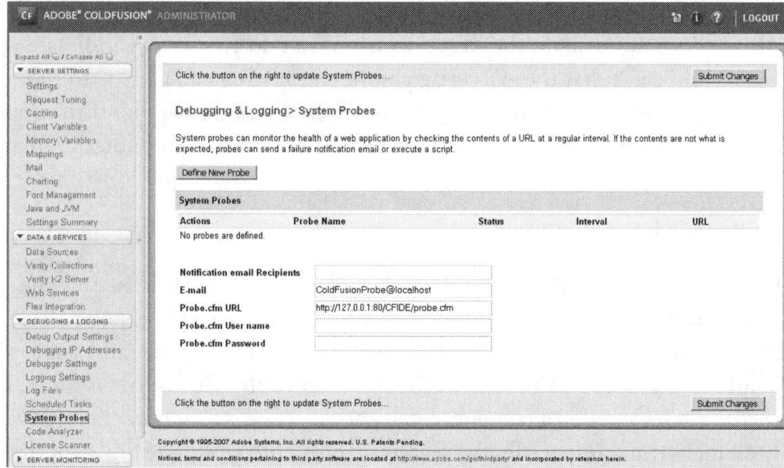

Figure 56.2
The System Probes screen before you've configured any probes.

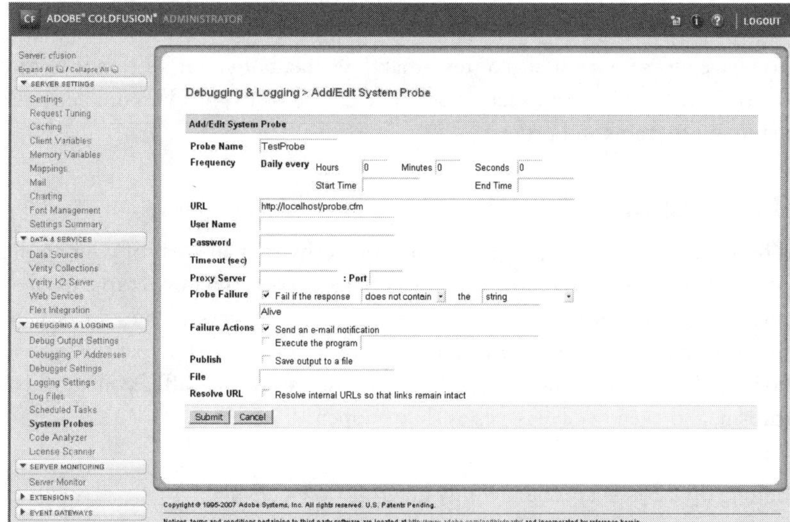

Figure 56.3
The configured content-match probe.

6. In the Probe URL box, enter the URL you want ColdFusion to verify. In the example in Figure 56.3, the URL is `http://localhost/probe.cfm`, indicating that ColdFusion should check a page called `probe.cfm`. In some situations you may want to probe parts of your site that are behind some sort of secure area. In this case you can also pass a username and password in the user name and password fields.

7. In the Timeout box, enter a timeout value of at least 30 seconds. If you have set ColdFusion in Server settings to time out requests after a certain number of seconds, you should use the same value here.

8. Choose the Probe Failure settings. In this example, the probe will fail if the response does not contain the `Alive` string. What do you want ColdFusion to do if the probe indicates that it can't verify your content? You can choose to send an email notification, execute a program, or log the error to a specific log file. If the content you want to match contains spaces make sure to surround the text with quotation marks in your ColdFusion Administrator.

9. Click the Submit button.

After you have set up the content match probe, when you click Submit and return to the System Probes page, it displays your content match with a status of Unknown. Test the probe by clicking its URL. If the probe succeeds, the status will be OK; if the probe fails, you'll get a Failed status. If ColdFusion displays a Failed status but you can verify that the site is functioning properly (in other words, you have set up a content match and the page is rendering correctly), edit the probe and verify all the settings (especially the search string). Often a simple typo will make the difference between success and failure statuses on a functioning site. However, if ColdFusion displays a Failed status, and the page does not render correctly or at all when you browse it, you know you have set up a successful content-match probe.

You have just set up a basic content-match probe, but you might want to monitor other components of your Web application, such as database connectivity, SMTP connectivity, and availability of external programs and processes.

Other Probes

There are several other probes to help you verify that all areas of your application are working properly. By writing a simple ColdFusion page, you can connect to a database and run a query, then return a specific recordset. If the recordset can be retrieved, you know the database server is working properly. Or you can write an extensive ColdFusion page that performs a complete check on your application's components. ColdFusion server probes offer you another great tool to monitor, inform, and even resolve issues as they happen.

Setting Up a System Probe to Verify External Connectivity

Let's look at how we can setup a system probe to check for database connectivity. The easiest way to do this is to just create a simple query; it does not even have to return anything, inside a CFTRY block. If the page cannot connect to the database for any reason, it will throw an exception and return "Error"; otherwise, it will return "Success." Listing 56.1 shows an example of a simple database probe.

Listing 56.1 `probe.database.cfm`—Simple Database Connectivity Probe

```
<cftry>
     <cfquery name="probeDB" datasource="OWS">
          Select contacts.FirstName
               From contacts
               Where  contacts.FirstName ='Ben'
     </cfquery>
```

Listing 56.1 (continued)

```
<cfcatch type="database">
     Error!
</cfcatch>
     Success
</cftry>
```

Save this probe somewhere in your Web root. You will need to make sure the data source `ows` is configured and setup in your ColdFusion Administrator. Now just follow the same steps as you would to configure the content probe. Here is a short summary again:

1. Click the Define New Probe button to create a new probe.
2. Enter the frequency with which you want ColdFusion to load the page. For this example an hour is sufficient. Then add a star time and if you want a finish time.
3. In the Probe Name box, select a unique name for this probe that describes what you are testing: for example `owsdatabaseprobe`. In the URL box, select the path to the `probe.database.cfm` file.
4. Set the Probe Failure settings to fail if it does not contain the string Success, then select the e-mail notification.
5. Click Submit Changes. You have now set up the probe.

You should now see your probe under the list of System Probes in the ColdFusion Administrator. You should also see four icons next to the name of your system probe. The second icon allows you to immediately run the probe so you can test it and when you move your mouse pointer over it you should see Run Task. Select this icon to run the probe. If you have configured everything correctly you should not get a notification. If anything wrong with the database connection then you will.

You can configure all system probes to send emails when a probe fails. Monitoring the System Probes page in ColdFusion Administrator at all times is virtually impossible. Setting up email alarms is an essential way to remain up-to-date regarding the availability of your Web servers. It also helps you gather trend information to make educated choices on strengthening site availability. In the System Probes page, enter a list of email recipients to receive probe notifications separating each email using a semicolon, and then click Submit Changes.

By combining different kinds of probes with email alarm notification, you can get a pretty good idea of your Web application's availability in real time. After you start to notice performance trends, you are ready to start looking for server bottlenecks.

NOTE

All probes run as scheduled tasks, so creating too many probes or setting them with high frequencies (such as every second) will adversely affect the system's performance.

The ColdFusion Server Monitor

In previous versions of ColdFusion, monitoring the state of your ColdFusion server and troubleshooting required the use of specialized tools such as SNMP, JVM profilers, and specialized log parsers. With the introduction of ColdFusion 8, Adobe has provided a powerful new tool, the ColdFusion Server Monitor, a Flex-based application that lets you see in, real time, server requests, thread usage, queries, memory usage, errors, and much more.

The ColdFusion Server Monitor allows you to set intervals for gathering information, filter out information you are not interested in, take snapshots of a period in time, and generate reports. The Server Monitor also allows you to create a variety of alerts to specific events, such as hung threads and JVM's reaching a memory threshold and to perform specific actions on events, such as send an email or kill a thread.

To start using the ColdFusion Monitor, follow these steps:

1. Go to the ColdFusion Administrator and select the Server Monitoring tab.
2. Select Server Monitor. When you are asked to select either the normal Server Monitor or the Multiple Server Monitor, select Launch Server Monitor.

From here you should see something like Figure 56.4, which is the default monitor view called the Overview; it shows a dashboard summary of a variety of metrics and reports. Select Start Monitoring, Start Profiling, and Start Memory Tracking; the monitor will now start collecting data and providing information to the graphs in the Overview.

Figure 56.4

The ColdFusion Server Monitor Overview.

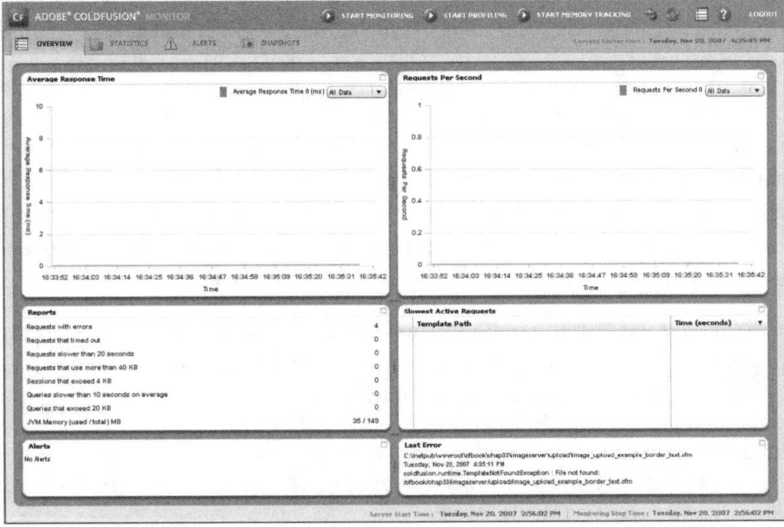

Each of the buttons in the Overview allows you to monitor specific parts of your ColdFusion Server, as described in Table 56.4.

TIP

Because the Server Monitor is a separate application, you can call it by going to `http://[your server name or ip]/CFIDE/administrator/monitor/launch-monitor.cfm`.

Table 56.4 ColdFusion Server Monitoring Options

OPTION	DESCRIPTION
Start Monitoring	Collects all requests, including active requests, slowest requests, active sessions, cumulative server usage, highest hit counts, template cache status, request throttle data, requests that timed out, requests with errors, and server alerts. You can filter out data by defining filters in Filter Settings in the monitor settings.
Start Profiling	Collets tag and function timing information for the Slowest Requests report; CFML stack trace for the Active Requests report; and information about active queries, slowest queries, cached queries, and query cache status, database pool status, and the most frequently run queries.
Start Memory Tracking	Collects data on memory usage, including total memory usage, most memory-intensive queries, most memory-intensive sessions, memory usage by all application and server scopes, and profiling information on the largest variables in the Requests by Memory Usage report, if profiling is enabled.

You also, using the Settings button in the Overview, define how often data is collected, whether to include the ColdFusion Administrator in monitoring, what data to exclude, and specific paths to exclude or include in monitoring. This capability is extremely helpful when you want to focus on just a specific application or area within an application that is causing problems.

As you can see, the monitor allows access to a large amount of server information that in previous versions of ColdFusion was hard to access. With the Server Monitor, you can use the monitor dashboard or Overview screen to drill down into a number of reports; select any report item and double-clicking it to go to the Statistics detail view for that item. For example, double-clicking Request with Errors under Reports in the Overview takes you to the Statistics > Errors > Requests with Errors view. From there, you can see the entire request with errors listed by template path, error count, and last occurrence. By double-clicking the error template, you can see a detail view of the error, as shown in Figure 56.5.

Now that you have seen a little of how the monitor works, let's look at it in more detail.

NOTE

A number of other tools, such as seefusion and fusion reactor, provide functionality and benefits that the built-in Server Monitor does not provide.

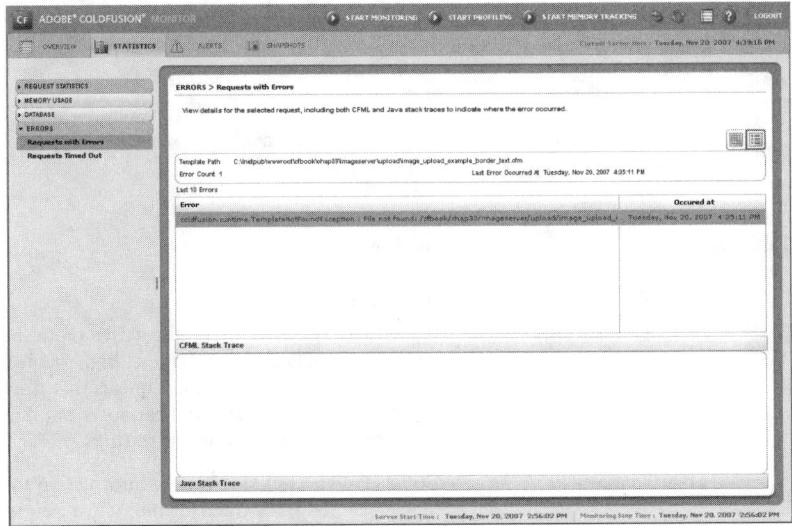

Figure 56.5

Example of the detail of a specific request error.

Starting Monitors

You will note that some items in reports show no information. This is in part because monitoring is not enabled for these items, or *collectors* (we will now refer to all discrete items in the report that generate statistics as collectors). If you look at the Server Monitor, you see three green buttons, each of which starts a specific type of monitoring. Even if you do not enable any of them, some of the reports and charts still track data. These reports are always active by default and generate essentially no overhead. They reflect data to which ColdFusion inherently has access. The rest of the reports and collectors will not generate data unless you start that monitor, profiler, or tracker by selecting Start.

Although the default reports generate almost no overhead on the targeted the basic Server Monitor, activated by selecting Start Monitoring, and the profiler, activated by selecting Start Profiler, do generate some overhead on the ColdFusion server. The memory tracker, activated by selecting Start Memory Tracking, will generate serious overhead and can, under certain conditions, cause problems with the targeted server, so make sure not to turn on your various monitors (especially the memory tracker) when you are doing performance testing or on production machines that you are not actively trying to troubleshoot.

Now let us look at how you can use the ColdFusion Monitor to help with common ColdFusion issues.

Tracking Memory Utilization

Almost all ColdFusion developers have at one time or another wondered how variables such as `session` and `application` are affecting their applications and the system memory. You can get a lot of information simply by going to the Statistics > Request Statistics > Active Sessions report. You can view application and server variables in use using Statistics > Memory Usage > Application Scope Memory Usage and Server Scope Memory Usage, respectively. If you do this on a server that is not under load, you can see that each of variables shows a size value of 0KB, but simply double-clicking a variable allows you to drill down and see a detail view, which shows the variable name, value, and size in bytes.

You can drill down into both application and session variables, but session variables also have another optional report: a chart of active sessions over time. This report can be immensely helpful in debugging strange session behavior.

You have even more insight into how your application is using memory when you enable the memory monitor by selecting Start Memory Tracking. When you enable this monitor, you can see each request's memory usage and even how a specific scope (`var`, `session`, `application`, and so on) and type are using that memory.

Under Statistics > Memory Usage are a number of useful reports:

- **Memory Usage Summary.** This report shows a graph of estimated memory usage by memory scopes on the server, including the server scope, application scope, and session scope. This report can give you a general idea of how much memory the JVM is using (see Chapter 58, "Scaling with J2EE," for more information on the JVM) as well as which scopes are using the most memory.
- **Requests by Memory Usage.** This report lists requests using the most memory. You can view a list or a detailed view.
- **CF Threads by Memory Usage.** This report lists the threads using the most memory.
- **Queries by Memory Usage.** This report lists the queries using the most memory. This report provides great insight into what is generally the greatest bottleneck in any ColdFusion Application: the database. This report allows you to quickly identify queries that may need tuning or caching.
- **Sessions by Memory Usage.** This report lists the sessions that use the most memory.
- **Application Scope Memory Usage.** This report lists the application scopes that use the most memory. The detail list shows application scope variables that use the most memory.
- **Server Scope Memory Usage.** This report shows server scope variables using the most memory.

Through careful use of these reports, you can measure the impact of code changes and find bugs that are creating memory leaks or causing other problems. You can also use the Memory Usage Summary report to help tune your JVM.

Monitoring the Database

As stated before, one of the biggest bottlenecks in any ColdFusion application is the database, and it is often particularly hard to troubleshoot, monitor, and debug ColdFusion interactions with the database. The ColdFusion Server Monitor, though, provides a number of reports to assist you; choose Statistics > Database. These reports are as follows:

- Active Queries. This report shows all active queries that take longer to load than the threshold specified on the Slowest Queries report. You can view a list or a detailed view.
- Slowest Queries. This report provides the Slowest Queries report and the Slowest Queries by Average report (as different tabs). Before you use this report, you need to select Start Monitoring and Start Profiling. Each report shows queries along with the template name and line number. The Slowest Queries report shows specific instances of a query that is slow, along with the SQL statement for the query. The detail view includes the SQL statement.
- Slowest Queries by Average. This report shows, by average, which queries are slow. This report and the Slowest Queries report can be invaluable in identifying performance issues.
- Cached Queries. This report lists cached queries as a list or detailed view for an individual query.
- Query Cache Status. This report shows a graph of the cached queries, the estimated memory that the query cache consumes, and the query cache-to-hit ratio. Performance increases as the query cache-to-hit ratio increases.
- Pool Status. This report lists ColdFusion's data sources, whether an application on the server is using a data source, and the number of connections.
- Most Frequently Run Queries. This report shows which queries were executed the most. This report provides a great way to see which queries are the best candidates for tuning.

A common way to use database reports is to find the slowest, largest, and most commonly run queries in your application. Starting from a performance baseline in your testing environment, you should run your load tests while using the ColdFusion Server Monitor to look at each of these reports; then identify which queries you may want to tune. Always try to correlate your most frequently run queries with your slowest queries and tune the queries that are both slow and constantly run to get the most impact from your tuning efforts.

Monitoring ColdFusion Errors

To create a high-performance application, you want to remove as many application errors as possible. In the past, ColdFusion developers have had a hard time debugging ColdFusion applications as errors are generated under production usage because you usually have to either turn on debugging in the ColdFusion Administrator (which has a huge impact on performance) or mine the log files on the ColdFusion server. Worse is when you have users reporting problems with your server and you cannot easily correlate their problems with your error logs. The ColdFusion Server Monitor can assist here as well. By selecting Start Profiling and then choosing Statistics > Errors, you can get access to two reports that will help you track down problems in requests:

- Requests with Errors. This report lists requests generating errors by template path and last occurrence. Double-clicking the error allows you to drill down to see the most recent error, time of the error, error message, CFML stack trace, and Java stack trace.
- Requests Timed Out. This report shows which requests have timed out by template path and last occurrence. Double-clicking the request allows you to see a detail view that shows the path of the template, number of times the request timed out, most recent response time, last time of request, last estimated request size, and CFML stack trace.

Using the ColdFusion Server Monitor to monitor your errors as they happen on the server can save you an immense amount of time trying to correlate log files. Combining the error reports with your other reporting options can help you more quickly understand the nature of a problem. For instance, if you are seeing a large number of timed-out requests along with Java out-of-memory errors, you can turn on your memory tracking monitor to see if your Java heap is full. You then can look at your memory usage summary to see whether your application scope is taking an abnormal amount of memory and, if so, by clicking Application Scope Memory Usage, exactly which application variable is causing the problem.

Using Server Statistics for Tuning

ColdFusion Server Monitor also allows you to see a large number of common performance metrics and statistics that usually would require you to use a more traditional performance monitor. You can see these statistics reports by choosing Statistics > Request Statistics. The reports are as follows:

- Active Requests. This report shows all active requests that take longer to load than the request interval specified in the ColdFusion Server Monitor settings (the icon near the help question mark at the upper right of the application). Requests include all browser requests, Web Services, gateways, and Flash Remoting. You can double-click a request or select a detail view or click the icon for a detail view and see the template path, request type, thread name, time, client IP, memory used by the request, CFML stack trace, and all the scope variables. To see all request graphs in one view, click Chart. The graph shows requests the server is currently processing and queued requests.
- Active ColdFusion Threads. This report lists all currently active threads launched by `CFTHREAD`. You can double-click the thread to see a detailed view or click the graph icon to see a graph of active threads.
- Slowest Requests. This report lists the slowest requests by template path and response time in seconds specified by the Request Slower Than threshold in this report, which allows you to define the number of seconds. You can control the list size using the List Up To field to set the number of requests to view in this report. You can double-click a request and see a detailed view including the template path, time executed, request size in

kilobytes, response time for the request, average response time for that template, minimum response time, and maximum response time, as well as request scope variables, the top-10 slowest tags and functions in that request, and the CFML stack trace.

- Slowest ColdFusion Threads. This report lists the slowest ColdFusion threads by spawned template path and average response time specified exactly as in the Slowest Requests report.
- Active Sessions. This report shows all the active sessions by session ID, client IP, application name, and session size in kilobytes. You can view the report as a list, detailed view, or graph of active sessions. The graph displays the active sessions and the number of users logged in to the server.
- Cumulative Server Usage. This report summarizes the requests that have cumulatively used the most CPU time as determined by the average response time for the request and its total number of hits. Very fast templates may be listed at the top of this report if they are the most commonly called templates, or if you use Fusebox you may see only `index.cfm` files listed here. The detailed view of this report provides the template path of the request, total CPU time used as a percentage, number of hits, last time of the request, last response time, average execution time, minimum execution time, maximum execution time, last request size in kilobytes, and average request size in kilobytes. You can also see a graph of request-versus-CPU usage.
- Highest Hit Counts. This report shows the requests that have the highest hit count by template path, hit count, average execution time in seconds, and average request time in kilobytes. You can also view this report as a graph.
- Template Cache Status. This report presents two graphs showing information about the ColdFusion Template cache (the template cache is where the ColdFusion server stores compiled CFM and CFC templates in memory). The first graph shows the number of cache hits over time and the cache-to-hit ratio, which is the number of cache hits in relation to the number of cache misses. *Cache hits* refers to the templates retrieved from the cache. *Cache misses* refers to the templates that must be compiled before being placed in the cache. A server that is performing well should have a high cache-to-hit ration. The second graph shows whether the template total cache-to-hit ratio is low; if your template cache is close to the same size as the cache size set in the server settings in the ColdFusion Administrator, you should consider increasing the size of the cache by going to Server Settings > Caching in the ColdFusion Administrator.
- Request Throttle Data. This report lists all requests that the ColdFusion server throttles because not enough memory is available to handle them as defined in Server Settings > Settings in the ColdFusion Administrator. These requests are then pushed into the ColdFusion server queue.

As you can see, the ColdFusion Server Monitor request statistics provide a very granular and detailed view of how the application is performing at any time and over time. The capability to use reports such as Slowest Requests to monitor which requests and templates might be bottlenecks and then dive into the request and see exactly which tags and functions along the request execution path are taking the most time is an incredibly powerful tool.

The Server Monitor also allows you to see over time which parts of your site are consuming the most resources or are the most active in receiving hits, helping you make decisions about whether you need to increase your cache size, whether you may need to change the number of threads for a particular service, and more. As you will see in the next section, you can use the ColdFusion Server Monitor not only to obtain information when you actively use the monitor but also to receive notification when the ColdFusion server has some sort of problem—for example, when response times start exceeding 20 seconds—and even to take action, such as killing threads or running code you have defined.

ColdFusion Monitor Alerts and Snapshots

One of the most powerful features of the ColdFusion Server Monitor is the capability to create alerts that essentially allow you define specific events or thresholds that occur on the ColdFusion server and an action to be taken when the event or threshold is reached. The ColdFusion Server Monitor alerts can be reached by going to the monitor and selecting the Alerts tab. The Alerts view simply shows you all the alerts that have happened by alert type, alert status, time, and alert message. To define new alert conditions, select Alert Configuration.

You can enable and configure four types of alerts:

- **Unresponsive Server.** When enabled, this alert is triggered when threads do not respond within a time defined by you in the Busty Thread Time field. The Hung Thread Count is the number of threads executing that exceeded the Busy Thread Time threshold before the event triggered. All four alerts allow you to select the same five actions: send email, dump a snapshot, kill threads running longer than a interval defined by you in seconds, reject any new requests, and execute a custom CFC.
- **Slow Server.** When enabled, this alert is triggered when the response time threshold is below the average response time of requests on the server. You can define the response time in seconds in the Response Time Threshold field. You can trigger the same actions for this alert as you can with the Unresponsive Server alert.
- **JVM Memory.** When enabled, this alert is triggered when the ColdFusion JVM uses more memory that the threshold defined by you in megabytes in the JVM Memory Threshold field. Unlike with the other alerts, you can perform an additional action: garbage collection (see Chapter 58 for more information on the JVM and garbage collection).
- **Timeouts.** When enabled, this alert is triggered when the request timeout count defined in the Timeouts Count field is within the time internal in seconds defined in the Time Interval field. You can perform the same actions on this alert as for the Unresponsive Server alert.

For all of these alerts, you can define the email address for alerts to be sent to on the Email Settings tab. Alerts are especially powerful in that they allow you to create custom event handlers in the form of CFCs; such an event handler, for instance, might email multiple people, or not send an email notice until the specific alert has been raised more than once (for example, 10 times in an hour for a slow server). If you want to use your own CFCs, all you need to do is add the path to the CFC in the Processing CFC field of the alert. Furthermore, when creating custom CFCs for alerts, you need to use two functions, `onAlertStart()` and `onAlertEnd()`, which accept a structure as an argument and do not return anything. They are defined like this:

- **`onAlertStart()`.** This function is called when the alert is triggered and is passed a structure that contains all the information about the settings for the alert that was activated.
- **`onAlertEnd()`.** This function is called when the alert is not valid any more, and a structure is passed to this function that contains the alert settings when the alert was disabled.

Another option you can perform in an alert or by choosing Snapshots > Trigger Snapshot is to take a snapshot. A snapshot is literally a snapshot in time of your ColdFusion server's health in regard to:

- Number and type of requests
- JVM memory usage
- Server, application, and session scope memory usage
- Throttle queue size and memory usage
- Information about cached queries
- Status of the database pool
- Java stack trace

All of this information is critical in understanding what may have caused an alert and in helping you with your debugging.

Although the ColdFusion Server Monitor provides a number of ways to check the health of your server, monitor your server, and manage your server and stay aware of possible worrisome events, the ColdFusion developers at Adobe realize that there may be other things that you, as the ColdFusion server administrator, want that the ColdFusion Server Monitor does not provide. For these cases, you can use the Server Monitor API.

Server Monitor API

Adobe has, as with other parts of the ColdFusion Administrator, opened an API for the ColdFusion Server Monitor, allowing server administrators to programmatically perform server monitor tasks using `servermonitor.cfc`. There are too many methods for `servermonitor.cfc` to cover in this book, but you can easily view the API by opening your browser and going to `http://localhost/`

CFIDE/adminapi/servermonitoring.cfc. Using the API is just like working with any other CFC except that you have to pass your ColdFusion Administrator login password to the CFC, as shown in Listing 56.2.

Listing 56.2 getApplicationScopeMemory.cfm—Viewing Application Scope Memory Usage

```
<cfscript>
  // Login to the ColdFusion Administrator.
   adminObj = createObject("component","cfide.adminapi.administrator");
   adminObj.login("youradminpassword");

   // Instantiate the Server Monitor object.
   myObj = createObject("component","cfide.adminapi.servermonitoring");

   //  Get the data
   memData = myObj.getAllApplicationScopesMemoryUsed();
</cfscript>

<!---  Application Scope Memroy Usage  --->
Application Scope Memroy Usage :<br />
<cfdump var="#memData#">
```

As you can see in Listing 56.2, all we did is create an instance of the ColdFusion Administrator CFC, call the login method, create an instance of the Server Monitor CFC, call the getAllApplicationScopesMemoryUsed() function, which returns a structure, and then use CFDUMP to display the data. While this example is somewhat trivial, you are constrained in no way other than your specific requirements and creativity since the full API is exposed to you.

Deciding What to Do Next

After you have a good grasp of your site's current performance, you can start looking for bottlenecks and performance issues. Every ColdFusion site is unique in one way or another, so it is hard to generalize about specific symptoms and their relationships to performance problems. One site may have a custom integration routine that downloads Web orders to an order processing system. Another site may have integrated ColdFusion with an Open Market transaction server. Many sites need to interface with a legacy mainframe database or with third-party applications. If you have examined all the non-ColdFusion bottleneck possibilities and still need to improve your ColdFusion server's performance, you have two options: optimizing the code, or adding more servers.

Some Issues to Consider When Looking for Performance Problems

A typical ColdFusion-driven site is fairly complex. Many factors, such as databases and network layout, contribute to performance. Given the possible number of these factors, your bottleneck is likely to lie outside ColdFusion or to indirectly depend on ColdFusion.

A good step, if you are experiencing performance problems, is to examine closely using the Server Monitoring tool the pages that users were requesting at the time of the problem. If you use the Server Monitoring tool and cannot find any issues with your application code, queries, and so on, then perhaps the issue is outside the ColdFusion server. There are a number of issues that can cause performance problems for your application outside of ColdFusion itself. Let's look at a list of possible bottleneck points on a typical ColdFusion server that . you should examine before you consider scaling.

Typical Bottlenecks

You should consider several possible sources of bottlenecks:

- **Web-Server Bandwidth**. Check to see how much bandwidth your network provider allocates for your site. If you have substantial traffic, a bottleneck might be caused if the provider institutes a cap on bandwidth (called *bandwidth throttling*), or if the networking equipment in place poses physical limitations on bandwidth.
- **Web-Server Performance**. Preset limits to simultaneous HTTP requests can create a bottleneck.
- **Other Processes Running on the Same Server**. Each additional process uses critical CPU and memory, even if it is just a small amount. These tiny amounts can accumulate quickly and impact performance. Conduct an audit of your server: If you are running Windows, use the Task Manager to determine how many processes are running and how they are affecting your resources. If you are running Unix operating systems, run the appropriate command to view open processes (for example, `ps ax` on Linux).
- **Hard Drive Speed**. This is not just for `<cffile>`; ColdFusion must pull templates off the disk if they are not in cache. Don't forget your `application.cfm` files and `<cfinclude>` files. Even if you are caching templates, ColdFusion still checks the file on disk to see whether it has been modified, unless you specifically tell ColdFusion to trust cache files.
- **Network Latency**. If you are communicating with other machines on the local network, latency generally should not be an issue. However, if you are communicating with machines on remote networks, or if communications travel through switches or routers—especially at varying speeds—check the response time of each machine with which you are communicating. You can do this with a simple ping command to get the response time of a particular machine or by using the traceroute command (`tracert` on Windows) to determine whether any slow hops exist between you and the target machine.
- **Database Server Performance**. While using the Server Monitor to check for long-running or poorly executing queries is important, often to get the best performance from a ColdFusion application using a database, you will need to optimize the database itself using indexes, views, and so on.
- **JDBC Configuration**. Your Server Monitor can point to issues with your database performance, but often you will need to tune your database connection pool. Tune your maximum simultaneous connections and cached queries settings. Sometimes using different JDBC drivers will result in improved performance, or even just upgrading to the latest version of a driver will help.

- **<cfmail>, <cfftp>, <cfhttp>.** The performance of other servers (SMTP, FTP, HTTP, and such) may affect the performance of your application. The Internet latency to get there and back may be a bottleneck. Create a system probe to determine whether one of these servers is timing out, or you can write a `.cfm` page to report each server's response times.

Understanding all the bottlenecks in your application is crucial to understanding what you actually need to monitor so that you can actually figure out what is wrong with your application. Although the ColdFusion Server Monitor provides the capability to gain deep insight into how your ColdFusion Server is performing, there are a number of other things that may be affecting your application that the monitor cannot provide information for. In these cases, you need to use other tools to understand what might be affecting your system as a whole. Furthermore, sometimes you have to dig through log files to find the real culprit, which may be faulty drivers, bugs in the JVM, or a host of other issues that cannot be resolved by better coding, selecting a few options, or making some minor changes. The good news is that most important bottlenecks in a ColdFusion application end up being physical limitations of hardware, your network, and so on, and at that point you can look to methods of scaling your application to overcome these bottlenecks.

➜ For more about how to do this, look at Chapter 57, "Scaling with ColdFusion," and Chapter 58.

CHAPTER 57

Scaling with ColdFusion

IN THIS CHAPTER

In the first two chapters of this book, you learned about high availability and about monitoring system performance. In the two chapters following this one, you'll learn about scaling with Java and managing session state in a cluster. Here in this chapter we'll concentrate on what you need to know about scaling with ColdFusion 8.

We'll cover scaling considerations, writing ColdFusion 8 applications that will scale, keeping server data in sync, the differences between hardware and software load balancing options, scaling with ColdFusion Load Balancing, and scaling with hardware-based load-balancing devices. When looking at scaling options and strategies with ColdFusion 8, we'll focus on your (the developer's) point of view. This chapter highlights what you can do to build highly scalable ColdFusion 8 applications that can be deployed on one, two, or many ColdFusion 8 servers.

The Importance of Scaling

One way to define scaling is as "the ability to enlarge or reduce a design." In the computer science world, scaling applies generally to growing an application to handle more traffic, tasks, and transactions—but that is not the only definition. For this reason, we're going to focus on the issue of scaling as the ability to grow your ColdFusion application to handle a larger load, process more transactions, and work more easily overall.

Generally, when you look at scaling ColdFusion applications, there are several distinct areas to consider. These areas are:

- Hardware (your application server, database server, etc.)
- Software (how you design and build and deploy your application)
- Infrastructure (the network, switches, routers, and hardware load balancing systems)
- Special scaling systems (third-party caching tools, proxy servers, and other methods of scaling an application that stand apart from the main system)

Since scaling is such a substantial topic, this chapter addresses only the most common aspects of scaling. This chapter's purpose is to give you a working understanding of some of the major factors and considerations involved in scaling a application. Before you embark on developing a large-scale, high-availability system yourself, you need to be thoroughly comfortable with all the subject material in this chapter or consult someone who is.

Almost all accepted best practices and approaches to scaling ColdFusion, and Web applications in general, involve clustering which we touched on in Chapter 55, "Understanding High Availability." Clustering does not only offer the possibility for failover but is generally the easiest method for scaling an application horizontally. In this case horizontally means the addition of servers while vertically means the increasing of servers resources through the addition of things like CPUs and more memory.

Clustering allows you to create a group of servers that act like a single system. Most modern clustering approaches take advantage of hardware, software, and networking strategies that allow you to easily add or remove servers to an existing cluster without having to experience any downtime.

Running one Web site on one server is relatively straightforward: You know that every Web request goes to the same Web server software and ColdFusion 8 service, with the same settings and environment. But as soon as you add a second server, you are faced with a host of technical challenges. The following sections examine some of the implications. Later in this chapter, we'll review some of the principal technologies that enable you to effectively distribute your traffic across multiple servers, and how such technologies are implemented.

Scaling Considerations

There are many issues to consider when you're building a clustered environment. Proper planning of your application architecture is important, as well. Many factors are involved, and laying out a plan before purchasing and building your clustered environment can save you many headaches later. Questions you may want to ask include:

- **How many servers do you need?** The number of servers will depend on how much traffic you expect and how Web site functionality is distributed in your server farm.
- **What types of servers and operating systems do you want to deploy?** Choosing servers and operating systems depends on many factors, including your team's skill sets and experience in these areas.
- **How do you balance traffic between the servers?** The methods that you select for load balancing may affect your choice of load balancer. You may want users to stay on one machine for the length of their session. Failover and server monitoring are other considerations when balancing traffic in a cluster.
- **How will you keep the Web site content in sync among all the servers, and how will you deploy the Web site?** This is potentially one of the most troublesome areas in Web site maintenance. Not only do you need to keep Web site content in sync, but each server requires periodic configuration changes, patches, and hot fixes to be deployed as well.

We'll try to answer some of these questions by breaking the Web site infrastructure into major elements and then discussing their implementation. These major elements include tiered application architecture, server and hardware components, and cluster load balancing.

What do you have when you have a Web site? You have a server or servers with operating systems, files, directories, configurations, hardware, and software. Your environment may be tiered, consisting of the Web server, application server, and a separate database server. Let's discuss this tiered application architecture first.

Tiered Application Architecture

One of the most common approaches to scaling a system is *tiering*. What tiering means is to logically or physically separate and encapsulate a set of processes or functionality. Generally when you are looking to scale a system, you want to consider physical tiering where you separate specific system functions physically, by putting them on their own machines or clusters. For example, most simple ColdFusion applications are *three-tiered applications*, where the browser is the client tier, the Web server and ColdFusion are the application tiers, and a database is the data tier. Complex applications can have any number of tiers, and it's not uncommon see authentication tiers, business object tiers, and others. This sort of architecture is usually called a *physical architecture*, in that the actual physical separation of software systems is represented on specific groups of servers or hardware.

Figure 57.1 shows a three-tiered Web site architecture where ColdFusion 8 is installed in the application server tier. This configuration can be accomplished by installing ColdFusion 8 on a supported J2EE application server platform. For more about deploying ColdFusion 8 on J2EE, see Chapter 58, "Scaling with J2EE."

Figure 57.1

Three-tiered server farm with ColdFusion 8.

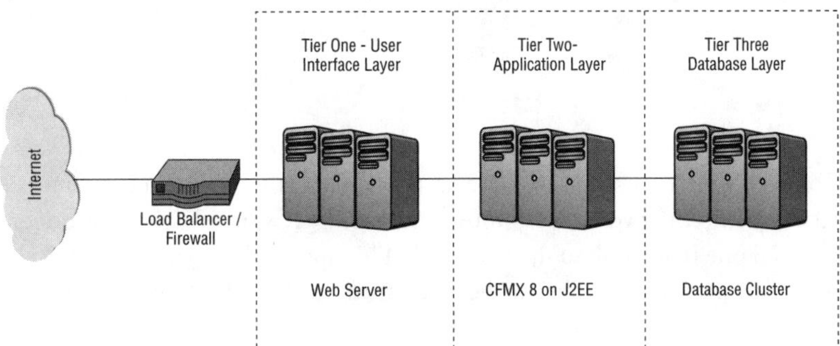

Front-End Servers Vs. Back-End Servers

When creating your system infrastructure, it's important to design with security in mind. One of the best ways to do this is to limit public exposure to only those systems that absolutely need to be exposed, such as Web servers, and nothing else. This public set of servers and the network are often referred to as the *front end*; servers on the private network are referred to as the *back end.*

The front end is the network segment between the public Internet and your Web cluster. The front end should be optimized for speed. Place a switched segment with lots of bandwidth in front of your Web servers. Your two primary goals on the front end are to avoid collisions and to minimize the number of hops (intervening network devices) between your Web servers and the public Internet. If you are using hardware-based load balancing, you could have a hardware load balancer in front of your front-end network.

The back end is the network segment between your Web cluster and your supporting servers. Because your support servers need to talk only to your Web servers and your LAN, you don't need to make this segment directly accessible to the public Internet. In fact, you might do better to deliberately prevent any access to these machines from the public Internet by using private IP addresses or a firewall. Doing so enables you to take advantage of useful network protocols that would be a security risk if they were made available to the public Internet. In addition, be sure to spend some time trying to minimize collisions on your back-end network. A configuration like this might look like that in Figure 57.2. You have either a single firewall that separates the public from the private system or—better yet—a firewall in front of your Web servers and another one in front of your back-end servers, which are connected to the public server via a trusted connection.

Figure 57.2

This figure shows how a firewall can separate servers available to the public Internet from database servers and others systems on the back-end or private internal network.

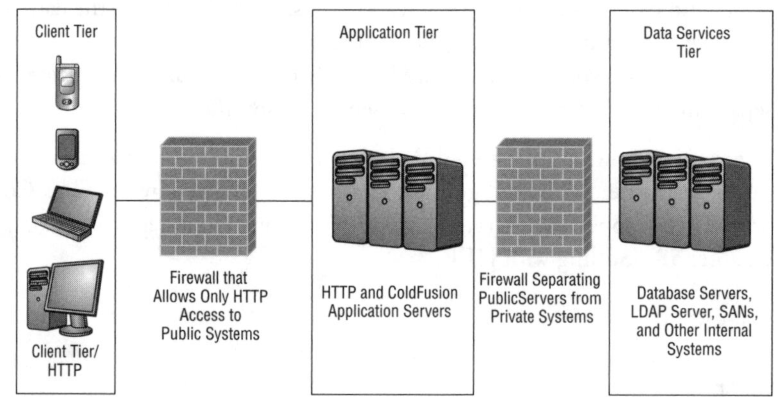

To protect the back-end servers from unwanted traffic, you can implement *dual-homed servers*. This strategy employs two network interface cards (NICs) in a Web server: one that speaks to the front end and one that speak to the back end. This approach improves your Web server's network performance by preventing collisions between front-end and back-end packets.

NOTE

If you choose to dual-home your Windows 2000 servers, you must contend with a particularly nasty problem known as dead gateway detection. Your server must detect whether a client across the Net has ended communications even though the request has not been fulfilled. This problem commonly occurs when a user clicks the Stop button on a Web browser in the middle of a download and goes somewhere else. If errors occur, Windows 2000 will eventually stop responding. The solution to this problem in Windows is an advanced networking topic and beyond the scope of this book. You can find information on this subject at the Microsoft Web site at `www.microsoft.com/`. The concept in general is covered in RFC-816. The full text of this RFC is available on many public sites throughout the Internet.

In a dual-homed configuration, depending on which type of load balancing you are using, you can use private, nonroutable IP addresses to address machines on the back-end server farm (see Figure 57.2). Using private nonroutables introduces another layer of complexity to your setup but can be a significant security advantage.

Server and Hardware Components

Several considerations regarding server and hardware configurations crop up when you attempt to scale your site. These issues include the number of CPUs per box, the amount of RAM, and the hard drive speed and server configuration in general.

If your server is implemented with one CPU, turning it into a two-CPU system does not double your performance, even if the two processors are identical. Depending on the hardware, your operating systems, and your application, you should expect only about a 60 percent performance increase. Adding a third CPU increases the performance even less, and the fourth CPU gives an even smaller boost. This is true because each additional CPU consumes operating system resources simply to keep itself in sync with the others. Also, not every operating system or application can effectively and efficiently take advantage of multiple CPUs. Generally, if a two-processor machine is running out of processor resources, you're better off adding a second two-processor machine than adding two processors to your existing machine. To illustrate, see Figure 57.3, which shows performance gains when adding up to four CPUs on one server. Notice that the performance gains are not linear. Each additional CPU has less improvement than the preceding CPU.

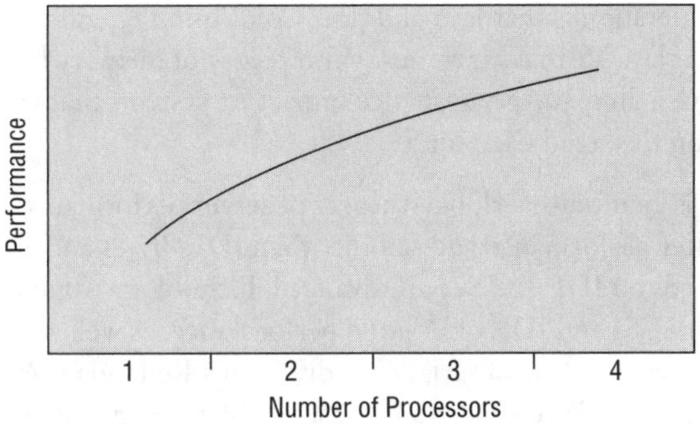

Figure 57.3

Performance gains by adding CPUs to a server are not linear.

You might ask why you would want a two-processor machine at all. Why not use four single-processor machines instead? In an abstract measure of processor utilization, you might be right. But you also must deal with problems of user experience. Even though you're not using 100 percent of the second processor on the server, you are getting a strong performance boost. With this increase, a page that takes 2 seconds to process on a one-processor box might take just over 1 second to process on a two-processor box. This can be the difference between a site that feels slow and a site with happy users. Another point in favor of two-processor machines: Many server-class machines, with configurations that support other advanced hardware features necessary for a robust server, support dual processors as part of their feature sets. If you're investing in server-class machines, adding a second processor before adding a second server can be cost effective.

Adobe has worked with Intel and Microsoft to greatly improve multiple processor performance in Windows. If you are using Windows 2000 Server, Advanced Server, DataCenter Server, Windows 2003, or Vista you will see a far better performance improvement with additional processors than you would with Windows 2000. If you are developing a new site and you haven't yet chosen a Windows-based operating system, look into Windows 2003 for better performance.

Unix environments, on the other hand, are designed to take advantage of multiple processors and use them efficiently; ColdFusion profits from the extra processing power Unix environments provide. To determine how to scale a Unix environment (that is, whether to add processing power or another server), make your best judgment using your performance-testing data. Bear in mind, however, that although adding a few more processors will definitely increase your Unix site's performance, if you have only one Web server and that server goes down, no amount of processors will beat having an additional machine for redundancy.

Linux has become especially popular among ColdFusion 8 developers and hosting companies. ColdFusion 8 performs extremely well on Red Hat Linux, as well as some other, but unsupported, distributions.

RAM is another hardware issue to consider. The bottom line is that RAM is cheap, so put as much RAM in each machine as you can afford. I recommend at least 4 GB of RAM. Additional RAM allows for more cached database queries, templates, and memory-resident data. The more RAM you have, the more information you will be able to cache in memory rather than on disk, and the faster your site will run.

Another memory consideration is that Java and thus ColdFusion 8 tend to be more memory intensive due to the nature of Java Virtual Machines. With plenty of memory that you can assign to your JVM heap, you can have a dramatic performance impact on systems that you expect to experience high usage. For more on this, read Chapter 58.

Hard-disk drive speed is an often-overlooked aspect of server performance. Traditionally, SCSI drives have offered better performance and stability than IDE drives and are usually recommended. Recently, however, speeds on IDE and Serial Advanced Technology Attachment (SATA) drives have greatly improved. Both SCSI and IDE offer good performance, as well as high availability in the case of drive failure; the same is true of serial ATA drives in a Redundant Array of Independent Drives (RAID) on a dedicated drive controller. Most production-level RAID controllers enable you to add RAM to the controller itself. This memory, called the first-in, first-out (FIFO) cache, allows recently accessed data to be stored and processed directly from the RAM on the controller. You get a pronounced speed increase from this type of system because data never has to be sought out and read from the drive.

NOTE

If you use virtualization (virtual machine software such as VMware–`http://vmware.com`) it is especially important to have fast hard drives since virtual machines perform significant drive input and output. For optimal performance, get the fastest possible hard drives you can.

If you use a RAID controller with a lot of RAM on board, you also should invest in redundant power supplies and a good uninterruptible power system (UPS). The RAM on the RAID controller is written back to the hard disk only if the system is shut down in an orderly fashion. If your system loses power, all the data in RAM on the controller is lost. If you don't understand why this is bad, imagine that the record of your last 50 orders for your product were in the RAM cache, instead of written to the disk, when the power failed. The more RAM you have on the controller, the greater the magnitude of your problem in the event of a power outage.

Many people believe that all servers should make use of RAID, but it often makes more sense to use RAID only on systems that are actually doing substantial data storage and file I/O, such as database servers. Often, a whole application layer is actually designed to run in an application server cluster's RAM; thus, minimal RAID or even mirrored drives might make sense. This decision will in large part be dictated by your application design, architecture, and available budget.

The type of load-balancing technology you use has a big impact on the way you build your system. If you are using load-balancing technology that distributes traffic equally to all servers, you want each of your systems to be configured identically, depending on that tier. (Your Web servers will likely have much different hardware requirements than your database servers.) Most dedicated load-balancing hardware can detect a failed server and stop sending traffic to it. If your system works this way, and you have some extra capacity in your cluster, it's acceptable for each box to be somewhat less reliable because the others can pick up the slack if it goes down. But if you're using a simple load-balancing approach such as round-robin DNS (RRDNS), which can't detect a down server, you need each box to be as reliable as possible because a single failure means some of your users cannot use your site.

Because you want your users to have a uniform experience on your site, regardless of which server responds to their requests, keep your system configurations as close to identical as possible. Unfortunately, because of the advanced complexity of today's operating systems and applications, this consistency is a lot harder to accomplish than it sounds. Identical configurations also help to alleviate quality assurance issues for your Web site. If your servers are not identical, your Web site may not function the same way on the different servers. This condition makes managing your Web site unnecessarily complex. If you must have different servers in your configuration, plan to spend extra time performing quality assurance on your Web applications to ensure that they will run as expected on all servers in the cluster.

Considerations for Choosing a Load-Balancing Option

Before deploying your clustered server farm, consider how you want your servers to handle and distribute load, as well as what your budget is. Also take into account how much traffic you expect to handle and how much that traffic will grow. There are a variety of approaches for handling and distributing load, including dedicated load-balancing hardware, load-balancing software, and RRDNS. Software and hardware load-balancing systems employ user-request distribution algorithms, which can distribute user requests to a pre-specified server, to a server with the least load, or through other methods. A round-robin configuration passes each user request to the next available server. This is sometimes performed regardless of the selected server's current load. Round-robin configurations may involve DNS changes. Consult with your network administrator when discussing this option.

Round-Robin DNS

The RRDNS method of load balancing takes advantage of some capabilities that are the result of the way the Internet's domain name system handles multiple IP addresses with the same domain name. To configure RRDNS, you should be comfortable with making changes to your DNS server.

CAUTION

Be careful when making DNS server changes. Making an incorrect DNS change is roughly equivalent to sending out change-of-address and change-of-phone-number forms to incorrect destinations for every one of your customers and vendors, and having no way to tell the people at the incorrect postal destination or the incorrect phone number to forward the errant mail back to you. If you broadcast incorrect DNS information, you could cut off all traffic to your site for days or weeks.

Simply put, RRDNS centers around the concept of giving your public domain name (`www.mycompany.com`) more than one IP address. You should give each machine in your cluster two domain names: one for the public domain, and one that lets you address each machine uniquely. See Table 57.1 for some examples.

Table 57.1 Examples of IP Addresses

SERVER	PUBLIC ADDRESS	MACHINE NAME	IP ADDRESS
#1	www	Web1	192.168.64.1
#2	www	Web2	192.168.64.2
#3	www	Web3	192.168.64.3

When a remote domain-name server queries your domain-name server for information about `www.mycompany.com` (because a user has requested a Web page and needs to know the address of your server), your DNS server returns one of the multiple IP addresses you've listed for `www.mycompany.com`. The remote DNS server then uses that IP address until its DNS cache expires, upon which it queries your DNS server again, possibly getting a different IP address. Each sequential request from a remote DNS server receives a different IP address as a response.

Round-robin DNS is a crude way to balance load. When a remote DNS gets one of your IP addresses in its cache, it uses that same IP address until the cache expires, no matter how many requests originate from the remote domain and regardless of whether the target IP address is responding. This type of load balancing is extremely vulnerable to what is known as the *mega-proxy problem*.

Internet service providers (ISPs) manage user connections by caching Web site content and rotating their IP addresses among users using proxy servers. This allows the ISP to manage more user connections than it has available IP addresses. A user on your e-commerce site may be in the middle of checking out, and the ISP could change its IP addresses. The user's connection to your Web site would be broken and their cart will be empty. Similarly, an ISP's cached content may point to only one of your Web servers. If that server crashes, any user who tries to access your site from the ISP is still directed to that down IP address. The user's experience will be that your site is down, even though you might have two or three other Web servers ready to respond to the request.

Because DNS caches generally take one to seven days to expire, any DNS change you make to a RRDNS cluster will take a long time to propagate. So in the case of a server crash, removing the down server's IP address from your DNS server doesn't solve the mega-proxy problem because the IP address of the down server is still in the ISP's DNS cache. You can partially correct this problem by setting your DNS record's time to live (TTL) to a very low value, so that remote DNSs are instructed to expire their records of your domain's IP address after a brief period of time. This solution can cause undue load on your DNS, however. Even with low TTL, an IP address that you remove from the RRDNS cluster might still be in the cache of some remote DNS for a week or more.

RRDNS should really only be considered for applications that need not be highly available or that do not require real failover, and are often best for systems with relatively static content. Most system designers do not even consider RRDNS a real solution to load balancing, especially in light of the plentiful software-based load balancing solutions (such as ColdFusion Load Balancing). We have included RRDNS in this discussion for the sake of completeness, as well as to make you aware of all the options available to system developers and designers.

User-Request Distribution Algorithms

Most load-balancing hardware and software devices offer customizable user-request distribution algorithms. Based on a particular algorithm, users will be directed to an available server. Hardware and software load-balancing systems offer a number of sophisticated features besides load balancing, depending on the product and vendor. Work with a knowledgeable resource to pick a product for your specific system.

User-request distribution algorithms can include the following:

- Users are directed to the server with the least amount of load or CPU utilization.
- Clustered servers are set up with a priority hierarchy. The available server with the highest priority handles the next user request.
- Web site objects can be clustered and managed when deployed with J2EE. Objects include Enterprise JavaBeans (EJBs) and servlets.
- Web server response is used to determine which server handles the user's request. For example, the fastest server in the cluster handles the next request.

The distribution algorithms listed above are not meant to be a complete list, but they do illustrate that many methods are available to choose from. They offer very granular and intelligent control over request distribution in a cluster. Choosing your load-balancing device may depend on deciding among these methods for your preferred cluster configuration.

Session State Management

Another load-balancing consideration is session-aware or "sticky" load balancing. Session-aware load balancing keeps each user on the same server as long as their session is active. This is an effective approach for applications requiring that a session's state be maintained while processing the user's requests. It fails, however, if the server fails. The user's session is effectively lost and, even if it fails over to an alternate server in the cluster, the user must restart the session and all information accumulated by the original session will no longer exist. Storing session information centrally among all clustered servers helps alleviate this issue. See Chapter 59, "Managing Session State in Clusters," for more information on implementing session state management.

Failover

Consider how you want your application to respond when a server in the cluster fails. Consider how you want to deal with loss of state information, and how you might create a state management system that is impervious to loss of a specific Web server or even a database server. An effective strategy will allow seamless failover to an alternate server without the user's knowing that a problem occurred. Utilizing a load-balancing option with centralized session state management can help maintain state for the user while the user's session is transferred to a healthy machine. Understanding the capability of your hardware and networking infrastructure and designing with specific capabilities in mind can make application developers' jobs much easier. It's important to include system administrators, system designers, and networking professionals in the cycle of application and software design.

Failover considerations also come into play with Web site deployment. You can shut down a server that is ready for deployment without having to shut down your entire Web site, enabling you to deploy to each server in your cluster, in turn, while maintaining an active functioning Web site. As each server is brought back into the cluster, another is shut down for deployment.

Mixed Web Application Environments

If your Web site consists of mixed applications and application servers, choosing your load-balancing solution becomes even more difficult. Let's take an example where your current Web site is being rewritten and transformed from an ASP (Active Server Page) Web site to a ColdFusion (CFML) Web site. Your current Web site is in the middle of this transformation, and ASP pages are co-existing with CFML pages. Not all load-balancing solutions will be able to effectively handle server load at the application level. Some will be able to handle load at the Web-server level only. In addition, session state management may not work as planned. Because ASP session and ColdFusion sessions are not necessarily known between the two systems, you may want to implement session-aware load balancing in this "mixed" environment. This type of session-aware load balancing could consist of cookies or other variables that both applications can read.

How to Write ColdFusion 8 Applications That Scale

Pay special attention to scaling issues when you are writing applications for a clustered environment. Poorly written code can suffocate any Web site, no matter how much hardware you throw at it. Successful building of applications that scale follows good coding techniques, concentrating on writing clean, well-thought-out code. Scalable code is well organized, modular in nature, structured, and free of common bottlenecks.

Code Organization

A stable and scalable application typically is the end product of careful design and planning *before* any code is written. Good software comes from good planning, and following common Software Design Life Cycle methodologies. Some attributes of good code are easy to spot: being well organized, sufficiently commented, and easy to follow. Your software should also be thoroughly documented—most people don't associate this necessity with scaling, but there is nothing worse than trying to grow, extend, and manage software over its life cycle without proper documentation.

Before you begin to write any if your application's code, design a directory structure that matches the requirements of your specific application. For example, suppose you're building a large application that makes use of a large number of images and static content. Rather than creating an image directory on each server, you might want to link to content on a separate cluster of file servers or proxy servers. You'll also want to design with encapsulation and reuse in mind. Try to employ as many of ColdFusion 8's new features as possible to create loosely coupled applications that have few dependencies on other files, allowing easier management and less complicated application changes over time.

Always decide beforehand on specific coding standards and conventions that will be enforced. This not only allows other developers to collaborate more easily, but acts as system documentation for you and future developers in maintaining the system. Along with coding conventions, consider using a specific application-development methodology or framework such as Fusebox (`www.fusebox.org`), Mach-II (`www.mach-ii.org`), or Model-Glue (`http://www.model-glue.com`), especially for large projects. Established methodologies allow groups to work together with less difficulty, and they often solve many common problems faced by most applications. Not every application will be a good fit for public methodologies, and you'll have to consider the particular skills of your team as well as the application's requirements before making that decision.

NOTE

Most ColdFusion frameworks add some overhead to your applications' performance, but the benefits offered by good design, clear organization, and a standard approach to coding often make up for the small impact on performance. At the same time, you should constantly performance-test your applications when using frameworks to make sure the framework and the way you are using it stay within acceptable performance benchmarks.

Modularity

Modular code helps promote code reuse. Code that is used many times in an application, such as a CFC for authentication, should become more stable over time as developers fix bugs and tweak it for performance. Modular code is also much easier to test, and there are a number of useful testing tools to help developers' unit-test CFCs. Well-written modular code follows good coding practices and helps you to avoid common bottlenecks. It also eases development efforts because developers do not have to rewrite this code every time they need similar functionality.

Multithreading and Asynchronous Processing

ColdFusion 8 introduces some new ways to scale applications. Not only is ColdFusion 8 faster, it now allows you to control threads at a more granular level, allowing you to select parts of code or even CFCs in which you want multiple threads executing simultaneously (for more on threads see Chapter 30, "Managing Threads," in *Adobe ColdFusion 8 Web Application Construction Kit, Volume 2: Application Development*). If you have an application that has code or components that do not execute sequentially or where multiple actions should take place at the same time, use of the new `<CFTHREAD>` tag can radically increase performance and scalability.

Another similar approach is to use gateways, introduced in ColdFusion 7, to pass asynchronous tasks outside the Web tier. This approach is particularly useful for integration tasks, scheduled operations, and so on. The use of gateways and `<CFTHREAD>` can remove many of the performance bottlenecks in common ColdFusion applications.

Streamlined, Efficient Code

Implementing best practices for Web site development is an important discipline for developers building highly scalable applications. The following example illustrates that point. The code attempts to find the name of the first administrator user. Each administrator user has a security level of 1. The code queries all users and loops through the record set searching for the first administrator record and returns their names:

```
<cfquery name="getAdminUser" datasource="db_Utility">
 SELECT * FROM tbl_User
</cfquery>

<!--- Loop until you find first user with security level of 1 --->
<cfloop query="getAdminUser">
 <cfif trim(getAdminUser.int_Security) IS 1>
 <cfset AdminName = getAdminUser.vc_name>
 </cfif>
</cfloop>

Admin User Name: <cfoutput>#AdminName#</cfoutput>
```

This example demonstrates inefficient code that can slow your application if this piece of code sustains many requests. In addition, even after it finds the first administrator record, it does not stop looping through the returned user record set. What if the user table contained thousands of records? This code would take a long time to process and consume valuable system resources.

Here's a more efficient version for finding the first administrator record and returning the name:

```
<cfquery name="getAdminUser" datasource="db_Utility">
 SELECT TOP 1 vc_name FROM tbl_User WHERE int_security = 1
</cfquery>

<cfif getAdminUser.RecordCount GT 0>
 <cfset AdminName = getAdminUser.vc_name>
</cfif>

Admin User Name: <cfoutput>#AdminName#</cfoutput>
```

This code is much more efficient and easier to understand. The query isolates only the records and columns that need to be used in the code. It will only return one record if any records have a security level of 1.

NOTE

As important as efficiency is, do not fall into the trap of trying always to write the best and most efficient code possible. Often developers will sacrifice readability, modularity, and maintainability for the sake of performance; as a general rule, this is a huge mistake. Focus on writing good, solid, maintainable code. When you do, your application will be easy to scale via the addition of more hardware–which is always cheaper and easier to budget for, and has fewer consequences than spending too much time rewriting code to get minor performance gains.

Avoiding Common Bottlenecks

The preceding example illustrated a simple way to write more efficient code. Let's look at other coding bottlenecks and discuss ways to avoid them.

Querying a Database

When writing queries to retrieve data for output on the screen or into form variables, pay careful attention to the number of records to be returned and the structure of the SQL itself. A bottleneck, common to complex queries, results from a query returning more records than are required and using only a subset of the returned records. Such a query should be rewritten to return only the required records.

In addition, database software is much more efficient at processing database requests than ColdFusion is. For a highly scalable Web site, it's best to create views for selecting data, and stored procedures for inputting, adding, and deleting data to and from the database. Design your ColdFusion templates to call these views and stored procedures to interact with the database. Asking the database server to perform this kind of work is much more efficient and tends to stabilize performance.

Here is an example of a poorly coded set of queries to retrieve data. This code is not scalable and will adversely affect Web site performance. Notice that the same table is queried twice to return different data. One query, in this case, would be sufficient:

```
<cfquery name="getUser" datasource="db_Utility">
 SELECT vc_name FROM tbl_User WHERE int_userID = 26
</cfquery>

<cfset userName = getUser.vc_name>

Hello <cfoutput>#userName#</cfoutput>

some more code here ......

<cfquery name="getUserInfo" datasource="db_Utility">
 SELECT int_userid, vc_username, vc_password, vc_email, dt_createdate FROM tbl_User
WHERE vc_name = '#userName#'
</cfquery>

Here is the information you requested:<br>

<cfoutput query="getUserInfo">
 Your User ID: #int_userid#<br>
 Your User Name: #vc_username#<br>
 Your Password: #vc_password#<br>
```

```
 Your Email: #vc_email#<br>
 Date you joined: #dt_createdate#
</cfoutput>
```

As you can see, only one query need be called to return this data. This is a common mistake.

Absolute Path, Relative Path, and Other Links

One of the more common problems when working with ColdFusion is confusion about when to use the absolute or relative path for a link. Both methods can be employed, but you must be cognizant of the impact of each approach when you are coding for a clustered environment. Here are a couple of questions to ask before utilizing absolute or relatives paths in your application:

- **Will the link be moved at any point in time?** If the answer is yes, an absolute path will be a more viable option, since it is assumed that the new path can be mapped on the Web server to be the same mapping as before.
- **Does the path exist under the current subdirectory?** If the answer is yes, then relative path mapping will work.

NOTE

Relative path is relative to the current template. Absolute path is the path relative to the root of the Web site.

Hard-coding links will cause problems with clustered machines. Say that you have an upload facility on your Web site that allows users to upload documents. The code needs to know a physical path in order to upload the documents to the correct place. Server 1 contains the mapped drive E pointing to the central file server where all the documents are stored. The file server has an `uploadedfiles` directory located on its D drive, so the path can be set to `e:\uploadedfiles`. But Server 2 does not contain a mapped drive named E pointing to the file server. If you deploy your code from Server 1 to Server 2, the upload code will break because Server 2 does not know where `e:\uploadedfiles` is. It's better to use Universal Naming Convention (UNC) syntax in the upload path: `\\servername\d\uploadedfiles`. Note that having one file server in the configuration described creates a single point of failure for your Web site.

NOTE

Universal Naming Convention (UNC) is a standard method for identifying the server name and the network name of a resource. UNC names use one of the following formats: `\\servername\netname\path\filename` or `\\servername\netname\devicename`.

Nesting Files Too Deeply

Nesting files using `cfinclude`, `cfmodule`, or any other mechanism is considered a valuable tool for developers in building complex applications. Nesting too many files with in other files, however, can cause code to become unmanageable and virtually incomprehensible. A developer working on a Web site where nesting is especially deep may eventually stop trying to follow all the levels of nesting and just attempt write new workaround code. This approach may cause the application to function in unexpected ways. Too many nested files in your code can also affect performance. In part, this is how ColdFusion compiles things like file includes and `cfmodule` calls but also just the number of functions and processes that a file made up of many nested files will call.

It is always better to try to simplify your code to encapsulate specific functions into highly cohesive units and to call as few operations as necessary per application request. Doing so will streamline the application, reduce nested layers, improve code readability, and increase performance. This all goes back to planning and designing *before* you code—nesting problems usually occur in applications whose requirements have changed over time.

Keeping Web Site Servers in Sync

Keeping Web sites in sync across multiple servers in a clustered environment has never been an easy task. Not only do you need to keep content and Web pages in sync, server settings need to be maintained as well. The Archive and Deploy capabilities in ColdFusion 8 provide improved Web site maintenance. We will discuss this functionality along with some other options in the following section.

What to Maintain?

When you are attempting to maintain your Web site across multiple servers, what do you need to maintain? This is sometimes a tough question to answer if you are not solely responsible for all of the Web servers, their operating systems, and Web applications. Typically these responsibilities are shared among several individuals, each with their own methods for maintaining settings. You might want to consider the following settings when you're attempting to keep your Web site servers in sync:

- Operating system and Web server software updates, service packs, security patches, and hot fixes
- Operating system configuration settings for services, Registry, installed software, mappings, and so on
- Web server configuration settings, including virtual path mappings, security settings, Web site configurations, and other Web server settings
- JDBC and database settings
- ColdFusion administrator settings
- HTML pages and images, CFML pages, and so on

Keeping up with all these different sets of configurations can be a gargantuan task requiring patience and attention to detail. There are several methods for performing these functions, but no one method performs all of them by itself. You may want to employ a combination of techniques for deploying and maintaining your clustered server farm. Here is a partial list of options:

- **FTP**. Copy files and directory structures from server to server. Disadvantages: Not automated, requires separate connections to each server, and only covers files and directories.

- **Deployment Software**. Purchase software that performs automated copying of files, directories, and other settings. Disadvantages: Might not offer all functionality required.
- **Roll Your Own**. Create your own program that gathers all required information and deploys to the cluster. Disadvantages: Requires time to write and test code. May not offer all functionality required.
- **ColdFusion 8 Archive and Deploy**. Built into ColdFusion 8 and is an easy method for deploying your Web site directories, content, and ColdFusion Administrator settings.

Archive and Deploy

ColdFusion 8 has several methods to deploy ColdFusion applications—including some new ones such as sourceless deployment, which lets you deploy your ColdFusion application without including the original source code! To read more about these exciting new features, refer to Chapter 60, "Deploying Applications."

Other Options

Many other options exist for deploying applications and copying files. None of these options will deploy ColdFusion 8 administrator settings, but they can deploy other information to your Web servers. Options include source-control software like Concurrent Version Control (CVS) the free open source de-facto standard for version control or Visual Source Safe from Microsoft. Visual Source Safe, for example, can deploy files and directories to servers by pulling the latest version from its database and copying to a working directory.

NOTE

If you are not using version control, you should. There is no good reason not to. Many excellent free and commercial version-control programs are available that are not only easy to use but can actually save you time developing software. More importantly, they will protect you from accidental overwrites, lost code, and various other hazards.

Other software, such as Robocopy from the Microsoft Windows Resource Kit, can copy files and directories by means of scripts. Using Robocopy is as simple as invoking it from the command line, specifying a target and source directory, and pressing Enter. Robocopy also supplies several useful command-line attributes that enable you to customize your replication system. Robocopy enables you to use UNCs so you can access content on NT servers across a network. After you determine your content-replication scheme, simply put your Robocopy command in a CMD file somewhere in the system path, and trigger it with the Windows 2000 Task Scheduler Utility.

Mirroring software such as Symantec's Ghost will create an exact image of your server and allow you to copy this image onto another server. This provides a complete solution for creating an exact copy of each server in your environment.

Setting up a dedicated file system on a back-end machine that contains your entire Web site is another alternative for synchronizing content. You would point the roots of each machine's Web server at that shared volume. If you have a fast network and the dedicated file system is highly optimized and reliable, this option can be efficient. You don't need to worry about sending copies of each file to each server. One risk, though, is that the file system will receive a huge amount of load, and it will become a single point of failure. Consider setting up a redundant clustered file system in case you suffer an extremely rare event such as a controller card failure. The major disadvantage of this approach is that accessing files over the network is always slower than accessing a drive on the same machine. You also have to worry about network collisions due to the high network traffic to this single file system.

While there are many solutions for deploying your Web site to multiple servers, none of them is a complete solution, and some will not run in environments other than Windows. There are several solutions for maintaining files and directories, but none of the options discussed here offers methods for keeping your operating systems and Web servers in sync, except Symantec's Ghost. ColdFusion 8's Archive and Deployment options provide a robust solution for synchronizing your ColdFusion environment in any server environment that ColdFusion 8 supports. This is a viable solution for the ColdFusion developer.

Multiple ColdFusion 8 Instances

One of the more interesting of ColdFusion 8's new functions and features is the capability to create multiple instances of the ColdFusion server directly from the ColdFusion Administrator. This feature is only available in the Enterprise version of ColdFusion installed in the multiserver configuration.

There are two major reasons why you might want to deploy multiple instances of ColdFusion on a server:

- **Application isolation**. Each instance of ColdFusion uses its own JVM and its own resources, and you can deploy separate applications each on its own instance of ColdFusion. If one application has problems that hit the server, other applications on their own instance will remain unaffected.
- **Load balancing and failover**. Multiple instances of ColdFusion can be set up and added to a cluster to provide failover and load balancing; if one instance fails due to application issues, the other instance will pick up the load. It's important to note that this only provides application-level failover. True high availability and failover will require hardware redundancy.

In ColdFusion 6, establishing multiple instances of the server required that you use J2EE deployment on top of a J2EE container, with multiple instances of the J2EE server; this could become complex and required multiple steps. Now, setting up and deploying multiple instances of ColdFusion could not be simpler.

To set up multiple instances of ColdFusion 8, first make sure you are running ColdFusion 8 in the multiserver configuration, which is the only option that supports the creation of instances and clusters from the ColdFusion Administrator.

NOTE

You can still manually create multiple instances of ColdFusion 8 using your specific J2EE server's create-and-deploy mechanism. You'll learn more about this in Chapter 58.

Let's walk through the steps of creating a new instance.

1. Log in to the ColdFusion Administrator. At the bottom of the navigation panel on the left, click to expand the Enterprise Manager menu. Click on Instance Manager to display the window shown in Figure 57.4.

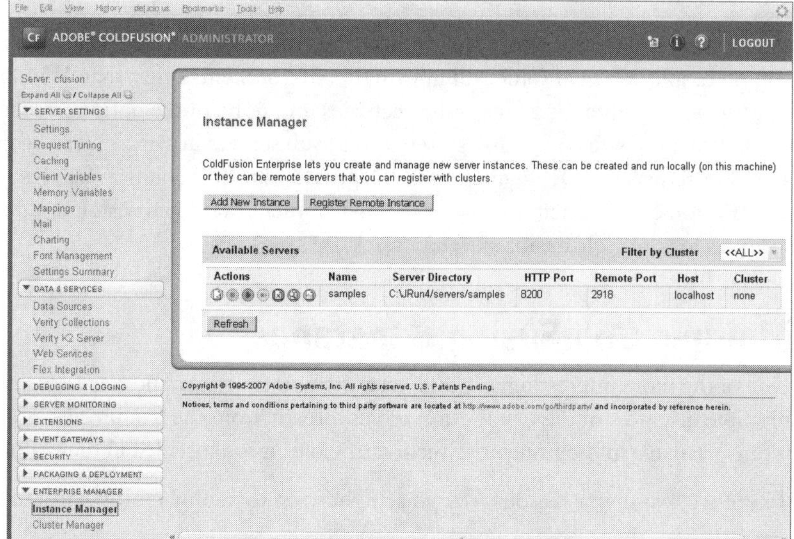

Figure 57.4

The ColdFusion 8 Administrator Instance Manager.

2. Select Add New Instance. You'll see the Add New ColdFusion Server window as shown in Figure 57.5.

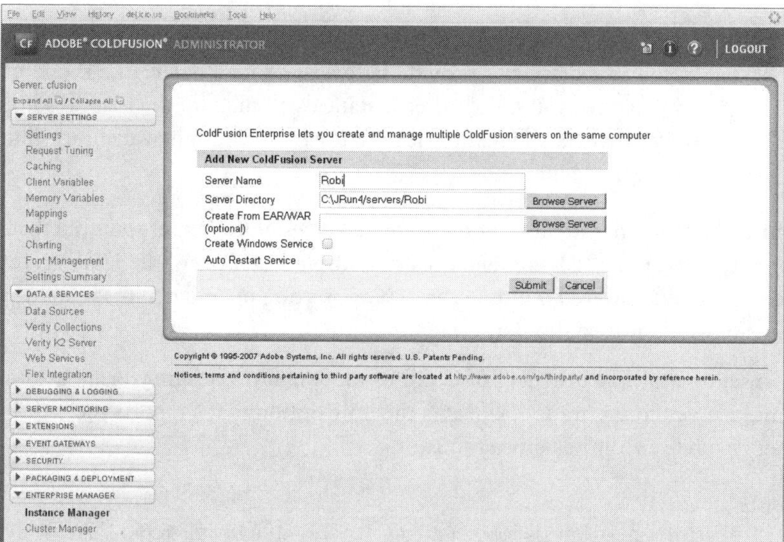

Figure 57.5

Adding a new instance of ColdFusion via the Instance Manager.

3. Fill in the form:

   Add the name for the server instance in the Server Name field.

   If you can want to use the default directory for the server instance ColdFusion should automatically fill it in for you (`jrun_root/servers/servername`); otherwise you will need to add the path to where you want the server instance.

   If you plan to deploy a ColdFusion application and its databases and various settings at that same time, you can use a Java Enterprise Archive (EAR) or Java Web Application Archive (WAR) file. You can add the path to your EAR or WAR and have ColdFusion deploy the application when it creates the instance. This is optional, and for this example we will leave it blank.

   There are two more optional settings, available only on Windows versions of ColdFusion 8. If desired, you can specify that you want the new instance to be created as a Windows server, and you can enable an auto restart for the instance.

4. After you have set all your options, click the Submit button. ColdFusion 8 starts to create a new instance of the server with all the options you have defined. This can take several minutes, during which you'll see a window like that in Figure 57.6.

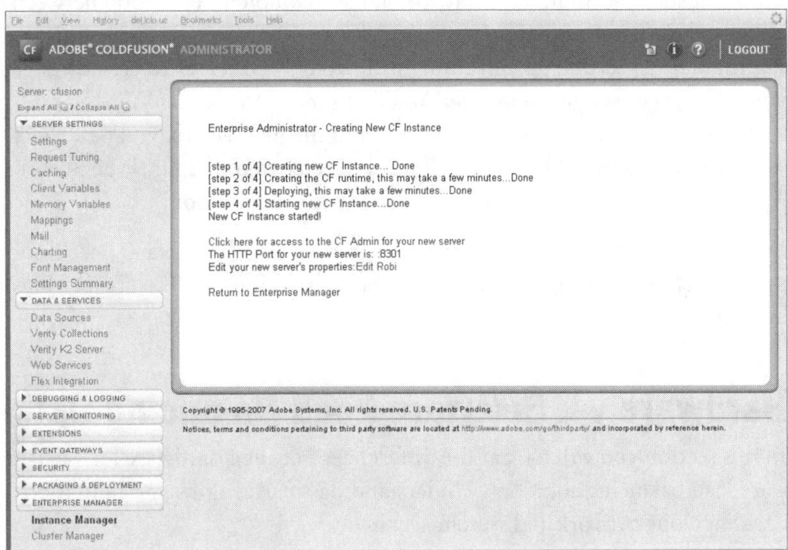

Figure 57.6
Creation and deployment of a new ColdFusion 8 instance.

5. After the new instance has been created, select Instance Manager again. You should see your new instance of ColdFusion 8, as shown in Figure 57.7.

   You can now also start and stop each instance of the ColdFusion 8 server from the JMC, the JRun Launcher, or by using the start and stop batch files from the command line:

```
jrun_root/bin jrun -start|-stop servername
```

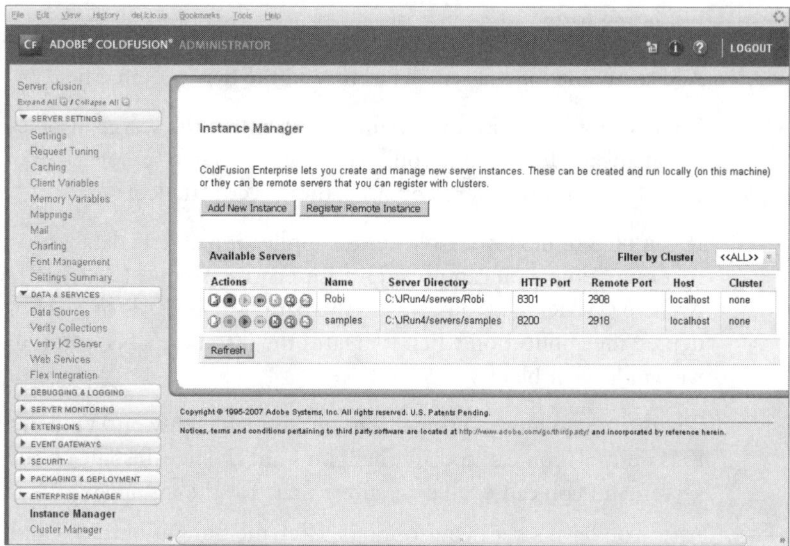

Figure 57.7

Instance Manager showing a view of multiple instances running.

To obtain application isolation, you'll also want to create a specific separate Web site and associate a specific instance with it. This way, you'll have complete separation between your applications and can even configure and set up your JVM for each instance (more on this in Chapter 58). For more information on setting up and configuring your Web server to create a separate Web site, refer to your Web server's documentation. You'll also need to use the Web Server Configuration Tool to then connect an instance of ColdFusion 8 to the new Web site. The various Web servers have their own procedures to do this, so you'll need to refer to the topic "Web Server Configuration for Application Isolation" in your ColdFusion 8 documentation.

Later, in the section "Scaling with ColdFusion 8 Load Balancing," we'll show you how to use multiple local or multiple remote instances of ColdFusion 8 to create a cluster for failover and load balancing.

Hardware vs. Software Load Balancing Options

In this section you will look at the differences between hardware load balancing solutions and software load balancing solutions. Understanding the strengths and limitations of each is crucial in deciding your network and system architecture.

ColdFusion 8 Load Balancing and Software-Based Load Balancing

In most software-based load-balancing methodologies, a service runs on each machine in a cluster. A machine designated as the primary cluster server distributes load to the other servers in the cluster. Should one server go down, the other machines in the cluster are notified by communication among the servers' cluster services, and the other machines act to absorb the extra load. One limitation of this approach is that it requires your Web servers to act as their own clustering agents.

ColdFusion 8 Enterprise Edition uses the integrated JRun clustering technology to provide load balancing and failover services. You can build and manage clusters right from the ColdFusion 8 Administrator. It can detect failed servers and busy applications, and provide redirection from these servers to other available servers. ColdFusion 8 Load Balancing uses HTTP redirection to balance load across a cluster as well as provide failover (see Figure 57.8). ColdFusion 8 Load Balancing runs on Windows, Solaris, and Linux platforms.

Figure 57.8
The Web Server Connector balances the load across the JRun servers in the cluster.

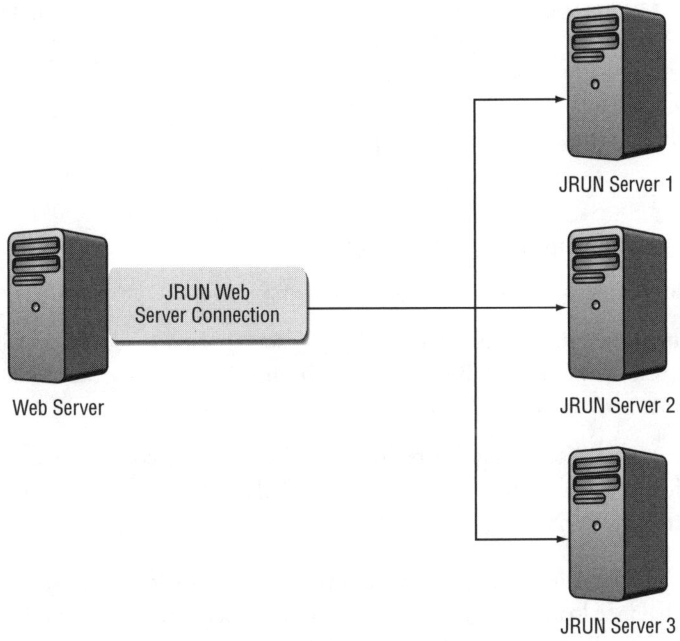

With ColdFusion 8 Load Balancing:

- Application and server load management for ColdFusion 8 applications is provided. Server failover is also provided, whereby requests to failed servers are redirected to other servers in the cluster.
- Session state management can be implemented so that users stay on the same server for the duration of their session.
- Application servers can be monitored and restarted if they fail.
- All servers in the cluster work together to manage HTTP requests, eliminating a point of failure for the system.
- Centralized configuration services for all nodes in the cluster are provided.

See Table 57.2 for the advantages and disadvantages of using ColdFusion 8 Load Balancing software-based load balancing.

Table 57.2 ColdFusion 8 Load Balancing Advantages and Disadvantages

ADVANTAGES	DISADVANTAGES
Tightly integrated with ColdFusion 8 and very easy to set up	Negates full proportional distribution of load
Provides for failover and content awareness	No intermediary between servers and load
Can perform session-aware clustering	Does not provide for network address translation (NAT) for security
Can work with RRDNS as a two-layer approach	Inexpensive
Included with ColdFusion 8 Enterprise	

Dedicated Load-Balancing Hardware

Hardware load balancers come in two basic flavors:

- **Server-based**. This is accomplished by server-class PCs with specialized load-balancing software. The most widely used load balancers on the market today are Cisco's `LocalDirector` and F5's BigIP series.
- **Content-switch-based**. Load balancers such as Cisco's CSS series combine the efficiency of a routing switch with load-balancing software that acts as an intelligent switching device.

Using dedicated load-balancing hardware is the most sophisticated way and, for large clusters, the best way to balance load across a cluster. Hardware-based load balancers sit in front of the Web servers and route all requests to them. Requests come in to a single IP address for your domain. The load-balancing hardware answers the request and mediates with individual Web servers to provide a response that appears to have originated from your domain's single public IP address. This form of distribution relies on complex algorithms to determine which Web server is "most available" at the time the request is presented. Usually this determination is made by a server polling for HTTP response time and, optionally, by the use of agents residing on the Web servers that make up your cluster. The agents report to the load-balancing hardware various aspects of your system's performance, such as CPU utilization, process utilization, and other vital machine statistics. Based on this data, the device routes the request to the most available server. Server failover is managed because a server fails polling tests and does not return any usable performance data via its agent.

Setting up load-balancing hardware is fairly complex. The arrangement is generally dual-homed (see the section "Tiered Application Architecture" in this chapter). Configuration requires fairly robust knowledge of TCP/IP networking principles, as well as the ability to absorb new concepts associated with the load-balancing hardware itself. For example, one downside to load-balancing hardware is the single-point-of-failure problem. To alleviate this issue, most manufacturers recommend that you purchase two boxes and set them up so that the second one can seamlessly take over for the first in case of failure. This backup box is known as a *hot spare*. You also need to address security and administration issues for your load-balancing hardware, just as you would for any other machine on your network.

NOTE

Only qualified routing technicians should set up hardware-based load balancing. Because these machines actually translate addresses, you can affect the operation of other routers on your network if you perform an incorrect installation or modification. In addition, network address translations (NATs) can affect the way your site functions after it is behind the load balancer.

Hardware-based load balancing provides an enhanced level of security because most of this hardware uses network address translation (NAT). This way, an administrator can use private, nonroutable IP numbers to address Web servers and can filter requests to those machines on specific ports at the NAT machine. For example, the NAT machine knows that 192.168.0.1 is a Web server behind the NAT. An instruction is given to the NAT machine that says a public address of 206.123.23.5 maps to 192.168.0.1 on port 80. Then, when a request comes to 206.123.23.5 on port 80, the NAT machine passes the request through to the back-end server. The user, however, never knows the true IP address of the server responding to the request, and a different server could be substituted for 192.168.0.1 by changing the mapping. Many hardware load-balancing solutions also offer sophisticated firewalls.

See Table 57.3 for the advantages and disadvantages of using a hardware load-balancing solution.

Table 57.3 Hardware-Based Load-Balancing Advantages and Disadvantages

ADVANTAGES	DISADVANTAGES
Provides true distribution of load based on server resources	Setup and administration require advanced networking knowledge
Acts as an added layer of security	Single point of failure; increased cost for purchasing the recommended hot spare
Provides for automatic failover to standby machines	Expensive
More reliable and better performing than software-based solutions	Expensive
Enables a single URL to access all machines behind load balance (more seamless to end user)	Expensive

Scaling with ColdFusion 8 Load Balancing

New to ColdFusion 8 Enterprise Edition is integrated load balancing and failover, with the capability to create and manage a cluster directly from the ColdFusion Administrator. ColdFusion 8 Load Balancing monitors your ColdFusion 8 servers and can redirect requests away from a server that is beginning to enter a busy state. When ColdFusion Load Balancing redirects requests to another server, it does so by redirecting them to the URL of another machine in the cluster. If your server is completely out of commission (that is, turned off), ColdFusion Load Balancing cannot communicate with it and therefore cannot redirect requests away from it.

Perhaps the most attractive aspect of using ColdFusion 8 Load Balancing for load-balancing solutions is its integration with ColdFusion 8. ColdFusion 8 Load Balancing is extremely easy to configure and set up, unlike many other software and hardware load-balancing solutions.

Understanding ColdFusion 8 Load Balancing

ColdFusion Load Balancing consists of server and client components. The server component runs on the ColdFusion 8 server. ColdFusion 8 Load Balancing Explorer is the client-management facility for building and managing clusters. Each of these components plays a critical role in the configuration and support of your ColdFusion 8 Load Balancing clusters. The server component manages the server's contact with the cluster. The client component allows management of the cluster, creation of alarms, and cluster monitoring.

CAUTION

Be sure to test your Web site when redirection occurs from one Web server to another. To function properly, your application may need to compensate for path variables or employ session-state management.

NOTE

Although you can have a cluster consisting of a mix of Unix-, Solaris-, and Windows-based servers running ColdFusion 8 Load Balancing, you must have at least one Windows machine to run the ColdFusion 8 Load Balancing Explorer, or to run ColdFusion 8 Load Balancing Web Explorer for Unix clusters.

Configuring a Load Balanced Cluster

Setup and configuration of ColdFusion 8 Load Balancing is very simple. But before we walk through the process, there are a few things you need to do before you deploy your cluster.

First, confirm that all instances of ColdFusion you want to cluster are set up identically, with exactly the same databases, code, mappings, and so on.

If you are going to use session failover, make sure you turn on J2EE sessions in the ColdFusion Administrator, and enable session replication for each server. This will allow your session data to be shared across systems in the cluster, so if one ColdFusion instance is unavailable, your users' requests will be routed to another free server without session data being lost.

NOTE

During session replication, all session data is copied to each server in the cluster every time the data is modified. In applications that store large amounts of data in the session scope, this data duplication will have a negative impact on performance. One way around it is to store data in client variables and use a database as the client storage mechanism.

Configuring a cluster of ColdFusion servers is uncomplicated, and for this example you can use the instances you created in the earlier section "Multiple ColdFusion Instances." If you have multiple remote servers, the same steps will be applicable.

1. Check that all ColdFusion server instances have been created and that applications and databases have been deployed.

2. Open the ColdFusion 8 Administrator, select Enterprise Manger in the navigation panel, and then select Cluster Manager. You'll see the window in Figure 57.9.

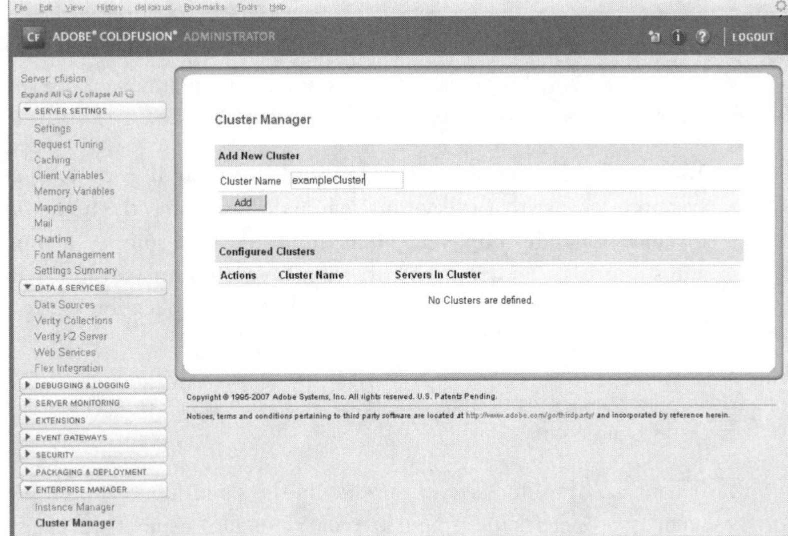

Figure 57.9

Adding a new cluster via the ColdFusion 8 Cluster Manager.

3. Name your cluster and click Add. Your cluster will be displayed in the Configured Clusters area.

4. Select your cluster and click the Edit icon next to the name. The Edit Cluster window is displayed (Figure 57.10).

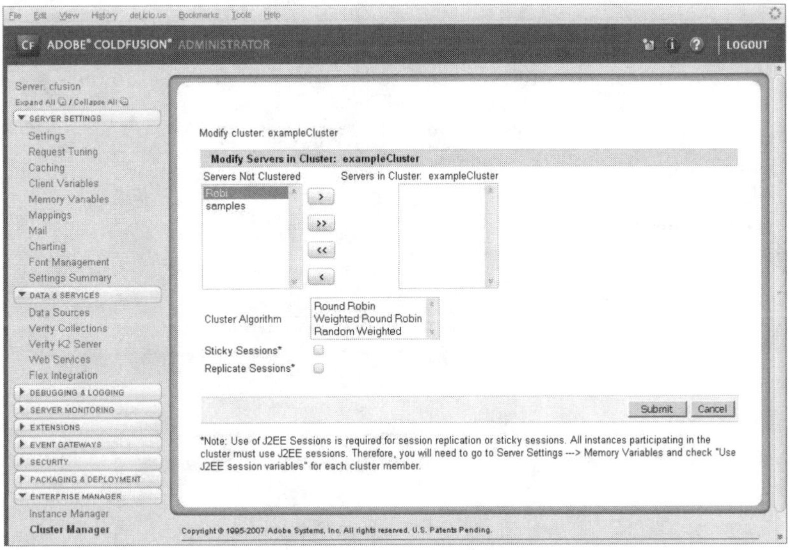

Figure 57.10

Editing a cluster in the ColdFusion 8 Cluster Manager.

5. Using the arrow buttons, add the instances you want to cluster.
6. If you want to share session information over the cluster, enable the Replicate Sessions option and select a cluster algorithm. Then click Submit.

NOTE

When you enable the Sticky Sessions option, the connector does not always route requests based strictly on the cluster algorithm. For more information, see Administrator Online Help.

7. You may need to restart each instance of JRun/ColdFusion 8. In addition, check your system to ensure that everything is functioning correctly. It's a good idea to check every instance of ColdFusion; verify that things like data sources, mappings, Verity Collections, and so forth are all deployed correctly. If you're using session replication, make sure each instance is also using J2EE sessions and session replication.

NOTE

ColdFusion components do not support session replication. When designing your ColdFusion applications, keep this in mind when you build persistence mechanisms.

8. If your ColdFusion 8 servers are *not* on the same subnet, you'll need to edit the JRun security properties file (found at `jrun_root/lib/security.properties`). Add the IP addresses of all the other servers in the cluster to the `jrun.trusted.hosts` property. If all your servers are on the same subnet, you can ignore this step.
9. Now bind your cluster to a Web site.

   Start the Web Server Configuration Tool (Start > All Programs > Adobe > ColdFusion 8 > Web Server Configuration Tool) or navigate to `jrun_root\bin\wsconfig.exe` and run the Tool.

   Select the Web site to which you want to connect. Instead of choosing a single server instance, select the cluster. See Figure 57.11 for an example.

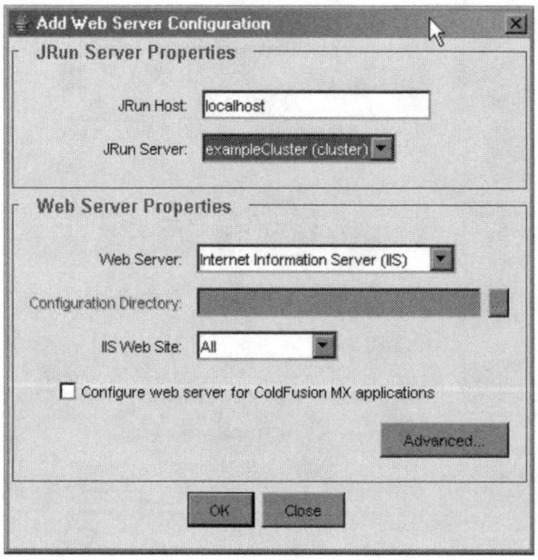

Figure 57.11

Deploy an existing archive with Web Server Connector Tool.

Ensure that you select the Configure Web Server for ColdFusion 8 Applications check box (in the GUI); or, if you're working from the command line, use the `-coldfusion` option.

For more help with this step, refer to the ColdFusion documentation for your specific Web server under the section Web Server Configuration.

10. Now go to each instance's `jrun.xml` file, which should be in `jrun_root\servers\cfusion\SERVER-INF\jrun.xml`. Make sure that the entry for the ProxyService `deactivated` attribute is set to `false`, like this:

    ```
    <attribute name="deactivated">false</attribute>
    ```

11. Finally, you can now test to see if your cluster is working correctly.

If your server is up and running and you want to take it out of the cluster for maintenance, you can simply remove the instance(s) for that server from the cluster via the ColdFusion 8 Administrator. When you're finished with maintenance, you can simply add the instance(s) back in. Or, if you want to add more ColdFusion 8 servers to the cluster, simply add them via the ColdFusion 8 Administrator. Nothing could be simpler.

TIP

You may notice that ColdFusion 8 allows you to weight ColdFusion servers for situations where you have systems with different resources–such as one server that has four CPUs and 4 GB of memory, compared with a server that has two CPUs and one gig of data. You can give the four-CPU server a higher weight, which will make the ColdFusion 8 Load Balancer refer a large percentage of server requests to that server.

Hardware Load-Balancing Options

Hardware load balancing, similar to software balancing with ColdFusion 8 Load Balancing, manages traffic within a Web cluster according to a specified load-balancing algorithm (such as round-robin, or least connections). However, unlike ColdFusion 8 Load Balancing, hardware-based load-balancing devices sit in front of the Web cluster, meaning that all traffic destined for the Web cluster must pass through the load-balancing device.

Suppose you are configuring a Cisco `LocalDirector` to load-balance the `www.mycompany.com` domain, which contains three Web servers and a database server. You would configure the load balancer with the IP address that corresponds, DNS-wise, to `www.mycompany.com`. This address is called the virtual Web server address. On the `LocalDirector`, you would also configure the addresses of the three Web servers behind the `LocalDirector` and a load-balancing algorithm, such as least connections. `LocalDirector` would assign users to the server with the least load. Figure 57.12 illustrates the basic network configuration of the load balancer.

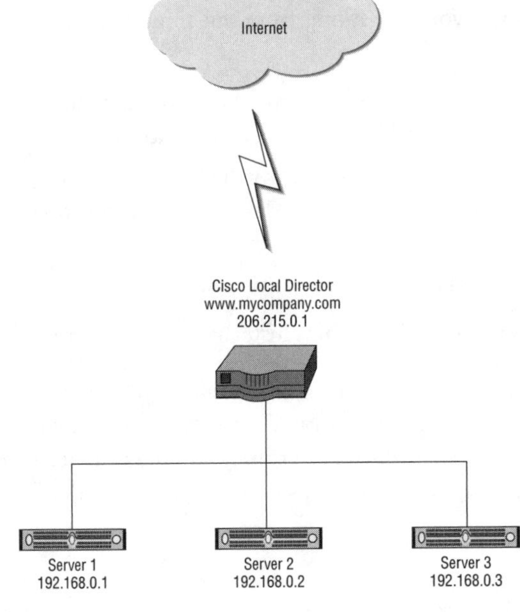

Figure 57.12
Cisco `LocalDirector` contains the virtual Web server `www.mycompany.com` directing traffic to three clustered servers.

`LocalDirector`

Cisco `LocalDirector` can be set up to maintain network address translation (NAT). This feature ensures that Web servers in a cluster are not directly accessible by a public IP address, thus ensuring security. In this model, `LocalDirector` maintains the IP address that corresponds to `www.mycompany.com`, but `LocalDirector` has another interface on a switch that is shared by the three Web servers. `LocalDirector` acts as the gateway for Web servers in a cluster.

NOTE

An advantage to hardware-based load balancing is that users never know that the site is behind a load balancer (servers are not required to have their own individual DNS names). This is especially useful when dealing with bookmarks. On a site balanced with ColdFusion 8 Load Balancing, users can easily bookmark `www1.mycompany.com` because that is the address displayed in their browser. This can cause difficulty if `www1.mycompany.com` has problems or is permanently taken offline.

Load-Balancing Algorithms

Adding hardware load balancing gives you flexibility in traffic management, but the load-balancing method or algorithm you choose will have impact on the efficiency of your site. The wide array of load balancers available vary slightly in their operations, but a few basic methods are described here as a guideline:

- **Round-Robin**. Similar to round-robin DNS, this load-balancing method assigns each server connections in the alternation fashion (the load balancer starts with Server 1 and assigns each user to the next server in order, and then starts again with Server 1). Unlike round-robin DNS, no traffic is directed to servers that have failed; these servers are automatically removed form the cluster until they have recovered. The basic round-robin method does not distribute traffic according to the number of server connections.

- **Round-Robin with Least Connections**. This method works in the same way as round-robin, but the load balancer monitors the number of connections each server has. As new users connect to the site, the load balancer sends the users to the server that has the fewest connections, even if that server is not next in the round-robin order.
- **Ratio**. This type of load balancing distributes traffic among servers based on a predetermined connection ratio. The ratio is set by the administrator and can be based on forecasted load for each server in the cluster. You might configure your cluster so that two servers handle five users each, to one user for the third server. This approach would allow the third server to handle back-end processing or secure-transaction processing.
- **Priority**. Similar to the ratio method, this method configures servers with a specific priority. Users are sent first to servers with a higher priority.
- **Fastest**. Traffic is sent to the server with the fastest response.

NOTE

The ratio and priority methods are useful when all servers in a cluster are not of equal performance capability.

Big IP

Another widely used series of load-balancing devices is F5's BigIP series. These devices are different from `LocalDirector`—rather than running Cisco's proprietary operating system, they run OpenBSD Unix, which has many security features inherent in its design. BigIP load balancers can be configured through a Web interface running SSL or by connecting to the BigIP server through secure shell (SSH). Because the BigIP is running OpenBSD, it can act as a load balancer, a packet filtering firewall, and a masquerading firewall. However, implementing these features has an impact on the efficiency of the devices.

If you are using F5's BigIP series, additional load-balancing algorithms called Observed and Predictive are available. The load balancer analyzes performance trends of the clustered servers over time. Traffic is distributed based on trend data collected.

Finishing Up

You've learned from this chapter that many pieces must come together in order to create highly scalable ColdFusion 8 Web sites. Discussing scaling considerations before building your clustered server farm will help alleviate headaches later. By understanding how your clustered Web site will handle user sessions and connect to the Internet and to back-end applications, you'll be better able to develop your applications so that they will scale well. Implementing the best load-balancing solution for your environment will minimize administration time later and provide your site's visitors with a pleasant user experience.

CHAPTER 58

Scaling with J2EE

IN THIS CHAPTER

ColdFusion 8 is a highly scalable Web application platform built on Java 2 Enterprise Edition (J2EE). J2EE is a set of standards that build on the Java 2 Standard Edition adding support for multi-tier enterprise application through support of technologies like Enterprise JavaBeans (EJB), JavaServer Pages (JSP), servlets, XML and Web Services, Java Messaging Service, and much more. J2EE gives developers more capability to reuse components, create Web Services, extend legacy applications, work with mobile devices, and expand enterprise interoperability. J2EE has become the de facto standard for developing large-scale enterprise-class Internet applications in part because of its multiplatform support.

Because ColdFusion 8 is built in Java on J2EE standards it offers exceptional capability to integrate with Java. You can easily work with Java classes, servlets, EJBs, or just about any other type of Java/J2EE service and resource from your ColdFusion applications.

ColdFusion is now more flexible than ever. It can be installed as a stand-alone solution or on supported J2EE application platforms. ColdFusion 8 comes in three flavors: ColdFusion 8 Server Edition, ColdFusion 8 Multi-Server Edition, and ColdFusion 8 for J2EE Application Server, including versions for Adobe JRun, Sun ONE Application Server, IBM WebSphere Server, and BEA WebLogic. ColdFusion no longer depends on the Web server for its support. Now ColdFusion can be installed as a tiered application server in a multi-tiered environment, providing more scalability and stability.

This chapter discusses the benefits of these new capabilities, how ColdFusion interacts with J2EE, interoperability between ColdFusion and Java application servers, ColdFusion on a supported J2EE platform, and scaling ColdFusion using J2EE architecture.

Benefits of Deploying ColdFusion on J2EE Application Server

There are many benefits of scaling ColdFusion onto a J2EE platform. Whether ColdFusion is deployed on the Adobe JRun, Sun ONE, IBM WebSphere, BEA WebLogic, JBoss, or another J2EE application server, you will benefit. ColdFusion 8 supports standards-based J2EE and inherits many capabilities from the underlying Java application server. It can support legacy infrastructure and enhance prior technology investments. This section and the next discuss many of these benefits.

Standards-Based

Since ColdFusion 8 is based on a well-defined, well-accepted, and strongly supported set of standards with a large vendor base, you have far more options available to you than developers on other platforms. As a ColdFusion developer you are not stuck with a specific J2EE vendor or operating system. ColdFusion 8 works on the major commercial J2EE servers as well as it can work with open source J2EE servers. ColdFusion 8 inherits Java's multiplatform support and works with every major operating system platform out there now, including Mac OS X.

Java's wide support and conformance to standards guarantees that ColdFusion developers will always have the freedom to choose the solutions that work best for them—not only which J2EE platform to use or which operating system, but which database, which Web server, which messaging system, or anything else they wish to use.

Multiple Platforms

There are several ways to install your ColdFusion 8 Server. ColdFusion 8 has three instillation varieties: ColdFusion 8 Stand-alone, ColdFusion 8 Multiserver, and ColdFusion MX for J2EE Application Server. These installation options are explained below as well as each of the major supported servers:

- **Stand-alone**. Install ColdFusion Server. This method allows the developer to utilize Java components in applications, including servlets, JSP pages, and EJBs.
- **Multiserver**. This option is only available to Enterprise license owners. This version of ColdFusion 8 automatically deploys ColdFusion on top of JRun 4.0 as a J2EE instance but allows you to create, delete, and manage JRun instances from the ColdFusion 8 Administrator. This method offers all the options of the stand-alone version as well as allowing you to manage instances from the ColdFusion Administrator instead of from the JRun administrator.
- **Adobe JRun 4.0**. Install ColdFusion for J2EE Application Server. Installing on JRun offers the same options as the stand-alone version with the administration functions of JRun.
- **Sun ONE Application Server 6.5**. Install ColdFusion for J2EE Application Server for Sun ONE. Installing on Sun ONE Application Server further extends the capabilities

within the enterprise by opening up options available on Sun ONE platforms, including native load balancing and Sun ONE components.

- **JBoss 4.0.5 and 4.2**. Install ColdFusion for J2EE Application Server for the popular Open Source JBoss 4.0 and up. JBoss allows ColdFusion proponents access to one of the best applications servers on the market without the high costs of most J2EE servers.
- **IBM WebSphere 5.0, 6.1, and 6.1 ND Application Server**. Install ColdFusion for J2EE Application Server for WebSphere. Installing on WebSphere provides features similar to Sun ONE and an alternative platform if your company is already deployed on WebSphere.
- **BEA WebLogic 8.1, 9.2, and 10 Application Server**. Install ColdFusion for J2EE Application Server for WebSphere. Installing on WebLogic provides features similar to other J2EE installs and an alternative platform if your company is already deployed on WebLogic.
- **Oracle Application Server 10*g***. Install ColdFusion for J2EE Application for Oracle Application Server 10*g*.

Although the above installations and installations types reference all the supported ways to install ColdFusion 8, it is possible to install ColdFusion 8 on J2EE servers others than those listed here. However, Adobe will not provide support or guarantees for any but the above J2EE servers.

Support for Legacy Infrastructure and Prior Investments

Most organizations have legacy infrastructure and have invested tremendous capital in building, deploying, and maintaining this infrastructure. Seldom does a CIO or CTO want to scrap these systems and perform complete overhauls of existing architectures. They merely want to improve upon these structures, provide better operability between disparate enterprise systems, and implement new features. They also want to develop these new applications utilizing standards-based tools.

ColdFusion allows developers and application architects to build applications that extend the enterprise and enhance existing functionality. ColdFusion code can use existing application servers, components, EJBs, and even existing JSP templates. Via its gateway functionality, ColdFusion 8 now can also work with a variety of messaging technologies such as JMS (Java Message Service) and MQ Series. The gateway feature allows you to integrate much more easily with new and legacy enterprise resource planning (ERP) applications such as SAP.

Integrating these systems can be accomplished by implementing ColdFusion applications, which push and pull data between disconnected systems. Data integrity is maintained by using components that have the application's business logic and database connectivity in place. This allows organizations to leverage existing systems, adding more capabilities to these systems without rebuilding from scratch.

Potential uses for ColdFusion in an enterprise include the following:

- Implement application integration to tie disparate systems together.
- Improve system functionality, and revive tired older systems by adding new features and requirements for today's business environment.
- Add new business process management (BPM) functions to applications. (BPM automates workflow management and process management, with checks and balances for providing data integrity, all in support of business processes.)
- Add business-to-business (B2B) connections to external business partners.
- Maximize new and existing investments in J2EE.

Inheritance of Multiplatform Interoperability

Because ColdFusion 8 is built on J2EE technology, the components of any application built using standards-based Java architecture are available to ColdFusion 8. In addition, ColdFusion 8 can potentially work with any existing infrastructure that supports Java within the enterprise. This makes ColdFusion a versatile tool for developers to use in solving common business problems, while providing methods for developing applications that can be run in many different environments.

Developers who use ColdFusion will not have to change tools in order to code on different platforms such as .NET and J2EE, and will be able to deploy Web applications on HP-UX, AIX, Linux, Solaris, and Windows.

Development Values of ColdFusion 8 on J2EE

We have already discussed some of the benefits of deploying ColdFusion 8 on J2EE. Developers also gain from using ColdFusion when deployed on top J2EE. ColdFusion 8 gives developers new tools to rapidly develop Java-based applications and to extend enterprise systems with new functionality at a fraction of the cost in time and resources when compared to straight Java development.

Deploying Rich Internet Applications in Java

ColdFusion 8 comes with many beneficial application services, including Flash Remoting, Flex Integration, charting and graphing, and full-text searching. These services are integrated into ColdFusion and can offer feature-rich interfaces with little effort for the developer. For example, you can very easily rapidly enhance applications by using Flex or Ajax-based forms—something that is difficult to do with Java alone. Or you can provide graphical components to portal interfaces for displaying analytical data in charts and graphs. Content-management systems can be extended with full-text searching capabilities, and management of these systems can be done with ColdFusion's advanced file-scripting techniques. With ColdFusion 8, rich user interfaces can be built that integrate with back-end components, thereby extending and enhancing the Java application layer.

NOTE

ColdFusion 8 allows unprecedented portal development for IBM's WebSphere Portal Server; see `http://labs.adobe.com/wiki/index.php/ColdFusion_Portlet_Toolkit`.

Extending the Platform

Today's businesses need to interact with their partners both internally and externally at "Internet speed." These demands cannot always be accomplished using existing tools in the allotted time. Many Java application servers come with prebuilt components for implementing the following:

- E-commerce
- User profiling and user experience management
- Business and application integration
- Strong cryptography and public-key integration and security
- Web services
- Portals
- Content management
- Business process management
- Customer relationship management
- Order processing and billing
- Legacy system integration

ColdFusion 8 inherits these components when it is deployed in the same tiered environment as the Java application server. Indeed, ColdFusion 8 can extend these components and add new features or enhancements. Deploying ColdFusion 8 on J2EE also allows applications to be built with more user-interface features, such as charting and full-text searching. ColdFusion can leverage existing Web services, components, JSP pages, Java servlets, and EJBs. New features and functionality can be added while maintaining data integrity and system security using existing business logic housed in the middle tier in EJBs, ColdFusion 8 components, or Java components.

ColdFusion 8 can add new services by building ColdFusion components. For example, let us say an e-commerce Web site allows users to create new orders, but no functionality exists for processing these orders through the supply chain. Using ColdFusion 8, build a component that is called when an order is placed and confirmed. The component will grab the order and move it to your order processing system. This component could also use ColdFusion gateway technology, discussed in Chapter 80, "Working with Gateways," to pass this information to the order processing system via JMS. The message could kick off a request to your order-processing system to complete order processing in the supply chain. JMS can implement a publish/subscribe architecture where orders are published. Message subscribers pick up the orders for further processing.

A BPM layer could be implemented to provide management for processing orders through the enterprise. The BPM layer could offer visibility of these orders to administrators and management, to ensure that the orders are processed correctly and efficiently. BPM enforces business rules and helps to make certain that data in the enterprise retains its integrity.

Business portals provide users with a one-stop shop for managing information in the enterprise. ColdFusion, with its many GUI features and services, can play a major role in portal application development. Use ColdFusion to build new Web services to expose business processes to a corporate portal, and to help monitor business health. These portal elements can be very dynamic using ColdFusion capabilities such as charts and graphs. ColdFusion can also call existing application components, pulling and displaying important business information into intuitive user interfaces.

Ease of Development

Developing applications for J2EE with ColdFusion gives you the power, scalability, and reliability of J2EE, without the complexity. ColdFusion can reuse Java application components, and it simplifies integration through ColdFusion's scripting language. Why reinvent the wheel when you can extend it instead?

The interoperability of ColdFusion, along with its powerful features, helps developers to build ColdFusion applications using prebuilt components. Also, Adobe has added capabilities for ColdFusion developers to build their own Java components. Other Java application servers can use ColdFusion 8's enhanced and much more interoperable Web services. ColdFusion pages can be called by JSP pages, and vice versa. This eases development of J2EE-based applications with ColdFusion's available services.

Leveraging Diverse Developer Skill Sets

Developers are like economists. Place 50 developers in a room and ask them to provide a solution for a relatively simple business problem, and you will more than likely receive 50 different responses. The good news is that having 50 options to choose from allows you to choose the best, most long-term solution for solving the problem.

This is true of ColdFusion as well. Over time, every developer will migrate to using a tool set that makes him or her more efficient and more flexible in developing solutions. This increases morale and employee longevity and, ultimately, productivity. If your business has decided to support J2EE technology, many of your developers—especially HTML and user interface designers—may feel slighted and will become less productive due to the huge learning curve with Java. Placing ColdFusion in their hands will help to eliminate this anxiety and allow for flexible, powerful development. Using ColdFusion in your J2EE architecture creates a larger tool set for your enterprise, increasing the potential for more viable solutions, both economically and time wise.

Using J2EE Built-In Security Features

J2EE application servers offer security features that are not inherently available in ColdFusion. These features provide enhanced capabilities to secure the entire Web architecture in a clustered environment. J2EE application servers can maintain security on many layers in the architecture.

IBM's WebSphere Application Server, for example, implements security at very granular levels utilizing existing LDAP-enabled directories, third-party authentication methods, and other services across the cluster. Security can be invoked for specific EJB methods or for specific Web site applications. This architecture allows centralized management and is efficient. All applications on the server can have security attached and deployed, thus providing a tighter, more closely controlled environment. This architecture helps strengthen security across the enterprise by enforcing controls at virtually every layer within the application.

Improving Web Site Scalability

Many methods are available for improving Web site scalability. Some of these methods, such as tiered infrastructure, may not necessarily involve deploying on J2EE, but can be implemented through careful planning with any Web site. This section concentrates on improving Web site scalability when deploying on J2EE.

Tiered Infrastructure

Traditional ColdFusion applications consisted of many pages of HTML and code that performed many functions, including user interface, application logic, and database queries. The ColdFusion Web pages would typically perform two of these functions—user interface and application logic. All HTML and ColdFusion Markup Language (CFML) code was placed into ColdFusion Web pages and displayed to the user. Application logic was also handled by CFML code, and all calls to the database server were initiated using the `<CFQUERY>` tag. ColdFusion Web pages would essentially handle all interaction between the user and the database. Figure 58.1 illustrates traditional two-tiered, page-based Web architecture.

ColdFusion 8 developers should be aware of the much greater flexibility that J2EE offers in separating the tiers of their application. Developers are not tied to a traditional two-tiered model but can slice their application to a very high level of granularity, allowing the use of hardware to isolate and scale the parts of the application that most need it. Splitting all functions of an application into its various components creates a more flexible, robust, scalable system that is easier to monitor and manage.

Figure 58.2 shows how a tiered architecture could be created for a highly scalable J2EE deployment involving ColdFusion. This example is meant to show one method and is not the only method that can be used for creating a scalable, tiered architecture. The edge server tier manages security, and monitors and distributes content for the Web site. The edge server can also be just a firewall providing security. Some J2EE vendors, like IBM, offer dedicated edge servers that live in front of the Web server and create another layer of Web site management services. Web servers provide HTTP connectivity and content. In the third tier, application servers provide dynamic content using CFML pages, Flash remoting, LCDS for Flex, JSP pages, servlets, and so forth. In the fourth tier, JavaBeans, EJBs, or ColdFusion components perform business logic functions, and access database servers and legacy information systems. All tiers can be load balanced and clustered for performance and stability. This creates a highly scalable Web infrastructure and increases the fault tolerance and reliability of enterprise applications.

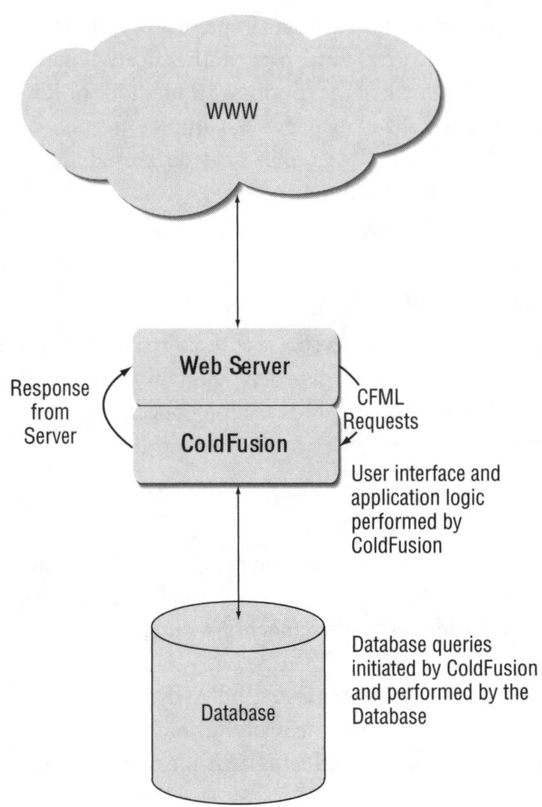

Figure 58.1

Traditional two-tiered page-based Web architecture.

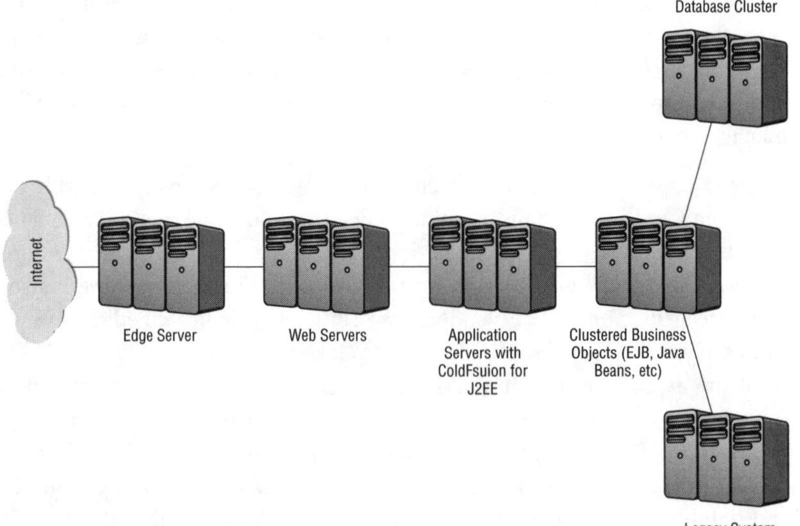

Figure 58.2

Multi-tiered J2EE Architecture with ColdFusion.

Native Load Balancing and Failover

Adobe JRun, Sun ONE Application Server, JBoss, Oracle Application Server, BEA WebLogic, and IBM WebSphere Application Server all offer native load-balancing support with their products. Load balancing can be performed at the Web server tier, the application server tier, or a combination of these tiers. Web server plug-ins and application server services control load balancing and failover. Choosing between load-balancing methods provides greater flexibility when designing for scalability. These J2EE application servers all have functions for creating redundancy on many levels within the Web site architecture, including components, systems, and for external network connectivity.

Adobe JRun offers native loading balancing and failover capabilities through the Jini service. Jini is a J2EE networking service that lets Java applications communicate easily with disparate distributed devices and objects. JRun clusters can be created and managed through the JRun Management Console (JMC). J2EE connectors are installed on the Web server to connect natively to the application server. These connectors can help maintain session state.

A combination of Web server and application load balancing can be utilized to provide further application partitioning and stability. Application servers provide services for connection pooling, Java Virtual Machine (JVM) pooling, object-level load balancing, and automated deployment.

JVM pooling is the process of creating multiple copies of an application server, components, JSPs, or servlets (sometimes called cloning). These clones can be run on the same physical machine or on several machines. JRun offers this option through the JMC to create any number of JRun instances. Using Jini, JRun services are *clusterable*; therefore, ColdFusion running on JRun is clusterable as well. Connection pooling is the process of maintaining relational database connections. Maintaining these connections increases the availability of database services.

Web server plug-ins or server applications can provide load balancing by monitoring workloads sending traffic to least-worked servers. This can be implemented by component, server, or a round-robin configuration. EJB components can be clustered across nodes within a single server or across several servers. User sessions can be maintained using sticky load balancing (session-aware) or through session clustering (session identifiers are stored centrally and available to all servers in the cluster).

Deployment and synchronization services make it easier than ever to deploy new Web site components automatically or manually using intuitive interfaces. Through techniques called "hot deploy," content and objects can be deployed while the service is live. JRun performs this deployment using built-in features in the JMC. New Web applications can be deployed onto clustered servers while maintaining client connectivity to the applications. This eliminates the need to take the entire Web site down during deployment.

Evaluating load-balancing and failover methods should be based on the needs of your Web site for performance, and on the experience and skills level of the developers and engineers involved in the process.

How ColdFusion Lives on Top of Java Server

ColdFusion 8 includes an embedded Java server based on JRun 4 technology. The infrastructure provides run-time services for ColdFusion Markup Language, Web services, and components. The ColdFusion application server relies upon the underlying JVM in order to serve ColdFusion pages and components. ColdFusion can now be deployed in the middle tiers of your Web site architecture. This leaves the Web server to host HTTP requests only, passing these requests to the application servers (ColdFusion on J2EE, for example) to process dynamic pages and run components. Splitting user-interface and business-logic functions into separate layers adds more stability and scalability to your Web site. Following the J2EE application model, ColdFusion can then run and expose Java components, Web services, JSP pages, and servlets.

One of the advantages of J2EE technology, properly implemented, is the modularity of design in components, servlets, and EJBs. Since ColdFusion is based on the Java platform, this is an important relationship. Applications can now be configured to run on tiers, where each tier provides specific functions. Understanding how to write your ColdFusion code in this tiered environment is important. A well-designed application, focusing on modularity, will scale well and improve the stability of the Web site. Some of these issues will be discussed in more detail in the section "Coding Implications from the Developer's Perspective." Managing session state is a complex process and even more complex in a multi-tiered mixed application server environment.

➜ Chapter 59, "Managing Session State in Clusters," discusses this topic at length.

When looking for bottlenecks in your applications deployed on multi-tiered J2EE installations, spend time understanding the layers or tiers that your application is invoking to perform work. Keep in mind that your application is now deployed in various layers, each layer focusing on specific tasks. For example, if the bottleneck is in an EJB, tweaking CFML that calls an EJB may not impact performance, but tweaking the poorly coded EJB will. In a multi-tiered environment, it's best to architect solutions with care before coding. Judicious choice of components to perform work is a prerequisite to gaining performance and scalability in multi-tiered solutions. This adds complexity to application development and precludes the "code and fix" mentality. Thoughtful and thorough planning will pay off when your Web site scales and performs properly.

Coding Implications from the Developer's Perspective

When deploying Web applications, coding implications arise in most any environment. Is the file I want accessible? Is the service or object I want available? Is the database connection available, or is the port I need to get through the firewall open and functioning? These considerations have not changed in ColdFusion 8. There are some things that ColdFusion 8 cannot control. It does do an excellent job of maintaining user sessions through client and session variables. And connecting to databases has been made easy with the ColdFusion Administrator.

When you introduce ColdFusion applications to a multi-tiered environment, there are several implications that need to be considered, including Java session variables, EJB pooling, JDBC database connections on the Java application server, and user security. The following sections offer some best-practices tips for building Java-enabled applications in ColdFusion.

J2EE Session Management

Even though you may have enabled Java session management in ColdFusion Administrator, you need to be aware of how sessions are managed in the Web site cluster. As mentioned before, Java application servers and Java Web server connector plug-ins offer different options for managing session variables, including

- *Persistent*, where session state is shared among all clustered servers and may exist after the browser is closed. Users can transfer between application servers without severing session information.
- *Sticky*, where session state is maintained by keeping the user on the same server throughout the session. The session is terminated when the user closes the browser. This is normally handled by the Web server cluster-managing device.

One of the great benefits of deploying ColdFusion 8 on J2EE is the interoperability of session-scoped variables between ColdFusion 8 and J2EE. Session scope can be shared between CFML and JSP pages. Therefore, session-scoped variables created in JSP pages are available to ColdFusion 8 components and CFML pages, and vice versa. Request and application scope variables can be shared between CFML and JSP as well. As a developer, you will want to be aware of how the J2EE application server, Java servlets, JSP pages, and components handle session variables. What is the timeout setting for session variables and does this timeout setting match the setting in ColdFusion 8? Are session variables released when finished using by a JSP page or Java component? Any CFML pages will be an extension of the J2EE application server environment. If there is interaction between CFML and JSP pages, it will be important to understand how session variables are managed by the server and in code.

When persistent session management is required, the user's session will be stored centrally in a database and will be available to every server in the cluster. Keep in mind that session management during failover still depends on the client's accepting a cookie, receiving a form variable, or using URL rewriting techniques to maintain state. Session state management methods are described in Chapter 59. If the server fails and the users do not have session data stored on the browser or in a cookie, the session will still be lost.

All Java Web server connector plug-ins for supported J2EE application servers discussed above offer session-aware load balancing. Session-aware load balancing for ColdFusion is described in Chapter 57, "Scaling with ColdFusion," and is similar to session-aware load balancing in J2EE architecture. This means that the session is "sticky" to the server. The user will remain on the server for the duration of the session. The session is terminated when the user closes the browser.

Both these methods are important for maintaining session state for Web applications such as shopping carts, where user information is stored as the user moves about the site and, hopefully, checks out. Maintaining the user's data is important for enhancing the user experience. Regardless of the method, you, the developer, need to be aware of how the session state is managed by the application server and should always check for its existence with every call to the session.

Scaling with ColdFusion and JRun

Scaling with ColdFusion MX for J2EE Application Server with JRun is very similar to scaling with ColdFusion. Indeed, as discussed in Chapter 57, ColdFusion 8 can use JRun's clustering functionality for both load balancing and failover. All JRun services are clusterable and JVM pooling can be invoked, creating a highly scalable Web site architecture. There are three levels of clustering available for ColdFusion on JRun: connector clustering, Web server clustering, and object clustering.

Connector clustering can be implemented by installing J2EE connectors on the Web servers, allowing them to natively connect to the application server. These connectors can help maintain session state. Session persistence is maintained through connecting to a centrally located database store using JDBC or through a shared file.

JRun clusters can be created and managed through the JRun Management Console (JMC). Deployment services are also provided. Steps to set up object clusters will be defined shortly.

Creating multiple instances of your JRun server will allow you to scale physically across multiple servers as well as on each server. Running multiple instances of JRun is called JVM pooling or cloning. Multiple instances of JRun are managed with the Web server connector plug-in. Three different algorithms for load balancing are offered: round robin, weighted round robin, and weighted random. If the JRun server fails, the connector automatically fails over to another JRun server in the cluster.

To create multiple JRun instances on one JRun server, open the JMC and click Create New Server, to open the window shown in Figure 58.3. Follow the wizard by inputting a unique server name, and click Create Server to create the server. Update the server URL and ports numbers, and click Finish. Adding this server to a cluster is described in the next section, "Configuring a JRun Cluster."

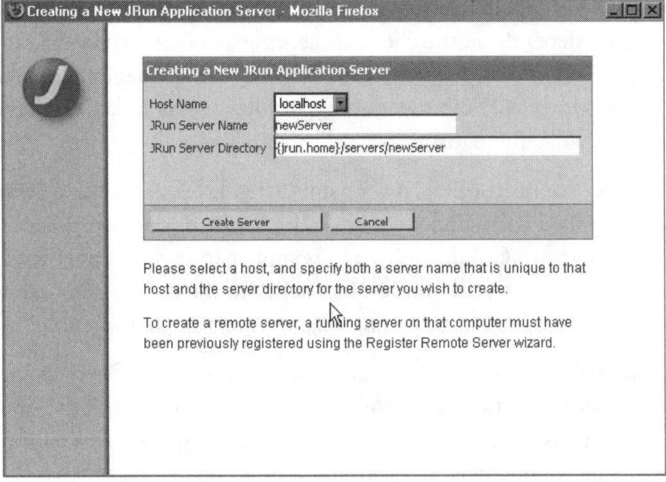

Figure 58.3

Creating a new server in JRun.

Object clustering uses the Jini lookup service. Each JRun server contains a service called the ClusterManager, which encapsulates the Jini lookup service. ClusterManagers work together in a peer-based fashion to provide cluster administration, thus eliminating the single-point-of-failure issue. Each service that is clustered can join the lookup service either by multicast or unicast IP packet methods. Multicasting allows a single IP packet to be received by multiple systems. This limits network traffic and makes one-to-many or many-to-many network services possible. Unicast is defined, as is the more traditional method for sending IP packets, in which each server sends an individual IP pack to each receiving server.

Configuring a JRun Cluster

To create a cluster with JRun, open the JMC. Click the Create New Cluster link to open the Creating a New JRun Cluster window (see Figure 58.4). Input the new cluster name; in this example, the cluster name is `mycompany`. Click Next, and in the next window select all servers to add to the cluster (see Figure 58.5). Click Next again, and the cluster is now set up, as shown in Figure 58.6.

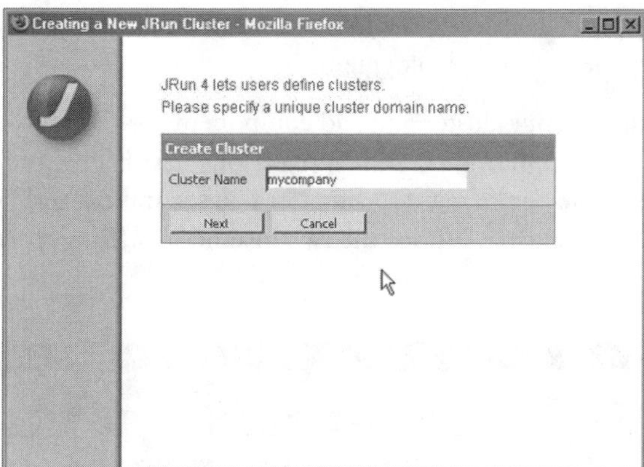

Figure 58.4
Creating a new JRun cluster.

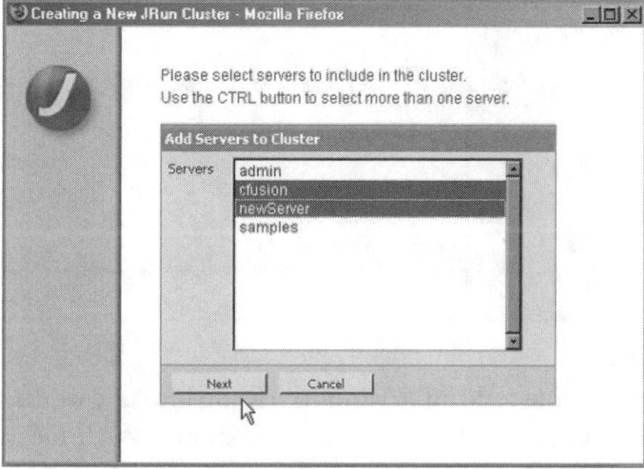

Figure 58.5
Add servers to the new cluster.

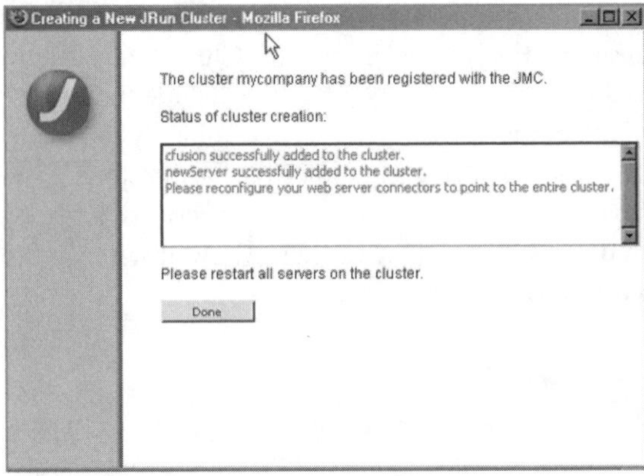

Figure 58.6
Cluster setup is complete.

Managing a JRun Cluster

After you have created your cluster using the JMC, you can work with your cluster to fine-tune its settings and to manage your Web site deployments.

You can refine the settings in your cluster and add components—see Figure 58.7 for cluster management options. Enterprise applications, Web applications, JavaBeans, and deployment settings can be added or changed. The deployment settings let you set and control how deployments are performed on servers in your cluster. Notice the two instances of JRun server: `default` and `newServer`.

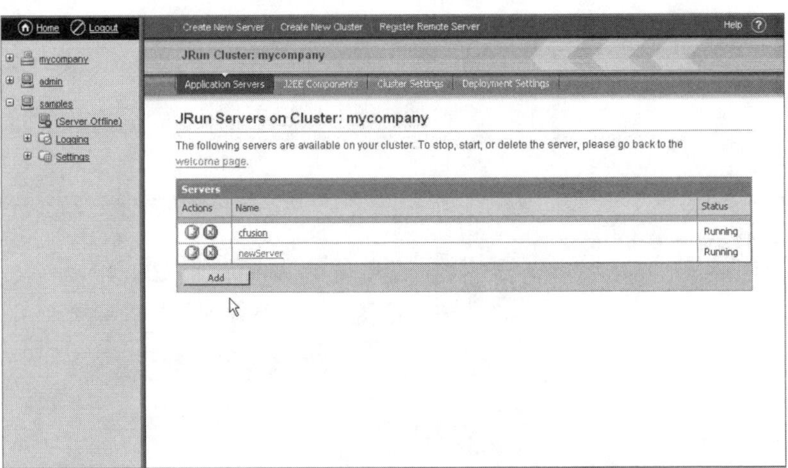

Figure 58.7
Cluster management options for `mycompany` in JRun.

To deploy your JRun applications, add an EAR or WAR file into one of the auto-deployment directories on one of the servers in the cluster. Creating an EAR or a WAR file is not explained here, but is covered in depth in Chapter 60, "Deploying Applications." In a live production environment, it's important to turn off the hot deployment feature on each server in the cluster, as shown in Figure 58.8. This is done to ensure that the deployment to each server is fully deployed when the server is restarted.

Restart each server in the cluster and verify the deployment. Click on the cluster name, and then click on J2EE components. On the summary page, you can view all deployed components.

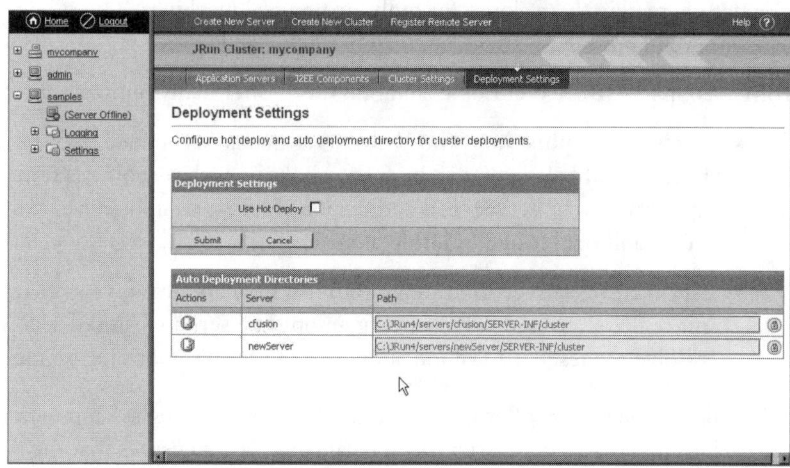

Figure 58.8

Deployment settings for `mycompany` cluster with hot deploy turned off.

NOTE

A WAR file is a J2EE Web application archive. An enterprise archive (EAR) file is a collection of WAR files, JAR files (EJBs), and other related files, including the application XML file.

Scaling with Other Java Application Servers

Integrated software load balancing and session management are some of the features offered by IBM WebSphere and Sun ONE application servers, as well as by Adobe JRun. Deploying your ColdFusion applications on servers running J2EE Application Server with ColdFusion offers many features that are not inherently present in ColdFusion itself. We will discuss some of their features and look at how they can affect scaling with ColdFusion.

Java application server architecture offers the concept of *application partitioning*. This architecture can be highly scalable because it splits the application's components into segments. These segments can be hosted on separate servers or sets of clustered servers. Application partitions can include HTML, CFML, JSP, servlets, and EJBs. A high-traffic Web site could be split into multiple tiers where each segment or tier resides on its own server or cluster of servers. For example, your Web server could be on one server, your ColdFusion 8 application could be deployed on another server, EJBs could have their own dedicated business logic server, etc. In some J2EE applications, heavy-use EJBs can even be split from other EJBs and hosted on dedicated servers, further augmenting the performance of the application.

Load balancing and session management are two important areas of concern for any Web site that requires high performance. J2EE application servers offer strong tool sets in these areas, with many options for tweaking applications for performance. WebSphere offers server-cloning features for creating multiple copies of an object such as an application server. With the application server, cloning can be performed by either vertical or horizontal cloning. Vertical cloning refers to creating multiple clones of an application server on the same physical machine. Horizontal cloning is the practice of creating these clones for multiple physical machines. This allows the application server to span several machines, enhancing load balancing and failover.

IBM WebSphere, BEA WebLogic, and Sun ONE offer many options for load balancing, including

- **Web server plug-ins**. The Web server manages the load on each application server. This type of load balancing can be set to choose which machine is sent requests for applications, by server load and response times, component load and response times, or in a traditional round-robin format.
- **Application server load management**. One application server or all application servers make decisions on load balancing among the set of clustered servers. This method can resolve requests in a fashion similar to the Web server plug-in method.

J2EE application servers offer various methods for performing session management. These methods include session-aware or sticky load balancing, which ensures that the user stays on the same server throughout the session. This is useful for maintaining state for a shopping cart application and cart checkout. Sessions can also be persistent through centralized management of the user's session. Both application servers described offer management interfaces for configuring session management across the cluster, making them viable options for preserving prior investments in J2EE architecture while moving to ColdFusion as a development platform.

NOTE

IBM has an excellent Web site for ColdFusion users who want to use WebSphere as their J2EE platform. If you're looking at or already using WebSphere as your J2EE platform, you'll want to bookmark and visit this site regularly: `http://www.ibm.com/developerworks/websphere/partners/Adobe/`.

Tuning the Java Virtual Machine

All Java applications rely on a Java Virtual Machine (JVM) to execute, and making sure your JVM is running as efficiently as possible is important so that your ColdFusion 8 applications work as efficiently as possible as well. In the next sections we are going to look at a high level how the JVM works, how garbage collection works, how to change and control the JVM, and how to monitor the JVM via log files and by visualizing the JVM so that you can tune the JVM for optimal performance.

Introducing the JVM

A JVM is an implementation of Sun's Java Virtual Machine specification, which defines an abstract machine or processor that is basically a software version of a hardware processor or CPU. The JVM spec also specifies an instruction set, a set of registers, a stack, a "garbage heap," and what is called a method area. Software companies (including Microsoft, BEA, and IBM), vendors, and others create JVMs for specific platforms, although by far the most popular is Sun's JVM. Once a JVM has been created for a given platform, any Java program (compiled Java source, or bytecode) can run on that platform. A JVM can either interpret bytecode one instruction at a time, mapping it to a real processor instruction; or it can further compile the bytecode for the real processor, using what is called a just-in-time (JIT) compiler, which radically improves performance.

NOTE

For a more detailed look at the Sun JVM specification, see `http://java.sun.com/docs/books/vmspec/`.

The JVM is the heart of any Java application and so must work as efficiently as possible. One of the main reasons a JVM may perform poorly is that it is not using memory efficiently. In general, the JVM is very efficient, but it can use some help in high-performance applications where it is expected to do a lot of work, manage a large number of objects, deal with large data sets, or simply operate as fast as possible. In this section we focus on some things you can do make your JVM excel for your specific application.

ColdFusion 8 ships with a series of default JVM attributes that are designed to work on almost any system or setup but are not the best configuration for every application. This is also true for almost every other J2EE application server, and knowledgeable J2EE system managers routinely profile and tune their J2EE servers based on their particular system and application operation parameters. When tuning your JVM, the first place to start is to figure out what the heap value for your JVM will be. Java applications make use of a garbage collection heap, which is a specialized memory structure. "The heap" is where all the objects of a Java program live. This means every ColdFusion page, CFC, session variable, and so on that becomes a Java object resides in the heap.

The JVM periodically performs "garbage collection" to remove or deallocate unused Java objects from the heap. Your heap value and settings determine in part how often and for how long garbage collection occurs. These settings are very important because, while garbage collection is happening, the JVM pauses and puts all other operations on hold. Usually garbage collection takes so little time that it has relatively no impact on performance, but in certain instances where there are few resources (for example, under high load), performance can take a hit during garbage collection.

If the heap value for your JVM is too low, you may see such things as the "`Java.lang.OutOfMemory`" error, ColdFusion server timeouts, poor response times under load, and what appear to be memory leaks. Furthermore, garbage collection may occur so often that it affects performance, which also leads to similar issues.

ColdFusion's default setting for the size of the JVM heap is 512 MB. (You'll find the JVM settings in `jvm.config`, in `server_root\bin`.) This is often sufficient for most applications, but if your application has a large amount of traffic, makes lots of large database queries, or otherwise requires more heap space, then you will want to set it higher. The easiest way to tell what your heap should be is by profiling your application using a product such as OptimizeIT (`http://www.borland.com/optimizeit/`) or JProfile (`http://www.ej-technologies.com/`). These programs help you easily determine the amount of memory your application is using and how it is using it. Another method is to use the ColdFusion server monitoring to land monitor the application under load. This way you can get a sense of memory usage even at peak times. If you find that the system is often using all the memory available to it, then you'll want to increase what you allocate to the heap.

Generally, if your server has substantial free memory, you'll want to assign it to the heap. A server with 2 GB of memory can afford a JVM heap maximum setting of 1024 MB. A good rule is to assign the JVM as much free memory as possible without causing the system to swap pages to disk. On production systems, you should also set the JVM heap's minimum to be the same as the maximum. This reduces periodic pauses of the JVM as it allocates more memory to itself, up to the maximum setting, and reduces what is called heap fragmentation.

NOTE

32-bit JVMs have a hard memory limit of 1.8 GB (see `http://www.adobe.com/go/tn_19359`), and in reality it is often hard to set the maximum heap to higher than 1.2 GB. If you find that you need even more memory, switching to 64-bit hardware, a 64-bit J2EE application server, and a 64-bit JVM will allow you to assign a maximum heap far higher (think hundreds of gigabytes).

So to set the maximum and minimum heap to 1 GB, you'd edit the `jvm.config` for each server instance that is running ColdFusion. On your J2EE server, look for `# Arguments to VM` and edit:

```
java.args=-server -Xmx512m
```

to read:

```
java.args=-server -Xmx1000m -Xms1000m
```

You don't want to touch the text `java.args=-server`, which is what Java expects to see to let it know that everything after that attribute comprises settings for the JVM. The `-Xmx` stands for heap maximum, and the `-Xms` stands for heap minimum.

TIP

Since the JVM is memory intensive, and memory is one of the largest bottlenecks for any Java application, always try to reasonably maximize memory on your servers. Memory is cheap, and having at least a gigabyte of memory available to your JVM heap will make a significant positive impact on performance.

Tuning Garbage Collection

Now that we have discussed what the JVM is and how to set the heap size, let's take a look at how to tune garbage collection. Generally the JVM does a good job of cleaning up all the unused objects in the heap, but if you have profiled your application, you can optimize the JVM for the specific application. In this section we'll describe some of the most common options and how to set them in `jvm.config`.

TIP

Incorrectly setting JVM attributes or even a simple typo can cause your J2EE server to fail to start. Simply replacing the `jvm.config` file with one that has the original settings will resolve this, so we suggest that you keep a copy of the original settings. Or, better yet, keep your `jvm.config` in a version control system with updates and notes every time you change the file.

Before we start discussing specific garbage collection options, let us take a closer look at heap memory usage and garbage collection. In this section, you will encounter some special Java terminology that will be important not only for understanding the garbage collection but also the garbage collection log files. If you plan to read more about tuning the JVM, you'll need an understanding of these terms.

The JVM breaks up the heap into pools or buckets of memory, into which are assigned Java objects that have specific life expectancies; after these periods of time end, the objects need to be cleaned up. These memory buckets are called *generations*, based on the life expectancy of their occupants. There are three major generations: *young*, *tenured*, and *perm* (for permanent, which is actually a special type of tenured generation). Objects that reside in the young generation are typically only going to last for, say, the life cycle of a ColdFusion page request. Objects with longer life expectancy, such as a cached query or even the classes that make up ColdFusion itself, would reside in the tenured generation. The perm generation contains objects that make up the actual JVM. Figure 58.9 will give you an idea of the heap's generations.

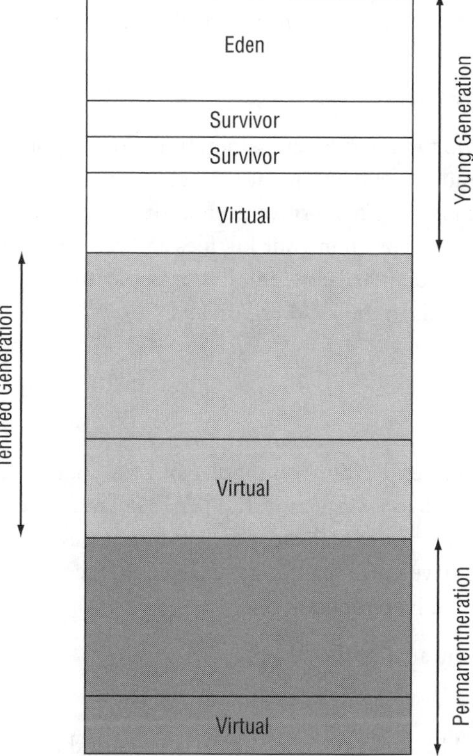

Figure 58.9

The heap is divided into the young, tenured, and permanent generations.

The young generation is probably the most important. It is made of three segments, *eden* and two *survivor* spaces. Eden is where Java objects are initially created and assigned and, if they are not immediately cleaned up, they are assigned to one of the survivor spaces. Survivor objects that are still needed are then copied to the tenured space. The young generation setting is, after the heap size, probably the most important setting and has the greatest impact on performance. The more memory assigned to the young generation, the less minor garbage collection has to be done by the JVM. This has a potential drawback: The greater your young generation, the smaller your tenured generation can be. This means the JVM has to more often do major garbage collection, which essentially pauses the JVM while it cleans up the tenured space. Depending on your application and the amount of memory available, this is usually not a problem.

You can use several attributes to control the young generation. Probably the most important of these are NewSize and MaxNewSize, which essentially function like minimum and maximum limits. You may notice the absence of these settings in jvm.config (they are optional). If they do not exist, the JVM tries to figure out the best settings dynamically, and it usually does a decent job. However, by experimenting with these settings you can often greatly improve performance.

Setting NewSize and MaxNewSize to be identical is just like setting Xms and Xmx for the heap to reduce the JVM's workload. Generally, setting the young generation to 25 percent of the total heap works well, but you'll need to test these settings to find the best size for your particular system and application. For example, to set the young generation size to 100 MB, add these strings to the Java arguments (java.args) string:

```
-XX:NewSize=100m -XX:NewMaxSize=100m
```

Finally, it is important to mention the permanent generation. Some applications, including ColdFusion 8, dynamically create and load a hefty quantity of classes into memory. With large ColdFusion applications, this can be an issue. This is often seen in situations where the "Java.lang.OutOfMemory" error crops up in your log files and can be easily solved by increasing the maximum permanent generation (MaxPermSize). For example, to increase maximum permanent generation size to 256 MB, add this to the JVM arguments:

```
-XX:MaxPermSize=256m
```

Selecting a Collector

The next most important thing after deciding on the size of your young generation is determining what garbage collection method to use. Generally, the JVM's default collector is fine—especially if your server has a single CPU—but other collectors can offer performance increases in these situations, as well as on servers that have more than one CPU. There are three different types of collectors: throughput, concurrent, and incremental.

The *throughput* collector is set by adding the string:

```
-XX:+UseParNewGC
```

to the JVM arguments string. This collector is a parallel version of the default young generation collector and is especially useful on servers with many CPUs and a large young generation.

TIP

The throughput collector is especially powerful on systems with many processors because, unlike the default collector, you can have the throughput collector use multiple threads for garbage collection. You can do this by adding the string -XX:ParallelGCThreads=<desired number> after -XX:+UseParallelGC, where desired number is usually the number of CPUs on the server.

The *concurrent* collector is set by adding the string:

```
-XX:+UseConcMarkSweepGC
```

after the JVM arguments string. This one is often called the "low pause" collector, in that it pauses the application for very short periods while it does collection on the tenured generation. You can also add a parallel version of the young generation collector, by adding this combination of parameters:

```
-XX:+UseConcMarkSweepGC -XX:+ParNewGC
```

to the JVM arguments string. If you decide to use this option, you'll need to delete the `-XX:+UseParallelGC` collector; this is usually the default collector that ships with ColdFusion's `jvm.config` file.

Finally, there is the *incremental* collector, which performs many small collections on the tenured generation but in most cases is slower than the default collection setting. You can set the incremental collector by adding:

```
-Xincgc
```

to the JVM arguments string.

All these collectors give you alternatives to the ColdFusion's default collector, but changing the default collector is the last thing you should attempt—only after increasing your heap size and tuning your young generation. After you have made those changes, you can try changing the collector to see if any of the optional collectors will increase performance.

Testing and Tuning

Now that you understand how memory is allocated, how to assign memory to the heap and the various generations, and how to assign specific garbage collections methods to the JVM, you should test your application. The simplest way to do this is generally to use your testing suite to put the application under load and monitor the effects of the new settings on application performance. If you do not see increases in throughput, try a different approach.

Another approach, especially if you are seeing intermittent errors or performance issues, is to dump the output of garbage collection to your logs. You do this by simply adding these parameters to your JVM arguments:

```
-XX:+PrintGCDetails -XX:+PrintGCTimeStamps -XX:+PrintHeapAtGC
```

- The `-XX:+PrintGCDetails` tells ColdFusion to print out garbage collection details.
- The `-XX:+PrintGCTimeStamps` tells it to add timestamps (which can be really useful in debugging so that you can correlate problems to specific times).
- The `-XX:+PrintHeapAtGC` will print out detailed information on the generations. By default, ColdFusion will output this data to `serverinstance_root\runtime\logs\<servername>-out.log`.

If you would like to log the garbage collection data to its own file, you can also add `-Xloggc:<filename>`, where `filename` is chosen by you.

- The output from the garbage collection will look something like this:

```
11948.248: [Full GC  {Heap before GC invocations=248:
Heap
 def new generation   total 49088K, used 4735K [0x10010000, 0x13010000, 0x13010000)
  eden space 49024K,   9% used [0x10010000, 0x104afda0, 0x12ff0000)
  from space 64K,   0% used [0x12ff0000, 0x12ff0000, 0x13000000)
  to   space 64K,   0% used [0x13000000, 0x13000000, 0x13010000)
 concurrent mark-sweep generation total 999424K, used 28683K [0x13010000,
0x50010000, 0x50010000)
 concurrent-mark-sweep perm gen total 65536K, used 22628K [0x50010000, 0x54010000,
0x58010000)
```

At first this might be intimidating and hard to read, but look at it carefully and it will start to make sense. Let us break it down. The first line marks specific events in seconds from when ColdFusion was started. In this example, a full garbage collection was started. Next comes detailed information about the various generations in the heap. Notice the first one, the `new` generation, which is the same thing as young generation; it has a total of 49088K allocated to it but is only using 4735K of the memory. The next two lines after the eden space are the `from` and `to`, which are essentially the survivor spaces; they are totally empty.

The next line shows that the `concurrent` garbage collection method was used, that the total heap was 999424K (1 gigabyte), and only 28683K was used. The last line shows that the `concurrent` collector was used on the permanent generation and that its size was 65536K, with only 22628K used.

As you can see, the output from the garbage collection is not too difficult to understand, but it can be difficult to read and determine what actions you need to take just from looking at a few lines in your log files. There are garbage collection log file readers such as HP's HPjtune (`http://www.hp.com/products1/unix/java/java2/hpjtune/index.html`), a free tool that reads garbage collection log files you have created and provides a variety of visual reports that may make your job easier. You should look into a tool like this in that you can look at log files from a week of actual usage and get a much better sense of how your system is behaving. Many of the more sophisticated commercial products also have built-in garbage collection analysis tools. If you find yourself often having to tune the JVMs of your application, then an investment in one of these will be well worth the money.

Not surprisingly, many ColdFusion developers as well as system administrators would rather not learn the JVM specification by heart. That said, knowing how the JVM functions and how to tune it will greatly increase your ability not just to troubleshoot possible errors and performance problems, but to squeeze the maximum performance from your ColdFusion applications.

Summary

J2EE has become the de facto standard for robust enterprise application development due to its maturity, breadth of functionality, superior technology, and stability. In this chapter we have looked at how you can leverage the innate functionality of J2EE to create sophisticated many-tiered architectures, set up multiple instances, cluster JRun instances, and tune the very heart of every J2EE application, the Java Virtual Machine. By learning more about the J2EE application platform and its inner workings, savvy ColdFusion 8 application developers and system administrators can scale ColdFusion applications to handle even the most complex and demanding of jobs.

CHAPTER 59

Managing Session State in Clusters

IN THIS CHAPTER

What Is Session State?

The Web is a stateless environment. Every HTTP request or response to your Web server opens a connection, but after the action has completed, the connection is closed. These requests and responses contain no information to tell the server to associate a request with previous or subsequent requests. *Session state* is the process of associating a series of HTTP requests and responses with a unique user, and keeping a set of variables for that session.

NOTE

A user session, not to be confused with a `session` variable, is defined as a related series of HTTP requests and responses for a particular user. Each session has a lifetime, typically the length of time the user's browser is actively connected to the Web site.

ColdFusion gives you several powerful tools for managing session state. These tools range from flexible manipulation of browser-based cookies to a full set of `CLIENT`- and `SESSION`-based variables. This chapter discusses these methods, but you should note that each method of session-state management poses some serious implications. When you manage state, you force the Web to do something it wasn't originally built to perform. Managing session state becomes especially complex if you are planning to scale your ColdFusion application across multiple ColdFusion servers.

In this chapter, you will learn how to manage state in a clustered environment using various techniques, including ColdFusion `CLIENT` variables, ColdFusion `SESSION` variables in conjunction with a `SESSION`-aware load-balancing solution, and storing user information in client-side cookies. You will also learn about Java `SESSION` variables, which have a number of advantages over traditional ColdFusion session variables. Managing state can be difficult and detailed, depending on which option you choose. Choose carefully: If you are basing your application on saving state, clustered environments introduce a whole new set of issues. Each of the techniques described in this chapter involve different coding methods. It is important to determine the appropriate strategy for your application early in the development process, preferably before coding begins.

The History of Managing State

In the early days of the Internet (way back in 1995), CGI programmers set up a roll-your-own method of maintaining client state. They used the HTTP protocol's built-in syntax for passing `name-value` pairs, either in the URL (with a `GET` request) or after the main body of the HTTP request (with a `POST` request, usually from a form). With care, a CGI programmer could hand the same `name-value` pairs from page to page of a site via URLs and forms. The problem with this method is that it creates very long URL strings, which can become unmanageable and would not work properly in some browsers.

Enter Cookies

Netscape defined the cookie as part of Netscape 1.0, which stored `name-value` pairs on the user's machine rather than forcing Web developers to remember to pass `name-value` pairs on every page. These cookies were passed to the server automatically with every HTTP request to the Web site, which set the cookie.

Always the subject of heated debate, cookies soon became the persistent variable favorite of Web application developers. One key advantage is that cookies can persist; you can configure them to stay on the user's machine from session to session instead of expiring at the end of the current session. This allows a Web developer to give a user a permanent (and unique) identifier or even store important data on the user's machine.

Cookies have continued to gain popularity and remain a key tool for developers to utilize when managing client state.

Why Maintain State?

Today's sophisticated Web applications require state. Users expect more than what yesterday's static HTML-based Web sites could provide. This requires that Web sites interact with the client; therefore, they cannot function without some form of session state management.

Various state uses include the following:

- Maintaining information for the user during a user session
- Recognizing a returning user
- Enhancing the usability and functionality of a Web site
- Reducing page-load times and requests to a database server
- Maintaining user sessions across multiple Web servers

As an example, an e-commerce site requires a way to link users with their cart items as they interact with the Web site. This link must be maintained as the user places new items in the shopping cart and successfully checks out. Other examples include enhanced usability from a Web site, such as remembering a customer the next time they visit the site, or pushing specific content to users based on their previous interactions with the site.

Today's Web developers need to be able to track a user through a series of requests, and ideally associate information with that user's session, as shown here:

```
<cflock scope="SESSION" Type="EXCLUSIVE" timeout="2">
 <cfif NOT isDefined("SESSION.AuthLevel")>
 <cfset SESSION.AuthLevel = 0>
 </cfif>
</cflock>
```

Instead of authenticating a user from scratch with every HTTP request, you can store the user's permissions in some form of session state. The session can then read these variables, rather than performing a database query with each page request. Page-build time and stress on the database can both be reduced. This approach is inherently more scalable and provides better functionality.

Load-balanced environments typically include multiple servers configured to appear identical to the users. Not only does state need to be maintained between the Web site and users, it also needs to be maintained when a user is moved from one server to another. Users are redirected from one server to the next based on available server resources. This setup creates a situation in which the Web developer cannot assume that visitors will use the same machine each time they visit the site.

Options for Managing Session State

There are several methods for managing client state with a clustered ColdFusion solution, including the following:

- Embedding parameters into `URL` or `FORM` post variables
- Cookies
- `SESSION` variables
- `CLIENT` variables
- J2EE session management
- Hardware-based session management
- Hybrid solutions (some combination of the above)

All of the solutions listed here work to some degree in a clustered solution, but require careful implementation to ensure that they function properly.

A Little About Server-Side ColdFusion `CLIENT`, `APPLICATION`, `SERVER`, and `SESSION` Variables

Applying the old saying "What's past is prelude" is perhaps the best way to understand ColdFusion's implementation of `SESSION` variables. ColdFusion doesn't replace HTTP `name-value` pairs or cookies, but it does automate the process of identifying users and sessions; you can therefore concentrate on your session-dependent applications instead of the mechanics of maintaining a session.

All server-side ColdFusion variable storage and retrieval depends on the existence of two variables, CFID and CFTOKEN. These two parameters define a unique identity for the user and reference variables stored in one of several places on the ColdFusion server. CFID and CFTOKEN are most commonly implemented as cookies, but you can use ColdFusion sessions without cookies by relying on HTTP name-value pairs. Again, you need to pay close attention to detail, making sure the URLs passed among pages in your application include these pairs.

Uniquely identifying the user is only half the value. To leverage session management fully, you must be able to store information about the user on the server. Since version 4, ColdFusion has offered several methods for storing server-side variables. The various types shown here enable you to define layers of persistent variables:

- SERVER variables are global variables, stored in RAM, that are available to any ColdFusion page on the currently running server. SERVER variables are visible to all sessions.
- APPLICATION variables are similar to SERVER variables but are specific to the current ColdFusion application, as specified in the NAME parameter of the <cfapplication> tag. APPLICATION variables are visible to all sessions.
- CLIENT variables are unique to the current user and persist across sessions. They can be stored in several locations, including a central database (for more on this subject, see "Using a Central CLIENT Variable Repository" later in this chapter), within cookies, or in the server's Registry.
- SESSION variables act much like CLIENT variables, but they are stored on the server in RAM and expire at the end of a user's session, based on a predetermined timeout.

If you have only one ColdFusion server, it doesn't matter that SERVER, APPLICATION, and SESSION variables are stored in RAM or that CLIENT variables are often stored in the server's Registry. But what happens if you have two ColdFusion servers? A SESSION variable that's stored in RAM on Server 1 isn't visible to a ColdFusion page on Server 2. You don't want the user to have to maintain a separate session for each of your servers; you want the user to have a single session with your entire site. How can you take advantage of SESSION and CLIENT variables in a scaled environment? Later in "Using a Central Client Variable Repository" and "Hardware-Based Session Management" you will learn several ways to solve this problem.

Embedding Parameters in a URL or a FORM Post

There are many reasons for passing session state information among Web pages using URL parameters or FORM variables. Passing these variables from page to page can offer cross-application support—Web pages running on different servers or different application-server platforms. These methods can also eliminate the need to use SESSION variables or client cookies.

Client variables, CFID and CFTOKEN, can be used to help maintain session state. You can append the variables to the URL on each page request, and ColdFusion will automatically recognize and use the variables. Listing 59.1 shows the most common way to do this by including the variables in the URL.

Listing 59.1 `addtokens.cfm`—Appending `CFID` and `CFTOKEN` to the URL String

```
<cfapplication sessionmanagement="yes" name="chap59">

<cflock type="EXCLUSIVE" timeout="10" scope="SESSION">
      <cfset SESSION.mySessionVar = "Advanced ColdFusion 8">
</cflock>

<cflocation url="somepage.cfm?cfid=#cfid#&cfidtoken=#cftoken#">
```

What you would see in your browser URL when you append the `CFID` and `CFTOKEN` variables is something like this:

```
http://localhost/somepage.cfm?cfid=300&cfidtoken=13296302
```

NOTE

`CFLOCATION` allows you to do this automatically as well by using the `ADDTOKEN attribute` like this: `<cflocation url="somepage.cfm" addtoken="Yes">`.

Another much easier method to embed URL session information specifically in situations where you wish to maintain state is by using the function `URLSessionFormat()`. This function checks to see if a user's client accepts cookies and if it does not it automatically appends all client identification information to the URL. To use it in the above listing all you would have to do is change the `CFLOCATION` tag URL like this:

```
<cflocation url="#URLSessionFormat("MyActionPage.cfm")#">
```

Embedding information in URL strings can be a security risk. Aside from the issue of passing potentially sensitive information about the user (such as a password) in cleartext, using a URL to pass `CFID` and `CFTOKEN` without another layer of user verification can potentially allow a hacker to highjack a user's account. Furthermore, appending and maintaining state information manually in a URL string is difficult. It is equally difficult and time consuming to pass information from page to page using `FORM` variables. You must expend painstaking effort to make sure all `FORM` elements and URL strings are sending the correct information to the CGI or script.

TIP

For more on best practices when passing information in URLs, please refer to `http://www.adobe.com/go/tn_17255` and be sure to keep up on security threats to ColdFusion and to Adobe products in general by keeping an eye on `http://www.adobe.com/support/security/`

Cookies

Cookies are probably the most popular method for maintaining state and are one of the simpler methods to implement, as illustrated in Listing 59.2. Cookies are stored on the client, and therefore any server in the domain can use them. This allows state management in a clustered environment. Cookies can be persistent or session-based. Persistent cookies exist beyond the user's session and typically have an expiration date. Session-based cookies automatically expire after the user closes the browser.

Listing 59.2 `login.cfm`—Login Form to Authenticate Users and Return Them to the Originating Page

```
<!---
Page Name: login.cfm
Description: Authenticate the user and their password.
 Return successful logins to original page.
--->
<cfparam name="URL.originURL" default="#CGI.script_name#?#CGI.query_string#">
<cfparam name="FORM.username" default="">
<cfparam name="errMsg" default="">

<cfif isDefined("FORM.submit")>
<cfquery name="qryLogin" datasource="OWS">
 SELECT contacts.FirstName,contacts.LastName, contacts.userRoleID,
UserRoles.UserRoleName
 FROM Contacts , UserRoles
  WHERE Contacts.userRoleID = UserRoles.UserRoleID and Contacts.UserLogin =
'#form.userName#' AND Contacts.UserPassword='#form.UserPassword#'
 </cfquery>

        <cfif qryLogin.recordCount EQ 1>
        <cfcookie name="fullname" value="#qryLogin.FirstName# #qryLogin.LastName#">
        <cfcookie name="userSecurity" value="#qryLogin.UserRoleName#">
        <cflocation url="#FORM.originURL#">
        <cfabort>
        <cfelse>
        <cfset errMsg = "Incorrect login information: Please try again">
        </cfif>
</cfif>

<cfoutput>
        <form action="#CGI.script_name#" method="post" name="login">
        <table width="250" cellpadding="3" cellspacing="0" border="1"
align="center">
               <tr bgcolor="navy">
               <td>
               <font face="verdana" size="2" color="white">
               <b>Login</b>
               </front>
               </td>
               </tr>
               <tr>
               <td>
               <font face="verdana" size="2" color="000000">#errMsg#</font>
               <br><b>UserName:</b><br>
               <input type="text" name="userName"
value="<cfoutput>#FORM.userName#</cfoutput>" maxlength="25">
               <br><b>Password:</b><br>
               <input type="password" name="userPassword" maxlength="25">
               <br><br>
               <input type="submit" name="submit" value="submit">
               <input type="hidden" name="originURL" value="#URL.originURL#">
               </td>
               </tr>
        </table>
        </form>
</cfoutput>
</body>
</html>
```

Listing 59.2 shows a processing template for a login form. In this case, there are different classes of users—administrators and normal users. The distinguishing factor is what permissions they have to the system. In this code, the first time users request `somepage.cfm`, they are redirected to the login page (Figure 59.1).

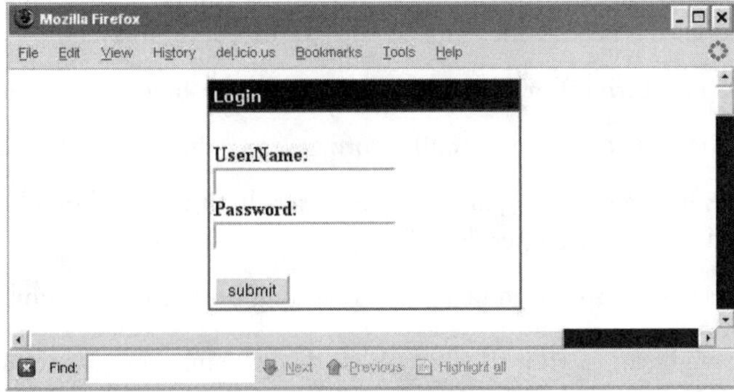

Figure 59.1
A login form.

After a successful login, two cookies are set for the user's full name and security level (Figure 59.2).

Figure 59.2
After a user has successfully logged in, a welcome message greets the person and shows his or her security level.

If you have debugging turned on, you may see something like this in your browser under `Cookie Variables`:

```
CFID=7877
CFTOKEN=42428018
FULLNAME=Ben Forta
USERSECURITY=User
```

You can use these cookies throughout the site to interact with the user.

You can invoke security by applying the logic shown in Listing 59.3 in other Web pages. This example uses the `somepage.cfm` template to call the login form if the `fullname` cookie does not exist, to ensure that the user has logged in before seeing this page.

Listing 59.3 `somepage.cfm`—Snippet of Template to Call Login Form If Cookie Does Not Exist

```
<!--- Check if the user has logged in --->
<cfif structKeyExists(COOKIE, "fullname")>
 <!--- proceeed --->
<b>Welcome back - <cfoutput>#COOKIE.fullname#</cfoutput></b><br>
Your security level is - <cfoutput>#COOKIE.userSecurity#</cfoutput>
```

Listing 59.3 (CONTINUED)

```
<cfelse>
 <cfparam NAME="originURL" DEFAULT="#CGI.script_name#?#CGI.query_string#">
 <cflocation URL="/login.cfm?originURL=#urlEncodedFormat(originURL)#">
 <cfabort>
</cfif>
```

Consider the following issues with using cookies to store session state:

- Clients may turn off or filter cookies using cookie-blocking software.
- Clients may be behind a firewall or proxy server that prevents cookie transmission.
- Cookies have a size limit, and most browsers limit the total number of stored cookies to 300 and allow only 20 per domain.
- Cookies may be stored in plain text, revealing private information about the user.

Because a user might access your site from more than one machine or browser (or might experience a system crash that wipes out cookies), it's usually best to store a minimal user identifier in a cookie and keep critical data on the server side.

It is possible to track a user's state through an application by carrying the variables along on the client side, either in `name-value` pairs in the URL or in a client-side cookie. Information stored in cookies can be either `name-value` pairs or complex WDDX packets (see Chapter 47, "Using WDDX," online), storing a structure of information about the user. Carrying this data around in the URL is a painstaking, difficult-to-maintain practice, and even the most intrepid Web developer should think twice before going down this road. The upside of this strategy is that it does not matter to the system whether a user is redirected to another machine. All the information the script needs is contained in the URL referencing it.

Storing this information in cookies is easier to implement and allows storage of complex data structures in the form of WDDX packets. You can further simplify this scheme by specifying cookies as the default repository for `CLIENT` variable storage in ColdFusion Administrator. The downside of using cookies is that because they are maintained solely on the client side, an enterprising user can hack the application by modifying the cookies.

The following sections examine ColdFusion-specific solutions for implementing session-state management.

`SESSION` Variables vs. `CLIENT` Variables

ColdFusion offers two methods for developers to maintain session state when running on the traditional ColdFusion application server platform: `CLIENT` variables and `SESSION` variables. This section discusses the benefits and risks of using these two variables for implementing session state in a clustered environment.

To use `CLIENT` or `SESSION` variables, ColdFusion sets two values for each user: `CFID`, a sequential client identifier, and `CFTOKEN`, a random-number client-security token. These two variables will uniquely identify a user to ColdFusion and help maintain state.

SESSION variables exist in memory on the server that initiated the session with the user. This is an issue in a clustered Web site. The user's session will be lost upon transfer to another server in the cluster. The new server will not know about the prior session and will start a new session with the user. SESSION-aware load balancing can resolve this problem by keeping a user on the same server throughout the session (see the discussion of this topic in "Keeping the User on the Same Machine" later in this chapter). This server becomes a single point of failure, and you risk the server's crashing and losing the user session.

CLIENT variables can exist in three ways: in the server's Registry, in a database, or in cookies. To use CLIENT variables in a clustered environment, you should store them either in a centrally located database or as cookies to share among all servers in the cluster. Keep in mind that there are serious problems with storing CLIENT variables in the Registry. On high-volume sites, storing too many persistent variables in the Registry will eventually overflow the Registry, causing instability and server crashes. If you must store CLIENT variables in the Registry, set the purge setting in ColdFusion Administrator to a low value to reduce the possibility of filling up your Registry.

NOTE

Adobe strongly discourages customers from storing CLIENT variables in the Registry–even in a single-server environment. If you're not careful, you'll end up adding large amounts of data to the Registry in the form of stored CLIENT variables. Because the Registry was not intended to work as a relational database, this data can overwhelm the Registry quickly and cause system instability or crashes.

TIP

It might be tempting to set the purge value to 0, but this actually causes ColdFusion to attempt to purge the client values every millisecond; see http://www.adobe.com/cfusion/knowledgebase/index.cfm?id=2621e228.

Storing CLIENT variables in a database is easy to administer and is outlined later in this chapter (see "Using a Central CLIENT Variable Repository"). This is the recommended method for maintaining CLIENT variables. It allows the Web site to scale and will let all servers in the cluster access the same CLIENT store.

If the user will not accept cookies, maintaining state with CLIENT or SESSION variables will be difficult. Writing CFID and CFTOKEN as session-based cookies may appease users who are filtering cookies. Session-based cookies offer an alternative and are not persistent, existing only as long as the user session exists. Listing 59.4 illustrates how to code this work-around. By setting the client cookie attribute to No, ColdFusion does not automatically store the variables to cookies; you need to set them manually in code. For this example make the following client-management settings in the Application.cfm template.

Listing 59.4 Application.cfm—Settings for Client Management with Session-Based Cookies

```
<cfapplication name="MXusers"
 clientmanagement="Yes"
 setclientcookies="No">
<!--Set the client cookies as session-based cookies -->
<cfcookie name="cfid" value="#CLIENT.cfid#">
<cfcookie name="cftoken" value="#CLIENT.cftoken#">
```

You can use the CLIENT-management methods described above to manage SESSION variables as well, except that you can't store SESSION variables in a central database.

Keeping the User on the Same Machine

One popular method for managing session state in a scaled environment is to direct a user to the server that's currently most available (as in least utilized) and to have the user continue to interact with the same server for the duration of the session. You can accomplish this approach through either a software-based solution SESSION-aware clustering, or hardware-based solutions.

NOTE

This solution is most prevalent for session-management solutions involving SESSION variables.

Although this method is certainly valid, obvious limitations exist when you're trying to use your server resources to their fullest. For example, User 1 might make a quick stop at your site and only request three simple requests from Server 1 during his or her session. User 2 could be a seasoned user who requests 10 requests from Server 2, including a complex database transaction, during the session. As a result, Server 2 is far busier than Server 1, even though both servers have handled one session.

You can't maintain complete balance. The advantage of SESSION-aware clustering is that you can accomplish it much more simply (and inexpensively) than truly session independent clustering.

Using a Central CLIENT Variable Repository

ColdFusion has the capability to store client information in a central database. This feature creates an effective way to save state across clustered Web servers. If you store CLIENT variables in a central database, any of your ColdFusion servers with access to this database can use the same pool of CLIENT variables.

After you establish your central database, you can set parameters on clients from any of your front-end ColdFusion servers. They remain accessible even if a user switches from one machine to another as long as you continue to pass CFID and CFTOKEN or some other unique identifier. Because CLIENT variables can persist from session to session, you now have a collection of information for each user that can be accessed whenever the user visits your site. Given the simplicity of such a setup, this is a good strategy for many applications—it anticipates the need to scale across multiple servers, even if you don't need to do so right away.

NOTE

Client variables function much like Session variables and if your users refuse to enable cookies on their web browsers then you must pass the CFID and CFTOKEN using one of the methods described earlier in "Embedding Parameters in a URL or a Form Post."

When you decide on this strategy, you must configure your ColdFusion servers to take advantage of the database. Assuming you've already set up a central database server, and you only need to configure your ColdFusion servers to use that database for client storage, here's how to get started:

1. Create a blank database to store your client data.

NOTE

If you're using `CLIENT` variables in a clustered environment, you must first set the default storage mechanism for `CLIENT` variables to be either `COOKIE` or a JDBC data source. Using a client-server database for the central database is preferred.

2. On all your ColdFusion servers, create a data source in ColdFusion Administrator pointing to that central database.
3. In the ColdFusion Administrator, select Client Variables in the Server Settings section.
4. Choose the data source from the pull-down menu and click the Add button
5. On the next screen, check the Create Client Database Tables check-box. This will create the required tables for `CLIENT` variable storage in the database.

NOTE

If this is the first time you've used your database for client storage, on the first ColdFusion server for which you configure `CLIENT` variable storage, select Create Client Database. On subsequent ColdFusion servers, do not select this option when you configure `CLIENT` variable storage. This option actually creates tables named `CDATA` and `CGLOBAL` in your database to store the `CLIENT` variable physically.

NOTE

Make sure to enable the option `Purge Data for Clients That Remain Unvisited for xx Days` on only one of the machines in the cluster. You'll apply unnecessary load to the database server if you have multiple machines performing the periodic deletes.

6. Put the following code in the `application.cfm` files of your application:

   ```
   <cfapplication name="MXusers" clientmanagement="Yes" clientstorage="cfMXvars">
   ```

   In this code, `cfMXvars` refers to the database we created to hold your client variables.
7. Use `CLIENT`-scoped variables in your application to reference persistent data. For example, you could do something like Listing 59.5.

Listing 59.5 `getlastaccess.cfm`

```
<cfapplication
        name="MXusers" clientmanagement="Yes" clientstorage="cfMXvars">

<cfif isDefined("CLIENT.LastAccess")>
        <cfoutput>You were last here on #CLIENT.lastAccess#.</cfoutput>
<cfelse>
        <cfset client.LastAccess = dateFormat(Now())>
        <cflocation url="somepage.cfm">
</cfif>
```

All this simple code does is check the `CFID` and `CFTOKEN` cookies on a user's client and see if they match values in the database. If they do, then `CLIENT.LastAccess` is defined and retrieved based on the `CFID` and `CFTOKEN`.

After you complete these steps, all `CLIENT` variables are stored in the data source. As long as you've configured all your Web servers to use the central database, you don't need to worry about which server receives a given user's request. Even if your environment is not clustered, it is still best to store CLIENT variables in a central database because of the dangers of using the Registry.

Also, for higher-traffic sites, you may wish to select Disable Global Client Variable Updates. In general, try leaving updates enabled and load-test your system; then disable them and load-test your system to see how much the change actually affects your specific application's performance. You should also keep this approach in mind when designing your code if you plan to use client variables such as LVISIT (the last date and time that the client with that CFID loaded a page) and HITCOUNT (the number of page impressions by a particular client). If you do select Disable Global Client Variable Updates, you may break your code.

Java Sessions

Java session management offers an alternative to traditional ColdFusion SESSION variables. J2EE session management uses a session-specific identifier called jsessionid. Using Java sessions in ColdFusion, you can share sessions between ColdFusion and other Java applications, including JavaBeans, JavaServer Pages (JSPs), JSP custom tabs, and Java servlets. This sharing offers many possibilities for extending your ColdFusion application with Java, as you will see in Chapter 78, "Extending ColdFusion with Java."

There is another reason to use J2EE session variables instead of normal session variables: security. ColdFusion uses the same client identifiers for the Client scope and the standard Session scope. Since CFToken and CFID values are used to identify a user over a period of time, they are generally saved as cookies on the client browser. These cookies persist until the client's browser deletes them, which can amount to a considerable length of time. This creates a security risk because a hacker can get access to these variables over a period of time and then spoof or pretend to be a user and gain unauthorized access to sites or systems. Although this is very unlikely, it is still possible and thus a major security consideration. Using J2EE SESSION variables partially counters this risk. The J2EE session-management mechanism creates a new session identifier for each session and does not use either the CFToken or the CFID cookie value.

Configuring a ColdFusion server to use Java sessions could not be simpler and requires only two steps. First, you need to modify the settings in ColdFusion Administrator. Go to the Memory Variables settings page in ColdFusion Administrator. Select both the Use J2EE Session Variables and Enable Session Variables checkboxes. Next, insert the following code into Application.cfm to enable session management in your application:

```
<cfapplication name="MXusers"
 clientmanagement="Yes"
 sessionmanagement="Yes"
 setclientcookies="Yes">
```

ColdFusion will now set the SESSION.SESSIONID variable to jsessionid. You can view the new session ID by using CFDUMP to output it. It should look something like this:

```
7430f3c7f41b376530924e4220d3f3a505b1
```

SESSION.SESSIONID now consists of jsessionid, and SESSION.URLTOKEN consists of a combination of CFID, CFTOKEN, and jsessionid. SESSIONID no longer utilizes the variable application name.

When you use session management and client management, but not Java sessions, the SESSIONID value looks like this:

```
MXUSERS_8877_42428018
```

Notice how the SESSIONID is configured with a combination of the application name, CFID, and CFTOKEN. You can test this yourself by using the <cfdump> tag to dump the contents of both the client structure and the session structure.

Serializing ColdFusion Components

One of the new features of ColdFusion 8 is the capability to serialize ColdFusion Components, allowing you to save them to files, stream them over the Internet, or more important for this chapter, share them across session scopes in a J2EE cluster (see Chapter 58, "Scaling with J2EE," for more on setting up a ColdFusion cluster). ColdFusion does this by taking advantage of Java's serialization API (see Chapter 78 for information about how you can use Java to serialize CFCs to a file).

This capability is especially useful if you regularly put CFCs in the session scope in your application because it allows you to share CFCs in a session even if one of your servers in a cluster goes down. To set this up, you first need to make sure that you have J2EE sessions turned on (see "Java Sessions" earlier in this chapter).

CFC serialization lets you use J2EE session replication to automatically replicate sessions across a cluster, giving you access to the CFCs in session scope on any server in a cluster. This feature supports most ColdFusion variables, including structures, in a replicated session scope.

NOTE

At the time of writing, arrays in CFCs were not supported for session replication.

You can also preserve and access data in a CFC in the event of session failover (if a machine in the cluster fails and other machines then have to pick up its load and state). ColdFusion structures stored within the session scope are available in the session scope, even after failure of the server. For example, if you are running multiple ColdFusion instances to balance server load, you can store useful data, including CFCs, within the session so that you can access the data across all the pages that are served in that session.

Enabling CFC serialization in easy. All you have to do is set the CFC in your session scope like this:

```
<cfset cfccomponent = CreateObject("component", "myShoppingCart")>
<cfset session.userCart = myShoppingCart>
```

Then, from any machine, you can check a specific CFC, like this:

```
<cfset check = session.userCart.verifyDATA(CartID)>
```

Hardware-Based Session Management

Some hardware load-balancing devices, such as Cisco LocalDirector, offer sticky management of cookie states. The load balancer works in concert with the Web server to create session-based cookies. These cookies create a session for the user. Both the load balancer and the Web server can manipulate and read them.

Some load balancers can operate in Cookie-Rewrite, Cookie-Passive, or Cookie-Insert modes. In the Cookie-Rewrite mode, the Web server creates the cookie, and the load balancer will rewrite it. Cookie-Passive mode looks for a cookie set by the Web server but will not create a cookie of its own. It attempts to learn the cookie to manage session state. If no cookie is present, Cookie-Passive mode will not depend on a cookie to maintain state. Cookie-Insert mode allows the load balancer to create a cookie and set it on the client. In this mode, the load balancer first looks for a cookie; if no cookie is present, this mode connects to the client and creates a cookie.

Some load balancers offer other persistence modes to manage a user session, including Secure Socket Layer (SSL), preferred server, and source. These configurations maintain `SESSION`-aware sessions and provide secured connections to load-balanced servers. Talk to your network or system administrators about what options are available in your hardware solution in order to determine what makes the most sense for your specific application.

Hybrid Solutions

Today's Web sites are complex applications, consisting of many pages and relying on sophisticated techniques to provide content and feature-rich user interfaces. Typically you cannot use one method for managing session state for the Web site, and so the viable solution becomes some combination of the techniques discussed in this chapter. This introduces complexities beyond the focus of this chapter, but I will offer some plausible solutions.

Obviously one hybrid solution involves using cookies and `CLIENT` or `SESSION` variables in combination to manage session state. Two cookies are stored on the client to identify the user to the server.

Other hybrid solutions include using cookies or `SESSION` variables to identify the user and storing all session information in a centrally located database. A cookie is polled for a user identifier that is used to query the database. This is practical for an e-commerce site, which creates a unique identifier for each user and stores all shopping cart and checkout information in a database. Each time the shopping cart information is requested, the database is queried to populate the information on the page.

You can also use J2EE session management on the ColdFusion MX application server and utilize this `sessionid` to access user information, such as username and password.

Web sites can dynamically push content to users based on their preferences or characteristics, by associating a unique identifier stored in a `SESSION` variable and relating this to information residing in a database.

The potential uses for session state are endless, and every developer will have a preferred method for managing and using state in Web applications. Optimal session-state management in a clustered environment complicates the issue, but you can overcome these difficulties by carefully structuring and applying these techniques in designing your Web site.

CHAPTER 60

Deploying Applications

IN THIS CHAPTER

Deployment Options

The ability to write, compile, and package application code and application-specific settings on one system, then deploy that package on disparate systems is a powerful part of the J2EE architecture. ColdFusion is a certified J2EE application. ColdFusion 8 provides three methods for deploying applications to other ColdFusion servers:

- **ColdFusion Archives (CAR)**. Packaging ColdFusion application code, server settings, data sources, and other elements into CAR files.
- **J2EE Archives (EAR/WAR)**. Packaging ColdFusion applications as Enterprise Application Archives (EAR) or Web Application Archives (WAR) for deployment on J2EE application servers.
- **ColdFusion Compiler (`cfcompile` Utility)**. Compiling ColdFusion templates into Java bytecode.

The two archive options are configurable via the ColdFusion Administrator. The ColdFusion Compiler is a command-line tool.

ColdFusion Archives

Adobe introduced CAR files with the Archive and Deploy feature of ColdFusion 5 Enterprise. These ColdFusion Administrator (CFAM) tools provide administrators with a simple means of quickly backing up ColdFusion server configuration settings and application files for archiving purposes or later deployment. The interface is very flexible, allowing you to create as many CAR files as you want and to choose which settings and files you want to archive. For example, you can choose to archive all of the ColdFusion server settings in one CAR file, or create independent CAR files for each setting (data sources, scheduled tasks, and so forth), or simply back up your application files or custom tags. Although these powerful tools were carried over into ColdFusion 8, they still remain one of the least-used administration features.

TIP

ColdFusion 8 will deploy CAR files created with ColdFusion MX versions 6.x and 7.x. However, because of configuration differences in ColdFusion 8, Adobe recommends using the Migration stage of the Configuration Wizard to import settings from previous versions, and then using the ColdFusion Archive and Deploy tools to create a ColdFusion 8 CAR file. See the ColdFusion 8 release notes for known issues related to deployment of CAR files, at `http://www.adobe.com/support/documentation/en/coldfusion/8/releasenotes.pdf`.

CAR files have an archive format similar to WAR and/or ZIP files. CARs contain all the files related to the ColdFusion application and server. In each CAR file are two XML property files containing WDDX data structure: `archive_properties.xml` and `server_settings.xml`. The `archive_properties.xml` file holds descriptors for the archive definition, including archive variables that help with deployment on different machines. The `server_settings.xml` file holds descriptors for each ColdFusion server setting.

There are three steps to deploying applications with archives:

1. Define the archive.
2. Build the archive.
3. Deploy the archive.

Defining the Archive

You define an archive by giving it a name and then selecting the settings and/or files you want to archive. You will use the archive name when you want to deploy or update the archive. Begin creating your archive definition by accessing the ColdFusion Archives (`.car`) window in the Packaging and Deployment section of the ColdFusion Administrator.

NOTE

All ColdFusion wizards require a browser with JavaScript enabled.

NOTE

The ColdFusion Archives option is not available in the ColdFusion Standard Edition.

1. Start the Archive Wizard:

   Open the ColdFusion Administrator. Expand the Packaging and Deployment section (if necessary) in the left navigation frame, and click the ColdFusion Archives link (Figure 60.1).

   In the ColdFusion Archives window, enter a name for your archive in the Archive Name text field and click Create. Archive names can contain only letters, numbers, dots, underscores, and dashes. The archive name appears in the Current Archive Definition List, and the Archive Wizard appears (Figure 60.2).

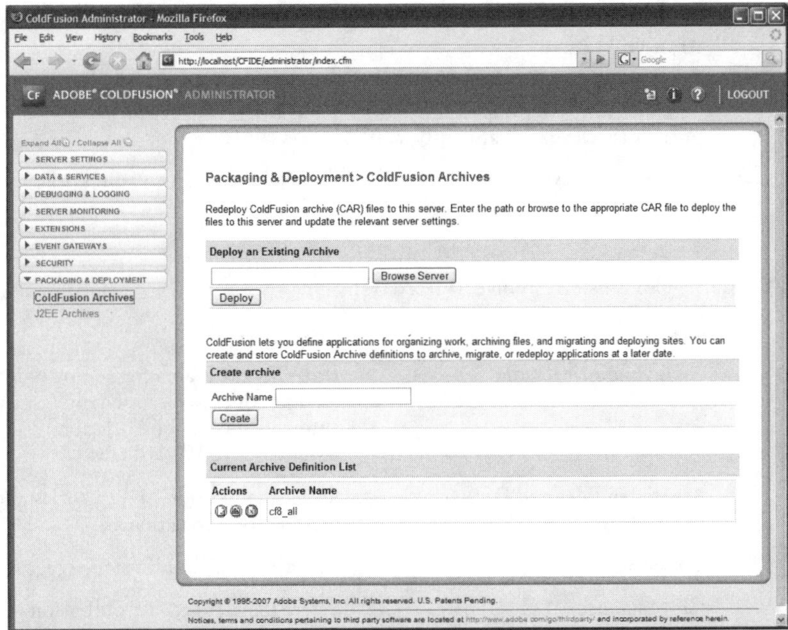

Figure 60.1

The ColdFusion Archives (`.car`) window.

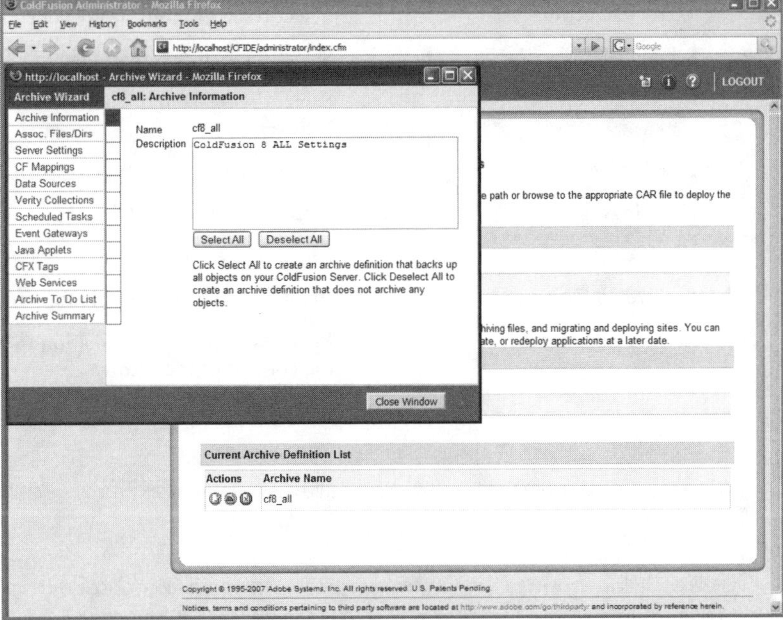

Figure 60.2

The Archive Wizard.

NOTE

Pop-up blockers may prevent the Archive Wizard windows from appearing; click the archive name to launch the wizard. Consider either disabling the pop-up blocker or allowing pop-ups for the ColdFusion 8 Administrator.

2. In the Archive Wizard, specify the data to archive. Table 60.1 describes the tabs in the Archive Wizard.

   On tabs containing check boxes, your selections are saved after you click the mouse button (`onclick` JavaScript event).

3. When you have finished selecting the archive options, click Close Window. Your archive definition is now complete.

Table 60.1 ColdFusion Archive Wizard Tabs

TAB	DESCRIPTION
Archive Information	Provides a text area for adding a description for the archive. Also provides Select All and Deselect All buttons for automatically enabling/disabling all the options available on other Archive Wizard tabs.
Associated Files and Directories	Select the location of directories and files to include and exclude from the archive.
Server Settings	Select general ColdFusion server settings to archive.
CF Mappings	Select the registered ColdFusion mappings to archive.
Data Sources	Select the registered ColdFusion data sources to archive.
Verity Collections	Select the registered Verity collections to archive.
Scheduled Tasks	Select the registered automated tasks to archive.
Event Gateways	Select the registered ColdFusion event gateway instances to archive.
Java Applets	Select the registered applets to archive.
CFX Tags	Select the registered CFX tags to archive.
Web Services	Select the registered Web Services to archive.
Archive To Do List	Itemize tasks to perform before/after deploying an archive.
Archive Summary	Provides summary information to help you quickly identify the content of the archive.

TIP

Make sure you import any third-party files, drivers, or certificate stores when creating archive definitions.

TIP

Creating a ColdFusion archive after initially configuring server settings (e.g., data sources, caching, mappings, etc.) is a good way to create a re-deployable server baseline. Creating or updating archives as settings undergo change is also a good way to create server snapshots. Creation of a snapshot is also helpful when creating new server instances for use with JRun clustering.

Modifying the Definition

Should you need to modify the archive definition, follow these steps:

1. Open the ColdFusion Administrator, expand Packaging and Deployment, and open the ColdFusion Archive window.
2. Find your archive definition name in the Current Archive Definition List.
3. Start the Archive Wizard by clicking either the name of your archive, or the adjacent Edit Archive Definition icon (the one on the far left).
4. In the Archive Wizard, make the desired changes on the tabs containing the options you want to modify (see Table 60.1).
5. When you have finished modifying the options, click Close Window.

Deleting the Definition

To delete an existing archive definition, do the following:

1. Open the ColdFusion Administrator, expand Packaging and Deployment, and open the ColdFusion Archives window.
2. In the Current Archive Definition List, click the Delete Archive icon (the one at the far right) next to the archive name you want to delete.
3. A message window appears asking you to confirm the delete operation (Figure 60.3). Click OK to confirm. The ColdFusion Archives window refreshes and the deleted archive is removed from the Current Archive Definition List. Or click Cancel to cancel the delete operation.

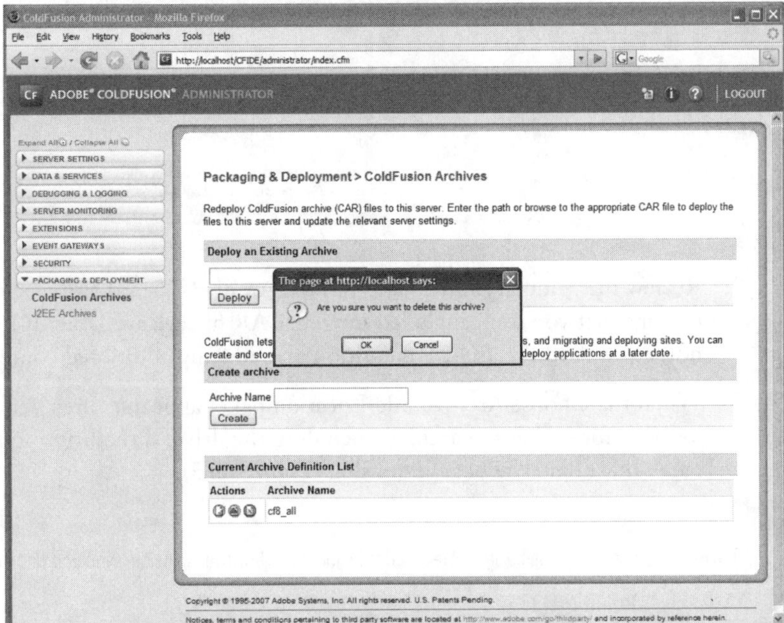

Figure 60.3

Confirming the deletion of the ColdFusion archive definition.

Building the Archive

An archive's definition identifies the objects to be included in the archive. You use it to build your CAR file for deployment. Follow these steps to build an archive:

1. Start the Archive Wizard:

   Open the ColdFusion Administrator. Expand the Packaging and Deployment section (if necessary) in the left navigation frame, and click the ColdFusion Archives link.

   In the ColdFusion Archives window's Current Archive Definition List, click the Build Archive icon (the middle one) next to the archive name you want to build. The Archive Wizard appears (Figure 60.4).

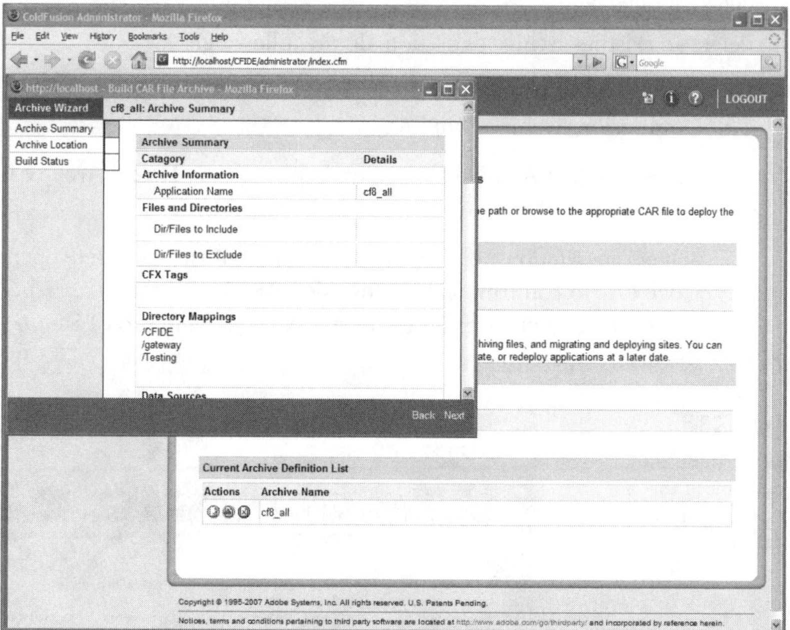

Figure 60.4

Building the archive using the Archive Wizard.

2. Review the summary information in the Archive Wizard and ensure that all of the options that you want included in your CAR file are available. If they are, click Next. If not, go back to the archive definition and add any additional content.

3. When the Choose Archive File Location panel appears, enter a full system path to the location for saving the archive, including the drive, directory, and file name. The file name must have the `.car` extension (Figure 60.5).

TIP

The file name and archive name are not required to be the same; however, consider synchronizing these names for administration ease.

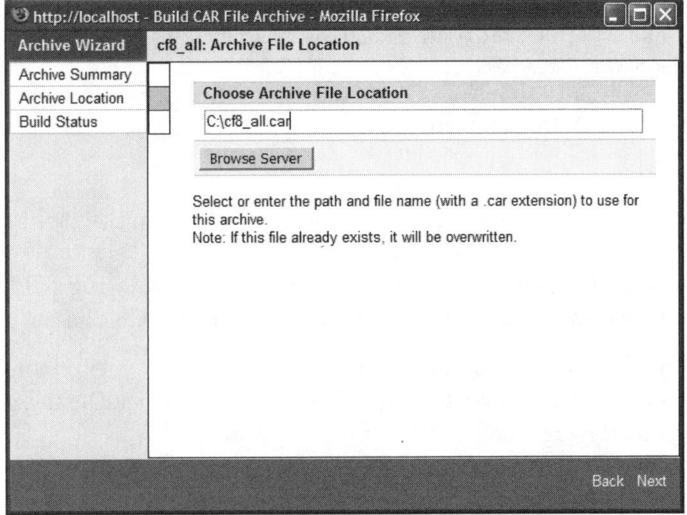

Figure 60.5

Specify a location and file name with a `.car` extension for the archive file.

4. Click Next to start building the archive. The Archive Wizard will display one of the following messages when the operation completes: "Build Successful" or "Build completed with errors, Please check logs for more information."
5. Click OK to close the message window. If the build had errors, you can browse the status messages in the Build Status panel.

TIP

For large or complex archives, the "Build Successful" alert box may actually appear while ColdFusion is still building the physical archive file. You will know that the physical archive file is completely built when the Next button in the Archive Wizard changes to Close.

6. Click Close to close the Archive Wizard.

Your archive is now built. You should browse the file system and verify that the physical CAR file exists in the location you specified in the Archive Wizard. You can view the contents of the CAR file by using an archive utility such as WinZip. If the build operation completed with errors (and you cannot see the error in the Status panel), check the source of the problem in the CAR archive log (`cfroot\logs\car_archive_FILENAME.log`).

Deploying the Archive

Now that you have built the physical CAR file, you are ready to deploy it on another ColdFusion server.

NOTE

Avoid deploying archives created in ColdFusion MX 6.x and 7.x that contain Java and JVM settings, Locking settings, or Verity collections. All other settings can be safely deployed on ColdFusion 8. Do not deploy archives created in ColdFusion 8 on ColdFusion MX 6.x systems.

TIP

ColdFusion 8 uses the RSA JSafe Crypto libraries for encrypting and decrypting password strings. You may need to reenter the passwords for some data sources deployed from ColdFusion MX CAR files.

1. Access the Archive Wizard.

TIP

The window title bar says "Deploy Wizard," but the menu item title says "Archive Wizard." This is bug ID 70779.

Open the ColdFusion Administrator. Expand the Packaging and Deployment section (if necessary) in the left navigation frame, and click the ColdFusion Archives link.

In the Deploy an Existing Archive section, browse to or enter a full system path to the location of the archive (CAR file) in the text field. Click Deploy, and the Deploy Wizard appears (Figure 60.6).

NOTE

If pop-up blockers prevent the Deploy Wizard windows from appearing, consider either disabling the pop-up blocker or allowing pop-ups for the ColdFusion 8 Administrator.

Figure 60.6

Deploying the archive.

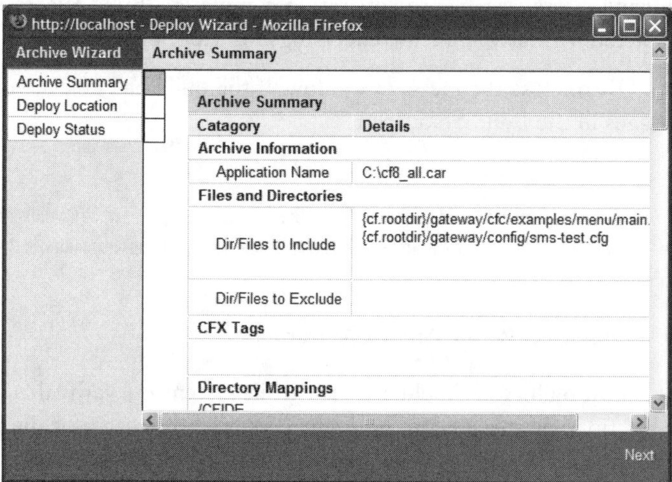

2. Review the summary information in the Deploy Wizard and ensure that the available options in the CAR file are what you want deployed on this ColdFusion server. (The Archive Summary tab may take a while to display for larger/more complex archives.) When you're ready, click Next to continue.

3. On the Deploy Location panel modify the Directory Path Translation entries as necessary. You will only see paths listed if the archive includes files and directories (such as application code, Verity collections, and so on). Also be sure to note any pre-restore to-do items listed on the screen.

4. Click Deploy to restore the archive. The Archive Wizard will display one of the following messages when the operation completes: "Deploy Successful" or "Deploy completed with errors, Please check logs for more information".

5. After reviewing the post-restore to-do list, click OK to close the message window. If the deployment had errors, you can browse the status messages in the Deploy Status panel.

TIP

For large or complex archives, the "Deploy Successful" alert box may actually appear while ColdFusion is still restoring the physical archive file. You will know that the archive is completely restored when the Next button in the Archive Wizard changes to Close.

6. Click Close to close the Archive Wizard.

The archive has been restored to the ColdFusion server. You should go through the ColdFusion Administrator and file system to verify that the settings were applied and files were added. If the deploy operation completed with errors (and you cannot see them in the Status panel), check the source of the problem in the CAR deploy log (`cfroot\logs\car_deploy_FILENAME.log`).

J2EE Archives

ColdFusion is a certified J2EE application capable of being deployed as an EAR or WAR file on J2EE application servers. Deploying ColdFusion MX on J2EE application servers required multiple administration steps, including creating the ColdFusion application server instance, configuring data sources, deploying application code, and more. ColdFusion MX 7 introduced the capability to package the ColdFusion server and application code into a single J2EE Archive for deployment from within the ColdFusion Administrator.

This J2EE Archive feature is different from the J2EE configuration option of the ColdFusion 8 installer. The installer's J2EE configuration option will only create a base ColdFusion 8 application server as an EAR or WAR file. The J2EE Archive feature, in contrast, allows you to package your ColdFusion application code (CFM, CFC, and CFR files) in an archive file with a configured ColdFusion 8 application server. In this way, it combines parts of the installer's J2EE configuration with the ColdFusion Archive feature.

Defining J2EE Archives

Following are the steps to define a J2EE archive:

1. Open the ColdFusion 8 Administrator. Expand the Packaging and Deployment section (if necessary) in the left navigation frame, and click the J2EE Archives link.

2. In the J2EE Archives window, enter the name for your archive in the Archive Name text field in the Add New Archive section (Figure 60.7). Archive names must be alphanumeric. You cannot use any non-alphanumeric characters such as punctuation, currency symbols, etc. When you're done, click Add.

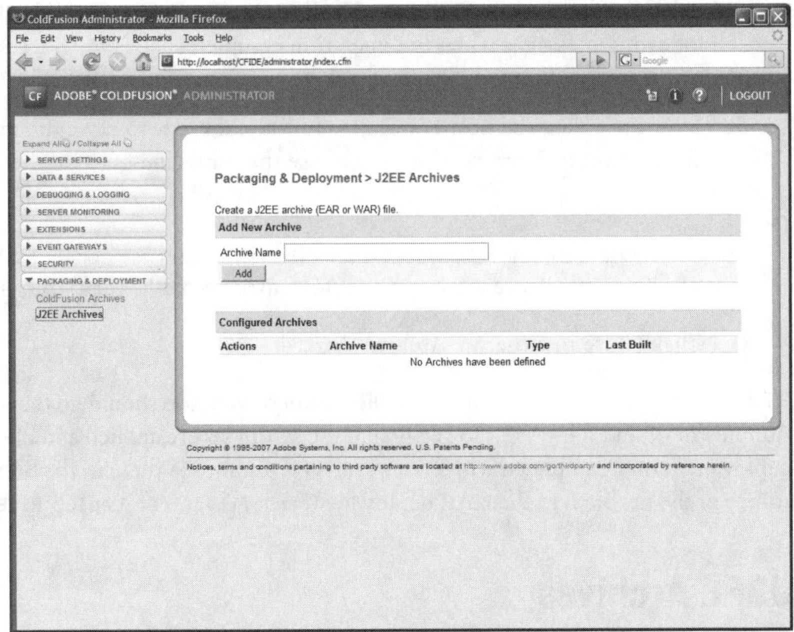

Figure 60.7

The J2EE Archives window.

NOTE

Avoid using `cfusion` as an archive name. When choosing the EAR/WAR configuration during installation, the installer creates a `cfusion.ear` or `cfusion.war` file. If you name your J2EE archive `cfusion`, the J2EE archive feature will create the same file names and this may cause confusion.

3. In the Add/Edit J2EE Archive window that appears (Figure 60.8), specify settings for your archive. These include the application code directory, a destination directory for the compiled archive file, the archive type, a context root (if necessary), ColdFusion data sources to include, and so on. Table 60.2 describes the available options.
4. Click Submit. ColdFusion will compile an EAR or WAR file using the options you have selected and save it in the distribution directory. The J2EE Archives window reappears with the new archive definition listed under Configured Archives (Figure 60.9).

TIP

The default distribution directory for the compiled J2EE archive is `cfroot/packages/{archive_name}` for ColdFusion server configurations, and `cf_web_root/WEB-INF/cfusion/packages/{archive_name}` for ColdFusion J2EE configurations. Consider saving your archive files outside of the ColdFusion directory structure and web root, in another partition. Secure your archive files with standard operating system security.

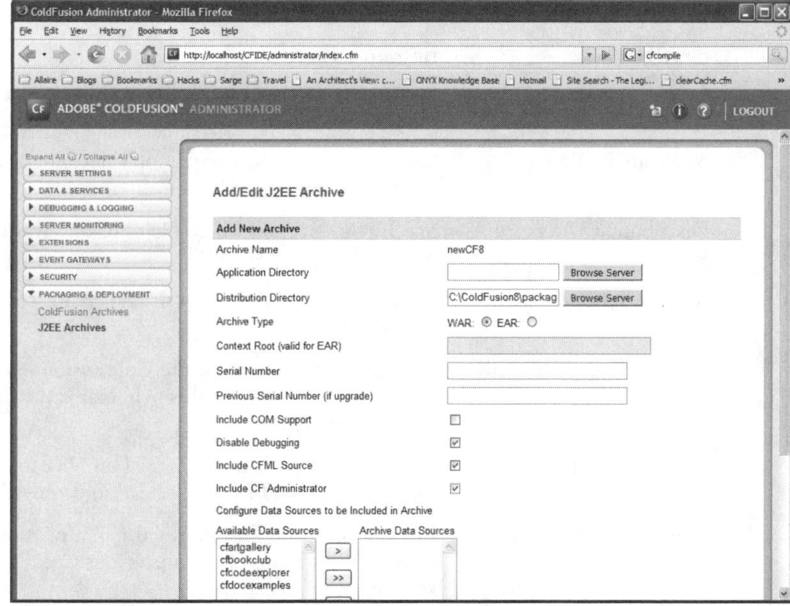

Figure 60.8

Use the J2EE Archives Add/Edit window to create or modify the archive definition.

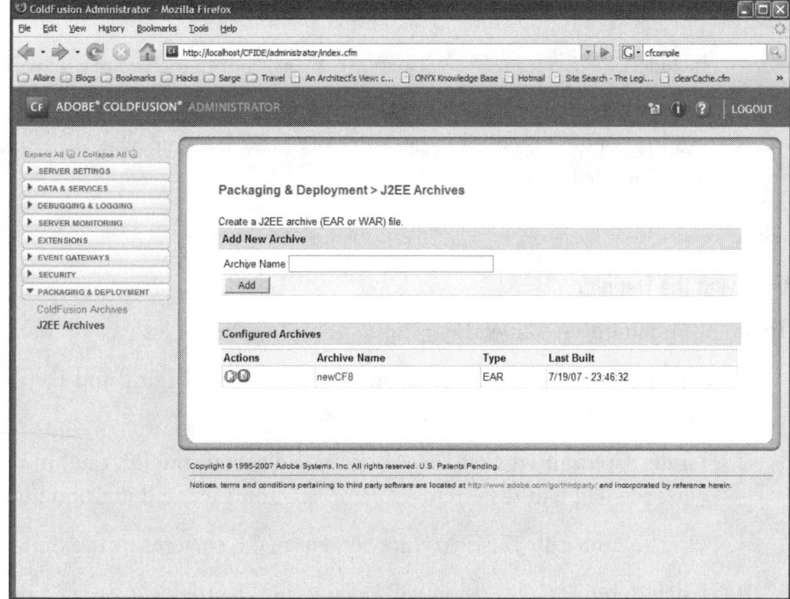

Figure 60.9

The created archive appears in the Configured Archives list.9.

Table 60.2 J2EE Archive Options

OPTION	DESCRIPTION	REQUIRED?
Archive Name	Specify the name for the J2EE Archive (which will also be used as the EAR or WAR file name).	Yes
Application Directory	Specify the directory containing the ColdFusion application code (CFM, CFC, and so on).	Yes
Distribution Directory	Specify the location where ColdFusion saves the compiled EAR or WAR file.	Yes
Archive Type	Select whether ColdFusion should create a WAR or EAR file.	Yes
Context Root (EAR only)	Specify a context root for the ColdFusion application. If you leave this field blank, the default context root (/) is used.	No
Serial Number	Enter a valid ColdFusion 8 serial number to use for the archived ColdFusion application deployed.	No
Previous Serial Number	Enter a valid ColdFusion MX 6.*x*, 7.*x*, or 8.*x* serial number if upgrading from a previous ColdFusion version.	
Include COM Support	Select if you want to include COM support.	No
Disable Debugging	Select to disable debugging in the archived ColdFusion application.	No
Include CFML Source	Specify whether or not to include the source.	No
Include CF Admin		No
Configure Data Sources to be Included in Archive	Select the data sources to include in the archive.	No

Modifying the Definition

To modify a definition, follow these steps:

1. Open the ColdFusion Administrator, expand Packaging and Deployment (if necessary), and open the J2EE Archives window.
2. Under Configured Archives, click the Edit icon (the left one) in the Actions column, or click the name in the Archive Name column for the definition you want to edit.
3. On the Add/Edit J2EE Archive screen, make changes to the options you want to modify.
4. Click Submit. ColdFusion will recompile the archive, save it in the Distribution Directory, and return to the J2EE Archives window.

Deleting the Definition

1. Open the ColdFusion Administrator, expand Packaging and Deployment (if necessary) , and open the J2EE Archives window.
2. In the J2EE Archives window, click the Delete icon (the right one) in the Actions column, or click the name in the Archive Name column for the definition you want to delete.
3. A message window appears asking you to confirm the delete operation. Click OK to confirm that you want to delete the archive. The J2EE Archives screen refreshes, and the archive is removed from the Configured Archives list. Or, click Cancel to cancel the operation. The archive name will remain in the Configured Archives list.

J2EE Archive Definition Considerations

Keep the following in mind as you create your J2EE archive definition:

- **Archive File Size**. The typical archive file size is approximately 100 MB. Ensure that the partition containing the destination directory has enough space to accommodate this size requirement. The total archive file size is ultimately affected by the size of the application directory and the selected options; for example, including COM support, ColdFusion Administrator, or ColdFusion source.
- **Archive File Type**. Not all J2EE application servers require the same archive file type. It's important to consider the archive file deployment requirements of your J2EE application server when defining and deploying the archive file. For example, IBM WebSphere will require that you deploy your ColdFusion application as an EAR, but servers such as BEA's WebLogic, JBoss, and the SunOne Application Server will let you deploy the same application as a WAR.
- **Application Code**. All files (CFM, CFC, CFR, HTM, JPG, and so on) in the specified application directory will be included in the archive. If you do not specify the Include CFM Source Option, then all ColdFusion files (files with `.cfm`, `.cfc`, and `.cfr` extensions) will be compiled to Java bytecode.

  Although you can specify any local partition for the application directory, the files in this directory will be deployed beneath the ColdFusion application root directory (such as `/cfusion.war/myTemplate.cfm`). This could cause application errors after deployment if the code contains links to external directories or depends on Web server mappings.
- **CF Custom Tags**. All templates in the global custom tags directory (`cfroot\CustomTags`) are automatically included in the archive file. This is a potential security risk and also adds to the archive file size. Consider removing tags from the global custom tags directory (including subdirectories) before defining the archive if you do not want them deployed on a new system.

- **Serial Number**. J2EE deployment is a ColdFusion Enterprise feature. If a serial number is omitted or invalid in the archive definition, then the deployed ColdFusion Application will revert to a Trial Edition. You can upgrade to the Enterprise Edition after deployment by entering a valid Enterprise serial number, using the ColdFusion Administrator or the Administrator API. See Chapter 66, "Using the Administrator API," for details.
- **COM Support**. COM support is only available for Windows systems. If there is a possibility that the archive will be deployed on a non-Windows system, do not include COM support.
- **ColdFusion Administrator**. Even if you choose not to include the ColdFusion Administrator in your archive definition, parts of the CFIDE directory structure are still included to enable other functionality, such as CFFORM and the Administrator API. See Chapter 66 for details on the Administrator API.

Deploying the Archive

The created J2EE archive contains a ColdFusion Server Enterprise edition in J2EE configuration. Use your J2EE application server's deployment features to deploy your archive. For example, the ColdFusion 8 Multiserver configuration allows you to create and manage multiple servers using the Enterprise Manager feature in the ColdFusion Administrator. You can combine the Instance Manager feature with the J2EE archive feature to deploy customized ColdFusion applications from within the ColdFusion Administrator. See Chapter 58, "Scaling with J2EE," for more information.

TIP

When creating a new ColdFusion instance, the Instance Manager automatically deploys a copy of the currently running ColdFusion application server (Administrator settings, CF mappings, data sources, verity collections, and so on). If you want to deploy a customized ColdFusion application instance, use the J2EE archive feature to package a ColdFusion application as an EAR file. Create a new ColdFusion instance, and enter your EAR file in the Create From EAR/WAR option.

J2EE Archive Deployment Considerations

Keep the following in mind when deploying your J2EE archive:

- **Mappings**. The ColdFusion mappings in the archived application point to directories on the computer used to create the archive. You must use the ColdFusion Administrator or Administrator API to modify the ColdFusion mappings on your newly deployed server if those directories do not exist on that server.
- **CFX Tags**. ColdFusion CFX tag support may not be enabled on the deployed system. You need to ensure that the `cfroot/WEB-INF/cfusion/lib` directory is added to the JVM's native library path (`java.library.path`) to enable CFX support.
- **Verity**. The Verity mappings of the original ColdFusion server that created the archive will also be in the EAR/WAR. You must ensure that Verity is enabled on the deployment computer and that the archived settings are suitable for it.

TIP

If Verity is not enabled on your system, run the platform-specific Verity search server installer. See "Installing the Verity Search Server Separately" section of the Installing and Using ColdFusion help manual at `http://livedocs.adobe.com/coldfusion/8/htmldocs/00000014.htm#1202283`.

Use the ColdFusion Administrator or the Administrator API to modify the Verity settings once Verity is deployed. See Chapter 66 for details on the Administrator API.

ColdFusion Compiler

The ColdFusion Compiler compiles ColdFusion templates (CFM, CFC, and CFR) into Java bytecode. Adobe provides a command-line interface to the compiler (`cfcompile.bat` on Windows; `cfcompile.sh` on Unix). The script is located in the `cf_root/bin` (server configuration) or `cf_webapp_root/WEB-INF/cfusion/bin` (J2EE configurations) directory.

You can use this utility for:

- Converting ColdFusion source code into Java bytecode for sourceless deployment of ColdFusion templates
- Precompiling ColdFusion templates into Java class files

The basic syntax for calling the `cfcompile` script is as follows:

```
cfcompile [-deploy] webroot [directory-to-compile] [output-directory]
```

It is preconfigured with the options necessary to compile source code into Java bytecode for sourceless deployment, and for compiling ColdFusion templates into Java class files.

Compiling Sourceless Templates

The capability to deploy sourceless ColdFusion templates is one of the most anticipated ColdFusion 8 features. *Sourceless* means you can deploy your ColdFusion templates (CFM, CFC, and CFR files) as Java bytecode and distribute them without changing the template names or paths. The templates will contain unreadable Java bytecode but will run as if they contained CFML. This makes source code distribution more secure and protects the intellectual property contained in the files. For more information on the security of sourceless deployment, see the "Encrypting ColdFusion Templates" section of Chapter 65, "Security in Shared and Hosted Environments."

Use the `cfcompile` utility with the `-deploy` option to convert the source code of your ColdFusion templates to Java bytecode. The utility will make a copy of your original template and compile the CFML to Java bytecode. The template containing the Java bytecode will be written to the specified destination directory, leaving unchanged your original CFML templates. The `cfcompile` executable is located in the `cf_root/bin` (server configuration) or `cf_webapp_root/WEB-INF/cfusion/bin` (J2EE configurations) directory. Use the following command to compile your templates to Java bytecode:

```
cfcompile -deploy webroot directory-to-compile output-directory
```

Table 60.3 describes the `cfcompile` parameters for creating sourceless templates.

Table 60.3 `cfcompile` **Script Options for Sourceless Deployment**

OPTION	DESCRIPTION	REQUIRED?
`webroot`	Specify the fully qualified path to the web server root directory (for instance, `C:\ColdFusion8\wwwroot or C:\Inetpub\wwwroot`).	Yes
`directory-to-compile`	Specify the fully qualified path to the directory containing the templates to be compiled. This directory must be under the specified `webroot` directory. If omitted, ColdFusion will compile all ColdFusion templates in the specified `webroot` directory.	Yes
`output-directory`	Specify the fully qualified path to the destination directory that will contain the compiled deployable files. This cannot be the same directory as the source directory.	Yes

Precompiling ColdFusion Templates

As you may know, the ColdFusion server compiles each ColdFusion template into Java bytecode when the template is initially requested—that is, the first time after a server restart. When the "Save class files" option in ColdFusion Administrator is enabled, the compiler writes the bytecode into Java `.class` files on the disk and then copies the bytecode into memory (the Template Cache); otherwise, the bytecode is written directly to the Template Cache. This compilation process increases the initial page request. ColdFusion will continue serving the template from the Template Cache, so that only the initial request takes the compilation hit. Combining this technique with the Trusted Cache option can dramatically improve site performance. Adobe recommends saving the class files only for production servers.

Use the following command to compile ColdFusion templates (CFM, CFC, and CFR files) into Java class files:

```
cfcompile webroot directory-to-compile
```

Table 60.4 summarizes the script options.

Table 60.4 `cfcompile` **Script Options for Precompiling** `.class` **Files**

OPTION	DESCRIPTION	REQUIRED?
`webroot`	Specify the fully qualified path to the Web server root directory (for instance, `C:\ColdFusion8\wwwroot or C:\Inetpub\wwwroot`).	Yes
`directory-to-compile`	Specify the fully qualified path to the directory containing the templates to be compiled. This directory must be under the specified `webroot` directory. If omitted, ColdFusion will compile all ColdFusion templates in the specified `webroot` directory.	Yes

TIP

Notice that the `directory-to-compile` must be within the specified `webroot`. If you want to compile templates outside of the actual `webroot` to class files–such as templates in a Web server virtual directory called `Testing`–then specify that directory as the `webroot` and omit the `directory-to-compile` parameter: `cfcompile C:\Testing`.

The compiled class files are stored in the `cf_root/wwroot/WEB-INF/cfclasses` (server configuration) or `cf_webapp_root/WEB-INF/cfclasses` (J2EE configurations) directory. The files are renamed using a unique syntax:

```
cf + filename + hash code + .class
```

ColdFusion uses the following to derive this file name:

- The `filename` is extracted from a Java File object created from the canonical file name (for example, `C:\Testing\hasher.cfm`) with the following substitutions:

  Included slashes (`/`) in the file name are replaced with a double underscore (__).

  Any characters that are illegal in a Java identifier are replaced with their equivalent two-digit hexadecimal number; for example, a period (`.`) becomes `2e`.
- The `hash code` represents the hash code value created by the Java File object (`java.io.File`). The hash code is generated by calling the `hashCode` method; refer to the Java documentation at `http://java.sun.com/javase/6/docs/api/java/io/File.html#hashCode()`.

  If the value returned by `hashCode()` is negative, it is exclusive-or'd with 0xFFFFFFFF to get the value ColdFusion uses.

TIP

You will also see `.class` files with a dollar sign (`$`) in the name followed by a function name, as in `cfApplication2ecfc639310892$funcONREQUESTSTART.class`. The `$` represents the compiled ColdFusion user-defined function (UDF) calls within the file. This is more common for ColdFusion Components (CFC) files, but they will occur for any ColdFusion template containing UDF calls.

ColdFusion Template Deployment Considerations

At first glance, the difference in the command syntax for compiling your ColdFusion templates to `.class` files as compared with compiling to sourceless code is the `-deploy` option. However, the *real* difference is the process by which the code is compiled. When precompiling (or not using the `-deploy` option), the compiler translates the CFML into Java bytecode and writes the bytecode to a `.class` file. When creating sourceless templates, the compiler implements the ColdFusion run-time service, translates the CFML into Java bytecode, and then creates a new template (with the same name as the original) and writes the bytecode into that template. Implementing the run-time service allows the compiler to check the code for syntax errors—as if the code were called from the browser. The compiler will fail and return if there are any errors in your code. The error and stack trace are recorded to the ColdFusion exception log (`cfroot\logs\exception.log`).

TIP

The `-deploy` option will catch compilation errors, but some run-time errors will not occur until after deployment. For example, "Template not found" errors for `cfinclude` will not occur until the deployed file is run on the deployed system.

Adobe provided the `cfcompile` script with ColdFusion for precompiling `.class` files. Some developers have tried deploying these files on other systems. Adobe does not recommend deploying compiled `.class` files, however, because they are largely dependent on the underlying directory structure of the source server. Some of the class files might actually work on the deployment server. Adobe created the `-deploy` option to enable the secure deployment of ColdFusion templates.

Customizing the `cfcompile` Script

You can customize the `cfcompile` script file that ships with ColdFusion 8, or build your own. Table 60.5 provides a complete list of ColdFusion Compiler options. The `cfcompile` script preconfigures some of these options for you. Examine the preconfigured values to ensure that the script will run on your system.

TIP

You can compile individual files by specifying the fully qualified path to the file instead of just the directory path. For example: `cfcompile C:\InetPub\wwwroot C:\InetPub\wwwroot\index.cfm`.

Table 60.5 ColdFusion Compiler Command Options

OPTION	DESCRIPTION	REQUIRED
`cfroot`	The fully qualified path to the ColdFusion root directory (such as `C:\ColdFusion8` or `/opt/coldfusion8`).	Yes
`d` or `deploy`	Compile templates for sourceless deployment.	Yes for Sourceless Deployment
`deploydir`	The fully qualified path to the directory that will contain the compiled deployable files. This cannot be the same directory as the source directory.	Yes for Sourceless Deployment
`f` or `force`	Force compilation.	No
`g` or `debug`	Enable debug symbols.	No
`help`	Displays usage information and available options.	No
`srcdir`	The fully qualified path to the directory containing the templates to be compiled. This directory must be under the specified `webroot` directory. If omitted, ColdFusion will compile all ColdFusion templates in the specified `webroot` directory.	Yes
`webinf`	The fully qualified path to the ColdFusion `WEB-INF` directory.	Yes
`webroot`	The fully qualified path to the Web server root directory (such as `C:\ColdFusion8\wwwroot` or `C::\Inetpub\wwwroot`).	Yes
`v` or `verbose`	Display compiler performance statistics.	No

With the options in Table 60.5, you can create your own compiler script using syntax similar to the following:

```
java -cp "c:\ColdFusion8\runtime\lib\jrun.jar;C:\ColdFusion8\wwwroot\WEB-
INF\lib\cfmx_bootstrap.jar;C:\ColdFusion8\wwwroot\WEB-INF\lib\cfx.jar" -
Dcoldfusion.classPath=C:/ColdFusion8/lib/updates,C:/ColdFusion8/lib
-Dcoldfusion.libPath=C:/ColdFusion8/lib coldfusion.tools.CommandLineInvoker
Compiler -cfroot C:\ColdFusion8 -webinf C:\ColdFusion8\wwwroot\WEB-INF
-webroot C:\ColdFusion8\wwwroot -deploy -srcdir C:\Testing\deploy -deploydir
C:\Testing\source -v
```

This command will compile all the ColdFusion templates (CFM, CFC, and CFR files) in the `C:\Testing\deploy` directory and save the Java bytecode versions in the `C:\Testing\source` directory. The original files in `C:\Testing\deploy` will retain the original CFML in a human-readable format.

NOTE

The ColdFusion Compiler is hard coded to accept only the default ColdFusion file extensions (`.cfm`, `.cfc`, and `.cfr`) for deployment. The capability to compile additional file name extensions is not fully exposed via the command-line interface. If you configure your ColdFusion server to process other extensions (such as `*.cfx`), you will have to specify the fully qualified path to the individual files instead of just the directory path. For example, to create a sourceless version of `index.cfx`, you will need to call

```
cfcompile -deploy C:\InetPub\wwwroot C:\InetPub\wwwroot\index.cfx C:\Testing\source
```

If you try using a wildcard (as in `C:\InetPub\wwwroot\*.cfx`), only the first file is compiled. See the "Setting the File Name Extension" section in Chapter 65 for details on adding additional ColdFusion file name extensions.

Choosing the Right Deployment Option

Adobe provides three methods for deploying your ColdFusion applications. You have to decide the appropriate method for your configuration and the target environment. For example, if you need to simply back up your current configuration as part of a contingency plan for hardware failure, you might choose to create a ColdFusion archive (`.car`). This will allow you to re-create the ColdFusion settings and redeploy any code and other files. Or maybe you are an IS manager who needs the ability to deploy multiple ColdFusion server instances on a departmental IBM WebSphere server. The J2EE archive (`.EAR`) makes more sense for you. Or perhaps you are an independent developer interested in selling your custom tags or components without having your code reverse-engineered into the original CFML. Then surely you will opt for sourceless deployment.

Table 60.6 should help you determine the appropriate deployment option.

Table 60.6 Deployment Options

REQUIREMENTS	COLDFUSION ARCHIVE (.car)	J2EE ARCHIVES	SOURCELESS DEPLOYMENT
Existing ColdFusion 8 Server	x		x
Existing J2EE Application Server		x	
Integrate with J2EE Application Server deployment functionality		x	
Integrate with the ColdFusion 8 multiserver configuration Instance Manager	x		
ColdFusion 8 Enterprise license for archive creation	x		
ColdFusion 8 Enterprise license for archive deployment	x	x	
Configure within ColdFusion 8 Administrator	x	x	
Configure from the command line			x
Create archive files	x	x	
Deploy a full ColdFusion 8 Application server		x	
Optionally include ColdFusion 8 Administrator	x	x	
Optionally include specific ColdFusion Server settings	x		
Optionally include specific Data Sources	x	x	
Optionally include specific Event Gateways, Scheduled Tasks, Verity Collections, etc.	x		
Optionally include files from different server directories	x		
Deploy CFML Source Code	x	x	
Deploy ColdFusion templates as Java bytecode		x	x

PART X

Ensuring Security

CHAPTER 61

Understanding Security

IN THIS CHAPTER

It is important to understand that security risks are inherent to any application running on a networked machine. This remains true of all Internet applications. The risks do not apply only to the code, database, servers, and infrastructure of the application. The risks are just as real to end users because they often use the applications to enter sensitive information, which then needs to be transmitted back to the servers. In this time of increasing cyber-terrorism, protecting sensitive data should be a chief priority for Web applications.

Security Risks

The reality of Internet applications is that each piece of data being transmitted from the client to the server and back to the client passes through equipment on several different networks. In multi-tiered systems, the client-server paradigm is extended to include application servers, databases, and other heterogeneous systems. Each of these represents a point where the data passing between a user and the server could potentially be compromised.

To minimize the risk of data being compromised in this fashion, many Internet applications are built using Secure Socket Layers (SSL) over the HTTPS protocol. Using this technology, data sent between the server and browser (client) is encrypted (the bit depth of encryption can vary among brands and versions of the browsers), making it much more difficult for outsiders to read this data.

NOTE

Although encryption can make users' data more difficult to steal, technologies exist that, given enough time and processing power, can decrypt any encrypted strings. Nevertheless, the stronger the encryption used, the longer it will take a malicious user to decrypt it.

Encryption schemes are good protection from eavesdroppers; however, by themselves, they do not completely guard your data and back-end systems from malicious users. It is commonplace for Web sites/applications to accept end-user input from browsers (input such as forms and/or URL parameters) and pass it directly to the database (or other back-end systems). The application must validate such browser input to ensure only valid data reaches the database.

In many cases, there are pages or whole sections of a Web site that only authorized users can view. These pages require a protection system to which users can identify themselves (log in) and have the system check whether they are authorized to view the requested page. These login routines can be handled either at the operating system/Web server level or within the application itself.

A final concept in Internet security is access control. Through the use of firewalls, it is possible to restrict certain machine communication (as determined by IP or MAC addresses) with specific parts (ports) of other machines. With a well-established set of firewall rules, it is possible to limit public access to machines and offer the application's infrastructure a higher degree of security. For example, it is not uncommon for network administrators to establish firewall rules that only allow access to the database servers from the ColdFusion server. Because the public cannot access this machine directly, it makes it much more difficult for malicious users to compromise the company's data.

What Is ColdFusion's Concern and What Is Not

Application architects must consider security early in the design process. For example, in a typical e-commerce application you generally have a database, application server, and web server delivering content and accepting orders from disparate clients. Architects must consider all possible points of penetration that may lead to data compromise, including:

- **Data Level**. Application data is the most crucial and delicate part of any system. It must be protected from contamination and theft—by authorized and unauthorized users. Database administrators protect data integrity with user accounts, resource permissions, encryption, etc.
- **Web Server Level**. The Web server is the public interface into a network. These interfaces need guarding against unauthorized access and data theft. Administrators typically guard Web servers against intrusion and limit Web server resources with access permissions. SSL, firewalls, and virtual private networks (VPNs) can protect a Web server connection from eavesdropping.
- **Application Server Level**. Application servers are middleware that connect two or more disparate systems—typically a Web server and database, mail, or directory servers. Application server connections can be protected via SSL and VPNs. The application server has built-in security to protect its own resources. Developers code their own security paradigm (e.g., roles-based) or extend others (e.g., operating system, Web server, etc.) to provide authorization and authentication within applications.
- **Operating System (OS) Level**. All clients and servers—Web servers, database servers, phones and PDAs, and so on—run some form of operating system. Operating systems also provide user access controls to protect resources. Some operating systems are capable of encrypting entire file systems.
- **Network Level**. Network systems require software and hardware security measures. Network devices require physical security typically in a secured network operations center (NOC). Network connections are protected with firewalls (hardware and software), VPNs, WEP/WPA, filtering, and access control policies.

Although it provides some base functionality in many of these areas for securing Internet applications, the ColdFusion 8 Application Server is not intended to solve all security issues at every level. It can offer application-level security by defending applications against security risks in four areas: encryption, validation, authentication, and authorization. Let's examine ColdFusion's role in these areas.

Encryption

Encryption is the process of applying a random key and an algorithm to plaintext data (called cleartext) to produce encrypted data (called ciphertext) that is unreadable or meaningless to third parties who do not have the key for decryption. Several places throughout an application can benefit from encryption. One of these is the transmission of sensitive data between a browser and the server. Another is the storage and transfer of data within an application.

Encryption between servers and browsers is best handled by the Web server through the use of Secure Socket Layers (SSL). ColdFusion 8 offers the `Encrypt()`, `EncryptBinary()`, `Decrypt()`, `DecryptBinary()`, and `Hash()` functions, which are useful for encrypting sensitive information before it is written to a database, cookie, or URL variable. These functions are not replacements for SSL.

NOTE

The encryption functions are useful for encrypting strings only after ColdFusion has processed them. None of these functions can operate on strings sent by client browsers to the Web server.

Cleartext Risks

Packet sniffers are software used for troubleshooting network issues. They work by displaying the contents of data packets traveling along a network. Although they are necessary network administration tools, in the wrong hands packet sniffers can expose sensitive data. As previously mentioned, any data sent across the Internet usually passes across the hardware of several network along the path to the data's destination. If anyone is running a packet sniffer on any of the network segments, the data's contents will become visible to those networks. To counter this risk, a number of encryption schemes have been created. Their purpose is to make sniffed packets unreadable.

NOTE

No encryption scheme can make text or packets truly unreadable. Given enough time and computing power, any encryption can be broken. Encryption schemes serve to make text unreadable to the naked eye and to make it harder to decrypt.

ColdFusion Encryption Functions

A common mistake about ColdFusion is that it lacks strong encryption capabilities. ColdFusion 8 includes five functions for string encryption: `Encrypt()`, `EncryptBinary()`, `Decrypt()`, `DecryptBinary()`, and `Hash()`. Versions of ColdFusion prior to MX 7 used an XOR-based algorithm—a 32-bit pseudorandom key (based on a developer-provided seed), and UUencoding for `Encrypt()` and `Decrypt()`. The `Hash()` function used the MD5 algorithm in a one-way hash to create a fixed-length, 32-byte hexadecimal string from variable-length string. No matter the size of the original string, the resulting hash was always 32-bytes.

NOTE

XOR stands for exclusive-or. It is a bitwise or Boolean operator which returns true (or one) if its operands have different values, and false (or zero) if the values are the same. UUEncode (or Unix to Unix Encoding) is a method of converting binary data to ASCII for sending across the Internet.

ColdFusion MX 7 provided support for the Sun Java Cryptography Extension (JCE). This allowed developers to use the default and third-party JCE provider algorithms in the ColdFusion encryption functions. CFMX 7 also added two binary encoding methods: Base64 and Hex. ColdFusion 8 Enterprise edition now includes the RSA BSafe Crypto-J library (version 3.6) to provide FIPS-140 Compliant Strong Cryptography. The result is stronger encryption strings for greater security by allowing developers to specify different algorithms, feedback modes, and padding methods.

TIP

ColdFusion 8 embeds the Sun 1.6.0_01 JVM, which includes the JCE by default. Should you want to change JVMs for ColdFusion, ensure that your JVM of choice includes the JCE–and that the SunJCE provider is the default provider.

TIP

For unlimited-strength cryptography, download the JCE Unlimited Strength Jurisdiction Policy Files 6 located under Other Downloads at `http://java.sun.com/javase/downloads/index.jsp`. Back up the `current local_policy.jar` and `US_export_policy.jar` files in `cf_root/runtime/jre/lib/security` and replace them with the `.jar` files in the downloaded `jce_policy-6.zip` file.

How `Encrypt()` and `Decrypt()` Work

`Encrypt()` works by using a symmetric key–based algorithm, which means the same key used to encrypt the string must be used to decrypt it. A string encrypted this way is only as secure as the key. If the key is compromised, the string can be decrypted by anyone possessing it. Also remember that if the key is lost, the data cannot be decrypted.

When specifying the default algorithm (`CFMX_COMPAT`), `Encrypt()` uses an XOR-based algorithm to create a pseudo-random 32-bit key based on the specified key. Encrypted data can be much larger (potentially as much as three times as large) as the original string. Use the following syntax for `CFMX_COMPAT` algorithm:

```
encrypt(string, key)
```

To enable strong encryption, specify a Block or Password-Based Encryption algorithm. You also need to specify the appropriate optional parameters for the algorithm you want to use. Block encryption ciphers are symmetric-key encryption algorithms that encrypt fixed-length blocks (usually 64- or 128-bits) of plaintext data into same-length blocks of *ciphertext*. They require binary keys of specific lengths and may require an Initialization Vector (IV). Use the `GenerateSecretKey` function to create a unique key of the appropriate length. You can manually create binary keys, but you have to ensure that the keys are the correct length for the specified algorithm. This may mean changing the algorithm's default encryption mode and padding methods. ColdFusion will automatically create an appropriate Initialization Vector for the specified algorithm. You may also create one manually and pass it to the `IVorSalt` parameter, but you need to ensure the correct block size for the algorithm.

CAUTION

The values ColdFusion generates for the Initialization Vector with the `generateSecretKey` function should suffice for most encryption schemes. ColdFusion will automatically prepend a secure, random Initialization Vector onto the encrypted data. However, if you create your own IV, ColdFusion will not include it with the encrypted data, and you have to keep track of it throughout the application. The `generateSecretKey` function returns a Base64-encoded binary key of the default length for the specified algorithm that is created using a secure random number generator. It can only be used for the CFMX_Compat and Block Encryption algorithms.

For a list of Sun Provider algorithms in Java 6, see Java Cryptography Architecture Sun Providers Documentation at `http://java.sun.com/javase/6/docs/technotes/guides/security/SunProviders.html`.

Password-Based Encryption (PBE) uses passwords or passphrases as keys. For PBE algorithms, ColdFusion will automatically generate a binary salt value. A salt is a random string that is prepended to the specified passphrase and hashed over a number of iterations in order to create the encryption key. ColdFusion will automatically create a secure, random 8-byte salt value and use an iteration count of 1000. You can create your own binary salt value and pass it to the `IVorSalt` parameter. Specify your own count to the `iterations` parameter.

Use the ColdFusion `Decrypt()` function to decipher a string that has been encrypted with the `Encrypt()` function. `Decrypt()` and `Encrypt()` are mirror functions in that they require the same arguments (see the section "`Encrypt()` and `Decrypt()` Parameters" later in this chapter). Remember that ColdFusion's encryption is symmetric—you must use the same key to encrypt and decrypt the string. If you use strong encryption (a Block or PBE algorithm) to encrypt the string, then you need to use the same key (seed) or password (salt), algorithm, and `IVorSalt` and `iterations` values to decrypt it. Listing 61.1 shows an example of the use of strong encryption with `Encrypt()` and `Decrypt()`.

Listing 61.1 `encrypter.cfm`—The `Encrypt()` and `Decrypt()` Functions at Work

```
<cfsetting enablecfoutputonly="yes">
<!---####
Name of file: encypter.cfm
Description: Demonstrates strong algorithms used in Encrypt() and Decrypt()
functions.
Sarge (sarge@adobe.com) www.adobe.com/go/sarge_blog
Date created: February 9, 2005
Date modified: July 25, 2007
 ####--->
<cfsetting enablecfoutputonly="no">
<!DOCTYPE HTML PUBLIC -//W3C//DTD HTML 4.0 Transitional//EN>
<html>
<head>
    <title>ColdFusion 8 Encryption Test</title>
</head>
<body>
```

Listing 61.1 (continued)

```
<h2>ColdFusion 8 Encrypter</h2>
<cfform id="encrypter" name="encrypter">
<table border="0">
<tr><td>String: </td><td><cfinput type="text" id="plainText" name="plainText"
size="25" required="yes" message="You must provide a string to encrypt."></td></tr>
<tr><td>Key:</td><td><input type="text" id="key" name="key" size="25"
disabled></td></tr>
<tr><td>Algorithm:</td>
<td><cfselect id="algo" name="algo"
onChange="if(algo.value.indexOf('PBE')){key.disabled=true} else
{key.disabled=false}">
<option value="AES">AES</option>
<option value="Blowfish">Blowfish</option>
<option value="DES">DES</option>
<option value="DESEDE">Triple DES</option>
<option value="PBEWithMD5AndDES">Password With DES</option>
<option value="PBEWithMD5AndTripleDES">Password With TripleDES</option>
<option value="PBEWithSHA1AndDESede">PBEWithSHA1AndDESede</option>
<option value="PBEWithSHA1AndRC2_40">PBEWithSHA1AndRC2_40</option>
</cfselect></td></tr>
<tr><td>Encoding:</td>
<td><cfselect id="encode" name="encode">
<option value="UU">UUencode</option>
<option value="Base64">Base64</option>
<option value="Hex">HEX</option>
</cfselect></td></tr>
<tr><td> </td><td><input type="submit" name="Submit"
value="Submit">  <input name="Reset" type="Reset"></td></tr>
</table>
</cfform>
<br />
<a href="index.cfm">Back to index</a>

<cfsetting enablecfoutputonly="yes">
<cfif isDefined('FORM.algo')>
    <!---#### Set a default key value in case user does not submit one or Block
Encryption is used. ####--->
<!---#### Detect Password Based Encryption algorithms. ####--->
    <cfif UCase(Left(FORM.algo,3)) EQ "PBE">
<!---#### Create a default key for Password Based Encryption algorithm. ####--->
        <cfif NOT len(trim(FORM.key))>
            <cfset variables.key = "My secret password string" />
            <cfset variables.autoKey = true />
         <cfelse>
            <cfset variables.key = trim(FORM.key) />
            <cfset variables.autoKey = false />
         </cfif>
    <cfelse>
    <!---#### Use generateSecretKey to create a secure, random key for the chosen
Block Encryption algorithm. ####--->
        <cfset variables.key = generateSecretKey(FORM.algo) />
        <cfset variables.autoKey = true />
    </cfif>

    <!---#### Perform encryption with default ColdFusion Compatible algorithm
(CFMX_Compat). ####--->
```

Listing 61.1 (continued)

```
    <cfset variables.compatText = encrypt(FORM.plainText, variables.key) />

    <!---#### Perform encryption/decryption with strong algorithms. ####--->
    <cfset variables.cipherText = encrypt(FORM.plainText, variables.key, FORM.algo,
FORM.encode) />
    <cfset variables.origText = decrypt(variables.cipherText, variables.key,
FORM.algo, FORM.encode) />
    <cfoutput>
    <hr>
    <table border="0">
    <tr><th align="left">Original String:</th><td>#FORM.plainText#<br></td></tr>
    <tr><th align="left">Key (Auto Generated:
#yesNoFormat(variables.autoKey)#):</th><td>#variables.key#<br></td></tr>
    <tr><th align="left">CFMX_Compat Encrypted:</th><td
style="color:##FF0000">#variables.compatText#</td></tr>
    <tr><th align="left">#FORM.algo# Encrypted:</th><td
style="color:##009900">#variables.cipherText#</td></tr>
    <tr><th align="left">Encoding:</th><td
style="color:##009900">#FORM.encode#</td></tr>
    <tr><th align="left">Decrypted:</th><td
style="color:##0099CC">#variables.origText#</td></tr>
    </table>
    </cfoutput>
</cfif>
<cfsetting enablecfoutputonly="no">
</body>
</html>
```

The code in Listing 61.1 displays a form that allows the user to submit a string to encrypt, a password or seed value, the encryption algorithm, and encoding. The string is encrypted using the seed, algorithm, and encoding values. The Block Encryption algorithms will use `generateSecretKey()` to create a secure, random key. Only the `CFMX_Compat` and PBE algorithms will use the submitted seed/password value. The decrypt function requires that all parameters have the same values used to encrypt the string. Finally, the original string, encrypted string, encoding, and decrypted string are output (Figure 61.1).

TIP

`GenerateSecretKey()` creates a secure key of default length for the specified algorithm. ColdFusion 8 adds an optional `keysize` parameter for specifying the number of bits for the key length. ColdFusion will throw an error if you specify a `keysize` value that is too large for the specified algorithm.

NOTE

The embedded 1.6.0_01 JVM uses the `/dev/urandom` device by default to seed the PRNG (pseudo-random number generator) used by the Java `SecureRandom()` calls that generate secure, random values.

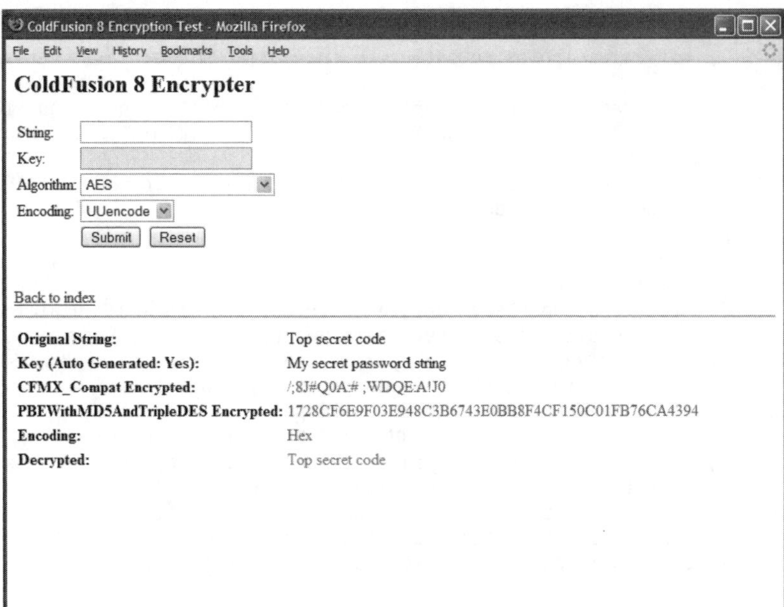

Figure 61.1

The `Encrypt()` and `Decrypt()` functions are useful for setting sensitive data into a cookie because a user won't need to interact with it directly, but it will be sent as cleartext (with some exceptions) on each request to the site.

`Encrypt()` and `Decrypt()` Parameters

Listing 61.1 illustrates how to use `Encrypt()` and `Decrypt()` to secure plaintext data. This section will describe the parameters for these functions. Both have two required parameters: `string` and `key`. The first required parameter is the plaintext/ciphertext string to be encrypted/decrypted; the second is a key or seed value used to encrypt/decrypt the string. There are four optional parameters: `algorithm`, `encoding`, `IVorSalt`, and `iterations`. Here is the syntax for each function:

```
Encrypt(string, key, [algorithm ,encoding ,IVorSalt ,iterations])
Decrypt(string, key, [algorithm ,encoding ,IVorSalt ,iterations])
```

Following are descriptions of the parameters for `Encrypt()` and `Decrypt()`.

`string`

Required. This is the plaintext string to encrypt, or ciphertext string to decrypt. (Always interpreted as a UTF-8 string for ColdFusion.)

`key`

Required. This is the encryption key (seed) or password (salt). Can be:

- A string used as a seed to generate a 32-bit encryption key for the CFMX_COMPAT algorithm.

- A key in the format for the specified Block Encryption algorithm; use the `GenerateSecretKey` function to generate the appropriate key.
- The password or passphrase for the specified Password Block Encryption algorithm.

`algorithm`

Optional. This is the algorithm used to encrypt/decrypt the string. ColdFusion includes a backward-compatible algorithm as well as the default algorithms supported by the SunJCE provider:

- Backward-Compatible algorithm: CFMX_COMPAT (default). Algorithm used in previous ColdFusion versions. This is the least-secure option.
- Block Encryption algorithms:

  AES. The Advanced Encryption Standard specified by U.S. National Institute of Standards and Technology (NIST) Federal Information Processing Standard (FIPS) 197.

  ARCFOUR. The RC4 symmetric block encryption algorithm.

  Blowfish. The Blowfish algorithm defined by Bruce Schneier.

  DES. The Data Encryption Standard algorithm defined by NIST FIPS-46-3.

  DESEDE: The "Triple DES" algorithm defined by NIST FIPS-46-3.

  RC2: The RC2 symmetric block encryption algorithm defined by RFC 2268.

  ColdFusion 8 Enterprise edition includes the following RSA BSafe Crypto-J library algorithms:

  DESX: The extended Data Encryption Standard symmetric encryption algorithm.

  RC4: The RC4 symmetric encryption algorithm.

  RC5: The RC5 encryption algorithm.
- Password-Based Encryption (PBE) algorithms:

  PBEWithMD5AndDES. A password-based version of the DES algorithm; uses an MD5 hash of the specified password as the encryption key.

  PBEWithMD5AndTripleDES.* A password-based version of the DES-EDE algorithm; uses an MD5 hash of the specified password as the encryption key. (This algorithm requires Sun Unlimited Strength Jurisdiction Policy Files for Java 6.)

  PBEWithSHA1AndDESede.* A password-based version of the DES-EDE algorithm; uses a SHA-1 hash of the specified password as the encryption key.

  PBEWithSHA1AndRC2_40.* A password-based version of the 40-bit RC2 algorithm; uses a SHA1 hash of the specified password as the encryption key.

ColdFusion 8 Enterprise edition includes the following RSA BSafe Crypto-J library algorithms for use with `encrypt()/decrypt()`:

PBEWithSHA1AndRC2. A password-based version of the RC2 algorithm; uses a SHA-1 hash of the specified password as the encryption key

PBEWithHmacSHA1AndDESede. A password-based version of the DES-EDE algorithm; uses an HMAC-SHA-1 hash of the specified password as the encryption key.

NOTE

*Requires the Sun JCE Unlimited Strength Jurisdiction Policy Files for Java 6.

TIP

If an algorithm is in both the Sun JCE and Crypto-J, ColdFusion will use the one provided by Crypto-J.

encoding

Optional; you must specify the `algorithm` parameter in order to use `encoding`. This is the binary encoded representation of the encrypted string. Can be:

- `Base64`. The IETF RFC 2045 Base64 algorithm.
- `Hex`. Hexadecimal byte values represented by the characters 0–9 and A–F.
- `UU`. (default) The UUencode algorithm.

IVorSalt

Optional; you must specify the `algorithm` parameter in order to use `IVorSalt`. This is Initialization Vector or Salt, for Block or PBE algorithms, respectively.

- **Block Encryption algorithms.** The binary Initialization Vector value to use with the algorithm. The algorithm must contain a feedback mode other than ECB (Electronic Code Book).
- **Password-Based Encryption algorithms.** The binary salt value added to the specified password and hashed into the encryption key.

iterations

Optional; this is the number of times to hash the password and salt to produce the encryption key for PBE algorithms. Must be a positive, nonzero number (default value is 1000). You must specify the `algorithm` parameter with a PBE algorithm in order to use `iterations`.

CAUTION

You will receive the following error if you try to use some of the stronger algorithms (for example, PBEWithMD5andTripleDES) or key size lengths:

coldfusion.runtime.Encryptor$InvalidEncryptionKeyException: The key specified is not a valid key for this encryption: Illegal key size.

ColdFusion's `Hash()` Function

The other function in ColdFusion for obfuscating data is `Hash()`. `Hash()` provides one-way encryption, meaning there is virtually no way to decrypt a string after it has been hashed. In previous versions of ColdFusion, this worked by taking using the MD5 algorithm to convert a plaintext into a 32-byte, hexadecimal string. In ColdFusion 8, the `Hash()` function also leverages the message digests supplied by the SunJCE provider. The syntax for `Hash()` is:

```
Hash(string[, algorithm[, encoding]] )
```

Following are descriptions of the parameters and algorithms for `Hash()`.

`string`

Required. This is the plaintext string to hash.

`algorithm`

Optional. This is the algorithm used to decrypt the string. ColdFusion includes a backward-compatible algorithm, as well as the default algorithms supported by the SunJCE provider:

- CFMX_COMPAT. (default) Algorithm used in previous ColdFusion versions. This is the least-secure option. (Same as MD5 algorithm.)
- MD2. The MD2 algorithm; generates a 32-byte, hexadecimal string.
- MD5. (default) The MD5 algorithm; generates a 32-byte, hexadecimal string. (Same as CFMX_COMPAT algorithm.)
- SHA. The original SHA-0 (Secure Hash Standard) algorithm specified by NIST FIPS-180; generates a 40-character string.
- SHA-1. The SHA-1 algorithm specified by NIST FIPS-180-2; generates a 40-character string.
- SHA-256. Uses SHA-256 algorithm specified by FIPS-180-2; generates a 64-character string.
- SHA-384. Uses SHA-256 algorithm specified by FIPS-180-2; generates a 96-character string.
- SHA-512. Uses SHA-256 algorithm specified by FIPS-180-2; generates an 128-character string.

ColdFusion 8 Enterprise edition includes the following RSA BSafe Crypto-J library algorithms for use with `hash()`:

- SHA-224: The 224-bit secure hash algorithm defined by FIPS 180-2 and FIPS 198.
- HMAC-MD5: The hash message authentication code calculated using the MD5 hash algorithm.

- HMAC-RIPEMD160: The hash message authentication code calculated using the RACE Integrity Primitives Evaluation Message Digest 160-bit message digest algorithm and cryptographic hash function.
- HMAC-SHA1: The hash message authentication code calculated using the 160-bit secure hash algorithm defined by FIPS 180-2 and FIPS 198.
- HMAC-SHA224: The hash message authentication code calculated using the 224-bit secure hash algorithm defined by FIPS 180-2 and FIPS 198.
- HMAC-SHA256: The hash message authentication code calculated using the 256-bit secure hash algorithm defined by FIPS 180-2 and FIPS 198.
- HMAC-SHA384: The hash message authentication code calculated using the 384-bit secure hash algorithm defined by FIPS 180-2 and FIPS 198.
- HMAC-SHA512: The hash message authentication code calculated using the 512-bit secure hash algorithm defined by FIPS 180-2 and FIPS 198.

TIP

If an algorithm is in both the Sun JCE and Crypto-J, ColdFusion will use the one provided by Crypto-J.

`encoding`

Optional; you must specify the `algorithm` parameter in order to use `encoding`. The `encoding` used when converting the string into byte data; used by the hash function. Default is UTF-8 (or the value specified by the `defaultCharset` entry in `cfroot\lib\neo-runtime.xml`. Must be a value recognized by the JRE.

TIP

The encoding value is ignored when using the CFMX_COMPAT algorithm, which always produces a hexadecimal string. Specify the MD5 algorithm if you want to use a hash similar to CFMX_COMPAT but produce a different encoded string.

Listing 61.2 shows how to use the `Hash()` function.

Listing 61.2 `hasher.cfm`—Encrypting with the `Hash()` Function

```
<cfsetting enablecfoutputonly="yes">
<!---####
Name of file: hasher.cfm
Description: Demonstrates strong algorithms used in the Hash() function.
Author name and e-mail: Sarge (sarge@sargeway.com) www.sargeway.com/blog
Date created: February 9, 2005
Date modified: July 25, 2007
 ####--->

<!---#### Set the default encoding. ####--->
<cfparam name="FORM.encode" default="UTF-8" type="string">
<!---#### Create a object to hold all of the charsets available to the JVM.  ####---
>
<cfobject type="java" name="cs" class="java.nio.charset.Charset" action="create">
```

Listing 61.2 (continued)

```
<cfset variables.charSets = cs.availableCharsets()>
<cfsetting enablecfoutputonly="no">
<!DOCTYPE HTML PUBLIC -//W3C//DTD HTML 4.0 Transitional//EN>
<html>
<head>
 <title>ColdFusion 8 Hash Test</title>
</head>
<body>
<h2>ColdFusion 8 Hasher</h2>
<cfform name="hasher">
<table border="0">
<tr><td>String: </td><td><cfinput type="text" name="plainText" size="25"
required="yes" message="You must provide a string to hash."></td></tr>
<tr><td>Algorithm:</td><td><cfselect name="algo">
<option value="MD2">MD2</option>
<option value="MD5">MD5</option>
<option value="SHA">SHA-1</option>
<option value="SHA-256">SHA-256</option>
<option value="SHA-384">SHA-384</option>
<option value="SHA-512">SHA-512</option>
</cfselect></td></tr>
<tr><td>Encoding:</td>
<td><cfselect name="encode">
<cfoutput>
<cfloop collection="#charSets#" item="set">
<option value="#charSets[set]#" <cfif findNoCase(FORM.encode,
set)>selected</cfif>>#charSets[set]#</option>
</cfloop></cfoutput>
</cfselect></td></tr>
<tr><td> </td><td><input type="submit" name="Submit"
value="Submit">  <input name="Reset" type="Reset"></td></tr>
</table><br />
</cfform>
<a href="index.cfm">Back to index</a>
<cfsetting enablecfoutputonly="yes">
<cfif isDefined('FORM.algo')>
    <!---#### Perform the hash using submitted algorithm and encoding. ####--->
    <cfset variables.theHash = hash(FORM.plainText, FORM.algo, FORM.encode)>
    <cfoutput>
    <hr>
    <table border="0">
    <tr><th align="left">Original String:</th><td>#FORM.plainText#<br></td></tr>
    <tr><th align="left">CF Hash:</th><td
style="color:##FF0000">#hash(FORM.plainText)#</td></tr>
    <tr><th align="left">#FORM.algo# Hash:</th><td
style="color:##009900">#variables.theHash#<br></td></tr>
    <tr><th align="left">Hash Length:</th><td
style="color:##0099CC">#len(Trim(variables.theHash))# characters</td></tr>
    <tr><th align="left">Encoding:</th><td
style="color:##009900">#FORM.encode#</td></tr>
    </table>
    </cfoutput>
</cfif>
<cfsetting enablecfoutputonly="no">
</body>
</html>
```

The code in Listing 61.2 shows how to hash a string with strong algorithms (Figure 61.2). Because it provides one-way encryption, `Hash()` creates a fingerprint of the original string. This is most useful for storing sensitive data into a database in such a way that if the database security is compromised, the data remains safe. You can then compare a hash of a user-submitted string to the fingerprint in the database. This is particularly useful for things like passwords:

```
<cfquery name="checkuser" datasource="#dsn#">
  SELECT userID FROM user
  WHERE username ='#FORM.username#'
  and password ='#Hash(FORM.password, FORM.algorithm)#'
</cfquery>
```

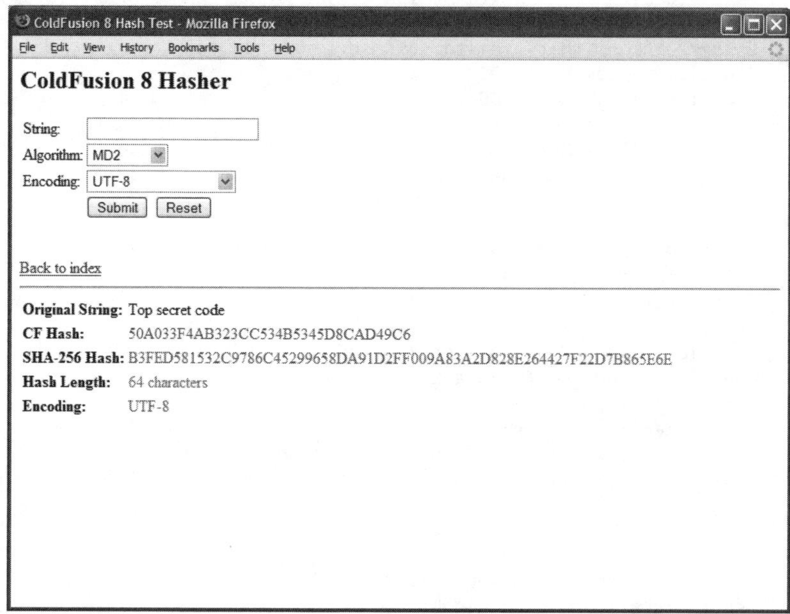

Figure 61.2

The original ColdFusion-compatible, and strong-algorithm-hashed string output from Listing 61.2. Encoding display will vary depending on system-supported character sets.

TIP

As with the `Encrypt()` and `Decrypt()` functions, you must use the same algorithm when comparing hashed strings.

Of course, neither `Hash()` nor `Encrypt()` will protect data being sent from the client's browser to the server. For this, you'll need to use SSL. SSL is a commonly used protocol for securing message transmission across the Internet. It operates between the Application (HTTP) and Transport (TCP) layers of the OSI (Open Systems Interconnectivity) model. SSL clients are included as part of most major browsers, including Microsoft Internet Explorer and Mozilla Firefox, and the SSL protocol is built into (or can be added to) most modern Web servers. SSL uses the public-and-private key encryption system from RSA (`www.rsasecurity.com`), which also includes the use of digital certificates. As such, the responsibility of securing data as it travels across the Internet is not the responsibility of the ColdFusion Application Server.

Forcing a Page Request to Use SSL

Although ColdFusion has no part in the SSL handshake (it is strictly a function between the browser and Web server), an astute developer can take precautions to ensure that secure pages are only accessed via SSL:

```
<CFIF FindNoCase("off", CGI.HTTPS) or NOT len(trim(CGI.HTTPS))>
  <CFLOCATION URL="https://#cgi.server_name##cgi.script_name#?#cgi.query_string#">
  <CFABORT>
</CFIF>
```

This code begins by checking the CGI `HTTPS` variable. This variable is set to `on` when a connection is SSL. If `CGI.HTTPS` is set to `off`, the `<CFLOCATION>` tag redirects the user to the same page using the HTTPS protocol rather than HTTP.

SSL Liabilities

Although SSL is great for encrypting communications between the client and Web server, handling the encrypting and decrypting puts an enormous burden on the Web server, impeding performance. For this reason, it's important only to use SSL when sensitive data is being passed. SSL accelerators are a hardware-based solution that off-loads the SSL processing from the Web server, which can vastly improve performance. Unfortunately, these accelerators can be quite expensive and are often too costly for use in many applications.

Securing ColdFusion in Distributed Mode

If you are concerned about snooping on your wire, consider encrypting the connections between the major parts of your application: the Web server, ColdFusion server, and database server. Typically, the Web server and ColdFusion application server reside on the same machine, so you only need to worry about the network connection to the database. However, ColdFusion is capable of running in Distributed mode, where the Web server is on a completely separate machine. In this configuration, you may also want to encrypt the connections between all machines: ColdFusion to Web server, ColdFusion to database server, and Web server to database server.

You can do this with SSL, with hardware, or with a Virtual Private Network (VPN). As mentioned in "SSL Liabilities," SSL communications tend to be slow, and hardware accelerators are expensive. VPNs are widely used in server farms, where each machine has at least two NICs—one with a publicly accessible IP Address, the other with a private address. All internal inter-server communication happens on the private address—the VPN.

➜ For more information on configuring ColdFusion in Distributed mode (versions 6.x-7), see the "Running Macromedia ColdFusion in Distributed Mode" article in Macromedia ColdFusion Developer Center, at www.adobe.com/support/coldfusion/administration/cfmx_in_distributed_mode/.

Browser Validation

The Web server is responsible for securing data from prying eyes as it traverses the Internet to the browser. However, the Web server cannot guarantee the integrity of the data exchanged between the client and the back-end system. Hackers can still compromise sites running SSL. Because it is the doorway to the back-end systems, protecting the site from these attacks is ColdFusion's job.

Cross-site scripting, tampered form and URL values, and contaminated file uploads are methods used by hackers and script bunnies to attack your site. Validating all browser input is the most effective panacea for these attacks. ColdFusion provides several function and tag countermeasures. These countermeasures should be a fundamental part of every methodology for securing ColdFusion applications.

Cross-Site Scripting (XSS)

In February 2000, CERT (`www.cert.org`), DoD-CERT (`www.cert.mil`), et al., created the term *cross-site scripting (XSS)* to describe the injection of code by one source into the Web pages of another source. This attack involves using cookies, form and URL parameters, and other valid HTML to upload JavaScript, ActiveX, or other executable scripts into an unsuspecting Web site, enabling arbitrary code to run against the client's browser and/or the Web server.

➜ For the Adobe Security Bulletin on Cross-Site Scripting, see ASB00-05 at `http://www.adobe.com/devnet/security/security_zone/asb00-05.html`. For Adobe's list of best practices for validating browser input, see TechNote Article 17502 at http://www.adobe.com/go/tn_17502.

Cross-site scripting works because the Web server accepts non-validated input from the browser, and processes or redisplays the malicious code. Because the server uses the non-validated input to dynamically generate Web pages, the server treats the embedded script as if it came from a trusted source—namely itself—and runs it in the security context of the server's own pages. So in this vein, a hacker can inject malicious code into a secured (SSL) site, and dupe a consumer into sending their credit card information to their personal server.

The original CERT advisory (`www.cert.org/advisories/CA-2000-02.html`) lists the following example code:

```
<A HREF="http://example.com/comment.cgi? mycomment=<SCRIPT>malicious code</SCRIPT>">
Click here</A>
```

Changing the HTML character set, inserting database queries into cookies, sending hexadecimal character shell commands, and other Web-server-specific attacks are examples of recent XSS attacks.

The first line of defense against cross-site attacks is to update your Web server software. Web server vendors update their products (with hot fixes or service packs) and introduce new tools as the vendors are made aware of vulnerabilities. Examples of such tools are Microsoft's IIS Lockdown and URLScan Security tools (`www.microsoft.com/technet/security/tools/default.mspx`).

In terms of code, Adobe recommends using the following techniques in your CFML:

- Use `CFHEADER` to define a character set in HTML output.
- Use built-in CFML tags such as `CFARGUMENT`, `CFPARAM`, `CFQUERYPARAM`, `CFPROCPARAM`, `CFSWITCH`, `CFIF-CFELSE`, `CFLOCATION`, `CFHEADER`, `CFHTMLHEAD`, etc.

- Use built-in functions such as `HTMLCodeFormat`, `HTMLEditFormat`, `URLEncodedFormat`, `URLDecode`, `ReplaceList`, `REReplace`, `REReplaceNoCase`, `SetEncoding`, `StripCR`, `IsJSON`, `IsValid`, `IsXML`, etc.
- Properly scope all variables.
- Escape and replace special characters and tags content in Java.
- Use the `Scriptprotect` setting, described in the next section.

The `Scriptprotect` Setting

ColdFusion MX 7 introduced the `Scriptprotect` attribute to protect ColdFusion variables from cross-site scripting attacks. The XSS protection mechanism is a customizable regular expression ColdFusion applies to one or more specified scopes. When enabled, ColdFusion applies the script protection at the beginning of the request during application setting processing. If one of the filtered words (object, embed, script, applet, or meta by default) is submitted as a tag in the specified scopes, ColdFusion replaces all occurrences with the text `InvalidTag`. However, the filtered words are allowed as regular text.

The `Scriptprotect` regular expression is defined in the `CrossSiteScriptPatterns` entry in the `cf_root\lib\neo-security.xml` (server configuration) or `cf_root\WEB-INF\cfusion\lib\neo-security.xml` (J2EE configuration):

```
<var name="CrossSiteScriptPatterns">
  <struct type="coldfusion.server.ConfigMap">
    <var name="&lt;\s*(object|embed|script|applet|meta)">
      <string>&lt;InvalidTag</string>
    </var>
  </struct>
</var>
```

For backward compatibility, ColdFusion 8 script protection is disabled by default. There are three places to enable it: the ColdFusion Administrator, in `Application.cfc`, and in the `CFAPPLICATION` tag:

- The Enable Global Script Protection option in the ColdFusion Administrator Settings window enables XSS protection for the entire server.
- In the `Application.cfc`, set the `scriptProtect` variable in the `This` scope; for example: `this.scriptProtect=Form`.
- To use the `CFAPPLICATION` tag, specify the scopes you want to protect in the `scriptProtect` attribute.

NOTE

The Administrator setting sets the serverwide default value, but the `scriptProtect` variable and attribute override the Enable Global Script Protection setting at the application level.

Table 61.1 lists valid values for the `Application.cfc` variable and `CFAPPLICATION` tag attribute.

Table 61.1 Values for the `Scriptprotect` Variable/Attribute

VALUE	DESCRIPTION
`None`	Provides no protection for any scopes
`All`	Protects CGI, cookie, form, and URL variables
Comma-delimited list	Protects variables specified in the list

TIP

ColdFusion's XSS script protection can be applied to all ColdFusion scopes. However, this places additional processing overhead on the server. For this reason, when you specify a value of `All` to the `scriptProtect` variable/attribute, or if you enable it globally in the Administrator, only the commonly attacked scopes are protected (CGI, cookie, form, and URL).

CAUTION

Although ColdFusion's `scriptProtect` attribute is a great first line of defense, it does not protect against all forms of XSS attacks. Be sure to review your application's specific needs to determine whether `scriptProtect`, `scriptProtect` and another method, or just another method alone meets the specific security needs of your application.

Form and URL Hacks

Form and URL hacking are favorites in cross-site attacks. HTML forms are the chief interfaces used to collect data from clients, used for shopping carts, search engines, application/site security, guest books, and more. Because the browser renders the form as cleartext HTML, malicious users can download the form, modify the fields, and then submit the form from another server.

URL parameters typically drive dynamic Web pages. URL hacking involves manipulating the URL query string to alter the intended behavior of the rendered Web page. Developers typically evaluate one or more parameters in the URL query string to determine the content of the requested Web page. Perhaps the best example of this is search-engine result pages—changing one of the values in the URL query string usually changes the displayed results.

An attack known as *SQL injection* or *SQL poisoning* is the most prevalent version of form and URL hacking. Hackers use SQL injection to manipulate databases by submitting additional SQL statements in form fields and/or URL query strings. The additional SQL is usually something damaging like `DROP TABLE Users WHERE 1=1`. You can imagine the effects of completely removing a Web site's users table.

Since databases are the heart of most Web sites today, form and URL validation is paramount to ensure data integrity and site security. Web servers—hence regular HTML—offer little to no defense against these attacks. Again, it is ColdFusion's responsibility to protect the data it sends to the back-end systems, and ColdFusion provides several tags and functions that perform the job well.

Validation Techniques

Traditionally, ColdFusion offers the following data validation techniques:

- Decision functions

- Client- and server-side form validation
- Variable data-typing with CFARGUMENT, CFPARAM, CFQUERYPARAM, and CFPROCPARAM

ColdFusion MX 7 extended the validation techniques by adding more algorithms, options, and functions. This section introduces some of these changes. However, for greater detail see Chapter 13, "Form Data Validation," in *Adobe ColdFusion 8 Web Application Construction Kit, Volume 1: Getting Started*.

To stop the majority of URL hacks, begin with the same methods highlighted in the Cross-Site Scripting section. Leverage the CF decision functions to stop SQL injections and similar hacks, specifically the following: `IsBinary()`, `IsBoolean()`, `IsDate()`, `IsDefined()`, `IsJSON()`, `IsNumeric()`, `IsNumericDate()`, `IsSimpleValue()`, `IsXML()`, `LSIsDate()`, and `LSIsNumeric()`. The `IsValid()` function combines the functionality of most of the decision functions. In addition to testing regular expressions and numeric ranges, `IsValid()` can validate any legitimate ColdFusion format including: array, binary, Boolean, creditcard, date/time/eurodate/U.S. date, email, float/integer/numeric, guid, query, range, `regex`, `ssn`, string, struct, telephone, URL, uuid, `variableName`, XML, and U.S. ZIP code.

TIP

Use `IsValid()` as the function equivalent of the CFPARAM tag.

ColdFusion 8 extends the built-in client-and server-side form validation. You can create XML and Flash forms with extended validation algorithms.

- The CFFORM tag provides client-side JavaScript for form-field validating in the browser.
- The CFINPUT tag now provides the `mask` and `validateat` attributes. The `mask` attribute allows developers to create character patterns to control user data input in text fields. The `validateat` attribute specifies where data validation occurs. It accepts one or more of the following values in a comma-separated list: `onBlur`, where validation occurs in the browser when the form field loses focus; `onSubmit`, where validation occurs in the browser before the form is submitted; and `onServer`, where validation occurs on the server.

For server-side form validation, ColdFusion MX 7 also extended the existing hidden form-field validation support with an additional 12 validation rules. It also changes the special rule identifiers to suffixes beginning with `_cf`, but continues to support the original syntax for backward compatibility. The `onServer` value for the CFINPUT `validateat` attribute produces the same server-side validation rules as the hidden form-field method.

TIP

Both `validateat=onServer` and hidden form fields provide the same validation rules. However, use hidden form fields if you want to apply multiple validation rules to a single form field, or if you want to provide server-side validation for regular form fields.

Client- and server-side validation each has its pros and cons, but they share one common fatal flaw: They rely on code in the client. CFFORM (and related tags) generate form fields and the JavaScript code that evaluates them in the browser. ColdFusion's server-side validation relies on hidden form fields for the validation rules. Savvy hackers will save the rendered HTML forms and remove the JavaScript and/or hidden form fields, thus bypassing all validation.

TIP

A nice method of protection against user-modified form submittals is to code conditional logic that compares the `CGI.HTTP_HOST` and `CGI.HTTP_REFERER` values. For example:

```
<cfif  NOT FindNoCase(CGI.HTTP_HOST, CGI.HTTP_REFERER)>
Invalid Form submittal
<cflocation url="byebye.cfm">
</cfif>
```

If this code returns false, then you know the form was submitted from an external server.

A combination of client- and server-side validation is the best protection. However, be sure to also code your own CFML to perform data typing before sending values to back-end systems. Use proper variable scoping and tags such as `CFARGUMENT`, `CFPARAM`, `CFPROCPARAM`, and `CFQUERYPARAM` to ensure that the correct variable exists and is of the correct type. Use `IF-ELSE` and `SWITCH-CASE` blocks to apply conditional logic and set default values.

Working with validation techniques requires more effort on your part—but considering the potential aftermath of a hack, an ounce of prevention....

File Uploads

The attacks described in this section center around affecting your site by directly manipulating your code and data. Allowing users to upload files directly to your Web server potentially exposes your entire system and network to harm. Electronic libraries and head-hunter sites are examples that typically allow file uploads. If unchecked, hackers can freely upload viruses, worms, Trojan horses, and so on, to your Web server, which can spread to your server farm, and eventually cripple your entire network.

The best defense against harmful file uploads is to avoid uploads altogether. If this feature is a vital part of your application's functionality, however, use antivirus software to stop the infection of worms and Trojan horses. Limit upload features to authenticated users. Only allow uploads of certain file types and lengths, and to a separate physical server running antivirus software.

ColdFusion is not an antivirus program, but you can write CFML that controls the destination, MIME type, and size restrictions and that sets the attributes of uploaded files. Adjust the Maximum Size of Post Data value in the ColdFusion 8 Administrator Settings screen. You can also code your own security routine in CFML that will limit uploading to authenticated users, as shown in Listing 61.3.

Listing 61.3 `uploader.cfm`—Limiting File Upload to Authorized Users

```
<cfsetting enablecfoutputonly="yes">
<!---####
Name of file: uploader.cfm
```

Listing 61.2 (continued)

```
Description of the script: Displays cookies values captured from one site and set in
the URL of the local site.
Author name and e-mail: Sarge (sarge@sargeway.com) www.sargeway.com/blog/
Date created: February 9, 2005
Date modified: July 25, 2007
####--->
<cfsetting enablecfoutputonly="no">
<!DOCTYPE HTML PUBLIC -//W3C//DTD HTML 4.0 Transitional//EN>
<html>
<head>
<title>ColdFusion 8 Image Upload Test</title>
</head>
<body>
<h2>ColdFusion 8 Image Uploader</h2>
<!---#### Check user's authorization to upload. ####--->
<cfif NOT IsUserInRole("publisher")>
<cfinclude template="loginform.cfm">
<a href="index.cfm">Back to index</a><cfabort>
<cfelseif IsDefined("FORM.upload")>
<cfparam name="variables.uploaddir" default="j:\otherserver\images">
<cftry>
<!---#### Restrict upload size. ####--->
<cfif CGI.CONTENT_LENGTH gt 1024>
<cfthrow message="Your image file is bigger than 1mb. try again!">
<cfelse>
<cffile accept="image/jpeg; image/gif" action="upload" attributes="readonly"
destination="#variables.uploaddir#" filefield="form.newImage" nameconflict="error">
<cfif cffile.fileWasSaved>
<cfoutput><span style="color:##00FF00">#cffile.clientFileName# successfully
uploaded!</span></cfoutput>
</cfif>
</cfif>
<cfcatch type="any">
<cfoutput>
<strong>message:</strong> #cfcatch.message#<br>
<strong>detail:</strong> #cfcatch.detail#<br>
</cfoutput>
</cfcatch>
</cftry>
</cfif>
<cfform id="imageUpload" name="imageUpload" method="post" action="#CGI.SCRIPT_NAME#"
enctype="multipart/form-data">
<cfinput type="file" id="newImage" name="newImage" size="25" message="You must
choose an image to upload!" required="yes">
<cfinput type="submit" id="upload" name="upload" value="Upload!">
</cfform>
<a href="index.cfm">Back to index</a>
</body>
</html>
```

Authentication and Authorization

Securing sensitive areas of an application, such as administrative pages, prevents unauthorized access to protected functionality. This is done through an access control system with user authentication and authorization. *Authentication* is proving the user is who they say they are. *Authorization* is determining which resources the authenticated user can access.

Such security models vary vastly from the simple—where authentication consists of a single username and/or password for all users—to the detailed—where user-authentication access control throughout the Web site is very granular. There are even single sign-on models in which logging into one application allows users to access a variety of other applications. Single sign-on models typically authenticate users with identity tokens, ranging from electronic technologies such as Smart Cards and X.509 certificates, to the more advanced biometric technologies such as fingerprinting and facial recognition.

You can create feature-rich access control paradigms with just ColdFusion and a database, or you can integrate ColdFusion with a third-party security system for added out-of-the-box functionality. Whether custom built or out-of-the-box, many applications today use robust "role-based" security models, where users are grouped together based on their roles for an application.

Databases are the storage facilities for these role-based group memberships. The database can be a simple RDBMS (Relational Database Management System) such as Oracle or SQL Server, or an LDAP (Lightweight Directory Access Protocol) server such as Active Directory, Novell, or Sun ONE, or even a simple flat-file system like the NT SAM. The access permissions or groups are properties in the database to which individual user IDs are added.

Imagine the Web site of an eZine that publishes new articles and columns daily. We can group the four authors who provide the initial content into a role called Author. When these authors submit their articles, the Editor group is responsible for reviewing the submissions and either approving or rejecting them. In this simple scenario, it is easy to see the benefits of being able to apply permissions to groups of users, rather than having to reenter the same data to assign the permission to each individual user.

Suppose the eZine is using an LDAP for user management and it contains the two groups—Editor and Author. Individual employees are added to these groups. The eZine could also leverage an X.509 user certificate system to provide access control throughout the publishing section of its site. (X.509 user certificates are SSL certificates that guarantee the user's identity.) Since LDAP entries typically contain certificate properties, they will integrate nicely with the eZine's LDAP.

➜ For more information on X.509 certificates see `http://www.ietf.org/html.charters/pkix-charter.html`.

Now when editors or authors access the publishing section of the site—secured with SSL, of course—the Web server challenges them to authenticate using their certificates. The CN ("common name" or LDAP version of username) in the certificate is compared to users' LDAP entries. If an entry matches, the security code retrieves the user's group memberships, authorizing him or her to access the appropriate parts of the publishing section.

This eZine example illustrates the power of the user authentication and authorization system to provide access control to resources within your site. In general, it's a good practice to use network and OS/Web server–level access controls to protect any sensitive sections of a Web site, in addition to any application-level controls. If you decide to use ColdFusion to provide access control, it's a good idea to use SSL to secure the login page. This way, malicious users will not be able to easily "sniff" the username and password combination sent during the authorization. You should also make a point of using the `Application.cfc` file of the secured directory to ensure that all accessed pages require an authenticated user. A popular technique is utilizing ColdFusion `session` variables to store the authenticated user's login and permissions.

TIP

The use of ColdFusion `session` variables may require proper scope-level locking. See "Using Persistent Data and Locking" in the *ColdFusion Developers Guide* in your ColdFusion 8 documentation.

CHAPTER 62

Securing the ColdFusion Administrator

IN THIS CHAPTER

Administrator Security Options

The ColdFusion Administrator is the browser-based interface for configuring the ColdFusion server environment. The Administrator is traditionally secured by a single password (Figure 62.1). ColdFusion 8 extends this security, allowing user-based access to Administrator functionality, including sandboxes (discussed in detail in Chapter 64, "Creating Server Sandboxes") and the Administrator API. The ColdFusion 8 Administrator security options are:

- **Administrator**. Choose the authentication type and set the default password for ColdFusion Administrator access.
- **RDS**. Choose the authentication type and set the default password for Remote Development Services access to ColdFusion.
- **Resource/Sandbox Security**. Configure security restrictions for designated areas of ColdFusion sites. Chapter 64 discusses sandbox security in detail.
- **User Manager**. Create users and passwords and assign access rights to administrator resources and sandboxes.

Figure 62.1

The ColdFusion 8 Administrator is secured by a root username and password.

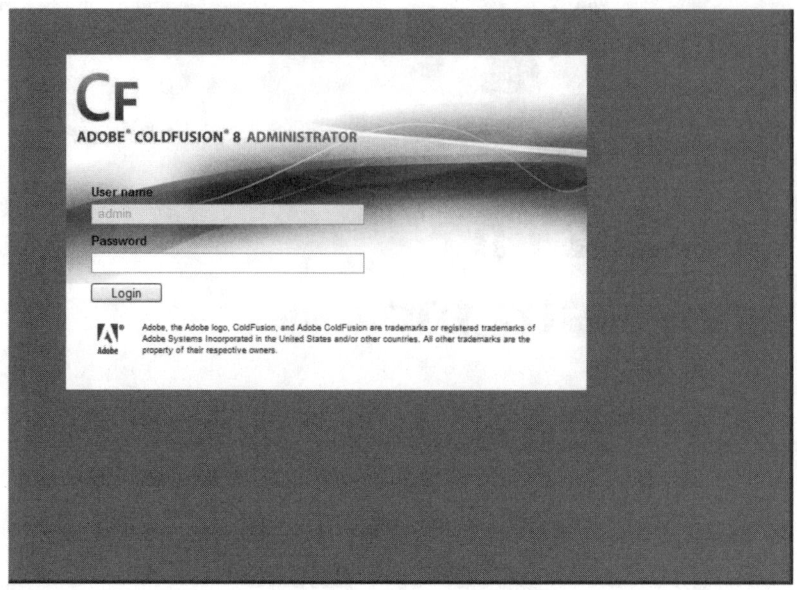

Administrator Page

To access the Administrator security options page, click the Administrator link in the Security section in the left navigation pane of the ColdFusion Administrator. This screen is divided into two sections: ColdFusion Administration Authentication and Root Administrator Password (Figure 62.2).

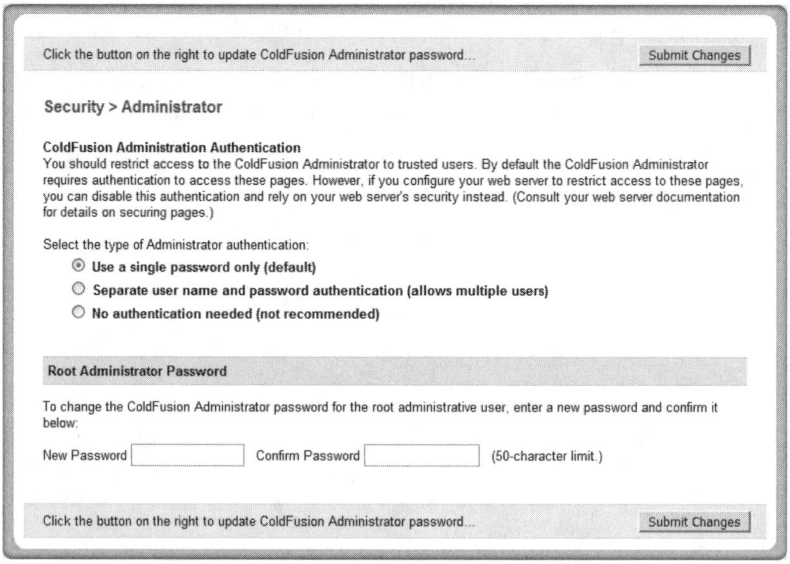

Figure 62.2

Use the Administrator page to configure the Administrator authentication type and password.

Click the button on the right to update ColdFusion Administrator password... Submit Changes

Security > Administrator

ColdFusion Administration Authentication

You should restrict access to the ColdFusion Administrator to trusted users. By default the ColdFusion Administrator requires authentication to access these pages. However, if you configure your web server to restrict access to these pages, you can disable this authentication and rely on your web server's security instead. (Consult your web server documentation for details on securing pages.)

Select the type of Administrator authentication:

- **Use a single password only (default)**
- **Separate user name and password authentication (allows multiple users)**
- **No authentication needed (not recommended)**

Root Administrator Password

To change the ColdFusion Administrator password for the root administrative user, enter a new password and confirm it below:

New Password Confirm Password (50-character limit.)

Click the button on the right to update ColdFusion Administrator password... Submit Changes

ColdFusion 8 provides three types of authentication to the Administrator:

- **Use a Single Password Only (Default)**. Select this option to enable the default ColdFusion Administrator security behavior. The Administrator uses either the administrator password configured during installation, or the one entered in the Root Administrator Password section.
- **Separate User Name and Password Authentication (Allows Multiple Users)**. Select this option to enable the use of individual usernames and passwords for access to the Administrator (discussed later in this chapter). When this option is selected, the User Name text field is enabled in the ColdFusion 8 Administrator login screen (Figure 62.3).

Figure 62.3

The username field is enabled when multiple users are allowed.

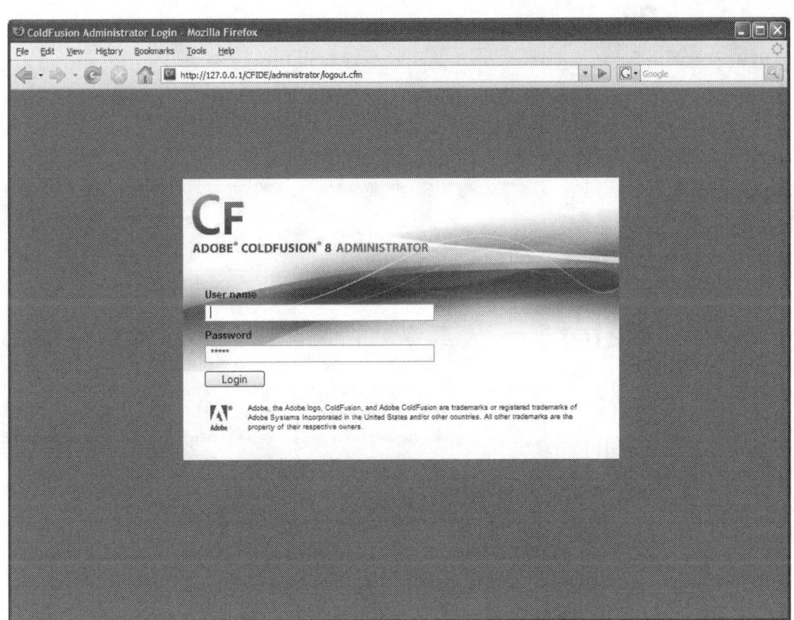

- **No Authentication Needed (Not Recommended)**. Select this option to disable ColdFusion Administrator security. This option completely removes authentication challenges to the ColdFusion Administrator.

NOTE

The ColdFusion Administrator password and authentication options also govern Administrator API access. The Administrator API is discussed in Chapter 66, "Using the Administrator API."

TIP

Adobe does not recommend disabling the ColdFusion Administrator password. Leaving the Administrator unsecure severely jeopardizes the integrity of the entire ColdFusion server configuration.

The form fields in the Root Administrator Password section allow you to configure and confirm a new root administrator password. The root administrator password is used for the single-password authentication type. The default root administrator password is configured during ColdFusion installation. Enter a password in the New Password text field and enter the same password in the Confirm Password text field. Click Submit Changes to commit the new password.

TIP

Although single-password authentication is a less secure option, configuring a stronger, complex string for the root password will provide greater security.

RDS Page

You access the RDS security options page by clicking the RDS link under the Security section in the left navigation pane of the ColdFusion Administrator. This screen is divided into two sections: RDS Authentication and RDS Single Password (Figure 62.4).

Figure 62.4

Use the RDS page to configure the RDS authentication type and password.

Click the button on the right to update RDS Password...
Submit Changes
Security > RDS
RDS authentication
You should restrict access to RDS to trusted users. By default RDS requires authentication. However, you may disable this authentication and rely on your web server's security instead.
Select the type of RDS authentication:
Use a single password only (default)
Separate user name and password authentication (allows multiple users)
No authentication needed (not recommended)
RDS Single Password
To change the single RDS password, enter a new password and confirm it below:
New Password
Confirm Password
(50-character limit.)
Click the button on the right to update RDS Password...
Submit Changes

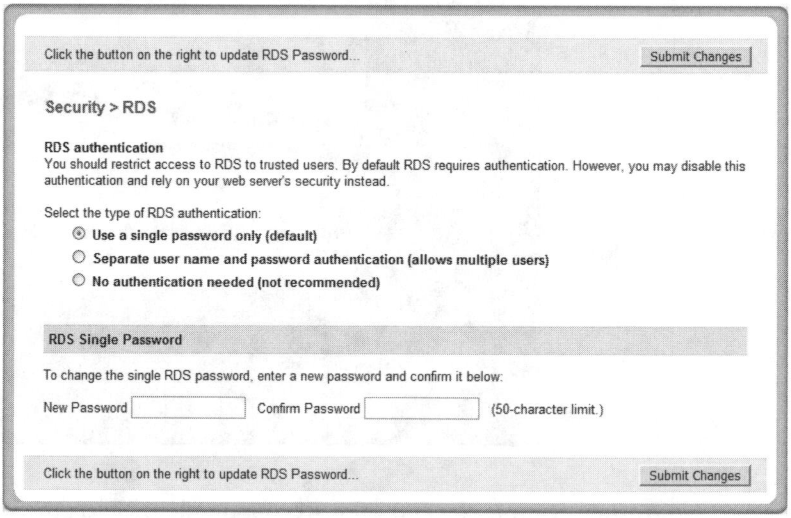

ColdFusion 8 provides three types of authentication for RDS:

- **Use a Single Password Only (Default).** Select this option to enable the default RDS security behavior. Remote Development Services uses either the RDS password configured during installation or the one entered in the RDS Single Password section.
- **Separate User Name and Password Authentication (Allows Multiple Users).** Select this option to enable the use of individual usernames and passwords for RDS access. Configure the usernames and passwords on the User Manager page, discussed later in this chapter.
- **No Authentication Needed (Not Recommended).** Select this option to disable RDS security. This option completely removes password access to RDS.

TIP

Adobe recommends disabling RDS for production systems. See tech note tn_17276, Disabling/Enabling ColdFusion RDS on Production Servers, at `http://www.adobe.com/go/tn_17276`. Best practice is to configure a strong RDS single password whether or not RDS is disabled.

The form fields in the RDS Single Password section allow you to configure and confirm a new RDS password. The RDS single password is used for the RDS single-password authentication type. The default RDS password is configured during ColdFusion installation. Enter a password in the New Password text field and enter the same password in the Confirm Password text field. Click Submit Changes to commit the new password.

User Manager Page

The ColdFusion 8 Administrator includes the new User Manager page for configuring user-based Administrator and RDS access. You access this page from the User Manager link in the Security section of the left navigation pane in the ColdFusion Administrator.

User-based access allows administrators to create individual user accounts with individual passwords and then assign various roles to those accounts. By default, there are no configured user accounts. To enable user-based access, you must first create user accounts and passwords, assign roles to those accounts, and enable the Separate User Name and Password Authentication Administrator or RDS authentication type.

The User Manager screen is divided into three sections: User Authentication, User RDS and Administrator Access, and User Sandboxes. At a minimum, you must configure a username and password for the User Manager.

The User Authentication section is where you configure the individual usernames and passwords for user-based access. Enter an alphanumeric string of five characters or more for a username. Enter and confirm a string of five characters or more for the user password.

The User RDS and Administrator Access section is where you add roles for user accounts. Select the Allow RDS Access check box to grant RDS access for a user. The user will be required to enter both a username and password in the IDE. Select the Allow Administrative Access check box to allow the user account to access the Administrative functionality. When this option is selected, the Administrator Console and API Access and API Access Only radio buttons are enabled. By default, all Administrator roles are prohibited—you must move roles to the Allowed Roles list to enable them for a user.

The User Sandboxes section allows you to assign access to configured sandboxes to the user account. All sandboxes on the server are prohibited by default. You must manually grant access to sandboxes.

Creating a New User

Here's how to create a new user:

1. Access the User Manager by clicking the User Manager link in the Security section of the left navigation pane in the ColdFusion Administrator.

2. Click the Add User button (Figure 62.5).

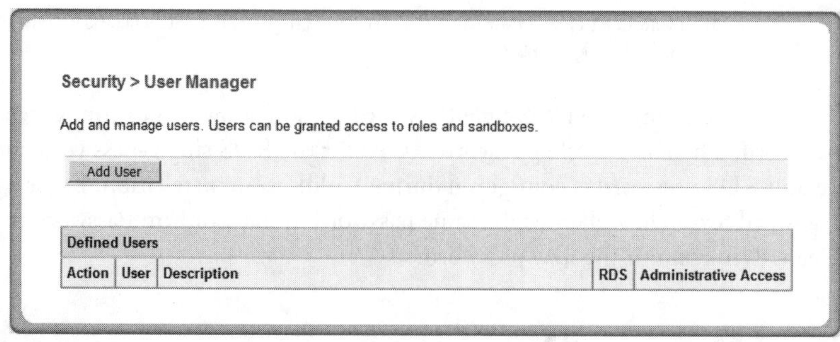

Figure 62.5
Click Add User to begin creating a new user.

The User Manager page appears (Figure 62.6).

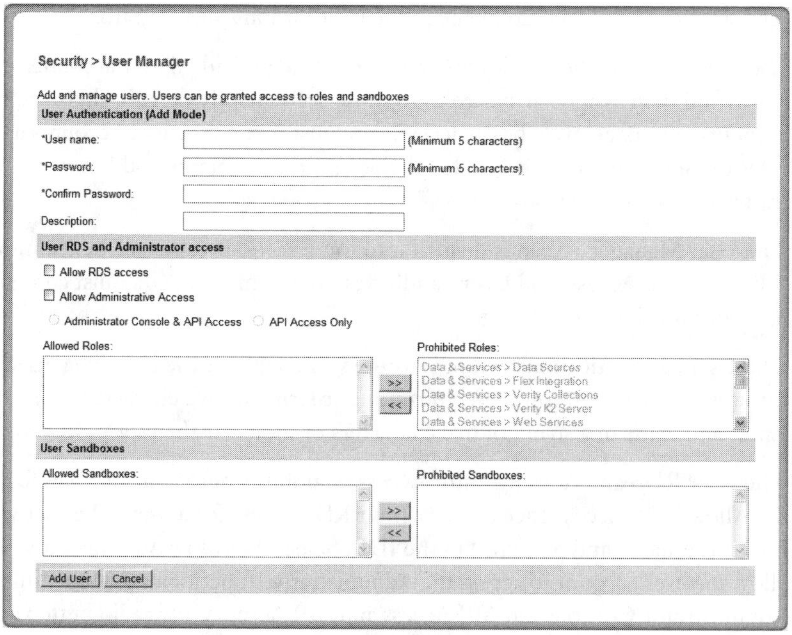

Figure 62.6
Use the User Manager page to create user accounts and assign roles and sandboxes.

Security > User Manager

Add and manage users. Users can be granted access to roles and sandboxes

User Authentication (Add Mode)

*User name: (Minimum 5 characters)

*Password: (Minimum 5 characters)

*Confirm Password:

Description:

User RDS and Administrator access

Allow RDS access

Allow Administrative Access

Administrator Console & API Access API Access Only

Allowed Roles: Prohibited Roles:

Data & Services > Data Sources
Data & Services > Flex Integration
Data & Services > Verity Collections
Data & Services > Verity K2 Server
Data & Services > Web Services

User Sandboxes

Allowed Sandboxes: Prohibited Sandboxes:

Add User Cancel

3. In the User Authentication section, enter a username and enter and confirm a password. You can also enter a description if you like.

TIP

If you submit a username that is same as the configured root user, you will receive this error message: `Unable to create user: You are attempting to create a user with the same ID as the root user.` To change the root user, see tech note kb402459, ColdFusion 8: How to Change the Root Administrator Username, at `http://www.adobe.com/go/kb402459`.

4. In the User RDS and Administrator Access section, do the following:

   - To grant the user RDS permissions, check the box for Allow RDS Access. If the Separate User Name and Password Authentication type is not enabled for RDS authentication, you will receive an alert message (Figure 62.7).

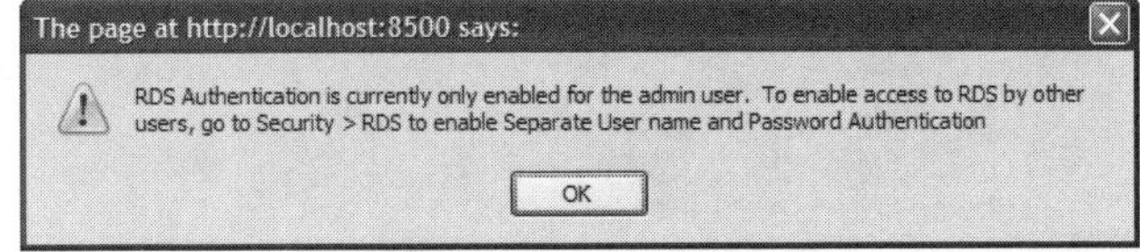

Figure 62.7 Separate User name and Password Authentication required for user-based RDS access.

   - To grant the user access to Administrator resources, check the box for Allow Administrative Access. If the Separate User Name and Password Authentication type is not enabled for Administrator authentication, you will receive an alert message (Figure 62.8).

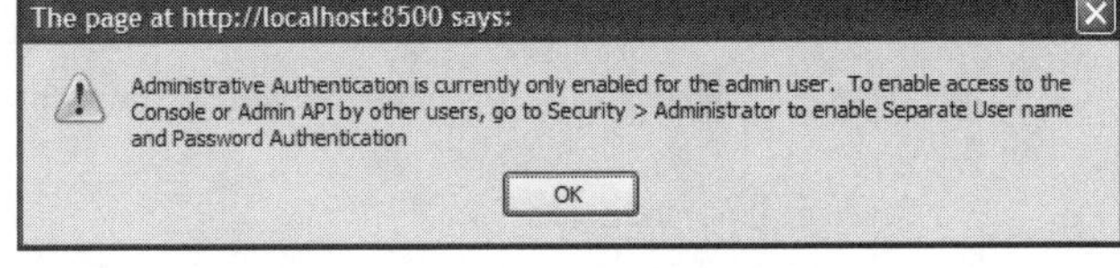

Figure 62.8 Separate User name and Password Authentication required for user-based Administrator access.

   - Decide whether to grant Administrator console and API access, or API access only and select the radio button next to the appropriate option.
   - Highlight the roles in the Prohibited Roles list that you want to grant to the user account and click the left-pointing arrows button (<<) to move them to the Allowed Roles list.

5. In the User Sandboxes section, if there are sandboxes configured on the server, highlight the ones in the Prohibited Sandboxes list that you want to grant to the user account and click the left-pointing arrows button (<<) to move them to the Allowed Sandboxes list.

6. Click the Add User button at the bottom of the screen (Figure 62.9).

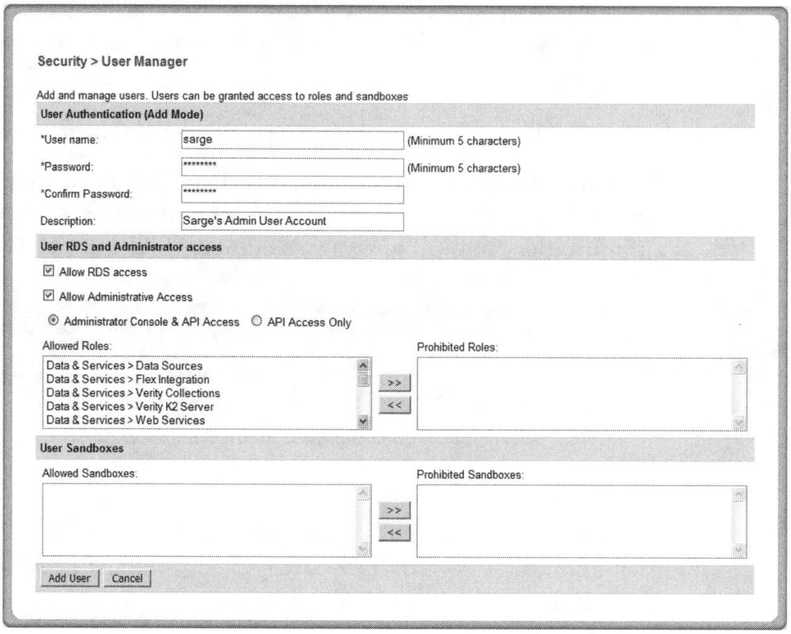

Figure 62.9

Defining a new user role for Administrator and RDS access.

Your user is now added to the Defined Users list on the User Manager page (Figure 62.10).

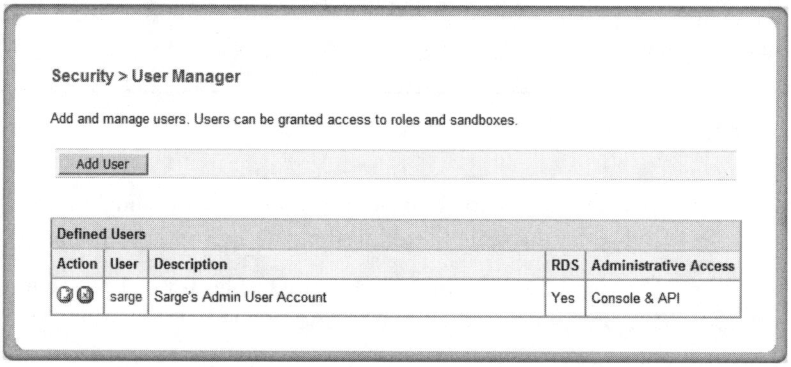

Figure 62.10

New user is added to the Defined Users list.

To edit existing user definitions, click either the edit icon (at the far left) or the user's name. Make your modifications and then click the Edit User button.

CHAPTER 63 ColdFusion Security Options

IN THIS CHAPTER

As you have seen in Chapter 61, "Understanding Security," Adobe ColdFusion has an important role in application security. Security should start at the physical level (server hardware) and move up to the application level (operating system, Web server, application server, and so on). Each operating system provides fundamental access control over its resources (files, directories, and shares), and most Web servers today allow for some native method of user authentication and authorization. A well-secured application uses the inherent capabilities of the operating system and the Web server.

ColdFusion Security Framework

Besides the operating system and Web server security services, administrators also have ColdFusion's security framework available to them. The migration to the Java platform means a change in ColdFusion's security infrastructure by leveraging the JAAS (Java Authentication and Authorization Service).

NOTE

ColdFusion MX introduced a new security framework that completely replaced the Advanced Security system of previous versions. As a result, the following tags and functions are obsolete: `<cfauthenticate>`, `<cfimpersonate>`, `AuthenticatedContext()`, `AuthenticatedUser()`, `IsAuthenticated()`, `IsAuthorized()`, and `IsProtected()`. However, current versions of ColdFusion will allow you to create user-defined functions (UDFs) with the same names as these obsolete security functions.

ColdFusion offers security in the following areas

- **Development security** provides protection for the Administrator and Remote Development Services (RDS) access via Adobe Dreamweaver, HomeSite+, or the CFEclipse RDS plug-in.

- **Runtime security** provides protection in the follow areas:
  - **Resource**. ColdFusion Sandbox security controls access to a subset of tags and functions, data sources, files and directories, and host IP addresses.
  - **User**. ColdFusion provides user authentication, allowing you to secure application functionality based on a user's role (or group membership).

This portion of the chapter focuses on development security. Other CFML security enhancements are discussed in Chapter 61, and resource security (the server sandbox) is covered in Chapter 64, "Creating Server Sandboxes."

Development Security

ColdFusion's security implementation begins with the ColdFusion Administrator. The Security section of the Administrator allows you to configure the following security options: ColdFusion Administrator, RDS, Resource/Sandbox, and User Manager. By default, ColdFusion protects Administrator and RDS (if installed) access with the passwords entered during installation. The Administrator page (Figure 63.1) allows you to choose the authentication type or enter and confirm a new Administrator password.

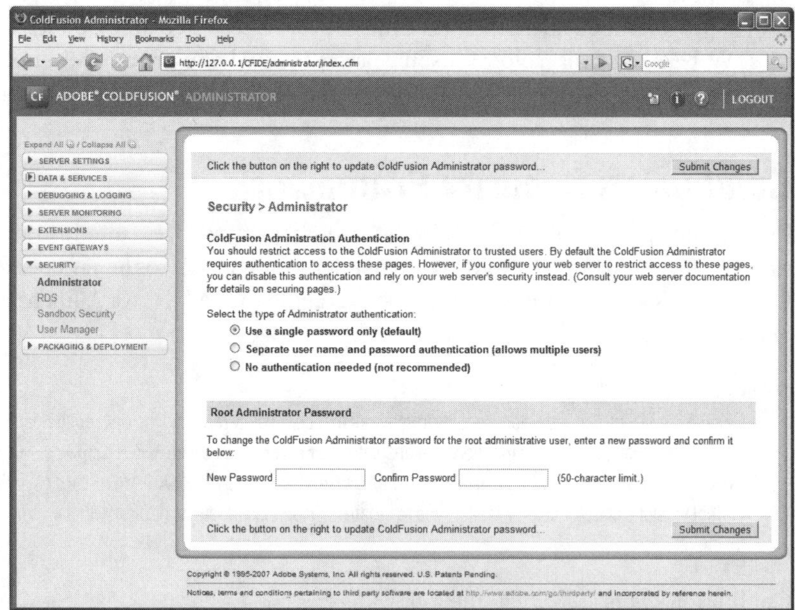

Figure 63.1

Use the ColdFusion Administrator Security page to determine the authentication type and change the Administrator password. To completely disable the password, select "No authentication needed."

Figure 63.2 shows the RDS page, which is used to control visual tool access to ColdFusion. The RDS page also allows you to choose the RDS authentication type or enter and confirm a new RDS password. Disabling RDS security means that you must rely on the Web server and individual database servers for file and data source security.

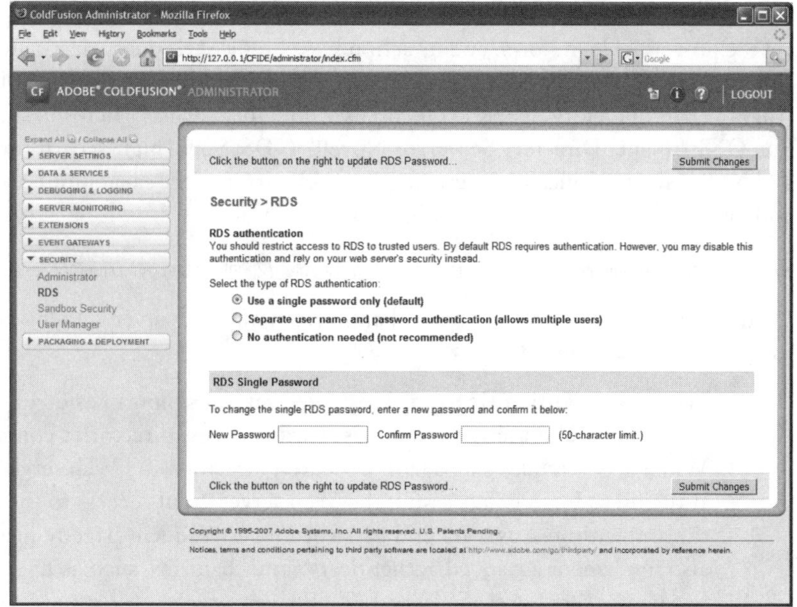

Figure 63.2

Use the RDS Security page to control the password for Dreamweaver, HomeSite+, CFEclipse, or ColdFusion Studio access, or to completely disable RDS security.

CAUTION

Disabling either the Administrator or RDS password can open devastating holes in your application. Disable the Administrator password only if you are using Web server ACLs for access control to the `CFIDE` directory and its children. Although Adobe recommends completely disabling RDS on production systems, you should always enable the RDS password on all systems. For steps to disable RDS, see the "Disabling RDS on Production Servers" section of Chapter 65, "Security in Shared and Hosted Environments."

ColdFusion 8 allows administrators to provide customized user access to the ColdFusion Administrator, the Administrator API, and RDS. For more details on ColdFusion 8's User Manager, see Chapter 62, "Securing the ColdFusion Administrator."

User Security

User security provides granular application control beyond that of the operating system and Web server. The operating system controls local and share access to files and directories—for example, NTFS permissions. The Web server's ACLs grant access to files and directories containing code, based upon an authenticated user's credentials. However, neither the Web server nor the operating system allows you to natively extend the system's security framework beyond the page level to the elements within your code (HTML, CFML, images, Web services, and so on). ColdFusion's user security provides the authentication and authorization features that extend access control to the element level, allowing you to programmatically decide what functionality displays in a page.

About Authentication

You should already be familiar with authentication and authorization. Authentication is the process of validating a user's identity. The typical paradigm is a username/login ID and password stored in a user table of a back-end relational database (RDBMS). A user submits a username and password via the proverbial login form, and its action page fires a SQL query that matches the user's input with the entries in a user table. Some enterprise solutions replace the RDBMS with an LDAP (Lightweight Directory Access Protocol) user directory such as Microsoft's Active Directory, the Sun ONE/iPlanet Directory Server, or Novell's NDS. Some high-security sites even utilize LDAP and X.509 client certificates, leveraging the Web server's SSL capabilities. ColdFusion provides tags and functions for easy integration with all these solutions.

➜ For information on integrating ColdFusion with LDAP see Chapter 72, "Interacting with Directory Services."

ColdFusion recognizes two methods of authorization: Web server authentication and application (programmatic) authentication.

- **Web server authentication**. Most Web servers support basic HTTP authentication, requiring a valid username and password to access directories containing application files. When a user requests a page in a secured directory, the Web server presents a login form. If the user's login is successful, the Web server grants access to the directory and caches the authenticated user ID and password for subsequent page requests. Web servers can also implement advanced authentication mechanisms, such as Digest authentication and Secure Sockets Layer (SSL) or HTTPS.
- **Application authentication**. Application authentication relies on application code and logic to perform roles-based authentication. In this method, it's the application that displays the login form and authenticates the user against the application's own user directory (usually a database or LDAP). Upon a successful login, the application checks the user's credentials and grants access to the appropriate application resources.

About Authorization

Authorization ensures that the authenticated user has the appropriate credentials to access resources. Roles—group memberships defined in a user directory—dictate which users have access to what resources. This is undoubtedly a familiar model. Consider the personnel structure of a typical Web department:

- Network administrators
- Systems administrators
- Database administrators
- Web developers

Each individual in the department falls into one of these roles. Each role has access to particular sections of the network infrastructure, database, Web server, and so forth. Indeed, each role has specific responsibilities and duties. Similarly, applications define roles and assign them to users. These roles control what a user can do or can access within the application. Applications then acquire the authenticated user's ID and roles from the user directory at login, storing them for the duration of the user's session.

In ColdFusion, the `<cflogin>` and `<cfloginuser>` tags provide the authentication functionality, and the `GetAuthUser()` and `IsUserInRole()` functions perform authorization. ColdFusion 8 adds `getUserRoles()`, `isUserInAnyRole()`, `isUserLoggedIn()`, and `verifyClient()` security functions.

Security Tags and Functions

As previously mentioned, ColdFusion includes tags and functions with which to implement security and access control. Table 63.1 describes the ColdFusion security tags and functions.

Table 63.1 ColdFusion Security Tags and Functions

TAG OR FUNCTION	DESCRIPTION
`<cflogin>`	Provides a container for user authentication code. Used with the `<cfloginuser>` tag to validate a user login against an LDAP, database, or other user repository.
`<cfloginuser>`	Identifies the authenticated user to ColdFusion by specifying the user's ID, password, and `roles`. Requires the `name`, `password`, and `roles` attributes. Specify a comma-delimited list to the `roles` attribute. ColdFusion evaluates whitespace in this attribute, so be careful not to add spaces after commas.
`<cflogout>`	Logs the current authenticated user out of ColdFusion by completely removing the user's authenticated ID (session) and roles. When this tag is not used, ColdFusion automatically logs users out when their sessions time out.
`<cffunction>`	The `roles` attribute restricts function execution to authenticated users in the specified roles. The `secureJSON` attribute determines whether to prepend a security prefix to JSON-formatted return values. The `verifyClient` attribute determines whether to require remote function calls in ColdFusion Ajax applications to include an encrypted security token.
`<cfntauthenticate>`	Authenticates a username against the Windows domain in which the ColdFusion server is running. This tag can optionally retrieve the authenticated user's group memberships as well. This tag was added in ColdFusion MX 7.
`GetAuthUser()`	Returns the authenticated user's ID. By default it returns the `username` value specified in `<cfloginuser>`; if this is blank, it returns the value of `CGI.Remote_User`.
`GetUserRoles()`	Returns the list of roles for the authenticated user.
`IsUserInAnyRole()`	Returns true if the authenticated user is a member of any role listed in the string passed to the function.
`IsUserInRole()`	Returns `true` if the authenticated user is a member of the specified roles. Use a comma-delimited list to check multiple role assignments.
`IsUserLoggedIn()`	Returns `true` if the user is authenticated.

Authenticating with <cflogin>

Code all of your authentication logic between `<cflogin>` tags—including database username/password lookups, Windows authentication, LDAP logins, and so forth. The `<cflogin>` tag creates a container for storing user security information—the `CFLOGIN` scope. This scope contains two variables: `CFLOGIN.name` and `CFLOGIN.password`. These two variables are populated with a user's login ID and password when any of the following occurs:

TIP

Authentication logic between `<cflogin>` tags can also be calls to external components, and not just in-line CFML.

- A form is submitted containing input fields with the special `j_username` and `j_password` names. For example:

```
<input type="text" name="j_username">
<input type="password" name="j_password">
```

- An Adobe Flash Remoting `gatewayConnection` object is sent containing the `setCredentials()` method.

TIP

For an example of how to authenticate via Flash Remoting, see Adobe TechNote 18684, "How to pass login credentials to `cflogin` via Flash Remoting" at `http://www.Adobe.com/go/tn_18684`.

- A request contains an Authorization Header with a username and password sent via HTTP Basic authentication.
- A request contains an Authorization Header with a hashed username and password sent via Digest or NTLM authentication. In this case, `CFLOGIN.name` contains the username sent by the Web server, but `CFLOGIN.password` is set to an empty string.

CAUTION

Username and password are sent in cleartext using a simple login form. Flash Remoting sends the username/password over the binary-encoded AMF (Action Message Format) protocol. HTTP Basic authentication sends the username and password in a Base64-encoded string with each request. Consider using SSL (HTTPS) to secure the username and password when authenticating with these methods.

The `<cflogin>` tag accepts three optional attributes:

- `IdleTimeout`. Specifies a maximum time interval for inactivity (the period between page requests) before logging out the user. The default value is 1800 seconds (30 minutes). This attribute is ignored if the `loginStorage` attribute is set to `Session` in the `<cfapplication>` tag or `Application.cfc`.
- `ApplicationToken`. An application-specific identifier used to restrict the `CFLOGIN` scope to the current application. This defaults to the current application name—specified in the `<cfapplication>` tag or with the `THIS.name` variable in `Application.cfc`—and prevents cross-application logins. ColdFusion 8 allows you to specify the same `applicationToken` value for multiple applications.

NOTE

Normally you won't need to specify ApplicationToken as ColdFusion will use the default value `CFAUTHORIZATION_applicationname`; however, ColdFusion allows unnamed applications for J2EE compatibility. ColdFusion uses the `ApplicationToken` value to help keep the user's login valid for only the current directory and its subdirectories. To secure code in other directories or applications, specify an identical application name in `ApplicationToken`.

- `CookieDomain`. Specifies the domain for which the login cookies are set. This prevents cross-site cookie attacks and is useful in clustered environments.

If authentication is successful, specify the authenticated user's user ID, password, and roles to the `<cfloginuser>` tag to log the user into the ColdFusion application. The `IsUserLoggedIn()` function returns true. The `GetAuthUser()` function returns the user ID specified in `<cfloginuser>`. The `IsUserInRole()` function checks the specified role against the list of roles specified in `<cfloginuser>`.

TIP

If Web server security is used instead of ColdFusion security (`CFLOGIN`), `GetAuthUser()` returns the value of `CGI.Remote_User`, which is set by the Web server. If using both Web server security and `CFLOGIN`, pass the Web server's authenticated user ID (for instance, `CGI.Remote_User` or `CGI.Auth_User`) to the `<cfloginuser>` name attribute to keep Web server security and ColdFusion security in synch. The `IsUserInRoles()` function requires `<cfloginuser>`.

Storing Login Information

Login credentials are stored either in a cookie or in the `Session` scope, as determined by the `LoginStorage` value as either an `Application.cfc` initialization variable or in the `<cfapplication>` attribute. By default, `<cflogin>` sets a non-persistent cookie in the user's browser, called `cfauthorization_`*`applicationName`*. The cookie value is a Base64-encoded string containing the user ID, password, and application name. This in-memory cookie is not written to disk (for example, the `cookies.txt` file) and is destroyed when the browser closes.

Because ColdFusion sends this cookie with every request, users must allow in-memory cookies in their browsers. If the browser disables cookies, then the effect of the `<cfloginuser>` tag exists only for the current page request. In this scenario, ColdFusion allows you to code the `<cfloginuser>` outside of the `<cflogin>` tag in every template you want to secure, in order to persist the login information across page requests.

When storing login information in the `Session` scope, ColdFusion stores the Base64-encoded user ID, password, and application name in the `SESSION.cfauthorization` variable. ColdFusion stores this variable in its internal memory space and uses the browser's session cookies (`CFID` and `CFTOKEN`, or `JSESSIONID`) for user identification. This is more secure than using cookies for login storage because ColdFusion does not pass `SESSION.cfauthorization` with every page request. The user's login and session share the same timeout value—and ColdFusion ignores the `IdleTimeout` `<cflogin>` attribute.

NOTE

The configured session timeout value replaces `idleTimeout` when `loginStorage=session`.

To use the `Session` scope to store login information, ensure the following:

- Session Management is enabled in the ColdFusion Administrator
- Session Management is enabled in the `Application.cfc` or `<cfapplication>`
- `LoginStorage=Session` is specified in either the `Application.cfc` or `<cfapplication>`

TIP

With `SetDomainCookies` enabled in `Application.cfc` or `<cfapplication>`, the `SESSION.cfauthorization` login variable is available to all members in a server cluster.

Best Practice: ColdFusion Sessions and `CFLOGIN`

Session scope variables are held in ColdFusion memory space. Storing the `CFLOGIN` authorization variable (`SESSION.cfauthenticate`) in the `Session` scope (`LoginStorage=Session`) will persist the value for the duration of the user's session. If the user closes the browser without logging out with `CFLOGOUT`, the authorization value will still persist in ColdFusion memory until the `Session` scope is cleared when the session times out or the server is restarted. If another user logs in with the same Session ID (`CFID` and `CFTOKEN` or `JSESSIONID`) as the authenticated user, that user can impersonate the previously authenticated user.

ColdFusion identifies browser sessions by cookies and URL parameters. A ColdFusion Session ID comprises the `CFID`, `CFTOKEN`, and Application name (`applicationName_CFID_CFTOKEN`). When J2EE Sessions are enabled, the Session ID is the `JSESSIONID` value. A ColdFusion session can be impersonated by passing existing Session ID values on the URL or in cookies.

The following are best-practice steps to prevent session impersonation:

- Use the `verifyClient` function and `Application.cfc/<cfapplication>` attribute to force ColdFusion to require the encrypted security token for ColdFusion Ajax client requests.
- Enable J2EE session management and use `JSESSIONID`:
    - `JSESSIONID` is a randomly generated, alphanumeric string created as a non-persistent cookie.
    - Use `GetPageContext().GetSession().InValidate()` to clear J2EE Session data, including the login information (`SESSION.cfauthenticate`).
- For ColdFusion session management:
    - Use a UUID for `CFTOKEN`. Enable UUID for `CFTOKEN` in the ColdFusion Administrator Settings page.
    - Ensure CFID and CFTOKEN are created as non-persistent values. See Adobe TechNote 17915 at `http://www.adobe.com/go/tn_17915`.
    - Do not allow Session variables to pass on the URL. These values are not browser specific like cookies.

- When logging out the user, ensure that `<cflogout>` is called as well as `StructClear(Session)`. `StructClear(Session)` clears all session variables except the `SESSIONID` and `SESSION.cfauthenticate` values.
- Use the `OnSessionStart` method in the `Application.cfc` to clear any existing `SESSIONID` values (from URL or cookie).
- Call `<cflogout>` in the `OnSessionEnd` method to ensure the logged-in user is logged out when the session ends.
- When creating user sessions inspect `CGI.HTTP_REFERER` to ensure the request is coming from with the application.

Logging Out

There are several ways to log out users and remove their login information from ColdFusion. The primary method is to use the `<cflogout>` tag. ColdFusion MX did a poor job of destroying session information after a user logged out. Table 63.2 lists the circumstances in which ColdFusion logs out the current user and destroys the `<cfloginuser>` authentication credentials.

Table 63.2 ColdFusion User Logout

DESCRIPTION	LoginStorage=Cookie	LoginStorage=Session
Application fires `<cflogout>`	x	x
The `<cflogin>` `IdleTimeout` value is reached	x	N/A
The user closes all browser windows	x	N/A
The ColdFusion session ends	N/A	x

CAUTION

`<cflogout>` does not clear the login information if you authenticate users via Web server security or the HTTP Authorization header. These security paradigms continue to send authentication information to ColdFusion until all browser windows are closed. Therefore, until all browser windows are closed, the `CFLOGIN` scope may persist beyond user logout, providing a window of opportunity for another user to impersonate the first user.

Executing `<cflogout>` when using `LoginStorage=Session` removes the `SESSION.cfauthorization` variable from the `Session` scope, but does not end the current user's session. Therefore, if you want to log the user out and completely clear his or her session, you must code logic that calls `<cflogout>` and `StructClear(Session)`:

```
<cfif IsDefined('URL.Logout') and URL.Logout>
  <cflogout>
  <cfset StructClear(Session)>
</cfif>
```

TIP

Calling `StructClear(Session)` will not generate a new session id but it will completely empty the SESSION structure.

Basic ColdFusion Login Example

The following code demonstrates a single-page login mechanism. Three templates are involved: `Application.cfm`, `loginForm.cfm`, and `index.cfm`. The `loginForm.cfm` template contains a simple login form—username and password fields—that passes the special `j_username` and `j_password` to the `<cfloginuser>` tag in the `Application.cfm`. The user must authenticate with the login form in order to access the `index.cfm`. The `Application.cfm` contains all the authentication and authorization logic in the body of `<cflogin>`. Listings 63.1 through 63.3 display this basic login code example (using "admin" and "password" for the username and password, respectively).

Listing 63.1 `Application.cfm`—ColdFusion Login Structure

```
<cfsilent>
<!---####
 File name: Application.cfm
 Description: Demonstrates coldfusion user security with <CFLOGIN>, <CFLOGINuser>,
and <cflogout> Tags.
 Assumptions: None
 Author name and e-mail: Sarge (sarge@sargeway.com) www.sargeway.com/blog/
 Date Created: July 24, 2002
 Change Log: Updated July 27, 2007
####--->

<cfapplication name="OWS" sessionmanagement="yes"
sessiontimeout="#createTimeSpan(0,0,0,30)#" loginstorage="session">
<!---#### Display a nice title in the browser title bar ####--->
<cfhtmlhead text="<TITLE>ColdFusion: User Security Test</title>">

<!---#### If the logout url variable is passed, log off the current user, then
return to the login screen. ####--->
<cfif IsDefined('URL.logout') and URL.logout>
 <cflogout>
 <cfset StructClear(Session)>
 <cfinclude template="loginForm.cfm"><cfabort>
</cfif>

<!---#### call <cflogin> to create the CFLOGIN scope/container. Idle time is set to
30 minutes or 1800 seconds. ####--->
<cflogin idletimeout="1800">

  <!---#### CFLOGIN.name and CFLOGIN.password automatically assume the j_username
and j_password values from the login form.
  If you use some other field naming conventions, you will have to manually set
CFLOGIN.name and CFLOGIN.password equal to the corresponding values.
 ####--->
  <cfif IsDefined("CFLOGIN.name") and Len(Trim(CFLOGIN.name)) and
Len(Trim(CFLOGIN.password))>

    <!---#### Authenticate the user. for this example, the only valid user is
"admin," whose password is "password." CompareNoCase will return a
 zero (0) if the two strings are identical.
####--->
    <cfif NOT CompareNoCase('admin', Trim(CFLOGIN.name)) and
 NOT CompareNoCase(Trim(CFLOGIN.password), "password")>
```

Listing 63.1 (continued)

```
      <!---#### Pass the authenticated user's user name, password, and role to
<CFLOGINUSER> ####--->
      <cfloginuser name="#CFLOGIN.name#" password="#CFLOGIN.password#"
roles="admin">
    <cfelse>
      <cfset REQUEST.badlogin = "true">

      <!---#### if the login fails, return to the login form. ####--->
      <cfinclude template="loginForm.cfm"><cfabort>
    </cfif>
  <cfelse>
    <!---#### if the login fails, return to the login form. ####--->
    <cfinclude template="loginForm.cfm"><cfabort>
  </cfif>
</CFLOGIN>
</cfsilent>
```

The `Application.cfm` checks to see if a user is logged in, and redirects the request to the login page (`loginform.cfm`) if needed.

Listing 63.2 `loginForm.cfm`—Sample Login Form

```
<cfsetting enablecfoutputonly="yes">
<!---####
 File name: loginForm.cfm
 Description: Login form for the ColdFusion user security example.
 Demonstrates how to use the special j_username and j_password field names for the
<cflogin> tag.
 Assumptions: None
 Author name and e-mail: Sarge (sarge@sargeway.com)
 Date Created: July 24, 2002
 Change Log: Updated February 20, 2005
####--->
<cfsetting enablecfoutputonly="no">
<!doctype html public "-//w3c//dtd html 4.01 transitional//en">
<html>
<body>
<p>Please enter your login information:</p>
<!---#### If the user submits a bad login, display a friendly message ####--->
<cfif IsDefined('REQUEST.badlogin')><span style="color: red">Your login information
was invalid!</span></cfif>
<!---#### Use cfform to provide client-side javascript validation on the user name
form field. ####--->
<cfform action="index.cfm" method="post">
<table border="0">
  <tr>
    <td>User Name:</td>
    <td><cfinput type="text" name="j_username" message="You must enter a user name!"
required="yes"></td>
  </tr>
  <tr>
    <td>Password:</td>
    <td><cfinput type="password" name="j_password" message="You must enter a
password!" required="yes"></td>
  </tr>
```

Listing 63.2 (CONTINUED)

```
    <tr>
      <td> </td>
      <td><input type="reset"> | <input type="submit" name="logon" value="Login"></td>
    </tr>
  </table>
  </cfform>
  </body>
  </html>
```

The `loginForm.cfm` template contains the actual form that submits the username and password. These are processed by the `Application.cfm` when the form is submitted. The code in `Application.cfm` will allow processing to continue with `index.cfm` if authentication is successful; otherwise, the login form will redisplay.

Listing 63.3 `index.cfm`—Securing a Template with `GetAuthUser()` and `IsUserInRole()`

```
<cfsetting enablecfoutputonly="yes">
<!---####
 File Name: index.cfm
 Description: Index page secured by <cflogin> in the Application.cfm. This
 page also shows how to use the ColdFusion security functions:
 GetAuthUser() and IsUserInRole.
 Assumptions: None
 Author name and e-mail: Sarge (sarge@sargeway.com)
 Date Created: July 24, 2002
 Change Log: Updated February 20, 2005
####--->
<cfsetting enablecfoutputonly="no">
<!doctype html public "-//w3c//dtd html 4.01 transitional//en">
<html>
<body>
  <!---#### Use the GetAuthUser function to display the authenticated id ####--->
  <p><b>Welcome, <span style="color: green"><cfoutput>#GetAuthUser()#</span>
</cfoutput>!</b></p>
  <!---#### Use the IsUserInRole function to add conditional logic based on the
user's group membership (role). ####--->
<cfif IsUserInRole("admin")>
  <p>Based on your login ID, you are permitted to access this section of the
site.</p>
Please proceed to the <a href="index.cfm" title="This link is for demonstration
purposes only">Administrator's section</a>.
  <!---#### Display the log out link. ####--->
  <p><a href="index.cfm?logout=yes">Log Out</on></p>
</cfif>
</body>
</html>
```

ColdFusion Login Wizard Extension

ColdFusion 8 includes several powerful extensions for Dreamweaver that enhance ColdFusion development. One of these is the Login Wizard. The Login Wizard allows developers to quickly create login forms and well-formed ColdFusion components that leverage the ColdFusion security framework. Developers can either use templates created by the ColdFusion Login Wizard to secure their application directories, or incorporate the code within the templates into the developer's own security paradigms.

Download the ColdFusion 8 Update for Dreamweaver from the ColdFusion 8 Developer Tools section on the Adobe Web site at `http://www.adobe.com/go/cf_extensions`. After you double-click the executable file (`cf8_tags_for_dw.mxp`), the Adobe Extension Manager opens and installs the extensions into Dreamweaver.

NOTE

The ColdFusion Login Wizard requires a Dreamweaver site configured with RDS access to ColdFusion. ColdFusion 8 allows individual usernames and passwords for RDS access—see Chapter 62. Adobe recommends disabling RDS for production systems.

To start the ColdFusion Login Wizard, open Dreamweaver and connect to a site definition that uses RDS, open or create a ColdFusion template, and open the Commands menu and select ColdFusion Login Wizard. Figure 63.3 shows the wizard's Welcome screen.

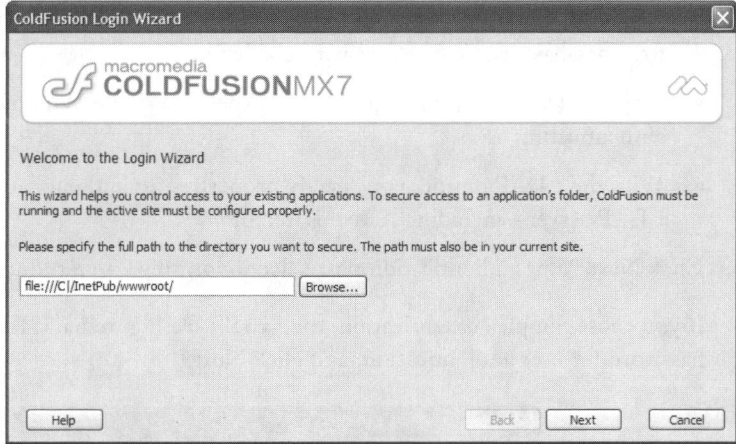

Figure 63.3

Welcome to the Dreamweaver ColdFusion Login Wizard.

Then follow these steps to create security templates:

1. With the ColdFusion Login Wizard open, enter or browse to the full directory path that you want to secure. Click Next.

TIP

The wizard requires an open file in a Dreamweaver site that uses an RDS connection to ColdFusion. The opened file must be in the currently selected site definition. You cannot use an FTP and RDS Server type of Dreamweaver site with the ColdFusion Login Wizard.

2. On the Authentication Type screen (Figure 63.4) that opens next, select the type of authentication you want to employ. Then choose whether you want the wizard to create a ColdFusion login page or a browser pop-up dialog box as a user login interface.

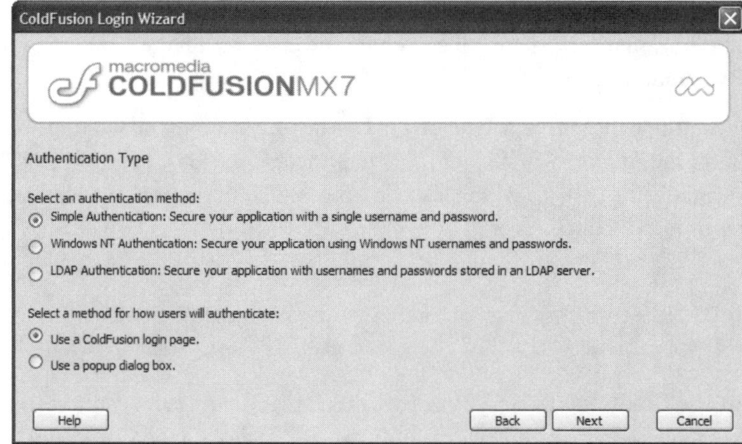

Figure 63.4
Specify an authentication type and the type of login form to present the user.

- The Simple option provides a standard challenge for a single username and password. Choose this option for a simple security test and/or to provide a template for a database user name/password challenge.
- The NT Domain option allows you to specify a single Windows domain for authenticating users.
- With the LDAP option, you specify properties for authenticating users against an LDAP server—including Active Directory.

3. Click Next. Your authentication type selection in step 2 determines the next screen:

   If you chose Simple authentication, then you'll see Figure 63.5. Enter a username and password for user authentication, and click Next.

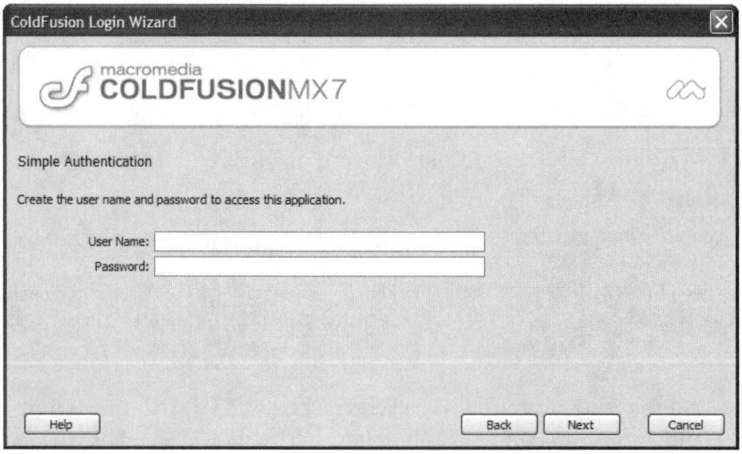

Figure 63.5
Enter a username and password for simple authentication.

If you chose NT Domain authentication, you'll see Figure 63.6. Enter the Windows domain to use for user authentication, and click Next.

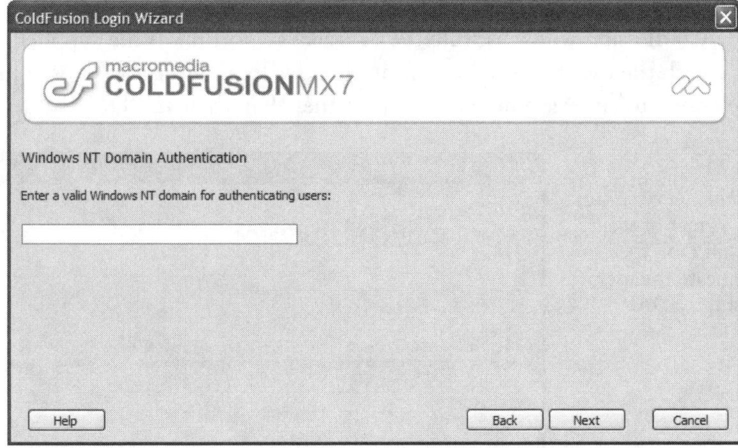

Figure 63.6
Enter the Windows domain to use for authentication.

If you chose LDAP authentication, you'll see Figure 63.7. Enter the LDAP server information and proper bind DN for an administrative user. Click Verify LDAP Server or click Next. If verification is successful, you can continue on to step 4; if it is unsuccessful, modify the information in one or more of the fields and then re-verify.

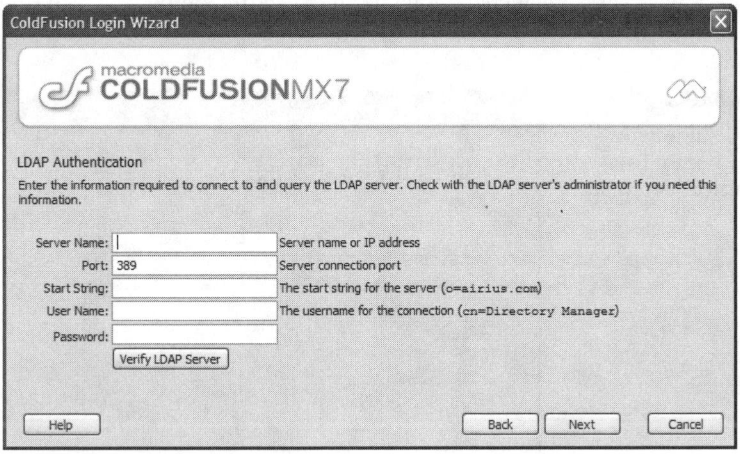

Figure 63.7
Enter the values necessary to authenticate to the LDAP server.

TIP

The wizard will not let you continue until you successfully verify your LDAP settings. The typical causes of failure are an improper Start String, Username, or Password. View your LDAP server logs (if available) to help you debug the bind attempts made during verification.

Click Next when you're ready. You'll see the LDAP Authentication Query String screen (Figure 63.8). Enter the query string format used to authenticate the user. The query string format should be similar to `cn={username},ou=People,dc=company,dc=com`.

ColdFusion will substitute the `{username}` portion of the supplied query string format with the user name submitted in the user login interface (chosen in step 2). This allows users to enter a simple username rather than their full DN.

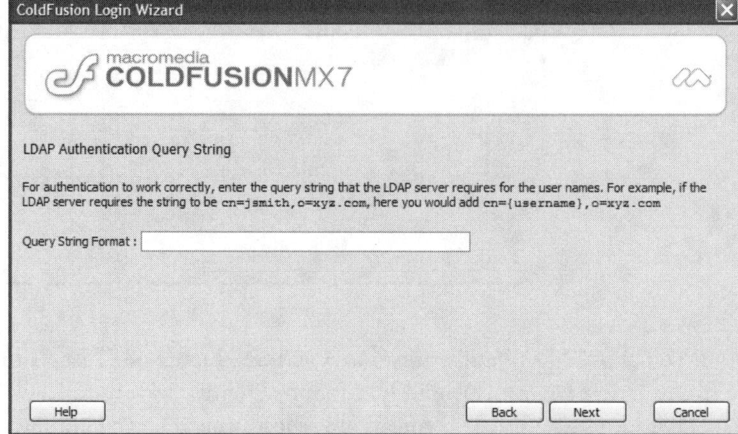

Figure 63.8

Enter the query string, in the format of the user's full DN, used to authenticate the user against the LDAP server.

4. Click Next. Then click Done on the Wizard Complete screen (Figure 63.9) to close the wizard.

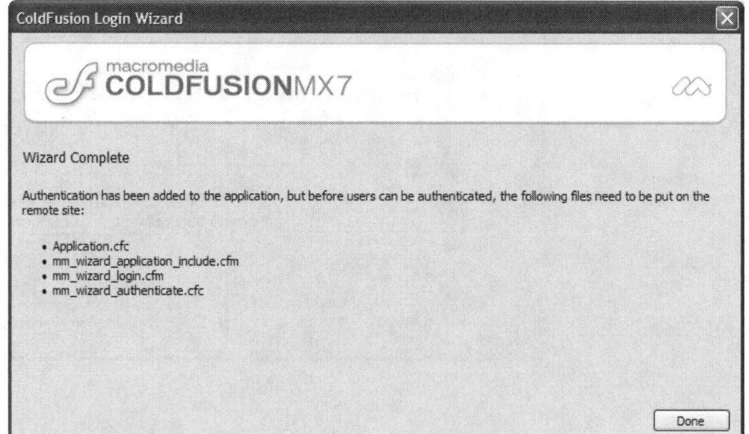

Figure 63.9

The ColdFusion Login Wizard has completed successfully.

The Login Wizard creates four ColdFusion files:

- **`Application.cfc`.** This file starts the ColdFusion Application Framework. If the file does not exist, it is created with an `OnRequestStart` method containing a `<cfinclude>` tag that specifies the `mm_wizard_application_include.cfm`, and a simple logout form that displays with every page request for the authenticated user. If the `Application.cfc` already exists, the wizard creates the `OnRequestStart` method if one does not exist. If the `OnRequestStart` already exists, it should simply add the `<cfinclude>`.
- **`mm_wizard_application_include.cfm`.** The Login Wizard records in this file the authentication parameters entered into the wizard fields. These parameters are passed as arguments to the methods in `mm_wizard_authenticate.cfc` component.
- **`mm_wizard_authenticate.cfc`.** This component contains all the code to perform authentication and authorization, including the `<cflogin>` container. It contains the following methods:
  - **Authentication methods for each authentication type**: Simple (`simpleauth`), NT Domain (`ntauth`), and LDAP (`ldapauth`). These methods validate the submitted username and password and return whether or not the authentication was successful. All authentication methods are generated—including those not chosen in the wizard.
  - **`performLogin` method**: This method contains the `<cflogin>` container that presents the login challenge, calls the appropriate authentication method, and logs the authenticated user in with `<cfloginuser>`.
  - **`logout` method**: Calls `<cflogout>` and logs out the current user. It also calls the `closeBrowser` method if Browser Dialog Box was selected as the challenge method in the wizard. The call to `closeBrowser` prevents the browser from continuing to send old login information after the call to `<cflogout>`.
  - **`closeBrowser`**: This method uses JavaScript to prompt the user to close the browser and/or closes the browser to complete the logout process.
- **`mm_wizard_login.cfm`.** The login form presented to the user if ColdFusion login was chosen in the wizard.

TIP

`Application.cfc` overrides any `Application.cfm` templates in the same directory path. Consider moving your application logic in `Application.cfm` to the application event handlers in `Application.cfc`. See the "Migrating from Application.cfm to Application.cfc" section of the chapter "Designing and Optimizing a ColdFusion Application" in the ColdFusion 8 Developer's Guide help manual at `http://livedocs.adobe.com/coldfusion/8/htmldocs/appFramework_15.html#1191454`.

The code generated by the wizard can be used as is for the most part; however, it has some shortcomings that you should customize before putting it into production:

- The `Application.cfc` contains no initialization variables, including application name, `LoginStorage`, `SessionManagement`, `SessionTimeout`, `SetClientCookies`, or the like. You should code these variables to strengthen your security paradigm.
- Consider changing the `simpleAuth` authentication method to perform a database query using the submitted username and password instead of a simple string comparison. Use the `Hash()` function to strengthen the security of passwords in the database. See Chapter 61 for more information on the ColdFusion 8 `Hash()` function.
- The authentication methods contain simplified code and may not work without modification. For example, the LDAP code queries for an attribute named `"roles"`, which is probably not valid for most LDAP servers.
- The authentication methods only return Boolean values in ColdFusion structures that indicate whether authentication failed. Modify the code to populate the structure with the authenticated user's roles, as well.
- All authenticated users are granted a single role: user. Modify this hard-coded `<cfloginuser>` value in the `performLogin` method to dynamically accept roles returned from the authentication methods.
- The wizard allows you to specify a Browser dialog box, but it does not allow you to specify the authentication realm. Modify the default Basic Realm values in the `<cfheader>` tag in the `performLogin` method.
- The wizard creates a default error message for login failures, but it does not create code for handling any exceptions, such as domain controller access failures or LDAP failure codes.

TIP

Choosing the right login challenge is important. Select Browser Dialog Box if you are integrating with Web server authentication, or chose NT Domain as the authentication type. Use a ColdFusion login page for database and LDAP logins, because a database and LDAP won't be able to validate the Basic Realm of the WWW Authentication header passed by the Browser dialog box.

ColdFusion Login Wizard Example

The following example uses the templates generated by the ColdFusion Login Wizard to perform authentication against a Windows domain. Listing 63.4 shows the `mm_wizard_login.cfm`, which displays the login form. The `Application.cfc` in Listing 63.5 has been modified with the coding of the `THIS.name` variable, to set the application name. The `mm_wizard_include.cfm` in Listing 63.6 records the parameters entered into the wizard fields and passes them to the `mm_wizard_authenticate.cfc`. The `simpleauth` and `ldapauth` methods have been removed from the `mm_wizard_authenticate.cfc` in Listing 63.7. The `ntauth` method has been modified to return the authentication structure returned from the `<cfntauthenticate>`, which is used to log in the user.

Table 63.3 lists the `<cfntauthenticate>` attributes; Table 63.4 lists the fields in the returned structure.

TIP

If you're familiar with performing authentication and authorization in your `Application.cfm`, move the `<cflogin>` container into the `OnRequestStart` method of the `Application.cfc`.

Table 63.3 `<cfntauthenticate>` Attributes

ATTRIBUTE	DESCRIPTION	REQUIRED
`username`	A username to authenticate against the specified domain.	Yes
`password`	The password for the specified username.	Yes
`domain`	Windows domain to authenticate against. ColdFusion must be running on a server within the specified domain.	Yes
`result`	Variable name for the return structure. Default value is `cfauthenticate`.	No
`listGroups`	Boolean indicating whether or not to return a list of domain groups to which the authenticated user belongs. Default value is `no`.	No
`throwOnError`	Boolean indicating whether or not to throw an exception if user authentication fails.	No

Table 63.4 Fields in the `<cfntauthenticate>` Structure

FIELD	DESCRIPTION
`auth`	Boolean indicating whether the user is authenticated.
`groups`	Comma-delimited list of groups in the specified domain to which the user belongs. This field is only returned if the `ListGroups=yes`.
`name`	The same value as the `username` attribute.
`status`	Authentication status. Returns one of the following: `success` means the username is found in the domain and the password is valid; `UserNotInDirFailure` means the username is not found in the specified domain; `AuthenticationFailure` means the username is found, but the password is invalid.

Listing 63.4 `mm_wizard_login.cfm`—ColdFusion Login Wizard's Login Form

```
<cfsetting enablecfoutputonly="yes">
<!---####
 File name: mm_wizard_login.cfc
 Description: Login form created by the ColdFusion Login Wizard.
 Assumptions: None
 Author name and e-mail: Sarge (sarge@sargeway.com)
 Date Created: February 22, 2005
####--->
<cfsetting enablecfoutputonly="no">
<cfparam name="errorMessage" default="">
```

Listing 63.4 (continued)

```
<!--- output error message if it has been defined --->
<cfif len(trim(errorMessage))>
  <cfoutput>
  <ul>
    <li><font color="FF0000">#errorMessage#</font></li>
  </ul>
  </cfoutput>
</cfif>

<!--- This is the login form, you can change the font and color etc but please keep
the username and password input names the same --->
<cfoutput>
<h2>Please Login using #args.authtype# authentication.</h2>

   <cfform  name="loginform" action="#CGI.script_name#?#CGI.query_string#"
method="Post">
      <table>
         <tr>
            <td>username:</td>
            <td><cfinput type="text" name="j_username" required="yes" message="A
username is required"></td>
         </tr>
         <tr>
            <td>password:</td>
            <td><cfinput type="password" name="j_password" required="yes" message="A
password is required"></td>
         </tr>
         </table>
      <br>
      <input type="submit" value="Log In">
   </cfform>
</cfoutput>
```

Listing 63.5 `Application.cfc`—ColdFusion Login Wizard's `Application.cfc` File

```
<!---####
  File name: Application.cfc
  Description: Template created by the ColdFusion Login Wizard that handles
application events.
  Assumptions: None
  Author name and e-mail: Sarge (sarge@sargeway.com)
  Date Created: February 22, 2005
####--->
<cfcomponent>
  <!---#### Application initialization variables. ####--->
  <cfset THIS.name = "ows">
  <cffunction name = "onRequestStart">
    <cfargument name = "thisRequest" required="true"/>
    <cfinclude template="mm_wizard_application_include.cfm">
    <cfif GetAuthUser() NEQ "">
      <cfoutput>
        <cfform
action="mm_wizard_authenticate.cfc?method=logout&loginType=#args.authLogin#"
method="Post">
          <cfinput type="submit" name="Logout" value="Logout">
```

Listing 63.5 (continued)

```
         </cfform>
       </cfoutput>
     </cfif>
   </cffunction>
</cfcomponent>
```

Listing 63.6 `mm_wizard_include.cfm`—ColdFusion Login Wizard's Decision File

```
<cfsetting enablecfoutputonly="yes">
<!---####
  File name: mm_wizard_application_include.cfm
  Description: Template created by ColdFusion Login Wizard that records
authentication information from the wizard fields and passes them to the
mm_wizard_authenticate.cfc
  Assumptions: None
  Author name and e-mail: Sarge (sarge@sargeway.com)
  Date Created: February 22, 2005
####--->
<cfsetting enablecfoutputonly="no">
<!--- MM WIZARD CODE: BEGIN   --->
  <!--- Set the NT Authentication Logic parameters --->
  <cfset args = StructNew()>
  <!--- Authentication Type ---->
  <cfset args.authtype = "NT">
  <!--- Domain Name ---->
  <cfset args.domain = "Sargeway">
  <!--- Login type--->
  <cfset args.authLogin = "CFlogin">
  <!--- Login Page ---->
  <cfset args.loginform = "mm_wizard_login.cfm">
  <!--- Call the CFC to perform the authentication --->
  <cfinvoke component="mm_wizard_authenticate" method="performlogin">
    <cfinvokeargument name="args" value="#args#">
  </cfinvoke>
<!--- MM WIZARD CODE: END --->
```

Listing 63.7 `mm_wizard_authenticate.cfc`—ColdFusion Wizard's Authentication File

```
<!---####
  File name: mm_wizard_authenticate.cfc
  Description: Modified ColdFusion Login Wizard template that performs user
authentication and login.
  Assumptions: This template only performs Windows authentication -- all other
authentication methods are removed.
  Author name and e-mail: Sarge (sarge@sargeway.com)
  Date Created: February 22, 2005
####--->
<cfcomponent>
  <!---- ////////////////////////////////////////////////////////--->
  <!---- NT Domain Authentication                          --->
  <!---- ////////////////////////////////////////////////////////--->
  <cffunction name="ntauth" access="private" output="false" returntype="struct"
hint="Authenticate against a NT domain">
    <cfargument name="nusername" required="true" hint="The username">
    <cfargument name="npassword" required="true" hint="The password">
```

Listing 63.7 (continued)

```
    <cfargument name="ndomain" required="true" hint="The domain to authenticate
against">
    <!---#### Modify the <cfntauthenticate> by setting listgroups=yes ####--->
    <cfntauthenticate
      username="#arguments.nusername#"
      password="#arguments.npassword#"
      domain="#arguments.ndomain#"
      result="authenticated"
      listgroups="yes">
    <cfreturn authenticated>
  </cffunction>

  <!---- ///////////////////////////////////////////////////////--->
  <!--- This method performs the <cflogin> call and in turn  --->
  <!--- calls the actual authentication method               --->
  <!---- ///////////////////////////////////////////////////////--->
  <cffunction name="performlogin" access="public" output="true" hint="Log a user in
using either NT authentication.">
  <cfargument name="args" type="struct" required="true" hint="These are the
parameters setup by the Login Wizard">
    <cflogin>
      <cfif NOT IsDefined("cflogin")>
        <cfinclude template="#args.loginform#"><cfabort>
      <cfelse>
        <cftry>
          <cfinvoke method="ntauth"
            returnvariable="result"
            nusername="#cflogin.name#"
            npassword="#cflogin.password#"
            ndomain="#args.domain#" >
          <cfcatch>
            <cfset errorMessage = "Your login information is not valid.<br>Please
Try again">
            <cfinclude template="#args.loginform#"><cfabort>
          </cfcatch>
        </cftry>
      </cfif>
      <!--- validate if the user is authenticated --->
      <cfif result.auth eq "YES">
      <!--- if authenticated --->
        <cfloginuser name="#cflogin.name#" password="#cflogin.password#"
roles="#result.groups#">
      <cfelse>
        <!--- if not authenticated, return to login form with an error message --->
        <cfset errorMessage = "Your login information is not valid.<br>Please Try
again">
        <cfinclude template="#args.loginform#"><cfabort>
      </cfif>
    </cflogin>
  </cffunction>

  <!---- ///////////////////////////////////////////////////////--->
  <!--- Logout  --->
  <!---- ///////////////////////////////////////////////////////--->
  <cffunction name="logout" access="remote" output="true" hint="Log the user out.">
```

Listing 63.7 (continued)

```
  <cfargument name="logintype" type="string" required="yes" hint="The login type
used to login.">
    <cfif isDefined("form.logout")>
      <cflogout>
        <cfif arguments.logintype eq "challenge">
          <cfset foo = closeBrowser()>
        <cfelse>
          <!--- replace this URL to a page logged out users should see --->
          <cflocation url="http://www.Adobe.com">
        </cfif>
    </cfif>
  </cffunction>

  <!---- ///////////////////////////////////////////////////////--->
  <!--- Close Browser  --->
  <!--- To ensure the header authentication information --->
  <!--- has been thouroughly flushed the browser should be closed --->
  <!---- ///////////////////////////////////////////////////////--->
  <cffunction name="closeBrowser" access="public" output="true" hint="Close the
browser to clear the header information.">
    <script language="javascript">
      if(navigator.appName == "Microsoft Internet Explorer") {
        alert("The browser will now close to complete the logout.");
        window.close();
      }
      if(navigator.appName == "Netscape") {
        alert("To complete the logout you must close this browser.");
      }
    </script>
  </cffunction>
</cfcomponent>
```

CHAPTER 64

Creating Server Sandboxes

IN THIS CHAPTER

Chapter 63, "ColdFusion Security Options," introduced the security options available in Adobe ColdFusion: development security (Remote Development Services, or RDS) and run-time security—resource (data sources, files, and so on) and user (or programmatic) security. This chapter discusses resource security.

Resource security controls access to ColdFusion resources based on template locations. By applying a set of rules at the directory level to limit access of the CFML in the underlying templates at run time, you create a specific area in which the code can operate. Securing resources in this manner is known as *sandbox security*, and it is configured in the ColdFusion Administrator.

Understanding Sandboxes

Sandbox security takes its name from its real-world counterpart: Just as children are allowed to build anything they please within the confines of a sandbox, developers can be restricted to write and read code only within a virtual sandbox. In the case of ColdFusion Server, developers can be restricted to a set of directory structures—the virtual sandbox. This way, two different companies that each have an application hosted on the same server will not be able to read or write to each other's directories.

Sandbox security applies restrictions on the directories in which ColdFusion templates exist. Permissions of parent directories propagate to subdirectories (their children). Sandboxes defined for subdirectories override the sandbox settings on parent directories. This enables administrators of shared hosted environments to set up a root sandbox for each application and create personalized sandboxes on subdirectories within the parent sandboxes, without compromising the security of sandboxes for the other hosted sites. Examine the following directory structure:

- `C:\ColdFusion8\wwwroot\ows`
- `C:\ColdFusion8\wwwroot\ows\Actors`
- `C:\ColdFusion8\wwwroot\ows\Actors\Female`

In this hierarchy, the `Actors` and `Female` directories automatically inherit any sandbox restrictions defined for the `ows` directory. The `Female` directory would inherit any sandbox restrictions defined for the `Actors` directory, leaving the `ows` sandbox intact.

Sandbox definitions restrict access to the following resources:

- **Data sources:** Defined ColdFusion data source connections
- **CF tags:** A subset of ColdFusion tags
- **CF functions:** A subset of ColdFusion functions
- **Files and directories:** File and directory pathnames on the server
- **Servers and ports:** Server IP addresses and ports accessible by Internet Protocol tag calls to third-party resources

NOTE

Read and Execute access to the files and subdirectories of the `cf_web_root/CFIDE/adminapi` directory must be allowed in order to use the Administrator API when sandbox security is enabled.

Understanding File and Directory Permissions

ColdFusion 8 uses the Java security model for its file and directory permissions. An asterisk (`\*`) represents all the files in the parent directory and a list of subdirectories, but not the files in those subdirectories. A backslash followed by a dash (`\-`) indicates all the files in the parent directory, a list of subdirectories, *and* all the files in those subdirectories.

Table 64.1 illustrates the inheritance patterns of files and directories.

Table 64.1 File and Directory Inheritance

PATHNAME	AFFECTED FILES AND DIRECTORIES
C:\ColdFusion8\wwwroot\ows*	C:\ColdFusion8\wwwroot\ows C:\ColdFusion8\wwwroot\ows\index.cfm C:\ColdFusion8\wwwroot\ows\Actors
C:\ColdFusion8\wwwroot\ows\-	C:\ColdFusion8\wwwroot\ows\index.cfm C:\ColdFusion8\wwwroot\ows\Actors\index.cfm C:\ColdFusion8\wwwroot\ows\Actors\Female\index.cfm
C:\ColdFusion8\wwwroot\ows	C:\ColdFusion8\wwwroot\ows

Table 64.2 illustrates the effect of permissions on files and directories.

Table 64.2 File and Directory Permissions

PERMISSION	RESULT FOR FILES	RESULT FOR DIRECTORIES
Read	Can view the file	Can list all files in the current directory
Write	Can write to the file	Does not apply
Execute	Can execute the file	Does not apply
Delete	Can delete the file	Can delete the directory

Setting read permissions on the pathname `C:\ColdFusion8\wwwroot\ows\Actors\*` produces the following results:

- All files in `C:\ColdFusion8\wwwroot\ows\Actors` can be listed.
- All files in `C:\ColdFusion8\wwwroot\ows\Actors\Female` can be listed.
- `C:\ColdFusion8\wwwroot\ows\Actors\index.cfm` can be read.

Changes in ColdFusion MX

Previous versions of ColdFusion (4.x through 5.0) leveraged the Netegrity SiteMinder API for sandbox security as a part of ColdFusion's Advanced Security framework. Though still a directory-based access control mechanism, sandboxes in this framework came in two flavors: operating system and ColdFusion. An operating system sandbox—available only on Windows-based systems—protected OS-level resources by assigning privileges to Windows domain members. ColdFusion sandboxes protected resources by assigning privileges through security contexts. A security context contained policies and rules that defined access control to resources: applications, data sources, tags and functions, user objects, and so on. Administrators then added users and/or groups from a user directory (LDAP, NT SAM, or ODBC) to the policies in order to govern access.

ColdFusion MX simplified the entire resource-security paradigm by eliminating the dependency of user directories and security contexts. This adds flexibility to the framework, making it independent of users and completely directory based. Tag restrictions and the unsecured tag directory are now a part of sandbox security, giving you more structured control over dangerous tags without inhibiting functionality within ColdFusion Administrator. Administrators can even limit the access of IP tags (such as `<cfftp>`, `<cfhttp>`, and `<cfldap>`) to specific server IPs and ports.

Changes in ColdFusion MX 7

ColdFusion MX 7 added `<cfdocument>` and `<cfreport>` to the list of available tag restrictions. It also added `GetGatewayHelper()` and `SendGatewayMessage()` functions to the list of available function restrictions. The most significant change to sandbox/resource security introduced in ColdFusion MX 7 is the ability to restrict access to the `CreateObject` function by type. Administrators are now able to restrict access to COM, Java, or Web services without disabling access to ColdFusion components via the `CreateObject` function.

In ColdFusion MX, developers were able to access undocumented administrator functions with `<cfobject>` and `CreateObject()` calls; for example:

```
<cfscript>
  factory = createObject('java','coldfusion.server.ServiceFactory')
</cfscript>
```

Adobe recommends disabling `<cfobject>` and `CreateObject()` in shared or untrusted environments, and recommended granting access to shared Java objects via `<cfinvoke>` (see Adobe Security Bulletin MPSB04-10 at `http://www.adobe.com/devnet/security/security_zone/mpsb04-10.html`). Disabling `<cfobject>` and `CreateObject` meant you couldn't use them to integrate safely with COM or Web Services objects.

ColdFusion MX 7 allows administrators to secure their servers against developers hacking at administrative functionality via Java objects, without limiting COM and Web Services integration. Adobe also tightened this loophole by automatically restricting the corresponding object types in the `<cfobject>` tag when access to COM, Java, or Web Services objects is disabled via `CreateObject()`.

Changes in ColdFusion 8

There are no major changes to sandboxing in ColdFusion 8, other than an updated list of tags and functions to protect.

ColdFusion Edition Differences

The Enterprise editions of ColdFusion Server allow administrators to create several sandboxes. The Standard edition allows only the root sandbox configuration (Resource Security) (Figure 64.1). The Developer edition is a fully functional limited-IP edition, intended for local development, to help developers learn how to build applications with ColdFusion. Because it is fully functional, administrators can also configure additional sandboxes with the Developer edition.

NOTE

Adobe ColdFusion Server is available for download as a fully functional 30-day Trial edition. At the end of 30 days, it becomes the limited-IP Developer edition.

Security Defaults

Resource or sandbox security is disabled by default in ColdFusion and must be enabled via the ColdFusion Administrator (Figure 64.2). Administrator password protection and RDS password protection are enabled by default and configured with the passwords you used during the installation process. See Chapter 62, "Securing the ColdFusion Administrator," for more information.

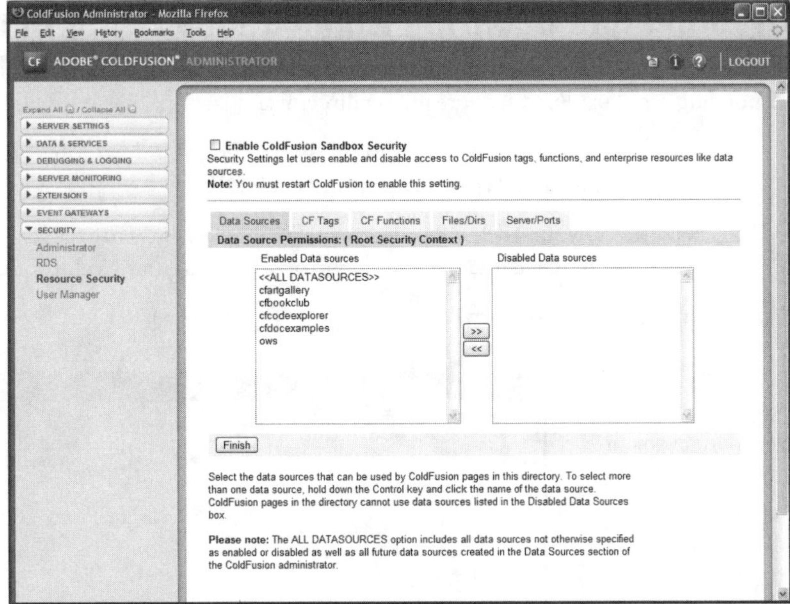

Figure 64.1

Only the root sandbox exists in the ColdFusion Standard edition.

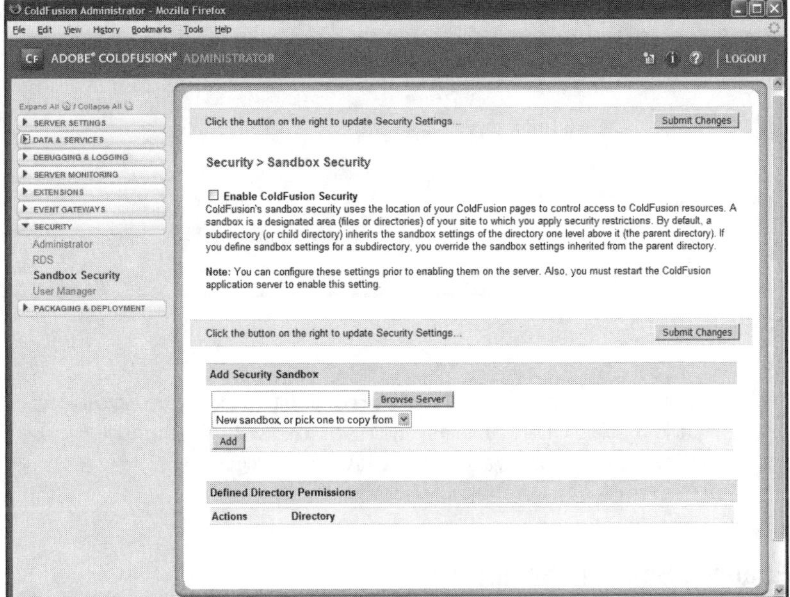

Figure 64.2

Sandbox security is disabled by default in ColdFusion Administrator.

Creating and Securing Applications Using Sandboxes

To demonstrate sandbox security, we'll create a directory in the Web root called `Blackbox` and a corresponding sandbox. First, let's create the directory:

1. For Unix systems, open a console/terminal. For Windows, open Windows Explorer: Click Start > Run. Type `Explorer` and click OK.
2. Navigate to your Web root directory. For Unix: `/opt/coldfusion8/wwwroot/`. For Windows: `C:\ColdFusion8\wwwroot\` (or wherever your Web root exists).
3. Create a new directory called `Blackbox` (Figure 64.3).

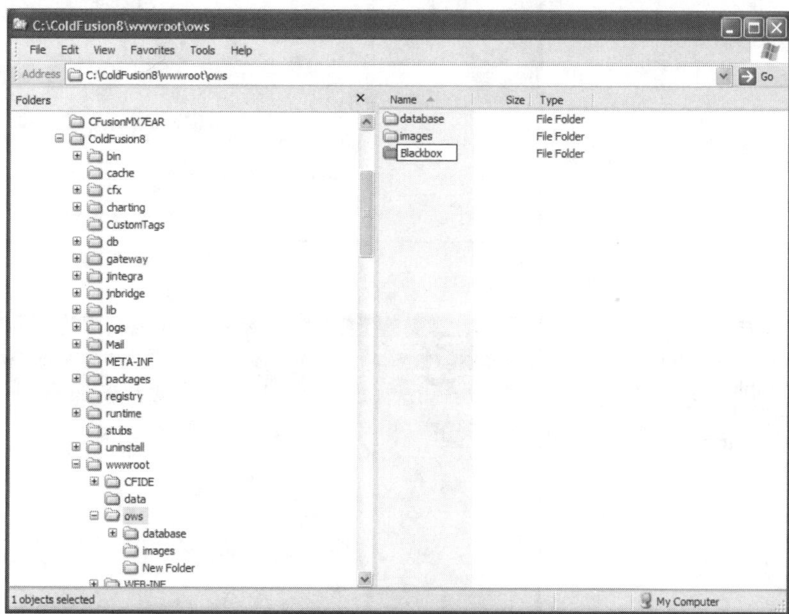

Figure 64.3

Create a directory named `Blackbox` in your Web root.

TIP

ColdFusion must be able to access the `Blackbox` directory. If you add this directory outside of your default Web root, you may need to add a ColdFusion mapping using the ColdFusion Administrator Mappings page. Because this example is using ColdFusion's stand-alone Web server, you may also need to add a virtual mapping in your `cf_root\wwwroot\WEB-INF\jrun-web.xml` file. Remember, this is Java, so all settings are case-sensitive!

Enabling Sandbox Security

Now that we have a directory on the Web server to hold the application code that we want to secure, we need to enable sandbox security. Remember, ColdFusion does not enable sandbox (or resource) security after installation. This allows developers full reign over all resources on the server. Follow these steps to enable sandbox security:

1. Open ColdFusion Administrator.

CAUTION

To enable Sandbox security in the Multiserver and J2EE configurations, the underlying application server deploying ColdFusion must have a security manager (`java.lang.SecurityManager`) running with the following JVM arguments specified:

```
-Djava.security.manager
-Djava.security.policy="cf_root/WEB-INF/cfusion/lib/coldfusion.policy"
-Djava.security.auth.policy="cf_root/WEB-INF/cfusion/lib/neo_jaas.policy"
```

2. Expand the Security section in the left navigation pane (if it's not already expanded.
3. Click the Sandbox Security link.
4. Check the box next to Enable ColdFusion Security in the window on the right. Click Submit. The page should refresh and display the success message (Figure 64.4).

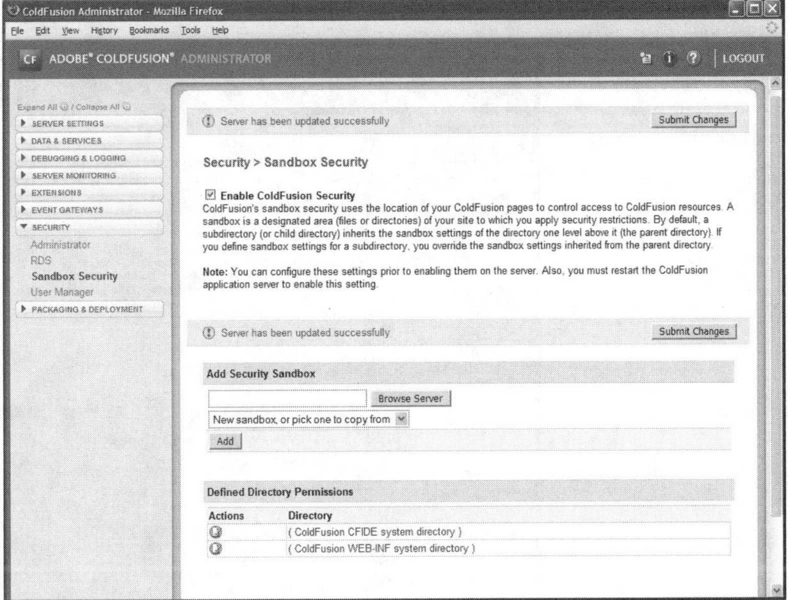

Figure 64.4

You must manually enable sandbox security using the Sandbox Security page.

5. Restart ColdFusion.

TIP

If the link in the Security section of the Administrator navigation pane says "Resource Security," you have the ColdFusion Standard edition and will not be able to configure additional sandboxes.

Notice that after you enable sandbox security, ColdFusion automatically creates the two sandboxes (shown in Figure 64.4):

- ColdFusion CFIDE system directory
- ColdFusion WEB-INF system directory

You can edit these two internal, system-level sandboxes, but you cannot delete them.

NOTE

If you have the Standard edition, the root security context is your sandbox (shown in Figure 64.1). This enables you to apply server-level security.

Adding a Sandbox

Follow these steps to add a sandbox:

1. On the Sandbox Security page, enter the directory for your sandbox in the Add Security Sandbox field. Remember, sandboxes are directories, so either browse to or enter the absolute path to the `Blackbox` directory (Figure 64.5). In the selection box, choose New Sandbox.

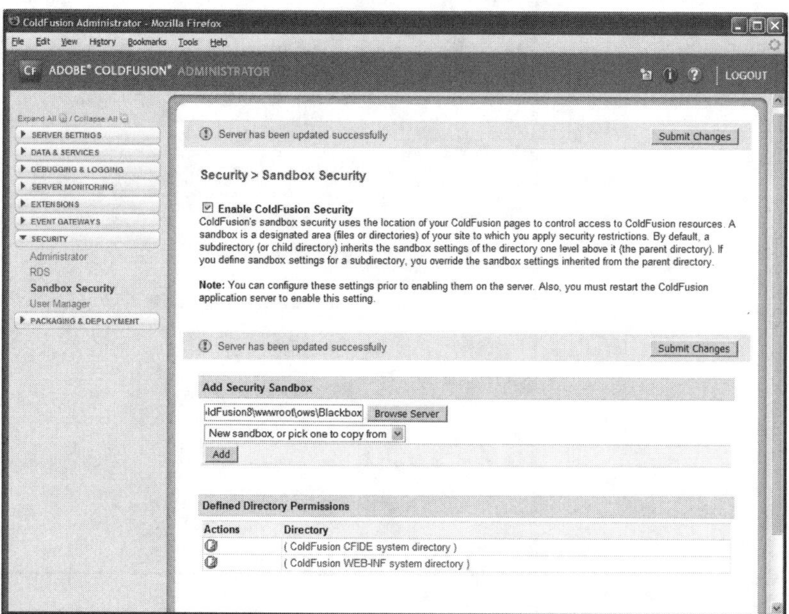

Figure 64.5

Enter the absolute path to your new sandbox directory.

TIP

If you already have a sandbox set up, you can copy its settings to your new sandbox by selecting the existing one in the selection box.

2. Click Add. Your sandbox is added to the Defined Directory Permissions list (Figure 64.6).

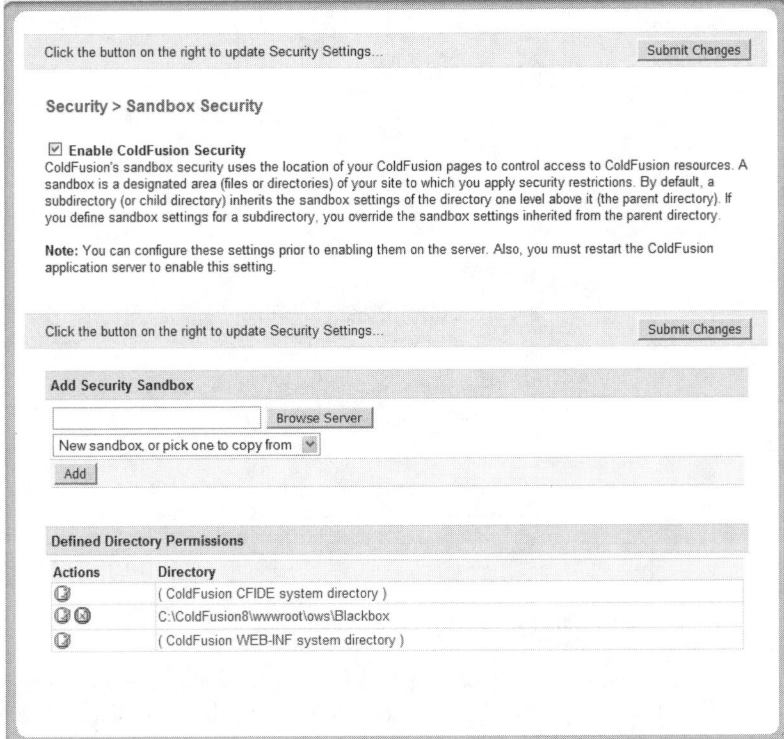

Figure 64.6
Click Add to include your new sandbox in the list of Defined Directory Permissions.

Configuring Your Sandbox

Remember that you must manually enable sandbox security. You must also manually create resource permissions for your new sandboxes. If you chose to apply an existing sandbox's configuration to your new sandbox, some of those settings will be designated for you. Follow these steps to configure your new sandbox:

1. Access the Sandbox Security page in the ColdFusion Administrator.

2. In the list of Defined Directory Permissions, click the name of your sandbox or click the Edit icon next to it. This opens the Security Permissions screen (Figure 64.7).

3. The Security Permissions page opens to the Data Sources tab. All pages in your sandbox have full access to all configured data sources on your server. To disable a data source, select it in the Enabled Data Sources list on the left, and click the right arrow to move it to the Disabled Data Source window on the right.

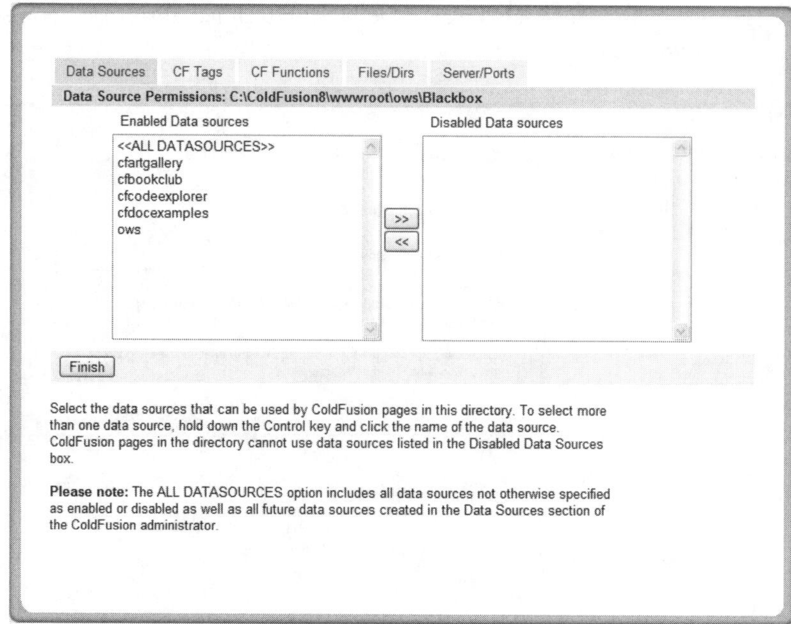

Figure 64.7

Use the Security Permissions page to add resource permissions for your sandbox.

NOTE

The `<<all datasources>>` option means every existing data source–whether enabled or disabled–and all future data sources.

4. Select the CF Tags tab. All pages in your sandbox have full access to all ColdFusion tags. To disable tags, highlight the tags in the Enabled Tags list on the left, and click the right arrow. For our `Blackbox` sandbox example, we want to disable the `<cfdirectory>` tag (Figure 64.8).

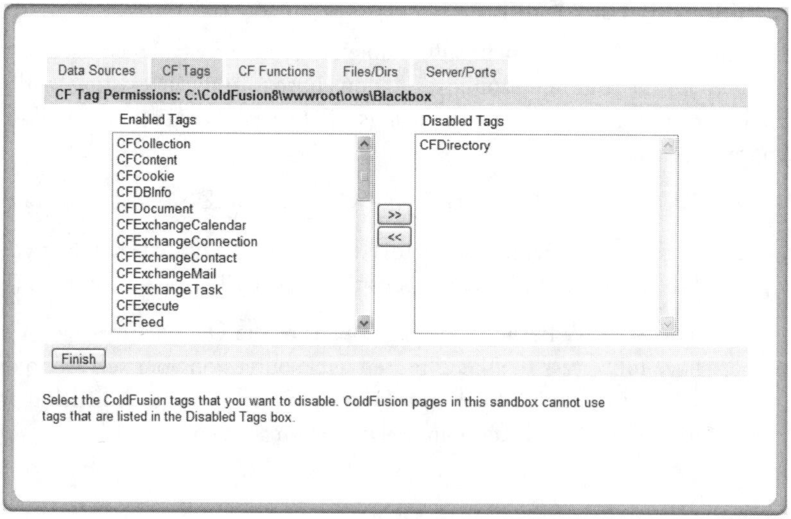

Figure 64.8

Disable access to the `<cfdirectory>` tag.

5. Select the CF Functions tab (Figure 64.9). All pages in your sandbox have full access to every ColdFusion function. To disable functions, highlight the functions in the Enabled Functions list on the left, and click the right arrow.

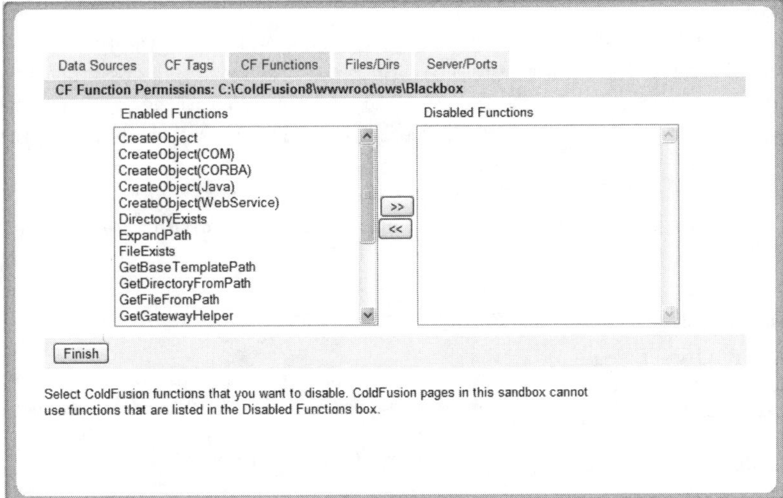

Figure 64.9

Disable access to functions on the CF Functions tab.

6. Select the Files/Dirs tab. Use this tab to grant permissions to files and directories, instead of disabling permissions as on other tabs. There are two file paths that are secured by default (Figure 64.10). Verify that these paths are correct.

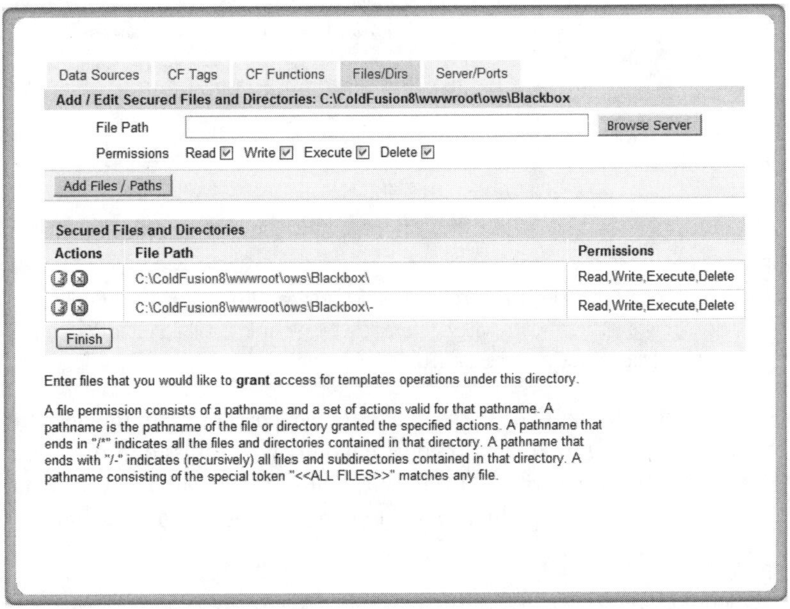

Data Sources | CF Tags | CF Functions | Files/Dirs | Server/Ports

Add / Edit Secured Files and Directories: C:\ColdFusion8\wwwroot\ows\Blackbox

File Path [ ] Browse Server

Permissions Read ☑ Write ☑ Execute ☑ Delete ☑

Add Files / Paths

Secured Files and Directories

Actions	File Path	Permissions
	C:\ColdFusion8\wwwroot\ows\Blackbox\	Read,Write,Execute,Delete
	C:\ColdFusion8\wwwroot\ows\Blackbox\-	Read,Write,Execute,Delete

Finish

Enter files that you would like to **grant** access for templates operations under this directory.

A file permission consists of a pathname and a set of actions valid for that pathname. A pathname is the pathname of the file or directory granted the specified actions. A pathname that ends in "/*" indicates all the files and directories contained in that directory. A pathname that ends with "/-" indicates (recursively) all files and subdirectories contained in that directory. A pathname consisting of the special token "<<ALL FILES>>" matches any file.

Figure 64.10

The Files/Dirs tab grants permissions for files and directories within the sandbox.

- To secure a new file or directory, enter the absolute path in the File Path box, or click the Browse Server button to navigate to it. To edit an existing file or directory, click the pathname or the Edit button next to it in the Secured Files and Directories list.

NOTE

Notice the character after the trailing backslash (or slash, for Unix) in the pathname. If there is no character, it means access permissions are valid for the current pathname only. An asterisk (`*`) indicates access permissions on all files in the current directory and a list of subdirectories–but not the files in those subdirectories. A dash (`-`) indicates recursive access permissions on all files in the current directory and any subdirectories. The special token `<<all files>>` added to the pathname matches any file in that path.

- In the File Path box, choose the permissions you want to grant for the pathname. For example, configure Read and Execute permissions for the `directory.cfm` template (Figure 64.11).

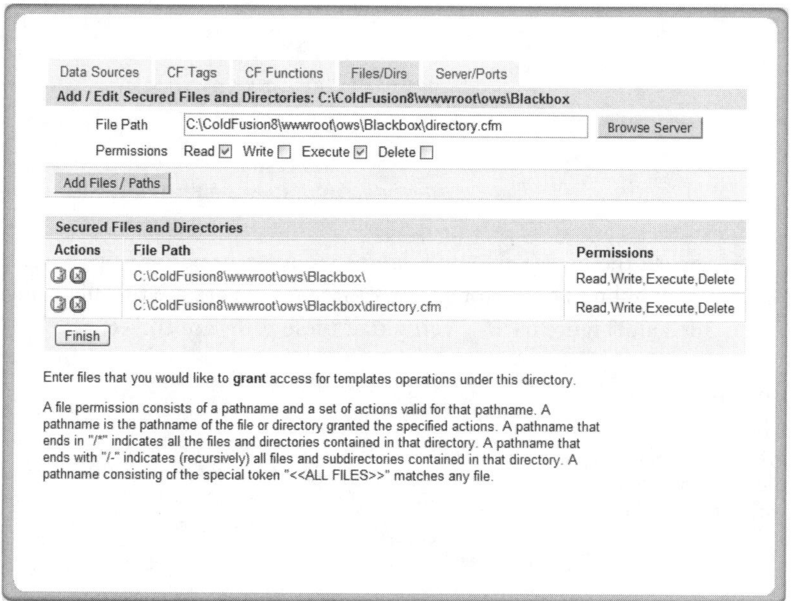

Figure 64.11

Add Read and Execute permissions for the `directory.cfm` template in our sandbox.

TIP

You must explicitly grant file/directory permissions for any area of the server you want ColdFusion tags and directories to access–including those outside of your sandbox. For example, if you want to enable access to D:\, you must enter D:\ in the File Path box, select the appropriate permissions, and click Add Files/Paths.

- Click Add Files/Paths to add the new pathname in the Secured Files and Directories list (Figure 64.12). If you are modifying permissions for an existing secured pathname, the button will read Edit Files/Paths. ColdFusion throws an error (Figure 64.13) if you try to add a pathname without configuring any permissions.

TIP

Be careful not to click Finish before you apply your permissions for the pathname. If you do, you'll be returned to the Sandbox Security Permissions page and your settings won't be saved.

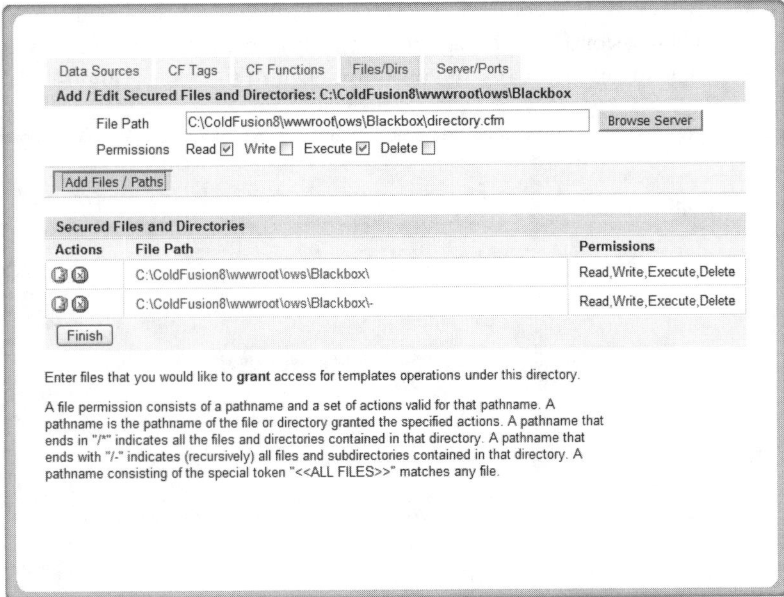

Figure 64.12

Add the pathname to the Secured Files and Directories list.

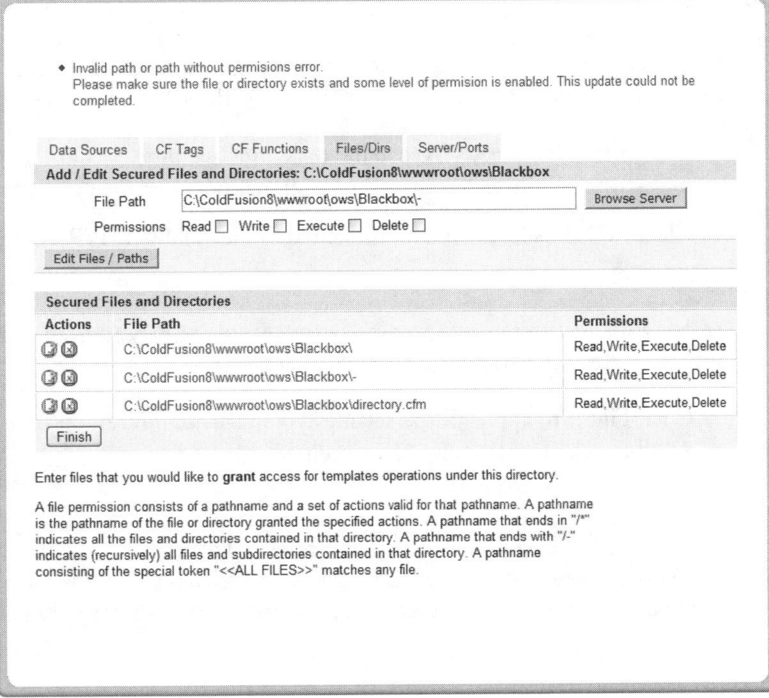

Figure 64.13

You must enter a valid pathname and select some level of permissions, or you'll get an error.

7. Select the Servers/Port tab. Here you can restrict the IP addresses and ports used by the ColdFusion Protocol tags `<cfftp>`, `<cfhttp>`, `<cfldap>`, `<cfmail>`, and `<cfpop>`. By default, all server IPs and ports are open to these tags (Figure 64.14).

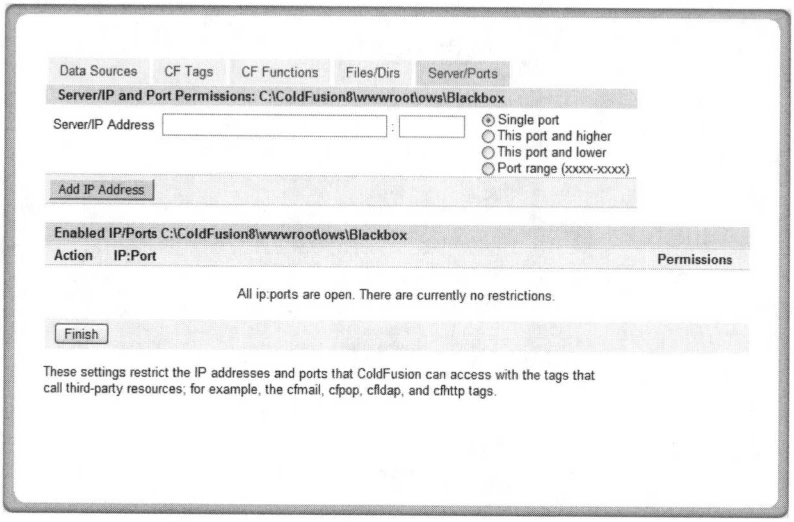

Figure 64.14

All IP addresses and ports are open by default.

TIP

Server IP address and port restrictions are useful for shared hosted environments where multiple virtual servers are configured on different ports for a single IP. See Chapter 65, "Security in Shared and Hosted Environments," for details.

8. Enter the IP address, server name (`www.example.com`), or domain (`example.com`) you wish to restrict. Additionally, choose an optional port or range of ports to block access.

9. Click Add IP Address to add the entry to the Enabled IP/Ports list.

NOTE

IP address and port restrictions do not inhibit a user's ability to browse sites. Rather, they prohibit ColdFusion templates within a sandbox from accessing servers and/or ports that are not listed.

10. Click Finish to apply all the settings you have configured on each tab and return to the Sandbox Security Permissions screen.

NOTE

You should disable JSP integration for your ColdFusion sandboxes. ColdFusion restricts resource access for all CFM, CFML, CFC, and CFR requests it receives for templates in its sandbox. JSP requests have the capability to bypass this security and access the resources blocked by the sandbox. Remove any `.jsp` mappings from your Web server-ColdFusion configuration.

The Blackbox Sandbox Example

Now that you have configured the `C:\ColdFusion8\wwwroot\ows\Blackbox` sandbox, let's put it into action. If you remember, we restricted access to the `<cfdirectory>` tag for all templates in the `C:\ColdFusion8\wwwroot\ows\Blackbox` directory and subdirectories. The code in Listing 64.1 attempts to use `<cfdirectory>` to list the files in the current directory.

Listing 64.1 `directory.cfm`—List the Files in the Current Directory Path

```
<cfsetting enablecfoutputonly="yes">
<!---####
  File name: directory.cfm
  Description: Demonstrates ColdFusion sandbox and tag restrictions using
<cfdirectory>.
  Assumptions: Creation of a Sandbox that restricts <cfdirectory>. Run this
  file from the sandbox.
  Author name and e-mail: Sarge (ssargent@Adobe.com)
  Date Created: July 17, 2002
  Change Log:
####--->
<cfsetting enablecfoutputonly="no">
<html>
<head>
 <title>Blackbox Sandbox Security</title>
</head>
<body>
 <!---#### Create a variable to hold the current directory path ####--->
 <cfset VARIABLES.CurrentDir = GetDirectoryFromPath(CGI.CF_Template_Path)>

 <!---#### Pass the currentdir variable to the cfdirectory tag with Action=list
####--->
  <cfdirectory action="list"
       directory="#VARIABLES.CurrentDir#"
       name="blacklist">
  <h2>Listing of <cfoutput>#VARIABLES.CurrentDir#</cfoutput></h2>

  <!---#### <cfdirectory> returns a query object. Use <cftable> to display the query
object result set. ####--->
  <cftable query="blacklist" colheaders htmltable border>
    <cfcol text="#name#" header="File Name" align="left">
    <cfcol text="#size#" header="File Size" align="center">
    <cfcol text="#type#" header="File Type" align="center">
    <cfcol text="#datelastmodified#" header="Date Last Modified">
  </cftable>
</body>
</html>
```

Figure 64.15 shows the error that results when the code in Listing 64.1 runs within the sandbox. Try creating a subdirectory in `C:\ColdFusion8\wwwroot\Blackbox`, and run the `directory.cfm` template. You should see the same error, because the default directory mappings in the sandbox (`C:\ColdFusion8\wwwroot\Blackbox\-`) are recursive.

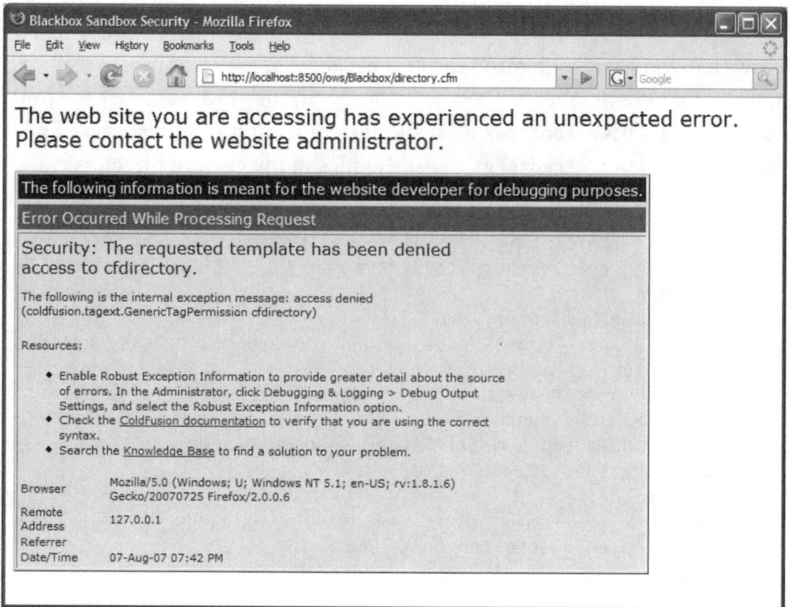

Figure 64.15

Sandbox security denies access to `<cfdirectory>`.

Return to the sandbox definition and enable access to the `<cfdirectory>` tag. Now the directory listing displays correctly, as shown in Figure 64.16.

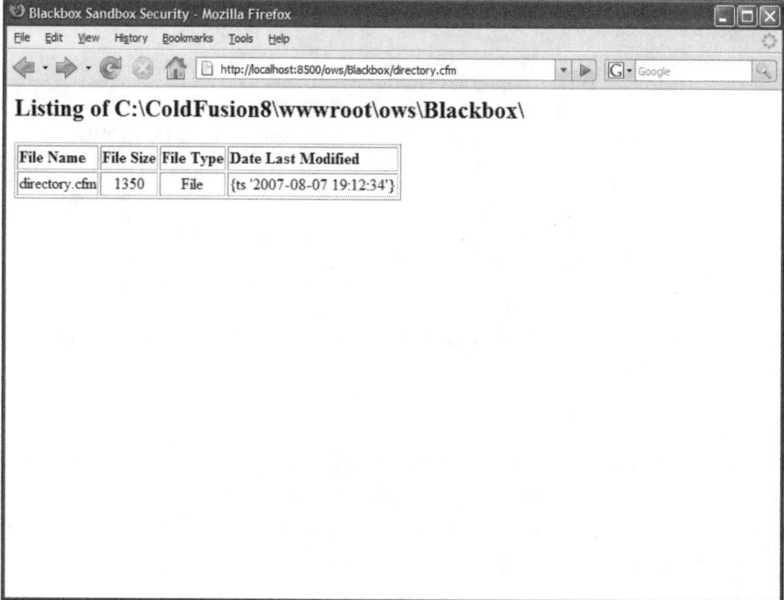

Figure 64.16

Sandbox security allows access to `<cfdirectory>`.

CHAPTER 65

Security in Shared and Hosted Environments

IN THIS CHAPTER

One benefit of ColdFusion is that it allows hosting providers to house several ColdFusion applications on the same server. This capability comes with a number of inherent risks that come to light when several users have access to the same server. ColdFusion has many powerful features that can be used to control and manage the server, file system, and other network resources such as databases, and these features can be used maliciously unless access to them is not appropriately restricted.

CFML-Based Risks

ColdFusion's language is filled with feature-rich functions and tags capable of accessing the system's hard drive, Registry, and network resources. Improper or malicious use of many of these tags and functions by unauthorized developers (or hackers) could compromise the server, thereby compromising the data of other sites hosted on the same box.

To mitigate this risk, ColdFusion enables server administrators to restrict developer access to several tags and functions. Table 65.1 shows the ColdFusion 8 tags and some of the risks associated with them. Table 65.2 shows the associated risks of ColdFusion 8 functions.

Table 65.1 ColdFusion Tags and Their Associated Risks

TAG	POTENTIAL RISK
CFCOLLECTION	Can be used to modify or delete collections
CFCONTENT	Can be used to download files outside of Web root
CFCOOKIE	Can be used to write cookies to client browsers
CFDBINFO	Can be used to gather information about data source and database objects
CFDIRECTORY	Can be used to delete, move, and otherwise affect files and directories

Table 65.1 (continued)

TAG	POTENTIAL RISK
CFDOCUMENT	Can be used to create FlashPaper and PDF objects
CFEXCHANGECALENDAR	Can be used to modify Microsoft Exchange calendar events
CFEXCHANGECONNECTION	Can be used to create connections to Microsoft Exchange servers
CFEXCHANGECONTACT	Can be used to modify Microsoft Exchange contact records
CFEXCHANGEMAIL	Can be used delete messages on Microsoft Exchange servers
CFEXCHANGETASK	Can be used to modify Microsoft Exchange tasks
CFEXECUTE	Can be used to execute arbitrary programs from the command line
CFFEED	Can be used to create or read RSS and Atom feeds
CFFILE	Can be used to upload, delete, rename, or overwrite files
CFFTP	Allows users to transfer files between one machine and a remote FTP site
CFGRIDUPDATE	Can be used to update ODBC data sources from within `CFGRID`
CFHTTP	Can be used to perform `GET` and `POST` operations against external servers—including file uploads, and form, query, and cookies posts
CFHTTPPARAM	Specifies the parameters to use for `CFHTTP` operations
CFIMAGE	Can be used to manipulate images
CFINDEX	Can be used to modify Verity indexes
CFINSERT	Can be used to insert data into data sources
CFINVOKE	Can be used to instantiate components and Web services and call their methods
CFLDAP	Can be used to access LDAP servers
CFLOG	Can be used to mask evidence of an attempted hack
CFMAIL	Can be used to email files on the system
CFPOP	Can be used to read email files
CFOBJECT	Can be used to create and access COM, component, Java, CORBA, and Web service objects
CFOBJECTCACHE	Can be used to clear all cache queries on the server
CFQUERY	Can be used to execute malicious SQL against databases
CFPDF	Can be used to manipulate PDF documents
CFPRINT	Can be used to send PDF pages in automated batch jobs to a printer
CFREGISTRY	Can be used to read and set Registry keys
CFREPORT	Can be used to execute ColdFusion and Crystal Reports report documents
CFSCHEDULE	Can be used to manipulate the ColdFusion scheduling engine

Table 65.1 (continued)

TAG	POTENTIAL RISK
`CFSEARCH`	Can be used to search collections
`CFSTOREDPROC`	Can be used to execute stored procedures on databases
`CFTHREAD`	Can be used to create autonomous streams of execution
`CFTRANSACTION`	Can be used to erroneously commit or roll back database transactions
`CFUPDATE`	Can be used to update data in a data source

Table 65.2 ColdFusion Functions and Their Associated Risks

FUNCTION	POTENTIAL RISK
`CreateObject`	Can be used to create and access .NET, COM, component, Java, CORBA, and Web services objects (can be restricted individually)
`DirectoryExists`	Can be used to inspect the file system to discover whether directories exist
`ExpandPath`	Can be used to resolve real pathnames
`FileExists`	Can be used to inspect the file system to discover whether a file exists
`GetBaseTemplatePath`	Can be used to determine the absolute path of an application's base page
`GetDirectoryFromPath`	Can be used to determine an absolute path
`GetFileFromPath`	Can be used to extract a file name from an absolute path
`GetGatewayHelper`	Can be used to access Java `GatewayHelper` objects
`GetPrinterInfo`	Can be used to inspect printers
`GetProfileString`	Can be used to extract information from an initialization file
`GetTempDirectory`	Can be used to find the system's `temp` directory
`GetTempFile`	Can be used to create temporary files on the system
`GetTemplatePath`	Deprecated function; same risk as `GetBaseTemplatePath`
`SendGatewayMessage`	Can be used to send data across gateways
`SetProfileString`	Can be used to modify initialization files

ColdFusion administrators can restrict access to all the tags and functions listed in Tables 65.1 and 65.2. Tag and function restrictions are part of sandbox security, discussed in Chapter 64, "Creating Server Sandboxes."

Securing ColdFusion ServiceFactory

ColdFusion ServiceFactory is a collection of objects that expose the integrated services of the ColdFusion environment. It is one of the undocumented features of ColdFusion provided by the underlying Java API. There are many blog postings and articles detailing how to use the ServiceFactory to manipulate ColdFusion objects, including data sources and scheduled tasks. The Administrator API was created to provide developers with safe, secure access to the ServiceFactory features without providing direct access to the ServiceFactory objects themselves. See Chapter 66, "Using the Administrator API," for more information on Administrator API methods.

NOTE

Although access to the ServiceFactory is legitimate coding and there are a number of sites and articles that explain how to mimic ColdFusion Administrator functions (such as the disabling of data sources), Adobe officially supports only issues originating from the Administrator API.

The only way to secure the ServiceFactory in previous versions of ColdFusion was to disable access to Java objects with `createObject()` and `<cfobject>` with sandboxing. ColdFusion 8 now gives administrators a means to secure the ServiceFactory. The ColdFusion 8 Administrator Settings screen includes the Disable Access to Internal ColdFusion Java Components option. Enable this option to prevent unauthorized access to the ServiceFactory's objects.

Securing RDS

A task crucial in shared hosting environments is securing the file system. ColdFusion Remote Development Service (RDS) is a powerful feature that lets users read and write to the file system, as well as work with ColdFusion data sources. However, in a shared environment, it is not wise to allow developers of one application to have access to the files or data sources for another application. One way to protect access this is to disallow (or disable) RDS access to the server and allow developers to access the server over FTP. This approach requires that hosting providers set up an FTP account for each application and specify its root as the application's Web root.

NOTE

Disabling RDS is not a full solution to securing a hosting environment. This action must be accompanied by restriction of tag use, such as the use of `<cfregistry>`, `<cffile>`, and `<cfdirectory>` tags, all of which can be used to gain unauthorized access to resources on the server. Again, tag restrictions are a part of the server sandbox configuration.

RDS offers great benefits to developers; however, these services also introduce new security risks. To deal with this, ColdFusion offers a development security model, discussed in Chapter 63, "ColdFusion Security Options." It is always recommended to disable RDS access on production servers.

Enabling RDS Password Security

ColdFusion restricts RDS access via Dreamweaver, HomeSite+, the ColdFusion ReportBuilder, and the CFEclipse RDS plug-in with password security. Enabling RDS is a ColdFusion installer option. Single-password security is the default authentication for RDS. ColdFusion 8 also provides user-based RDS authentication for a more flexible security paradigm.

➜ Chapter 62, "Securing the ColdFusion Administrator," discusses how to enable RDS security options.

Disabling RDS on Production Servers

ColdFusion implements RDS as a servlet mapped in the `web.xml` file. It is strongly recommended that server administrators disable the RDS services on servers that are not being explicitly used for development, and on servers that do not require remote access to files and databases.

CAUTION

Administrators should be aware that disabling the RDS services will also disable several Java applets in the ColdFusion Administrator, including the applet used to configure a file-based data source. If this functionality is required, you'll have to temporarily enable RDS, modify the Server configuration, and disable RDS again.

To disable RDS in ColdFusion, do the following:

1. Stop ColdFusion.
2. Back up the `web.xml` file.

   On Windows, the path is `cf_root\wwwroot\WEB-INF\web.xml`.

   On Unix systems, the path is `cf_root/wwwroot/WEB-INF/web.xml`.

   For the Multiserver and J2EE configurations, the path is `cf_web_root/WEB-INF/web.xml`.
3. Open the original file in an editor, and comment out the `RDSServlet` mapping:

   ```
   <!--
     <servlet-mapping id="coldfusion_mapping_9">
       <servlet-name>RDSServlet</servlet-name>
       <url-pattern>/CFIDE/main/ide.cfm</url-pattern>
     </servlet-mapping>
   -->
   ```
4. Start ColdFusion.

NOTE

For more information on enabling and disabling the RDSServlet, see Adobe Tech Note 17276, Disabling/Enabling ColdFusion RDS on Production Servers, at `http://www.adobe.com/go/tn_17276`.

Applying ColdFusion Sandbox Security

ColdFusion's sandbox security applies directory-based restrictions to limit application access to ColdFusion resources: data sources, tags, functions, and so on. Use sandboxes to partition the shared-host environment into separate directory hierarchies that allow multiple applications to run securely on a single-server platform. Create a separate directory for each application. Then, apply rules that restrict access to the application's own files and data sources.

When enabled, ColdFusion automatically creates sandboxes for the `CFIDE` and `WEB-INF` directories. This ensures the security of internal system-level templates—including the ColdFusion Administrator. After installation, administrators of shared-hosted environments should immediately create a

ROOT sandbox (Figure 65.1). The following configuration will remove all resource privileges on the server:

- **Data Sources.** Disable access to all data sources.
- **CF Tags.** Disable access to all tags.
- **CF Functions.** Disable access to all functions.
- **Files/Dirs.** Remove all secured file and directory mappings.
- **Servers/Ports.** Restrict access to the loopback IP address.

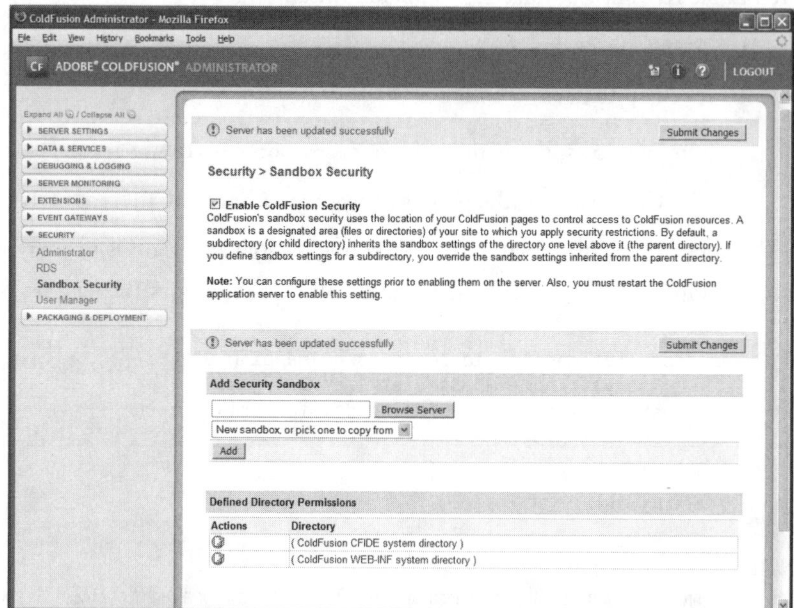

Figure 65.1

Create sandboxes for the root directories on all drives/partitions.

Disabling access to all data sources, tags, and functions on the root or system drive completely protects this drive from ColdFusion. Removing all pathnames from the Secured Files and Directories prohibits ColdFusion templates from accessing all files, directories, and subdirectories (and any files therein) on the server. The combination of removing access to the Internet Protocol tags (such as `<cfhttp>`, `<cfftp>`, `<cfmail>`, etc.) and restricting access to the loopback address prevents templates from accessing third-party servers.

➔ Chapter 64 explains how to implement ColdFusion sandbox security.

Securing Multiple Server Configurations

ColdFusion 8 is a J2EE application. The ColdFusion 8 Enterprise Edition is deployable on multiple J2EE application server instances. Supported J2EE application servers include Macromedia

JRun, BEA WebLogic, IBM WebSphere, and JBoss. Running ColdFusion in multiple instances on J2EE application servers provides scaling through application isolation and server clustering/failover. You can combine multiple server instances with multi-homed Web servers to provide complete application and Web site isolation.

NOTE

For information on configuring application isolation with multi-homed Web servers, see "Enabling application isolation" in the Configuring and Administering ColdFusion manual at `http://livedocs.adobe.com/coldfusion/8/htmldocs/clustering_1.html`.

The ColdFusion MX 7 Enterprise Edition in Multiserver configuration introduced the ability to configure JRun server instances and automatically deploy an instance of ColdFusion to those JRun instances from within the ColdFusion Administrator. Administrators can combine this feature with the J2EE Archives feature to deploy packaged ColdFusion applications that contain the application server, application files (`.cfm`, `.cfc`, `.cfr`, etc.), and server settings (data sources).

➔ Chapter 60, "Deploying Applications," provides more details on packaging ColdFusion application servers as J2EE Archives. Chapter 58, "Scaling with J2EE," discusses configuring multiple instances with the ColdFusion Instance Manager.

Running multiple instances of ColdFusion on J2EE application servers provides the following security benefits:

- Each ColdFusion instance is isolated so that each can have dedicated server resources, including JVM, simultaneous requests, memory, caching, data sources, and so on.
- Applications can be isolated to leverage individual server instances and individual Web server instances.
- Application isolation prevents problems (bottlenecks, memory leaks, and the like) in one application from affecting in other applications.
- Application isolation increases sandbox security by extending restrictions to an application instance.
- Clustered instances provide failover, which can help maintain the user session integrity for sensitive data such as shopping carts during catastrophic application failure.

Configuration Issues for Multi-homed Web Servers

Most ISPs operate in a multi-homed environment—a server containing multiple virtual Web server instances, each with a separate Web root. This is also known as multi-hosting; a server hosts multiple domain names on a single IP address. In these configurations, each virtual server has a different Web root and domain name, but a single ColdFusion server answers requests for all virtual servers. When configuring ColdFusion in these environments beware of the following issues, which are discussed in the sections that follow:

- Running the stand-alone ColdFusion Web server
- Cached Web server paths enabled

- ColdFusion Administrator access
- Access to the `cfform.js` file

NOTE

Most of the information in this section describes issues with multi-homed configurations affecting ColdFusion MX 6.0. These issues were corrected in the 6.1 release. The information in this section may prove useful for administrators upgrading from ColdFusion MX 6.0 to 8, or who have a misconfigured 6.1 installation.

Problems with the Stand-Alone Web Server and Web Server Path Caching

The ColdFusion MX 6.0 stand-alone Web server ran by default after an install. ColdFusion MX 6.1 fixed this issue; however, it is still considered a best practice to install ColdFusion using the stand-alone Web server, and then enable external Web server support after completing the Configuration Wizard.

The stand-alone Web server runs on port 8500 by default. Keep in mind that running the stand-alone server in addition to your production Web server adds overhead and potential security risks via port 8500.

TIP

If it detects an existing ColdFusion server bound to port 8500, the ColdFusion 8 stand-alone Web server may bind to port 8501. This allows both versions to run simultaneously. If port 8501 is taken, the stand-alone server will continue to search incrementally until it finds an open port.

ColdFusion MX 6.0 also enables template path caching by default to optimize performance. On multi-homed servers, template path caching may cause the incorrect display of all templates with relative paths similar to their respective Web server roots. For example, ColdFusion will cache the first request for `http://www.mysite.com/products/index.cfm`, and any subsequent calls to `http://www.yoursite.com/products/index.cfm` will display the cached `/products/index.cfm` page results for `www.mysite.com` because the relative paths are similar. This problem was corrected in ColdFusion MX Updater 2, but administrators should still be wary of this issue.

TIP

See the Adobe ColdFusion Release Notes (`http://www.adobe.com/support/documentation/en/coldfusion/releasenotes.html`) for more information on these and other issues.

You can shut down the stand-alone Web server and disable Web server path caching either in the `cf_root\runtime\servers\coldfusion\SERVER-INF\jrun.xml` (Server configuration) or in `jrun_root\servers\cfusion\SERVER-INF\jrun.xml` (Multiserver configuration). Use the following steps to modify the `jrun.xml` file:

1. Back up the `jrun.xml` file.
2. To turn off the stand-alone Web server, navigate to the `WebService` service class declaration and set the deactivated attribute to `true`:

   ```
   <attribute name="deactivated">true</attribute>
   ```

3. To disable Web server path caching, navigate to the `ProxyService` service class declaration and ensure the `cacheRealPath` attribute to `false`:

```
<attribute name="cacheRealPath">false</attribute>
```

TIP

The `cacheRealPath` value is already set to false in ColdFusion versions MX 7.0.2 and 8.

4. Stop and restart ColdFusion.

Issues with ColdFusion Administrator Access

The ColdFusion Administrator should only be accessed from one Web server instance. This keeps administration simple and helps augment the ColdFusion Administrator security. Because all ColdFusion Administrator instances modify the same configuration files in the Server configuration, having multiple instances can cause unforeseen problems leading to server instability or failure. However, should access to the ColdFusion Administrator be required from virtual sites, create a virtual mapping to the originally installed `CFIDE` directory. You can also create local `CFIDE` directories for individual virtual servers and copy to them the code from the original `CFIDE`; this does, however, add an additional administration step of keeping the code in sync.

➜ Chapter 62 discusses ColdFusion Administrator security options. Chapter 66 discusses access to ColdFusion Administrator functionality is via the ColdFusion Administrator API.

TIP

You can use the Web Server Configuration Tool's `-cfwebroot` option, to allow access to the `CFIDE` directory under the specified Web root when configuring virtual server integration with ColdFusion.

Access to `CFIDE/scripts`

ColdFusion 8 includes support for default client-side JavaScript routines used by `<cfform>` validation, cascading style sheets for control layouts, and Ajax functionality. The default location for these libraries is `CFIDE/scripts`. If this folder is not available to all virtual servers, `<cfform>` validation and Ajax functionality will fail. If application logic in any of the virtual servers will use `<cfform>`, `<cfajaximport>`, and so on, take one of the following actions:

- Modify the Default ScriptSrc Directory value on the ColdFusion Administrator Settings page.
- Map a virtual directory from the virtual server instance to the original `CFIDE/scripts` folder.
- Copy the original `CFIDE/scripts` folder to the virtual server's Web root.
- Specify the URL (relative to the Web root) of the directory containing the ColdFusion JavaScript source files in the `ScriptSrc` attribute for `<cfform>` and/or `<cfajaxproxy>`.

TIP

You can have only one `scriptSrc` attribute in a page.

NOTE

If you use specify a directory to the `scriptSrc` attribute, that directory must have the same structure as the `/CFIDE/scripts` directory. The directory specified in the `scriptSrc` attribute overrides the directory configured in the ColdFusion Administrator. See Chapter 13, "Form Data Validation," in *Adobe ColdFusion 8 Web Application Construction Kit, Volume 1: Getting Started,* for more information on `<cfform>`. See Chapter 15, "Beyond HTML Forms: ColdFusion-Powered Ajax," also in Vol. 1, for more information on ColdFusion's Ajax controls.

Configuring ColdFusion for Multiple Hosts

The ColdFusion installer utilizes the JRun 4 Web Server Configuration tool (`wsconfig`) to install the connector into the Web server. The connector is a filter that intercepts ColdFusion template requests from the Web server and passes them to the ColdFusion engine. The `wsconfig` tool (`cf_root\runtime\bin\wsconfig.exe` in Server configuration and `jrun_root\bin\wsconfig.exe` in Multiserver configuration on Windows; `cf_root/runtime/bin/wsconfig` in Server configuration and `jrun_root/bin/wsconfig` in Multiserver configuration on Unix) has a GUI and a command-line interface.

Previously when installing on multi-homed servers, the ColdFusion MX 6.0 installer configured only the first virtual server instance. For IIS, this is usually the Default Web Site, and for Sun ONE it is the first configuration directory (in alphabetical order). Since Apache's virtual host configuration is contained in one file (`apache_root\conf\httpd.conf`), the installer correctly configures all Apache virtual hosts.

Although later versions of the installer now correctly configure multi-homed Web servers, you may still need to configure the remaining virtual sites for the IIS and Sun ONE server platforms—and any new additions. The following sections explain how to do this.

TIP

Think of the connector as the Web server stub in ColdFusion 4.*x* and 5.0.

Microsoft IIS 5.*x*, 6.0, and 7.0

To properly integrate with ColdFusion, you must make these configuration changes to your IIS server:

- Add the ColdFusion file name extensions (`.cfm`, `.cfc`, `.cfr`, and so on).
- For IIS 5.*x*, create the JRun Connector Filter ISAPI filter and create the JRunScripts virtual directory.
- For IIS 6.0 and 7.0, configure a IIS wildcard application mapping for ColdFusion.

NOTE

ColdFusion MX 6.1 was the first version to officially support Windows 2003 and IIS 6.0. If you are upgrading from ColdFusion MX 6.1, the ColdFusion 8 installer should properly configure your IIS for multi-homing.

Creating the JRun Connector ISAPI Filter and the JRunScripts Virtual Directory

The ColdFusion installer uses the wsconfig tool to implement these changes. However, the ColdFusion MX installer only added the ISAPI filter and JRunScripts virtual directory to the default Web site. These need to be configured at the WWW Master Property sheet level in order to propagate to all sites (existing and new). Because the ColdFusion file name extensions are mapped at the WWW Master Property sheet level, the individual virtual servers properly handle all ColdFusion template requests.

NOTE

In IIS 6.0 and 7.0, the JRun Connector Filter ISAPI filter is replaced by wildcard application mapping to provide connection to the Flash Remoting gateway.

For IIS 5.*x*, you need to configure a JRunScripts virtual directory for each of your virtual sites. Adobe has created batch files in the `cf_root\bin\connectors` directory for removing and adding the Web server (Apache, IIS, and iPlanet/Sun ONE) connectors. Follow these steps to correct your IIS 5.*x* configuration:

1. Stop the World Wide Web Publishing Service via the Services applet or the Internet Services Manager.
2. Run the `cf_root\bin\connectors\Remove_ALL_connectors.bat` to remove the misconfigured ISAPI filter.

   The `Remove_ALL_connectors.bat` file will remove all configured connectors for all Web servers on the machine—Apache, IIS, and iPlanet/Sun ONE. You can modify this file by replacing the `-uninstall` with `-remove` and supplying the appropriate `-ws <server name>`, and `-site <site name>` or `-dir <config directory>` parameters. See Table 65.3 for more command-line options, and consult the ColdFusion online documentation for a complete overview at `http://livedocs.adobe.com/coldfusion/8/htmldocs/help.html?content=webservmgmt_5.html`.

NOTE

You can also use the `wsconfig` GUI tool to remove the IIS mappings.

3. Run the `cf_root\bin\connectors\IIS_connectors.bat` to properly reconfigure *all* existing sites.

NOTE

The `IIS_connectors.bat` will configure all virtual sites for ColdFusion. You may have virtual sites that should not have access to ColdFusion, or you may have sites that integrate with JRun 4. Since you need to have ColdFusion properly configured at the WWW Master Property sheet level, you can run the `IIS_Unconfigure_one_Site.bat` file for each site for which you wish to remove ColdFusion access.

4. Restart the World Wide Web Publishing Service.

Adding the ColdFusion Extensions

Newly created virtual servers will inherit the ColdFusion file name extension mappings and ISAPI filter. However, you may need to manually configure the JRunScripts virtual directory for IIS 5.*x* using the following steps:

1. Start the Virtual Directory Creation Wizard for your newly added virtual site:
   a. Open the Internet Service Manager.
   b. If the new server isn't already open, click the + next to the server name.
   c. Right-click the new virtual site name and select New > Virtual Directory.
   d. Click Next.
2. Enter `JRunScripts` as the Alias. Click Next.

TIP

`JRunScripts` is case sensitive. Please ensure that you use the correct mixed-case capitalization.

3. Browse to or type in the path to the directory containing the `jrun.dll` (for example, `cf_root\runtime\lib\wsconfig\1`). Click Next.
4. Only check the boxes next to Execute (such as ISAPI applications or CGI). Clear all other check boxes (Figure 65.2), and click Next.

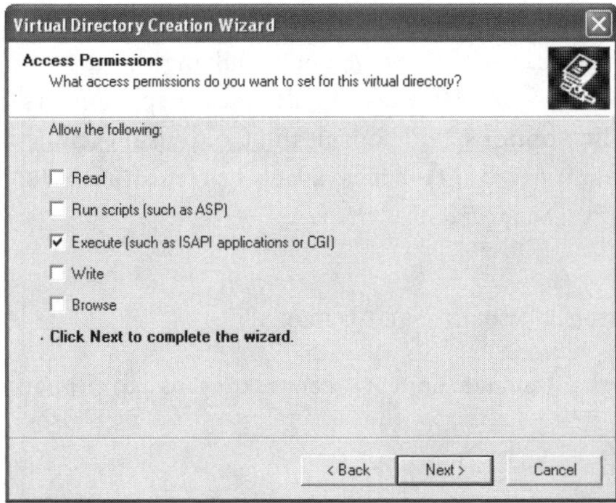

Figure 65.2
Enable Execute permissions only for JRunScripts.

5. Click Finish. The Wizard will close, and your new JRunScripts virtual directory should be selected (Figure 65.3).

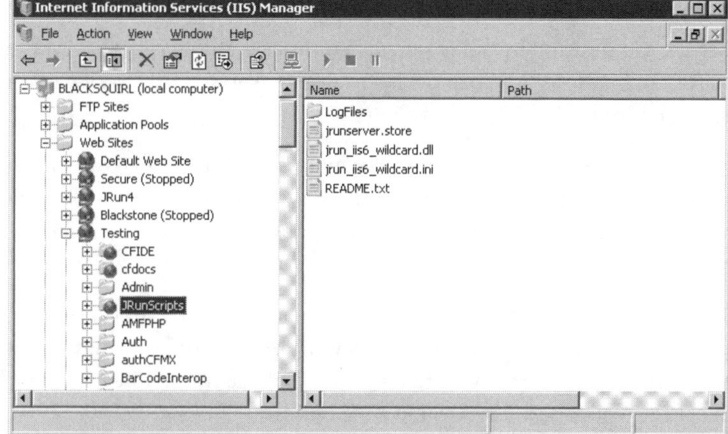

Figure 65.3

New JRunScripts directory after completing the wizard.

6. Right-click the JRunScripts virtual directory and select Properties.
7. Click Remove. Your properties sheet should have Application Name disabled, the virtual server name as the starting point, and Scripts and Executables as the execute permissions (Figure 65.4).

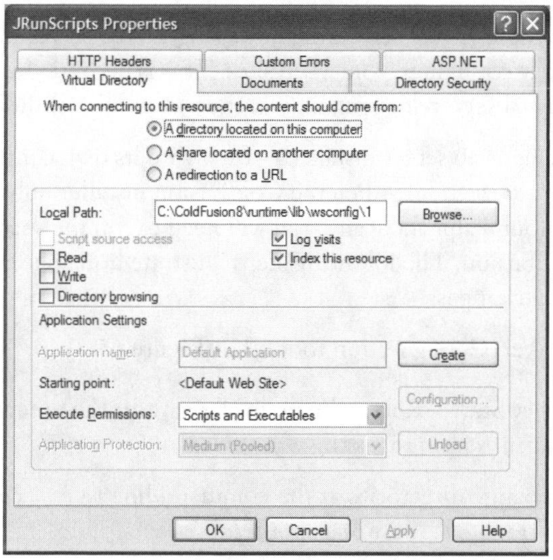

Figure 65.4

Final view of the JRunScripts properties sheet Virtual Directory tab.

JRunScripts Properties
HTTP Headers | Custom Errors | ASP.NET
Virtual Directory | Documents | Directory Security
When connecting to this resource, the content should come from:
A directory located on this computer
A share located on another computer
A redirection to a URL
Local Path: C:\ColdFusion8\runtime\lib\wsconfig\1 Browse...
Script source access
Read
Write
Directory browsing
Log visits
Index this resource
Application Settings
Application name: Default Application Create
Starting point: <Default Web Site>
Execute Permissions: Scripts and Executables
Configuration...
Application Protection: Medium (Pooled) Unload
OK Cancel Apply Help

8. Click OK to close the properties sheet.

You'll need to repeat these steps each time you add a new virtual server.

Sun Java System Web Server

Whether the ColdFusion installer actually configures all of your Sun Web servers depends on how they are set up. Sun 6.1 and 7.0 allow for multiple Web servers via two configurations: virtual servers, and multiple Web server instances.

You configure virtual servers on a single IP address and port of an individual, installed Web server instance. All of the virtual server's configuration parameters are stored in the `server.xml` file in the configuration directory of the Web server instance—for example, `sunone_root\https-<server_id>\config\server.xml`.

Web server instances are typically installed on a particular IP address—although they can work on different ports with the same IP address, as well. In addition, they have their own autonomous configuration directory (`sun_root\ https-<server_id>\config`). They exist for backwards compatibility with earlier Netscape/iPlanet/Sun ONE builds.

Multiple virtual servers configured per Web server instance is Sun's preferred way to implement multi-hosting.

NOTE

> Kiss it! If you want centralized management of your multi-homed configuration, install a single Sun instance on a static IP address, and configure multiple virtual instances. ColdFusion will correctly install the connector to integrate with all your virtual hosts. See the Sun Java System Web Server 7.0 Administrator's Guide for more information about the recommended Sun configuration.

If you have configured multiple virtual servers against a single Web server instance, then the ColdFusion installer has properly configured your Web sites. This is because the configuration parameters for each individual virtual server are contained in the `server.xml` of the Web server instance.

If you have installed multiple Web server instances—each with its own configuration directory (`sun_root\https-<server_id>\config`)—then the ColdFusion installer only configured the first configuration directory it found alphabetically. You will need to run the `wsconfig` tool to properly install connectors for ColdFusion. The following steps illustrate how to use the `wsconfig` tool GUI to make your configuration changes:

1. Start the JRun 4 Web Configuration tool GUI (Figure 65.5):

   On Windows, select Start > Run and type in the path to the executable: `cf_root\runtime\bin\wsconfig.exe`

   On Unix/Linux, change directories at the command line to `cf_root\runtime\jre\bin`, and enter `./java -jar ../../lib/wsconfig.jar`.

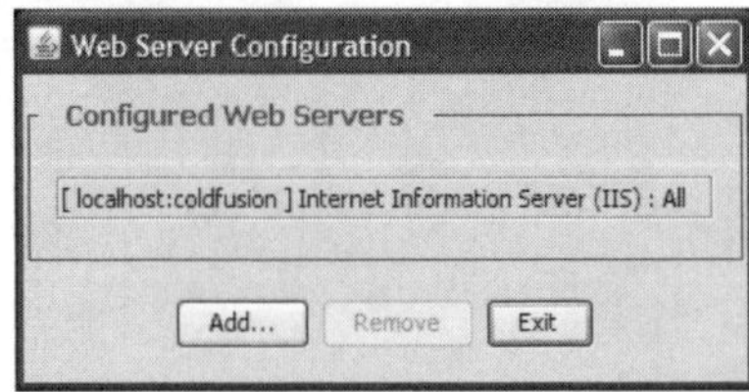

Figure 65.5

The JRun 4 Web Server Configuration tool.

TIP

Notice that the configuration directory of the one instance configured by the installer is already present in the `wsconfig` tool window.

2. Click Add. The Add Web Server dialog box opens (Figure 65.6).

Figure 65.6

Point to your Sun ONE server's configuration directory.

3. Choose Sun ONE Web Server (iPlanet) in the drop-down list for Web Server. Then enter or browse to the configuration directory path of one of your installed servers.
4. Check the box next to Configure Web Server for ColdFusion 8 Applications.
5. Click OK, and click Yes at the response (Figure 65.7).

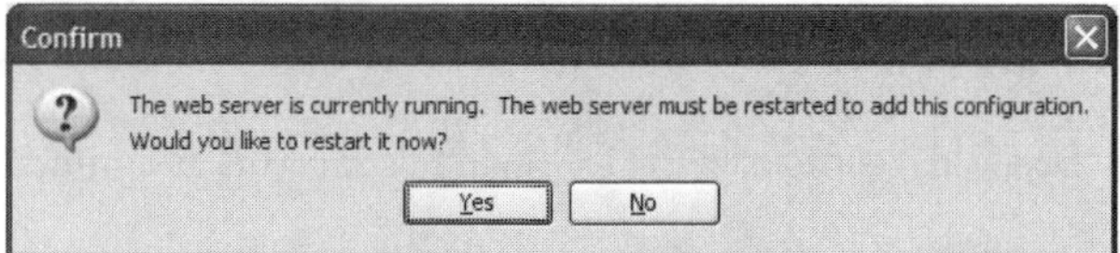

Figure 65.7

Restart the iPlanet Web server instance.

6. The JRun 4 Web Server Configuration window returns (Figure 65.8). The Configured Web Servers list now displays the configuration directory path of your newly configured Sun ONE server instance.

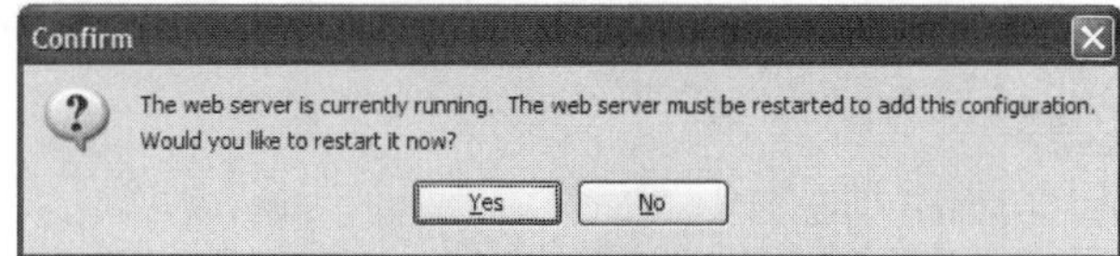

Figure 65.8

Congratulations! You have configured your Web server instance.

7. Click Add to repeat the process for your remaining Web server instances.

NOTE

For each Web server instance, you'll have to go to the Sun ONE Server Manager and apply the configuration file edits. Click the Apply button to restart the Web server.

Other Issues

The following sections provide additional best practice information for all ColdFusion environments. The previous sections describe configuration issues specific to shared and hosted environments. The security issues in the following section also affect dedicated environments. These issues are not specific to any operating system platform or Web server configuration.

Running ColdFusion as a User

ColdFusion services run as the privileged local system account user by default on Windows systems. This may provide a higher level of access to system resources than security policies permit. Administrators may need to change the user account for the ColdFusion services. The ColdFusion installer requests a user account for ColdFusion on Unix-based systems, so this is rarely a problem. To run ColdFusion as a specific user account, first create the user account (adding it to the appropriate groups). Apply the following permissions for the ColdFusion user account:

NOTE

The following instructions refer to ColdFusion 8 installations. For previous ColdFusion installations see Tech Note 17279, Running ColdFusion as a Specific User, at `http://www.adobe.com/go/tn_17279`.

- `Modify` (or `Read & Execute`, `List Folder Contents`, `Write`, and `Delete` on Windows; `Read`, `Write`, `Execute`, and `Delete` or `MOD 777` on Unix) permissions on the entire cf_root directory structure
- `Read` and `Execute` permissions on all Web content (`.cfm`, `.cfc`, images, etc.)

On Windows, give the ColdFusion user the following user rights assignments:

- Log on as a service
- Deny log on locally
- Deny log on through terminal services

Use the following steps to start ColdFusion with the new account:

TIP

Ensure the file permissions are set before starting ColdFusion with the new account.

Windows 2000, XP, 2003, and Vista

1. Open the Services applet: select Start menu > Settings > Control Panel > Administrative Tools > Services.

2. Double-click the ColdFusion 8 Application Server service.
3. On the General tab, click Stop to stop the service if it is running.
4. On the Log On tab, select the radio button next to "This account:"
5. Browse to the ColdFusion user account.
6. Enter and confirm the password for the ColdFusion user account (Figure 65.9).

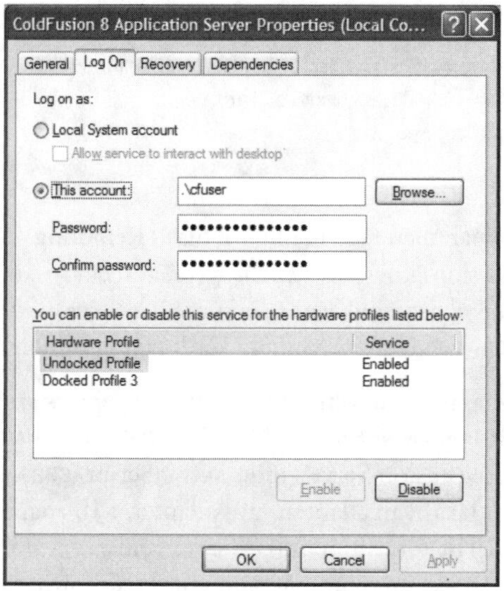

Figure 65.9

Enter the username and password for the ColdFusion user account.

7. Click Apply.
8. On the General tab, click Start.
9. Click OK to close.

TIP

Consider using the same user account for the ColdFusion 8 .NET service.

Unix systems (Unix, Linux, and Mac OS X)

1. Stop ColdFusion if it is running.
2. Back up the `cf_root/bin/coldfusion` file.
3. Edit the `cf_root/bin/coldfusion` file and replace the `RUNTIME_USER` entry with the name of the new ColdFusion account.
4. Save the file.
5. Start ColdFusion.

Adobe Flex and LiveCycle Integration

Flash Remoting MX (`http://www.adobe.com/products/flashremoting/`) integration was introduced in ColdFusion MX as a means to build rich Internet applications using Flash movies and ColdFusion objects. ColdFusion MX 7 introduced Flash-based form controls, and MX 7.0.2 introduced Adobe Flex integration (see Chapter 35, "Understanding ColdFusion-Powered Flex," in *Adobe ColdFusion 8 Web Application Construction Kit, Volume 2: Application Development*). ColdFusion 8 offers improvements on these existing functions and introduces LiveCycle Data Services ES integration.

NOTE

ColdFusion MX 7.0.2 included Flex Data Services and a subset of the Flex server to provide Flash form functionality. ColdFusion 8 includes a full Flex 2.0 server, including the Flex compiler (`mxmlc.jar`).

Flash Gateway Adapters

ColdFusion MX 6.*x* used `web.xml` parameters to configure Flash Remoting. The `web.xml` parameters for ColdFusion MX 7 and later versions now point to the `gateway-config.xml` file for configuration of the Flash gateways. Both `web.xml` and `gateway-config.xml` are in `cf_root/wwwroot/WEB-INF` (Server configuration) or `cf_web_root/WEB-INF` (Multiserver and J2EE configurations).

There are several Flash service adapters, but only the following adapters are enabled by default: Pageable Resultset (`PageableResultsetAdapter`), ColdFusion (`ColdFusionAdapter`), ColdFusion Component (`CFCAdapter`), and ColdFusion Server-Side ActionScript (`CFSSASAdapter`). You can enable the other service adapters (JavaBean adapter, Java adapter, EJB adapter, Servlet adapter, and ColdFusion Web Services adapter) by uncommenting them in `gateway-config.xml`. For example, to enable the ColdFusion Web Services adapter, uncomment the following line:

```
<adapter>coldfusion.flash.adapter.CFWSAdapter</adapter>
```

Flash Gateway Security

The `gateway-config.xml` also configures security for the Flash gateways. The `<security>..</security>` container is where you configure security settings. It contains three child tags: `<login-command>`, `<show-stacktraces>`, and `<whitelist>`.

The `<login-command>` tag provides access to the login module (`LoginCommand`) for customized authentication. The integrated Flash and Flex services provide login adaptors for Macromedia JRun, Apache Tomcat, Oracle Application Server, BEA WebLogic, and IBM WebSphere. The default configured adapter for Flash Remoting and Flash forms is `flashgateway.security.JRunLoginCommand`; for Flex the default is `flex.messaging.security.JRunLoginCommand`.

Administrators should configure the appropriate module for their application servers. The options are:

- Oracle (`OracleLoginCommand`)
- Tomcat (`TomcatLoginCommand`)
- Weblogic (`WeblogicLoginCommand`)
- WebSphere (`WebSphereLoginCommand`)

To change the application server module, modify the <class> and <server-match> values. For example, to enable the Tomcat login adaptor specify:

```
<class>flashgateway.security.TomcatLoginCommand</class>
<server-match>Tomcat</server-match>
```

NOTE

The Flex security adaptors are found in /WEB-INF/flex/services-config.xml. The adaptor syntax is a single tag: <login-command class="flex.messaging.security.JRunLoginCommand" server="JRun"/>. You can uncomment multiple security adaptors for Flex. For more information on customized authentication, see http://livedocs.adobe.com/flex/201/html/ent_services_config_097_15.html.

TIP

The custom authentication adapters are not commonly used by ISPs, but this information may prove useful to ColdFusion administrators who house several departmental Web sites or applications on the ColdFusion server.

The <show-stacktraces> tag determines whether stack traces are sent to the client. Stack traces are useful for diagnosing applications, but they provide a potential security risk if they are displayed in production. The default setting is false, and administrators should keep the default for production and shared environments.

The <whitelist> entry is a list of remote sources accessible via Flash gateways. Administrators can use the <whitelist> entry to restrict access to certain ColdFusion-based services. ColdFusion-based services are actually directories that are treated like Java packages; for example: the C:\ColdFusion8\wwwroot\ows\Blackbox directory is specified as ows.Blackbox.*. The default whitelist enables access to all ColdFusion-based services (or *). Administrators should change the default to lock down Flash gateways.

To add whitelist restrictions, modify the <source> attribute of the <whitelist> entry in the <security> section of gateway-config.xml. You can specify more than one <source> attribute. Here is the syntax:

```
<whitelist>
   <source>ows.Blackbox.*</source>
</whitelist>
```

TIP

The /WEB-INF/cfform-gateway-config.xml file contains configuration settings for the Flash forms gateway, including all of the <security> parameters mentioned in this section.

Disabling JSP Functionality

ColdFusion includes support for JavaServer Pages (JSP) functionality by leveraging the underlying J2EE application server. However, ColdFusion's security sandboxes cannot restrict access to JSP functionality. For this reason, Adobe recommends disabling JSP support in multi-hosted environments (see security bulletin MPSB02-04 at http://www.adobe.com/devnet/security/security_zone/mpsb02-04.html.)

Use the following steps to disable JSP functionality within ColdFusion:

1. Stop ColdFusion.
2. Back up the `default-web.xml` file. This is located in `cf_root\runtime\servers\coldfusion\SERVER-INF` (Server configuration) and `cf_web_root\ servers\server_name\SERVER-INF` (Multiserver configuration).
3. Open the original file in a text editor, and delete or comment out the servlet-mapping entry for `*.jsp` as follows:

```
<!--
  <servlet-mapping>
    <servlet-name>JSPServlet</servlet-name>
    <url-pattern>*.jsp</url-pattern>
  </servlet-mapping>
-->
```

4. Save and close the file.
5. Start ColdFusion.

Securing the `CFIDE` Directory

The `CFIDE` directory path is known as the ColdFusion administration directory. The default path to `CFIDE` is `webroot/CFIDE` for external Web server integration and `cf_root/wwwroot/CFIDE` when using the internal Web server. The subdirectories in the `CFIDE` contain key ColdFusion functionality which may break if removed from the `CFIDE` directory. The following describes some of the subdirectories and the functionality each houses:

- `adminapi`. The `adminapi` directory houses the ColdFusion 8 Administrator API code used for programmatic access to ColdFusion Administrator functionality. The ColdFusion Administrator itself implements some of the Admin API components. This directory cannot be moved because the components require the `/CFIDE/adminapi` directory path and the `/CFIDE` ColdFusion mapping in the administrator. The `/CFIDE` ColdFusion mapping is not configurable.The Administrator API is discussed in Chapter 66.
- `administrator`. The `administrator` directory houses the ColdFusion administrator browser application. This directory cannot be moved because it depends on the `/CFIDE` mapping and the Admin API code.
- `classes`. The `classes` directory houses the Java code (applet and JRE plug-in) used for `cfgrid`, `cfslider`, and `cftree` Java controls. This directory cannot be moved.
- `componentutils`. The `componentutils` directory houses the ColdFusion Component Explorer (`cfcexplorer`), which allows inspection of ColdFusion components. This directory cannot be moved.
- `scripts`. The `scripts` directory houses the JavaScript, Flash components, and style sheets used for `<cfform>` and Ajax support. This code is used to perform client-side validation, create Flash Forms, generate Ajax controls, and apply XML skins. This directory can be

moved anywhere on the server and can be pointed to in the ColdFusion Administrator or the `scriptsrc` attributes of `<cfform>` and `<cfajaximport>`.

- `wizards`. The `wizards` directory houses components used by the ColdFusion 8 Login Wizard extension for Dreamweaver. This directory cannot be moved.

The following are best practices for securing the `CFIDE` directory without limiting the functionality of its subdirectories:

- Keep the directory structure intact. Do not remove any of the subdirectories from `CFIDE`.
- Either configure ColdFusion to use the internal Web server during installation—install `CFIDE` within the ColdFusion root directory (for example, `cf_root\wwwroot\CFIDE`)—or move the entire `CFIDE` directory structure to a separate document root for your external Web server
- Create a virtual Web server or virtual directory to access `CFIDE`.

TIP

If you move the `CFIDE` directory, modify the `/CFIDE` entry in the `cf_root/lib/neo-runtime.xml` file and restart ColdFusion. Point it to the absolute path where you are moving `CFIDE`. ColdFusion must be able to reach this path.

- Apply OS and Web server permissions.
- Protect access to the ColdFusion Administrator.
- Leverage the Admin API to provide limited ColdFusion Administrator functionality to users.
- Only allow access to the ColdFusion Administrator via the internal Web server or a secure Web server instance. Using the internal Web server requires enabling it manually and restarting ColdFusion. Since using the internal Web server is not recommended in Production, create a secure Web server instance. Secure the instance with a protected IP address, and only turn the instance on for administrative purposes.
- When creating sandboxes for applications, only provide read and execute access to the classes and scripts subdirectories.

TIP

If access to the ColdFusion Administrator is needed from multiple virtual sites, do not copy the `CFIDE` directory to each Web server instance. Instead, configure virtual directory mappings to the `CFIDE` directory for those server instances.

Limiting Session Timeout Values

Session-scope variables are held in ColdFusion memory space until the session timeout value is reached (or they are cleared with either `structClear()` or `structDelete()`). The timeout is the period of inactivity between browser clicks. The Maximum Session Timeout value on the ColdFusion Administrator Memory Variables page defaults to two days. This is too long to let session variables remain in memory.

Developers can enable application-specific session timeouts with the `SessionTimeout` `Application.cfc` variable and `<cfapplication>` attribute; however, the Administrator setting is the absolute maximum for the server. In other words, any coded `SessionTimeout` value greater than the Administrator setting is ignored.

Limit the Maximum Session Timeout to 30–60 minutes. Remember that the timer restarts with every page request. It is a security hazard to let stale sessions linger on your server—this gives hackers time to impersonate authenticated users. The Maximum Session Timeout is an administrator's only control over developers' `Session` scope variables.

Sessions can become invalid when enabling J2EE Session Management and if the Session Timeout value (in the Administrator or in developer's code) is greater than the J2EE Session Timeout value. Synchronize the ColdFusion Administrator's Maximum Session Timeout and J2EE Session Timeout values. The J2EE Session Timeout value is configurable in the `session-timeout` value in the `web.xml` descriptor file found in `cf_root/WEB-INF/` (Server configuration) or `cf_web_root/WEB-INF` (Multiserver/J2EE configuration). Read Adobe Tech Note 19190 at `http://www.adobe.com/go/tn_19109` for more information.

CAUTION

The session settings affect the entire server. If J2EE Session Management is enabled in the ColdFusion Administrator, then it is enabled for every application on the server. This means ColdFusion uses the `jsessionid` value to uniquely identify browser sessions instead of `CFID` and `CFTOKEN`. ColdFusion will still send the `CFID` and `CFTOKEN` cookie values, but `SESSION.SessionID` becomes the `jsessionid` value. This may break some applications that rely on `CFID` and `CFTOKEN` as the session identifier. For more details consult the ColdFusion documentation or Tech Note 18232, How to Enable J2EE Session Management in ColdFusion, at `http://www.adobe.com/go/tn_18232`.

Removing Help Docs and Example Applications

For production systems, Adobe recommends not installing the ColdFusion help documentation (`cfdocs` directory) and the example applications (`gettingstarted` directory). The help documentation and example applications are installed if you select the Getting Started, Tutorials & Documentation option on the Sub-component Installation screen of the ColdFusion 8 installer. Although the example applications display only for the local host (127.0.0.1), it is nevertheless recommended that they not be installed. If you have these folders installed on your production servers, remove them immediately.

Setting Debugging Restrictions

Debugging output is invaluable for diagnosing errors during application development; however, it opens severe security holes on production systems by publicly displaying too much information. In development environments, ColdFusion administrators should restrict access to specific IP addresses. ColdFusion restricts debugging output to the local host IP by default (Figure 65.10). Administrators should completely disable Request Debugging Output and Robust Exception Information on production systems (Figure 65.11).

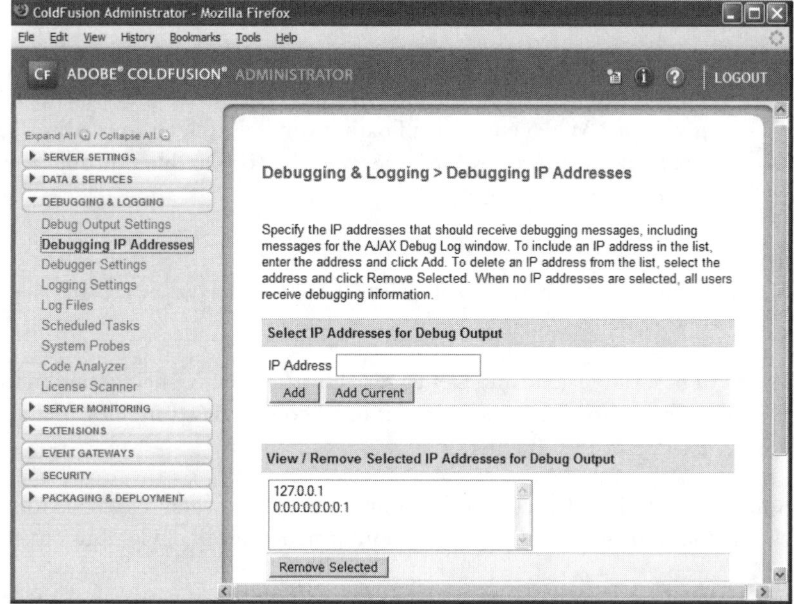

Figure 65.10

Enter IP addresses for which you want to receive debugging output. The loopback address is added by default.

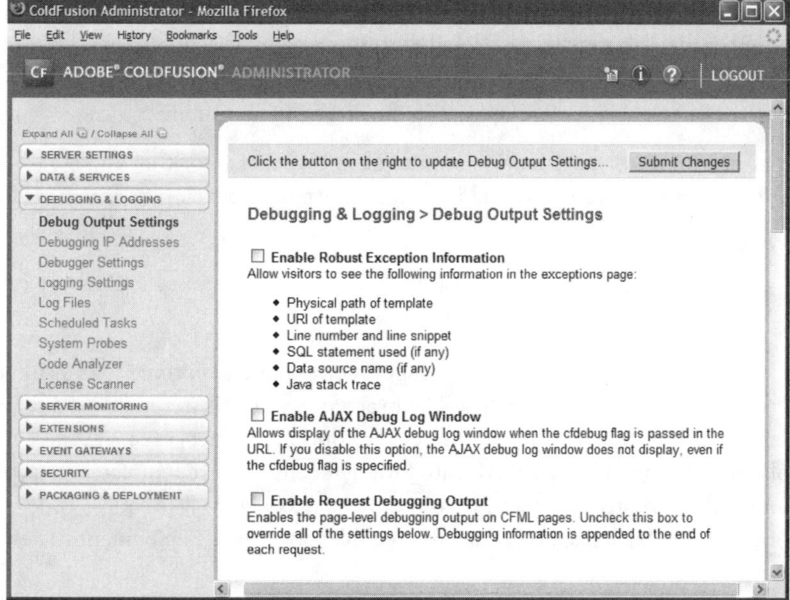

Figure 65.11

Clear the check box next to Enable Debugging and click Submit Changes.

TIP

ColdFusion checks every IP address against the debugging IP list, which can slow pages down if the list becomes too big. Ideally, debugging access should be limited to just the local host or loopback address–127.0.0.1.

ColdFusion 8 introduces two new debugging tools:

- The Ajax Debug Log window provides insight into the Ajax functionality in a ColdFusion template running in the browser. It is invoked by passing `cfdebug` as a `URL` parameter. When enabled, a floating window appears in the browser showing error and customizable messages for JavaScript objects. Disable this option in production and hosted environments.

TIP

At the time of publication, the Ajax Debug Log window cannot be disabled via `<cfsetting showdebugoutput="false">`.

- The ColdFusion Line Debugger allows interactive debugging in the Eclipse IDE. This plug-in allows developers to set breakpoints, view variables, and step through code within Eclipse or Flex Builder.

Administrators should disable both options in production and hosted environments. See Chapter 52, "Using the Debugger," online, for more information on all of ColdFusion's debugging options.

Encrypting ColdFusion Templates

Previous versions of ColdFusion use the `CFENCODE` utility to encrypt the ColdFusion templates on the server. This utility, found in `cf_root\bin`, does not offer strong encryption, but it does make templates legible only to ColdFusion itself. To use `CFENCODE`, simply call it from the command line and pass a template name or path as an argument. If you specify a directory to encode, pass the `/r` parameter to encrypt all templates in the directory and subdirectories.

The rub on `CFENCODE` is that it uses a weak encryption algorithm and is easily broken. Also, there is also a known crack for it available on the Internet, so developers are offered minimal protection.

CAUTION

You will not be able to read encoded templates, so save the original unencoded templates in a secured place–preferably on another server.

ColdFusion MX 7 introduced a stronger method of encrypting ColdFusion templates using the `cfcompile` command-line utility. The `cfcompile` utility is normally used to precompile ColdFusion templates into Java class files. The `-deploy` option instructs `cfcompile` to copy ColdFusion templates and convert their CFML into Java bytecode. Unlike templates encrypted with `CFENCODE`, a template encrypted by `cfcompile` can only be decoded to Java source code, and not back to the original CFML. This level of security enables sourceless deployment of developer code.

TIP

For more information on sourceless deployment, see the "ColdFusion Compiler" section of Chapter 60, "Deploying Applications."

Handling Error Messages

Errors are a part of every application. ColdFusion errors give malicious hackers an abundance of information about your server and application, including file names, server paths, and database structures. ColdFusion has a tag-based, structured exception-handling mechanism for managing run-time application errors—`<cftry>`, `<cfcatch>`, `<cferror>`, `<cfthrow>`, and so on. However, this means depending on developers to properly code for errors. ColdFusion offers another solution: administrators can configure global templates for error handling, in the event that developers neglect to properly code for application errors. These templates are

- The *Missing Template Handler* executes when ColdFusion fails to find a template.
- The *Site-wide Error Handler* executes when ColdFusion encounters errors in a page request that are not handled by a coded Try-Catch block or `<cferror>`.

Configure both the Missing Template and Site-Wide Error handlers in the ColdFusion Administrator Settings page (Figure 65.12).

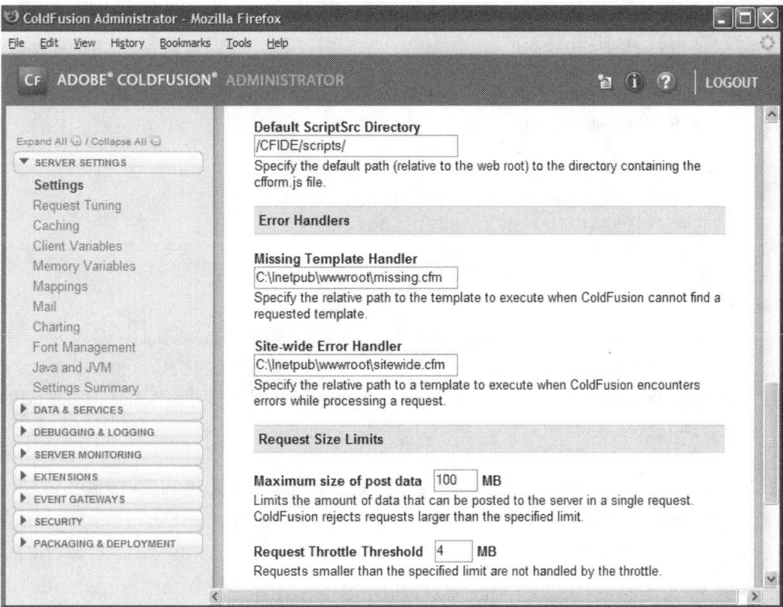

Figure 65.12

Specify paths to your Missing Template and Site-Wide Error handlers in the ColdFusion Administrator's Settings page.

TIP

ColdFusion 8 introduces the Request Queue Timeout Page option for specifying an HTML page that is displayed if queued requests time out. This page is displayed instead of an HTTP 500 Request Timeout error.

Setting Custom Tag Paths

Remove the default Custom tag path `cf_root\CustomTags`. This path is known to every experienced ColdFusion user and is accessible by all templates, including those restricted by sandboxes. The ColdFusion Sandbox file and directory permissions may not apply to all the tags in the custom tag paths. For example, a custom tag may exist in the global custom tags directory that may enable base template access to some unrestricted functionality. The best policy is to create custom tag directories within individual application sandboxes, and then require developers to use `<cfmodule>` and `<cfimport>` to access their custom tags.

TIP

ColdFusion looks for custom tags in the same directory as the calling template first, then in the global `cf_root\CustomTags` directory and its subdirectories, and finally in directories specified in the Custom Tags screen of the ColdFusion Administrator.

Setting the File Name Extension

The default file name extension for ColdFusion templates is `.cfm`. Consider changing this to another extension to help mask the fact that you have a ColdFusion site. Be careful to change the Web server file mappings to match your new ColdFusion extension. To change the extension mapping for ColdFusion, change the servlet mappings for `.cfm` in the `cf_root\wwwroot\WEB-INF\web.xml` file. The following entries change the ColdFusion extension from `.cfm` to `.cfx`:

```
<servlet-mapping>
  <servlet-name>CfmServlet</servlet-name>
  <url-pattern>*.cfx</url-pattern>
</servlet-mapping>

<servlet-mapping>
  <servlet-name>CfmServlet</servlet-name>
  <url-pattern>*.cfx/*</url-pattern>
</servlet-mapping>
```

CAUTION

If you change the file name extension of your ColdFusion templates, you may not be able to use the `cfcompile` utility for sourceless deployment. The version of `cfcompile` that ships with ColdFusion 8 is hard-coded to work on files with the default ColdFusion extensions: `.cfm`, `.cfc`, and `.cfr`. See the "ColdFusion Compiler" section of Chapter 60 for more information on `cfcompile`.

The best way to change the ColdFusion extension mappings for your Web server is to use the `wsconfig` command-line tool: `cf_root\runtime\lib\wsconfig.jar`. If your Web server is already configured for ColdFusion, you must first remove the connector. Use the sample code in Table 65.3 to remove the ColdFusion configuration for all your Web server instances.

TIP

Enter the commands in Tables 65.3 and 65.4 as single-line commands.

NOTE

You can only use the GUI `wsconfig` tool to reconfigure IIS. The GUI tool does not allow you to specify mappings for Apache or iPlanet.

TIP

You can remove all Web server connectors by specifying the `-uninstall` option without the `-dir <config directory>` or `-site <site name>` options.

To reconfigure your Web servers with the new ColdFusion extension, use the appropriate code in Table 65.4.

Table 65.3 `WSCONFIG` **Command-Line Removal Options**

WEB SERVER	COMMAND
IIS	`cf_root\runtime\bin\wsconfig.exe -remove -server coldfusion -ws IIS -site sitename -v`
Apache	On Windows: `cf_root\runtime\bin\wsconfig -remove -server coldfusion -ws Apache -dir [path to httpd.conf]` On Unix: `./cf_root/runtime/bin/wsconfig -remove -server coldfusion -ws Apache -dir [path to httpd.conf] -v`
Sun ONE/iPlanet/Netscape	On Windows: `cf_root\runtime\bin\wsconfig.exe -remove -server -ws sunone|iplanet|nes -dir [path to config] -v` On Unix: `./cf_root/runtime/bin/wsconfig -remove -server -ws sunone|iplanet|nes -dir [path to config] -v`

Table 65.4 `WSCONFIG` **File Mapping Options**

WEB SERVER	COMMAND
IIS	`cf_root\runtime\bin\wsconfig.exe -server coldfusion -ws IIS -site sitename -coldfusion -map .cfx -v`
Apache	On Windows: `cf_root\runtime\bin\wsconfig -server coldfusion -ws Apache -dir [path to httpd.conf] -coldfusion -map .cfx -v` On Unix: `./cf_root/\runtime\bin\wsconfig -server coldfusion -ws Apache -dir [path to httpd.conf] -coldfusion -map .cfx -v`
Sun ONE/iPlanet/Netscape	On Windows: `cf_root\runtime\bin\wsconfig -server coldfuion -ws sunone|iplanet|nes -dir [path to conf directory] -coldfusion -map .cfx -v` On Unix: `cf_root/runtime/bin/wsconfig -server coldfusion -ws sunone|iplanet|nes -dir [path to conf directory] -coldfusion -map .cfx -v`

Adding the Default Document

The *default document* is the file the Web server displays when a template name is missing from the URL—for example, `www.mysite.com/`. If this template is not configured, your Web server either returns a 403 Forbidden Access error or it lists the contents of the current directory. Consult your Web server documentation for information on configuring the default document.

Staying Informed

As always, it is important to stay on top of security issues because the landscape changes daily. We strongly recommend watching—frequently—the Web sites of the makers of your operating system, Web server, and application server frequently. Here is a partial list of the security sections for some of the more popular vendors:

- Adobe: `http://www.adobe.com/devnet/security/`
- Microsoft: `http://www.microsoft.com/security/default.mspx`
- Sun: `http://www.sun.com/software/security/`
- RedHat: `www.redhat.com/security/`
- Netscape: `channels.netscape.com/ns/browsers/security.jsp`
- Apache: `httpd.apache.org/security_report.html`

CHAPTER 66

Using the Administrator API

IN THIS CHAPTER

Understanding the Admin API

ColdFusion MX 7 introduced programmatic access to most ColdFusion Administrator functionality. The Administrator API (Admin API) is a set of ColdFusion Components (CFCs). These CFCs have methods that allow completion of Administrator tasks without accessing the ColdFusion Administrator (`/CFIDE/administrator/index.cfm`). ColdFusion 8 extends the Admin API with additional administrator methods.

The Administrator API CFCs are located in the `cf_web_root/CFIDE/adminapi` directory. You'll find 12 CFCs (13 in Multiserver configuration) and an `Application.cfm`. The CFCs represent the functional areas of the Administrator: Server Settings, Data & Services, Debugging & Logging, Server Monitoring, Extensions, Event Gateways, Security, and Enterprise Manager. The following are descriptions of the Admin API components and their functionality:

- `accessmanager.cfc`. Provides methods for authorizing user access to Admin API methods. The root administrator user account (admin) is used by default if the separate username and password is not enabled for either Administrator or RDS security. Chapter 62, "Securing the ColdFusion Administrator," details separate user access to ColdFusion Administrator.
- `administrator.cfc`. Provides login and logout functions, and management of settings in the Migration and Setup Wizard. You must call the `login` method before calling any other methods in the Admin API. This component will typically be used only for API authentication; there is nominal need to access Migration and Setup Wizard settings.

- `base.cfc`. The base object with common methods (such as `dump`) inherited by all other Admin API CFCs. This component should not be accessed directly. Its methods are available via the other components.
- `datasource.cfc`. Provides ColdFusion data sources management. Allows you to add, delete, and modify data source properties, including the setup of third-party drivers. This component provides the functionality of the Data Sources page in the Data & Services section of the Administrator. It is a potentially dangerous component because it can expose all DSNs (data source names) on the server.
- `debugging.cfc`. Provides management of settings for ColdFusion debugging and logging. This component provides the functionality of the CF Administrator Debugging & Logging section.
- `eventgateway.cfc`. Provides event gateway management. This component provides the functionality of the CF Administrator Event Gateways section.
- `extensions.cfc`. Provides custom tag, ColdFusion mapping, CFX, applet, CORBA, and Web services management. This component provides the functionality of the CF Administrator's Extensions section and the Web Services page of the Data & Services section. This component provides access to global resources, such as CF mappings, Web services, etc.
- `flex.cfc`. Provides management of Flex data services options. This component provides the functionality of the ColdFusion Administrator's Flex Integration page in the Data & Services section.
- `mail.cfc`. Provides management of ColdFusion mail settings. This component provides the functionality of the Mail Settings page in the CF Administrator Server Settings section.
- `runtime.cfc`. Provides management of runtime settings for caching, charting, configuration, fonts, and other settings. These are configuration settings found in the CF Administrator's Server Settings section. They are system-wide settings and should not be exposed to all users.
- `security.cfc`. Provides management of Administrator and RDS passwords, and sandbox security. This component provides the functionality of the CF Administrator Security section.
- `serverinstance.cfc`. Starts, stops, and restarts JRun server instances. This component provides the functionality of the CF Administrator Enterprise Manager section only available for ColdFusion 8 Multiserver configuration.
- `servermonitor.cfc`. Provides an API for accessing ColdFusion 8 Server Monitor functionality. See Chapter 56, "Monitoring System Performance," for more information about using the ColdFusion 8 Server Monitor.

Building Custom Admin Consoles

Most ISPs or hosting companies provide site owners with a control panel for their site. A control panel is an application that provides site administration to the site owners, including domain management, FTP access, database administration, and bandwidth statistics. Conversely, intranet and other shared-host administrators are less inclined to provide site administration features to their customers. There is usually some sort of change review process that takes place before these administrators will implement even the slightest DSN change for developers. This is where the Admin API fits into the process.

The Admin API allows ISPs to extend their current control-panel applications to allow site owners to have customized ColdFusion administration. Some control-panel applications may already leverage the ColdFusion `ServiceFactory` to provide the same functionality; however, the Admin API is the preferred—and only supported—method. It also enables intranet administrators to provide end-user access to ColdFusion Administrator functionality without compromising security. This eliminates some of the overhead in change-control processes and facilitates the development life cycle.

The Façade Component

To properly and securely extend the Admin API to users, custom modules should be built that provide minimal exposure to its methods. These modules should implement a *façade* design pattern. In *Design Patterns: Elements of Reusable Object-Oriented Software* (Addison-Wesley 1995), the "Gang of Four" (Erich Gamma, Richard Helm, Ralph Johnson, and John Vlissides) state the following as the purpose of the façade:

"Provide a unified interface to a set of interfaces in a subsystem. Façade defines a higher-level interface that makes the subsystem easier to use."

For custom admin consoles, the façade is a ColdFusion component that interfaces with the Admin API modules (Figure 66.1). Code the façade component to expose only the Admin API methods that make sense for the customer. For example, suppose a customer has a dedicated server and you want to allow this customer to manage custom tags, data sources, and debugging IP restriction. You would code a component that would interface with those Admin API modules. Listing 66.1 illustrates a façade component that limits access just to creating an Apache Derby data source, and adding an IP address to the debugging IP restriction list.

Figure 66.1

A façade pattern for accessing the Admin API components.

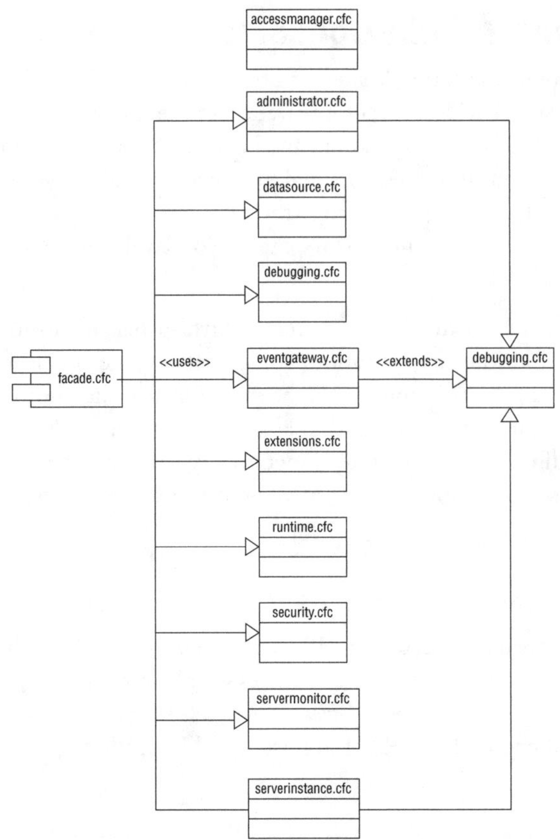

Listing 66.1 `façade.cfc`—Façade Access to Admin API

```
<cfcomponent displayname="Facade" hint="Provides custom interface to the Admin API">
<!---####
  File name: facade.cfc
  Description: Template that provides access to Admin API methods
  Assumptions: Access to the Admin API code base (/CFIDE/adminapi)
  Author name and e-mail: Sarge (ssargent@ sargeway.com)
  Date Created: February 28, 2005
####--->
  <cffunction name="login" access="remote" returntype="any" output="false"
hint="Authenticate user to the Admin API">
    <cfargument name="adminUser" type="string" required="true">
    <cfset adminObj= CreateObject("Component",
"CFIDE.adminapi.administrator").login(ARGUMENTS.adminUser)>
    <!---#### Return an instance of the facade object ####--->
    <cfreturn THIS>
  </cffunction>

  <cffunction name="logout" access="remote" returntype="void" output="false"
hint="Logout user from the Admin API">
```

Listing 66.1 (continued)

```
    <cfset adminObj= CreateObject("Component",
"CFIDE.adminapi.administrator").logout()>
  </cffunction>

  <cffunction name="getDatasources" access="remote" returntype="struct"
output="false" hint="Returns structure of DSNs">
    <cfargument name="dsnname" required="no" hint="Name of a data source to
retrieve">

    <cfobject name="dsnObj" component="CFIDE.adminapi.datasource">
    <cfif IsDefined("ARGUMENTS.dsnname")>
      <cfreturn dsnObj.getDatasources(ARGUMENTS.dsnname)>
    <cfelse>
      <cfreturn dsnObj.getDatasources()>
    </cfif>
  </cffunction>

  <cffunction name="getIPList" access="remote" returntype="any" output="false"
hint="Returns a list of IP in the Debug Restriction List">
    <cfobject name="debugObj" component="CFIDE.adminapi.debugging">
    <cfreturn debugObj.getIPList()>
  </cffunction>

  <cffunction name="setIP" access="remote" returntype="void" output="false"
hint="Adds IP to Debug Restriction List">
    <cfargument name="debugip" required="no" type="string" hint="List of one or more
IP Address to add to the debugging list.">
    <cftry>
      <cfobject name="debugObj" component="CFIDE.adminapi.debugging">
      <cfif IsDefined("ARGUMENTS.debugip")>
        <cfset debugObj.setIP(ARGUMENTS.debugip)>
      <cfelse>
        <cfset debugObj.setIP(debugObj.getCurrentIP())>
      </cfif>
      <cfcatch>
        <cfthrow detail="#CFCATCH.detail#" message="#CFCATCH.message#">
      </cfcatch>
    </cftry>
  </cffunction>

  <cffunction name="setMSAccessUnicode" access="remote" returntype="any"
output="true" hint="Creates a new DSN">
    <cfargument name="name" required="yes" type="string" hint="ColdFusion data
source name">
    <cfargument name="databasefile" required="yes" type="string" hint="Fully
qualified path to the database file">
    <cfargument name="driver" required="no" type="string" default="MSAccessJet"
hint="JDBC driver for this DSN">
    <cfargument name="class" required="no" type="string"
default="com.inzoom.jdbcado.Driver" hint="Fully qualified JDBC driver class name">
    <cfargument name="username" required="no" type="string" default=""
hint="Database username">
    <cfargument name="password" required="no" type="string" default=""
hint="Database password">
```

Listing 66.1 (continued)

```
    <cfargument name="encryptpassword" required="no" type="boolean" default="true"
hint="Encrypt password stored in neo-query.xml">
    <cfargument name="description" required="no" type="string" hint="Data source
description">
    <cfset var success = "false">
    <cfset var dbObj = "">

    <cfscript>
    try {
       dbObj = createObject("component", "CFIDE.adminapi.datasource");
      if (not dbObj.verifyDSN(ARGUMENTS.name)) {
        dbObj.setMSAccessUnicode(argumentCollection=ARGUMENTS);
        success=dbObj.verifyDSN(ARGUMENTS.name);
      } else {
        throw("Sorry but that data source name (#ARGUMENTS.name#) already exists!",
"Application");
      }
    }
    catch (Any ex) {
      throw(ex.message, ex.type, ex.detail);
    }
    </cfscript>
    <cfreturn success>
  </cffunction>

  <cffunction name="throw" access="private" returntype="void" output="false"
hint="Throws errors in cfscript block">
    <cfargument name="message" required="yes" default="" hint="Error message to
display">
    <cfargument name="type" required="no" default="any" hint="Type of exception
thrown">
    <cfargument name="detail" required="no" default="" hint="Description of
exception">
    <cfargument name="errorCode" required="no" default="" hint="Custom error code">
    <cfargument name="extendedInfo" required="no" default="" hint="Custom error
information">

    <cfthrow message="#ARGUMENTS.message#" type="#ARGUMENTS.type#"
detail="#ARGUMENTS.detail#" errorcode="#ARGUMENTS.errorcode#"
extendedinfo="#ARGUMENTS.extendedInfo#">
  </cffunction>
</cfcomponent>
```

The `facade.cfc` provides an interface to the Admin API. Administrators make this component available to their users in a secured area of the server. Keeping the `facade.cfc` in a secure area helps minimize the risk of unauthorized or malicious access. In this example, the `facade.cfc` enables users to create a data source and modify the debugging IP restriction list. The following uses the `facade.cfc` to add the current IP address to the debugging list:

```
<cfobject name="REQUEST.myAdminObj" component="ows.chapter66.façade">
<cfset REQUEST.myAdminObj.setIP()>
```

The `facade.cfc` in Listing 66.1 illustrates one method of exposing only a subset of the Admin API. Limiting the functionality in the façade prevents unintentional systemwide damage or disclosure of sensitive data. The ColdFusion Component Explorer shows the methods and properties of the `facade.cfc` (Figure 66.2).

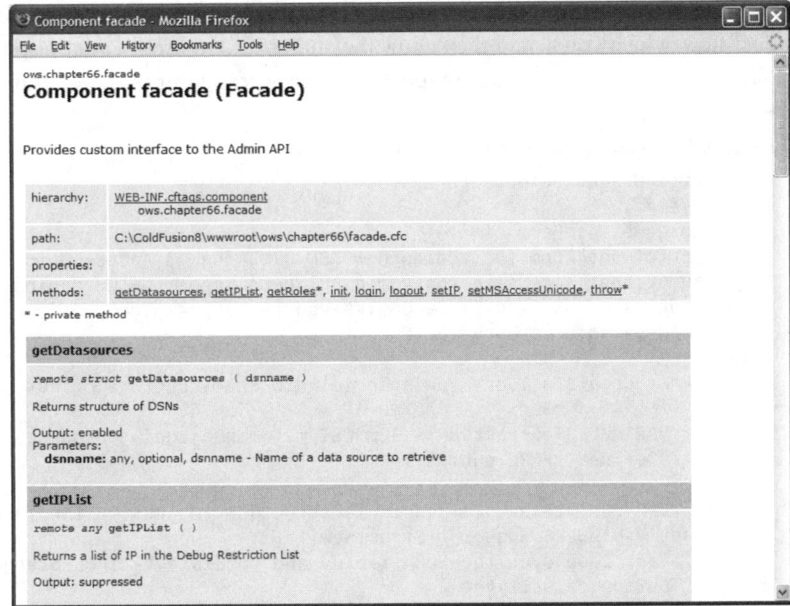

Figure 66.2

Component Explorer view of the façade component (`facade.cfc`).

TIP

Best practice is to secure the Admin API directory with a sandbox and only allow access to it from the custom module.

The front-end to the `facade.cfc` is a simple self-submitting form that accepts settings from the user. The form processes the user input and makes the appropriate call to the façade methods. For example, to create a new DSN based on submitted values, the form action code calls as follows:

```
<cfif isDefined('FORM.submit')>
  <cfset VARIABLES.argCol = StructNew()>
  <cfloop index="i" list="#FORM.fieldNames#">
    <cfif NOT FindNoCase("submit", i)>
      <cfset StructInsert(VARIABLES.argCol, i, FORM[i])>
    </cfif>
  </cfloop>
  <cfset
REQUEST.myAdminObj.setMSAccessUnicode(argumentCollection=#VARIABLES.argCol#)>
```

Similarly, here is a call to register an IP address for debugging:

```
<cfif isDefined('FORM.submit')>
    <cfset REQUEST.myAdminObj.setIP(FORM.ip)>
  <cfelseif isDefined('FORM.currentIP')>
    <cfset REQUEST.myAdminObj.setIP()>
</cfif>
```

Listings 66.2 and 66.3 show the completed forms for the IP and DSN functionality. You can add as much complexity or simplicity to your admin console as you want. For example, you could develop a front-end that leverages an LDAP to provide authentication and authorization. You could also extend the LDAP entries to store properties (such as a list of CFXs, DSNs, and mappings) for individual sites, which you would then allow the authenticated user to administer for their site. The main idea is to have one façade component as the access point to the Admin API.

Listing 66.2 `dsnForm.cfn`—Adding a Data Source

```
<cfsetting enablecfoutputonly="yes">
<!---####
  File name: dsnForm.cfm
  Description: Form for adding new DSN with the MS Access Unicode driver
  Assumptions: Access to the Admin API code base (/CFIDE/adminapi) via facade.cfc
  Author name and e-mail: Sarge (ssargent@ sargeway.com)
  Date Created: February 28, 2005
####--->
<!---#### Create a local variable to hold the structure of current ColdFusion DSNs.
####--->
<cfset VARIABLES.currentDSN = REQUEST.myAdminObj.getDatasources()>
<cfif isDefined('FORM.submit')>
<cftry>
  <!---#### Create a local variable structure to pass to the facade method. ####--->
  <cfset VARIABLES.argCol = StructNew()>
  <!---#### Loop over the FORM fields and populate VARIABLES.argCol, removing the
submit button value. ####--->
  <cfloop index="i" list="#FORM.fieldNames#">
    <cfif NOT FindNoCase("submit", i)>
      <cfset StructInsert(VARIABLES.argCol, i, FORM[i])>
    </cfif>
  </cfloop>
  <!---#### Call the facade method to create the DSN, it will throw an error if it
fails or the DSN is a duplicate. ####--->
  <cfset
REQUEST.myAdminObj.setMSAccessUnicode(argumentCollection=#VARIABLES.argCol#)>
  <cfcatch type="any">
  <cfoutput><h3 style="color: red">#CFCATCH.message#</h3></cfoutput>
  </cfcatch>
</cftry>
</cfif>
<cfsetting enablecfoutputonly="no"><!---#### Display form to accept input for DSN.
####--->
<cfform method="post" name="dsnForm" format="xml" skin="Blue" width="450"
preservedata="yes">
    <cfformitem type="html"><span class="header">Complete the form to create a new
Microsoft Access Unicode DSN. Check the table below the form to ensure the DSN does
not already exist.</span></cfformitem>
    <cfformgroup type="vertical">
      <cfinput name="name" label="Name" required="yes" type="text" size="15">
      <cfinput type="text" name="databasefile" size="25" label="Database File"
tooltip="Fully qualified path to the database file" required="yes">
      <cfinput name="username" label="Username" required="no" type="text">
      <cfinput name="password" label="Password" type="password">
    </cfformgroup><cftextarea name="description" label="Description"></cftextarea>
    <cfformgroup type="horizontal">
```

Listing 66.2 (continued)

```
      <cfinput type="submit" name="submit" value="Create">
      <cfinput type="reset" name="reset" value="Reset">
    </cfformgroup>
</cfform>
<cfsetting enablecfoutputonly="no">
<!---#### Display currently configured DSNs ####--->
<p><table id="DSNs" border="0">
<caption align="top" style="font-size:medium; font-weight:bold; color:
#00A3DD;">Current ColdFusion Data Sources</caption>
<tr><th>Name</th><th>Driver</th><th>Class</th></tr>
<cfoutput><cfloop
list="#ListSort(structKeyList(VARIABLES.currentDSN),"textnocase")#" index="d">
<tr><td>#d#</td><td>#VARIABLES.currentDSN[d].driver#</td><td>#VARIABLES.currentDSN[d
].class#</td></tr>
</cfloop></cfoutput>
</table></p>
```

Listing 66.3 `ipForm.cfm`—Adding an IP for Debugging

```
<cfsetting enablecfoutputonly="yes">
<!---####
  File name: ipForm.cfm
  Description: Form for adding IP addresses to the Debugging IP Restriction List
  Assumptions: Access to the Admin API code base (/CFIDE/adminapi) via facade.cfc
  Author name and e-mail: Sarge (ssargent@ sargeway.com)
  Date Created: February 28, 2005
####--->
<cftry><!---#### If an IP is submitted the pass it to the setIP method, otherwise
setIP uses the current IP. ####--->
  <cfif isDefined('FORM.submit')>
    <cfset REQUEST.myAdminObj.setIP(FORM.ip)>
  <cfelseif isDefined('FORM.currentIP')>
    <cfset REQUEST.myAdminObj.setIP()>
  </cfif>
  <cfcatch type="any"><!---#### Display any error messages. ####--->
    <cfoutput><h3 style="color: red">#CFCATCH.message#</h3></cfoutput>
  </cfcatch>
</cftry>
<cfsetting enablecfoutputonly="no">
<p>Add an IP address or submit the current IP address</p>
<cfform name="ipForm">
<table border="0">
<tr><td>IP Address</td><td><cfinput type="text" name="ip"></td></tr>
<tr><td><cfinput type="submit" name="submit" value="Submit"></td><td><cfinput
type="submit" name="currentip" value="Add Current"></td></tr>
</table>
</cfform>
<hr><!---#### Display a list of current IPs ####--->
<table border="0" width="250">
<tr><th>Current IP Addresses</th></tr>
<cfoutput><cfloop list="#REQUEST.myAdminObj.getIPList()#" index="i">
<tr><td>#i#</td></tr>
</cfloop></cfoutput>
</table>
```

Security Implications for the Admin API

Before using the ColdFusion Admin API, certain security implications need consideration. Administrators must understand the potential for allowing unfettered access to the ColdFusion Administrator. ColdFusion secures the ColdFusion Administrator with a single password, which administrators should not provide to users. Administrators must also enable access to the Admin API code directory: `/CFIDE/AdminAPI`. This directory is installed by default, and the API modules are hard-coded to look for this path.

ColdFusion `ServiceFactory`

Soon after ColdFusion MX was released, developers learned how to access the ColdFusion `ServiceFactory` object, by using `CreateObject()` and `<cfobject>` calls to `coldfusion.server.ServiceFactory`. This Java object gives developers complete access to all ColdFusion server objects, including the Data Source, Licensing, Runtime, and Security Services. It also allowed developers to bypass the ColdFusion Administrator to programmatically configure data sources, debugging, and so on. Hackers could also use it to disable the admin and RDS passwords and gain complete control over the server.

In response, Macromedia expanded the sandbox security restrictions in ColdFusion MX 7 for `CreateObject()`, allowing administrators to disable access to Java objects. This allowed administrators to use sandbox security to disable `ServiceFactory` access. Adobe improved `ServiceFactory` security in ColdFusion 8 by providing the Disable Access to Internal ColdFusion Java Components ColdFusion Administrator option. This option prevents unauthorized access to the internal ColdFusion objects while permitting developer access to other legitimate Java objects. Using this option with sandbox security and user-based administrator access, administrators have control over Admin API access.

NOTE

Under the hood, the Admin API components are invoking the `ServiceFactory`. So in effect, Adobe recommends using the Admin API and disabling all direct calls to the `ServiceFactory`.

TIP

For more information on ColdFusion 8 sandbox restrictions, see Chapter 64, "Creating Server Sandboxes."

Admin API Security Risks

The intent of the ColdFusion Admin API is to solve the challenge of extending ColdFusion Administrator functionality to developers/users without compromising security or exposing direct access to the `ServiceFactory`. There are valid reasons for providing this type of access—particularly for ISPs wanting to allow customers to create as many DSNs (data source names) as they need without the administrative overhead. However, providing this programmatic access potentially exposes serious security risks, such as the following:

- **Unauthorized access by hackers.** Hackers could potentially gain access to the Admin API through unsuspecting Web sites. If configured incorrectly, administrators may facilitate access to the Admin API through public Web services.

- **Malicious use by rogue developers**. Disgruntled developers may intentionally code back doors that provide access to the Admin API and thus to ColdFusion Administrator functionality. They may even disclose the security hole on public blogs, leading to attacks by other individuals.
- **Unintentional damage to systemwide settings**. Mistakes happen! Authorized users may unwittingly change systemwide server settings, causing instability or leading to other security risks. For example, an authorized user may want to add one of his or her Java libraries to ColdFusion's JVM classpath and implement a required JVM setting. If the wrong syntax is entered, the server could crash.
- **Inadvertent disclosure of sensitive server information**. Again, mistakes happen! Authorized access to the Admin API could lead to the leak of sensitive server information such as the admin password, DSN configurations, session data, and more. For example, an authorized user who may want to simply enable debugging for his or her IP address could actually enable debugging for all IPs. That would expose critical system information to remote clients.

Securing the Admin API

Fortunately, we can counter the aforementioned security risks with good security practices. Prevent unauthorized access and thwart rogue developers by securing the Administrator password, securing access to the Admin API directory, and limiting exposure to the Admin API methods. Developing custom modules with a good façade pattern that provides minimal exposure to Admin API methods will help prevent unintentional damage and inadvertent information disclosure.

ColdFusion Administrator Security

The ColdFusion Administrator implements password security by default. The password should be a strong string, such as a minimum of eight mixed-case, alphanumeric, and special characters. Customers and users should not have access to this root password. Keep the password written down in a secured location.

The ColdFusion 8 Administrator and Admin API are securable via user-based roles. Use the ColdFusion 8 User Manager to create individual user accounts and tailor their access permissions. Access permission can be restricted to RDS, Administrator & Admin API, and Admin API only.

CAUTION

ColdFusion Administrator Security must be enabled in order to secure the Admin API with the Administrator password. If this is disabled, both the ColdFusion Administrator and Admin API are left wide open.

The `login()` method of the `administrator.cfc` and `accessmanager.cfc` methods provide access control. You must authenticate with `login()` before using any methods of the other API components. The `accessmanager.cfc` methods determine whether the authenticated user is in the appropriate roles. The `login()` method allows the use of the RDS (remote development services) password for authentication by default. It is common for administrators to set the Administrator and RDS passwords to the same value. Best practice is to disable RDS access and configure user-based Administrator logins, and use the ColdFusion 8 User Manager to grant access rights to the Admin API and other Administrator functionality.

TIP

The ColdFusion 8 Dreamweaver Extensions and Eclipse plug-ins use the RDS password to access the Admin API.

NOTE

RDS provides secure remote access to files and data sources, and enables ColdFusion debugging. Adobe recommends disabling RDS on production servers to ensure security. See Adobe tech note 17276 at `http://www.adobe.com/go/tn_17276` for details on disabling RDS.

Securing the Admin API Directory

Ostensibly, the Admin API code directory is accessible to all application code by default. To prevent unauthorized attempts to access the Admin API methods from other application code, secure the `/CFIDE/AdminAPI` directory. The "Securing the `CFIDE` Directory" section of Chapter 65, "Security in Shared and Hosted Environments," recommends completely removing the `CFIDE` directory structure from the main Web root. Placing this directory on a separate, more secure Web root helps ensure `CFIDE`'s obscurity. Users will not easily be able to find the directory and, if they do, will be challenged for authentication in order to access it. You will want to restrict user access to Administrator functionality through authorized access to the Admin API code.

CAUTION

All application should run within sandboxes, especially in shared and hosted environments. Sandboxing creates directory structures to which the code has access. Any files or directories outside of a sandbox are protected from the code within. Therefore, ensure the sandboxes created for application code do not have access to the `/CFIDE/adminapi` directory. Only allow read and execute access to `/CFIDE/adminapi` for the custom admin console.

Securing the Façade Component

Recall that access to the Admin API is secured by the root ColdFusion Administrator and/or RDS password or by user-based administrator authentication. In addition, the API requires authentication via the `administrator.login()` method before calling all other API methods. This means either providing a challenge for the password, hard coding it, or passing it dynamically. Since users should never have access to the Administrator password (and RDS should be disabled on production systems), the only recourse is to hard-code the password somewhere in the custom admin module. The `Application.cfc` code in Listing 66.4 controls access to the example `facade.cfc` in Listing 66.1.

CAUTION

If you hard code the password or pass it as a variable, the value will show in the Java class files compiled by ColdFusion in `cf_root/WEB-INF/cfclasses` when the Save Class Files option is enabled in the ColdFusion Administrator. If hackers or users gain access to the class file, they can decode it and extract the Administrator password.

To prevent this scenario, disable the Save Class Files option, secure the `cf_root/WEB-INF/cfclasses` folder and contents with sandbox security and OS permissions. You can also place the password in a secure, external file and read it in at run time. For example, create an `admin.ini` file and use the `GetProfileString` function to retrieve the Administrator password:

```
REQUEST.myAdminObj.login(GetProfileString("C:\secured\admin.ini", "Admin Pass",
"password"))
```

This will safely pass the Administrator password to the `REQUEST.myAdminObj.login` method at run time, without exposing it as clear text in the Java class file.

Listing 66.4 `Application.cfc`—Securing Application Events

```
<cfcomponent>
  <!---####
    File name: Application.cfc
    Description: Template that handles application events
    Assumptions: None
    Author name and e-mail: Sarge (ssargent@ sargeway.com)
    Date Created: February 22, 2005
  ####--->
  <!---#### Application initialization variables. ####--->
  <cfscript>
    THIS.name = "CustomAdmin";
    THIS.loginStorage = "Cookie";
    THIS.scriptProtect = "CGI,Form,URL";
    THIS.sessionManagement = "yes";
    THIS.sessionTimeOut = CreateTimeSpan(0,0,5,0);
    VARIABLES.adminPasswd = "admin"; // CF Admin Password
  </cfscript>
  <cffunction name="onRequestStart" returntype="void">
    <cfargument name="thisRequest" required="true">
    <cfif IsDefined("Form.Logout") OR IsDefined("URL.Logout")>
      <cflock scope="session" timeout="30" throwontimeout="yes">
        <!---#### Log the user out of the Admin API. ####--->
        <cfif IsDefined('SESSION.myAdminObj')>
          <cfset SESSION.myAdminObj.logout>
          <!---#### Clear the facade object from the SESSION scope. ####--->
          <cfset StructDelete(SESSION, myAdminObj)>
        </cfif>
      </cflock>
      <!---#### Log the user out of ColdFusion. ####--->
      <cflogout>
    </cfif>
    <!---#### CFLOGIN structure for authentication code. ####--->
    <cflogin>
      <cfset REQUEST.loggedin = false>
      <cfif IsDefined("cflogin")>
      <!---#### Authenticate and login user to ColdFusion with appropriate roles.
####--->
```

Listing 66.4 (continued)

```
          <cfif not CompareNoCase('admin', Trim(CFLOGIN.name)) and
          not CompareNoCase(Trim(CFLOGIN.password), "password")>
            <cfloginuser name="#CFLOGIN.name#" password="#CFLOGIN.password#"
roles="admin,publisher">
            <cfset REQUEST.loggedin = "true">
          <cfelse>
            <cfset REQUEST.badlogin = "true">
            <cfset REQUEST.loggedin = "false">
            <!---#### If the login fails, return to the login form. ####--->
            <cfinclude template="loginform.cfm"><cfabort>
          </cfif>
        <cfelse>
          <cfinclude template="loginform.cfm"><cfabort>
        </cfif>
      </cflogin>
      <cfif Len(Trim(GetAuthUser()))>
        <!---#### If user is authenticated then create a SESSION-level object call to
the facade.cfc. ####--->
        <cflock scope="session" timeout="30" throwontimeout="yes">
          <!---#### Create the facade object only once per session. ####--->
          <cfif NOT IsDefined("SESSION.myAdminObj")>
            <cfset VARIABLES.adminPasswdFile = ExpandPath(.) & "\admin.ini">
            <!---#### Log the user into the Admin API. ####--->
            <cfset SESSION.myAdminObj = createObject("component",
"ows.chapter66.facade").login(GetProfileString(VARIABLES.adminPasswdFile,
"Admin_Pass", "password"))>
          </cfif>
          <!---#### Create a REQUEST scope pointer for use in other templates on
subsequent requests. ####--->
          <cfset REQUEST.myAdminObj = SESSION.myAdminObj>
        </cflock>
        <cfoutput>
          <!---#### Add Logout Button atop every page. ####--->
          <cfform name="Exit" action="index.cfm">
            <cfinput type="submit" name="Logout" value="Logout">
          </cfform>
        </cfoutput>
      </cfif>
    </cffunction>
    <cffunction name="onSessionEnd" returntype="void">
      <cfargument name="SessionScope" required="true">
      <cfargument name="ApplicationScope" required="false">
      <cflock scope="session" timeout="30" throwontimeout="yes">
        <cfif IsDefined("SESSION.myAdminObj")>
          <!---#### Ensure the user is logged out of the Admin API. ####--->
          <cfset SESSION.myAdminObj.logout>
          <!---#### Ensure the facade object is cleared from the SESSION scope. ####--
->
          <cfset StructDelete(SESSION, myAdminObj)>
        </cfif>
      </cflock>
      <!---#### Ensure the user is logged out of ColdFusion. ####--->
      <cflogout>
    </cffunction>
</cfcomponent>
```

Listing 66.4 shows the CF Admin password hard-coded in the `Application.cfc` (see the `VARIABLES.adminPasswd` variable). This is necessary for the façade to work. The code uses `VARIABLES.adminPasswd` to authenticate to the `facade.cfc`. Revisit the `facade.cfc` code in Listing 66.1. We can secure the method calls using the `<cffunction> roles` attribute. Specifying `roles="admin"` will require users to authenticate with the role of `admin` in order to run the facade methods. (This sample code provided for this chapter is already secured with `roles="admin"`.)

TIP

The `facade.cfc` methods in Listing 66.1 are also available as Web services by virtue of `access="remote"` in the `<cffunction>` calls. When `roles="admin"` is specified remote clients are also required to authenticate to ColdFusion as a user with the `admin` role in order to use the Web service.

The `Application.cfc` ensures only authorized ColdFusion users can access the `facade.cfc`. It forces users to a login form where they must enter authentication criteria. Upon successful authentication, `<cfloginuser>` logs the user into the ColdFusion security paradigm with the role of `admin`. If `GetAuthUser()` returns a value, an instance of the `facade.cfc` is created in the `SESSION` scope and authenticated to the Admin API:

```
<cfif NOT IsDefined("SESSION.myAdminObj")>
  <cfset SESSION.myAdminObj = createObject("component",
"ows.chapter66.facade").login(VARIABLES.adminPasswd)>
</cfif>
```

This `SESSION` scope object ensures authenticated access for every request during the user's session.

Next, provide a handle to the `SESSION` object in the `REQUEST` scope to eliminate any locking concerns:

```
<cfset REQUEST.myAdminObj = SESSION.myAdminObj>
```

Finally, the `Application.cfc` includes logout code to exit the Admin API, logout of ColdFusion, and destroying of the `SESSION` scope façade object:

```
<cflock scope="session" timeout="30" throwontimeout="yes">
      <cfif IsDefined("SESSION.myAdminObj")>
        <!---#### Ensure the user is logged out of the Admin API. ####--->
        <cfset SESSION.myAdminObj.logout>
        <!---#### Ensure the facade object is cleared from the SESSION scope
          ####--->
        <cfset StructDelete(SESSION, myAdminObj)>
      </cfif>
    </cflock>
    <!---#### Ensure the user is logged out of ColdFusion. ####--->
    <cflogout>
```

NOTE

Ensure that you log out from the Admin API (`administrator.logout()`) and from ColdFusion (`<cflogout>`). Place logout code in the `OnSessionEnd` method of `Application.cfc` to ensure logout is called when the user's session ends; that is, when the browser closes or session timeout is reached. See Chapter 63, "ColdFusion Security Options," for more information on `<cflogout>` and sessions.

Admin API Best Practices

The Admin API extends ColdFusion Administrator objects to end users. Like all things ColdFusion, Adobe makes it easy to use this extremely powerful functionality. Administrators can even use the Admin API to expose administrative functions as Web services, enabling remote administration of ColdFusion servers from any client. As always, security should be the primary concern. Implement the following best practices for using the Admin API.

Admin API Configuration

- Control the Administrator and RDS Passwords.

  Enable strong Administrator and RDS passwords; do not use the same string for both passwords.

  Keep the passwords secret.

  Disable RDS on production systems.

- Secure the Admin API directory (`/CFIDE/adminapi`).

  Create sandboxes for all application directories, and only enable access to the Admin API directory for the custom admin console. Console code needs only read and execute permissions on the Admin API files and folders.

  Enable operating system permissions. The ColdFusion user (usually LocalSystem on Windows, nobody on Unix) and administrator (or root) accounts should have full control. Only allow read and execute access for the Web server user and other authenticated users.

  Only allow access to the Admin API through custom console code.

Custom Console Coding Best Practices

Just a few custom console coding best practices include:

- Code custom admin modules that provide end-user access to the Admin API.
- Create methods with the same name as the API methods to avoid uncertainty.
- Limit the access to segments of Admin API features:

  No access to anything requiring restart.

  No access to the `security.cfc` or `runtime.cfc`.

  Limit access to serverwide settings: DSNs, mappings, debugging settings, and so on.

- Limit functionality to adding and modifying settings. All delete functionality should be done via the ColdFusion Administrator by administrators.

- Secure the custom admin modules:

  Leverage the roles' `<cffunction>` attribute to enforce user security.

  If you're hard-coding the ColdFusion Administrator password, pass it as a local variable to the `login()` method of `administrator.cfc`.

- Encrypt the custom admin console templates with the `cfcompile` utility. See the section on sourceless deployment in Chapter 60, "Deploying Applications," for details on using `cfcompile` to encrypt ColdFusion templates.

PART XI
Extending ColdFusion

CHAPTER 67

Using Server-Side HTTP and FTP

IN THIS CHAPTER

This chapter deals with two of the more popular transfer protocols used in Internet development today, HTTP and FTP. Transfer protocols by themselves are not associated to, nor do they specify ways that the protocols are to be used. This chapter highlights some of the more popular uses of these technologies from inside ColdFusion applications.

Think of transfer protocols as a standard way to communicate and move data from one place to another. Each protocol defines how the message format will be constructed, so that each device that looks to call to the message can react the same way to each of the commands. In addition to HTTP and FTP, these protocols include others that you have encountered or will learn about in other chapters in this book.

Overview

Prior to the release of ColdFusion MX, the discussion of HTTP eventually developed into discussions of *intelligent agents*—operations in which you're asking some outside process to perform a calculation and return some data. These operations can include calling a COM object, calling a stored procedure from a database, or using `<cfhttp>` to call another ColdFusion machine to do work for you. The simple determining factor is that the functionality resided outside of the application and that we needed to send information or make a request to some other machine to access it. The information returned is used for further processing or displayed without modification.

The brokering arrangements between servers were once custom written and specific to the needs of the application. However, both the Internet development environment we live in and ColdFusion have grown and made an industry standard of the technology required for communication among servers: It's called Web Services. Although an intelligent agent and a Web service can both accomplish the same functionality, the Web service is the preferred manner due to the supporting services and Web service–enabled applications currently available. The topic of Web Services will be covered in more detail in Chapter 68, "Creating and Consuming Web Services."

Web Services notwithstanding, it's important to understand what goes into creating an intelligent agent. An example of an intelligent agent would be using <cfhttp> to retrieve a page with stock values on it and then parsing out only the stock values, leaving the rest of the page unused. In this case, to use the stock values you would have to know the exact setup of the page you requested in order for the parsing algorithm to work. A safer use of an intelligent agent to get stock quotes would be to request the necessary stock quotes in an agreed-upon format, such as XML, so that you could avoid the constantly changing Web page parsing of the first example. This last option provides some standards-based ways of communicating, but it fails to provide the standard messaging that Web Services dictates.

<cfhttp>

The Hypertext Transfer Protocol (HTTP) is the most common and generalized method for transferring information across the Web from servers to clients (browsers) and back again. Although it usually is associated with Hypertext Markup Language (HTML), HTTP is basically unlimited in the types of files it can transfer. In fact, both Web Services and Adobe's Flash Remoting run on this protocol. Any file with a defined MIME (Multipurpose Internet Mail Extensions) type can be moved using this protocol. However, for large file transfer, it's recommended that you use FTP for transferring from server to server because of its optimization for this sort of action. FTP is covered in the "<cfftp>"section of this chapter.

Through the <cfhttp> tag, ColdFusion can make an internal call, using the HTTP protocol, to the Web server in the same way a Web browser would. Think of this arrangement as a virtual Web browser. Keeping that in mind, the <cfhttp> tag is susceptible to all the same errors to which a Web browser is susceptible.

Using the <cfhttp> tag, you can retrieve any Web page or Web-based file. The tag supports both the plain retrieval of information using the GET action, and an interactive retrieval (similar to a form posting) using the POST action. Again, remember that anything that can be done through a Web browser can be done through this tag. ColdFusion also supports HEAD, PUT, DELETE, OPTIONS, and TRACE methods. These will be discussed later.

The <cfhttp> tag provides a variety of options, such as simply displaying a requested page, interacting with pages to retrieve specialized content, and building a ColdFusion query from a delimited text file. (Code examples that demonstrate these options are shown in the section "Putting the <cfhttp> Tag to Use" later in this chapter.)

The standard tag syntax for <cfhttp> is as follows:

```
<cfhttp url="url" method="get">
```

When using the POST operations, the <cfhttp> must be terminated with a closing tag; </cfhttp>. The GET operation does not require this termination. The <cfhttp> tag's final behavior can be changed depending on the value of the attributes supplied to it during execution. Table 67.1 explains the attributes and their functions.

Table 67.1 Attributes of the `<cfhttp>` Tag.

ATTRIBUTE	DESCRIPTION
`url`	Required. Absolute URL of host name or IP address of server on which file resides. `url` must include protocol (`http` or `https`) and `hostname`. If the protocol is not supplied, ColdFusion will default to `http`. The URL can contain a port number, and if it does, this value overrides the `port` value.
`port`	Optional. The port number on the server from which the object is being requested. Default is `80` when using `http`, and `443` when using `https`. When used with `resolveURL`, the URLs of retrieved documents that specify a port number are automatically resolved to preserve links in the retrieved document.
`method`	Required. `GET`, `POST`, `HEAD`, `PUT`, `DELETE`, `OPTIONS`, `TRACE`. Use `GET` to retrieve a binary or text file or to build a query using the contents of a text file. Use `POST` to send information to a CGI program or server page for processing. `POST` operations require the use of one or more `<cfhttpparam>` tags. `HEAD` acts like `GET`, but only the header of the remote resource is returned. This is a handy way to test if a URL simply exists. Use `PUT` to store a file on a remote server. The server has to understand and accept the request. Use `DELETE` to remove a file from a remote server. Like `PUT`, the remote server has to accept the command. Use `TRACE` to ask the remote server simply to respond with your request. This could be used to examine your own request. Finally, `OPTIONS` will request the remote server to enumerate what features the server supports.
`username`	Optional. Submitted when a server requires a username for access.
`password`	Optional. Submitted when a server requires a password for access.
`name`	Optional. The name assigned to a query object when a query is to be constructed from a text file. Only used with `GET` and `POST` methods.
`columns`	Optional. Column names for a query. If no column names are specified, it defaults to the columns listed in the first row of the text file. Only used with `GET` and `POST` methods.
`firstRowAsHeader`	Optional. Determines how ColdFusion processes the first row of the query `recordset`: Defaults to `YES`. Only used with `GET` and `POST` methods.
`path`	Optional. Path to the directory (local) in which a file is to be stored. If a path is not specified in a `GET` or `POST` operation, the results are created in the `CFHTTP.FileContent` variable for output.
`file`	Optional. The file name in which the results of the specified operation are stored. The path to the file is specified in the `path` attribute. Defaults to the name of the file being requested in a `GET` operation only.
`delimiter`	Optional; required when creating a query. Valid characters are a tab or a comma. The default is a comma (`,`). Only used with `GET` and `POST` methods.

Table 67.1 (continued)

ATTRIBUTE	DESCRIPTION
`textQualifier`	Optional; required when creating a query. Indicates the start and finish of a column. Must be escaped when embedded in a column. If the qualifier is a quotation mark, it should be escaped as `""`. If no text qualifier appears in the file, specify a blank space as `" "`. The default is the double quotation mark (`"`).Only used with `GET` and `POST` methods.
`resolveURL`	Optional. `YES` or `NO`. Used for `GET` and `POST` operations. Default is `NO`. When set to `YES`, any link referenced in the remote page has its internal URL fully resolved and returned to the `CFHTTP.FileContent` variable so that the links remain intact. The following HTML tags, which can contain links, are resolved: `img src`, `a href`, `form action`, `applet code`, `script src`, `embed src`, `embed pluginspace`, `body background`, `frame src`, `bgsound src`, `object data`, `object classid`, `object codebase`, and `object usemap`.
`proxyServer`	Optional. Hostname or IP address of a proxy server, if required.
`proxyPort`	Optional. The port number on the proxy server from which the object is being requested. Default is `80`.
`proxyUser`	Optional. Username for the proxy server.
`proxyPassword`	Optional. Password for the proxy server.
`userAgent`	Optional. User agent request header. Defaults to "ColdFusion."
`throwOnError`	Optional. Boolean indicating whether to throw an exception that can be caught by using the `<cftry>` and `<cfcatch>` tags. The default is `NO`.
`redirect`	Optional. Boolean indicating whether to redirect according to a response header or to stop execution. The default is `YES`. If set to `NO` and `throwOnError` is set to `YES`, execution stops if `<cfhttp>` fails, and the status code and associated error message are returned in the variable `CFHTTP.StatusCode`. To see where execution would have been redirected, use the variable `CFHTTP.ResponseHeader[LOCATION]`. The key `LOCATION` identifies the path of redirection.
`timeout`	Optional. Value in seconds. When a URL timeout is specified in the browser, this setting takes precedence over the ColdFusion Administrator timeout, and ColdFusion uses the lesser of the URL timeout and the timeout passed in the `timeout` attribute, so that the request always times out before or at the same time as the page. If URL timeout is not specified, ColdFusion uses the lesser of the Administrator timeout and the timeout passed in the `timeout` attribute. If the timeout is not set in any of these, ColdFusion waits indefinitely for the `<cfhttp>` request to process. This attribute does not function with JDK 1.3.
`charset`	Optional. Defaults to `UTF-8`. A Java character-set name for the file or URL in a `GET` or `POST`. The following values are typically used: `UTF-8`, `ISO-8859-1`, `UTF-16`, `US-ASCII`, `UTF-16BE` and `UTF-16LE`.

Table 67.1 (CONTINUED)

ATTRIBUTE	DESCRIPTION
`getAsBinary`	Optional. Allows you to convert a response to binary. Possible values are `no`, `never`, `auto`, and `yes`. If `no`, and ColdFusion does not recognize the object as text, the result is converted into a ColdFusion object. This object can be displayed if the contents were text, but not identified as such by ColdFusion. If `never`, ColdFusion will always treat data returned as text, regardless of its MIME type. If `auto`, ColdFusion will convert the result to a binary object if it recognizes the response as binary data. Finally, `yes` will always convert the result to binary.
`result`	Optional. By default, the result of a `<cfhttp>` call is stored in a variable called `cfhttp`. The result attribute lets you specify the variable name of the result structure.
`multipart`	Optional. Instructs ColdFusion to send form data as multipart form data. Normally ColdFusion will send form data as `application/x-www-form-urlencoded`. Default is `no`.
`clientCert`	Optional. Specifies the full path to a PKCS12-format client certificate that will be sent with the request.
`clientCertPassword`	Password used to decrypt the client certificate.

Errors and Results for a `<cfhttp>` Call

As mentioned earlier, the `<cfhttp>` tag experiences all the same errors that a normal browser would, such as a 404 error when the requested page can't be found. In ColdFusion, a predefined error-handling routine is used to allow the program access and control to errors that happen throughout an application.

The `<cfhttp>` tag handles errors in two ways. One is through the ColdFusion error-handling framework, and the other is through suppression and population of a status code. The attribute that controls the mode that this tag runs through is `throwOnError`. When this attribute is set to `TRUE`, `<cfhttp>` will throw an error just like any other tag, thus enabling you to handle these errors inside the normal ColdFusion error-handling process of `<cftry>`/`<cfcatch>` or `<cferror>`.

When this attribute is `FALSE` (the default), ColdFusion suppresses any and all HTTP errors, including a 404 error, and populates the status code of this error inside the return structure (called `cfhttp` by default, unless overridden with the `result` attribute).

NOTE

When a delimited text file is converted into a query, errors generated in the process ignore the `throwOnError` attribute and throw a standard ColdFusion error.

Each request, regardless of whether it is a `POST` or a simple `GET`, creates the `cfhttp` structure that stores the outcome of the request. A quick way to look at the resulting `CFHTTP` structure is to display it through the `<cfdump>` tag preceding a `<cfhttp>` call. Table 67.2 shows the keys of the `CFHTTP` structure and how they are populated. Do not forget that you can change the name of this result structure by using the `result` attribute.

Table 67.2 The Keys of the `CFHTTP` Structure

KEY	DESCRIPTION
`charset`	The character set of the response.
`errorDetail`	Contains the error, if any, that occurred when performing the request.
`FileContent`	Returns the contents of the file for the text and MIME files.
`MimeType`	Returns the MIME type specified by the `Content-Type` header.
`ResponseHeader[KEY]`	Returns the response headers. If there is only one instance of a header key, the value can be accessed as a `simple` type. If there is more than one instance, the values are placed in an array within the `ResponseHeader` structure.
`Header`	Returns the raw response header.
`StatusCode`	Returns the HTTP error code and associated error string if the `throwOnError` is False.
`text`	ColdFusion will attempt to determine if the response was plain text. The `text` result will either be `Yes` or `No`, depending on whether ColdFusion recognizes the response as text.

Using the `<cfhttpparam>` Tag

Sometimes one Web site needs to interact with another Web site by passing it data. Setting the `<cfhttp>` method attribute to `POST` and passing each piece of data through a `<cfhttpparam>` tag accomplishes this. The `<cfhttpparam>` tag can pass a `HEADER`, `BODY`, `XML`, `FORMFIELD`, `COOKIE`, `FILE`, `URL`, or `CGI` variable to the URL specified in the `<cfhttp>` tag. It requires that it is placed between the start and end `<cfhttp>` tags. Do note that the passed values are URL encoded, so that special characters are preserved as they are passed to the server.

The syntax for the `<cfhttpparam>` tag is as follows:

```
<cfhttpparam name="name"
type="transaction type"
value="value"
file="filename" >
```

Table 67.3 shows the attributes for this tag.

Table 67.3 Attributes of the `<cfhttpparam>` Tag

ATTRIBUTE	DESCRIPTION
`name`	Required. A variable name for data being passed. Ignored for types `BODY` and `XML`.

Table 67.3 (continued)

ATTRIBUTE	DESCRIPTION
`type`	Required. The transaction type. Valid entries are `HEADER`, `BODY`, `XML`, `URL`, `FORMFIELD`, `COOKIE`, `CGI`, and `FILE`.
`value`	Optional; ignored for `type="File"`. Specifies the `HEADER`, `BODY`, `XML`, `URL`, `FORMFIELD`, `COOKIE`, `FILE`, or `CGI` variable being passed to the server. Must be a string or a type that ColdFusion can convert to a string for all types except `body`, which can be binary data.
`file`	Required for `type="File"`. Fully qualified local file name to be uploaded to the server. For example, `c:\temp\amazon.lst`.
`encoded`	Optional. Only applies for `type="FormField"` or `type="CGI"`. If set to true, the value will be URL encoded (default).
`mimeType`	Optional, Only applies for `type="File"`. Signifies the MIME type for the data in the file.

Putting `<cfhttp>` to Use

The `<cfhttp>` tag has unlimited uses—for example, it can be used as a simple request for a page, or as the cornerstone to a back-end agent that directs content to a user through email. Now that you have looked at the various attributes and syntax descriptions for the `<cfhttp>` tag, let's write some examples to demonstrate its various capabilities.

Using the `GET` Method

The first example demonstrates a simple `GET` operation. Listing 67.1 shows the CFML code necessary to use the `<cfhttp>` tag in a `GET` operation. This example fetches the index page from `http://www.wired.com` (a popular news site) and then displays the results.

Listing 67.1 `getwired.cfm`—Retrieving the Index Page from `www.wired.com` via the `<cfhttp>` Tag.

```
<!---
 Filename: getwired.cfm
 Purpose: Get the index page from Wired.com
--->

<cfhttp method="get" url="http://www.wired.com" resolveURL="yes">

<cfoutput>
#cfhttp.filecontent#
</cfoutput>
```

Figure 67.1 shows the output of the example, with the index page from `http://www.wired.com` fully displayed, including all its graphics and links.

Figure 67.1

Results from the main index page being pulled from the Wired site.

Looking through the code, you can see that the results of the request to the Web page are shown because the `cfhttp.filecontent` variable is output. In addition, the attribute `resolveURL` is set to `YES`, which tells ColdFusion to go into the results of the request and change all relative references into absolute references. For example, the images on the page are by default not hard coded to a specific location. Therefore, if we output the result of the request to the browser that requested the ColdFusion page containing the `<cfhttp>`, we won't be able to see the images because it would request that the images be embedded into the document using our server as the relative location.

Because resolving these locations is an extra step for ColdFusion, it is important to understand when it is appropriate to use this setting. Use it whenever you will be displaying the results of your internal HTTP request. On requests that are interacting for communication or data retrieval, this setting should be set to `NO`.

There are several cases where the results of a `<cfhttp>` request are not to be shown but instead stored locally. The next example demonstrates using `<cfhttp>` with the `GET` method to save the results to a file. To accomplish this, the `path` and `file` attributes are specified with the directory and file name to which the results are to be saved. If the `file` attribute is left blank, it defaults to the name of the file being requested.

In this next example, the `cfhttp.FileContent` variable doesn't contain the results of the request; instead, it contains a message that the results are stored in the specified file. To display the outcome of the request, the `<cffile>` tag would be needed to read the contents of the download file into a variable and then display the results. The modified template is shown in Listing 67.2.

Listing 67.2 getwired2.cfm—Using <cfhttp> with the GET Method to Download a File

```
<!---
 Filename: getwired2.cfm
 Purpose: Get the index page from Wired.com and save it
--->

<cfhttp method="get" url="http://www.wired.com"
 file="wiredindex.html" path="#expandPath('.')#" resolveurl="YES">

<cffile action="READ" variable="httpfile"
        file="#expandPath('./wiredindex.html')#">

<cfoutput>
#httpfile#
</cfoutput>
```

This technique is more commonly used to download documents and images from the Internet when other protocols, such as FTP, are not available.

TIP

Coupling the `get` method with the upload capability of a `<cffile>` and forms is a quick way to create your own FTP-style client. Use `<cfhttp>` to pass between servers and `<cffile>`/`<cfcontent>` to upload and download files (although you would want to watch the size of the files).

The output from this listing is the same as Listing 67.1. When running the example, you will notice that many of the links are broken. This is because the `resolveURL` attribute is ignored when the `path` and `file` attributes are specified. A quick work-around for saving a result HTML file with resolved links is to request the file as shown in Listing 67.1, and save the results found in the `cfhttp.filecontent` with `<cffile>`. The limitation has no effect when the technique is used to save a document or an image locally, as shown in the next example.

The preceding example (Listing 67.2) used the `GET` method to display and save the output of a standard Web page. The next example demonstrates the use of the `<cfhttp>` tag to download a binary file, such as an image or word document, from a remote Web server. For most binary files, the only method you can use to access them is `GET`. Using an unsupported method such as `POST` creates a "405 Method Not Allowed" HTTP error. Listing 67.3 shows this example and demonstrates the use of the `<cfdump>` tag to display the resulting `cfhttp` structure.

Listing 67.3 getbinary.cfm—Using <cfhttp> with the GET Method to Download a Binary File

```
<!---
 Filename: getbinary.cfm
 Author: Raymond Camden (ray@camdenfamily.com)
 Purpose: Get an image and save it
--->

<!--- get the base URL using our UDF --->
<cfset theURL = getBaseURL()>

<!--- add in our gif --->
<cfset theURL = theURL & "/excite_logo.gif">
<cfoutput>
```

Listing 67.3 (continued)

```
<p>
Getting #theURL#
</p>
</cfoutput>

<cfhttp method="get" url="#theURL#" resolveURL="YES"
 path="#getDirectoryFromPath(getCurrentTemplatePath())#"
 file="excite_logo_copy.gif">

<cfdump var="#cfhttp#">
```

The image file used in this example (`excite_logo.gif`) and all the code listings are included online. The UDF used in this example, `getBaseURL()`, is defined in the `Application.cfc` file, also included online. All this UDF does is translate the current request URL to a base URL (essentially, the current URL minus the filename).

Building on this functionality, you could create a tool that enables you to download binary documents through HTTP by dynamically specifying the `url`, `file`, and `path` attributes. In this dynamic situation, the MIME type of the binary file requested might need to be examined in order to filter adequate file types. Looking at the resulting `<cfhttp>` structure, we would find this in the `cfhttp.MimeType` variable. The results of Listing 67.3 are shown in Figure 67.2.

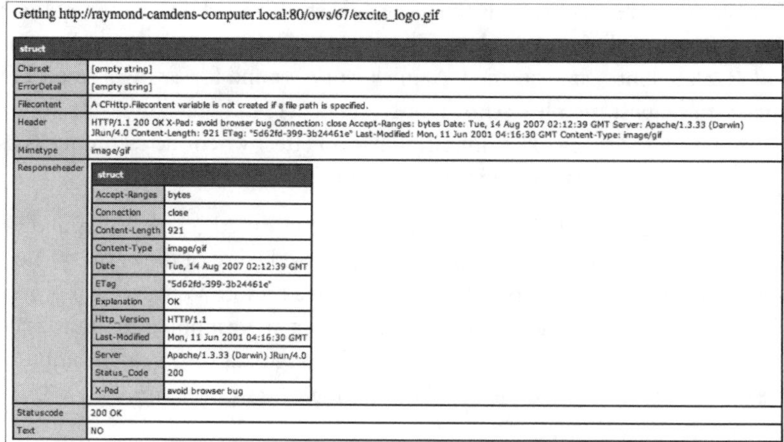

Figure 67.2 Output from the `<cfhttp>` tag after downloading a binary file using the `GET` method.

Building a Query from a Text File

HTML is a poor way of passing and storing data for use by other systems. By having the data stored in an agreed-upon format, sharing information between servers is much easier. One of the formats that can be used is a delimited text file. With the `<cfhttp>` tag, using the `GET` method, you can read a delimited text file and create a query object from it. Listing 67.4 contains the sample code necessary to perform this action.

Listing 67.4 `getauthors1.cfm`—Using `<cfhttp>` to Build a Query Using a Text File

```
<!---
 Filename: getauthors1.cfm
 Purpose: Get the authors data
--->

<html>
<head>
 <title>CFHTTP QUERY TEST</title>
</head>
<body>

<cfhttp method="GET"
 url="#getBaseURL()#/authors.txt"
 name="authors" delimiter="," textQualifier="""">

<table border>
<tr>
<th align="left">Last Name</th>
<th align="left">First Name</th>
</tr>
<cfoutput query="authors">
<tr>
<td align="left">#authors.lastname#</td>
<td align="left">#authors.firstname#</td>
</tr>
</cfoutput>
</table>
</body>
</html>
```

Several attributes must be used to have the `<cfhttp>` tag read the text file and create a query object. Setting the `name` attribute to the desired variable name indicates that you want the file pointed to by the URL attribute to be converted into a query object. In the example in Listing 67.4, the query object is called `authors`.

The only requirements of the text file are that the values are delineated and that the text values are qualified. The `delimiter` attribute specifies the value that separates the text values. The default is a comma (`,`), which also happens to be the most common. The typical file name extension for a comma-separated file is `.csv`. Because the text values can hold the delineating character, they need to be surrounded by some type of text qualifier. The `textQualifier` attribute is used to specify the value or values that surround all the text values. The default is a double quotation mark (`"`).

By default, the first row of the text file is reserved for the column headers, even if none is present. To signal that this isn't the case, the attribute `firstRowAsHeaders` is used to signal whether to use the first row to determine the headers for the query. If this is set to `TRUE`, the query object will be created with a `column_x` pattern for its name. To set your own column headers, the `columns` attribute is used to specify the names of the columns in the text file. The `columns` attribute must contain a comma-separated list of column headers that are in the same sequence as the columns in the text file. For each column of data, there must be a representing column header. In Listing 67.4, we do not need to specify the columns because our text file has the column names in the first line. We do not need to specify `firstRowAsHeaders` either since it defaults to true.

Immediately after the `<cfhttp>` tag executes, a query object is available for manipulation. Figure 67.3 shows the output from this example.

To summarize, the `<cfhttp>` tag uses the following guidelines when possessing text files:

- The `name` attribute specifies the name of the query object that is created by ColdFusion.
- A delimiter is specified with the `delimiter` attribute. If the delimiter is contained within a field in the file, it must be quoted using the character specified in the `textQualifier` attribute.
- The first row of the text file is interpreted as the column headers by default. You can override this setting by using the `columns` attribute; however, the first column is still ignored. The only exception is when the `firstRowAsHeaders` attribute is used.
- When ColdFusion encounters duplicate column names, it adds an underscore (_) character to the duplicate column name to make it unique.

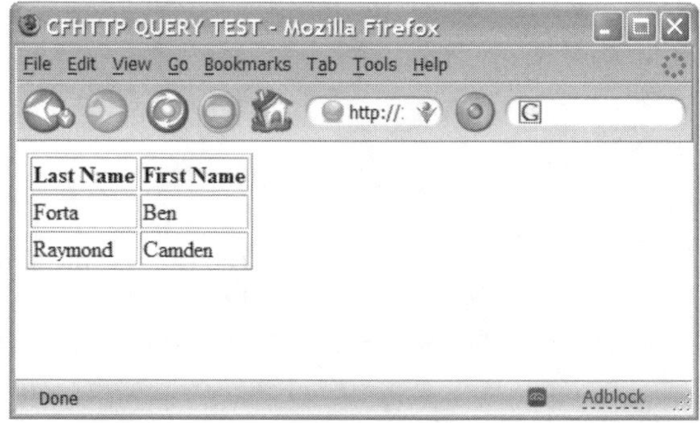

Figure 67.3

This output is the result of a query created using the `<cfhttp>` tag.

Using the `POST` Method

The `POST` method provides a way of interacting with other servers by letting you pass a wide variety of information for processing. Although the `GET` method does allow you to pass information as part of the URL's query string, it limits the type and quantity of information that can be passed to the server. The `POST` method, in contrast, enables you to create much richer interactive portals that feed both behind-the-scene agents as well as end users.

NOTE

Information passed through the `POST` method is embedded into the HTTP header of the request, whereas information passed through the `GET` method is embedded into the URL. Both forms will pass information, but the `POST` method is more structured and robust.

Eight types of variables can be passed through a POST method: URL, CGI, COOKIE, FORMFIELD, FILE, XML, HEADER, and BODY. The code in Listing 67.5 demonstrates the passing of most of these types of data. Note that when passing a file through <cfhttpparam>, instead of specifying the value attribute, you specify the file attribute, which contains the name of the file to be uploaded.

There is no restriction on the type of page the <cfhttp> tag can request. It can be another ColdFusion page, an ASP (Active Server Page), a PHP, or any other valid Web page. The variables passed are exposed exactly as if a browser were passing them. Because both CGI and URL variables can be passed in this manner, take care that you don't create a duplicate variable. Creating a duplicate variable overwrites the original values or appends the value into a string, depending on how the server handles the HTTP packet that is generated. As a general rule, never pass URL parameters through the URL attribute of the <cfhttp> tag; pass them only through <cfhttpparam>.

Listing 67.5 dopost.cfm—Using <cfhttp> with the POST Method

```
<!---
 Filename: dopost.cfm
 Purpose: Do a Post
--->

<!--- get the base URL using our UDF --->
<cfset theURL = getBaseURL()>

<!--- add in our file --->
<cfset theURL = theURL & "/dopostrequest.cfm">

<cfhttp method="POST" url="#theURL#">
 <cfhttpparam name="form_test" type="FormField" value="This is a form variable.">
 <cfhttpparam name="url_test" type="URL" value="This is a URL variable.">
 <cfhttpparam name="cgi_test" type="CGI" value="This is a CGI variable.">
 <cfhttpparam name="cookie_test" type="Cookie" value="This is a cookie.">
 <cfhttpparam name="filename" type="FILE"
 file="#getDirectoryFromPath(getCurrentTemplatePath())#excite_logo.gif">
 <cfhttpparam name="user-agent" type="header" value="FakeIE">
</cfhttp>
<cfoutput>
#cfhttp.filecontent#
</cfoutput>
```

As you can see, the code is pretty simple. The information is passed to the dopostrequest.cfm template. The code for this template is in Listing 67.6, and the results of the page are shown in Figure 67.4.

In Listing 67.6, the getHTTPRequestData() function is used to view the contents of the HTTP request data. This function returns a structure that describes and exposes the entire HTTP request packet. The content variable contains all the information passed in the body of the request packet in its native form. Because this example passes a file, this variable is transmitted in a binary format. To work with this binary value you have to issue a toString() function to convert it to a local variable. This function provides access to the full packet that makes up the HTTP request. Custom header information can be pulled out and used for items such as authentication or message routing.

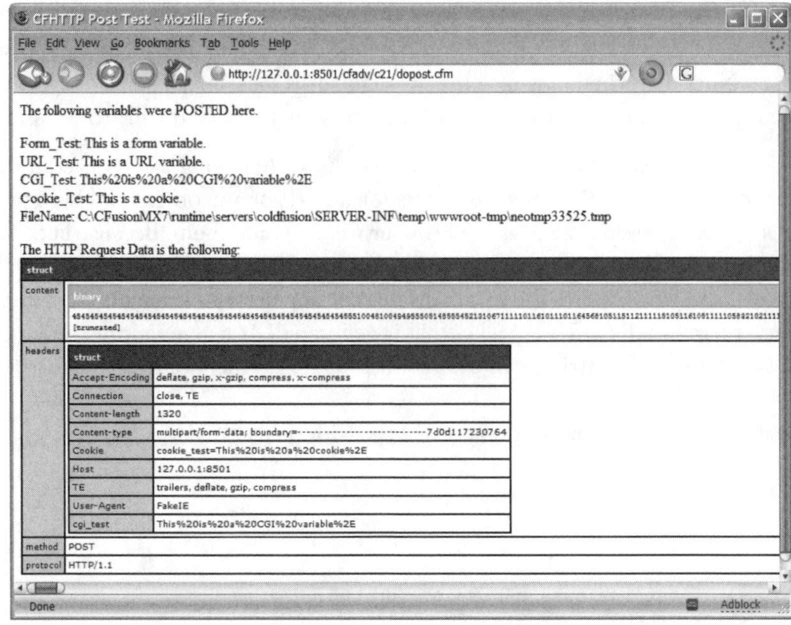

Figure 67.4

The `<cfhttp>` tag using the `POST` method produces this output.

Listing 67.6 `dopostrequest.cfm`—A Template That Processes the `<cfhttp>` `POST` Method Variables

```
<!---
 Filename: dopostrequest.cfm
 Purpose: Handle a post request
--->

<html>
<head>
 <title>CFHTTP Post Test</title>
</head>
<body>
 <cfoutput>
 The following variables were POSTED here.
 <p>
 Form_Test: #Form.form_test#<br>
 URL_Test: #URL.url_test#<br>
 CGI_Test: #CGI.cgi_test#<br>
 Cookie_Test: #COOKIE.cookie_test#<br>
 FileName: #form.filename#<br>
 </cfoutput>
 <p/>
 The HTTP Request Data is the following:
 <cfdump var="#GetHttpRequestData()#">
</body>
</html>
```

Creating Intelligent Agents with <cfhttp>

Now that you have experience with the basic features of the <cfhttp> tag, it's time to build your first intelligent agents. In this chapter we will discuss three types of agents. The first agent goes to http://www.barnesandnoble.com and requests a list of books written by this book's lead author, Ben Forta. This agent demonstrates how to interact with another site's functionality without modifying the results. The second agent searches for authors from your local site. In this example we'll interact with an actual agent that is expecting requests. The last example creates an agent that modifies external information for its own needs.

Regardless of the premise of the agent you build, you must address two issues. One is how it will interact with the other servers and applications. The second is how you work with the result of the server communication, realizing that each of the back-end communications can result in different formats.

Server Interaction with Intelligent Agents

An agent can make a request to any other Web server and for any page. In some cases, the agent will make a request to a site that is expecting agents to make requests, and other times the requests are made to a page that was created for its corresponding form page only. The challenge when requesting a page that is not set up for your agents is that your code is constantly changing to ensure that you are passing and requesting the correct page. (The Web Services concept was set up to provide a way to minimize this impact.)

The first agent you create passes information from your local server to the book search engine at http://www.barnesandnoble.com and then displays the results. The search engine is not aware of our agent. Because it isn't expecting any agents, it will undoubtedly change the search page to fit the needs of http://barnesandnoble.com. This situation illustrates the main problem with such agents: the target page can change its required variables at any time and therefore break the application.

However, we are not daunted. The first step in creating this agent is to go out to the book search engine's form page, http://search.barnesandnoble.com/booksearch/search.asp, and view the source. The goal is to understand what page does the actual querying and what values it expects. With the source of the page exposed, we note the form variables it expects (ATH, for the author) and the search-processing file (http://search.barnesandnoble.com/booksearch/results.asp).

With these values we can create a ColdFusion template that interacts with the search-processing page. The results from the search query are loaded into the CFHTTP.FileContent variable. Listing 67.7 shows the code used for this agent. For this example, the author name has been hard-coded, but this can quickly be adapted to take an author from a form value or database field.

Listing 67.7 searchbn.cfm—Passing Information to the www.barnesandnoble.com Book Search Engine

```
<!---
 Filename: searchbn.cfm
 Purpose: Search barnesandnoble.com
--->
```

Listing 67.7 (CONTINUED)

```
<cfhttp method="get" url="http://search.barnesandnoble.com/bookSearch/results.asp"
 resolveURL="YES" redirect="yes"
 userAgent="Mozilla/4.0 (compatible; MSIE 5.5; Windows NT 5.0)"
 timeout="10">

 <cfhttpparam name="ath" type="formfield" value="BEN FORTA">

</cfhttp>

<cfoutput>
#CFHTTP.fileContent#
</cfoutput>
```

When using the `<cfhttp>` tag to extract HTML from remote Web servers that don't expect agents, you should exercise caution from an intellectual property perspective. The code in Listing 67.7 is simple, yet it demonstrates the power of the `<cfhttp>` tag. By researching the form fields necessary to drive search engines, you can add powerful functionality to your ColdFusion templates.

The `redirect`, `useragent`, and `timeout` attributes of the `<cfhttp>` tag can be of key importance when you need to communicate with the outside world. As servers face an increasingly intense bombardment of requests from search engines, many sites are starting to filter requests based on the setting of the `User-Agent` value of the header.

When the requests are made through the `<cfhttp>` tag, the default of the user agent is either the name of the Java JVM you are using or ColdFusion. By providing the `userAgent` attribute, we can mask our request to look like it came from a different source—in our example, a Mozilla-compliant browser. Also, in response to constant changes in site structures, another popular approach has been redirecting requests from an old page location to the new location of the page. If `redirect` is set to `TRUE`, the request will flow through various redirects until it finds the necessary page. Otherwise, it will cause an error.

The redirects that are accomplished under the single `<cfhttp>` tag can be found in the `CFHTTP` structure on the `responseHeader[LOCATION]` key. This will give you access to where the request was routed. The `<cfhttp>` tag allows a maximum of only four redirects for a given request.

The last attribute to focus on is `timeout`. Because the requests are going external to our application, we lose control of the performance of each request. So if a given request is slow, the performance of our application is affected. The `timeout` attribute determines how long, in seconds, ColdFusion should wait before it terminates the request.

NOTE

You can set the timeout for a given request in the URL, the `<cfhttp>` tag, or the ColdFusion Administrator. These are the rules for how a request timeout is figured out: The URL variable `requesttimeout` can be used to set the maximum time in seconds that the request can take if a `timeout` attribute is specified in the `<cfhttp>` tag the lesser of the two values. If no URL variable is specified, then it is the lowest of either the setting in the ColdFusion Administrator, or the `<cfhttp>` tag.

If no timeout is set in the URL, the `<cfhttp>` tag, or the ColdFusion Administrator, ColdFusion processes requests synchronously, meaning that ColdFusion waits indefinitely for `cfhttp` requests to process.

This raises one more point of interest. When any timeout value is set, ColdFusion will go ahead and create a separate thread to process the new HTTP request. Thus your single request to the ColdFusion page turns into two requests in ColdFusion. No timeout means that the same request does all the work.

Note that you must enable the timeout set in the ColdFusion Administrator in order for the ColdFusion Administrator timeout and the URL timeout to take effect.

Another use of this technique would be to find local Social Security offices, weather, stocks, and so on. Figure 67.5 shows the output from this example.

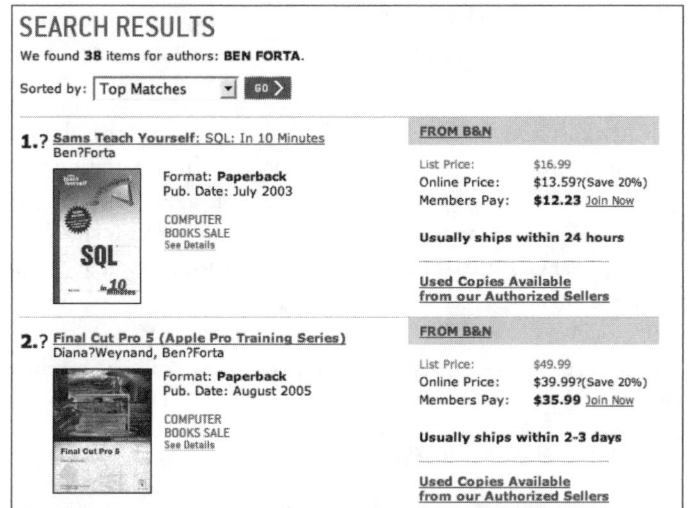

Figure 67.5

The Barnes & Noble book search engine, with data provided by the `<cfhttp>` tag, produces this output.

The results passed back from this example are in HTML. Although this doesn't pose a problem to your application, if the results are going to be embedded directly into the page it makes separating the data elements from the visual elements virtually impossible. And since the data that is exposed back from our agents will more than likely be used outside of the visual representation another site needs, this poses a problem. But bringing these back-end HTTP agents to another level requires either a heavy amount of parsing or having the data returned in a standard format, such as XML or WDDX. We will look at both these options over the next two examples.

CAUTION

It is important to emphasize that using any sort of parsing to extract data or reformat an HTML document is not recommended. This technique is commonly referred to as screen scraping. It is risky because of the danger of change in the returned HTML. Both parsing mechanisms rely on some type of pattern or set HTML being in place. If this changes, the whole parsing routine could have to change.

Another problem with screen scraping has to do with the need to avoid changing other parts of the HTML document (such as JavaScript) that are necessary for the HTML to work correctly. Removing either the JavaScript or the element that it needs can cause the resulting HTML page to throw errors. XML is the solution for worry-free passing of data back to an agent.

Interacting with Planned Agents

The second agent we're studying in this section acts against an author search engine created just for agents. These types of interactions are the most stable because the parameters used don't frequently change. Because these pages are not visible by browsing the Web site, you must have an arrangement with the particular Web site so that you know the locations and the parameters necessary for processing files.

The author search agent is pretty straightforward: It displays a self-posting form that collects the desired first and last names to search for. The specified first and last names are then passed to the author search processing page. Unlike the preceding example, in which the content was passed back in HTML form, here the resulting information tends to be more structured when you interact with an agent.

In this example, the resulting feedback is an XML document. Just as when you are trying to tap into an external site, the prerequisite for starting to construct the integration is to understand exactly where the agent is located and what is expected. Here the agent is looking for an author's first and last name. Listing 67.8 shows the code used in this second agent. It should be noted that in our examples we use several CGI variables that may or may not be available depending upon which Web server we are using.

Listing 67.8 `AuthorSearch.cfm`—Passing Information to the Author Search Processing Page

```
<!---
 Filename: AuthorSearch.cfm
 Purpose: Search against an XML file.
--->

<cfif isDefined("form.search")>

  <!--- Get authors by first and last name --->
  <cfhttp url="#getBaseURL()#/authorSearchPort.cfm" method="POST">
    <cfhttpparam name="firstname" type="formfield" value="#FORM.firstname#">
    <cfhttpparam name="lastname" type="formfield" value="#FORM.lastname#">
  </cfhttp>

  <cfset results = xmlParse(trim(cfhttp.FileContent))>
  <html>
  <head>
  <meta http-equiv="Content-Type" content="text/html; charset=utf-8">
  <title>Author Results</title>
  </head>

  <body>
  <h2>Author Results</h2>
  <hr>
  <cfif structKeyExists(results.Authors, "name")>
    <cfloop from="1" to="#arrayLen(Results.Authors.name)#" index="i">
    <table>
    <tr>
```

Listing 67.8 (CONTINUED)

```
        <th align="left">Author Name:</th>
        <cfoutput><td>#Results.Authors.name[i].lname.XmlText#,
        #Results.Authors.name[i].fname.XmlText#</td></cfoutput>
        </tr>
        </table>
        <hr>
        </cfloop>
     </cfif>
     </body>
     </html>

    <cfelse>
      <!DOCTYPE HTML PUBLIC "-//W3C//DTD HTML 4.0 Transitional//EN">

      <html>
      <head>
      <title>Author Search</title>
      </head>

      <body>
      <h1>Author Search Form</h1>
      <cfoutput>
      <form action="#cgi.path_info#" method="post">
      </cfoutput>
      <table>
      <tr>
      <td>First Name:</td>
      <td><input type="text" name="firstName" size="40"></td>
      </tr>
      <tr>
      <td>Last Name:</td>
      <td><input type="text" name="lastName" size="40"></td>
      </tr>
      <tr>
      <td></td>
      <td><input type="submit" name="search" value="Search"></td>
      </tr>
      </table>
      </form>

      </body>
      </html>
    </cfif>
```

Figure 67.6 shows the results of the search for "Raymond Camden." The file with which Listing 67.8 interacts, `authorSearchPort.cfm`, is included at this book's Web site. This document receives the form data and searches against a static XML document, `storedauthors.xml`, also included at the Web site. What's nice is that the remote client, Listing 67.8, doesn't even need to care. All it needs to know is what to send and what to expect back.

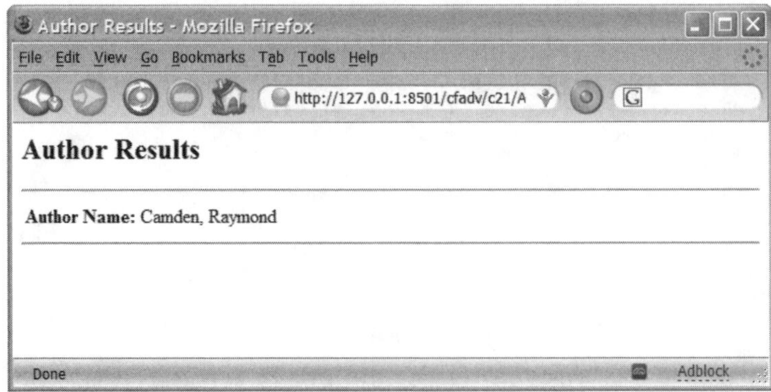

Figure 67.6

A search for "Raymond Camden" based on data provided by the `<cfhttp>` tag produced this output.

Summarizing the `<cfhttp>` Tag

The preceding examples showed how to use the `<cfhttp>` tag to interact with remote Web servers. The capability to create queries using text files demonstrates the power of data sharing as well as exposes a different method of receiving data and processing it using ColdFusion. To create intelligent agents, you must build upon the server interaction capabilities of the `<cfhttp>` tag to pull information and use it for internal processing. With the ability to upload and download files, and interaction with CGI applications such as search engines or other ColdFusion templates, `<cfhttp>` provides yet more tools to use during your application design.

`<cfftp>`

The other transfer protocol this chapter examines is the File Transfer Protocol (FTP). FTP is a streamlined mechanism for transferring files from one computer to another. Because both ASCII and binary transfers are supported by the FTP protocol, it is a de facto way of distributing software and files across the Internet. This protocol is not used as a means to interact with other servers for processing, as HTTP is used. Rather, FTP provides a mechanism for delivery or pulling across the Internet.

In ColdFusion, the `<cfftp>` tag is used to implement FTP operations. In its default configuration, the `<cfftp>` tag caches connections for reuse within the same template.

Operations using the `<cfftp>` tag are divided into two types:

- Connection operations
- File and directory operations

Connection Operations with `<cfftp>`

The syntax used in connection operations for the `<cfftp>` tag is as follows:

```
<cfftp action="action"
 username="username"
```

```
password="password"
server="server"
timeout="timeout in seconds"
port="port"
connection="name"
proxyServer="proxyserver"
retryCount="number"
passive="YES/NO"
stopOnError="Yes/No"
fingerprint="fingerprint"
key="path to key"
passphrase="passphrase"
secure="YES/NO"
result="cfftp">
```

This form of the `<cfftp>` tag is used to establish or close an FTP connection. No file manipulation can occur without a valid connection to the FTP server. Connections to the server can be made with each and every request by providing all the connection information for each request or by establishing a named connection and referring it in the `connection` attribute. If a connection is established, all subsequent requests can be referred to by the connection name in the `connection` attribute.

The attributes that control the behavior of the `<cfftp>` tag during the establishment or closure of a session are shown in Table 67.4.

Table 67.4 `<cfftp>` Tag Attributes

ATTRIBUTE	DESCRIPTION
`action`	Required. Determines the FTP operation to perform. Use `open` to open an FTP connection. Use `close` to close an FTP connection.
`actionparam`	Optional. Used when action is `quote`, `site`, or `acct`. This attribute sets the command when `quote` or `site` is used for an action and specifies account information for the `acct` action.
`username`	Required to open the session. Username to pass to the FTP server.
`password`	Required to open the session. Password to log in the user specified in `username`.
`server`	Required to open the session. The FTP server to connect to, such as `ftp.myserver.com`.
`timeout`	Optional. Value in seconds for the timeout of all operations, including individual data-request operations. Defaults to 30 seconds.
`port`	Optional. The remote TCP/IP port to connect to. The default is `21` for FTP.
`connection`	Optional. Name of the FTP connection. Used to cache the FTP connection information or to reuse a previously opened connection.
`proxyServer`	Optional. A string that contains the name of the proxy server(s) to use if proxy access was specified.
`retryCount`	Optional. Number of retries until failure is reported. Default is `1`.

Table 67.4 (continued)

ATTRIBUTE	DESCRIPTION
stopOnError	Optional. YES or NO. When YES (the default), halts all processing and displays an appropriate error. When NO, three variables can be checked to determine success: CFFTP.Succeeded—either YES or NO. CFFTP.ErrorCode—the error number (see Table 67.9.). CFFTP.ErrorText—message text explaining the error type.
passive	Optional. YES or NO. Indicates whether to enable passive mode. Set to YES if ColdFusion is behind a firewall.
fingerprint	Optional. A 16-bit unique identifier in the form of ssh-ds.ssh-rsa. Used for secure FTP connections.
key	Optional. Absolute path to the private key for the user. Used for secure FTP connections.
passphrase	Optional. Used to authenticate the key. Used for secure FTP connections.
secure	Optional. YES or NO. Used to enable secure FTP connections.
result	Optional. Defaults to cfftp. The result of the FTP operation is stored in a variable called cfftp. The result attribute lets you specify another variable name to use.

Listing 67.9 shows a simple template that establishes an FTP connection.

Listing 67.9 ftp1.cfm—Establishing an FTP Connection

```
<!---
 Filename: ftp1.cfm
 Purpose: Do a simple FTP operation
--->


<cfftp action="open" username="anonymous" password=""
server="ftp.mozilla.org" connection="mozilla" stoponerror="No">

<cfif cfftp.succeeded>

  <cfoutput>
  FTP Operation Successful: #CFFTP.succeeded#<br>
  FTP Return Value: <pre>#CFFTP.returnValue#</pre>
  </cfoutput>
  <cfftp action="close" connection="mozilla" stoponerror="No">

<cfelse>

  <cfoutput>
  FTP Error Code: #CFFTP.ErrorCode#<br>
  FTP Error Text: #CFFTP.ErrorText#<br>
  </cfoutput>

</cfif>
```

This simple example opens an FTP connection to Mozilla's FTP server, checks the status, and then closes the connection.

NOTE

`<cfftp>` can be used to push and pull files only on servers that have an FTP service running.

During a connection, the `<cfftp>` tag always requires the `username` and `password` attributes. When you need to use anonymous access to an FTP site, set `username` to `anonymous` and `password` to `blank`.

Looking at the first example, notice that the second `<cfftp>` didn't have to specify the `server`, `username`, or `password` attribute. This opened a cached connection in the first `<cfftp>`, enabling you to perform a series of file and directory operations without the overhead of opening and closing a connection. This is accomplished by the `connection` attribute when the FTP connection is established. All subsequent calls to the `<cfftp>` tag in the same template use the same `connection` name. Using this name forces `<cfftp>` to automatically reuse the connection information, which results in faster connections and improves file transfer performance.

NOTE

If you're using a cached connection, you do not have to specify the `username`, `password`, and `server` attributes for your file and directory operations.

The scope of the connection in the first example is local to the current template. To cache connections across multiple pages, you must set the `connection` attribute to a persistent scope, such as `session` or `application`. Even though it can maintain a connection across multiple pages, it is recommended that you keep it open only for the duration of your requests. Managing the number of unique connections to the FTP server is critical because most FTP servers allow a set number of concurrent connections at any one time. Having a persistent connection to the FTP server effectively ties up one of the connections to the server

Depending on the FTP server you are connecting to, making changes to cached connection settings, such as changing `retryCount` or `timeout`, will require shutting down and reestablishing the connection.

File and Directory Operations with `<cfftp>`

After you establish an FTP connection, you can perform various file and directory operations to send files to the server or receive files and directory listings from the server. Table 67.5 shows the attributes for file and directory operations.

Table 67.5 `<cfftp>` File and Directory Operation Attributes

ATTRIBUTE	DESCRIPTION
`action`	Required if the connection is not already cached using the `connection` attribute. Determines the FTP operation to perform. It can be one of the following: `ChangeDir`, `CreateDir`, `RemoveDir`, `ListDir`, `GetFile`, `PutFile`, `Rename`, `Remove`, `GetCurrentDir`, `GetCurrentURL`, `ExistsDir`, `ExistsFile`, `Allo`, `Quote`, `Site`, or `Exists`.
`username`	Required if the connection is not already cached.

Table 67.5 (continued)

ATTRIBUTE	DESCRIPTION
password	Required if the connection is not already cached.
server	Required if the connection is not already cached.
connection	Optional. Name of the FTP connection. Used to cache the FTP connection information or to reuse a previously opened connection.
name	Required for action=ListDir. Specifies the query object in which results will be stored.
asciiExtensionList	Optional. Semicolon-delimited list of file extensions that forces ASCII transfer mode when transferMode=""Autodetect"". The default list is txt; htm; html; cfm; cfml; shtm; shtml; css; asp; and asa.
transferMode	Optional. The FTP transfer mode. Valid entries are ASCII, Binary, and Auto. The default is Auto.
failIfExists	Optional. YES or NO. Defaults to YES. Specifies whether a GetFile operation will fail if a local file of the same name exists.
directory	Required for action=ChangeDir, CreateDir, ListDir, and ExistsDir. Specifies the directory on which the operation will be performed.
localFile	Required for action=GetFile and PutFile. Specifies a file on the local file system.
remoteFile	Required for action=GetFile, PutFile, and ExistsFile. Specifies the filename of the FTP server.
item	Required for action=Exists and Remove. Specifies the file, object, or directory for these actions.
existing	Required for action=Rename. Specifies the current name of the file or directory on the remote server.
new	Required for ACTION=Rename. Specifies the new name of the file or directory on the remote server.
stopOnError	Optional. YES or NO. When YES (the default), halts all processing and displays an appropriate error. When NO, three variables can be checked to determine success: CFFTP.Succeeded—YES or NO. CFFTP.ErrorCode—the error number (see Table 67.9). CFFTP.ErrorText—the message text explaining the error type.
proxyServer	Optional. A string that contains the name of the proxy server (or servers) to use if proxy access was specified.
passive	Optional. YES or NO. Indicates whether to enable passive mode.
result	Optional. Defaults to CFFTP. Determines the name of the result structure from the FTP operation.

Table 67.6 shows the attributes required for <cfftp> actions when a cached connection is used. If a cached connection is not used, the username, password, and server attributes must also be set.

Table 67.6 `<cfftp>` Required Attributes Shown by Action

ACTION	ATTRIBUTE
Acct	actionparam
Allo	None
ChangeDir	directory
Close	None
CreateDir	directory
Exists	item, remoteFile
ExistsDir	directory
ExistsFile	remoteFile
GetCurrentDir	None
GetCurrentURL	None
GetFile	localFile, remoteFile
ListDir	name, directory
Open	None
PutFile	localFile, remoteFile
Quote	actionparam
RemoveDir	item
Remove	item
Rename	existing, new
Site	actionparam

Errors and Results for a `<cfftp>` Call

Each FTP request, regardless of success or failure, results in `CFFTP` variables. (Remember, however, that you can rename this variable by using the `result` attribute.) The value of these variables depends in part on the action requested. The `CFFTP` is represented as a ColdFusion structure for manipulation. Table 67.7 lists the `CFFTP` variables available and their possible values. Because the value of `CFFTP.ReturnValue` is dependent on the type of action, see Table 67.8 for an explanation of what that value means.

Table 67.7 `CFFTP` Variables

KEY	DESCRIPTION
CFFTP.Succeeded	Boolean specifying whether the action was successful.
CFFTP.ErrorCode	The error number returned by the `<cfftp>` tag.

Table 67.7 (continued)

KEY	DESCRIPTION
CFFTP.ErrorText	Message text that explains the error code thrown. Do not use error code embedded in the CFFTP.ErrorText variable for the conditional statements; instead, use CFFTP.ErrorCode.
CFFTP.ReturnValue	General holding variable used by various <cfftp> actions to store resulting parameters. See Table 67.8 for values based on an action. For actions not listed, the value is the same as the CFFTP.ErrorText variable.

Table 67.8 Values of the CFFTP.ReturnValue Variable

<cfftp> ACTION	VALUE OF CFFTP.ReturnValue
GetCurrentDir	String value containing name of the current directory
GetCurrentURL	String value containing the current URL
ExistsDir	YES or NO
ExistsFile	YES or NO
Exists	YES or NO

Error handling with the <cfftp> tag can be done through the traditional error-handling framework of ColdFusion or through checking the status code on the resulting CFFTP scope. The attribute stopOnError is used to determine which mode you are running in. With its value set to TRUE, it will raise an error upon failure. However, this option is not recommended for handling errors with <cfftp> for two reasons. First, the errors are not as descriptive as the status errors returned through the CFFTP structure; second, no CFFTP structure is created if <cfftp> throws the error itself. Therefore, stopOnError should only be set to True if you want to just stop the page right there and do nothing with the error itself.

The other way to handle errors is to set the stopOnError value to False. This causes ColdFusion to suppress the normal error handling and instead record the error into several CFFTP variables. To verify the success of the request, simply query the CFFTP.Succeeded variable. This is a Boolean value that determines whether the request was successful. Due to the granularity of the information provided in this structure, this is the recommended way to handle errors when you want to handle the error at all programmatically.

TIP

If you want to fold errors from a <cfftp> call into the error-handling framework of ColdFusion, use the <cfthrow> tag to raise the error. To populate its attributes, use the keys of the resulting CFFTP structure.

Table 67.9 shows the possible error codes and their text descriptions.

Table 67.9 `<cfftp>` Error Codes

ERROR CODE	DESCRIPTION
0	Operation succeeded.
1	System error (operating system or FTP protocol error).
2	Internet session could not be established.
3	FTP session could not be opened.
4	File transfer mode not recognized.
5	Search connection could not be established.
6	Invoked operation valid only during a search.
7	Invalid timeout value.
8	Invalid port number.
9	Not enough memory to allocate system resources.
10	Cannot read contents of local file.
11	Cannot write to local file.
12	Cannot open remote file for reading.
13	Cannot read remote file.
14	Cannot open local file for writing.
15	Cannot write to remote file.
16	Unknown error.
17	Reserved.
18	File already exists.
19	Reserved.
20	Reserved.
21	Invalid retry count specified.

Putting `<cfftp>` to Use

The core functionality of the `<cfftp>` tag is transferring files quickly across multiple servers. The potential for this base functionality to assist your applications is limited only by your imagination. The `<cfftp>` tag can be used to create an FTP interface to your Web sites; to asynchronously syndicate data out to an affiliate site in the form of an HTML or XML document; and to pull a list of available software to download from another Web site and display to users. The rest of this section demonstrates a few of the capabilities of this robust tag.

Displaying Available Files

The code in Listing 67.10 performs directory operations using the `<cfftp>` tag while connected to Mozilla's FTP site. This code retrieves a file listing and displays the results. It also uses ColdFusion's error handling by setting the `throwOnError` attribute to `YES`, and leverages connection caching to maintain a connection to the server during directory and file operations.

Listing 67.10 `ftp_listdir.cfm`—Displaying a File Listing Using the `<cfftp>` Tag

```
<!---
 Filename: ftp_listdir.cfm
 Purpose: Do a simple FTP operation and show the files
--->


<!--- Connect to the Mozilla FTP server --->
<cfftp action="open" username="anonymous" password=""
server="ftp.mozilla.org" connection="moz" stopOnError="yes">


<cfftp connection="moz" action="changeDir" directory="/pub/mozilla.org">
<cfftp connection="moz" action="getCurrentDir" stopOnError="yes">

<cfoutput>
<p>
FTP Directory Listing of the following directory on Mozilla's directory:
#CFFTP.returnvalue#.
</p>
</cfoutput>

<!--- Get a list of files from the directory --->
<cfftp connection="moz" action="ListDir" directory="#CFFTP.returnvalue#"
name="dirlist" stopOnError="Yes">
<hr>
<table border>
<tr>
<th>Name</th>
<th>Path</th>
<th>URL</th>
<th>Length</th>
<th>LastModified</th>
<th>Is Directory</th>
</tr>
<tr>
<!--- Output the results of the directory listing --->
<cfoutput query="dirlist">
<td>#dirlist.name#</td>
<td>#dirlist.path#</td>
<td>#dirlist.url#</td>
<td>#dirlist.length#</td>
<td>#dateFormat(dirlist.lastmodified)#</td>
<td>#dirlist.isDirectory#</td>
</tr>
</cfoutput>
</table>

<!--- close connection --->
<cfftp action="close" connection="moz" stopOnError="yes">
```

Let's step through the code example. The first thing that happens is that a named connection to the Mozilla FTP server (`ftp.mozilla.org`) is established under the name `"Moz"`. This allows all other FTP requests to use this name in their `connection` attribute instead of specifying the connection information in each request. Next, the current directory is changed to `/pub/mozilla.org`. After this, a `getCurrentDir` action is run to confirm that the directory was changed. Then a `ListDir` action is run to get the contents of the directory. The result of the directory listing is stored as a query object in the variable specified in the `name` attribute, which in our example is `"dirlist"`. After grabbing the directory listing, the results are output into an HTML table by using `<cfoutput>`. Figure 67.7 shows the output from this example.

Figure 67.7

The `<cfftp>` directory listing.

FTP Directory Listing of the following directory on Mozilla's directory: /pub/mozilla.org.

Name	Path	URL	Length	LastModified	Is Directory
OJI	/pub/mozilla.org/OJI	ftp://ftp.mozilla.org/pub/mozilla.org/OJI	4096	05-Jun-02	YES
README	/pub/mozilla.org/README	ftp://ftp.mozilla.org/pub/mozilla.org/README	1144	03-Jul-01	NO
addons	/pub/mozilla.org/addons	ftp://ftp.mozilla.org/pub/mozilla.org/addons	65536	13-Aug-06	YES
bouncer	/pub/mozilla.org/bouncer	ftp://ftp.mozilla.org/pub/mozilla.org/bouncer	4096	14-Aug-06	YES
calendar	/pub/mozilla.org/calendar	ftp://ftp.mozilla.org/pub/mozilla.org/calendar	4096	02-Jun-05	YES
camino	/pub/mozilla.org/camino	ftp://ftp.mozilla.org/pub/mozilla.org/camino	4096	11-Jul-07	YES
cck	/pub/mozilla.org/cck	ftp://ftp.mozilla.org/pub/mozilla.org/cck	4096	16-Oct-06	YES
chimera	/pub/mozilla.org/chimera	ftp://ftp.mozilla.org/pub/mozilla.org/chimera	4096	10-Jul-04	YES
data	/pub/mozilla.org/data	ftp://ftp.mozilla.org/pub/mozilla.org/data	4096	31-Aug-01	YES
directory	/pub/mozilla.org/directory	ftp://ftp.mozilla.org/pub/mozilla.org/directory	4096	19-Jun-07	YES
extensions	/pub/mozilla.org/extensions	ftp://ftp.mozilla.org/pub/mozilla.org/extensions	106496	04-Mar-07	YES
firebird	/pub/mozilla.org/firebird	ftp://ftp.mozilla.org/pub/mozilla.org/firebird	4096	16-May-03	YES
firefox	/pub/mozilla.org/firefox	ftp://ftp.mozilla.org/pub/mozilla.org/firefox	4096	26-Apr-07	YES
ftp	/pub/mozilla.org/ftp	ftp://ftp.mozilla.org/pub/mozilla.org/ftp	4096	22-Feb-06	YES
grendel	/pub/mozilla.org/grendel	ftp://ftp.mozilla.org/pub/mozilla.org/grendel	4096	07-Aug-99	YES
js	/pub/mozilla.org/js	ftp://ftp.mozilla.org/pub/mozilla.org/js	4096	09-Aug-07	YES
l10n-kits	/pub/mozilla.org/l10n-kits	ftp://ftp.mozilla.org/pub/mozilla.org/l10n-kits	4096	22-Oct-04	YES
ls-lR	/pub/mozilla.org/ls-lR	ftp://ftp.mozilla.org/pub/mozilla.org/ls-lR	1868178	17-Sep-03	NO
ls-lR.gz	/pub/mozilla.org/ls-lR.gz	ftp://ftp.mozilla.org/pub/mozilla.org/ls-lR.gz	169159	17-Sep-03	NO
minimo	/pub/mozilla.org/minimo	ftp://ftp.mozilla.org/pub/mozilla.org/minimo	4096	15-Sep-05	YES
mozilla	/pub/mozilla.org/mozilla	ftp://ftp.mozilla.org/pub/mozilla.org/mozilla	4096	27-Oct-05	YES

When requesting a directory listing, the results are stored in a query object. The `name` attribute of the `<cfftp>` is set to the name of the query object that is to be created. After it is created, the query object can be manipulated just as if it were created with `<cfquery>`. Information about each file or subdirectory found in the specified directory is stored in a separate row in the query. The columns of the created query object are shown in Table 67.10.

Table 67.10 `<cfftp>` Query Object Definitions

COLUMN	DESCRIPTION
`Name`	Name of the file or directory.
`Path`	File path (without drive designation).
`URL`	Complete URL of the file or directory.
`Length`	Number indicating the size of the file.
`LastModified`	Date/Time value indicating when the file or directory was last modified.
`Attributes`	String indicating attributes of the file or directory.
`IsDirectory`	Boolean value indicating whether the element is a directory.
`Mode`	Applies only to Solaris and HP-UX. Permissions. Octal string.

Using <cfftp> to Download a File

The <cfftp> tag can be used to download a file from an FTP server to your local machine. Listing 67.11 shows the code used to download a file, which in this case is the README file for the ftp.mozilla.org server. In this example the stopOnError is set to FALSE, so the CFFTP variables are checked for success. If the file type (binary or ASCII) is known ahead of time, transferMode can be specified ahead of time. If it is not known, the default of auto should be used.

Listing 67.11 ftp_getfile.cfm—Code to Download a File Using <cfftp>

```
<!---
 Filename: ftp_getfile.cfm
 Purpose: Do a simple FTP operation and get a file
--->

<cfftp action="open" username="anonymous" password=""
server="ftp.mozilla.org" connection="moz" stopOnError="yes">

<cfftp connection="moz" action="changeDir" directory="/pub/mozilla.org">

<cfftp connection="moz" action="GetFile"
 localfile= "#getDirectoryFromPath(getCurrentTemplatePath())#\welcome.txt"
 remotefile="README" stopOnError="No"
 transfermode="BINARY" failIfExists="No">

<cfoutput>
FTP Operation Return Value: #CFFTP.ReturnValue#<br>
FTP Operation Successful: #CFFTP.Succeeded#<br>
FTP Operation Error Code: #CFFTP.ErrorCode#<br>
FTP Operation Error Message: #CFFTP.ErrorText#<br>
</cfoutput>
```

Using <cfftp> to Upload a File

The <cfftp> tag can also be used to push a file to an FTP server from your local machine. Listing 67.12 shows the code used to push a file. Again, if the file type (binary or ASCII) is known ahead of time, the transferMode can be specified ahead of time. If it is not known, the default autoDetect should be used. This listing uses an FTP server local to the machine itself. You will need to modify the settings in order for the listing to work.

Listing 67.12 Using <cfftp> to Upload a File

```
<cfset ftpServer = "127.0.0.1">
<cfset username="foo">
<cfset password="moo">

<cfftp action="open" username="#username#" password="#password#"
server="#ftpServer#" connection="mycon" stopOnError="yes">

<!--- The file to put up. --->
<cfset localFile = getDirectoryFromPath(getCurrentTemplatePath()) &
    getFileFromPath(getCurrentTemplatePath())>
```

Listing 67.12 (continued)

```
<cfoutput><p>Moving up #localFile#</p></cfoutput>

<cfftp action="putfile" stopOnError="yes" connection="mycon"
  localFile="#localFile#"
  remoteFile="#getFileFromPath(getCurrentTemplatePath())#"
  transfermode="autoDetect">

<cfoutput>
FTP Operation Return Value: #CFFTP.ReturnValue#<br>
FTP Operation Successful: #CFFTP.Succeeded#<br>
FTP Operation Error Code: #CFFTP.ErrorCode#<br>
FTP Operation Error Message: #CFFTP.ErrorText#<br>
</cfoutput>

<cfftp action="close" connection="mycon" stopOnError="yes">
```

The template begins by specifying the settings for the FTP server, username, and password. As mentioned earlier, you will need to modify these values in order for this script to work. A connection is opened using these settings. Next, we create a variable, `localFile`, that points to this template itself. This file is uploaded to the remote server using the same name as the local file (although without the directory). After the file is uploaded, the values in the `CFFTP` struct are displayed. Lastly, the connection is closed.

When you interact with a server and manipulate files or directories, security becomes an issue. You can do a couple of things to minimize your exposure during FTP communication. First, if you are not looking to have public anonymous access, move the FTP from port 21 (the default) to a different port. This is then broadcast only to your partners who need to use the site. Second, restrict certain functionality and directories to certain user accounts, so that you only expose what is absolutely necessary for each user. The `<cfftp>` tag has the `username`, `password`, and `port` attributes, which can all be used to deal with this issue.

Secure FTP Connections

ColdFusion 8 adds a long-requested feature to the `<cfftp>` tag: secure FTP support. To enable a connection to a secure FTP server, simply add the `secure="YES"` attribute to a `<cfttp>` tag. Optional attributes added to the tag include `fingerprint`, `key`, and `passphrase` (covered in Table 67.4). Outside the connection attributes, your interactions with the FTP server will remain the same.

Summarizing the <cfftp> Tag

The preceding examples demonstrate how to use the `<cfftp>` tag to transfer and view files across networks. Though using FTP is simple, the options it provides as it becomes a reaction to a needed business process make it a significant addition to ColdFusion.

CHAPTER 68

Creating and Consuming Web Services

IN THIS CHAPTER

Understanding Web Services

At its very simplest, a *Web Service* is a Web-based application that can communicate and exchange data with other such applications over the Internet without regard for application, platform, syntax, or architecture. The Web Services technology provides a new, standardized way of communicating between—and integrating with—applications that connect to the Internet. Web Services are made possible by industry standards such as the Transport Content Protocol/Internet Protocol (TCP/IP) and Hypertext Transfer Protocol (HTTP). Web Services use additional agreed-upon standards such as XML for representing structured data; Simple Object Access Protocol (SOAP) for communicating data; Web Services Description Language (WSDL) for describing data and services; and Universal Description, Discovery, and Integration (UDDI) for locating published Web Services in public or private registries.

Due in part to the attention Web Services has received, some of the biggest names in the IT industry are making these applications an important component in their platform architecture:

- Microsoft reinvented its entire company around the .NET application architecture, of which XML Web Services is a significant part.
- IBM is striving to deliver the standards-based platforms needed to build and manage enterprise Web Services and integrated applications.
- BEA has incorporated significant support for Web Services in its flagship WebLogic Java Application Server.

Architecture is only one piece of the puzzle. Web Services possess many capabilities that have the technology and business world excited. If a single “killer app” exists for the Web Services concept, it is probably in the arena of corporate integration. Linking business units, divisions, or related entities that utilize incompatible legacy platforms can be an extremely difficult job. Companies will often use a single vendor in an attempt to simplify Enterprise Application Integration (EAI) projects.

Web Services isn't a replacement for EAI, but may end up being the genesis of new and better EAI systems in the future. Web Services can streamline the integration of new applications among vendors, partners, and customers without the need for the centralized or proprietary software of EAI. Middleware is sometimes needed to bridge legacy applications and a Web Services interface. This middleware is not proprietary and need only support a limited set of protocols, such as XML and SOAP, in order to interact with the rest of the Web Services world. This allows disparate systems within a company to communicate with each other more easily than before and can also allow communication among incompatible systems across companies. This can significantly lower the cost of doing business, especially with companies that have adopted technology different from your own.

To get to where we are today, we need to look back at the evolution of the Web to see how the Web Services concept is a natural next step.

Evolution of the Web

In the beginning, people used their Internet browsers to access static information from university libraries or read brochures at commercial Web sites. Such was the earliest era of the Web. Soon every company needed to establish a "Web presence." The Internet at that time was something for people to "see." Figure 68.1 shows the type of interaction during that period.

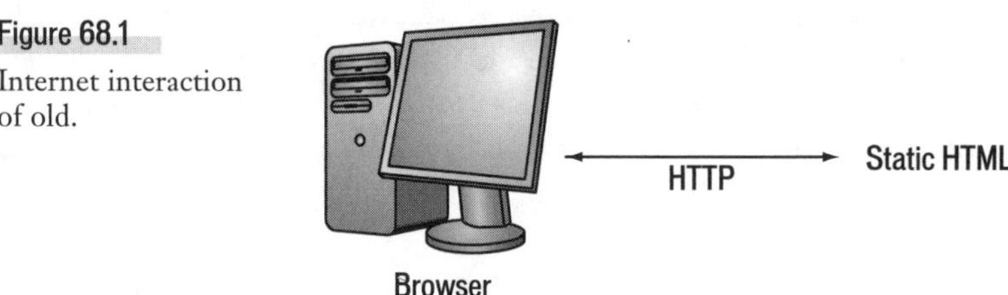

Figure 68.1
Internet interaction of old.

Eventually people began using their browsers to interact. Message boards and email became more mainstream. Companies began to develop applications that provided useful functions, as opposed to the simple brochureware that had been so prevalent. These newer applications included e-commerce and customer service, as well as business intranets. The Internet was becoming something to "do." Figure 68.2 shows an interaction typical of today.

With the advent of Web Services, the Internet may soon be seen just as much for interapplication communication as for e-commerce. In the not-too-distant future, virtually all business applications should be able to communicate and interact with all other applications via Web Services using industry-standard protocols. The Internet will simply "be." Figure 68.3 shows a multitude of possible interactions available through and because of Web Services.

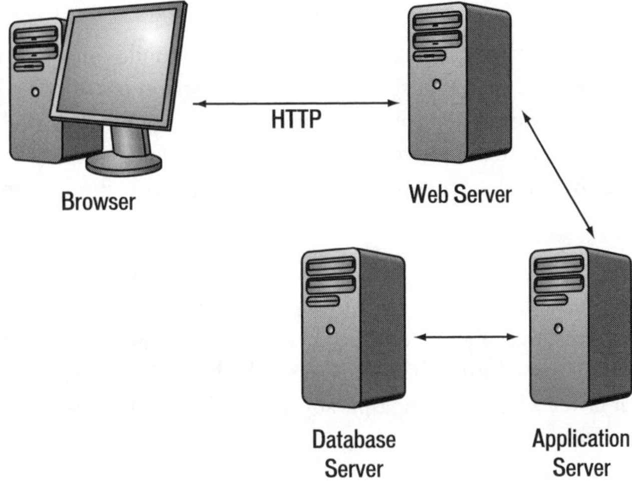

Figure 68.2
Internet interaction today.

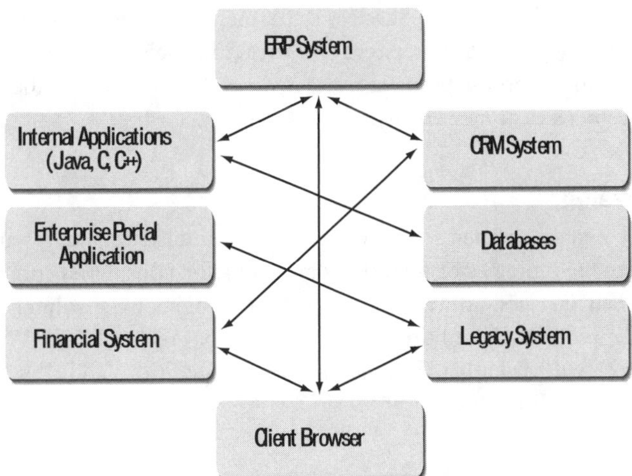

Figure 68.3
Possible Internet interactions.

Business Models

Web Services are attractive to businesses because they foster better communication within companies, and between companies and their customers and suppliers. As markets tighten and businesses need the capability to link up their systems quickly with those of other companies, Web Services may give them the edge they need to survive.

There are many models for integrating Web Services technology into the enterprise. Here is a list of a few examples of these common business models.

Provider Model

The Web Services provider model describes a company that builds an application enabling the company to provide a value-added business service to other companies. As a Web Service, the company can provide this service to any company capable of communicating via baseline protocols. This is advantageous because the provider can widen its base of potential customers while increasing efficiency and providing better customer service through enhanced communication with customers.

Consumer Model

The Web Services consumer model describes a company that uses existing Web Services by incorporating them into new applications the company is building. This allows it to get its products or services to market faster while reducing operational and startup expenses.

Syndication Model

The partner or syndication model describes a company that sells a product using its own outlets and makes the product available via Web Services to partners who can sell the product themselves or bundle complementary products or services together. This helps increase market penetration, and allows the repackaging of products and services in an almost infinite number of ways while taking advantage of a partner's customer loyalty.

Core Technologies

Web Services is based on an open set of ever-expanding industry standards and protocols. While more than a dozen technologies or methodologies could be considered core to the distributed architecture of Web Services, only a few of these technologies are absolutely central. Among these are HTTP, XML, and SOAP. Additionally, two descendent technologies, WSDL and UDDI, standardize the syntax for describing a Web Service and its operations and allow for the querying and cataloging of corresponding files.

HTTP (Hypertext Transfer Protocol)

HTTP is a communications protocol for exchanging information over the Internet. It is the common transport mechanism that allows Web Service providers and consumers to communicate.

XML (Extensible Markup Language)

XML is similar to HTML in that it uses tags to describe and encode information for transmission over the Internet. HTML has preset tags that define how information is displayed. XML lets you create your own tags to represent not only data but also a multitude of data types. This ensures accurate data transmission among Web Service providers and consumers.

SOAP (Simple Object Access Protocol)

SOAP is a lightweight protocol for the exchange of information in a distributed environment. SOAP can be used in messaging systems or for invoking remote procedure calls. It is based on XML and consists of three logical parts:

- A framework for describing what is in a message and how to process it
- A set of encoding rules for interpreting application-defined data types
- A convention for representing remote procedure calls and responses

SOAP handles the onerous job of translating data and converting data types between consumers and Web Service providers.

WSDL (Web Services Description Language)

WSDL defines an XML-based syntax for describing network services as a set of endpoints that accept messages containing either document- or procedure-related information. See the "WSDL" section coming up.

UDDI (Universal Description, Discovery, and Integration)

UDDI defines a SOAP-based Web Service for locating WSDL documents. UDDI was proposed by IBM and Microsoft and is supported by many other software vendors. Public UDDI registries allow you to *publish* your Web Services and query existing WSDL documents. ColdFusion 8 does not directly support UDDI, so you must register a service or search a registry manually.

NOTE

For more information on UDDI, visit `http://www.UDDI.org`. To search existing UDDI registries, visit `http://uddi.microsoft.com/`, `http://www.ibm.com/services/uddi/`, and `http://www.xmethods.net/`.

WSDL

Web Services Description Language (WSDL) is an XML-based language specification that defines Web Services and describes how to access them.

WSDL is used to explain the details needed to invoke a Web Service over the Internet. WSDL defines XML syntax for describing services between a set of endpoints, usually a client and server, that exchange messages. This documentation can then act as a road map for automating the details of a Web Service. WSDL describes the service interaction rather than the formats or network protocols used to communicate. It simply defines the endpoints and their data, regardless of the implementation detail. Early Web Services existed without SOAP or WSDL and required constant communication among developers creating and consuming Web Services. They needed to know what parameters and data types a Web Service's function required, as well as how to encode and decode XML so as to convert one platform's complex data types to another's.

Thankfully, today's ColdFusion developers do not need to concern themselves with such intricacies, or the need to write documentation by hand, because ColdFusion 8 generates WSDL automatically. To view the generated WSDL for a ColdFusion component deployed as a Web Service, append the string `?wsdl` to the component's URL. The WSDL document is then displayed in your Web browser.

The intent of this section is to give ColdFusion developers with little knowledge of Web Services architecture enough WSDL knowledge to recognize common WSDL syntax, to understand the MX-generated WSDL for a ColdFusion component, and to invoke a Web Service by hand with only a WSDL document as a guide. Table 68.1 describes 11 tag elements that make up a WSDL document.

Table 68.1 WSDL Document Elements

NAME	DESCRIPTION
`definitions`	Defines XML namespaces that you use to avoid naming conflicts between multiple Web Services. This is the root element of a WSDL file.
`types`	Defines data types that are used by the service's messages.
`message`	Defines the data transferred by a Web Service operation, typically the name and data type of input parameters and return values.
`portType`	Defines one or more operations provided by the Web Service.
`port`	Defines an operation and its associated inputs and outputs.
`operation`	Defines an operation that can be invoked remotely.
`input`	Specifies an input parameter to the operation using a previously defined message.
`output`	Specifies the return values from the operation using a previously defined message.
`fault`	Defines an optional error message returned from an operation.
`binding`	Specifies the protocol used to access a Web Service, including SOAP, HTTP GET and POST, and MIME.
`service`	Defines a group of related operations.

These WSDL tag elements are important because they define everything about a WSDL document and therefore everything about a Web Service. Some of the tag elements are useful only if you are dealing with a complex data type that ColdFusion doesn't understand, or if you are going to parse the returned XML on your own. Nevertheless, being able to recognize elements within a WSDL document will give you all the information you need to invoke the available methods of any Web Service.

Listing 68.1 shows a sample WSDL layout containing descriptions about the sections of a WSDL document, and information on the tags within it. This document does not exist on the book's Web site. It is simply presented here as an example.

Listing 68.1 Sample WSDL Layout

```
<?xml version="1.0" encoding="UTF-8" ?>
<!--
 This is the WSDL declaration tag, which defines the XML version and
 encoding format being used. It is the only tag in XML that does not
 have an end tag.
-->
<wsdl:definitions>
<!--
 As the Root element of a WSDL file, the opening <wsdl:definitions> tag
 defines all applicable XML namespaces to avoid naming conflicts
 between identically named XML tags
-->
 <wsdl:types>
 <!--
 The <wsdl:types> tag defines platform-neutral data type
 definitions from the XML Schema specification. These are the
 data types that are used for messages.
 -->
 </wsdl:types>
 <wsdl:message>
 <!-- Code describing WSDL "message"
 The <wsdl:message> tag defines the communication data elements.
 Each message consists of one or more logical <wsdl:part> tags.
 <wsdl:part> tags contain name and WSDL date type information and
 are similar to the parameters of a method call in Java or
 function call in C++ or ColdFusion.
 -->
 </wsdl:message>
 <wsdl:portType>
 <!-- Code describing WSDL "port"
 The <wsdl:portType> tag defines operations (functions) that can
 be called within a Web Service, and the messages (input & output
 parameters) that are involved. You can think of a portType as
 being somewhat similar to a class in Java or C++. In fact, a
 portType is almost exactly like a CFC in that it contains methods
 but can't be instantiated and doesn't have member variables. An
 operation is extremely similar to a function in a structured
 programming language such as C or ColdFusion.
 -->
 </wsdl:portType>
 <wsdl:binding>
 <!--
 Code within the opening and closing <wsdl:binding> tag
 defines the WSDL "binding" of data types for all input
 and output parameters as well as to their encoding style.
 -->
 </wsdl:binding>
 <wsdl:service>
 <!--
 Within a <wsdl:service> tag is a <wsdl:port> port, which defines
 the connection point to a Web Service and its SOAP binding.
 -->
 </wsdl:service>
</wsdl:definitions>
```

Now that we have looked at the layout of WSDL and definitions of the tag elements that make up a document, we need to examine a simple WSDL document and get familiar with its syntax. To give us something for comparison with our WSDL document, here is an extremely simple ColdFusion Component (CFC) that is being deployed as a Web Service. Listing 68.2 shows the Number-To-String Conversion Web Service.

Listing 68.2 `NumericString.cfc`—Number-to-String Conversion Web Service

```
<!---
DATE: 06/01/02
AUTHOR: Brendan O'Hara (bohara@etechsolutions.com)
WEB SERVICE: NumericString.cfc
DESCRIPTION: ColdFusion CFC deployed as a Web Service to return
a passed-in integer into its String representation.
ARGUMENTS: name="numberNumeric" type="numeric"
required="false" default="0"
--->

<!--- Here is a display name for the CFC/WS with a hint. --->
<cfcomponent displayname="NumericString" output="false"
             hint="Converts a number to its String representation">

<!--- Here is the only function in the CFC. We know it is deployed as a
Web Service because its access variable is set to "remote" --->
<cffunction name="IntegerToString" returnType="string" output="false"
            access="remote">
  <!--- Here is the argument variable --->
  <cfargument name="numberNumeric"     type="numeric" required="true">
  <cfset var returnString = "">

  <!--- Here is the "logic" of the CFC Web Service --->
       <cfswitch expression="#arguments.numberNumeric#">
              <cfcase value="0"><cfset returnString = "Zero"></cfcase>
              <cfcase value="1"><cfset returnString = "One"></cfcase>
              <cfcase value="2"><cfset returnString = "Two"></cfcase>
              <cfcase value="3"><cfset returnString = "Three"></cfcase>
              <cfcase value="4"><cfset returnString = "Four"></cfcase>
              <cfcase value="5"><cfset returnString = "Five"></cfcase>
              <cfcase value="6"><cfset returnString = "Six"></cfcase>
              <cfcase value="7"><cfset returnString = "Seven"></cfcase>
              <cfcase value="8"><cfset returnString = "Eight"></cfcase>
              <cfcase value="9"><cfset returnString = "Nine"></cfcase>
              <cfdefaultcase>
                <cfset returnString = "What am I a mathematician?">
              </cfdefaultcase>
       </cfswitch>
  <!--- Now we return the returnString variable --->
  <cfreturn returnString>
</cffunction>

</cfcomponent>
```

This is a ColdFusion Component that is being deployed as a Web Service. We know this because the `access` variable of at least one function is set to `Remote`. When we examine this CFC, we notice it contains a single function: The `IntegerToString` function takes one argument named `numberNumeric`, which is of `numeric` type and is required.

When `IntegerToString` is called, the passed value `numberNumeric` is evaluated in a `<cfswitch>` tag's `expression` statement. The corresponding `<cfcase>` tag sets the variable `returnString` with the appropriate string representation of the `numericNumber` variable. Finally, the `returnString` is returned to the Web Service caller by the `<cfreturn>` tag. To display the WSDL for this CFC Web Service, we append the string `?wsdl` to the CFC's URL.

NOTE

We will go further into the creation of Web Services in the next section. For additional information on CFCs, read Chapter 27, "Creating Advanced ColdFusion Components," in *Adobe ColdFusion 8 Web Application Construction Kit, Volume 2: Application Development.*

Now that we have an understanding of what our Web Service/CFC does, we need to go through the WSDL line by line and study the syntax. Let's examine the fraction of a WSDL definition in Listing 68.3.

Listing 68.3 `NumericString.cfc`—`portType` and Operation from the WSDL

```
<wsdl:portType name="NumericString">
  <wsdl:operation name="IntegerToString" parameterOrder="numberNumeric">
    <wsdl:input message="impl:IntegerToStringRequest"
name="IntegerToStringRequest"/>
    <wsdl:output message="impl:IntegerToStringResponse"
name="IntegerToStringResponse"/>
    <wsdl:fault message="impl:CFCInvocationException"
name="CFCInvocationException"/>
  </wsdl:operation>
</wsdl:portType>
```

On the first line of our WSDL code block, we notice that the `portType` matches the name of the `.cfc` file and really represents the `.cfc` and the Web Service. In Java or object-oriented terms, you can think of the `portType` as being similar to a Java class. A `port` or `portType` defines the operations provided by a Web Service and their associated inputs and outputs.

An `operation` in WSDL, and therefore in Web Services, is very similar in function to a method name in Java or a function name in C++. The `operation` in the second line of our sample code defines the `IntegerToString` operation.

Directly below the operation definition are our `wsdl:input`, `wsdl:output`, and `wsdl:fault` tags. `wsdl:input` and `wsdl:output` contain a predefined message and aren't that helpful in determining what our Web Service is doing or what we would need to do to call it. The `wsdl:fault` tag catches errors and outputs the applicable error message. The `message` and `part` tags really define the input parameters and the return value of our function. Listing 68.4 shows that WSDL snippet.

Listing 68.4 `NumericString.cfc`—The `message` and `part` Tags from Our WSDL

```
<wsdl:message name="IntegerToStringRequest">
  <wsdl:part name="numberNumeric" type="xsd:double"/>
</wsdl:message>

<wsdl:message name="IntegerToStringResponse">
  <wsdl:part name="IntegerToStringReturn" type="xsd:string"/>
</wsdl:message>
```

Listing 68.4 shows the two `wsdl:message` tags that map to our single operation `IntegerToString`. First is the `IntegerToStringRequest` message, which contains the `wsdl:part` tags. These tags are very important to recognize, because they define the input parameter variables and their WSDL data types.

NOTE

WSDL uses data types as they are defined in the XML Schema specification.

You have probably already guessed at the message-naming convention. For a request message, the message name is a concatenation of the `operation` name and the word `Request`; for example, `IntegerToStringRequest`. The `wsdl:part` tag's name is the same as the input parameter or argument for the CFC. In this case, it is `numericNumber`, which is a `numeric` ColdFusion type but maps to a `xsd:double` data type in WSDL. The `wsdl:message` and `wsdl:part` in this example are of the `Request-response` operation type. This is by far the most common operation in a Web Service, but it is not the only one possible. Table 68.2 describes possible operation types within a WSDL document.

Table 68.2 Operation Types in WSDL

NAME	DESCRIPTION
`Request-response`	The Web Service can receive a request and return a response.
`Solicit-response`	The Web Service can send a request and wait for a response.
`One-way`	The Web Service can receive a message.
`Notification`	The Web Service can send a message.

The standard and most common operation type is `Request-response`. If an application server such as ColdFusion has a scheduled task that runs regularly, the server can handle it as a `Solicit-response` Web Service connected to a `Request-response` Web Service on the other end. `One-way` and `Notification` types are less common; they are used more often in messaging-based or asynchronous Web Services. We will discuss asynchronous Web Services briefly in the "Best Practices" section of this chapter. For `Request-response` operations, a Boolean value of `true` may be returned simply to confirm that a sent request message has indeed been received.

Now let's take a look at the entire WSDL document in Listing 68.5.

Listing 68.5 `NumericString.cfc`—The WSDL for Our Simple Web Service

```
<?xml version="1.0" encoding="UTF-8"?>
<wsdl:definitions targetNamespace="http://ows.68/"
  xmlns="http://schemas.xmlsoap.org/wsdl/"
  xmlns:apachesoap="http://xml.apache.org/xml-soap"
  xmlns:impl="http://ows.68ows.68/"
  xmlns:intf="http://ows.68ows.68/"
  xmlns:soapenc="http://schemas.xmlsoap.org/soap/encoding/"
  xmlns:tns1="http://rpc.xml.coldfusion/"
  xmlns:wsdl="http://schemas.xmlsoap.org/wsdl/"
  xmlns:wsdlsoap="http://schemas.xmlsoap.org/wsdl/soap/"
  xmlns:xsd="http://www.w3.org/2001/XMLSchema">
<!--WSDL created by Macromedia ColdFusion MX version 7,0,0,89494-->
  <wsdl:types>
    <schema targetNamespace="http://rpc.xml.coldfusion/"
xmlns="http://www.w3.org/2001/XMLSchema">
      <import namespace="http://schemas.xmlsoap.org/soap/encoding/"/>
      <complexType name="CFCInvocationException">
        <sequence/>
      </complexType>
    </schema>
  </wsdl:types>

  <wsdl:message name="IntegerToStringResponse">
    <wsdl:part name="IntegerToStringReturn" type="xsd:string"/>
  </wsdl:message>

  <wsdl:message name="IntegerToStringRequest">
    <wsdl:part name="numberNumeric" type="xsd:double"/>
  </wsdl:message>

  <wsdl:message name="CFCInvocationException">
    <wsdl:part name="fault" type="tns1:CFCInvocationException"/>
  </wsdl:message>

  <wsdl:portType name="NumericString">
    <wsdl:operation name="IntegerToString" parameterOrder="numberNumeric">
      <wsdl:input message="impl:IntegerToStringRequest"
name="IntegerToStringRequest"/>
      <wsdl:output message="impl:IntegerToStringResponse"
name="IntegerToStringResponse"/>
      <wsdl:fault message="impl:CFCInvocationException"
name="CFCInvocationException"/>
    </wsdl:operation>
  </wsdl:portType>

  <wsdl:binding name="NumericString.cfcSoapBinding" type="impl:NumericString">
    <wsdlsoap:binding style="rpc"
                      transport="http://schemas.xmlsoap.org/soap/http"/>
      <wsdl:operation name="IntegerToString">
        <wsdlsoap:operation soapAction=""/>
        <wsdl:input name="IntegerToStringRequest">
          <wsdlsoap:body encodingStyle="http://schemas.xmlsoap.org/soap/encoding/"
                         namespace="http://ows.68ows.68/" use="encoded"/>
        </wsdl:input>
```

Listing 68.5 (continued)

```
            <wsdl:output name="IntegerToStringResponse">
              <wsdlsoap:body encodingStyle =
                            "http://schemas.xmlsoap.org/soap/encoding/"
                            namespace="http://ows.68ows.68/" use="encoded"/>
            </wsdl:output>

            <wsdl:fault name="CFCInvocationException">
              <wsdlsoap:fault encodingStyle =
                             "http://schemas.xmlsoap.org/soap/encoding/"
                             name="CFCInvocationException"
                             namespace="http://ows.68ows.68/" use="encoded"/>
            </wsdl:fault>

          </wsdl:operation>

      </wsdl:binding>

      <wsdl:service name="NumericString">

        <wsdl:documentation xmlns:wsdl="http://schemas.xmlsoap.org/wsdl/">
        Converts a number to its String representation
        </wsdl:documentation>

        <wsdl:port binding="impl:NumericString.cfcSoapBinding"
                   name="NumericString.cfc">
          <wsdlsoap:address location =
                           "http://127.0.0.1:8501/ows.68ows/68/NumericString.cfc"/>
        </wsdl:port>

      </wsdl:service>

    </wsdl:definitions>
```

Now that we have a general idea of what is going on, let's try to figure out what we would need to know from the WSDL document in order to invoke our example Web Service. The first thing we need is the URL for the WSDL document. We used this previously to get the WSDL to display in our browser. Next, we need to determine what the input parameters are and what their data types are. We know from the single `<wsdl:part>` tag within the `IntegerToStringRequest` message that the only input parameter is named `numberNumeric`, and its XML Schema data type is `xsd:double`. We now know everything needed in order to call the `IntegerToString` method of the `NumericString` Web Service. We will review this more in the section on "Consuming Web Services."

NOTE

To learn more about the WSDL specification, visit the World Wide Web Consortium's WSDL note at `http://www.w3.org/TR/wsdl`.

We have analyzed the elements of WSDL and described how they relate to a Web Service. In the next two sections, we will refer back to the knowledge gained here to understand what a WSDL document looks like for a Web Service that we have created, and how to consume a Web Service using nothing but its WSDL documentation as a guide. With the descriptive power of WSDL, it is substantially easier to access remote applications and databases as if they were local.

Creating Web Services

Creating Web Services that can be consumed by different platforms allows ColdFusion to communicate with a client over the Internet. The resulting Web Service can expose internal information to the rest of a company's platforms or to platforms from a partner company that can communicate via the protocols we have previously discussed.

In ColdFusion, we create Web Services using ColdFusion Components. We can deploy a prebuilt CFC as a Web Service or we can create a CFC specifically for the purpose of deploying it as a Web Service. Either way, in order to create and deploy Web Services we need to understand the basics of CFCs and how they operate.

NOTE

For more information on ColdFusion Components, read Chapter 27.

Components

By now we hope you have found the time to read up on and experiment with ColdFusion Components (CFCs), which take an objectlike approach to grouping related functions and encapsulating business logic. If you have any experience with CFCs, you should have no trouble following the relatively simple examples in this section. Let's first review Listing 68.6, which contains the `SimpleCreditRating.cfc`, so we can understand how this ordinary ColdFusion Component can become a powerful Web Service.

Listing 68.6 `SimpleCreditRating.cfc`—Web Service with a Simple Data Type

```
<!---
DATE: 06/01/02
AUTHOR: Brendan O'Hara (bohara@etechsolutions.com)
WEB SERVICE: SimpleCreditRating.cfc

DESCRIPTION: ColdFusion CFC deployed as a Web Service to return
a Credit Rating "string" for a passed-in Social Security number
which is a string represented by the argument "SSN".
--->

<cfcomponent output="false">

<!--- We define the CFC's single function that retrieves the credit
 rating for a passed-in Social Security number and returns it --->
<cffunction name="getCreditRating" returnType="string" output="false"
            access="remote">
  <!--- The GetCreditRating function takes a single
        argument SSN of type string, which is required --->
  <cfargument name="SSN" type="string" required="yes">
  <!--- var scope the result --->
  <cfset var result = "">

  <!--- This is where the logic would normally go. --->
  <cfset result = randRange(500,900)>

  <!--- Then the CreditRating is returned --->
```

Listing 68.6 (CONTINUED)

```
    <cfreturn result>
</cffunction>

</cfcomponent>
```

The `SimpleCreditRating` CFC starts with a `<cfcomponent>` tag, which wraps the component's content. Then the `<cffunction>` tag with a name and return type defines a single function that retrieves the credit rating for a passed Social Security number. The optional `access` attribute is set to `remote`, which exposes this CFC to the world as a Web Service. The `getCreditRating` function takes a single argument named SSN, which is of type `string` and is required. We create a credit rating by simply using the `randRange()` function. (In practice, there would be some real logic here.) The credit rating is then returned to the Web Service client.

NOTE

The `<cffunction>` attribute `Required` is ignored when a CFC is called as a Web Service. For a Web Service, all arguments are required. Because ColdFusion doesn't support method overloading, you need to define different method names for all possible parameter combinations. These methods can call a private function within the CFC that does the processing and allows for defaults.

Now we have a simple CFC-based Web Service, which we can publish and allow to be called by Web Service clients across the Web. Those clients looking to find someone's credit rating need only have that person's Social Security number. Let's examine the ColdFusion-generated WSDL for the Web Service in Listing 68.7.

Listing 68.7 `SimpleCreditRating.cfc`—WSDL Display with Simple Data Type

```
<?xml version="1.0" encoding="UTF-8"?>
<wsdl:definitions targetNamespace="http://ows.68ows.68/"
                  xmlns="http://schemas.xmlsoap.org/wsdl/"
                  xmlns:apachesoap="http://xml.apache.org/xml-soap"
                  xmlns:impl="http://ows.68ows.68/"
                  xmlns:intf="http://ows.68ows.68/"
                  xmlns:soapenc="http://schemas.xmlsoap.org/soap/encoding/"
                  xmlns:tns1="http://rpc.xml.coldfusion/"
                  xmlns:wsdl="http://schemas.xmlsoap.org/wsdl/"
                  xmlns:wsdlsoap="http://schemas.xmlsoap.org/wsdl/soap/"
                  xmlns:xsd="http://www.w3.org/2001/XMLSchema">
<!--WSDL created by Macromedia ColdFusion MX version 7,0,0,89494-->
<wsdl:types>
  <schema targetNamespace="http://rpc.xml.coldfusion/"
          xmlns="http://www.w3.org/2001/XMLSchema">
    <import namespace="http://schemas.xmlsoap.org/soap/encoding/"/>
    <complexType name="CFCInvocationException">
      <sequence/>
    </complexType>
  </schema>
</wsdl:types>

<wsdl:message name="getCreditRatingResponse">
  <wsdl:part name="getCreditRatingReturn" type="xsd:string"/>
</wsdl:message>
```

Listing 68.7 (continued)

```
<wsdl:message name="getCreditRatingRequest">
  <wsdl:part name="SSN" type="xsd:string"/>
</wsdl:message>

<wsdl:message name="CFCInvocationException">
  <wsdl:part name="fault" type="tns1:CFCInvocationException"/>
</wsdl:message>

<wsdl:portType name="SimpleCreditRating">
  <wsdl:operation name="getCreditRating" parameterOrder="SSN">
    <wsdl:input message="impl:getCreditRatingRequest"
                name="getCreditRatingRequest"/>
    <wsdl:output message="impl:getCreditRatingResponse"
                 name="getCreditRatingResponse"/>
    <wsdl:fault message="impl:CFCInvocationException"
                name="CFCInvocationException"/>
  </wsdl:operation>
</wsdl:portType>

<wsdl:binding name="SimpleCreditRating.cfcSoapBinding"
              type="impl:SimpleCreditRating">
  <wsdlsoap:binding style="rpc"
                    transport="http://schemas.xmlsoap.org/soap/http"/>
  <wsdl:operation name="getCreditRating">
    <wsdlsoap:operation soapAction=""/>
    <wsdl:input name="getCreditRatingRequest">
      <wsdlsoap:body encodingStyle="http://schemas.xmlsoap.org/soap/encoding/"
                     namespace="http://ows.68ows.68/" use="encoded"/>
    </wsdl:input>
    <wsdl:output name="getCreditRatingResponse">
      <wsdlsoap:body encodingStyle="http://schemas.xmlsoap.org/soap/encoding/"
                     namespace="http://ows.68ows.68/" use="encoded"/>
    </wsdl:output>
    <wsdl:fault name="CFCInvocationException">
      <wsdlsoap:fault encodingStyle="http://schemas.xmlsoap.org/soap/encoding/"
                      name="CFCInvocationException"
                      namespace="http://ows.68ows.68/" use="encoded"/>
    </wsdl:fault>
  </wsdl:operation>
</wsdl:binding>

<wsdl:service name="SimpleCreditRatingService">
  <wsdl:port binding="impl:SimpleCreditRating.cfcSoapBinding"
             name="SimpleCreditRating.cfc">
    <wsdlsoap:address
             location="http://127.0.0.1:8501/ows.68ows/68/SimpleCreditRating.cfc"/>
  </wsdl:port>
</wsdl:service>

</wsdl:definitions>
```

Now when we look at this WSDL document, it should quickly be apparent what is important. On the line with the first `<wsdl:operation>` tag, we see the operation `getCreditRating`, which is the method clients will wish to invoke. On the next line we see that the input message is `getCreditRatingRequest`, which is displayed on the first line with a `<wsdl:message>` tag. It has a single `<wsdl:part>` tag named `SSN`, which is of data type `xsd:string`. The message `getCreditRatingResponse` describes the `return` variable and its data type.

Our relatively simple CFC is now a powerful Web Service that can be used by businesses around the world to access credit ratings for potential customers before deciding to extend credit to them. Listing 68.8 shows an example of ColdFusion consuming the `SimpleCreditRating` Web Service; this action will also be reviewed later in this chapter.

Listing 68.8 `TestSimpleCreditRating.cfm`—Invocation Example with Simple Data Type

```
<!---
DATE: 06/01/02
AUTHOR: Brendan O'Hara (bohara@etechsolutions.com)
WEB SERVICE: TestSimpleCreditRating.cfm

DESCRIPTION: Test the CFC.
--->

<!--- Construct the URL dynamically --->
<cfif not findNoCase("https", cgi.server_protocol)>
  <cfset theURL = "http://">
<cfelse>
  <cfset theURL = "https://">
</cfif>

<!--- Add the server and current path --->
<cfset theURL = theURL & cgi.server_name & ":" & cgi.server_port &
       cgi.script_name>

<!--- Now remove this file's name, which is at the end --->
<cfset theURL = listDeleteAt(theURL, listLen(theURL,"/"), "/")>

<cfinvoke webservice="#theURL#/SimpleCreditRating.cfc?wsdl"
          method="getCreditRating" returnvariable="creditRating">
  <cfinvokeargument name="SSN" value="000000001"/>
</cfinvoke>

<cfoutput>The result is: #creditRating#</cfoutput>
```

Most of this script simply creates the `theURL` variable. This allows the script to run on any Web server and any directory. The script assumes that it lies in the same directory as the Web Service. Once the URL is figured out, the script simply uses the `<cfinvoke>` tag to call it.

Now let's take a look at a similar CFC that takes a `struct` data type. While a `struct` is similar to a number of data types in C++ and Java, it does not exactly match any of those defined in the XML Schema used by WSDL and SOAP for data-type representation and conversion. Listing 68.9 shows the Credit Rating Web Service, which for its only argument takes a `map` or ColdFusion structure as the data type for its only argument.

Listing 68.9 `MapCreditRating.cfc`—Web Service with `struct` or `map` Data Type

```
<!--- DATE: 06/01/02
AUTHOR: Brendan O'Hara (bohara@etechsolutions.com)
```

Listing 68.9 (continued)

```
WEB SERVICE: MapCreditRating.cfc

DESCRIPTION: ColdFusion CFC deployed as a Web Service to return
a Credit Rating string for a passed-in "Person" struct.

ARGUMENTS: name="Person" type="struct" required="yes"
--->
<cfcomponent output="false">

<!--- We define the CFC's single function that retrieves the credit
 rating for a passed-in "Person" and returns it --->
 <cffunction name="getCreditRating" output="false" returnType="string"
            access="remote">
  <!--- The getCreditRating function takes a single argument
        called "Person" of type struct, which is required --->
  <cfargument name="Person" type="struct" required="yes">
  <!--- var scope the result --->
  <cfset var result = "">

  <!--- This would be real logic here --->
  <cfset result = len(arguments.person.ssn) * randRange(50,100)>

  <!--- Then the CreditRating is returned --->
  <cfreturn result>
</cffunction>

</cfcomponent>
```

Other than the data type change, the only thing new here is the fake logic used to return the credit rating. The problem we face is this: When clients other than ColdFusion call this Web Service, they will need additional information to convert the arguments to a data type that ColdFusion expects and understands. Let's look at a portion of the generated WSDL for the `mapCreditRating` Web Service to see what we are talking about. It is displayed in Listing 68.10.

Listing 68.10 `MapCreditRating.cfc`—WSDL Portion with `struct` or `map` Data Type

```
<wsdl:types>
  <schema targetNamespace="http://xml.apache.org/xml-soap"
          xmlns="http://www.w3.org/2001/XMLSchema">
    <import namespace="http://ows.68ows.68/"/>
    <import namespace="http://rpc.xml.coldfusion/"/>
    <import namespace="http://schemas.xmlsoap.org/soap/encoding/"/>
    <complexType name="mapItem">
           <sequence>
             <element name="key" nillable="true" type="xsd:anyType"/>
             <element name="value" nillable="true" type="xsd:anyType"/>
           </sequence>
    </complexType>
    <complexType name="Map">
      <sequence>
        <element maxOccurs="unbounded" minOccurs="0" name="item"
                 type="apachesoap:mapItem"/>
      </sequence>
    </complexType>
  </schema>
```

This map complex type is generated by all uses of the struct data type in <cffunction> arguments. You will notice that both the key and value can be of any data type. A call to this Web Service will work if it comes from a ColdFusion page, but it's not the most platform-independent way of accepting structured data. Because ColdFusion doesn't predefine data types for all variables, we need to be aware of data types that may be problematic. The struct or map data type common to ColdFusion is not exactly represented in the XML Schema that SOAP uses for automatic data-type translation. Another unsupported data type is query. That is why we need to limit the use of unsupported data types in Web Services when interacting with other platforms.

Defining Complex Data Types

Web Services may be significantly more complex than our "simple" example, and their input parameters may be custom or unsupported data types. A Web Service may need to accept multiple fields, or a single field containing a complex data type, in order to process the called function and return data to the caller. Object-oriented languages such as Java, C++, and C# have direct mappings from their complex data types to the XML Schema data types used by SOAP and WSDL. Unfortunately, ColdFusion doesn't have direct mappings to many of these complex data types. What it does have is the capacity to let you define your own complex data types using CFCs and the <cfproperty> tag.

Listing 68.11 shows a CFC completely empty of content except for <cfproperty> tags.

Listing 68.11 CreditPerson.cfc—Complex Data Type for Use with a Web Service

```
<!---
DATE: 06/01/02
AUTHOR: Brendan O'Hara (bohara@etechsolutions.com)
COMPONENT: CreditPerson.cfc

DESCRIPTION: ColdFusion CFC deployed as a complex data type for
use with Web Services. No functions. No arguments.

--->

<cfcomponent>
  <cfproperty name="FirstName" type="string">
  <cfproperty name="Lastname" type="string">
  <cfproperty name="Address" type="string">
  <cfproperty name="City" type="string">
  <cfproperty name="State" type="string">
  <cfproperty name="ZipCode" type="string">
  <cfproperty name="SSN" type="string">
</cfcomponent>
```

The <cfproperty> tag is used in order for Web Services to define a complex data type. In ColdFusion this would be a structure, but because a struct is not a supported data type, we use another CFC without arguments to define the structure of our complex data type. The Credit Rating CFC Web Service using a complex data type is shown in Listing 68.12.

Listing 68.12 `ComplexCreditRating.cfc`—Web Service with Complex Data Type

```
<!---
DATE: 06/01/02
AUTHOR: Brendan O'Hara (bohara@etechsolutions.com)
WEB SERVICE: ComplexCreditRating.cfc

DESCRIPTION: ColdFusion CFC deployed as a Web Service to return
a Credit Rating "string" for a passed-in "Person", which is a Complex
Data Type which is defined in the CFC Person.cfc.

ARGUMENTS: name="SSN" type="string" required="yes"
--->

<cfcomponent output="false">

<!--- We define the CFC's single function that retrieves the credit
 rating for a passed-in "Person" and returns it --->
<cffunction name="GetCreditRating" returnType="string" output="false"
            access="remote">
  <!--- The GetCreditRating function takes a single argument
        called "Person" of type struct, which is required --->
  <cfargument name="person" type="CreditPerson" required="yes">
  <!--- var scope the result --->
  <cfset var result = "">

  <!--- This would be real logic here --->
  <cfset result = len(arguments.person.ssn) * randRange(50,100)>

  <!--- Then the CreditRating is returned --->
  <cfreturn result>
</cffunction>

</cfcomponent>
```

When the `type` attribute in the `<cfargument>` tag is not a recognized type, the attribute is assumed to be the name of a ColdFusion Component. The CFC is converted to a complex data type when represented in WSDL. This will take extra work to extract and convert the data on the client side, so the attribute should be used only when it is clearly advantageous.

Take a look at the generated WSDL, and notice that the complex type is represented differently than our `struct` and `map` examples—even though the processing in the CFC Web Service is virtually identical. Listing 68.13 shows the WSDL for our `ComplexCreditRating` Web Service.

Listing 68.13 `ComplexCreditRating.cfc`—WSDL Display with Complex Data Type

```
<?xml version="1.0" encoding="UTF-8"?>
<wsdl:definitions targetNamespace="http://ows.68ows.68/"
                  xmlns="http://schemas.xmlsoap.org/wsdl/"
                  xmlns:apachesoap="http://xml.apache.org/xml-soap"
                  xmlns:impl="http://ows.68/"
                  xmlns:intf="http://ows.68/"
                  xmlns:soapenc="http://schemas.xmlsoap.org/soap/encoding/"
                  xmlns:tns1="http://rpc.xml.coldfusion/"
                  xmlns:wsdl="http://schemas.xmlsoap.org/wsdl/"
                  xmlns:wsdlsoap="http://schemas.xmlsoap.org/wsdl/soap/"
```

Listing 68.13 (continued)

```
                  xmlns:xsd="http://www.w3.org/2001/XMLSchema">
<!--WSDL created by Macromedia ColdFusion MX version 7,0,0,89494-->
<wsdl:types>
  <schema targetNamespace="http://ows.68/"
          xmlns="http://www.w3.org/2001/XMLSchema">
    <import namespace="http://rpc.xml.coldfusion/"/>
    <import namespace="http://schemas.xmlsoap.org/soap/encoding/"/>
    <complexType name="creditperson">
      <sequence>
        <element name="SSN" nillable="true" type="xsd:string"/>
       <element name="address" nillable="true" type="xsd:string"/>
       <element name="city" nillable="true" type="xsd:string"/>
       <element name="firstName" nillable="true" type="xsd:string"/>
       <element name="lastname" nillable="true" type="xsd:string"/>
       <element name="state" nillable="true" type="xsd:string"/>
       <element name="zipCode" nillable="true" type="xsd:string"/>
      </sequence>
    </complexType>
  </schema>

  <schema targetNamespace="http://rpc.xml.coldfusion/"
          xmlns="http://www.w3.org/2001/XMLSchema">
    <import namespace="http://ows.68/"/>
    <import namespace="http://schemas.xmlsoap.org/soap/encoding/"/>
    <complexType name="CFCInvocationException">
      <sequence/>
    </complexType>
    </schema>
</wsdl:types>

<wsdl:message name="GetCreditRatingRequest">
  <wsdl:part name="person" type="impl:creditperson"/>
</wsdl:message>

<wsdl:message name="GetCreditRatingResponse">
  <wsdl:part name="GetCreditRatingReturn" type="xsd:string"/>
</wsdl:message>

<wsdl:message name="CFCInvocationException">
  <wsdl:part name="fault" type="tns1:CFCInvocationException"/>
</wsdl:message>

<wsdl:portType name="ComplexCreditRating">
  <wsdl:operation name="GetCreditRating" parameterOrder="person">
    <wsdl:input message="impl:GetCreditRatingRequest"
                name="GetCreditRatingRequest"/>
    <wsdl:output message="impl:GetCreditRatingResponse"
                 name="GetCreditRatingResponse"/>
    <wsdl:fault message="impl:CFCInvocationException"
                name="CFCInvocationException"/>
  </wsdl:operation>
</wsdl:portType>

<wsdl:binding name="ComplexCreditRating.cfcSoapBinding"
              type="impl:ComplexCreditRating">
```

Listing 68.13 (continued)

```
<wsdlsoap:binding style="rpc"
                  transport="http://schemas.xmlsoap.org/soap/http"/>
<wsdl:operation name="GetCreditRating">
  <wsdlsoap:operation soapAction=""/>
  <wsdl:input name="GetCreditRatingRequest">
    <wsdlsoap:body encodingStyle="http://schemas.xmlsoap.org/soap/encoding/"
                   namespace="http://ows.68/" use="encoded"/>
  </wsdl:input>
  <wsdl:output name="GetCreditRatingResponse">
    <wsdlsoap:body encodingStyle="http://schemas.xmlsoap.org/soap/encoding/"
                   namespace="http://ows.68/" use="encoded"/>
  </wsdl:output>
  <wsdl:fault name="CFCInvocationException">
    <wsdlsoap:fault encodingStyle="http://schemas.xmlsoap.org/soap/encoding/"
                    name="CFCInvocationException"
                    namespace="http://ows.68/" use="encoded"/>
  </wsdl:fault>
</wsdl:operation>
</wsdl:binding>

<wsdl:service name="ComplexCreditRatingService">
  <wsdl:port binding="impl:ComplexCreditRating.cfcSoapBinding"
          name="ComplexCreditRating.cfc">
    <wsdlsoap:address location=
                  "http://127.0.0.1:8501/ows/68/ComplexCreditRating.cfc"/>
  </wsdl:port>

</wsdl:service>

</wsdl:definitions>
```

This example provides significantly more information than does the WSDL generated for our ColdFusion `struct` or `map` example. The `map` had undefined `key` values and an undefined number of elements in the `map`, so someone trying to call our Web Service from only the WSDL would have no clue what parameters were required and what their true data types should be. Our custom complex data type, however, defines the elements in the structure and their associated types. In this case they are all strings, but they could just as easily have all been different. This Web Service can work when called by a ColdFusion page, and with minimal adjustments and testing can be accessed by most other platforms.

Consuming Web Services

In the last section, we walked through the fundamentals of creating Web Services. As we discovered, Web Service creation in ColdFusion is exceptionally easy when we utilize the functionality inherent in ColdFusion components (CFCs). So how do we "consume" a Web Service from within ColdFusion? How do we utilize data from other ColdFusion servers or disparate platforms, such as Microsoft .NET and Oracle9*i*, running on other networks? As long as these Web Services are standards compliant, we should have no problem using them.

Consult the WSDL

The first step to consuming a Web Service is obtaining the URL of the WSDL document for the service you'll be using. To do this, consult a UDDI directory or the Web Service provider. The WSDL document contains all the information you will need to call the Web Service (methods, parameters, data types, expected return values, and so on). In Listing 68.14, let's take a look at part of the WSDL for our number translation Web Service from a previous section.

Listing 68.14 `NumericString.cfc`—Partial WSDL Display

```
<wsdl:message name="IntegerToStringResponse">
  <wsdl:part name="IntegerToStringReturn" type="xsd:string"/>
</wsdl:message>

<wsdl:message name="IntegerToStringRequest">
  <wsdl:part name="numberNumeric" type="xsd:double"/>
</wsdl:message>

<wsdl:portType name="NumericString">
  <wsdl:operation name="IntegerToString" parameterOrder="numberNumeric">
    <wsdl:input message="impl:IntegerToStringRequest"
                name="IntegerToStringRequest"/>
    <wsdl:output message="impl:IntegerToStringResponse"
                 name="IntegerToStringResponse"/>
    <wsdl:fault message="impl:CFCInvocationException"
                name="CFCInvocationException"/>
  </wsdl:operation>
</wsdl:portType>
```

As designed, this Web Service has an operation named `IntegerToString` that accepts a number as input and returns its textual name. The request message contains one input parameter, whose data type is `double`. The response message contains one output parameter of type `string`.

Invoking ColdFusion Web Services

Invoking a ColdFusion Web Service from within ColdFusion is extremely easy. There are two simple methods for accomplishing this: `createObject()/<cfobject>` and `<cfinvoke>`.

`createObject()/<cfobject>`

This function and tag can instantiate a Web Service similarly to a ColdFusion object, given the WSDL location. Once instantiated, all the developer has to do is call methods that the Web Service makes available with the correct parameters. Listing 68.15 shows a sample call.

Listing 68.15 `createobject_example.cfm`—`createObject()` Example Invocation

```
<cfscript>

/* Construct the URL dynamically */
if (not findNoCase("https", cgi.server_protocol))
  theURL = "http://";
else
```

Listing 68.15 (continued)

```
    theURL = "https://";

  /* Add the server and current path */
  theURL = theURL & cgi.server_name & ":" & cgi.server_port & cgi.script_name;

  /* Now remove this file's name, which is at the end */
  theURL = listDeleteAt(theURL, listLen(theURL,"/"), "/");


   // Initialize the input parameter
   num = "4";

   // Instantiate the Web Service
   ws = createObject("webservice", "#theURL#/NumericString.cfc?wsdl");

   // Call the Web Service's integerToString method
   result = ws.integerToString(num);
  </cfscript>

  <cfoutput>The number #num# as a string is #result#.</cfoutput>
```

As in the earlier example, the script begins by simply determining the current location of the file in the form of a URL. This lets us then call the Web Service in the current directory using a full URL. Since you may have copied this book's files to a nonstandard directory, calling the Web Service using a URL helps the code be more portable. Once we have figured out the URL, the `createObject()` function is called to create a reference to the Web Service. After that is done, we can invoke methods on the Web Service. In this case, we call the `integerToString` method to convert the number to a string.

<cfinvoke>

`<cfinvoke>` is an extremely powerful tag. It is recommended that you review the ColdFusion Tag Reference before implementing any `<cfinvoke>` calls because there are at least five ways to use it. Listing 68.16 shows two sample calls.

Listing 68.16 `cfinvoke_example.cfm`—`<cfinvoke>` Example Invocation

```
<!---
DATE: 12/30/04
AUTHOR: Raymond Camden (ray@camdenfamily.com)
--->

<!--- Construct the URL dynamically --->
<cfif not findNoCase("https", cgi.server_protocol)>
  <cfset theURL = "http://">
<cfelse>
  <cfset theURL = "https://">
</cfif>

<!--- Add the server and current path --->
```

Listing 68.16 (continued)

```
<cfset theURL = theURL & cgi.server_name & ":" & cgi.server_port &
       cgi.script_name>

<!--- Now remove this file's name, which is at the end --->
<cfset theURL = listDeleteAt(theURL, listLen(theURL,"/"), "/")>

<!--- Invoke the web service --->
<cfinvoke webservice="#theURL#/NumericString.cfc?wsdl"
          method="integerToString" numberNumeric="#randRange(0,9)#"
          returnVariable="result">

<cfoutput>Result of web service call: #result#</cfoutput>

<p>

<!--- now do a simple CFC call --->
<cfinvoke component="NumericString"
          method="integerToString" numberNumeric="#randRange(0,9)#"
          returnVariable="result">

<cfoutput>Result of component call: #result#</cfoutput>
```

Once again, the script starts by figuring out the current root URL. After that, we use `<cfinvoke>` to call the `NumericString` Web Service. We tell the tag which method to execute, and we pass in the `numberNumeric` attribute. Lastly, we tell the `<cfinvoke>` tag to return the result in a variable called `result`. The next use of `<cfinvoke>` calls the exact same code, except this time it is used as a ColdFusion component.

Complex Data Types

As we discussed previously, a *complex data type* can be described as a data type that represents multiple values. Arrays, record sets, and structures are good examples of complex data types. Although these are relatively easy to visualize and describe, representing them programmatically among different application servers on different platforms presents a formidable obstacle.

SOAP saves us from having to code our Web Services to accommodate every server's interpretation of every data type. This is accomplished by defining SOAP-specific data types that are a workable subset of common data types. The most that developers must do is plug their variables into the appropriate SOAP data types. Each application is responsible for translating to and from the SOAP data types.

CFML contains several of these complex data types. As part of consuming Web Services, you will need to know how ColdFusion converts WSDL-defined data types to ColdFusion data types and vice versa. In order to facilitate their uses in CFCs exposed as Web Services, ColdFusion maps certain objects to their corresponding SOAP data types completely behind the scenes. Table 68.3 shows this mapping.

Table 68.3 WSDL-to-ColdFusion Data Type Conversion

WSDL DATA TYPE	COLDFUSION DATA TYPE
`SOAP-ENC:double`	`numeric`
`SOAP-ENC:boolean`	`boolean`
`SOAP-ENC:string`	`string`
`SOAP-ENC:Array`	`array`
`xsd:base64Binary`	`binary`
`xsd:float`	`numeric`
`xsd:enumeration`	`string`
`xsd:dateTime`	`date`
`tns1:QueryBean*`	`query`
`void`	Nothing is returned
Other complex type	structure

* These types do convert between ColdFusion and other SOAP implementations and are not supported directly by WSDL.

Invocation with Dreamweaver

Dreamweaver reads the WSDL document when you register a Web Service so that it can generate the invocation code for you. You never have to read the WSDL yourself! Figure 68.4 shows the Dreamweaver user interface for invoking a Web Service.

Figure 68.4 Dreamweaver's user interface for invoking a Web Service.

You point Dreamweaver to a UDDI registry or directly at a WSDL document. Dreamweaver analyzes the WSDL and outputs the correct method calls for you as drag-and-drop snippets. These operations are done via the Components panel.

Invoking .NET Web Services

Microsoft's much-hyped .NET architecture has had a huge impact in the Web Services arena. Because .NET offers multiple languages to choose from (VB.NET, C#, and others), a large developer base, and simple Web Services development tools, many corporations are taking a serious look at standardizing on the Microsoft platform. As long as the Web Services that are created in .NET adhere to the established standards, any Web Services developed for .NET can be accessed easily from ColdFusion.

Listing 68.17 shows you the simplicity with which a ColdFusion page can invoke a Web Service built using Microsoft's .NET architecture.

Listing 68.17 `DotNetDaily.cfm`—Consuming a Microsoft .NET Web Service

```
<html>
<head>
  <title>DotNet Daily</title>
  <meta http-equiv="Content-Type" content="text/html; charset=iso-8859-1">
</head>
<body>

<cfinvoke webservice="http://www.xmlme.com/WSDailyNet.asmx?WSDL"
          method="getDotnetDailyFact" returnvariable="aString" />

<cfoutput>
Your Daily DotNet for #dateFormat(now(), "MM-dd-yyyy")#:<br>
#aString#
</cfoutput>

</body>
</html>
```

NOTE

You can sometimes tell from its extension what language or platform a Web Service is written in. The `.asmx` extension tells you that this Web Service has been written in .NET.

This Web Service's WSDL can be found at `http://www.Xmethods.net` along with a number of our example calls to other platforms' Web Services.

Invoking Java Web Services

ColdFusion 8 Enterprise Edition can run on top of Java Application Servers that have native Java support for Web Services. Java Web Services are usually in the remote procedure call (RPC)–style, though Java also supports message-style Web Services that implement a JMS (Java Messaging Service) message listener. In Java, an RPC Web Service is usually implemented by deploying a stateless session Enterprise JavaBean (EJB) as a Web Service. Clients invoke the Web Service by sending parameters via HTTP to a Web Service that executes the applicable method within the EJB and processes any return data. Please see the documentation for your Java Application Server for information about how to deploy a Web Service.

Database Web Services

The world of Web Services is not the domain of the Web application server alone. A number of relational databases can deploy Web Services, making them capable of exposing internal information to the outside world. Two of the top databases in the enterprise, Microsoft's SQL Server 2000 and Oracle's 9*i*, both have the capability to deploy Web Services (through add-ons and tool kits) and implement industry-standard protocols such as UDDI, WSDL, XML, and SOAP.

- **Microsoft SQL Server 2000**. SQL Server 2000 was the first database to provide native XML support, allowing HTTP queries and the retrieval of relational data in XML format. You can now build powerful Web Services using the SQLXML 3.0 tool kit. It is relatively simple to set up virtual directories, enable data access via HTTP, execute queries, and build Web Services.
- **Oracle9*i***. The Oracle9*i* Web Services framework provides for the development, management, and deployment of Web Services. Developers can leverage existing database content and functionality from the Oracle9*i* Application Server. This information can be delivered via Web Services to end-user Web or client-server applications.

Dealing with Generated WSDL

As you can probably imagine, the task of generating WSDL for a Web Service takes time. Because of this, ColdFusion caches the WSDL generated by the Web Service after the first time it is generated. There are two ways to deal with this. The ColdFusion Administrator provides a simple button you can use to refresh the WSDL generated by a Web Service call. Also, the `cfinvoke` tag supports a `refreshWSDL` attribute that you can use to force ColdFusion to refresh its WSDL definition.

Another useful addition to `cfinvoke` in ColdFusion 8 is `wsdl2JavaArgs`. If you are familiar with the WSDL2 Java tool that allows ColdFusion users to generate WSDL, you can specify a space-delimited set of arguments that will be passed to this tool when `cfinvoke` is used. Most folks will never need to use this attribute, though.

Working with SOAP Requests

ColdFusion offers a variety of ways to work with the SOAP requests and responses involved in Web Services. Let's start with a simple example. As discussed earlier, for a component to be used as a Web Service, it must have at least one method with `access="remote"`. This same method, however, can be called by other ColdFusion templates on the server. It can also be called via Flash Remoting. What if you want to ensure that the method is *only* called as a Web Service? ColdFusion has a function, `isSoapRequest()`, that returns `true` if the current method was executed as a Web Service. Listing 68.18 demonstrates a simple Web Service with a method that can only be called as a Web Service.

Listing 68.18 `justawebservice.cfc`—A Web-Service-Only Component

```
<cfcomponent>

  <cffunction name="test" returntype="string" access="remote">
        <cfif isSoapRequest()>
```

Listing 68.18 (continued)

```
            <cfreturn "Good call!">
      <cfelse>
        <cfthrow message="This method must be called as a web service.">
      </cfif>
         </cffunction>

</cfcomponent>
```

This component has only one method: `test`. The body of the method simply checks to see if it is being executed as a SOAP request. It does this using `isSoapRequest()`. If this function returns `true`, we return a simple string. If not, we use `<cfthrow>` to throw an error. The following code snippet demonstrates using the same component both as a Web Service and as a local CFC:

```
<!--- Construct the URL dynamically --->
<cfif not findNoCase("https", cgi.server_protocol)>
  <cfset theURL = "http://">
<cfelse>
  <cfset theURL = "https://">
</cfif>

<!--- Add the server and current path --->
<cfset theURL = theURL & cgi.server_name & ":" & cgi.server_port &
       cgi.script_name>

<!--- Now remove this file's name, which is at the end --->
<cfset theURL = listDeleteAt(theURL, listLen(theURL,"/"), "/")>

<!--- Call as a web service --->
<cfinvoke webservice="#theURL#/justawebservice.cfc?wsdl" method="test"
          returnVariable="result">
<cfoutput>#result#</cfoutput>

<p>

<!--- Call as a CFC --->
<cftry>
  <cfinvoke component="justawebservice" method="test" returnVariable="result">
  <cfoutput><p>#result#</cfoutput>
  <cfcatch>
    Sorry, but I couldn't call the method.
  </cfcatch>
</cftry>
```

As in the other templates we have used, the script begins by determining the current URL. Once past that, we invoke the Web Service method and then call the same method as a local CFC. Since we know this isn't going to work, we wrap it in a `<cftry><cfcatch>` block. When run, the Web Service will return a good result, while the local CFC invocation will throw an error.

Calling Web Services with Nillable Arguments

When building a method, any combination of arguments can be used to define its behavior. Some Web Services may define a method as having "nillable" arguments. This simply means the value can be null. However, ColdFusion doesn't allow you to create null values. Thus in earlier versions of

ColdFusion it was impossible to call these Web Services. A new argument, `omit`, can be used in `<cfinvokeargument>` to pass a null value to a Web Service. Listing 68.19 demonstrates a simple Web Service with an optional argument (this will act as a nillable argument).

Listing 68.19 `NillableWS.cfc`—Nillable CFC Example

```
<cfcomponent>

       <cffunction name="test" returntype="string" access="remote">
         <cfargument name="alpha" type="string" required="true">
         <cfargument name="beta" type="string" required="false">
         <cfargument name="carny" type="string" required="true">

         <cfreturn "Foo">
       </cffunction>

</cfcomponent>
```

This is an extremely simple Web Service. The test method has three arguments. The second argument, `beta`, is marked as optional. Listing 68.20 demonstrates how we can correctly call this Web Service.

Listing 68.20 `TestNillable.cfm`—Testing `NillableWS.cfc`

```
<!--- Construct the URL dynamically --->
<cfif not findNoCase("https", cgi.server_protocol)>
  <cfset theURL = "http://">
<cfelse>
  <cfset theURL = "https://">
</cfif>

<!--- Add the server and current path --->
<cfset theURL = theURL & cgi.server_name & ":" & cgi.server_port &
       cgi.script_name>

<!--- Now remove this file's name, which is at the end --->
<cfset theURL = listDeleteAt(theURL, listLen(theURL,"/"), "/")>

<cfinvoke webservice="#theURL#/NillableWS.cfc?wsdl" method="test"
          returnVariable="result">
  <cfinvokeargument name="alpha" value="foo">
  <cfinvokeargument name="beta" omit="yes">
  <cfinvokeargument name="carny" value="moo">
</cfinvoke>

<cfoutput>Result is #result#</cfoutput>
```

As with our numerous other examples, we begin by simply grabbing the current URL dynamically. We then invoke the `NillableWS` Web Service. This Web Service takes three arguments, with the middle argument, `beta`, being optional. By default, you cannot omit this argument, even though the method was defined as optional. With ColdFusion, however, we can pass in the argument and use `omit="yes"` to pass a null value to the Web Service. Think of this as a simple way of passing a null value, which ColdFusion doesn't natively support.

Best Practices

As with many new technologies, architectures, and strategies, Web Services has generated significant hype. The adoption rate for Web Services has grown to the point that it's now becoming clear there is some substance behind the excitement. Unlike many earlier technologies, Web Services has a chance to meet and perhaps even exceed the expectations surrounding it.

Along with the advantages of cross-platform compatibility come some drawbacks. Although the distributed computing environment of Web Services is widely recognized as the way of the future, it carries the baggage of network latency and additional translation time. The actual overhead of running a Web Service is not as bad as perceived, but it is a factor for system architects to consider when selecting parts of their systems to expose to the world. Careful testing and optimization can reduce this potential problem significantly. Here are several general principles to consider when programming and architecting Web Services:

- Use Web Services only when appropriate. Use ColdFusion Components when interoperability is unnecessary.
- Use coarse-grained Web Services. Do not call the same Web Service 10 times on a page. Call it once and use a query of queries to return the granular information for display. Return the appropriate amount of information based on the transaction overhead.
- Use stateless Web Services whenever possible.
- Limit the use of SSL, because the security feature has a considerable impact on performance. Try to encrypt data whenever possible.
- Limit the use of complex data types within a Web Service when interacting with other platforms.

Another practice that is highly recommended is the use of asynchronous Web Services.

Synchronous RPC-style operations let you know immediately whether an operation was successful. Performing synchronous operations across multiple processes is an all-or-nothing proposition. The initiating application must wait for the chain of `Request-response` operations, regardless of its length. When something goes down or a process fails, the application initiating the request must know to take some other course of action. On the other hand, asynchronous messaging allows a process to be concerned only with initiating a request, knowing that it will eventually receive a response asynchronously. This relieves the Web Service client from waiting for the invoked operation to respond. The `One-way` and `Solicitation` operation types are commonly used with asynchronous Web Services. These should be used for performance reasons, when available from Web Services providers, whenever immediate responses are not required.

Error Handling

In the "WSDL" section of this chapter, we briefly mentioned the `message` name `CFCInvokationException` that ColdFusion creates when generating the WSDL for your Web Service. This allows someone who calls a Web Service you have written to catch run-time or other errors while their code continues processing without the expected response from your Web Service.

Any Web Service can throw errors, which may or may not be critical to the page that is calling the service. If you use `<cftry>` and `<cfcatch>` or the `try, catch` `<cfscript>` equivalents, you can catch CFC, SOAP, and other errors in your application. If you don't catch these errors, they will be displayed in the browser. Unless you're testing the Web Service yourself, you probably don't want the error to be written to the screen. Catching errors in ColdFusion is not difficult, but it does take some effort. You can catch multiple types of errors that may all require various types of additional processing. You can also specify an error type of `any`, which acts as a catch-all to the ColdFusion `<cfcatch>` tag, as shown in Listing 68.21.

Listing 68.21 `trycatch_example.cfm`—Sample Use of `<cftry><cfcatch>` While Invoking a Web Service

```
<html>
<head>
  <title>Where in the world is Sven Svensson?</title>
  <meta http-equiv="Content-Type" content="text/html; charset=iso-8859-1">
</head>
<body>

<cftry>
  <cfinvoke method="HTMLSearchAddress" returnvariable="aString"
          webservice=
     "http://www.marotz.se/scripts/searchperson.exe/wsdl/ISearchSwedishPerson">
    <cfinvokeargument name="fName" value="Sven"/>
    <cfinvokeargument name="lName" value="Svensson"/>
    <cfinvokeargument name="address" value=""/>
    <cfinvokeargument name="zipCode" value=""/>
    <cfinvokeargument name="city" value=""/>
  </cfinvoke>
   <cfcatch type="any">
     <cfset astring = "Where in the world is Sven Svensson?">
   </cfcatch>
</cftry>

<cfoutput>#aString#</cfoutput>

</body>
</html>
```

Configuring in ColdFusion Administrator

The ColdFusion Administrator lets you register a Web Service with a name and URL. When you reference that Web Service later in your code, you won't have to specify the URL for the Web Service's WSDL file. Instead, the Web Service can be referenced using the name that points to the WSDL's URL. For example, anytime you invoke a Web Service registered as `ZipCodeWS` on a particular server, you reference it as `WebService="ZipCodeWS"`. The URL can then be changed to point to another URL without modifying the invocation code throughout the application. This represents a type of code encapsulation, which could also be done using `Application` or `Request` scope variables.

Security

Web Services rely on current technologies to implement security. These include SSL, IP filtering, and digital certificates. These techniques address some issues related to Web Services security but are far from comprehensive. A new standards body, the Web Services Interoperability Organization (WSI), is developing specifications for Web Services–specific security issues. These comprise a variety of platforms, applications, and programming languages. They include possible Web Services specifications such as HTTP-R, XML Encryption, and XML Digital Signature. ColdFusion Web Services security is usually handled programmatically within ColdFusion Components, but when sensitive data is communicated across HTTP, that may not be enough.

Security concerns may eventually lead to creation of firewalls for specific applications within the enterprises. Under such security policies, the contents of all communications would be inspected, including XML and SOAP messages.

Web Services security is incomplete at best and is clearly in its infancy. Existing methods of securing data and limiting access were not designed with interoperability and performance in mind.

CHAPTER 69 Working with Feeds

IN THIS CHAPTER

Feeling a bit overwhelmed? Join the club. With the variety of Web sites out there today, it can be hard to keep up with your favorite blogs and online magazines. Luckily, help is available: Really Simple Syndication (RSS) and Atom feeds. RSS and Atom feeds provide a simple way to keep users up to date with the changes in your Web site, and they let your own Web site aggregate information from other sites as well. You can use ColdFusion 8 to both create and consume feeds. Let's get started!

Why Use Feeds?

Feeds can help you keep on top of the latest content across the Internet by enumerating and showing you exactly what has changed at a Web site. For instance, you can use feeds to keep track of blogs. A blog is a collection of articles (or entries) that are typically organized chronologically, so a blog feed might list the last 10 articles written on the blog. Now suppose you are interested in 10 blogs. If each blog provides a feed, these feeds can be combined into one feed, providing you with a single list of all the blogs' entries ordered by date—in effect, an uber blog that contains all the content in one place. There are sites on the Internet that do this for you: for example, ColdFusion Bloggers, at `http://www.coldfusionbloggers.org`. This site aggregates more than 300 blogs at one site—a service possible only because each blog provides a feed for external sites to consume and list.

Feeds can also be used by desktop clients. For instance, Mozilla Thunderbird, an email client for both Windows and OS X, supports the download and display of feeds directly in the client, so that users can browse feeds just as they do email. Another example is Fresh, which is a feed reader built with AIR (the Adobe Integrated Runtime). You can download Fresh from the AIR samples page, at `http://labs.adobe.com/technologies/air/samples/`. Figure 69.1 shows Fresh in action.

Feeds can also be useful on e-commerce sites. Orange Whip Studios could provide a feed that lists all upcoming movie releases, for example. Orange Whip Studios could even provide one feed per movie category, so that one user could subscribe to an Action feed, for instance, while another user subscribes to a Comedy feed.

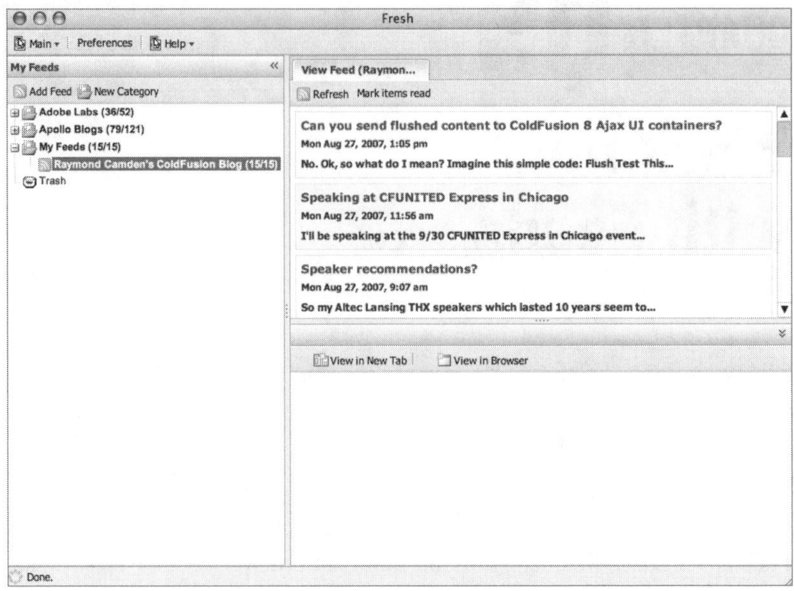

Figure 69.1

Fresh is an RSS and Atom feed aggregator built with Adobe AIR.

If you think this description of feeds sounds a bit like a description of Web services, you are correct. Both provide a way for a remote client to retrieve information from a Web site. Both use a format that can be universally understood because it follows a specification. (RSS and Atom have different specifications, which we will discuss later, but luckily you don't have to worry about this when consuming feeds with ColdFusion.) However, whereas Web services typically provide an interactive API (for example, a Web service may provide a way to update content), feeds are used only to read information.

Flavors of RSS and Atom

Feeds can be divided into two main categories: RSS and Atom. RSS has the longer history and covers multiple versions of specifications. Atom was partially created in response to some limitations and problems in RSS. Even though ColdFusion does its best to hide the flavor that a particular feed uses, you need to be aware of what types of feeds exist, especially because you must pick one when you create a feed. ColdFusion can read RSS 0.90, 0.91, 0.92, 0.93, 0.94, 1.0, and 2.0, and ColdFusion can create RSS 2.0 feeds. ColdFusion can read Atom versions 0.3 and 1.0, and ColdFusion can create Atom 1.0.

Later in this chapter, we discuss how these different versions affect how you create and read RSS feeds. The differences are important, so try to remember which type of RSS feed you are using.

NOTE

Many people refer to all feeds–both RSS and Atom–as RSS feeds.

Creating Feeds

ColdFusion 8 provides the new `<cffeed>` tag. This tag is used for both creating and reading (also known as consuming) RSS and Atom feeds. We will start by looking at how to create feeds. Table 69.1 lists the attributes of `<cffeed>` used when creating a feed.

Table 69.1 `<cffeed>` Tag Attributes Used in Creating Feeds

ATTRIBUTE	DESCRIPTION
`action`	Specifies the action that the tag will take. The value can be either `create` or `read`. Defaults to read.
`columnMap`	When you're using a query to create a feed, lets you specify a structure that maps your query columns to columns that match the RSS or Atom feed being created.
`name`	Specifies the name of a structure that contains entry and metadata information. Used if a query is not provided.
`outputFile`	Specifies either a full or relative path for storing the XML created by `<cffeed>`.
`overwrite`	Specifies a Boolean value that indicates whether `<cffeed>` should overwrite a file when using the `outputFile` option. The default value is false. ColdFusion will throw an error if `overwrite` is set to false and the file already exists.
`properties`	Specifies a structure of metadata for the feed. The keys used in this structure partially depend on the type of feed being created. Used in combination with the `query` attribute.
`query`	Specifies a query that will be used to populate the feed. Used in combination with the `properties` attribute.
`xmlVar`	Specifies the name of a variable that stores the created XML.

When creating a feed, your first task is to choose the feed type. As stated earlier, for ColdFusion you can choose either RSS 2.0 or Atom 1.0.

Next, you need to decide how the data will be provided to the feed. You have two options: Either one structure with both metadata and entry data can be passed via the `name` attribute, or a `properties` structure and `query` variable can be used. Because most people will be using database information for feeds, this chapter demonstrates only the latter approach.

Your last decision is to determine what metadata you want provided with the feed. This metadata can provide information about the feed as a whole, including the main site's URL, title, and description. RSS 2.0 in particular requires that certain items be included in the metadata.

Now take a look at an example. Listing 69.1 demonstrates a simple RSS 2.0-based feed.

Listing 69.1 `create1.cfm`—Creating an RSS 2.0 Feed

```
<!--- Struct to contain metadata --->
<cfset meta = structNew()>
<cfset meta.title = "Orange Whip Studio Films">
<cfset meta.link = "http://localhost/ows">
<cfset meta.description = "Latest Films">
<cfset meta.version = "rss_2.0">

<cfquery name="films" datasource="ows" maxrows="10">
select   filmid, movietitle, pitchtext, dateintheaters
from   films
order by dateintheaters desc
</cfquery>

<!--- create a mapping from films query to rss columns --->
<cfset cmap = structNew()>
<cfset cmap.publisheddate = "DATEINTHEATERS">
<cfset cmap.title = "MOVIETITLE">
<cfset cmap.content = "PITCHTEXT">

<cffeed action="create" properties="#meta#" query="#films#"
        columnMap="#cmap#" xmlVar="feedXML">

<cfcontent type="text/xml" reset="true">
<cfoutput>#feedxml#</cfoutput>
```

The listing begins with a series of variables set in a structure named `meta`. As you can probably guess, this is the metadata for the feed and describes the feed at a high level. The link would normally point to the Orange Whip Studio's home page.

Next a query is used to return the 10 latest films produced by OWS. This query contains columns that do not exactly match with the columns needed to create a feed. Therefore, we have to tell ColdFusion which columns in the query match the columns that the feed expects. For three columns, `publisheddate`, `title`, and `content`, we specify a column in the query. This creates the mapping. Note that there is a bug in the currently released version of ColdFusion 8: The names of the columns in the query must be capitalized or they will not be recognized.

Next the `<cffeed>` tag is used with the `create` option. The `meta` struct is passed in to define the metadata. The query is passed in to define the entries. The `columnMap` structure is passed to help define which columns in the query match the columns in the feed. The `xmlVar` attribute specifies which variable stores the result. The last two lines simply specify the proper content type and serve up the XML.

Figure 69.2 shows how this feed is rendered in Firefox.

This feed is missing something, though: links. Typically, a feed entry actually links to the item in question, whether it be a product page or a blog entry. Listing 69.2 is a modified version of Listing 69.1.

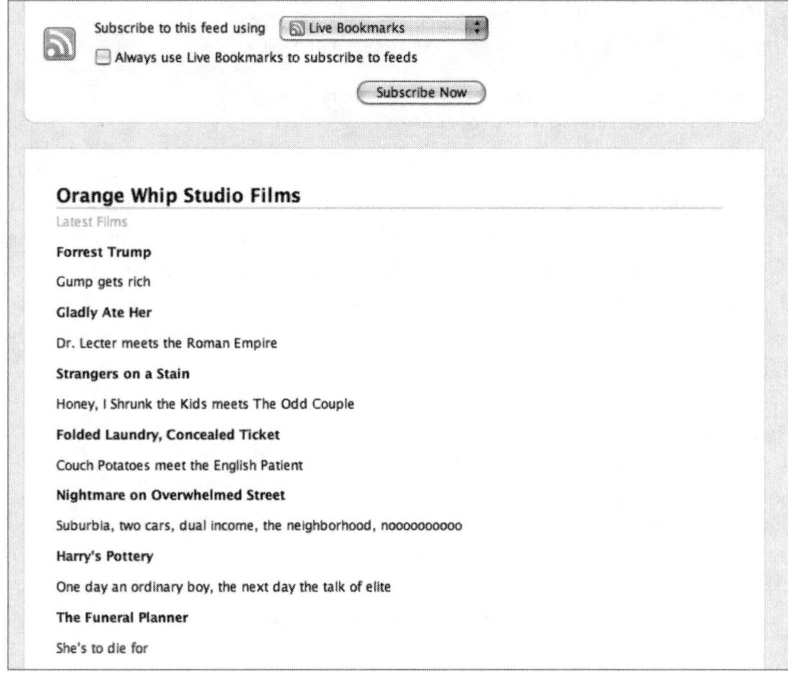

Figure 69.2 ColdFusion-powered feed displayed in Firefox.

Listing 69.2 `create2.cfm`—Creating an RSS 2.0 Feed with Links

```
<!--- Struct to contain metadata --->
<cfset meta = structNew()>
<cfset meta.title = "Orange Whip Studio Films">
<cfset meta.link = "http://localhost/ows">
<cfset meta.description = "Latest Films">
<cfset meta.version = "rss_2.0">

<cfquery name="films" datasource="ows" maxrows="10">
select    filmid, movietitle, pitchtext, dateintheaters
from    films
order by dateintheaters desc
</cfquery>

<cfset queryAddColumn(films, "rsslink", arrayNew(1))>
<cfloop query="films">
    <cfset querySetCell(films, "rsslink",
    "http://localhost/ows/film.cfm?id=#filmid#",currentRow)>
</cfloop>

<!--- create a mapping from films query to rss columns --->
<cfset cmap = structNew()>
<cfset cmap.publisheddate = "DATEINTHEATERS">
<cfset cmap.title = "MOVIETITLE">
<cfset cmap.content = "PITCHTEXT">

<cffeed action="create" properties="#meta#" query="#films#"
```

Listing 69.2 (continued)

```
          columnMap="#cmap#" xmlVar="feedXML">

<cfcontent type="text/xml" reset="true">
<cfoutput>#feedxml#</cfoutput>
```

Let's look at what has changed in this new version of the listing. After the initial query is run, the query is modified by hand. First a new column is added. This column, `rsslink`, will be used by the feed to generate a link for each entry. The query is looped over, and `querySetCell()` is used to specify a link for the film. Although this URL will not work, it will provide information to the feed to display a link. Because a column name is used that the feed recognizes, there is no need to specify it in the `columnMap` structure. Figure 69.3 demonstrates that Firefox recognizes the links and correctly adds them when displaying the feed.

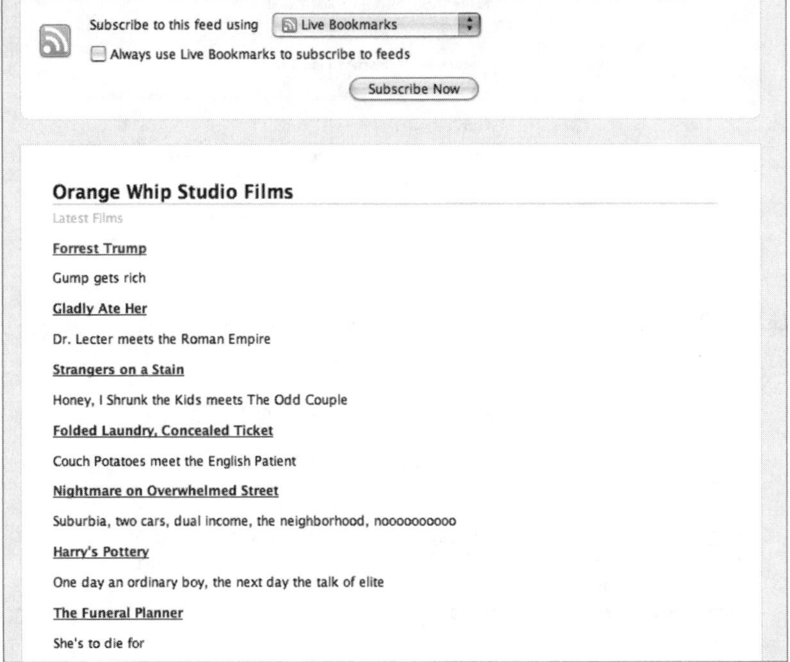

Figure 69.3 Another ColdFusion-powered feed displayed in Firefox.

The creation of Atom-based feeds is a bit more complex. The first difference is in the metadata. RSS feeds use simple values in the metadata, but the `title` and `link` values in Atom feeds are complex objects. The `title` value is a structure, and the `link` value is an array of structures. This complexity arises because Atom feeds can store more than just one simple title or link. The following code block shows the changes to the metadata required to build an Atom feed:

```
<!--- Struct to contain metadata --->
<cfset meta = structNew()>
<cfset meta.title = structNew()>
```

```
<cfset meta.title.value = "Orange Whip Studio Films">
<cfset meta.link = arrayNew(1)>
<cfset meta.link[1] = structNew()>
<cfset meta.link[1].href = "http://localhost/ows">
<cfset meta.description = "Latest Films">
<cfset meta.version = "atom_1.0">
```

Another difference is in the columns used to generate the Atom feed. Whereas the RSS feed uses a custom column named `rsslink`, the Atom feed uses a column named `linkhref`. Otherwise, though, the code is essentially the same. Listing 69.3 lists the Atom version of the feed.

Listing 69.3 `create3.cfm`—Creating an Atom Feed

```
<!--- Struct to contain metadata --->
<cfset meta = structNew()>
<cfset meta.title = structNew()>
<cfset meta.title.value = "Orange Whip Studio Films">
<cfset meta.link = arrayNew(1)>
<cfset meta.link[1] = structNew()>
<cfset meta.link[1].href = "http://localhost/ows">
<cfset meta.description = "Latest Films">
<cfset meta.version = "atom_1.0">

<cfquery name="films" datasource="ows" maxrows="10">
select    filmid, movietitle, pitchtext, dateintheaters
from    films
order by dateintheaters desc
</cfquery>

<cfset queryAddColumn(films, "linkhref", arrayNew(1))>
<cfloop query="films">
    <cfset querySetCell(films, "linkhref",
    "http://localhost/ows/film.cfm?id=#filmid#",currentRow)>
</cfloop>

<!--- create a mapping from films query to rss columns --->
<cfset cmap = structNew()>
<cfset cmap.publisheddate = "DATEINTHEATERS">
<cfset cmap.title = "MOVIETITLE">
<cfset cmap.content = "PITCHTEXT">

<cffeed action="create" properties="#meta#" query="#films#"
        columnMap="#cmap#" xmlVar="feedXML">

<cfcontent type="text/xml" reset="true">
<cfoutput>#feedxml#</cfoutput>
```

Reading Feeds

Now let's look at how to read feeds. Table 69.2 lists the attributes of `<cffeed>` used when reading feeds.

Table 69.2 `<cffeed>` Tag Attributes Used in Reading Feeds

ATTRIBUTE	DESCRIPTION
`action`	Specifies the action that the tag will take. The value can be either `create` or `read`.
`enclosureDir`	Specifies a relative or absolute path to save enclosures included in the feed. If the directory does not exist, ColdFusion throws an error. If the attribute is left blank, any enclosure in the feed will be ignored. To save enclosures in the current directory, use ".".
`ignoreEnclosureError`	Specifies whether ColdFusion should throw an error if an issue occurs while downloading enclosures. The default value is no.
`name`	Specifies the name of the variable for storing the result of the feed parsing. This structure will contain both the metadata and the entries.
`outputFile`	Specifies a full or absolute path and file name for storing the downloaded XML.
`overwriteEnclosure`	Specifies whether ColdFusion should overwrite an enclosure if a file with same name exists in the feed. ColdFusion throws an error if this attribute is set to no and the file already exists. The default is no.
`properties`	Specifies the name of a variable that stores the metadata of the feed. This variable will be a structure.
`proxyPassword`	Specifies the password if a proxy server is required for HTTP communication.
`proxyPort`	Specifies the port if a proxy server is required for HTTP communication.
`proxyServer`	Specifies the server if a proxy server is required for HTTP communication.
`proxyUser`	Specifies the username if a proxy server is required for HTTP communication.
`query`	Specifies the name of a query to create to hold the entries.
`source`	Specifies the URL of the feed to consume.
`timeout`	Specifies the number of seconds that ColdFusion should wait before timing out the request.
`userAgent`	Specifies the user agent to use when requesting the feed. The default is `ColdFusion`.
`xmlVar`	Specifies the name of a variable to create to store the downloaded XML.

Listing 69.4 shows how easy it is to read a feed.

Listing 69.4 `read1.cfm`—Reading a Feed

```
<cfset feedurl = "http://www.coldfusionjedi.com/rss.cfm">
<cffeed action="read" source="#feedurl#"
        properties="meta" query="entries">

<cfdump var="#meta#">

<cfoutput query="entries">
<p>
<a href="#rsslink#">#title#</a>
(#dateFormat(publisheddate)#)<br />
#content#
</p>
</cfoutput>
```

As you can see, there isn't much to this file. The first line specifies the URL of the feed: in this case, Raymond Camden's blog. Next, the `<cffeed>` tag is used to download the feed. The `properties` attribute specifies that the metadata should be stored in a structure named `meta`. The `query` attribute specifies that the entries should be stored in a query named `entries`. The `meta` structure is simply dumped to the screen. The `entries` query is looped over and displayed. The `rsslink`, `title`, `publisheddate`, and `content` columns are output. Figure 69.4 shows the result of this code.

Figure 69.4

The result of parsing a feed.

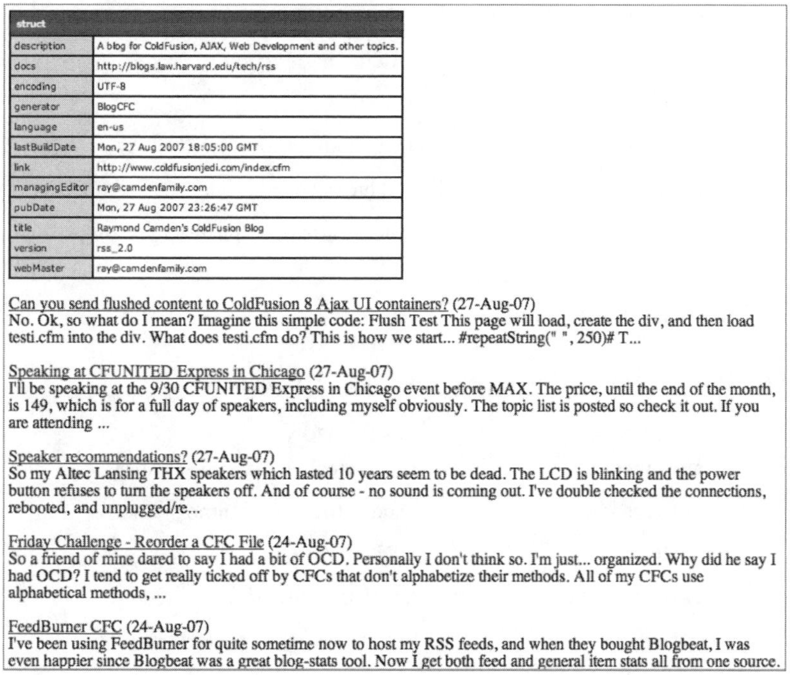

struct	
description	A blog for ColdFusion, AJAX, Web Development and other topics.
docs	http://blogs.law.harvard.edu/tech/rss
encoding	UTF-8
generator	BlogCFC
language	en-us
lastBuildDate	Mon, 27 Aug 2007 18:05:00 GMT
link	http://www.coldfusionjedi.com/index.cfm
managingEditor	ray@camdenfamily.com
pubDate	Mon, 27 Aug 2007 23:26:47 GMT
title	Raymond Camden's ColdFusion Blog
version	rss_2.0
webMaster	ray@camdenfamily.com

Can you send flushed content to ColdFusion 8 Ajax UI containers? (27-Aug-07)
No. Ok, so what do I mean? Imagine this simple code: Flush Test This page will load, create the div, and then load testi.cfm into the div. What does testi.cfm do? This is how we start... #repeatString(" ", 250)# T...

Speaking at CFUNITED Express in Chicago (27-Aug-07)
I'll be speaking at the 9/30 CFUNITED Express in Chicago event before MAX. The price, until the end of the month, is 149, which is for a full day of speakers, including myself obviously. The topic list is posted so check it out. If you are attending ...

Speaker recommendations? (27-Aug-07)
So my Altec Lansing THX speakers which lasted 10 years seem to be dead. The LCD is blinking and the power button refuses to turn the speakers off. And of course - no sound is coming out. I've double checked the connections, rebooted, and unplugged/re...

Friday Challenge - Reorder a CFC File (24-Aug-07)
So a friend of mine dared to say I had a bit of OCD. Personally I don't think so. I'm just... organized. Why did he say I had OCD? I tend to get really ticked off by CFCs that don't alphabetize their methods. All of my CFCs use alphabetical methods, ...

FeedBurner CFC (24-Aug-07)
I've been using FeedBurner for quite sometime now to host my RSS feeds, and when they bought Blogbeat, I was even happier since Blogbeat was a great blog-stats tool. Now I get both feed and general item stats all from one source.

How do we know that those query columns exist? Both RSS and Atom feeds specify different types of data, but the `<cffeed>` tag always creates the same columns.

NOTE

When a feed includes Dublin Core or iTunes extensions (discussed later in this chapter), additional columns may be returned.

Table 69.3 lists the columns used by RSS feeds.

Table 69.3 `<cffeed>` Query Columns Used by RSS Feeds

COLUMN	DESCRIPTION
`authoremail`	Author value
`categorylabel`	Category value
`categoryscheme`	Domain attribute of category value
`comments`	Comments value
`content`	Description value
`expirationdate`	Expiration date value (used only in RSS 0.93 feeds)
`id`	GUID value
`idpermalink`	isPermalink attribute of GUID value
`linkhref`	URL for enclosure value
`linklength`	Length attribute of enclosure value
`linktype`	Type attribute of enclosure value
`publishedDate`	Published date value
`rsslink`	Link value
`source`	Source value
`sourceurl`	URL attribute of source value
`title`	Title value
`uri`	`rdf:about` attribute for link value (used only in RSS 1.0 feeds)

Table 69.4 lists the columns used by Atom feeds.

Table 69.4 `<cffeed>` Query Columns Used by Atom Feeds

COLUMN	DESCRIPTION
`authoremail`	Email attribute of author value
`authorname`	Name attribute of author value
`authoruri`	URI attribute of author value
`categorylabel`	Label attribute of category value
`categoryscheme`	Scheme attribute of category value
`categoryterm`	Term attribute of category value
`content`	Content value
`contentmode`	Mode attribute of content value (used only in Atom 0.3 feeds)
`contentsrc`	Src attribute of content value

Table 69.4 (continued)

COLUMN	DESCRIPTION
contenttype	Type attribute of content value
contributoremail	Email attribute of contributor value
contributorname	Name attribute of contributor value
contributoruri	URI attribute of contributor value
createddate	Created value (used only in Atom 0.3 feeds)
id	ID value
linkhref	HREF attribute of link value
linkhreflang	HREFLang attribute of link value
linklength	Length attribute of link value
linkhref	HREF attribute of link value
linkrel	Rel attribute of link value
linktitle	Title attribute of link value
linktype	Type attribute of link value
publishedDate	Date published value (used only in Atom 0.3 feeds)
rights	Rights value (in Atom 0.3 feeds, this is the copyright value)
summary	Summary value
summarymode	Mode attribute of summary value
summarysrc	Normally blank; contains data in Atom 1.0 feeds where content is supplied for the summary element
summarytype	Type attribute of summary value
title	Title value
titletype	Type attribute of title value
updateddate	Updated value (used only in Atom 0.3 feeds)
xmlbase	xml:base attribute of content value

As mentioned earlier, every time you use the `<cffeed>` tag, all of these columns are returned—quite a bit of information. What you use will be based on what you need to display (or work with) and the type of feed you are using. The following is a complete list of all columns representing everything from Tables 69.3 and 69.4:

```
AuthorEmail, AuthorName, AuthorURI, CategoryLabel, CategoryScheme, CategoryTerm,
Comments, Content, ContentMode, ContentSrc, ContentType, ContributorEmail,
ContributorName, ContributorURI, CreatedDate, ExpirationDate, ID, IDPermalink,
LinkHref, LinkHrefLang, LinkLength, LinkRel, LinkTitle, LinkType, PublishedDate,
Rights, RSSLink, Source, SourceURL, Summary, SummaryMode, SummarySrc, SummaryType,
Title, TitleType, UpdatedDate, URI, XMLBase
```

Using Dublin Core and iTunes Extensions

Tables 69.3 and 69.4 list all the columns you can ordinarily expect to get when retrieving a feed, but there are two situations in which additional columns will be returned. Two extensions to the feed specifications are popular enough that Adobe provides support for them: the Dublin Core and iTunes extensions.

Dublin Core Extensions

Dublin Core extensions provide even more metadata information about a feed. ColdFusion supports the reading of Dublin Core extensions, but not the writing of them. If a feed contains Dublin Core extensions, the columns in Table 69.5 will be returned in addition to the normal columns.

Table 69.5 `<cffeed>` Query Columns Associated with Dublin Core Extensions

COLUMN	DESCRIPTION
`dc_contributor`	People or group responsible for writing content for the feed.
`dc_coverage`	The extent or range of the content.
`dc_creator`	People or group responsible for the feed.
`dc_date`	Date associated with the resource.
`dc_description`	Description of feed contents.
`dc_format`	File format or physical properties of the data.
`dc_identifier`	A unique identifier.
`dc_language`	Language for the feed.
`dc_publisher`	Person or group that publishers the feed.
`dc_relation`	Identifier of some related resource.
`dc_right`	Copyright or usage information.
`dc_source`	Pointer to the source of the feed data.
`dc_subject_taxonomyuri`	URI for taxonomy related to the subject.
`dc_subject_value`	Subject value.
`dc_title`	Title value.
`dc_type`	Type of data.

Listing 69.5 demonstrates a feed with Dublin Core extensions.

Listing 69.5 `read_dc.cfm`—Reading a Feed with Dublin Core Extensions

```
<cfset feedurl = "http://www.pheed.com/pheed/example.rss">
<cffeed action="read" source="#feedurl#"
   properties="meta" query="entries">

<cfdump var="#meta#">
<cfdump var="#entries#">
```

This listing fetches a feed that contains Dublin Core data. To see the Dublin Core extensions, view the result in your browser. Note that the metadata struct `meta` contains a key named `feedextension` that lists DublinCore. This lets you know that the feed does indeed contain Dublin Core extensions. Also note that the query `entries` contains the additional columns listed in Table 69.5.

iTunes Extensions

iTunes extensions were added to support podcasting. ColdFusion supports a subset of the total iTunes specification. This support applies to both the creation and reading of feeds. Feeds with iTunes extensions will have both additional query columns and additional metadata. Table 69.6 lists the new query and metadata columns.

Table 69.6 `<cffeed>` Query Columns and Metadata Properties Associated with iTunes Extensions

COLUMN OR PROPERTY	DESCRIPTION
`itunes_author`	Podcast artist name. Found in both the query and metadata.
`itunes_block`	Specification that the podcast should *not* be displayed. This property relies on the person reading the feed to obey the value. Found in both the query and metadata.
`itunes_duration`	The length of the podcast in seconds or in *HH:MM:SS* format. Found in the query.
`itunes_explicit`	Value that signifies that the content is explicit. Values can be `yes`, `no`, or `clean`. Found in both the query and metadata.
`itunes_keywords`	List of keywords or phrases that describe the podcast in comma-delimited format. Found in both the query and metadata.
`itunes_subtitle`	Short description for the podcast. Found in both the query and metadata.
`itunes_summary`	Longer description. Found in both the query and metadata.

In addition to these metadata properties and columns, the following items appear in the metadata only:

- `itunes_category`: A structure with two fields: `category` and `subcategory`. These relate specifically to the iTunes Music Store.
- `itunes_image`: An image URL for the podcast.
- `itunes_owner`: Information about the owner of the podcast. This contains two keys: `itunes_email` and `itunes_mail`.

Listing 69.6 demonstrates a sample iTunes feed.

Listing 69.6 `read_itunes.cfm`—Reading a Feed with iTunes Extensions

```
<cffeed source="itunes.xml" action="read"
   properties="meta" query="entries">

<cfdump var="#meta#">
<cfdump var="#entries#">
```

Again, the example is fairly simple. Note here that the source points to a local XML file (you can download this code from the Web site or copy it from `http://www.apple.com/itunes/store/podcaststechspecs.html#_Toc526931673`). As before, we dump the metadata properties and entries. If you view the result in your browser, you will see the iTunes extensions in both variables.

CHAPTER 70

Interacting with the Operating System

IN THIS CHAPTER

ColdFusion gives the developer many tools to interact with the operating system. These tools include functions and tags to manipulate files and directories using `<cffile>` and `<cfdirectory>`, execute applications on the server using the `<cfexecute>` tag, manipulate the system Registry using the `<cfregistry>` tag, and create and read Zip and JAR files using `<cfzip>`. This chapter shows how these tags can be used to interact with the file system and operating system. Another tag, `<cfNTAuthenticate>`, is covered in Chapter 23, "Securing Your Applications," online.

Introduction to <cffile>

`<cffile>` permits local file access through CFML templates. Files can be moved, copied, renamed, or deleted by using various action attributes for the `<cffile>` tag. Additionally, `<cffile>` provides mechanisms for reading and writing ASCII files with ColdFusion. By taking advantage of the `<cffile>` tag, you can produce complex applications with file manipulation using a single interface. The templates in which the `<cffile>` tag is used can be protected using native operating system security when the templates are stored in directories below the document root defined for the HTTP server. In addition to the ability to access the local file system, `<cffile>` provides the ability to upload files using the HTTP protocol.

The Varied Faces of <cffile>

The `<cffile>` tag performs different operations depending on the value of its `ACTION` attribute.

For moving, copying, or renaming files on the server's drives, it looks like this:

```
<cffile
 action="Copy or Move or Rename"
 source="c:\ LocationOnServer\ MySourceFile.txt"
 destination="c:\ AnotherLocationOnServer\ MyNewFile.txt">
```

For deleting a file on the server's drive, it looks like this:

```
<cffile
 action="Delete"
 file="c:\ LocationOnServer\ MyFileToDelete.txt">
```

For creating or adding to existing files on the server's drives, it looks like this:

```
<cffile
 action="Write or Append"
 file="c:\ LocationOnServer\ MyFile.txt"
 output="#ContentToSaveInFile#">
```

For reading a file on the server on the server's drive, it looks like this:

```
<cffile
 action="Read or ReadBinary"
 file="c:\ LocationOnServer\ MyFile.txt"
 variable="VariableNameToHoldContent">
```

Finally, for uploading a file from the browser machine to the server, it looks like this:

```
<cffile
 action="Upload"
 fileField="MyFormInput"
 destination="c:\ LocationOnServer">
```

NOTE

Because ColdFusion operates on the server, it has no direct access to the client file system, so it can't read, copy, delete, or do anything else to the files on the browser machine. The only file-related thing it can do is to accept file uploads from the browser, which must be explicitly initiated by the user. Keep this in mind when developing your applications.

As you can see, the `<cffile>` tag's attributes can be set to various values depending on the task at hand. Each attribute can be set dynamically using variables created via the `<cfset>` tag or with the values of query or form fields. (When using form fields, extreme care should be taken to ensure that security restrictions are in place to prevent malicious action as a result of dynamic file action.) Table 70.1 indicates the attributes and the valid values permitted for specific values of the `action` attribute.

NOTE

When using `FORM` fields, `URL` variables, or other user-entered data to set the attributes for the `<cffile>` tag, extreme caution should be used to ensure only valid entries are processed.

Table 70.1 `<cffile>` Tag `action` Attributes

ACTION	DESCRIPTION
`copy`	Copies a file from the location specified in `source` to the location specified in `destination`.
`move`	Moves a file from the location specified by `source` to the location specified in `destination`.
`delete`	Deletes the file specified by the `file` attribute.

Table 70.1 (continued)

ACTION	DESCRIPTION
rename	Renames the file specified in source and gives it the new name specified in destination.
read	Reads the contents of the text file specified by file to into the string variable specified by variable.
readBinary	Reads the contents of the binary file specified by file into a binary object variable specified by variable.
write	Writes the contents of the string specified in output to the file specified by file. If the file already exists, the existing file is completely replaced by the new one.
append	Writes the contents of the string specified in output to the file specified by file. If the file already exists, the new content is appended to the end of the existing content.
upload	Used to upload files. Accepts a file from the browser machine and saves it to the location on the server specified in destination. The fileField attribute must correspond to the name of an <input> form field of type="File". The nameConflict attribute controls what happens when a file with the same name already exists on the server.

NOTE

For all the actions that create files (Write, Append, Move, Copy, Rename, and Upload), you can also specify an attributes attribute to control the file's attributes on disk. For instance, when using action="Write" to create a new file, you could use attributes="ReadOnly" to make the new file be considered read-only.

NOTE

For Unix servers, you can also provide a mode attribute for actions that create completely new files (Write, Append, and Upload). This attribute gives you a way to control the chmod-style values for files.

Accessing the Server's File System

During application development you might need to perform local file system operations (local here refers to the Web server's file system): read or write ASCII files, or copy, move, rename, or delete various application files.

Reading and Writing Files

Using <cffile> to read and write ASCII files is fairly straightforward. For example, to read the file of the currently executing script, you could use code such as Listing 70.1.

Listing 70.1 SimpleFileRead.cfm—<cffile> Usage for Reading README.txt

```
<!---
 Filename: SimpleFileRead.cfm
 Edited By: Nate Weiss (NMW)
```

Listing 70.1 (continued)

```
 Purpose: Exhibits how to read and display the contents of a text file
--->

<!--- What is this file? --->
<cfset thisFile = expandPath(cgi.script_name)>
<!--- Read the contents of this file into a string variable --->
<cffile action="read" file="#thisFile#" variable="thisFileContent">

<!--- Display the value --->
<cfoutput>
 <table border="0" cellPadding="5" cellSpacing="0">
  <tr>
   <td style="background:navy;color:white;font-weight:bold">
    The first 1000 characters of this file are:
   </td>
  </tr><tr>
   <td bgcolor="silver">
    #htmlCodeFormat(left(thisFileContent, 1000))#
   </td>
  </tr>
 </table>
</cfoutput>
```

NOTE

`<cffile>` can read both ASCII and binary files. To read a binary file, the `action` attribute must be set to `ReadBinary`.

This is a simple yet powerful feature. The example in Listing 70.1 is trivial—it simply reads the contents of the current file on the server's drive, then displays the first 1000 characters on a Web page—but it serves as the basis for the power of reading files using `<cffile>`. After the `<cffile>` operation is completed, the contents of the file are available in the variable specified during the call (in this case, `thisFileContent`). If this file contained delimited data, it could be parsed using `<cfloop>` and various string functions.

Writing a file using `<cffile>` is just as easy. Listing 70.2 shows an example of writing a modified version of a file to disk.

Listing 70.2 `SimpleFileWrite.cfm`—`<cffile>` Usage to Alter a Text File

```
<!---
 Filename: SimpleFileWrite.cfm
 Author:  Nate Weiss (NMW)
 Purpose: Exhibits how to read, change, and re-write a text file
--->

<!--- Does the file exist? --->
<cfif fileExists(expandPath("./test.txt"))>
  <!--- Read the contents of the text file into a string variable --->
  <cffile action="read" file="#expandPath('./test.txt')#" variable="content">
<cfelse>
  <!--- Set it to a blank string --->
  <cfset content = "">
</cfif>
```

Listing 70.2 (continued)

```
<!--- Modify the contents of the variable --->
<cfset text = "File Modified using ColdFusion 8 on: ">
<cfset text = text & dateFormat(now(),"mm/dd/yyyy") & " at ">
<cfset text = text & timeFormat(now(),"h:mm:ss tt")>
<cfset revisedContent = content & text>

<!--- Write the contents of the variable back out to disk --->
<cffile action="write" file="#expandPath('./test.txt')#" output="#revisedContent#"
 addnewline="Yes">

<html>
<head>
 <title>&lt;cffile&gt; read/write Example</title>
</head>
<body>

<!--- Display the file's revised contents --->
<cfoutput>
 <table border="0" cellPadding="5" cellSpacing="0">
  <tr>
   <td style="background:navy;color:white;font-weight:bold">
    #expandPath("./test.txt")# was modified, as shown below:
   </td>
  </tr><tr>
   <td bgcolor="silver">
    #htmlCodeFormat(revisedContent)#
   </td>
  </tr>
 </table>
</cfoutput>
</body>
</html>
```

Listing 70.2 builds on the code in Listing 70.1. First, it uses the function `fileExists()` to see if our text file exists. If it does, it uses `<cffile>` to read the contents of `the file` into a variable. If it doesn't, it simply creates an empty string. Next, a new line is added to the end of the variable by concatenating a remark statement coupled with a date/time stamp to the contents of the variable. Lastly, `<cffile>` is called again to write the contents of the variable back out to disk. The resulting file output is displayed as it would be seen on disk.

NOTE

`<cffile>` with the `action` attribute set to `write` creates the file if it doesn't exist and overwrites the file if it does. Care should be taken to ensure that existing content isn't deleted inadvertently. If the contents of an existing ASCII file are to be kept, `<cffile>` should be used with the `action` set to `append`, which will concatenate the contents of the variable specified in the `output` attribute to the end of the disk file. The `fileExists()` function can be used to determine whether a `Write` or `Append` operation should take place.

NOTE

Using the `expandPath()` function is a handy way to turn relative paths into the absolute paths that `<cffile>` requires.

Copying, Moving, Renaming, and Deleting Files

The <cffile> tag provides the capability to perform local file operations such as copy, move, rename, and delete. Local in this example means local to the ColdFusion server—not local to the browser machine. These actions have the potential for causing severe damage to the file system. Security considerations should therefore be evaluated carefully before developing ColdFusion templates that provide the ability to copy, rename, move, or delete files.

NOTE

Security measures can vary by operating system and from one Web server to another. Consult documentation specific to the configuration of your Web server for detailed information about security issues.

To provide local file access, the <cffile> tag is used with the action attribute set to copy, move, rename, or delete. The destination attribute isn't required in the case of the delete action value; it is required in all other cases.

Listing 70.3 shows ColdFusion's capability to copy files on the local file system. The action attribute is set to copy; the source attribute is set to the name of the file that is to be copied. The destination attribute is set to the directory into which the file will be copied. The destination attribute also can specify a file name in addition to the directory name, which enables you to copy one file to another while changing the file name in the process.

Listing 70.3 SimpleFileCopy.cfm—Using <cffile> to Copy

```
<!---
 Filename: SimpleFileCopy.cfm
 Author: Nate Weiss (NMW)
 Purpose: Exhibits how to make a copy of a file on the server's drive
--->

<!--- Copy this file from one location to another --->
<cffile action="copy"
 source="#expandPath(cgi.script_name)#"
 destination="#expandPath(cgi.script_name)#.bak">

The file has been copied.
```

Listing 70.4 shows ColdFusion's capability to move files on the local file system. The action attribute is set to MOVE; the source attribute is set to the name of the file that is to be moved. The destination attribute is set to the directory into which the file will be moved.

Listing 70.4 SimpleFileMove.cfm—Using <cffile> to Move

```
<!---
 Filename: SimpleFileMove.cfm
 Edited By: Nate Weiss (NMW)
 Purpose: Exhibits how to move a file from one
       location to another on the server's drives
--->

<!--- Create a file we can move --->
<cfset newFile = expandPath("./tempFileToMove.txt")>
```

Listing 70.4 (continued)

```
<!--- Write it, even though it will be empty --->
<cffile action="write" file="#newFile#" output="">

<!--- Get the dir one up --->
<cfset newLocation = expandPath("../")>

<!--- Move a file from one location to another --->
<cffile action="move" source="#newFile#" destination="#newLocation#">
<cfoutput>The file (#newFile#) has been moved (#newLocation#).</cfoutput>
```

In Listing 70.4, a new file is created. This gives us something we can move later on. As before, we use the `expandPath()` function to help create absolute paths. Once the file is created, it is moved one directory up from the current script.

Listing 70.5 shows the use of the `DELETE` value of the `ACTION` attribute. The `ACTION` attribute is set to `DELETE`, and the `FILE` attribute is set to the name of the file you want deleted.

Listing 70.5 `SimpleFileDelete.cfm`—Using `<cffile>` to Delete

```
<!---
 Filename: SimpleFileDelete.cfm
 Author:  Nate Weiss (NMW)
 Purpose: Exhibits how to make a remove a file from the server's drive
--->

<!--- Create a file we can delete --->
<cfset newFile = expandPath("./tempFileToDelete.txt")>

<!--- Write it, even though it will be empty --->
<cffile action="write" file="#newFile#" output="">

<!--- Delete a file from the server's drive --->
<cffile action="delete" file="#newFile#">
<cfoutput>The file (#newFile#) has been deleted.</cfoutput>
```

NOTE

Use the `DELETE` action carefully. Access to templates that delete files should be carefully restricted.

Listing 70.6 shows `<cffile>` being used to `RENAME` an existing file.

Listing 70.6 `SimpleFileRename.cfm`—Using `<cffile>` to Rename

```
<!---
 Filename: SimpleFileRename.cfm
 Edited By: Nate Weiss (NMW)
 Purpose:  Exhibits how to rename a file on the server's drive
--->

<!--- Create a file we can move --->
<cfset newFile = expandPath("./tempFileToRename.txt")>

<!--- Write it, even though it will be empty --->
<cffile action="write" file="#newFile#" output="">
```

Listing 70.6 (CONTINUED)

```
<!--- renamed file name we will use --->
<cfset renamedFile = expandPath("./tempFileRenamed.txt")>

<!--- Rename a file on the server's drive --->
<cffile action="rename" source="#newFile#" destination="#renamedFile#">
<cfoutput>The file (#newFile#) has been renamed (#renamedFile#).</cfoutput>
```

Uploading Files

Browser-based file uploads in ColdFusion are provided through the `<cffile>` tag. This tag takes advantage of features available in most Web browsers that support file uploads using the HTTP protocol. The syntax of the `<cffile>` tag can be used with selected attributes to facilitate the uploading of files to the server.

NOTE

The method by which files are uploaded to the server using HTTP is documented in the Internet Request for Comment (RFC) 1867, which was available at `http://www.faqs.org/rfcs/rfc1867.html` at the time of this writing. RFC 1867 is the formal documentation of the HTTP file upload process. It specifies the concepts related to file uploads using MIME file extensions.

To upload a file from the browser machine to the server, the `<cffile>` tag is used like this:

```
<cffile
 action="Upload"
 fileField="myFormInput"
 destination="c:\ LocationOnServer"
 nameConflict="OVERWRITE"
 accept="image/gif">
```

Briefly, the meaning of each of these attributes is as follows:

- The `fileField` attribute must correspond to a special `<input>` field on an HTML form (you will see an example of this shortly, in Listing 70.7).
- The `destination` is the folder on the server where you want the file placed when the upload is complete.
- The `nameConflict` attribute controls what happens if there is already a file in the destination folder that has the same name as the file being uploaded.
- The `accept` attribute lets you control which types of files the user is able to upload (just images, just text files, and so on).

You must carefully consider a number of issues prior to writing the HTML/CFML necessary to process a file upload. First and foremost is security. The directory to which the files will be uploaded must be secure from outside view, and the templates used to perform the file operations must be protected from unauthorized access. Because the threat of computer viruses is increasing, you must take precautions to protect your system from malicious users. The second issue to examine is the reason you are providing file operations to the users. Is it necessary? Can it be accomplished using other means?

What If the File Already Exists on the Server?

It's often important for your server to be able to accept file uploads from multiple users at the same time. If the users are uploading files with the same file names (or file names that already exist on the server from prior uploads), you need to tell ColdFusion how to handle the situation using the `nameConflict` attribute. Table 70.2 lists the values you can supply to the `NAMECONFLICT` attribute.

Table 70.2 `nameConflict` Values for `<cffile> action="Upload"`

VALUE	MEANING
`nameConflict="Error"`	If a file with the same name already exists on the server, an error message is generated and page execution stops. Of course, you can catch and recover from the error using the `<cftry>` and `<cfcatch>` tags (discussed in Chapter 51, "Error Handling," online).
`nameConflict="Skip"`	If a file with the same name already exists on the server, the file upload operation is simply skipped. No error message is shown. Your code can examine the value of the `cffile.FileWasSaved` variable to detect whether the upload was actually skipped for this reason (see Table 70.3).
`nameConflict="Overwrite"`	If a file with the same name already exists on the server, the existing file is overwritten with the file being uploaded from the browser. Your code can look at the value of `cffile.FileWasOverwritten` to determine whether a file was actually overwritten when your code is actually used.
`nameConflict="MakeUnique"`	If a file with the same name already exists on the server, the file from the browser is saved with an automatically generated file name. This ensures that an uploaded file can always be saved without overwriting an existing file. Your code can use the `cffile.ServerFile` variable to determine the actual file name used (see Table 70.3).

Determining the Status of a File Upload

After a `<cffile>` operation is completed, information about the file is available in reference keys of the `cffile` structure. The `cffile` structure maintains status information about the most recent file operation completed or attempted. Keys in the `cffile` structure are referenced in the same manner as other ColdFusion variables (for example, `#cffile.ContentType#`). Table 70.3 identifies the attributes maintained and their meanings. The `<cffile>` tag also has a result attribute. This lets you specify the name of the structure returned from file upload operations. The value `cffile` is used by default.

Table 70.3 `cffile` Variables Available After a File Upload

KEY	EXPLANATION
`cffile.AttemptedServerFile`	The name ColdFusion tried to use when saving the file.
`cffile.ClientDirectory`	Client-side directory where the file was located.
`cffile.ClientFile`	Client-side file name (with extension).
`cffile.ClientFileExt`	Client-side file name extension without the period.
`cffile.ClientFileName`	Client-side file name (without extension).
`cffile.ContentSubType`	MIME content subtype of file.
`cffile.ContentType`	MIME content type of file.
`cffile.DateLastAccessed`	Returns the date and time the uploaded file was last accessed.
`cffile.FileExisted`	Did a file with the same name exist in the specified destination prior to upload, copy, or move? (Yes/No)
`cffile.FileSize`	Size of the uploaded file.
`cffile.FileWasAppended`	Was the file appended to an existing file by ColdFusion? (Yes/No)
`cffile.FileWasOverwritten`	Was an existing file overwritten by ColdFusion? (Yes/No)
`cffile.FileWasRenamed`	Was the uploaded file renamed to avoid a conflict? (Yes/No)
`cffile.FileWasSaved`	Was the file saved by ColdFusion? (Yes/No)
`cffile.OldFileSize`	Size of the file that was overwritten during an upload operation.
`cffile.ServerDirectory`	Directory on server where file was saved.
`cffile.ServerFile`	File name of the saved file.
`cffile.ServerFileExt`	Extension of the uploaded file without the period.
`cffile.ServerFileName`	File name without extension of the uploaded file.
`cffile.TimeCreated`	Returns the time the uploaded file was created.
`cffile.TimeLastModified`	Returns the date and time of the last modification to the uploaded file.

These variables are used in several of the examples below, specifically in Listing 70.8 and the examples that follow it.

Building an Upload Interface

Once you have decided to use `<cffile>` to upload a file, you can move on to the next step of the process, which is preparing the user interface. This requires the development of an HTML form, either through writing static HTML or by creating an HTML form using dynamic code generated via CFML. In either case, the form's structure is basically the same.

The next series of listings is used to create an add-on to the actor listings that will allow a photo to be linked to an actor record. First, the general syntax is shown, and then specific modifications to the actor templates are made.

Listing 70.7 shows the HTML code necessary to create a form that prompts the user for a file to be uploaded to the server (Figure 70.1). The user can use the Browse button to select a file from a file selection dialog box (Figure 70.2); the selected file name will be placed in the `TYPE="File"` input field (Figure 70.3), which will cause the file to be uploaded when the form is submitted.

Listing 70.7 `UploadForm.html`—HTML Form for File Upload Using `<cffile>`

```
<!---
 Filename: UploadForm.html
 Edited By: Nate Weiss (NMW)
 Purpose:  Simple file uploading example
--->

<html>
<head>
 <title>&lt;cffile&gt; Upload Demonstration - Example 1</title>
</head>

<body>
<h3>&lt;cffile&gt; Upload Demonstration - Example 1</h3>
<!--- Create HTML form to upload a file --->
<form action="UploadAction.cfm" enctype="multipart/form-data" method="post">
 <!--- File field for user to select or specify a filename --->
 <p>File to upload:<br>
 <input type="file" name="fileName" size="50"><br>

 <!--- Submit button to submit the form (and upload the file) --->
 <input type="submit" value="Upload the File">
</form>
</body>
</html>
```

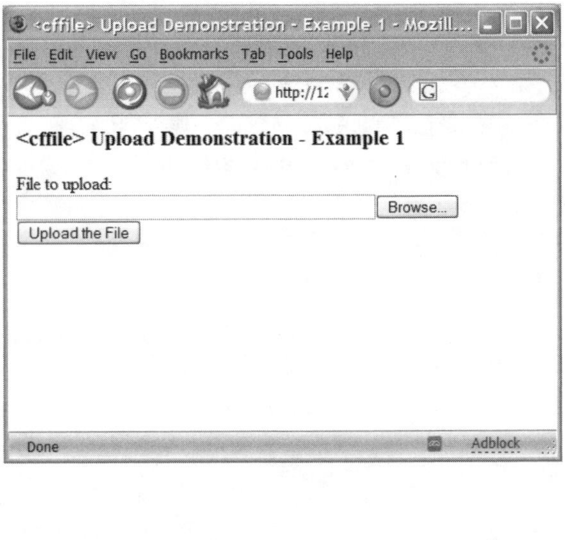

Figure 70.1

Example HTML form for file upload.

There are several important items in this form, all of which are necessary to perform a file upload:

- The `<form>` tag has a `enctype="multipart/form-data"` attribute, which is necessary for the browser to send the file to ColdFusion in a way that it can use.
- The addition of an `<input>` of `type="File"` tells the browser to process file selection using the standard user-interface functionality of the underlying operating system.
- The `<form>` tag's `action` attribute identifies which ColdFusion template will be used to process the file. That template will use the `<cffile>` tag with `action="Upload"`.
- The `method` attribute is set to `post`.

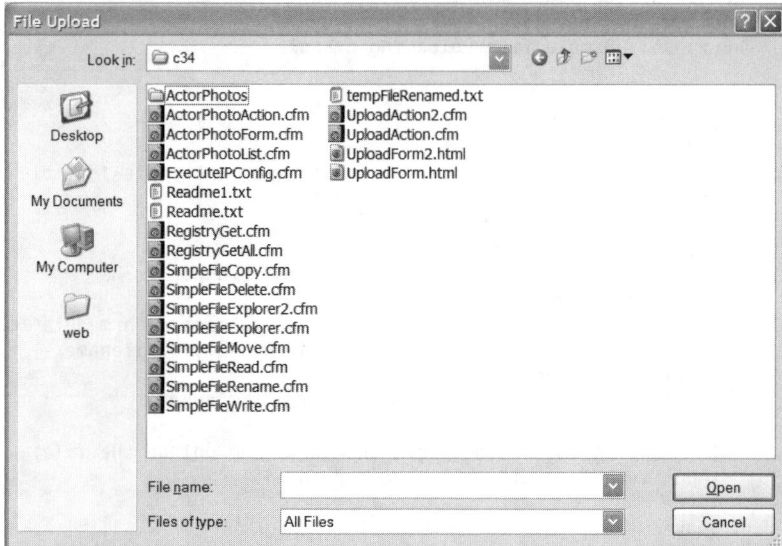

Figure 70.2

Example file selection dialog box.

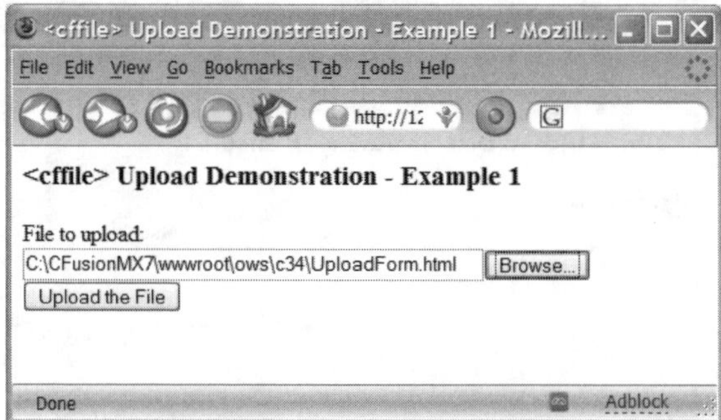

Figure 70.3

Example HTML form for file upload with selected file name.

The dialog box shown in Figure 70.2 is specific to the browser's operating system, and changes from one operating system to another. Figure 70.3 shows the HTML form with the text box filled with the selected file name.

When this form is submitted, the `form` tag's `action` attribute causes the selected file to be uploaded. Listing 70.8 shows the CFML code required to process the uploaded file. This example enumerates the values of the keys in the `cffile` structure after the file has been written to the file server. Details of the keys in the `cffile` structure can be seen in Table 70.3.

Listing 70.8 `UploadAction.cfm`—Processing an Uploaded File with ColdFusion

```
<!---
 Filename: UploadAction.cfm
 Edited By: Nate Weiss (NMW)
 Purpose:  Demonstrates how to accept a file upload from the browser machine
--->

<!--- Template to process uploaded files from user --->
<html>
<head>
 <title>&lt;cffile&gt; Upload Demonstration - Example 1</title>
</head>

<body>
<h3>&lt;cffile&gt; Upload Demonstration - Example 1</h3>

<!--- Accept the actual file upload --->
<!--- The file will be placed into the same folder as this ColdFusion page --->
<cffile destination="#getDirectoryFromPath(getBaseTemplatePath())#"
 action="upload" nameConflict="overwrite" filefield="fileName">

<!--- Output information about the status of the upload --->
<cfoutput>
 <p>
  &lt;cffile&gt; Tag File Upload Demonstration Results - Example 1<br>
  File Upload was Successful! Information about the file is detailed below
 </p>
 <table border="1">
  <caption><b>File Information</b></caption>
  <tr valign="top">
   <th align="left">File Name:</th>
   <td>#cffile.ServerDirectory#\ #cffile.ServerFile#</td>
   <th align="left">Content Type:</th><td>#cffile.ContentType#</td>
  </tr>
  <tr valign="top">
   <th align="left">Content SubType:</th>
   <td>#cffile.ContentSubType#</td>
   <th align="left">Client Path:</th>
   <td>#cffile.ClientDirectory#</td>
  </tr>
  <tr valign="top">
   <th align="left">Client File:</th>
   <td>#cffile.ClientFile#</td>
   <th align="left">Client FileName:</th>
   <td>#cffile.ClientFileName#</td>
```

Listing 70.8 (CONTINUED)

```
  </tr>
  <tr valign="top">
   <th align="left">Client FileExt:</th>
   <td>#cffile.ClientFileExt#</td>
   <th align="left">Server Path:</th>
   <td>#cffile.ServerDirectory#</td>
  </tr>
  <tr valign="top">
   <th align="left">Server File:</th>
   <td>#cffile.ServerFile#</td>
   <th align="left">Server FileName:</th>
   <td>#cffile.ServerFileName#</td>
  </tr>
  <tr valign="top">
   <th align="left">Server FileExt:</th>
   <td align="left">#cffile.ServerFileExt#</td>
   <th align="left">Attempted ServerFile:</th>
   <td>#cffile.AttemptedServerFile#</td>
  </tr>
  <tr valign="top">
   <th align="left">File Existed?</th>
   <td>#cffile.FileExisted#</td>
   <th align="left">File Was Saved?</th>
   <td>#cffile.FileWasSaved#</td>
  </tr>
  <tr valign="top">
   <th align="left">File Was Overwritten?</th>
   <td>#cffile.FileWasOverWritten#</td>
   <th align="left">File Was Appended?</th>
   <td>#cffile.FileWasAppended#</td>
  </tr>
  <tr valign="top">
   <th align="left">File Was Renamed?</th>
   <td>#cffile.FileWasRenamed#</td>
   <th align="left">File Size:</th>
   <td>#cffile.Filesize#</td></th>
  </tr>
  <tr valign="top">
   <th align="left">Old File Size:</th>
   <td>#cffile.OldFileSize#</td>
   <th align="left">Date Last Accessed:</th>
   <td>#dateFormat(cffile.DateLastAccessed,'dd mmm yyyy')#</td>
  </tr>
  <tr valign="top">
   <th align="left">Date/Time Created:</th>
   <td>
    #dateFormat(cffile.TimeCreated,'dd mmm yyyy')#
    #timeformat(cffile.TimeCreated,'hh:mm:ss')#
   </td>
   <th align="left">Date/Time Modified:</th>
   <td>
    #dateFormat(cffile.TimeLastModified,'dd mmm yyyy')#
    #timeformat(cffile.TimeLastModified,'hh:mm:ss')#
   </td>
  </tr>
```

Listing 70.8 (CONTINUED)

```
</table>
</cfoutput>
</body>
</html>
```

The CFML template shown in Listing 70.8 processes the uploaded file, stores it in the directory indicated in the `<cffile>` tag's `destination` attribute, and then prints out the contents of the keys in the `cffile` structure (Figure 70.4). Some of the `cffile` keys might not have values, depending on the attributes passed to the `<cffile>` tag.

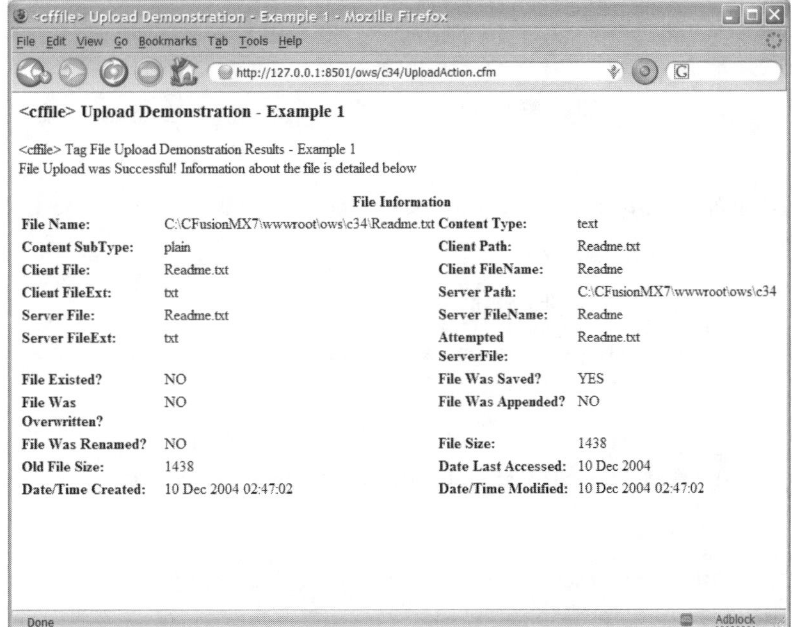

Figure 70.4

Example CFML output of uploaded file information

NOTE

Listing 70.8 uses the `getDirectoryFromPath()` and `getBaseTemplatePath()` functions to set the `destination` attribute to the directory portion of the currently executing template's file name. In other words, the uploaded file will be saved in the same folder that Listing 70.8 itself is stored in (probably the `ows/70` folder within your Web server's document root). This combination of functions can be used anytime. Earlier listings used `expandPath()`, which just goes to show that in ColdFusion, there are many ways to skin a cat.

Listing 70.9 shows an example that builds on the HTML/CFML code you just wrote; it demonstrates the use of variables to set the various attributes of the `<cffile>` tag. The HTML form has been modified by adding a radio button group that corresponds to the `nameConflict` attribute in the `<cffile>` tag (Figure 70.5).

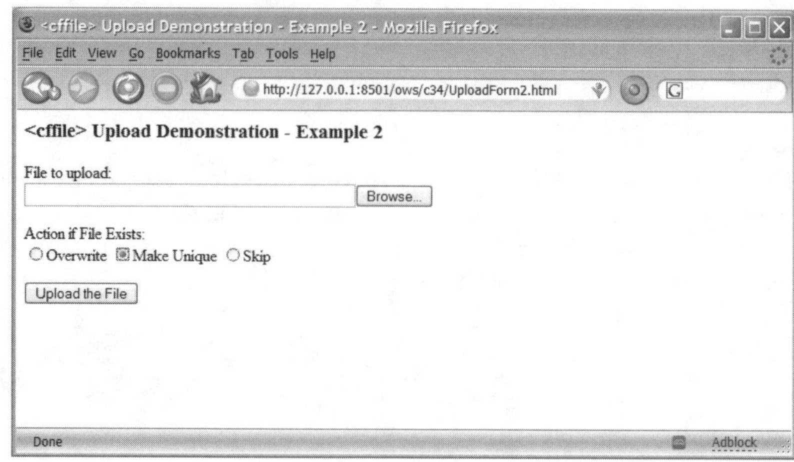

Figure 70.5 Providing further control over file uploads with form fields.

Listing 70.9 `UploadForm2.html`—Modification of HTML to Demonstrate Data-Driven Attribute Setting

```
<!---
 Filename: UploadForm2.html
 Edited By: Nate Weiss (NMW)
 Purpose:  Simple file uploading example
--->

<html>
<head>
 <title>&lt;cffile&gt; Upload Demonstration - Example 2</title>
</head>

<body>
<h3>&lt;cffile&gt; Upload Demonstration - Example 2</h3>

<!--- Create HTML form to upload a file --->
<form action="UploadAction2.cfm" enctype="multipart/form-data" method="post">
 <!--- File field for user to select or specify a filename --->
 <p>File to upload:<br>
 <input type="file" name="fileName" size="50"><br>
 <p>Action if File Exists:<br>
 <input type="radio" name="fileAction" value="overwrite" checked>Overwrite
 <input type="radio" name="fileAction" value="makeUnique">Make Unique
 <input type="radio" name="fileAction" value="skip">Skip
<!--- Submit button to submit the form (and upload the file) --->
 <p>
 <input type="submit" value="Upload the File">
</form>
</body>
</html>
```

NOTE

This book's Web site contains the `UploadAction2.cfm` action page that this form posts its data to. The `UploadAction2.cfm` file is exactly the same as the original version of the action page (Listing 70.8), except that the `nameConflict="Overwrite"` attribute has been replaced with `nameConflict="#FORM.fileAction#"`.

In the Figure 70.5 form screen shot, the Make Unique radio button is checked. With this option selected, if the same file is submitted, the server must create a unique name if the same file is uploaded the second time. The `cffile.FileWasRenamed` variable will reflect this with a value of `Yes` (Figure 70.6). In this case, I uploaded a file from my browser that had a file name of `Readme.txt`. The second time I uploaded it, the Make Unique behavior kicked in and saved the second version of the file with a file name of Readme1.txt.

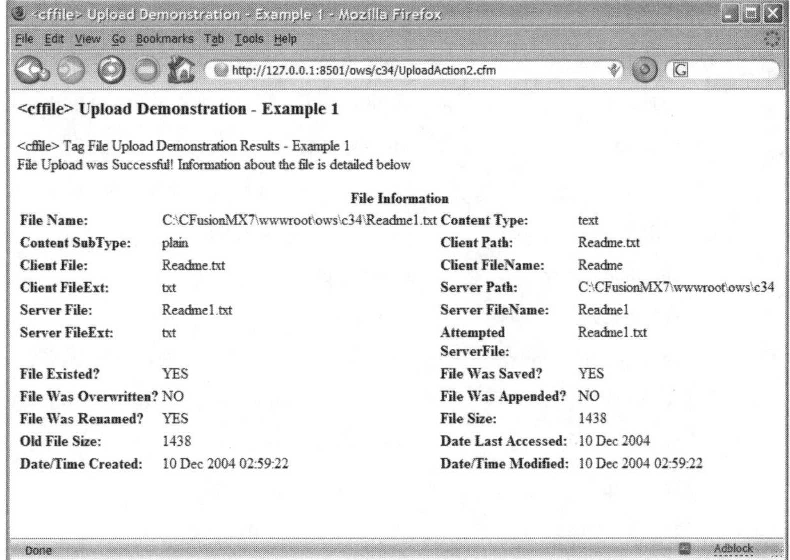

Figure 70.6

Example of output with user-specified `nameConflict` attribute.

The `<cffile>` tag in this example uses data passed from the form in the `FileAction` field to set the value of the `nameConflict` attribute. The field was referenced in the `<cffile>` tag as follows:

```
nameConflict="#FORM.fileAction#"
```

Any of the other attributes can also be set using `cfset` variables, `FORM` attributes, or `URL` attributes. Note, however, that setting the `source` or `destination` attribute based on user input can have far-reaching consequences. For security reasons, users should not be permitted to specify `source` or `destination` attributes using `text` input fields. For maximum security, the `source` and `destination` attributes should be set using only template-based code, which is conditionally executed.

Using File Functions

Although the `<cffile>` tag is useful for many file operations, ColdFusion 8 introduced numerous new file functions. These functions provide all the same actions as the `<cffile>` tag, and also include features brand new to ColdFusion. Table 70.4 lists all file-related functions. (Note that `fileExists()` is not new to ColdFusion 8.)

Table 70.4 File Functions

FUNCTION	PURPOSE
`FileClose`	Closes a file that was opened for reading.
`FileCopy`	Copies a file.
`FileDelete`	Deletes a file.
`FileExists`	Checks to see if a file exists.
`FileIsEOF`	When reading a file, determines whether you are at the end of a file.
`FileMove`	Moves a file.
`FileOpen`	Opens a file and returns a handler to the file.
`FileRead`	Reads a file or a file object.
`FileReadBinary`	Reads a binary file.
`FileReadLine`	Reads one line from a file.
`FileSetAccessMode`	Sets file access attributes for a file on a Unix or Linux system.
`FileSetAttribute`	Sets file attributes for a file on a Windows machine.
`FileSetLastModified`	Sets the last modified attribute for a file.
`FileWrite`	Writes content to a file.
`FileWriteLine`	Writes one line to a file.
`GetFileInfo`	Returns information about a file.

That's quite a few functions. Although most of these functions are pretty simple to understand, a few bring up a new concept in the ColdFusion language: file handlers. What is a file handler and why would we use one? Consider the `<cffile>` tag. When you tell it to read a file, ColdFusion reads the entire file into memory before letting you work with it. If you think of it, using `<cffile>` to read a large file could have a significant impact on your code's performance. What if there was a way to read in a file a bit at a time? The `FileRead` function allows just that. What about reading in a file line by line? Although this has always been possible with the `<cffile>` tag, you had to parse the file into lines yourself. With `FileReadLine`, this task is now considerably simpler. Listing 70.10 shows an example of this.

Listing 70.10 `filefuncs1.cfm`—File-Based Functions

```
<!---
 Filename: filefuncs1.cfm
 Author: Raymond Camden
 Purpose: Demonstrates file functions.
--->

<cfset fileToRead = expandPath("./SimpleFileWrite.cfm")>

<cfset fileOb = fileOpen(fileToRead)>

<cfdump var="#fileOb#">

<cfloop condition="not fileIsEOF(fileOb)">
    <cfset line = fileReadLine(fileOb)>
    <cfoutput>line: #htmlEditFormat(line)#<br /></cfoutput>
</cfloop>

<cfset fileClose(fileOb)>

<cfdump var="#fileOb#">
```

There is a lot going on here. Let's tackle this code line by line. First the code creates a variable, `fileToRead`, that points to one of the earlier file functions. Next the `fileOpen` function is used to open the file. It returns a variable that acts as a pointer or reference to the file. This object acts as a handler to the real file and allows you to perform various operations on it. When you open a file in this way, you have to tell ColdFusion what you will be doing with the file. We did not specify an action on this step so it assumed the default mode: `read`. The other possible values are `readBinary`, `write`, and `append`. The file object is displayed using `<cfdump>`, so you can see what it contains. The output shows various statistics about the file, but the important one is the status field, which you will see is marked as open.

Now for the file reading portion. A conditional loop uses the `fileEOF` function. EOF stands for end of file. The condition basically means "keep running until I notice I'm at the end of the file." Inside the loop, the contents of one line are stored in the line variable and printed to the screen. Next, the file is closed. This is a very important operation. Why? The `fileOpen` function creates a special connection to the physical file. If this connection is left open, the operating system could actually lock the file.

The last line uses `<cfdump>` to display the file object. The only thing of note here is the status value. It will now be labeled as closed to reflect the fact that the file was properly closed.

Getting File Information

Another useful feature added to ColdFusion 8 is the `getFileInfo()` function. In the past, the only way to get information about a file was with the `<cfdirectory>` tag (discussed later in the chapter). Although this tag would let you find out about a file, it was really meant to list multiple files. The `getFileInfo()` function gives you information about one file. Listing 70.11 presents an example of this.

Listing 70.11 `fileinfo.cfm`—Getting File Information

```
<!---
 Filename: fileinfo.cfm
 Author: Raymond Camden
 Purpose: Demonstrates fileInfo.
--->

<cfset info = getFileInfo(expandPath("./filefuncs1.cfm"))>

<table border="1">
    <tr>
        <th>Property</th>
        <th>Value</th>
    </tr>
    <cfloop item="key" collection="#info#">
    <tr>
        <cfoutput>
        <td>#key#</td>
        <td>#info[key]#</td>
        </cfoutput>
    </tr>
    </cfloop>
</table>
```

The first line of the listing shows an example of `getFileInfo()`. The tag takes an absolute path to a file name. The `expandPath()` function is used to determine the absolute path of the file used in Listing 70.10. The `getFileInfo()` function returns a structure of properties about the file, which Listing 70.11 displays in a table. Properties include various permissions (such as `canRead`), `size`, and other useful tidbits.

Reading Files with `<cfloop>`

We started this section talking about new file functions, but we will end it talking about an old tag: `<cfloop>`. ColdFusion 8 gives `<cfloop>` some nice new features, one of which is two different ways to loop over a file. The `<cfloop>` tag now includes a `file` attribute that lets the tag automatically loop over a file line by line, and as with the `fileRead` function, this is done by reading just one line from the file at a time. Another new attribute is `characters`, which lets you specify the number of characters to read from the file as opposed to reading one line at a time. Let's look at an example in Listing 70.12.

Listing 70.12 `cfloopfile.cfm`—Looping over a File

```
<!---
 Filename: cfloopfile.cfm
 Author: Raymond Camden
 Purpose: Demonstrates file functions.
--->

<cfset theFile = expandPath("./filefuncs1.cfm")>

<!--- Loop over by line --->
<cfloop file="#theFile#" index="line">
    <cfoutput>#htmlEditFormat(line)#<br /></cfoutput>
```

Listing 70.12 (CONTINUED)

```
</cfloop>

<p>
<hr/>
</p>

<!--- Loop over by chars --->
<cfloop file="#theFile#" index="block" characters="10">
    <cfoutput>#htmlEditFormat(block)#<br /></cfoutput>
</cfloop>
```

The listing begins by creating a variable that stores the full path to the file used in the previous listing. Next, `<cfloop>` is used to loop over the file. The `file` attribute points to the absolute path of the file to process, and the index value, `line`, will store one line of the file for each iteration of the loop. The next `<cfloop>` block also uses `<cfloop>` with a file, but notice the `characters` attribute. This tells the tag to read in 10 characters from the file at a time.

Manipulating Folders on the Server with `<cfdirectory>`

Just as `<cffile>` can be used to read, write, and manipulate files, `<cfdirectory>` can be used to manage directories on the server's drives. Like `<cffile>`, `<cfdirectory>` takes an `action` attribute that specifies the action to be performed.

Using `<cfdirectory>`

To create a directory, the tag is used like this:

```
<cfdirectory
 action="Create"
 directory="c:\ MyFolders\ MyNewFolder">
```

To delete a directory, just modify the `action`, like this:

```
<cfdirectory
 action="Delete"
 directory="c:\ MyFolders\ MyUnwantedFolder">
```

To rename a directory, use the tag like this:

```
<!--- To rename a directory --->
<cfdirectory
 action="Rename"
 directory="c:\ MyFolders\ MyExistingFolder"
 newdirectory="c:\ MyFolders\ MyNewFolderName">
```

Finally, to get a listing of the contents of a directory (that is, the files and subfolders that the directory contains), use the tag like this:

```
<cfdirectory
 action="List"
 directory="c:\ MyFolders\ MyExistingFolder"
```

```
sort="Name ASC"
filter="*.*"
name="myQueryName">
```

The supported actions for <cfdirectory> are listed formally in Table 70.5, and the tag's attributes are listed in Table 70.6.

Table 70.5 <cfdirectory> Actions

ACTION	DESCRIPTION
`create`	Creates the directory specified in the `directory` attribute.
`delete`	Deletes the directory specified in the `directory` attribute.
`rename`	Renames the directory specified in the `directory` attribute to the name specified in the `newDirectory` attribute.
`list`	Returns the contents of the directory specified in the `directory` attribute into a query named in the `name` attribute. An optional `filter` can be specified as well, as can a sort order and a `recurse` option.

Table 70.6 Additional <cfdirectory> Attributes

ATTRIBUTE	DESCRIPTION
`directory`	Required. Directory on which the action will be taken.
`mode`	Optional. Used in Unix versions of ColdFusion to set directory permissions when `action="Create"`. Ignored on Windows. Standard Unix octal values are accepted.
`newDirectory`	Required for `action="Rename"`. Ignored for all other actions. Specifies new name of directory.
`name`	Required for `action="List"`. Ignored for other actions. Specifies name of output query created by the action.
`filter`	Optional. Used with `action="List"` to filter the files returned in the query. An example is `*.txt`. Only one filter can be applied at a time. It's ignored for all other actions.
`sort`	Optional for `action="List"`. Ignored for other actions. Lists the columns in the query to sort the results with. Specified in a comma-delimited list. Ascending order is the default (`ASC`). Descending order is specified by the use of `DESC`. An example is `"dirname ASC, name DESC, size"`.
`recurse`	Optional for `action="List"`. Ignored for other actions. Lists not only the directory but subdirectories as well. When used, an additional column, directory, is added to the query. Defaults to false.
`listInfo`	Optional for `action="List"`. Ignored for other actions. Has two values: `all` and `name`. The default is `all` and signifies that all regular columns should be returned in the query. If `name` is used, only the name of the file in the directory is returned.
`type`	Optional for `action="List"`. Ignored for other actions. Has three possible values: `file`, `dir`, and `all`. If `file` is specified, only files are returned. If `dir` is specified, only directories are returned. The default value, `all`, means that both files and directories are returned.

Getting the Contents of a Directory

When you use `<cfdirectory>` with `action="List"`, ColdFusion creates a query record set object that contains information about the contents of the directory you specify in the `directory` attribute. The query object is returned to you with the variable name you specify in the `name` attribute. The query object contains one row for every file or subfolder within the directory. Additional rows will be returned if the `recurse` option is set to true. The columns of the query object are listed in Table 70.7. Remember that the `listInfo` attribute can restrict the columns returned to just the name.

So, for instance, if you provide `name="folderContents"` in a `<cfdirectory>` tag, you can refer to `folderContents.Name` to display the name of each file (or subfolder), and `folderContents.Size` to refer to its size on your server's drive.

NOTE

On Unix/Linux servers, there is also a `MODE` column that contains the octal value that specifies the permissions setting for the directory. For information about octal values, see the Unix man pages for the `chmod` shell command.

Table 70.7 Query Columns Populated by `<cfdirectory> action="List"`

COLUMN	DESCRIPTION
`Name`	The name of the file or folder, including the file extension (but not including the full directory path).
`Size`	The size of the file, in bytes.
`Type`	Whether the record represents a file or a folder. If the record represents a file, the value of the `TYPE` column will be File. If it represents a directory, the `TYPE` will be `Dir`.
`DateLastModified`	The date that the file was last modified, as a ColdFusion style date value. You can use this date with `dateFormat()`, `timeFormat()`, or any of the other date-related functions.
`Attributes`	The file's attributes (read-only, archive, and so on).
`Directory`	The file's directory. Only returned when the `recurse` option is used.

Building a Simple File Explorer

Listing 70.13 uses the `action="List"` attribute of `<cfdirectory>` to build a simple Web interface for exploring the files and subfolders within the `ows` folder in your Web server's document root. When you visit this page with your browser, you will see a drop-down list that includes the folders within the `ows` folder (Figure 70.7). When you select a folder from the list, the page reloads and the files in the selected directory appear. From there, you can navigate further to any of the selected folder's subfolders, or return to the previous folder using the Parent Folder option in the drop-down list (Figure 70.8).

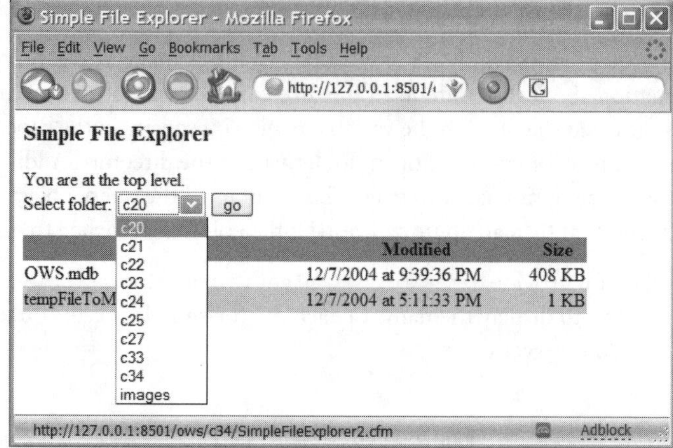

Figure 70.7

The directory listing provided by `<cfdirectory>` is exposed to the user as a drop-down list.

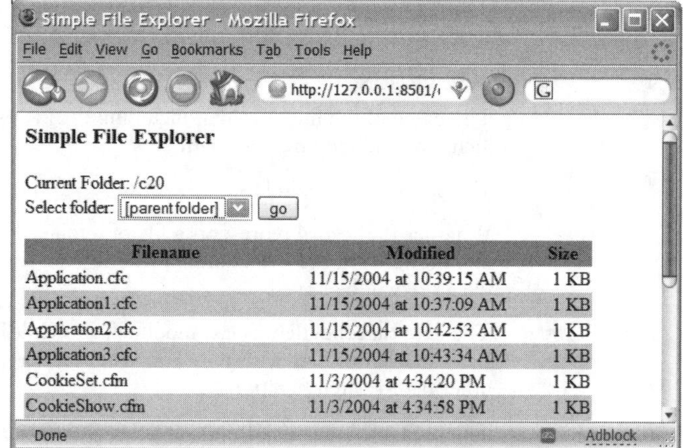

Figure 70.8

Users can view the files in the selected directory, or navigate up and down the folder structure.

NOTE

This example assumes that you are saving the example listings for this book's chapters in the recommended places. That is, the assumption is that there is a folder named `ows` in your server's Web document root, and that the example listings for Chapter 70 are in `ows/70`, the listings for Chapter 71 are in `ows/71`, and so on.

Listing 70.13 `SimpleFileExplorer.cfm`—Listing Files and Folders Within a Directory

```
<!---
 Filename: SimpleFileExplorer.cfm
     Author:  Nate Weiss (NMW)
     Purpose: Provides an interface for exploring files and subfolders
          within the ows root
--->

<!--- The user can explore this folder and any nested subfolders --->
<!--- Assume that the parent of the folder that contains this ColdFusion --->
```

Listing 70.13 (CONTINUED)

```
<!--- page (that is, the "ows" folder) should be considered explorable --->
<cfset baseFolder = expandPath("../")>

<!--- The SubfolderPath variable indicates the currently selected folder --->
<!--- (relative to the BaseFolder). Defaults to an empty string, meaning --->
<!--- that the BaseFolder will be current when the page first appears --->
<cfparam name="subfolderPath" type="string" default="">

<!--- This variable, then, is the full path of the selected folder --->
<cfset folderToDisplay = baseFolder & subfolderPath>

<!--- Get a listing of the selected folder --->
<cfdirectory directory="#folderToDisplay#" name="directoryQuery" sort="Name ASC"
 filter="*">

<cfoutput>
 <html>
  <head><title>Simple File Explorer</title></head>
 <body>
 <h3>Simple File Explorer</h3>

 <!--- Create a simple form for navigating through folders --->
 <form action="SimpleFileExplorer.cfm" method="post">

  <!--- Show the subfolder path, unless already at top level --->
  <cfif subfolderPath EQ "">
   You are at the top level.<br>
  <cfelse>
   Current Folder: #subfolderPath#<br>
  </cfif>

  <!--- Provide a drop-down list of subfolder names --->
  Select folder:
  <select name="subfolderPath" onchange="this.form.submit()">

   <!--- Provide an option to go up one level to the parent folder, --->
   <!--- unless already at the BaseFolder --->
   <cfif listLen(subfolderPath, "/") gt 0>
    <cfset parentFolder = listDeleteAt(subfolderPath, listLen(subfolderPath,
    "/"), "/")>
    <OPTION VALUE="#parentFolder#">[parent folder]</option>
   </cfif>

   <!--- For each record in the query returned by <cfdirectory> --->
   <cfloop query="DirectoryQuery">
    <!--- If the record represents a subfolder, list it as an option --->
    <cfif Type eq "Dir">
     <option value="#subfolderPath#/#Name#">#Name#</option>
    </cfif>
   </cfloop>
  </select>

  <!--- Submit button to navigate to the selected folder --->
  <input type="submit" value="go">
 </form>
```

Listing 70.13 (CONTINUED)

```
<!--- Use Query of Queries (In Memory Query) to get a subset of --->
<!--- the query returned by <cfdirectory>. This new query object --->
<!--- will hold only the file records, not any subfolder records --->
<cfquery dbtype="query" name="filesQuery">
 SELECT * FROM directoryQuery
 WHERE TYPE = 'File'
</cfquery>


<!--- If there is at least one file to display... --->
<cfif filesQuery.recordCount gt 0>
 <!--- Display the files in a simple HTML table --->
 <table width="500" border="0" cellPadding="1" cellSpacing="0">
  <tr bgcolor="cornflowerblue">
   <th>Filename</th>
   <th>Modified</th>
   <th>Size</th>
  </tr>

  <!--- For each file... --->
  <cfloop query="filesQuery">
   <!--- Use alternating colors for the table rows --->
   <cfif filesQuery.currentRow mod 2 eq 0>
    <cfset rowColor = "lightgrey">
   <cfelse>
    <cfset rowColor = "white">
   </cfif>
   <!--- Display the file details --->
   <tr bgcolor="#rowColor#">
    <!--- File name --->
    <td width="250">
     #Name#
    </td>
    <!--- File modification date and time --->
    <td width="200">
     #dateFormat(DateLastModified, "m/d/yyyy")#
     at
     #timeFormat(DateLastModified, "h:mm:ss tt")#
    </td>
    <!--- File size --->
    <td width="50" align="right">
     #ceiling(Size / 1024)# KB
    </td>
   </tr>
  </cfloop>
 </table>
</cfif>
</body>
</html>
</cfoutput>
```

First, the `expandPath()` function is used to create a variable called `baseFolder` that holds the path to the ows folder on your server's drive. The actual value of this variable when your page executes will likely be `c:\ coldfusion8\ wwwroot\ ows`, `c:\ inetpub\ wwwroot\ ows`, or something similar, depending on the Web server you're using. For common sense security reasons, the user will only be able to explore files and directories within the `baseFolder`. If you want the user to be able to explore some other folder, perhaps outside of your server's document root, you can hard-code the `baseFolder` variable with the location of that folder.

Next, the `<cfparam>` tag is used to declare a variable named `subfolderPath` and give it a default value of an empty string. This variable will indicate which subfolder within the `baseFolder` that the user wants to explore. If a URL or FORM parameter called `subfolderPath` is provided to the page, that value will be used; otherwise it's assumed that the page is appearing for the first time. If the user has selected the subfolder named images, then the value of `subfolderPath` will be `/images`.

The `folderToDisplay` variable is then created by concatenating the `baseFolder` together with the `subfolderPath`. This variable, then, holds the full path to the folder the user wants to explore; this is what will be supplied to the `<cfdirectory>` tag to obtain the contents of the folder. So if the user has selected the subfolder named images, the value of `folderToDisplay` will be `c:\ coldfusion8\ wwwroot\ ows\ images`, `c:\ inetpub\ wwwroot\ ows\ images`, or something similar, depending on what ColdFusion edition or Web server you are using.

Now the `<cfdirectory>` tag can be used to get a listing of all the files and subfolders within the selected folder. This will result in a query object called `directoryQuery`, which will contain the columns listed in Table 70.7.

Near the middle of this listing, a `<cfloop>` tag is used to loop over the `directoryQuery` query, generating an `<option>` tag for each subfolder within the current folder (as shown in Figure 70.7). Within the loop, a `<cfif>` test is used to only output options for rows where the `Type` column is set to `Dir`. This step is necessary because the query object may contain rows for subfolders and other rows for individual files. The `<cfif>` test effectively filters the query object so that only rows that represent folders are processed.

Another way to filter a directory query object by type (that is, to only include files or folders) is to use ColdFusion's Query of Queries feature (also called In Memory Query), discussed in Chapter 41, "More About SQL and Queries," online. This strategy is used in the second half of this listing, to create a filtered version of `directoryQuery` (called `filesQuery`) that only contains records for files, not subfolders. Once that's done, outputting the actual information about files is simple. A `<cfloop>` block is used to output the file information in a simple HTML table, displaying the values of each record's `Name`, `Size`, and `DateLastModified` columns. Note that the ordinary `dateFormat()`, `timeFormat()`, and `ceiling()` functions are used to display the data attractively.

Executing Programs on the Server with `<cfexecute>`

In the `<cfexecute>` tag, ColdFusion provides a simple, powerful tool for interacting with the operating system. It enables the execution of server processes at the command-line level.

NOTE

Executing processes on the server can have potentially disastrous consequences, so extreme care should be taken to control access to templates that use the `<cfexecute>` tag. Arbitrary user input of arguments to the tag should be prohibited.

Listing 70.14 shows the basic arguments for the `<cfexecute>` tag.

Listing 70.14 `<cfexecute>` Arguments

```
<cfexecute
 name="Application name"
 arguments="Command line arguments"
 outputFile="Output file name"
 variable="Variable to store result"
 timeout="Timeout interval in seconds">
```

Table 70.8 shows the definitions of the arguments and attributes for the `<cfexecute>` tag.

NOTE

On Windows systems, the `name` argument must contain the fully qualified path to the program to be executed, including the extension (e.g.: `C:\WINNT\SYSTEM32\IPCONFIG.EXE`).

Table 70.8 `<cfexecute>` Tag Syntax

ATTRIBUTE	DESCRIPTION
`name`	Required. The fully qualified name of the application to execute.
`arguments`	Optional. Command-line arguments to be passed to the program.
`outputFile`	Optional. File in which output of program will be written. If you don't provide this attribute or the `variable` attribute, the output of the program will be simply be included in the current ColdFusion page.
`variable`	Optional. Variable name in which output of program will be saved. If you don't provide this attribute or the `outputFile` attribute, the output of the program will be simply be included in the current ColdFusion page.
`timeout`	Optional. Indicates how long in seconds ColdFusion will wait for the process to complete. Values must be integers equal to or greater than 0.

If `arguments` is passed as a string, it is processed in the following ways:

- On Windows systems, the entire string is passed to the Windows process for parsing.
- In Unix, the string is tokenized into an array of arguments. The default token separator is a space; arguments with embedded spaces can be delimited by double quotes.

If `arguments` is passed as an array, it is processed as follows:

- On Windows systems, the array elements are concatenated into a string of tokens, separated by spaces. This string is then passed to the Windows process.
- In Unix, the elements of the `arguments` array are copied into a corresponding array of `exec()` arguments.

If `timeout` , `variable`, and `outputFile` are not provided as attributes to the tag, the resulting output from the executed process is ignored.

The `timeout` attribute is used to determine whether ColdFusion should execute the called process asynchronously (spawn process and continue) or synchronously (spawn process and wait). A value of `0` spawns the process asynchronously, with the ColdFusion execution picking up at the next line of CFML code immediately. Any positive integer value causes the process to be spawned synchronously, with ColdFusion waiting for `timeout` seconds before proceeding.

If errors occur during the process, exceptions are thrown that can be handled with `<cftry>` and `<cfcatch>` (as discussed in Chapter 51). These exceptions are:

- If the application name isn't found, an `Application File Not Found` exception is thrown.
- If the output file can't be opened, an `Output File Can't Be Opened` exception is thrown.
- If ColdFusion doesn't have permission to execute the process, a security exception is thrown.

Listing 70.15 shows an example of using the `<cfexecute>` tag to ping an IP address using the `ping` utility (Figure 70.9). This example was run on a Mac. To run it in Windows, you need to change the `name` attribute to point to the location where `ping.exe` is installed as well as change the `-c` argument to `-n`.

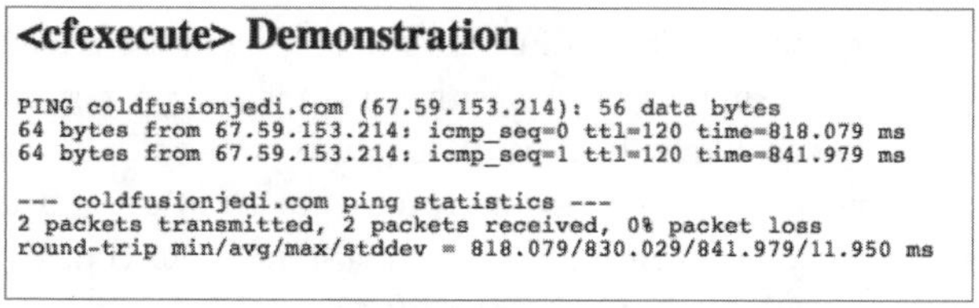

Figure 70.9

Output from the `<cfexecute>` example.

<cfexecute> Demonstration

```
PING coldfusionjedi.com (67.59.153.214): 56 data bytes
64 bytes from 67.59.153.214: icmp_seq=0 ttl=120 time=818.079 ms
64 bytes from 67.59.153.214: icmp_seq=1 ttl=120 time=841.979 ms

--- coldfusionjedi.com ping statistics ---
2 packets transmitted, 2 packets received, 0% packet loss
round-trip min/avg/max/stddev = 818.079/830.029/841.979/11.950 ms
```

Listing 70.15 `Execute.cfm`—`<CFEXECUTE>` Example Showing Output from `PING`

```
<!---
 Filename: Execute.cfm
 Edited By: Raymond Camden
--->

<html>
<head>
  <title>&lt;cfexecute&gt; Demonstration</title>
</head>
<body>

<h2>&lt;cfexecute&gt; Demonstration</h2>

<!--- Call the system utility, with output placed in the file --->
<cfexecute name="ping" arguments="-c 2 coldfusionjedi.com"
 timeout="15" variable="result" />

<!--- Display the contents of the file --->
<cfoutput>
 #htmlCodeFormat(result)#
</cfoutput>

</body>
</html>
```

The code in Listing 70.15 is fairly simple and straightforward. The first thing processed is the `<cfexecute>` tag. In this case, it runs the `PING` utility.

The `arguments` attribute is set to `"-c 2 coldfusionjedi.com"`, which tells the `PING` utility to ping `coldfusionjedi.com` two times. Lastly, the `timeout` attribute is set to 15 seconds, indicating that the process should be spawned in a synchronous fashion. The `variable` attribute tells `<cfexecute>` to store the result in a variable called `result`.

`<cfexecute>` provides a powerful set of functionalities, but its use should be carefully evaluated, because any server process has the potential to affect the stability of the server. There are many potential uses for `cfexecute`, including the capability to

- Submit batch processes to legacy command-line applications
- Use CF to communicate with external processes via the command line

Interacting with the System Registry Using `<cfregistry>`

If you are using a Windows server for ColdFusion, you may be interested in interacting with the registry. ColdFusion provides support for this with the `<cfregistry>` tag. However, working with the registry is almost *never* recommended, so although this book will tell you what the tag can do, no code samples will be provided. You are strongly urged to avoid any and all use of the registry. Not only can misuse bring down an entire machine, it also ties your code to Windows machines only, making moving your code to another server difficult.

ColdFusion's `<cfregistry>` tag allows you to get values, get a set of values, set values, and delete values.

Working with Zip Files

Back in the old days, before cable modems, T1 lines, and other high-speed connections, it sometimes took hours to download files. People began to compress and package files into containers that were typically smaller than the original file. These compressed files used many formats, but the most common format was `.zip`. Multiple files could be both compressed and stored together in one Zip file. Zips are still used today to make moving around or sharing large sets of files easier. Because Zip files can store both files and paths, they are very useful. ColdFusion provides features to make working with Zip files easier. Two tags, `<cfzip>` and `<cfzipparam>`, provide multiple ways of working with Zip files. Table 70.9 lists the actions available to `<cfzip>`.

NOTE

ColdFusion's `<cfzip>` tag works with JAR files as well as Zip files.

Table 70.9 <cfzip> Actions

ACTION	DESCRIPTION
`zip`	Creates a Zip file.
`unzip`	Expands a Zip file.
`list`	Lists the contents of a Zip file.
`read`	Reads a file from a Zip archive.
`readBinary`	Reads a binary file from a Zip archive.
`delete`	Deletes a file (or files) from a Zip archive.

Now that you know what you can do with Zip files, let's build a few examples.

Creating Zip Files

To create a Zip file, you need to begin by selecting what file or files will be zipped. Once you've decided what will be zipped, it is relatively easy to create the Zip file using `<cfzip>`. Table 70.10 lists the attributes specifically used when creating Zip files.

Table 70.10 <cfzip> Tag Attributes Used in Creating Zip Files

ATTRIBUTE	DESCRIPTION
`action`	Will be `zip` when creating Zip files.
`file`	Full path specification of the location where the Zip file will be created.
`filter`	Optionally filters the files added to a Zip file. For instance, this attribute could be used to add only the CFM files in a directory to a Zip file.
`overwrite`	If `overwrite` is set to true, then the operation will completely overwrite a Zip file if it already exists. If `overwrite` is set to false, the files will be added to the existing Zip file.
`prefix`	When adding files, `prefix` represents the subdirectory in which files are added to the Zip file.
`recurse`	Specifies whether ColdFusion should recursively add subdirectories and files to a Zip file. The default is true.
`source`	Source directory for the Zip operation. This attribute isn't required if the `<cfzipparam>` tag is used.
`storePath`	Specifies whether the path of the files added to a Zip file should be included in the Zip file. The default is yes. This attribute is useful for ensuring that extracted Zip files maintain the same folder structure as the original source.

Listing 70.16 is a simple example that creates a Zip file.

Listing 70.16 zip.cfm—<cfzip>Example

```
<!---
 Filename: zip.cfm
 Edited By: Raymond Camden
--->

<cfset zipFile = expandPath("./cfms.zip")>
<cfset source = expandPath(".")>

<cfzip file="#zipFile#" action="zip" source="#source#" filter="*.cfm">
```

The listing begins by creating two variables. The first variable, `zipFile`, is the full path and name of the Zip file that will be created. The second variable, `source`, is the folder that will be zipped. Last, the `<cfzip>` tag creates a Zip file based on the source variable. Notice that the filter specifies that only CFM files are included. When this listing is executed, the Zip file, `cfms.zip`, is created and will contain all the CFM files made earlier in this chapter.

Expanding Zip Files

We've created a Zip file; now let's see how easy it is to expand or extract Zip files. Table 70.11 lists the attributes used when expanding a Zip file.

Table 70.11 `<cfzip>` Tag Attributes Used in Expanding Zip Files

ATTRIBUTE	DESCRIPTION
`action`	Will be unzip when expanding Zip files.
`destination`	Full path specification to the location where the Zip file will be expanded.
`file`	Full path and file name of the Zip file to be expanded.
`filter`	An optional filter to restrict the files expanded from the Zip file.
`overwrite`	If true, files in the Zip file will overwrite files on the file system. If false, files will not be overwritten and will be skipped instead. The default value is false.
`recurse`	When unzipping, specifies whether subdirectories in the Zip file should also be extracted. The default is true.
`storePath`	Specifies whether directories in the Zip file should be re-created when they are extracted. The default value is true.

Listing 70.17 extracts files from a Zip file.

Listing 70.17 unzip.cfm—<cfzip>Unzip Example

```
<!---
 Filename: unzip.cfm
 Edited By: Raymond Camden
--->

<cfset zipFile = expandPath("./cfms.zip")>
<cfset destination = expandPath("./extract")>
```

Listing 70.17 (continued)

```
<cfif not directoryExists(destination)>
   <cfdirectory action="create" directory="#destination#">
</cfif>

<cfzip file="#zipFile#" action="unzip" destination="#destination#">
```

This listing is much like the previous one. We begin by creating a variable that points to the Zip file created in the earlier listing. Next, a variable is created for a subdirectory named `extract`. If this directory does not exist, it is created. Last, the `<cfzip>` tag is used to extract the Zip file into the destination folder.

Listing, Reading, and Deleting from Zip Files

What if you don't want to extract a Zip file, but simply want to see what is inside? The `<cfzip>` tag provides a list operation that displays all the entries in the file. Listing 70.18 shows an example.

Listing 70.18 `ziplist.cfm`—`<cfzip>List` Example

```
<!---
 Filename: ziplist.cfm
 Edited By: Raymond Camden
--->

<cfset zipFile = expandPath("./cfms.zip")>

<cfzip file="#zipFile#" action="list" name="files">

<cfdump var="#files#">
```

Once again, a variable is created to point to the Zip file created earlier. Next, the `list` action is used with `<cfzip>` to expand the Zip file into a query. Last, the query is dumped. Table 70.12 lists the columns created when a Zip file is expanded.

Table 70.12 `<cfzip>` Query Columns

COLUMN	DESCRIPTION
`comment`	A comment used when the Zip file was created.
`compressedSize`	The size of the file in the Zip archive.
`crc`	Checksum of the file.
`dateLastModified`	The last modified date of the file.
`directory`	Directory of the files in the Zip file. Remember that Zip files can represent multiple subdirectories.
`name`	Name of the file. This may also include a path based on the directory value.
`size`	The uncompressed size of the file.
`type`	The type of the entry.

Along with listing the contents of a Zip file, you can read individual files from a Zip file—useful for grabbing just a portion of a Zip file. The `<cfzip>` tag provides `read` and `readBinary` actions. The `read` action reads any simple file (such as a CFM or TXT file), and `readBinary` handles binary files (such as GIF and PDF). Listing 70.19 is an example that reads an individual file from a Zip file.

Listing 70.19 `zipread.cfm—<cfzip>Read` Example

```
<!---
 Filename: zipread.cfm
 Edited By: Raymond Camden
--->

<cfset zipFile = expandPath("./cfms.zip")>

<cfzip file="#zipFile#" action="read" entrypath="Execute.cfm"
       variable="data">

<cfoutput>#htmlCodeFormat(data)#</cfoutput>
```

As with the earlier listings, we begin by creating a variable to point to the Zip file. Next, the `<cfzip>` tag with `action="read"` is used. The `read` action requires an entry path. Remember that the entry path is both a file name and an optional folder name. In our example, we use `Execute.cfm`, which is at the root of the Zip file. Lastly, the `variable` attribute tells the tag where to store the contents of the file. Then the code is output using `htmlCodeFormat`.

Now that we've read a file from the Zip file, let's remove a file. Listing 70.20 demonstrates how to do this.

Listing 70.20 `zipdelete.cfm—<cfzip>Delete` Example

```
<!---
 Filename: zipdelete.cfm
 Edited By: Raymond Camden
--->

<cfset zipFile = expandPath("./cfms.zip")>

<cfzip file="#zipFile#" action="list" name="files">

<cfdump var="#files#" label="Before Delete">

<cfzip file="#zipFile#" action="delete" entrypath="Execute.cfm">

<cfzip file="#zipFile#" action="list" name="files">

<cfdump var="#files#" label="After Delete">
```

This listing begins like every other `<cfzip>` example: by creating a variable to point to `cfms.zip`. Next, the entries are listed out using the `list` action. The critical line is the `delete` action. Note again the use of `entrypath`. Last, the Zip file is listed again and dumped. If you view the result of this dump in your browser, you will see that the number of files decreases by one after the delete operation. Note that the `filter` attribute also works on delete operations, because the `entrypath` value can point to a folder. This would remove all files that match that folder, but the use of the `filter` attribute allows you to delete only certain types of files in a folder.

Working with `<cfzipparam>`

So far, our examples using Zip files have worked with one file or folder. The `<cfzipparam>` tag allows you to specify multiple files or directories when using `<cfzip>`. This tag can be used to add, delete, and extract resources to a Zip file. It also allows you to do something you can't do in the `<cfzip>` tag itself: add data from a ColdFusion variable, not a physical file. Table 70.13 lists the attributes of the `<cfzipparam>` tag.

Table 70.13 `<cfzipparam>` Attributes

ATTRIBUTE	DESCRIPTION
`charset`	Used to parse a string into binary data when performing a Zip operation and using the `content` attribute.
`content`	Data to store in the Zip file. You must use `entryPath` to specify the folder and file name for this content.
`entryPath`	Used to specify the folder and file of the content added to a Zip file.
`filter`	Allows an optional filter to applied to the action being performed on the Zip file.
`prefix`	String prepended to the Zip file.
`recurse`	Determines whether the current action is recursive.
`source`	Source file or folder used for Zip operations. If a source attribute is specified in the `<cfzip>` tag, then this source is relative.

Listing 70.21 shows one example of `<cfzipparam>`.

Listing 70.21 `zipparam.cfm—<cfzipparam>` Example

```
<!---
 Filename: zipparam.cfm
 Edited By: Raymond Camden
--->

<cfset zipFile = expandPath("./zp.zip")>

<cfzip file="#zipFile#" action="zip">
    <cfzipparam content="#repeatString('Simple Text',999)#"
                entrypath="simple.txt">
    <cfzipparam source="#expandPath('./unzip.cfm')#"
                entrypath="/sub/unzipfile.cfm">
</cfzip>

<cfzip file="#zipFile#" action="list" name="files">

<cfdump var="#files#">
```

We begin by creating a variable that represents the full path to a Zip file, this time named `zp.zip`. Next up is a `<cfzip>` tag. Notice that while `file` and `action` attributes are specified, no source is defined. The source will come from the two `<cfzipparam>` tags inside. The first creates a string using the `repeatString` function. This is used as the source for a file named `simple.txt` that is to be added to the Zip file. The next `<cfzipparam>` tag specifies a specific file. Notice though that when added to the Zip file, the file is renamed and added as a child of a subdirectory named `sub`. Both tags demonstrate that the contents of a Zip file need not have any relation to real files on your file system.

CHAPTER 71

Server-Side Printing

IN THIS CHAPTER

Imagine needing to print a document from ColdFusion to a printer attached to the server, whether attached directly to the server or accessible to it through the network. The document could be one created based on user input, such as a stock pick request to be printed in a warehouse when an order is placed, or an invoice printed in the Accounts Receivable department. Or it could be a frequently run report or nightly batch job. The problem is that the PDF file created or accessed by ColdFusion needs to be printed by the server, and preferably automatically and without human intervention.

ColdFusion 8 solves this problem of server-side printing simply and elegantly with the new `<CFPRINT>` tag and its related features.

In this chapter, we'll look at how `<CFPRINT>` enables the printing of PDF documents from ColdFusion. These can be static files or PDFs created using ColdFusion tags such as `<CFDOCUMENT>` and `<CFPDF>`. We'll also review related features such as the `getPrinterInfo()` function and the ColdFusion Administrator's System Information page, which allow us to retrieve information about available printers and their capabilities for use in `<CFPRINT>`, using `cfprint.log` and using `<CFTHREAD>`.

Overview

There are many ways to create PDF files in ColdFusion, whether in the latest release or in previous ones.

ColdFusion 8 makes it very easy to manipulate PDF documents using tags such as `<CFPDF>` and `<CFPDFFORM>`. You can even create interactive PDF forms with a combination of `<CFFORM>` and `<CFDOCUMENT>` or by way of Document Description XML (DDX) used by Adobe LiveCycle Assembler or the `<CFPDF>` tag.

ColdFusion 7 also introduced various means of creating PDFs, which you can continue to use in ColdFusion 8, including building them dynamically from CFML using `<CFDOCUMENT>` and with ColdFusion Report Builder and `<CFREPORT>`.

Further, developers have long found third-party solutions to help build PDFs. Also, static PDF files may exist or be created on the server by other means. They can be created by other processes on the server, or be placed on the server by some other operation, or even be uploaded to the server by end users.

Whatever the situation, a common requirement is the capability to print the document on a printer attached to the server, and `<CFPRINT>` makes this possible.

`<CFPRINT>` allows a developer to control the number of pages printed, the size of paper used for printing, whether to print in color, and more. In fact, you can control any printing options that a given printer supports, including stapling, multiple pages per side, rotation, orientation, scaling, and print quality. You can also provide a password for encrypted pages. And with the power of the new `<CFTHREAD>` tag, you can even spool a print task to be processed asynchronously so that the CFML page launching the print job need not wait for its completion and risk timing out.

Here are just a few possible scenarios that can make use of server-side printing:

- Generate order sheets when online orders are placed.
- Generate invoices, packing slips, testing documents, and legal documents.
- Manage electronic medical records and insurance claims and generate such documents on demand or as nightly reports.

One user described another scenario: Imagine a college (or similar institution) offering a means for its applicants to file online the necessary forms, references, cover letters, and so on; then all that information is printed for review when applications are considered.

Though the printer must be defined on or be accessible to the server running ColdFusion, it doesn't necessarily have to be physically attached to it. It could be connected via the network, including a WAN. This means it could enable:

- Printing to a remote printer in another location that is connected to the server network via IP address, such as a remote warehouse
- Printing to a broadcast printer, which in turn prints at several different workstation printers

Again, because we're talking about printing to a server-side printer and not an end-user's printer, this doesn't involve integration with the browser, which eliminates some common challenges. The simplicity of `<CFPRINT>` will be a welcome alternative to those who have previously created a concoction of steps such as use of `<CFEXECUTE>` and of batch files to open Acrobat Reader to effect PDF printing.

Using <CFPRINT>

The simplest form of syntax for `<CFPRINT>` is as follows:

```
<cfprint source="somefile.pdf">
```

The `source` attribute points to a file, and unlike other `<CFFILE>` actions, the `source` attribute can name either a relative or absolute path. A relative path would be relative to the page issuing the tag. The `source` attribute could also point to a variable holding the result of some previous ColdFusion tag that created, read in, or manipulated a PDF.

Printing to the Default Printer

The simplest form of `<CFPRINT>` sends the named file (or a variable value, if used) to the default printer—that is, the default printer for the operating system account running ColdFusion. How do you find out what that default printer is and how to refer to it? There are at least two ways.

First, the ColdFusion Administrator page, System Information, has a section called Printer Details that lists the default printer along with the names of all available printers. Also, the new function `getPrinterInfo()`can be called with the name of one of those printers as its argument, or it can be called with no argument, in which case it returns information about the default printer. In either case, the structure it returns contains several keys, one of which is the `printer` key, which displays the name of the selected printer.

Therefore, the following line of code can be used to quickly and easily show what the system reports to be the default printer, if any:

```
<cfdump var="#getprinterinfo().printer#">
```

The features for obtaining additional information about printers will be discussed further throughout this chapter.

Printing to Another Printer

Although the simple example just presented printed to the default printer, you can print just as easily to another printer if you know its name. You learned in the last section that the ColdFusion Administrator offers a way to see the names of available printers. If you have a printer on your server called HP LaserJet 2200 Series PCL 6, you can print the same document to it using this code:

```
<cfprint source="somefile.pdf" printer="HP LaserJet 2200 Series PCL 6">
```

If instead you want to print to an available network printer named NTN-2W-HP_BW02 as found on server s1001prn02, you can print to it by forming a UNC path for the server and printer, as follows:

```
<cfprint source="somefile.pdf" printer="\\s1001prn02\NTN-2W-HP_BW02">
```

NOTE

Printer names must be specified exactly as they are listed in ColdFusion Administrator.

Controlling Printer Capabilities

The examples just shown are indeed the simplest versions of the `<CFPRINT>` tag, but most printers offer a wide range of capabilities to more precisely control the appearance of the printed page.

Some of these capabilities are generic (number of copies to print, pages to print, and so on), and others are printer specific. This section introduces these kinds of printer control capabilities.

Primary <CFPRINT> Attributes

Table 71.1 presents the attributes of `<CFPRINT>` that apply to all printers.

Table 71.1 Attributes of the `<CFPRINT>` Tag

ATTRIBUTE	DESCRIPTION
`source`	Absolute or relative pathname to a PDF file or a PDF document variable
`attributeStruct`	ColdFusion structure that contains attribute key-value pairs
`color`	`yes` or `no` (defaults to `no`)
`copies`	Number of copies (defaults to `1`)
`fidelity`	`yes` or `no` (defaults to `no`)
`pages`	Page or pages to print (defaults to `all`)
`paper`	Options are `letter`, `legal`, `A4`, `A5`, `B4`, `B5`, `B4-JIS`, `B5-JIS`, and any media supported by the printer
`password`	PDF source file owner or user password
`printer`	String that specifies the printer name
`type`	`PDF`

Even though most of these options are generic and obvious, there are still some aspects of printer-specific behavior to notice. For instance, the default settings for some of the attributes listed in Table 71.1 may be printer dependent, and if you may try (mistakenly) to use attributes or values that are inappropriate, the available `fidelity` attribute can assist in protecting against such mistakes, as discussed in the next section.

Printer-Dependent Attributes

Your printer may support many more attributes than those listed in Table 71.1: options to control two-sided printing, stapling, reversal of the page order, and much more. These special attributes can be discovered using the `getPrinterInfo()` function.

Note, though, that you can't use these printer-dependent attributes on the `<CFPRINT>` tag. Instead, you must specify them by way of the `attributeStruct` attribute (and only by way of this attribute), as will be discussed later.

Example: Determining One Printer's Available Attributes

The following code dumps to the screen a structure that includes the attributes available for your default printer:

```
<cfdump var="#getprinterinfo()#">
```

Figure 71.1 shows some of the results on a system with a Brother MFC-8640D printer as the default.

Figure 71.1

Printer information available via <cfdump>.

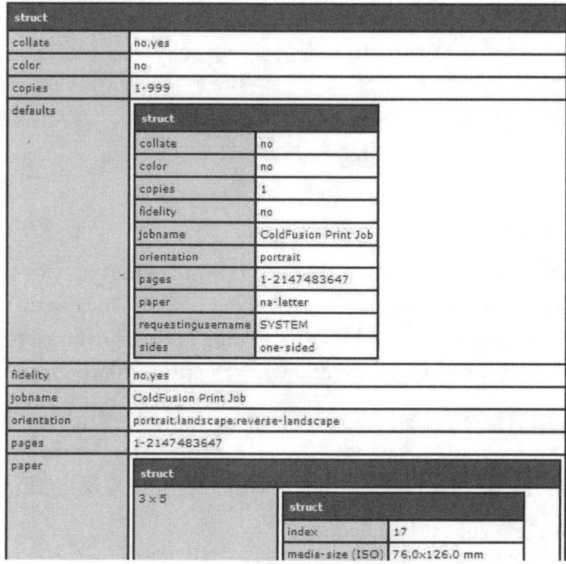

struct	
collate	no,yes
color	no
copies	1-999
defaults.collate	no
defaults.color	no
defaults.copies	1
defaults.fidelity	no
defaults.jobname	ColdFusion Print Job
defaults.orientation	portrait
defaults.pages	1-2147483647
defaults.paper	na-letter
defaults.requestingusername	SYSTEM
defaults.sides	one-sided
fidelity	no,yes
jobname	ColdFusion Print Job
orientation	portrait,landscape,reverse-landscape
pages	1-2147483647
paper.3 x 5.index	17
paper.3 x 5.media-size (ISO)	76.0x126.0 mm

In this example, we can see that the printer supports such additional attributes as `collate`, `jobname`, and `orientation`. The ColdFusion documentation (CFML Reference) for `<CFPRINT>` explains the purpose of many of these other attributes and their values.

Note that the some of the results of `getprinterinfo()`show different values even for attributes listed in Table 71.1 (such as for `paper`, which shows that the printer supports a `3x5` value, which was not listed previously).

We can also see in the dump a `defaults` structure nested within the result, and it shows defaults for both those attributes in Table 71.1 and the additional attributes unique to this printer.

Passing Printer-Dependent Attributes with `AttributeStruct`

Now that we have the available attributes for the capabilities of this printer, we can pass them to the `<CFPRINT>` tag, but we can't simply list them as attributes of the tag, as we can those in Table 71.1. Instead, these nonstandard attributes must be passed in using the special `attributeStruct` attribute. The following example will help demonstrate this concept.

If you want to print the first 16 pages of a document as two-sided on your printer, you can use the following:

```
<cfset aSet={sides="two-sided-long-edge",pages="1-16"}>
<cfprint source="somebook.pdf" attributeStruct="#aSet#">
```

Notice that we're creating a structure, called `aSet` (using the new feature in ColdFusion 8 to create structures implicitly rather than with `StructNew`). In it, we're placing two keys: the attributes `sides` and `pages` set to the desired values.

NOTE

Don't confuse this with another new feature in ColdFusion 8: `attributeCollection`. That's a separate feature for passing attributes to virtually any tag using a similar approach. Astute readers may notice that (unlike with `attributeCollection`) we can specify attributes for both `<CFPRINT>` and `attributeStruct`, in which case the attributes for the tag override those in the structure.

The `fidelity` Attribute

ColdFusion provides the flexibility to create and use attributes that may or may not be supported by a given printer, but this flexibility can also require management. Among the attributes listed in Table 71.1 is one whose purpose may not be self-evident: `fidelity`. This attribute indicates whether the attribute values specified must match exactly what the printer supports.

For instance, although `B4` is listed as a value for `paper` in Table 71.1, it's not listed as a valid value in the output the dump of the sample printer's supported `paper` values shown in Figure 71.1. If you specify `fidelity="yes"`, the print attempt will fail with a traditional ColdFusion error:

```
Error Occurred While Processing Request
Invalid media or paper for the cfprint tag.
Error: Media iso-b4 is not valid on Brother MFC-8640D Printer. Available media are
iso-a4,na-letter,na-legal,executive,iso-a5,iso-a6,iso-b5,iso-b6,na-number-10-
envelope,iso-designated-long,iso-c5,monarch-envelope,Organizer J,Organizer
K,invoice,A4 Long,3 x 5,folio,User Defined,iso-a3,tabloid,jis-b4,Automatic-
Feeder,top,MP Tray,manual
```

If you specify `fidelity="no"`, however, the printer will make a reasonable attempt to print the job using the provided settings. The `fidelity` attribute is optional and defaults to `no`.

Java Print Services and Attributes

Besides being dependent on the printer, the particular printer attributes supported also depend on the operating system and network printer server, if there is one, as well as Java Print Service (JPS), on which the `<CFPRINT>` tag is based. Many printers support attributes that are not accessible from JPS. For example, according to the ColdFusion documentation, "the JPS for a Macintosh OS X running JDK 1.5 supports the fewest printer attributes. Upgrading to JDK 1.6 adds some functionality, but finishing attributes are still not supported."

Additional <CFPRINT> Attributes

In addition to the list of tag attributes in Table 71.1 and any printer-specific attributes obtained via the `getprinterinfo()` function, a subset of the attributes for `<CFPRINT>` listed in the CFML Reference work even when `fidelity="yes"`, though they're not listed in the `getprinterinfo()` result. These include: `autoRotateAndCenter`, `pageScaling`, `reversePages`, and `usePDFPageSize`. See the CFML Reference for more details on the uses and values for these attributes.

Determining Available Printers

The section "Printing to the Default Printer" discussed how to determine and print to the default printer for your system, and the section "Printing to Another Printer" showed you how to print to another printer, whether on the computer running ColdFusion or on another server on your network. How do you determine what other printers are available?

Determining Available Printers

Of course, you can use your operating system–provided mechanisms to list available printers. If your application server runs on Windows, for instance, you can generally use Start > Printers and Faxes.

But you can also obtain the list of printers from the ColdFusion Administrator's System Information page, accessed by clicking the blue *i* icon at the top right of the Administrator screen, as shown in Figure 71.2. This figure also shows the portion of the report it displays, with the printers defined on this server listed at the bottom.

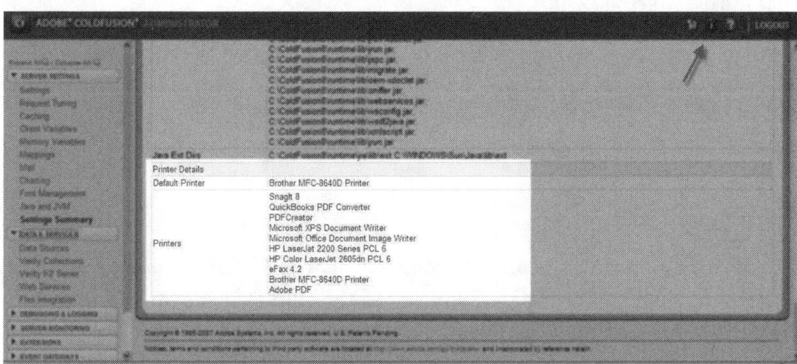

Figure 71.2

Available printers shown on the ColdFusion Administrator System Information page.

Note that this list shows only the printers' names, not their capabilities. For that, you must pass the printer name to the `getPrinterInfo()` function, like this:

```
<cfdump var="#getprinterinfo("HP LaserJet 2200 Series PCL 6")#">
```

This will result in a dump of a structure as shown in Figure 71.1.

TIP

You can also obtain the list of available printers programmatically. ColdFusion 8 does not (currently) provide a built-in function for this purpose, but Ben Forta has written a nifty custom tag that can provide the information. It relies on an undocumented `coldfusion.print.PrinterInfo` class in Java. As long as you've not disabled such internal Java objects (also a new option in ColdFusion 8), you can use this custom tag, which you can obtain at `http://www.cflib.org/udf.cfm?id=1782`.

What About Other Printers?

If you want to print to a printer that's not listed on the System Information page, you must add the printer using your operating system mechanism for adding printers. ColdFusion offers no means to do this independently.

As mentioned previously, however, if the printer is available on another printer on your network, you can print to that printer by forming a UNC path to name the server and printer, as shown in the section "Printing to Another Printer" earlier in this chapter.

Printer Permissions

Because ColdFusion relies on the operating system to control the available printers, it is also subject to security permissions that may be defined for the printers. Even if a printer is configured locally on the system, the printer will not be available if the account under which ColdFusion is running does not have the proper permissions.

By default, ColdFusion installs and runs as the Local System account (or "nobody" on Linux and Unix), which may not have printer access rights. For information on running ColdFusion as a specific user, see the following tech note: `http://www.adobe.com/cfusion/knowledgebase/index.cfm?id=tn_17279`.

Related Features

Before concluding coverage of `<CFPRINT>`, there are a few additional topics worth noting.

Print Log

Whenever you print a document using `<CFPRINT>`, ColdFusion logs the action (and some types of failures) to a `print.log` file that appears in the standard `<coldfusion>/logs` directory. You can also view the logs using the ColdFusion Administrator, on the Log Files page, in the Debugging and Logging section. For each printed file, two lines will be created, tracking the date, time, application name, and thread ID as well as details such as the following:

```
"Print job 'somebook.pdf' started.  Printer 'Brother MFC-8640D Printer'."
"Print job 'somebook.pdf' was sent to printer.  Printer: 'Brother MFC-8640D
Printer'.  Total pages: 2."
```

This log information can be very helpful when you're trying to diagnose printing problems or confirm successful printing.

Using <CFTHREAD>

Because the process of sending a print job to a printer (or more typically, to your operating system's print spooling service) may take some time, you can configure your code so that you don't need to wait for the completion of that process of sending the job to the printer. This is a great use for the new ColdFusion 8 tag <CFTHREAD>.

You can run a print job asynchronously (meaning without waiting for completion of its transmission to the printer or spool) by enclosing the <CFPRINT> tag within a <CFTHREAD> tag block, as the following example shows:

```
<cfthread name="print">
   <cfprint source="somefile.pdf" printer="\\s1001prn02\NTN-2W-HP_BW02">
</cfthread>
```

➜ See Chapter 30, "Managing Threads," in *Adobe ColdFusion 8 Web Application Construction Kit, Volume 2: Application Development*, for more details on <CFTHREAD>.

Printing Other than PDFs

As has been made clear from the beginning of this chapter, the <CFPRINT> tag can be used only to print PDF files. That may seem a severe limitation, and you may rightfully say, "What if I have some HTML or other content that I want to print?"

Remember that ColdFusion 7 introduced the <CFDOCUMENT> tag, which enables you to create a PDF file from HTML that you dynamically create using CFML.

And even if you don't have an existing PDF file that you need to print, recall that various tags in ColdFusion can create PDF files that you may want to print, including the results of ColdFusion Report Builder (with <CFREPORT>), <CFPDF>, <CFPDFFORM>, and more. See Chapter 32, "Working with PDF Files," in Vol. 2, *Application Development*, for more information.

CHAPTER 72

Interacting with Directory Services

IN THIS CHAPTER

One of the ongoing organizational tasks of any corporation is the structuring and maintenance of user and company information. This alone is a daunting process, and despite all the recent advances in collaboration technology, there still does not exist one single, standardized method that all corporations use to store this information.

For example, company A acquires company B and needs to combine information for users, departments, and other organizational entities. If each company is using a different method to store directory information, you can easily see the problem this creates. This type of disparity in corporate directory data was one of the underlying reasons, among others, for the creation of the Lightweight Directory Access Protocol (LDAP).

Understanding LDAP

LDAP (also referred to as LDAPv3) is a standard proposed by the Internet Engineering Task Force (IETF) that helps tie together directory structures from several of its predecessors, such as X.500 (DAP), into a more easily understood and interchangeable format. And although LDAP is still referred to as a proposed standard, the core features used for most development tasks have been, for the most part, unchanged over the past several years.

NOTE

Currently, LDAP is in its third version (RFCs 4511–4519), but many new enhancements are currently being proposed and debated by the IETF. To see frontline information regarding this process, visit the IETF Web site at `http://www.ietf.org/`.

The fact that large corporations such as Microsoft, Netscape, Sun, Oracle, and Novell now support LDAP is a compelling reason to begin learning it. In addition, many operating systems now work natively with LDAP, making it an important technology right now.

Directory Structures

To store information in an organized fashion, LDAP uses something called a Directory Information Tree (DIT). This tree is essentially a hierarchical map composed of entries and their corresponding attributes and values. An entry might be a department, division, or single user, and like any tree, LDAP starts at a single point (the root) and expands out into other branches or points until the end of the tree is reached. This type of structure allows LDAP to refer to entries in a unique manner, both quickly and efficiently. Directory trees can often be large and complex. Having a rough idea how this data is organized and accessed will give you a better chance of finding what you're looking for.

To perform a search, you can begin at any point within the directory tree, such as the root or at the department level. Each entry within the directory is called a Distinguished Name (DN), which is used to uniquely refer to that entry. To draw a parallel with RDBMS work, a DN is much like a primary key for an LDAP entry. A DN can be a single point within a directory, or it can represent a sequence of entries leading to a specific point in a directory.

Building a DN is one of the aspects of LDAP that confuses first-time users. Because of this, let's consider a parallel concept in JavaScript that shows how objects are accessed in JavaScript's Document Object Model (DOM). Follow the next example:

```
<script language="JavaScript">
 var objReference = document.forms[0].elements[0].value;
</script>
```

Even if your JavaScript skills aren't up to par, you can still follow that this example starts at the `document` level and drills down until it reaches a value within a form element. Along each step in the DOM, the parent object is kept as part of the object reference. This value is passed to the `objReference` variable, which can then be used later in the script.

This same type of "drill-down" process is used for LDAP as well, starting at the top and working down to the value you want to reference. At each step toward this value, you have to concatenate each branch's name and value pair, along with its parent branch's name and value pair, each separated by a comma. The following example shows what one DN might look like:

```
cn=Jeff Tapper, l=Astoria NY, ou=Development, o=Tapper Nimer and Associates Inc,
country=US
```

One key difference between JavaScript references and those in LDAP is the order in which items are listed. Notice in the example above that the most specific references appear first, and the references go up a level as you traverse farther to the right. In other words, the topmost branch is on the far right side of the DN, whereas the lowest—your destination within the tree—is on the left side of the DN.

Each branch has a name and value pair, such as `country=US`, and between each branch, you use a comma as a separator. The branch names in this example are merely samples; the next section explains real names and their meanings.

The completed DN now acts as a guide to the point in the directory tree that is required for your operation. Keep in mind that each entry within the example is a DN in and of itself, and when put together, these DNs can be thought of as a *DN sequence*.

Name Conventions

To access each DN within a directory tree, you need to use that DN's attribute name. Although potentially hundreds of attribute names may exist, the LDAP definition requires that all implementations provide the same basic set of entries. And depending on the LDAP software you're using, you may encounter inconsistencies from one implementation to the next. Most vendors, however, support the most basic and common directory schema. Table 72.1 shows the commonly used DN attributes and their corresponding meanings.

Table 72.1 DN Attribute Names and Meanings

ATTRIBUTE	MEANING
`c`	Country. A two-letter ISO 3166 country code, such as `US` or `GB`.
`l`	Locality. The name of a locality, such as a city, county, or other geographic region.
`st`	State. The full name of a state or province.
`street`	The physical address of the object to which the entry corresponds, such as an address for package delivery.
`o`	Organization. The name of an organization, such as a company name.
`ou`	Organizational unit. The name of an organizational unit, such as a department.
`title`	The title, such as Vice President, of a person in the organizational context.
`cn`	Common Name. This is the X.500 `commonName` attribute, which contains a name of an object. If the object corresponds to a person, it is typically the person's full name.
`sn`	Surname. This generally represents the family name, or last name, of a person.
`givenName`	This holds the part of a person's name that is neither the surname nor middle name. It is usually the person's first name.
`mail`	This represents the email address for the entry. Some LDAP servers use the `email` attribute instead.

Using `<cfldap>`

The capability to query LDAP servers is useful for ColdFusion developers. Many organizations use LDAP in one fashion or another as a companywide data repository. Exchange Server and ADSI (Active Directory Service Interface) are two examples (both from Microsoft) that provide developers an LDAP channel to this data.

ColdFusion 8 has introduced other mechanisms for interacting with the Exchange server; however, CFLDAP remains the most effective means of communicating with Microsoft Active Directory. Although there are other ways to retrieve this data, such as using `<cfobject>` and COM, `<cfldap>` provides a less complicated interface to the same data.

➜ See Chapter 75, "Extending ColdFusion with COM," for coverage of COM integration via `<cfobject>`, and Chapter 73, "Integrating with Microsoft Exchange," for information on the `CFExchange` tag.

Although it is ultimately up to you, the developer, to decide how you'll use `<cfldap>`, the following are some common uses:

- Creating interfaces for querying public LDAP servers, as for a local university.
- Creating interfaces for querying, updating, and deleting company directory entries for employees, departments, and the like. A company "phonebook" is one example of this.
- Creating interfaces to other data stored within an LDAP server. Company information is one of the many uses for LDAP.

Depending on the server you're accessing, you may need special privileges to perform certain actions, such as adding or deleting LDAP entries. Most public LDAP servers give anonymous access that allows you only to query the server.

For corporate uses, LDAP usually requires authentication with a username and password combination. Together, these restrict access to data that corresponds to the security level of the individual performing the operations. With LDAPv3, you can also use security certificates for authentication, as explained later in the section on the `SECURE` attribute.

Tag Overview

The `<cfldap>` tag, like most ColdFusion tags, has attributes for you to specify to indicate exactly how you intend to use it. Some attributes are required depending on the context of the tag, but in all cases there are several optional values you may set as well.

NOTE

The `<cfldap>` tag does not require a closing tag.

Table 72.2 shows the available attributes of the `<cfldap>` tag with corresponding descriptions for each. Some of these attributes require detailed descriptions, which follow the table.

Table 72.2 `<cfldap>` Tag Attributes and Descriptions

NAME	DESCRIPTION
`ACTION`	Optional. One of five possible actions for `<cfldap>` to perform. Values are `QUERY`, `ADD`, `MODIFY`, `MODIFYDN`, or `DELETE`. If none is specified, the default is `QUERY`.
`NAME`	Required if `ACTION="Query"`. This represents the name of the query object returned from the `<cfldap>` query.
`SERVER`	Required. The address hosting the LDAP server. Entries may be in the form of the server's IP address (that is, 127.0.0.1) or its DNS entry (that is, `ldap.server.com`).
`PORT`	Optional. The port to which LDAP is configured for listening. The default is 389.

Table 72.2 (CONTINUED)

NAME	DESCRIPTION
USERNAME	Required if `secure` attribute is set to `cfssl_basic`.
PASSWORD	Optional. The password used in conjunction with the `USERNAME` attribute for authentication.
TIMEOUT	Optional. the time, in seconds, allowed for the LDAP operation before timeout occurs. If none is provided, the default is 60 seconds.
MAXROWS	Optional. Used only with `ACTION="Query"`, this specifies the number of records to return from the LDAP query, similar to the `<cfquery>` tag. Note that this attribute does not work with all LDAP servers.
START	Required (and only used) if `ACTION="Query"`. This represents the DN starting point from which to begin the search within the Directory Information Tree (DIT).
SCOPE	Optional. Defines the scope for searching the DIT, starting at the value specified in the `START` attribute. Possible values are `Base`, `OneLevel`, or `SubTree`.
ATTRIBUTES	Required for `QUERY`, `ADD`, `MODIFY`, and `MODIFYDN` actions. When used with `QUERY`, it represents a comma-delimited list of return values used as columns in a query output; an asterisk (`*`) returns all values. For `ADD` and `MODIFY`, it represents a semicolon-separated list of add/modify values. For `MODIFYDN`, it represents the new DN for the entry and does not check for correct syntax.
FILTER	Optional. Used with `ACTION="Query"` to provide the search criteria for the query. The default filter is `objectClass=*`, which returns all values.
SORT	Optional. A comma-delimited list of attributes and sort directions by which to sort a query, as in `SORT="cn ASC, mail DESC"`.
SORTCONTROL	Optional. A comma-delimited list of sort control options for a query. Possible values are `asc`, `desc`, and `nocase`. Sorting, by default, is case-sensitive in ascending order (`asc`). The `desc` value sorts the query in descending order, and `nocase` discards case-sensitivity. Values can be used in tandem, as in `SORTCONTROL="nocase, desc"`.
DN	Required for `DELETE`, `ADD`, `MODIFY`, and `MODIFYDN` actions. Represents the Distinguished Name for the entry being operated on.
STARTROW	Optional. Used only with `ACTION="Query"`, this specifies the starting row for returning records. The default is 1.
MODIFYTYPE	Optional. Used only with `ACTION="Modify"`, this specifies the way to handle modifications within the attribute list. Possible values are `add`, `replace`, and `delete`. Default value is `"Replace"`.
REBIND	Optional. Boolean value indicating whether `<cfldap>` should rebind the referral callback and reissue the query via the referred address using the original credentials. Default value is `"no"`.
REFERRAL	Optional. Specifies the number of hops allowed in a referral. A zero value indicates `<cfldap>`'s capability to use referred addresses is disabled, and no data is returned.

Table 72.2 (continued)

NAME	DESCRIPTION
SECURE	Optional. Identifies the type of security to use, such as CFSSL_BASIC or CFSSL_CLIENT_AUTH, and additional information that is required by the corresponding security type. Possible field values are certificate_db, certificate_name, key_db, and keyword_db.
SEPARATOR	Optional. The character used to separate values in multivalue attributes. The default is a comma (,).
DELIMITER	Optional. The character used to separate name=value pairs. The default is a semicolon (;).
RETURNASBINARY	Optional. A comma- (or space) separated list of columns that are returned as a binary values.

NOTE

You can specify the RETURNASBINARY tag's attributes in an argumentsCollection attribute whose value is a structure. Specify the structure name in the argumentsCollection attribute and use the tag's attribute names as structure keys. Thus, these two specifications would return identical results:

```
<cfldap
       server="ldap.nyu.edu"
       action="QUERY"
       name="getStudents"
       attributes="ou,cn,mail"
       start="c=us"
       scope="SUBTREE"
       filter="ou=Tisch School of the Arts*">

<cfscript>
       stAtts = StructNew();
       stAtts.server = "ldap.nyu.edu";
       stAtts.action="QUERY";
       stAtts.attributes="ou,cn,mail";
       stAtts.name="getStudentsByAttr";
       stAtts.start="c=us";
       stAtts.scope="SUBTREE";
       stAtts.filter="ou=Tisch School of the Arts*";
</cfscript>
<cfldap argumentsCollection="#stAtts#"/>
```

Because some of <cfldap>'s attributes are a bit involved, the next few sections discuss in more depth how these attributes work.

The ACTION Attribute

ColdFusion's <cfldap> tag supports five distinct actions:

- QUERY
- ADD

- MODIFY
- MODIFYDN
- DELETE

QUERY is the default. The QUERY action allows you to return a query object (recordset) from an LDAP server. This can be used in the same way as any query object, such as one returned from the <cfquery> tag. Three variables, in addition to the query results, are available to the returned query object:

- RecordCount. The number of records returned from the query object.
- ColumnList. A comma-delimited list of column names in the query.
- CurrentRow. The current row index of the query being processed by an output mechanism, such as <cfoutput> or <cfloop>.

When ACTION is set to QUERY, you are also required to use the NAME, ATTRIBUTES, and START parameters. So at its simplest, your call to <cfldap> would look like:

```
<CFLDAP
 ACTION="QUERY"
 NAME="name of query"
 SERVER="server location"
 ATTRIBUTES="attribute list"
 START="starting location for the query">
```

NOTE

Unlike <cfquery>, the <cfldap> tag does not return the ExecutionTime variable when the ACTION is set to QUERY.

The ADD action is used to add entries to your LDAP server. This action requires the DN and ATTRIBUTES parameters. In this context, the DN is used to specify where to place the added entry in the DIT and should contain the full DN sequence. The ATTRIBUTES parameter is used to specify the name=value pairs to be added at the location specified in the DN parameter. Each name=value pair should be delimited with a semicolon (;), unless otherwise specified in the DELIMITER parameter.

The most basic form of an ADD action is as follows:

```
<CFLDAP
 ACTION="ADD"
 SERVER="server location"
 ATTRIBUTES="name=value; name2=value2; namen=valuen"
 DN="the distinguished name to add">
```

The MODIFY action allows you to modify attribute values for LDAP entries, one or more at a time. The only attribute that cannot be modified through this action is the DN, which is modified through the MODIFYDN action.

As with the ADD action, the MODIFY action's attributes are sent to the ATTRIBUTES parameter in semicolon-separated name=value pairs.

The following is the MODIFY action's basic required format:

```
<CFLDAP
 ACTION="MODIFY"
 SERVER="server location"
 ATTRIBUTES="name=value; name2=value2; namen=valuen"
 DN="the distinguished name of the entry to be modified">
```

The MODIFYDN attribute performs one specific function: It changes the Distinguished Name for an entry. To change the Distinguished Name, you must supply the original DN as well as the new DN replacement:

```
<CFLDAP
 ACTION="MODIFYDN"
 SERVER="server location"
 ATTRIBUTES="the new replacement DN value"
 DN="the original DN value being modified">
```

NOTE

Before you modify a DN entry, make absolutely sure that the syntax is correct. The MODIFYDN attribute of <cfldap> does not check the DN for syntax errors, and as a result, your entry may become malformed.

The only requirement for deleting an entry is the entry's Distinguished Name. Having this value allows <cfldap> to locate the entity you want to delete. After you delete an entry, it is gone, and because of this, you should make sure that the DN value is correct.

To delete an entry, use the following syntax:

```
<CFLDAP
 ACTION="DELETE"
 SERVER="server location"
 DN="the DN representing the entry to delete">
```

The SCOPE Attribute

When querying an LDAP server, <cfldap> provides a means to narrow that search—in addition to filtering—with three types of "branch" scopes. Each of these scopes dictates how the search is performed relative to the value entered in the START attribute. In other words, the START attribute is used as a starting point for the search, and the SCOPE value tells <cfldap> where to search from that starting point. These scopes are as follows:

- Base. If BASE is chosen, <cfldap> only searches the current branch specified in the START attribute. Any branches above or below this branch are not searched.
- OneLevel. To search a single level below the branch specified in the START attribute, use the OneLevel value. This only searches one level below the starting branch. Any branches above or more than one level below this branch are not searched.
- SubTree. This is the most commonly used value because it searches the entry specified in the START attribute as well as all branches beneath it. SubTree will not, however, search branches above the starting value. If you need to search branches higher up in the directory tree, simplify your starting value by making it more generalized.

Because of the recursive nature of the SubTree scope, performance may suffer with larger directory structures. As a result, you may want to use a drill-down approach when traversing a large directory, using the ONELEVEL scope in succession.

The MODIFYTYPE Attribute

When modifying an LDAP entry using ACTION="Modify", the MODIFYTYPE attribute allows you to specify which type of modification to perform. Having this capability allows you greater flexibility and control for modifying complex entries.

The following list provides detailed descriptions for each MODIFYTYPE and the action(s) it performs:

- Add. To add an attribute value to a multivalue entry, you can use the ADD modify type. The attribute(s) to be added should be listed in the ATTRIBUTES parameter as a semicolon-separated list, unless a different separator is specified in the SEPARATOR parameter.
- Delete. To delete a specific attribute from a multivalue entry, use the DELETE modify type. The value listed in the ATTRIBUTES parameter represents the value to delete if it exists.
- Replace. As the default modify type, the REPLACE value overwrites the existing attribute(s) specified in the ATTRIBUTES parameter.

NOTE

Attributes that already exist cannot be added using the MODIFY action. Additionally, entries that contain NULL values cannot be modified.

The SECURE Attribute

The SECURE attribute identifies which type of security to use in your LDAP calls. ColdFusion currently supports the CFSSL_BASIC only.

The format for CFSSL_BASIC authentication takes two values:

```
secure = "CFSSL_BASIC,certificate_db"
```

When using SECURE, keep the following in mind:

- The certificate_db value is the name or path to a valid (Netscape cert7.db format) certificate database file. This value is the default and need not be explicitly specified.
- The certificate_name represents the client certificate to send to the server.
- The key_db value is the name or path to a valid (Netscape key3.db format) file that contains the public or private key pair for the certificate.
- The keyword_db holds the password to the key database (key_db).
- If no path information is given for the certificate_db or key_db values, ColdFusion looks for them in the default LDAP directory.

Querying Public LDAP Servers

One of the easiest ways to begin using LDAP is by querying public LDAP directories. Although literally thousands of such directories exist, some of the better ones come from universities across the world. And because most of these directories allow anonymous access, you can easily query them.

Listing 72.1 queries an LDAP server at New York University.

Listing 72.1 `GetStudents.cfm`—Querying Public Servers

```
<!--- Query the LDAP server --->
<cfldap
       server="ldap.nyu.edu"
       action="QUERY"
       name="getStudents"
       attributes="ou,cn,mail"
       start="c=us"
       scope="SUBTREE"
       filter="ou=Tisch School of the Arts*"
       >

<!--- Display the query results --->
<TABLE BORDER="0" CELLSPACING="2" CELLPADDING="2">
 <TR>
 <TH COLSPAN="3">
 <cfoutput>
 A total of #GetStudents.RecordCount# records were found.
 </CFOUTPUT>
 </TH>
 </TR>
 <TR>
 <TH>Record</TH>
 <TH>Name</TH>
 <TH>e-mail</TH>
 <TH>Department</TH>

 </TR>
 <CFOUTPUT QUERY="GetStudents">
 <TR>
 <TD>#GetStudents.CurrentRow#</TD>
 <TD>#GetStudents.cn#</td>
 <TD><A HREF="mailto:#GetStudents.mail#">#GetStudents.mail#</A></TD>
 <td>#GetStudents.ou#</td>
 </TR>
 </CFOUTPUT>
</TABLE>
```

In this example, we told `<cfldap>` to return a query called `GetStudents` that contains the common name (`cn`) Department (`ou`), and email (`mail`) attributes. Each of these attributes is represented as a column name within the query. At this point, a lot of this may not make sense, but this example is intended to show you how simple a query can be and to have you try it on your own before you continue.

Interacting with Directories

For the examples in this chapter, most LDAP servers will support the conventions used. You may, however, run into situations where certain attributes or object classes do not work, depending on the LDAP software you're using. To understand more about the specific structure of your platform, check the documentation included with it.

Active Directories

Active Directory is an essential component of each version of Windows network architecture since Windows 2000. It behaves as a directory service to allow organizations to centrally manage information on users (including security information), as well as other network resources. Windows Domain Controllers each have an Active Directory service available, which provides access to the directory database. Using a standard CFLDAP tag, developers can integrate with this Active Directory to enable users to log into ColdFusion applications using their Windows network username and password. Listing 72.2 shows a simple example to authenticate users against an Active Directory.

Listing 72.2 `ldapAuth.cfm`—Authenticating a User with `<cfldap>`

```
<cflogin>
    <cfif NOT isDefined("Form.username")>
        <cfinclude template="login/login_form.cfm">
        <cfabort>
    <cfelse>
        <cftry>
           <cfldap action="QUERY"
              name="auth"
              attributes="cn"
              start="cn=users,dc=tapper,dc=net"
              server="localhost"
              port="389"
              username="#form.username#"
              password="#form.password#">
           <cfset isAuthenticated="yes">
           <cfcatch type="ANY">
              <cfset isAuthenticated="no">
           </cfcatch>
        </cftry>
        <cfif variables.isAuthenticated>
            <cfloginuser
                name="#Form.username#"
                password="#Form.password#"
                roles="Authenticated User">
        <cfelse>
            <cfinclude template="login/login_form.cfm">
            <h3>Your information is not valid.
            Please try again.</h3>
            <cfabort>
        </cfif>
    </cfif>
</cflogin>
```

In Listing 72.2, an LDAP query is done against a Microsoft Active Directory (AD) and is wrapped with a `<cflogin>` tag. By specifying the username and password as provided by the end user's form input, this query will run successfully only if those fields match a valid user's username and password from the AD. If either the username or password is incorrect, the AD will throw an error message. By wrapping the call with a `<cftry>` tag, we are able to catch the error message. The end result is that we have set a variable called `isAuthenticated` to either true if the query is able to run, or false if not. After the end of the `<cftry>` block, we check the value of `isAuthenticated`. If it is true, the user is logged in; otherwise, the user is redirected to the login form.

Querying Directories

One of the first things you need to know about any action within `<cfldap>` that requires authentication is how to use the `USERNAME` and `PASSWORD` attributes. The first common mistake is to enter the username by itself, as odd as that may sound. Often the full DN is required for the entry that represents the user, and the username:

```
USERNAME="cn=jtapper,cn=Recipients,ou=OWS,o=Orange Whip Studios"
```

Most of the time, however, you can just use the `cn` as the username, as in:

```
USERNAME="cn=jtapper"
```

So in this example, the username is actually `jtapper`, but the `USERNAME` attribute requires the `cn=` (common name) prefix.

The `PASSWORD` attribute, on the other hand, does not require any special considerations, so you simply enter it as it's written:

```
PASSWORD="jtapper_123"
```

NOTE

Depending on the vendor software you're using, the **USERNAME** attribute might require the full DN. Netscape Directory Server is one example of software that requires it. Check your LDAP documentation to see which method is used for your particular software package.

To take it a step further, you can run a query to gather the user's name and email address as follows:

```
<CFLDAP
 ACTION="QUERY"
 NAME="GetEmail"
 SERVER="localhost"
 USERNAME="cn=jtapper"
 PASSWORD="jtapper_123"
 SCOPE="SUBTREE"
 ATTRIBUTES="cn,mail"
 START=""
 FILTER="(uid=jtapper)">
```

In this example, you specify the `SUBTREE` scope that recursively checks all entries that contain a `cn` and `mail` attribute and that have a `uid` of `jtapper`. The last portion represents a filter; filters are discussed in more detail later in this section.

To output the data, you can use the value held in the NAME attribute as a query object reference. In other words, this is the value you put in the QUERY attribute of your <cfoutput> tag, as shown here:

```
<TABLE WIDTH="100%" BORDER="1" CELLSPACING="0">
 <TR>
 <TH>User (cn)</TH>
 <TH>Email</TH>
 </TR>
<CFOUTPUT QUERY="GetEmail">
 <TR>
 <TD>#cn#</TD>
 <TD>#mail#</TD>
 </TR>
</CFOUTPUT>
</TABLE>
```

If your goal is to list all email addresses for employees, you could easily modify the FILTER attribute to accommodate this:

```
filter="(uid=*)"
```

Here, the asterisk (*) acts as a wildcard character that tells <cfldap> to return all cn and mail entries with a uid.

In addition to the wildcard character, you can specify a wide range of filter sequences. Table 72.3 shows the allowed characters for filter strings with their descriptions, along with examples. The default filter, if none is provided, is objectClass=*.

Table 72.3 <cfldap> Search Filters and Descriptions Start Here

FILTER	EXAMPLE	DESCRIPTION
( )	(filter)	For non-comparative filters, parentheses are optional. For comparative filters, such as &, |, and !, parentheses are required.
*	uid=*	Any value. This example returns entries that contain *any* uid value.
=	c=US	An exact value match. This example returns values where the country is equal to US (United States).
~=	ou~=OWS	An approximate match. This example returns entries with organizational units (ou) that approximate OWS (Orange Whip Studios).
>=	sn>=tapper	Greater than or equal to. Alphabetically, this returns all values that would be ordered at or after the surname (sn) value of tapper.
<=	givenName<=dain	Less than or equal to. Alphabetically, this returns all values that would be ordered at or before the first name (givenName) value of dain.
&	(&(sn=An*)(cn=Da*))	Comparative AND. This example returns all entries that have a surname (sn) that starts with An *and* a common name (cn) that starts with Da.

Table 72.3 (continued)

FILTER	EXAMPLE	DESCRIPTION
|	`(|(sn=An*)(cn=Da*))`	Comparative `OR`. This example returns all entries that have a surname (`sn`) that starts with `An` *or* a common name (`cn`) that starts with Da.
!	`(!(cn=Jeff Tapper))`	Comparative `NOT`. This example returns all entries other than those whose common name (`cn`) is equal to `Jeff Tapper`.

Search filters can also contain multiple comparisons or any mixture of the filters seen in Table 72.3. To get all users in the `OWS` organizational unit (`ou`) with the last name Tapper or Forta, you can modify the filter as follows:

```
FILTER="(&(ou=OWS)(|(cn=Tapper)(cn=Forta)))"
```

To order the returned entries alphabetically, you can use the `SORT` attribute, as well:

```
FILTER="(&(ou=OWS)(|(cn=Tapper)(cn=Forta)))"
SORT="cn"
```

To obtain greater sort control, you could also specify the sorting as case-*in*sensitive (the default is case-sensitive) and in descending order:

```
FILTER="(&(ou=OWS)(|(cn=Tapper)(cn=Forta)))"
SORT="cn"
SORTCONTROL="nocase DESC"
```

If you know that the query will return hundreds of records, two additional attributes may be needed. The `TIMEOUT` attribute specifies the time, in seconds, to allow before the operation times out. Also, the `MAXROWS` attribute allows you to specify the maximum number of matching records to return:

```
FILTER="(&(ou=OWS)(|(cn=Tapper)(cn=Forta)))"
SORT="cn"
SORTCONTROL="nocase DESC"
TIMEOUT="10"
MAXROWS="100"
```

And finally, if you're using `<cfldap>` to page through hundreds of records, you may also want to consider using the `STARTROW` attribute, which allows you to return records from a specific row:

```
FILTER="(&(ou=OWS)(|(cn=Tapper)(cn=Forta)))"
SORT="cn"
SORTCONTROL="nocase DESC"
TIMEOUT="10"
MAXROWS="100"
STARTROW="#URL.StartRow#"
```

Here, the `#URL.StartRow#` variable would represent a value sent from a previous page's URL.

NOTE

Sorting is performed on the LDAP server and is only supported on servers compatible with LDAPv3.

Adding Entries

To add an entry to LDAP, you need to pay close attention to two special values: the DN for the entry, and the entry's `objectClass`. The object class is essentially an object map to the entry using the object class entries. The DN, on the other hand, is a similar type of map except that it uses the DN sequence. To gather both of these values, you can easily list all name and value pairs for a DN, one being the `objectClass`.

If, for example, you want to add a user to a specific group, you can use another user's attributes from that group as a guideline for adding the new user. See Listing 72.3 to see how this is accomplished.

Listing 72.3 `GetNameValues.cfm`—List Name/Value Pairs

```
<!--- Query for all (*) uid's --->
<CFLDAP ACTION="QUERY"
 NAME="GetNamesAndValues"
 SERVER="localhost"
 USERNAME="cn=jtapper"
 PASSWORD="jtapper_123"
 SCOPE="SUBTREE"
 ATTRIBUTES="*"
 START=""
 FILTER="(uid=*)">

<!--- Display all name/value pairs for each uid --->
<CFOUTPUT QUERY="GetNamesAndValues">
<TABLE WIDTH="100%" BORDER="1" CELLSPACING="0">
 <!--- Show the column headers only for the first record --->
 <CFIF CurrentRow EQ 1>
 <TR>
 <TH>Name</TH>
 <TH>Value</TH>
 </TR>
 </CFIF>
 <TR>
 <TD>#name#</TD>
 <TD>#value#</TD>
 </TR>
</TABLE>
</CFOUTPUT>
```

NOTE

Some software packages, such as Netscape Directory Server, return zero results if the `START` attribute is left blank. To resolve this, you can enter your company's organization as a minimum starting value.

By specifying an asterisk (*) for the `ATTRIBUTES` value, you're telling `<cfldap>` to return all attributes for all entries returned from the `FILTER` scope value. In this example, you used the `(uid=*)` filter to signify that you want all entries (*) that have a `uid` returned. The `objectClass` is now:

```
organizationalPerson, person, Top
```

and one of the DNs is:

```
cn=jtapper, cn=Recipients, ou=OWS, o=Orange Whip Studios
```

Having this list of available attributes allows you to build your ADD action construct. In Listing 72.4, you'll add "Ben Forta," along with his corresponding personal information values, to the Orange Whip Studios (OWS) organizational unit (ou) within the company.

Listing 72.4 AddEntry.cfm—Adding and Testing an Entry

```
<!--- Use the 'ADD' action to create a new entry --->
<CFLDAP ACTION="ADD"
 SERVER="localhost"
 USERNAME="cn=jtapper"
 PASSWORD="jtapper_123"
 ATTRIBUTES="objectclass=organizationalPerson, person, Top;
 cn=Ben Forta;
 sn=Forta;
 mail=Ben_Forta@orange-whip-studios.com;
 ou=OWS"
 DN="cn=ben_forta, cn=Recipients, ou=OWS, o=Orange Whip Studios">

<!--- Query to ensure the entry was added --->
<CFLDAP ACTION="QUERY"
 NAME="GetUser"
 SERVER="localhost"
 USERNAME="cn=jtapper"
 PASSWORD="jtapper_123"
 SCOPE="SUBTREE"
 ATTRIBUTES="dn,cn"
 START=""
 FILTER="(cn=ben_forta)">

<!--- Display the query results --->
<TABLE WIDTH="100%" BORDER="1" CELLSPACING="0">
 <TR>
 <TH>User (cn)</TH>
 <TH>DN</TH>
 </tr>
 <CFOUTPUT QUERY="GetUser">
 <TR>
 <TD>#cn#</TD>
 <TD>#dn#</TD>
 </TR>
 </CFOUTPUT>
</TABLE>
```

Because you used a filter of cn=ben_forta, all records with that cn are returned in the query object (which in this case is only a single record). The next section on modifying entries shows how you could easily add or change attributes for Ben's user entry.

NOTE

If you receive an Access Denied error message when adding entries, talk to your system administrator to ensure that you have sufficient access to perform the operation.

Modifying Entries

The trickiest part of learning <cfldap> is understanding how to modify entries. This section shows you several examples using each of the methods to modify entries, and because of this, it is also the most lengthy section in this chapter.

Through the <cfldap> interface, you can perform several modification tasks:

- Modify existing attribute values
- Modify entries by adding entries (such as groups and users)
- Modify entries by using the ModifyType attribute for better modification control
- Modify an entry's Distinguished Name through the MODIFYDN action

Most of these examples require a bit of trial and error, depending on how your LDAP server is configured. Exact behavior and syntax can vary based on the LDAP server being used and its configuration, so you may have to do some due diligence to learn more about the server you are using. With that information, you'll be on your way to creating robust applications using <cfldap>.

CAUTION

Be sure to test all modifications on a test server before using them in a production environment. LDAP is a trial-and-error process that requires substantial testing. A simple mistake can have enormous impact on the existing data's integrity.

Modifying Existing Attribute Values

As with adding entries, before you can modify an entry you must first know the DN for the entry. This is used to reference the entity you want to modify or delete. To gather this information, you'll perform a simple query using the uid attribute as shown in Listing 72.4.

Listing 72.5 gathers the DN as well as the user's common name (CN) and telephone number (telephoneNumber). The telephoneNumber field appears blank at this point. You'll modify that blank entry in a later example; first you need the DN.

Listing 72.5 GetDN.cfm—Running a Simple Query

```
<CFLDAP ACTION="QUERY"
 NAME="GetDN"
 SERVER="localhost"
 USERNAME="cn=jtapper"
 PASSWORD="jtapper_123"
 SCOPE="SUBTREE"
 ATTRIBUTES="dn,cn,telephonenumber"
 START=""
 FILTER="(uid=jtapper)">

<TABLE WIDTH="100%" BORDER="1" CELLSPACING="0">
 <TR>
 <TH>User (cn)</TH>
 <TH>DN</TH>
 <TH>Telephone</TH>
```

Listing 72.5 (continued)

```
 </TR>
 <CFOUTPUT QUERY="GetDN">
 <TR>
 <TD>#cn#</TD>
 <TD>#dn#</TD>
 <TD>#telephonenumber#</TD>
 </TR>
 </CFOUTPUT>
</TABLE>
```

The results of your query will return the `cn`, `dn`, and the `telephoneNumber` values. To restrict the number of results to a single user, you add a filter. And in this example, the `uid=jtapper` filter is used to return the values in the `ATTRIBUTES` parameter for the specific user.

After you have the DN for the entry you're modifying, you can run a second `<cfldap>` tag with the `ACTION` attribute set to `MODIFY`. The first query returned a DN of:

```
cn=jtapper, cn=Recipients, ou=OWS, o=Orange Whip Studios
```

which is what you'll use to modify the listing. For this next example, you'll change the telephone number value.

The first call to `<cfldap>`, as shown previously in Listing 72.4, gathers the DN. This value is required for any modifications you want to make. The second call uses the first call's DN as the value you supply to the DN attribute. Finally, one more `<cfldap>` call is used to requery the server, returning the newly modified results that contain the `telephoneNumber` value. See Listing 72.6 to get a better idea of how this works.

Listing 72.6 `ModifyTelephone.cfm`—Modifying an Entry

```
<!--- Update the 'telephoneNumber' value --->
<!--- The DN value is used from a previous CFLDAP call --->
<CFLDAP ACTION="MODIFY"
 SERVER="localhost"
 USERNAME="cn=jtapper"
 PASSWORD="jtapper_123"
 ATTRIBUTES="telephonenumber=(919) 555 - 5555"
 DN="#GetDN.DN#">

<!--- Run a query to gather the new results --->
<CFLDAP ACTION="QUERY"
 NAME="GetUserData"
 SERVER="localhost"
 USERNAME="cn=jtapper"
 PASSWORD="jtapper_123"
 SCOPE="SUBTREE"
 ATTRIBUTES="dn,cn,telephonenumber"
 START=""
 FILTER="(uid=jtapper)">

<!--- Display the new results --->
<TABLE WIDTH="100%" BORDER="1" CELLSPACING="0">
 <TR>
 <TH>User (cn)</TH>
```

Listing 72.6 (continued)

```
    <TH>DN</TH>
    <TH>Telephone</TH>
    </TR>
    <CFOUTPUT QUERY="GetUserData">
    <TR>
    <TD>#cn#</TD>
    <TD>#dn#</TD>
    <TD>#telephonenumber#</TD>
    </TR>
    </CFOUTPUT>
  </TABLE>
```

The telephone value is no longer blank. Running multiple calls to `<cfldap>` in one template is commonplace, just as you might run multiple `<cfquery>`s.

Modifying values is not restricted to a single value at a time; rather, you can make multiple modifications simultaneously with a single `<cfldap>` call, using a delimiter to separate each entry and its new value. Listing 72.7 shows how you would change the user's state as well as his street address.

Listing 72.7 `ModifyStreetState.cfm`—Updating Multiple Attributes

```
<!--- Update the 'street' and 'state' values --->
<CFLDAP ACTION="MODIFY"
 SERVER="localhost"
 USERNAME="cn=jtapper"
 PASSWORD="jtapper_123"
 ATTRIBUTES="st=NC; street=123 Orange Whip Lane"
 MODIFYTYPE="ADD"
 DN="cn=jtapper,cn=Recipients,ou=OWS,o=Orange Whip Studios">

<!--- Run a query to gather the new results --->
<CFLDAP ACTION="QUERY"
 NAME="GetDN"
 SERVER="localhost"
 USERNAME="cn=jtapper"
 PASSWORD="jtapper_123"
 SCOPE="SUBTREE"
 ATTRIBUTES="cn,street,st"
 START=""
 FILTER="(uid=jtapper)">

<!--- Display the new results --->
<TABLE WIDTH="100%" BORDER="1" CELLSPACING="0">
 <TR>
 <TH>User (cn)</TH>
 <TH>Street</TH>
 <TH>State</TH>
 </TR>
 <CFOUTPUT QUERY="GetDN">
 <TR>
 <TD>#cn#</TD>
 <TD>#street#</TD>
 <TD>#st#</TD>
 </TR>
 </CFOUTPUT>
</TABLE>
```

Modification by Adding Entries

One of the more difficult modification tasks of `<cfldap>` is modifying entries by adding additional entries. The next few examples show how to modify a group by adding a member to it.

To begin this example, you'll start by querying an existing group to which you want to add a member. The first part is used to ensure that the group does, in fact, exist. If not, you would throw an error:

```
<!--- This queries the group --->
<CFLDAP ACTION="query"
 NAME="GroupExists"
 SERVER="localhost"
 USERNAME="cn=jtapper"
 PASSWORD="jtapper_123"
 SCOPE="SUBTREE"
 ATTRIBUTES="uniquemember"
 START="cn=Marketing,cn=Recipients,ou=OWS,o=Orange Whip Studios">

<!--- If the group doesn't exist, throw an error message and abort --->
<CFIF NOT GroupExists.RecordCount>
 <CFTHROW MESSAGE="Group does not exist.">
 <CFABORT>
</CFIF>
```

At this point, you're checking to see whether the group exists where you want to place the new member(s). The value that defines whether it exists is the `#GroupExists.RecordCount#` variable. The `GroupExists` prefix is the name you assigned in the `NAME` attribute, which represents the name of the returned query object. If the group exists, you know that you can safely place a user into that group. Otherwise, you throw an error and abort processing.

The next step is to gather all users and their corresponding `uid` values for the existing group to which you want to add users. You can use the ColdFusion `ValueList()` function to create a list from all the `uid` values:

```
<!--- Get all uid's for the 'Marketing' group --->
<CFLDAP ACTION="query"
 NAME="GetUserList"
 SERVER="localhost"
 USERNAME="cn=jtapper"
 PASSWORD="jtapper_123"
 SCOPE="SUBTREE"
 ATTRIBUTES="uid"
 START="cn=Marketing,cn=Recipients,ou=OWS,o=Orange Whip Studios">

<!--- Create a list from the query's uid values --->
<CFSET UserList=ValueList(GetUserList.uid)>
```

For simplicity, the next section assumes that only two users are currently in the Marketing group (`cn=Marketing`), which are stored in the variable called `#UserList#`. Each element in the list is the user's `uid` value. To be sure, the `#UserList#` variable will be replaced with the actual list (`jtapper,bforta`):

```
<!--- Primer for the members list --->
<CFPARAM NAME="Members" DEFAULT="">
```

```
<!--- Loop through each uid using UserList --->
<CFLOOP LIST="#UserList#" INDEX="User">

 <!--- Get each user's DN from their uid --->
 <CFLDAP ACTION="query"
 NAME="GetUser"
 SERVER="localhost"
 USERNAME="cn=jtapper"
 PASSWORD="jtapper_123"
 SCOPE="SUBTREE"
 ATTRIBUTES="dn"
 START=""
 FILTER="(uid=#User#)">

 <!--- Create a semicolon-separated list of user DN's --->
 <!--- Each DN needs to have its commas escaped with another comma --->
 <CFSET Members= Members & "," & Replace(GetUser.dn, ",", ",,", "ALL")>

</CFLOOP>

<!--- Remove the leading comma from the Members list --->
<CFSET Members=RemoveChars(Members, 1, 1)>
```

The last section of code creates a list of lists. The outer list is a comma-separated list of all DNs for the group (Marketing). Within each DN (between each semicolon), another list contains an escaped comma-delimited list of attribute values for that DN (single user). Commas, in this context, must be escaped with a second comma so that `<cfldap>` does not mistake each DN's attributes as a separate entry. Had you not escaped these commas, none of the members—when you add additional members—would be unique, because each attribute would become a new member. In other words, it would create two members called `Marketing`, two members called `Recipients`, and so on.

The results of the `#Members#` variable contain all current Marketing users:

```
cn=jtapper,,cn=Recipients,,ou=OWS,,o=Orange Whip Studios;
cn=ben_forta,,cn=Recipients,,ou=OWS,,o=Orange Whip Studios
```

As you can see, each DN has its commas escaped, and each DN is separated by a single comma. It's always best to automate this process because this listing can become large.

In this example, you're going to add another user, John Doe, to the Marketing group. John Doe is currently not a member of any group—he's an entirely new user. Had John Doe already existed somewhere in the directory, adding him as a member of Marketing would not physically change his location in the directory. To physically move him, you would have to delete him from his current location and add him to another. By placing him in Marketing, you are merely adding him as a member of Marketing, but he could exist elsewhere in the directory structure. The hard-coded value for this user before escaping will be:

```
cn=john_doe,cn=Recipients,ou=OWS,o=Orange Whip Studios
```

After escaping the commas, the entry will look like this:

```
cn=john_doe,,cn=Recipients,,ou=OWS,,o=Orange Whip Studios
```

To update the members list for Marketing, you have to add John Doe to the current members list; be sure to add a comma between each entry:

```
<CFSET Members=Members & "," & "cn=john_doe,,cn=Recipients,,ou=OWS,,o=Orange Whip
Studios">
```

Finally, to update the current members of the Marketing group, you can replace the `uniqueMember` (all current members) list with the new `#Members#` list, which contains the newly added John Doe entry as well as all the preexisting members:

```
<CFLDAP ACTION="MODIFY"
 SERVER="localhost"
 USERNAME="cn=jtapper"
 PASSWORD="jtapper_123"
 ATTRIBUTES="objectclass=groupOfUniqueNames;uniquemember=#Members#"
 DN="cn=Marketing,cn=Recipients,ou=OWS,o=Orange Whip Studios">
```

While this is a tedious process, there is a far easier approach to making these modifications, with the use of the `ModifyType` attribute. The final code for these sections can be found encapsulated in the `LDAP.cfc` file shown in Listing 72.9 later in this chapter.

Modifying Entries with `ModifyType`

To help you appreciate the benefits of using the `ModifyType` attribute, the previous section demonstrated how cumbersome it can be to modify entries manually. Luckily, there is an easier way, by using the `ModifyType` attribute of the `<cfldap>` tag.

To recap, reread the section "The `MODIFYTYPE` Attribute" earlier in this chapter. The `add` modify type will look like the following:

```
<CFLDAP ACTION="MODIFY"
 MODIFYTYPE="ADD"
 SERVER="localhost"
 USERNAME="cn=jtapper"
 PASSWORD="jtapper_123"
 ATTRIBUTES="cn=john_doe,cn=Recipients,ou=OWS,o=Orange Whip Studios"
 DN="cn=Marketing,cn=Recipients,ou=OWS,o=Orange Whip Studios">
```

Had you added two users, you would separate each DN with a comma.

To replace entries, use the `replace` modify type.

CAUTION

Be careful that you do not overwrite existing entries with a single entry. The entries you supply to the `ATTRIBUTES` parameter will replace all existing entries for the DN specified.

For this example, you'll replace the current marketing users with a list of the old users plus a new user, John Doe. For this example, all the new users are placed in a variable called `#Members#`. Following is what the new users list will look like:

```
cn=jtapper,cn=Recipients,ou=OWS,o=Orange Whip Studios,
cn=ben_forta,cn=Recipients,ou=OWS,o=Orange Whip Studios,
cn=john_doe,cn=Recipients,ou=OWS,o=Orange Whip Studios
```

To replace the old members with the new, use the `replace` modify type:

```
<CFLDAP ACTION="MODIFY"
 MODIFYTYPE="REPLACE"
 SERVER="localhost"
 USERNAME="cn=jtapper"
 PASSWORD="jtapper_123"
 ATTRIBUTES="#Members#"
 DN="cn=Marketing,cn=Recipients,ou=OWS,o=Orange Whip Studios">
```

To delete an entry, use the `delete` modify type. This next example would delete the John Doe user from the Marketing group:

```
<CFLDAP ACTION="MODIFY"
 MODIFYTYPE="DELETE"
 SERVER="localhost"
 USERNAME="cn=jtapper"
 PASSWORD="jtapper_123"
 ATTRIBUTES="cn=john_doe,cn=Recipients,ou=OWS,o=Orange Whip Studios"
 DN="cn=Marketing,cn=Recipients,ou=OWS,o=Orange Whip Studios">
```

Modifying a Distinguished Name

Modifying a Distinguished Name (DN) requires `<cfldap>`'s `MODIFYDN` action. You cannot modify a Distinguished Name using the `MODIFY` action.

There are two values of interest when modifying a DN: the original DN and the replacement DN. The original DN is placed in the DN attribute, whereas the new replacement DN is placed in the `ATTRIBUTES` parameter as follows:

```
<CFLDAP ACTION="MODIFYDN"
 SERVER="localhost"
 USERNAME="cn=jtapper"
 PASSWORD="jtapper_123"
 ATTRIBUTES="cn=jane_doe,cn=Recipients,ou=OWS,o=Orange Whip Studios"
 DN="cn=john_doe,cn=Recipients,ou=OWS,o=Orange Whip Studios">
```

Deleting Entries

Deleting an entry is possibly the easiest action to perform using `<cfldap>`. Because of this, it is worth pointing out that after an entry is deleted, it's gone for good, and there isn't an "undo" mechanism.

The following code snippet shows the process of removing an entry from LDAP. The only requirements for doing so are having sufficient access as well as the DN of the entry you want to delete.

```
<CFLDAP ACTION="DELETE"
 SERVER="localhost"
 USERNAME="cn=jtapper"
 PASSWORD="jtapper_123"
 DN="cn=jtapper,cn=Recipients,ou=OWS,o=Orange Whip Studios">
```

After the code is run, the entry is gone. As a safeguard, you may want to create a database to hold "deleted" entries in the event that you need to restore an accidentally deleted entry. Using this concept, you would query the entry to gather all its Name/Value pairs, run an insert query, and then, if all goes well, run the LDAP deletion.

Listing 72.8 shows how to build a simple mailing list that enables you to send a message to every member in your LDAP directory. This example could be modified to filter specific groups or organizational units, or to enable you to specify filter options. The choices are unlimited.

Listing 72.8 `LDAPMailList.cfm`—Using LDAP to Create a Mailing List

```
<!--- Process code if the form was submitted --->
<CFIF IsDefined("FORM.Submit")>

 <!--- Simple form validation for each field --->
 <CFIF NOT Len(FORM.MessageTitle)>
 <CFTHROW MESSAGE="Please enter a message title.">
 </CFIF>
 <CFIF NOT Len(FORM.Message)>
 <CFTHROW MESSAGE="Please enter a message to send.">
 </CFIF>

 <!--- Run the LDAP query --->
 <CFLDAP ACTION="QUERY"
 NAME="LDAPMailList"
 SERVER="localhost"
 USERNAME="cn=jtapper"
 PASSWORD="jtapper_123"
 SCOPE="SUBTREE"
 ATTRIBUTES="cn,mail"
 START="">

 <!--- If records are returned, run CFMAIL --->
 <CFIF LDAPMailList.RecordCount>
 <CFMAIL FROM="list-serve@orange-whip-studios.com"
 TO="#mail#"
 SUBJECT="#Form.MessageTitle#"
 SERVER="mail.orange-whip-studios.com"
 QUERY="LDAPMailList">
Hello, #cn#

#FORM.Message#
 </CFMAIL>

 <!--- Feedback, sent --->
 <B>Your message was successfully sent.</B><P>

 <CFELSE>

 <!--- Feedback, failed --->
 <B>No records exist in the directory.</B>

 </CFIF>

</CFIF>

<!--- Form used to enter the mailing list contents --->
```

Listing 72.8 (continued)

```
<FORM ACTION="LDAPMailList.cfm" METHOD="post">
 Enter a title for the mailing:<BR>
 <INPUT NAME="MessageTitle" MAXLENGTH="200" SIZE="40"><P>

 Enter the message text:<BR>
 <TEXTAREA NAME="Message" COLS="40" ROWS="7"></TEXTAREA><P>

 <INPUT TYPE="Submit" NAME"Submit" VALUE="Send Message">
</FORM>
```

The first time you access the page, you will see a form that enables you to enter a title and content for the mailing. Clicking the Submit button posts the form values to the same page where processing the mailing begins.

The beginning of the ColdFusion code uses a simplified form of validation that checks whether a message and title are empty values; if they are, the `<CFTHROW>` tag is used to display an error message and the template aborts further processing.

If the validation passes, you make a call to the LDAP server requesting the `cn` and `mail` attributes for everyone. Because no filters are used, every entry containing a `cn` or `mail` attribute is returned as the `LDAPMailList` query. If records are returned, you use `<CFMAIL>`'s `QUERY` attribute to cycle once for each record in `LDAPMailList`. Upon template execution, a message is displayed indicating to you that the mailing was a success.

Building an LDAP CFC

Because we like to keep all data access logic in ColdFusion within CFCs, it makes sense to encapsulate all of our LDAP interactions into an LDAP CFC (see Listing 72.9). Each of the previous `<cfldap>` calls from this chapter were used to create this CFC.

Listing 72.9 `LDAP.cfc`—Creating an LDAP CFC

```
<cfcomponent>
    <cfscript>
        init();
    </cfscript>
    <cffunction name="init">
        <cfset serverAddr = "localhost">
        <cfset username="jtapper">
        <cfset password="jtapper_123">
        <cfset organization="Tapper Nimer and Associates, Inc.">
        <cfset ou="Tech">
    </cffunction>
    <cffunction name="getUsers" returnType="query" access="public">
        <cfargument name="filter" type="string" default="*">
        <cfargument name="start" type="string" required="true">

        <cfargument name="filterType" type="string"
            hint="AD for ActiveDirectory, LDAP for ADSI or LDAP">
        <Cfset var getEmail="">
        <cfif filterType eq "LDAP">
```

Listing 72.9 (continued)

```
            <cfset getEmail = getUsersByUID(filter,start)>
        <cfelseif filterType eq "AD">
            <cfset getEmail = getUsersByCN(filter,start)>
        </cfif>
        <cfreturn getEmail>
    </cffunction>
    <cffunction name="getUsersByUID" returnType="query" access="private">
        <cfargument name="filter" type="string" default="*">
        <cfargument name="start" type="string" required="true">
        <Cfset var getEmail="">
        <CFLDAP
             ACTION="QUERY"
             NAME="GetEmail"
             SERVER="#serverAddr#"
             USERNAME="cn=#username#"
             PASSWORD="#password#"
             SCOPE="SUBTREE"
             ATTRIBUTES="dn,cn,mail,objectclass"
             START="#attributes.start#"
             FILTER="(uid=#arguments.filter#)">
        <cfreturn getEmail>
    </cffunction>
    <cffunction name="getUsersByCN" returnType="query" access="private">
        <cfargument name="filter" type="string" default="*">
        <Cfset var getEmail="">
        <CFLDAP
             ACTION="QUERY"
             NAME="GetEmail"
             SERVER="#serverAddr#"
             USERNAME="cn=#username#"
             PASSWORD="#password#"
             SCOPE="SUBTREE"
             ATTRIBUTES="dn,cn,mail,objectclass"
             START="#attributes.start#"
             FILTER="(cn=#arguments.filter#)">
        <cfreturn getEmail>
    </cffunction>

    <cffunction name="getNameValuePairs" returnType="query">
        <cfargument name="start" type="string" required="true">
        <cfargument name="filterType" type="string"
            hint="AD for ActiveDirectory, LDAP for ADSI or LDAP"
            default="LDAP">
        <cfset var getNamesAndValues="">
        <cfif filterType eq "LDAP">
          <cfset getNamesAndValues=getNameValuePairsByUID(arguments.start)>
        <cfelseif filterType eq "AD">
          <cfset getNamesAndValues=getNameValuePairsByCN(arguments.start)>
        </cfif>
        <cfreturn getNamesAndValues>
    </cffunction>
    <cffunction
        name="getNameValuePairsByUID" returnType="query" access="private">
        <cfset var GetNamesAndValues="">
        <CFLDAP ACTION="QUERY"
```

Listing 72.9 (continued)

```
            NAME="GetNamesAndValues"
            SERVER="#serverAddr#"
            USERNAME="cn=#username#"
            PASSWORD="#password#"
            SCOPE="SUBTREE"
            ATTRIBUTES="*"
            START="#attributes.start#"
            FILTER="(uid=*)">
        <cfreturn getNamesAndValues>
    </cffunction>
    <cffunction
        name="getNameValuePairsByCN" returnType="query" access="private">
        <cfset var GetNamesAndValues="">
        <CFLDAP ACTION="QUERY"
            NAME="GetNamesAndValues"
            SERVER="#serverAddr#"
            USERNAME="cn=#username#"
            PASSWORD="#password#"
            SCOPE="SUBTREE"
            ATTRIBUTES="*"
            START="#attributes.start#"
            FILTER="(cn=*)">
        <cfreturn getNamesAndValues>
    </cffunction>

    <cffunction name="addUser" returnType="Boolean">
        <cfargument name="cn" type="string" required="true">
        <cfargument name="sn" type="string" required="true">
        <cfargument name="email" type="string" required="true">
        <cfargument name="uid" type="string" required="true">
        <cfargument name="objectClass" type="string" required="true">
        <cfargument name="dn" type="string"
            default="cn=#arguments.uid#, cn=Recipients, ou=#ou#, o=#organization#">
        <cftry>
            <CFLDAP ACTION="ADD"
                SERVER="#serverAddr#"
                USERNAME="cn=#username#"
                PASSWORD="#password#"
                ATTRIBUTES="objectclass=#arguments.objectClass#;
                    cn=#arguments.cn#;
                    sn=#arguments.sn#;
                    mail=#arguments.email#;
                    ou=#ou#"
                DN="#arguments.dn#">
            <cfcatch>
                <cfreturn false>
            </cfcatch>
        </cftry>
        <cfreturn true>
    </cffunction>
    <cffunction name="modifyUserSingleField" returnType="Boolean">
        <cfargument name="dn" type="string" required="true">
        <cfargument name="modifyField" type="string" required="true">
        <cfargument name="modifyValue" type="string" required="true">
        <cfargument name="modifyType" type="string" default="REPLACE">
```

Listing 72.9 (CONTINUED)

```
        <cftry>
            <CFLDAP ACTION="MODIFY"
               MODIFYTYPE="#arguments.modifyType#"
               SERVER="#serverAddr#"
               USERNAME="cn=#username#"
               PASSWORD="#password#"
               ATTRIBUTES="#arguments.modifyField#=#arguments.modifyValue#"
               DN="#arguments.DN#">
             <cfcatch>
                <cfreturn false>
            </cfcatch>
        </cftry>
        <cfreturn true>
    </cffunction>
    <cffunction name="modifyUserMultiField" returnType="Boolean">
        <cfargument name="dn" type="string" required="true">
        <cfargument name="modifyFieldArray" type="Array" required="true">
        <cfargument name="modifyValueArray" type="Array" required="true">
        <cfargument name="modifyType" type="string" default="REPLACE">
        <cfset var attributeString = "">
        <cftry>
            <cfloop from="1" to="#arrayLen(modifyFieldArray)#" index="i">
                <cfset attributeString = attributeString &
modifyFieldArray[i]&"="&modifyValueArray[i]&"; ">
            </cfloop>
            <CFLDAP ACTION="MODIFY"
                 SERVER="#serverAddr#"
                 MODIFYTYPE="#arguments.modifyType#"
                 USERNAME="cn=#username#"
                 PASSWORD="#password#"
                 ATTRIBUTES="#attributeString#"
                 DN="#arguments.DN#">
            <cfcatch>
                <cfreturn false>
            </cfcatch>
        </cftry>
        <cfreturn true>
    </cffunction>
    <cffunction name="deleteUser" returnType="Boolean">
        <cfargument name="dn" type="string" required="true">
        <cftry>
            <CFLDAP ACTION="DELETE"
                SERVER="#serverAddr#"
                USERNAME="cn=#username#"
                PASSWORD="#password#"
                DN="#attributes.dn#">
            <cfcatch>
                <cfreturn false>
            </cfcatch>
        </cftry>
        <cfreturn true>
    </cffunction>
    <cffunction name="modifyDN" returnType="Boolean">
        <cfargument name="newDN" type="string" required="true">
        <cfargument name="oldDN" type="string" required="true">
```

Listing 72.9 (continued)

```
            <cftry>
                <CFLDAP ACTION="MODIFYDN"
                    SERVER="#serverAddr#"
                    USERNAME="cn=#username#"
                    PASSWORD="#password#"
                    ATTRIBUTES="#attributes.newDN#"
                    DN="#attributes.oldDN#">
                <cfcatch>
                    <cfreturn false>
                </cfcatch>
            </cftry>
            <cfreturn true>
        </cffunction>
    </cfcomponent>
```

All of the methods of this CFC directly mirror the code used throughout this chapter. One key difference is that the queries are split, built to either filter based on UID (used by most standard LDAP servers) or by CN, which is more likely to be used by an Active Directory.

CHAPTER 73

Integrating with Microsoft Exchange

IN THIS CHAPTER

Many companies standardize on the Microsoft Exchange Server for calendaring, messaging, and contact and task management. Previous ColdFusion versions provided access to Exchange Server messaging via standard Internet Post Office Protocol 3 (POP3) and Simple Mail Transfer Protocol (SMTP) with `<cfpop>` and `<cfmail>`, respectively, and access to other Exchange Server objects via `<cfldap>`. ColdFusion 8 now provides a simpler Exchange Server interface for managing connections, calendar events, contacts, messages, and tasks.

➜ For information about `<cfmail>` and `<cfpop>`, see Chapter 21, "Interacting with Email," online. For information about integration of ColdFusion with LDAP, see Chapter 72, "Interacting with Directory Services."

ColdFusion Exchange Server Tags

Let's take a brief look at each of the new Exchange Server tags. Table 73.1 lists ColdFusion 8's six new Exchange Server tags and their usage.

Table 73.1 New ColdFusion 8 Exchange Server Tags

TAG	USE
`<cfexchangeconnection>`	Opens and closes persistent connections to the Exchange Server and retrieves information about mailbox subfolders.
`<cfexchangecalendar>`	Creates, retrieves, and manages calendar events.
`<cfexchangecontact>`	Creates, retrieves, and manages contacts.
`<cfexchangefilter>`	Provides filters for retrieving specific items for the `get` actions of the `<cfexchangecalendar>`, `<cfexchangecontact>`, `<cfexchangemail>`, and `<cfexchangetask>` tags.
`<cfexchangemail>`	Retrieves and manages mail messages. Does not send mail.
`<cfexchangetask>`	Creates, retrieves, and manages tasks.

NOTE

`<cfexchangefilter>` is the only child tag. All tags are container tags, but `<cfexchangeconnection>` should not contain any child tags.

<cfexchangeconnection>

Use `<cfexchangeconnection>` to open and close connections to Exchange Server or retrieve a list of mailbox subfolders. This tag's attributes provide connectivity to Exchange. Table 73.2 lists the `<cfexchangeconnection>` tag's attributes. Specifying the `connection` attribute determines the connection type: persistent or transient. See "Managing Exchange Server Connections" later in this chapter for more information about establishing persistent and transient connections.

TIP

You can create transient connections for the `<cfexchangeconnection>` `getSubfolders` action by omitting the `connection` attribute and specifying the required attributes for an `open` action.

Table 73.2 `<cfexchangeconnection>` Attributes

ATTRIBUTE	ACTION	REQUIRED	DESCRIPTION
`action`	N/A	Yes	One of the following actions to perform: `open`: Open a new persistent named connection. `close`: Close a named connection. `getSubfolders`: Get subfolder information of a specific folder.
`connection`	All	Yes, for `open` and `close` actions	The ID or name for the connection. Specify this ID to other tags used with open connections.
`ExchangeApplicationName`	`open` `getSubfolders`	No	Specifies the Exchange Server application name to use in the connection URL. Use only if IIS uses a name other than the default for the Exchange application (`exchange`).
`ExchangeServerLanguage`	`open` `getSubfolders`	No	The Exchange Server's language (default: English). An empty string can be specified if the language is unknown. For all values except English, ColdFusion will try to retrieve folders in the client's local language.

Table 73.2 (continued)

ATTRIBUTE	ACTION	REQUIRED	DESCRIPTION
`folder`	`getSubfolders`	No	The forward-slash (/) delimited path from the mailbox root to the folder containing the subfolders to retrieve. Default is the mailbox root. Use the `_xF8FF_` escape sequence to specify forward slashes in folder names.
`formBasedAuthentication`	`open` `getSubfolders`	No	A Boolean value indicating whether to display a login form and use form-based authentication for the Exchange connection. If the attribute value is `no` (default), and the Exchange Server returns a 440 error status (login timeout), ColdFusion automatically displays the login form and attempts to use form-based authentication.
`formBasedAuthenticationURL`	`open` `getSubfolders`	No	The URL to which to post the user ID and password when an Exchange Server uses form-based authentication. Use this attribute only if your Exchange Server does not use the default URL for form-based authentication. The default URL has the form `https://exchangeServer/exchweb/bin/auth/owaauth.dll`.
`mailboxName`	`open` `getSubfolders`	No	The Exchange mailbox ID to use for the connection. Specify this attribute to access a mailbox whose owner has delegated access rights to the account specified in the `username` attribute.
`name`	`getSubfolders`	Yes	A ColdFusion query variable name that contains information about retrieved subfolders.
`password`	`open` `getSubfolders`	No	The user's Exchange Server password.
`port`	`open` `getSubfolders`	No	The port used to connect to the Exchange Server (default: 80).

Table 73.2 (CONTINUED)

ATTRIBUTE	ACTION	REQUIRED	DESCRIPTION
`protocol`	`open` `getSubfolders`	No	The protocol to use for the connection: only either `http` or `https` (default: `http`).
`proxyHost`	`open` `getSubfolders`	No	The IP address or URL of a proxy host, if required for access to the network.
`proxyPort`	`open` `getSubfolders`	No	The port to connect to on the proxy host, usually port 80.
`recurse`	`getSubfolders`	No	A Boolean value: `true`: Retrieve information about all subfolders of the specified folder. `false` (default): Retrieve information about the top-level subfolders of the specified folder only.
`server`	`open` `getSubfolders`	Yes	The IP address or URL of the server providing access to Exchange.
`username`	`open` `getSubfolders`	Yes	The Exchange Server user ID.

The `getSubfolders` action returns a query containing information about the user's mailbox folders. If you omit the `folders` attribute, then information about the top-level mailbox folders is returned. Set the `recurse` attribute to `true` to get information about all sublevel folders. Table 73.3 lists the returned query columns. The following code block returns a query listing all Inbox subfolders:

```
<cfexchangeconnection name="myFolders" action="get" folder="Inbox"
recurse="true" server="#session.server#"
username="#SESSION.mailUser#" password="#SESSION.mailPasswd#" />
<cfdump var="#myFolders#">
```

NOTE

Mailbox folders can be accessed one at a time only. Loop over the returned query object to access messages and attachments in individual folders.

Table 73.3 `<cfexchangeconnection>` `getSubfolders` Query Columns

COLUMN	DESCRIPTION
`FOLDERNAME`	The subfolder name.
`FOLDERPATH`	The forward-slash (/) delimited path from the mailbox root to the subfolder, including the folder name (such as `Inbox/Archives`).
`FOLDERSIZE`	Size of the folder specified in bytes.

<cfexchangecalendar>

Use `<cfexchangecalendar>` to create, delete, get, and modify Exchange calendar events and retrieve or delete event attachments. A persistent or transient connection is required for this tag. Table 73.4 lists the `<cfexchangecalendar>` attributes.

Table 73.4 `<cfexchangecalendar>` Attributes

ATTRIBUTE	ACTION	REQUIRED	DESCRIPTION
`action`	N/A	Yes	One of the following actions to perform: `create`: Create an appointment or meeting event, including all-day events. `delete`: Delete one or more events. `deleteAttachments`: Delete an event attachment. `get`: Retrieve one or more events using a filters specified with `<cfexchangefilter>`. `getAttachments`: Retrieve attachments for a specific event. `modify`: Modify an existing event. `respond`: Respond to an event.
`attachmentPath`	`getAttachments`	No	The path to the directory in which ColdFusion will save attachments. If omitted, ColdFusion does not save any attachments. If using a relative path, the ColdFusion `temp` directory, as returned by `getTempDirectory()`, is the path root.
`connection`	All	No	The name of the Exchange Server connection specified in `<cfexchangeconnection>`. If omitted, you must create a connection by specifying the required `<cfexchangeconnection>` attributes in this tag.
`event`	`create` `modify`	Yes	A structure containing the event properties to set or modify, and their values. Surround the attribute value in hash marks (#).

Table 73.4 (continued)

ATTRIBUTE	ACTION	REQUIRED	DESCRIPTION
`generateUniqueFilenames`	`getAttachments`	No	A Boolean value (default: `no`) specifying whether to automatically generate unique file names for multiple attachments with the same file name. If `yes` is specified, ColdFusion appends an incrementing number to the file name (before the extension) of conflicting attachments.
`message`	`delete` `respond`	No	Optional message to send in the deletion or response notification.
`name`	`get` `getAttachments`	Yes	A ColdFusion query variable name that contains the retrieved events or information about the attachments that were retrieved.
`notify`	`delete` `respond`	No	Boolean value specifying whether to notify others of event changes.

`responseType`	`respond`	Yes	Must be one of the following:
			`accept`
			`decline`
			`tentative`

`result`	`create`	No	A variable name for the UID of the created event. Use this UID value in the `uid` attribute to specify that event for further actions other than `create`.

`uid`	`delete`
	`deleteAttachments`
	`getAttachments`
	`modify`
	`respond`
		Yes	Case-sensitive Exchange UID value(s) that uniquely identifies event(s) on which actions are performed.
			Only the `delete` action accepts a comma-delimited list of UID values; all other actions accept only a single UID value.

The `create` action creates calendar events. Use the `event` attribute to provide a structure that defines the calendar event: for example, attendees, duration, and reminders. Table 73.5 lists possible event items. Specify the `result` attribute to retrieve the UID of the created event. The following code creates a recurring birthday appointment:

```
<cfscript>
  stEvent.AllDayEvent = true;
  stEvent.isRecurring = true;
  stEvent.RecurrenceType = "YEARLY";
  stEvent.Subject = FORM.name&"'s Birthday";
  stEvent.StartTime = createDate(2007, 1, 9);
</cfscript>
<cfexchangecalendar action="create" event="#stEvent#"
   result="calendarID" server="#session.server#"
   username="#SESSION.mailUser#" password="#SESSION.mailPasswd#" />
<cfdump var="#calendarID#" />
```

TIP

To create an appointment, use the `create` action without specifying the `RequiredAttendees` or `OptionalAttendees` attribute.

Table 73.5 Calendar Event Properties

PROPERTY	DEFAULT	REQUIRED	DESCRIPTION
`AllDayEvent`	`false`	No, if `EndTime` is specified.	A Boolean value indicating whether this is an all-day event.
`Attachments`		No	One or more absolute paths to the files to send as attachments. Separate file paths with semicolons (;) on Windows, and colons (:) for Unix and Linux. Attachments are added to preexisting attachments when the `modify` action is used, and existing attachments are not deleted.
`Duration`		No	The duration of the event in minutes.
`EndTime`		No, if `AllDayEvent` is true	The end time of the event, in any valid ColdFusion date-time format.
`Importance`	`normal`	No	One of the following values: `high`, `normal`, `low`.
`IsRecurring`		No	A Boolean value indicating whether this event repeats. If true, you must specify a `RecurrenceType` element and elements to specify the recurrence details. Table 73.6 lists the recurrence fields.
`Location`		No	A string that specifies the event location.
`Message`		No	A string containing a message describing the event. The string can include HTML formatting.

Table 73.5 (CONTINUED)

PROPERTY	DEFAULT	REQUIRED	DESCRIPTION
`OptionalAttendees`		No	A comma-delimited list of mail IDs.
`Organizer`		No	A string that specifies the event organizer's name.
`Reminder`		No	The time (in minutes) before the event, to display a reminder message.
`RequiredAttendees`		No	A comma-delimited list of mail IDs.
`Resources`		No	A comma-delimited list of mail IDs for Exchange scheduling resources, such as conference rooms and display equipment.
`Sensitivity`		No	One of the following values: `normal`, `company-confidential`, `personal`, `private`.
`StartTime`		Yes	The start time of the event, in any valid ColdFusion date-time format. If you specify a date and time in this attribute and specify a `YEARLY` `RecurrenceType` value with no other recurrence attributes, the event recurs yearly at the day and time specified in this attribute.
`Subject`		No	A string that describes the event subject.

Table 73.6 Calendar Recurrence Types

ELEMENT	TYPE	DEFAULT	DESCRIPTION
`RecurrenceType`	All	`DAILY`	Used only if the `IsRecurring` attribute is true. Must be one of the following values: `DAILY`, `WEEKLY`, `MONTHLY`, `YEARLY`.
`RecurrenceNoEndDate`	All	`true`	A Boolean value; if true, the event recurs until changed or deleted. Mutually exclusive with `RecurrenceCount` and `RecurrenceEndDate`.
`RecurrenceCount`	All		The number of times the event recurs. Mutually exclusive with `RecurrenceEndDate` and `RecurrenceNoEndDate`.
`RecurrenceEndDate`	All		The date of the last recurrence. Mutually exclusive with `RecurrenceCount` and `RecurrenceNoEndDate`.

Table 73.6 (continued)

ELEMENT	TYPE	DEFAULT	DESCRIPTION
`RecurrenceFrequency`	`DAILY`, `WEEKLY`, `MONTHLY`	`1`	The frequency of the recurrence in days, weeks, or months, depending on the type. For example, for `DAILY` recurrence, a `RecurrenceFrequency` value of `3` schedules the event every three days.
`RecurEveryWeekDay`	`DAILY`		The recurrence of the event on every weekday, but not on Saturday or Sunday. Mutually exclusive with `RecurrenceFrequency`.
`RecurrenceDays`	`WEEKLY`		The day or days of the week on which the event occurs. Must be one or more of the following values in a comma-delimited list: `MON`, `TUE`, `WED`, `THU`, `FRI`, `SAT`, `SUN`. If you omit this field for a weekly recurrence, the event recurs on the day of the week that corresponds to the specified start date.
`RecurrenceDay`	`MONTHLY`, `YEARLY`		The day of the week on which the event occurs. Must be one of the following values: `MON`, `TUE`, `WED`, `THU`, `FRI`, `SAT`, `SUN`.
`RecurrenceWeek`	`MONTHLY`, `YEARLY`		The week of the month or year on which the event recurs. Valid values are `first`, `second`, `third`, `fourth`, `last`.
`RecurrenceMonth`	`YEARLY`		The month of the year on which the event recurs. Valid values are `JAN`, `FEB`, `MAR`, `APR`, `MAY`, `JUN`, `JUL`, `AUG`, `SEP`, `OCT`, `NOV`, `DEC`.

The `delete` action removes existing events from the server. You must specify one or more event UIDs in a comma-delimited list. ColdFusion will ignore any invalid UIDs and delete only events specified with valid ones. It will throw an error if all the UIDs are invalid.

The `deleteAttachments` action removes the specified existing attachment from the event on the server. You must specify a single event UID; multiple UIDs are not allowed.

The `get` action retrieves information about existing events. Use the `name` attribute to create a variable to contain the returned query. Use `<cfexchangefilter>` child tag to specify the event to retrieve.

TIP

Use the `get` action to retrieve the UID of events that you want to access with the `delete`, `deleteAttachments`, `getAttributes`, `modify`, and `response` actions.

The `getAttachments` action retrieves information about an existing event's attachments. You must specify a single event UID; multiple UIDs are not allowed. Use the `name` attribute to create a variable to contain the returned query.

NOTE

See the ColdFusion 8 LiveDocs for a description of the `get` and `getAttachment` returned query columns, at `http://livedocs.adobe.com/coldfusion/8/Tags_d-e_12.html`.

The `modify` action modifies existing events. You must provide the event's UID and an event item structure. You can modify only one event at a time; multiple UIDs are not allowed. Populate the event structure with only the event items that you want to modify. ColdFusion will add any specified attachments to existing event attachments. You must use the `deleteAttachments` action to delete existing attachments.

The `respond` action provides a response to meeting notifications sent with `<cfexchangemail>`. You must provide an `accept` or `tentatively accept` response to the meeting notification before the meeting will appear in your calendar and is accessible by `<cfexchangecalendar>`.

When using the `respond` action, you must specify a single event UID (multiple UIDs are not allowed) and the response type (`accept`, `reject`, or `tentatively accept`). You can also set a notification flag and send the creator a message.

<cfexchangecontact>

Use `<cfexchangecontact>` to create, delete, get, and modify Exchange contacts and retrieve contact record attachments. A persistent or transient connection is required when using this tag. Table 73.7 lists the `<cfexchangecontact>` attributes.

Table 73.7 `<cfexchangecontact>` Attributes

ATTRIBUTE	ACTION	REQUIRED	DESCRIPTION
`action`	N/A	Yes	One of the following actions to perform: `create`: Create a contact. `delete`: Delete one or more contacts. `deleteAttachments`: Delete a contact's attachment. `get`: Retrieve information about one or more contacts. `getAttachments`: Retrieve a contact's attachments. `modify`: Modify an existing contact.

Table 73.7 (continued)

ATTRIBUTE	ACTION	REQUIRED	DESCRIPTION
`attachmentPath`	`getAttachments`	No	The absolute path of the directory in which to save attachments. ColdFusion will create the directory if it does not exist. ColdFusion will not save any attachments if this attribute is omitted.
`connection`	all	No	The name of the Exchange Server connection specified in `<cfexchangeconnection>`. If omitted, you must create a connection by specifying the required `open` action `<cfexchangeconnection>` attributes in this tag.
`contact`	`create` `modify`	Yes	A structure containing the contact properties to set or change, and their values.
`generateUniqueFilenames`	`getAttachments`	No	A Boolean value (default: `no`) specifying whether to automatically generate unique file names for multiple attachments with the same file name. If `yes` is specified, ColdFusion appends an incrementing number to the file name (before the extension) of conflicting attachments.
`name`	`get` `getAttachments`	No	A ColdFusion query variable name that contains the retrieved contact records or information about the attachments that were retrieved.
`result`	`create`	No	A variable name for the UID of the created contact. Use this UID value in the `uid` attribute to specify that event for future actions on this new contact other than `create`.

`uid`	`delete`
	`deleteAttachments`
	`getAttachments`
	`modify`
		Yes	Case-sensitive Exchange UID value(s) that uniquely identifies contact(s) on which actions are performed.
			Only the `delete` action accepts a comma-delimited list of UID values; all other actions accept only a single UID value.

Use the `create` action to create a new contact. Use the `contact` attribute to specify a structure that defines the contact's properties: for example, first name, email address, and phone number. Table 73.8 lists possible contact properties. Specify the `result` attribute to retrieve the UID of the created contact. The following code accepts form values to create a new contact:

```
<cfscript>
  stContact.firstName = FORM.firstName;
  stContact.lastName = FORM.lastName;
  stContact.office = FORM.office;
</cfscript>
<cfexchangecontact action="create" contact="#stContact#"
   result="contactID" server="#session.server#"
   username="#SESSION.mailUser#" password="#SESSION.mailPasswd#"  />
<cfdump var="#contactID#" />
```

Table 73.8 Contact Properties

Assistant	Attachments	BusinessAddress	BusinessFax	Business-PhoneNumber
Categories	Company	Department	Description	DisplayAs
Email1	Email2	Email3	FirstName	HomeAddress
HomePhoneNumber	JobTitle	LastName	MailingAddressType	Manager
MiddleName	MobilePhoneNumber	NickName	Office	OtherAddress
OtherPhoneNumber	Pager	Profession	SpouseName	WebPage

The address fields (`BusinessAddress`, `HomeAddress`, and `OtherAddress`) require a structure containing the following keys:

- Street
- City
- State
- Zip
- Country

All other fields contain string data.

The `Attachments` field must contain the absolute file path names of any attachments to include in the contact. To specify multiple files, separate file paths with semicolons (;) for Windows and colons (:) for Unix and Linux.

The `Categories` field can have a comma-delimited list of the contact's categories.

The `DisplayAs` field defaults to FirstName, LastName if omitted.

The `delete` action removes contacts from the server. You must specify one or more contact UIDs in a comma-delimited list. ColdFusion will ignore any invalid UIDs and delete only contacts specified with valid ones. It will throw an error if all the UIDs are invalid.

The deleteAttachments action removes the specified existing contact's attachment. You must specify a single contact UID; multiple UIDs are not allowed.

The get action retrieves information about existing contacts. Use the name attribute to create a variable to contain the returned query. Optionally, use the <cfexchangefilter> child tag to filter the contacts to retrieve.

TIP

Use the get action to retrieve the UID of contacts that you want to access with the delete, deleteAttachments, getAttributes, and modify actions.

The getAttachments action retrieves information about an existing contact's attachments. You must specify a single contact UID; multiple UIDs are not allowed. ColdFusion retrieves the attachment and returns a query to the variable specified in the name attribute. If you omit the attachmentPath attribute, ColdFusion will retrieve only information about the attachment.

NOTE

See the ColdFusion 8 LiveDocs for a description of the get and getAttachment returned query columns, at http://livedocs.adobe.com/coldfusion/8/Tags_d-e_14.html.

The modify action modifies existing contacts. You must provide the contact's UID and a contact property structure. You can modify only one contact at a time; multiple UIDs are not allowed. Populate the event structure only with the event items you want to modify. ColdFusion will add any specified attachments to any existing attachments. You must use the deleteAttachments action to delete existing attachments.

<cfexchangefilter>

The <cfexchangefilter> tag provides parameters for filtering the results retrieved by the get action of <cfexchangecalendar>, <cfexchangecontact>, <cfexchangemail>, and <cfexchangetask>. Table 73.9 lists the <cfexchangefilter> attributes.

TIP

This tag is required only if you want to limit the number of items retrieved by the Exchange tag get actions. If you do not use <cfexchangefilter>, then ColdFusion will return the top 100 items by default.

Table 73.9 <cfexchangefilter> Attributes

ATTRIBUTE	REQUIRED	TAG	DESCRIPTION
name	Yes	All	The type of filter to use.
from	No	cfexchangecalendar cfexchangemail cfexchangetask	The start date or date and time to use for filtering. Can be in any valid ColdFusion date/time format. Mutually exclusive with the value attribute. If you specify a from attribute and omit the to attribute, the filter selects all entries on or after the date or time specified in this attribute.

Table 73.9 (continued)

ATTRIBUTE	REQUIRED	TAG	DESCRIPTION

`to`	No	`cfexchangecalendar`
		`cfexchangemail`
		`cfexchangetask`
			The end date or date and time to use for filtering. Can be in any valid ColdFusion date/time format. Mutually exclusive with the `value` attribute. If you specify a `to` attribute and omit the `from` attribute, the filter selects all entries on or before the date or time specified in this attribute.

`value`	No	All	A filter value for all non-date/time filters. Mutually exclusive with the `from` and `to` attributes. Empty strings cannot be used, or ColdFusion will throw an error.

`<cfexchangefilter>` is an optional child tag used only with the `get` action of `<cfexchangecalendar>`, `<cfexchangecontact>`, `<cfexchangemail>`, and `<cfexchangetask>`. It specifies filters for ColdFusion to match when retrieving items and attachments. The `name` attribute corresponds to the query object returned by the parent tag's `get` action. Only those items matching the filter are returned in a query to the variable specified in the parent tag's `name` attribute.

NOTE

For a detailed list of valid values for the `name` attribute, see the ColdFusion 8 LiveDocs at `http://livedocs.adobe.com/coldfusion/8/Tags_d-e_15.html`.

Other `<cfexchangefilter>` considerations include the following:

- ColdFusion returns a maximum of 100 items by default. You can specify a `maxrows` filter to increase or decrease the number of returned items. The value must be any integer greater than zero.
- The `value` attribute is mutually exclusive with the `from` and `to` attributes. If the `name` attribute specifies a field that takes text or numerical data, use the `value` attribute. If the `name` attribute specifies a field that takes a ColdFusion date/time object, use the `from` and `to` attributes to specify the range.
- In a date/time filter, you can omit either `to` or `from` to specify an open-ended range, such as all dates up to and including December 1, 2007.
- Date ranges are inclusive. The selected items include those with the specified `to` or `from` dates.
- ColdFusion performs literal string searches. You cannot use regular expressions, wildcards, or null values (empty strings). To find entries where a particular field has an empty value, get all entries and use a query of queries to filter the results to include only entries where the field is empty.

<cfexchangemail>

Use `<cfexchangemail>` to retrieve and delete Exchange messages and attachments. A persistent or transient connection is required for this tag. You can also retrieve meeting information, move messages, and set message properties. Table 73.10 lists the `<cfexchangecalendar>` attributes.

Table 73.10 `<cfexchangemail>` Attributes

ATTRIBUTE	ACTION	REQUIRED	DESCRIPTION
`Action`	N/A	Yes	One of the following actions to perform: `delete`: Permanently delete messages from the server. `deleteAttachments`: Delete a message's attachments. `get`: Retrieve one or more messages using a filter specified using `<cfexchangefilter>`. `getAttachments`: Retrieve attachments for a specified message. `getMeetingInfo`: Retrieve details about meetings for which you have a notification set, including meeting requests and cancellations. `move`: Move messages between folders, including the `Deleted Items` folder. `set`: Set the properties of a specific mail message.
`attachmentPath`	`getAttachments`	No	The path of the directory in which to save attachments. ColdFusion will create the directory if it does not exist. For relative paths, the directory root is the ColdFusion temporary directory, as returned by `getTempDirectory()`. Note that ColdFusion will not save any attachments if this attribute is omitted.
`connection`	All	No	The name of the Exchange Server connection specified in `<cfexchangeconnection>`. If omitted, you must create a connection by specifying the required `open` action `<cfexchangeconnection>` attributes in this tag.

Table 73.10 (CONTINUED)

ATTRIBUTE	ACTION	REQUIRED	DESCRIPTION
`destinationFolder`	`move`	No	The forward-slash (/) delimited path, relative to the root of the mailbox, of the folder to which to move the message or messages.
`folder`	All except `getMeetingInfo`	No	The forward-slash (/) delimited path, relative to the root of the mailbox, of the folder that contains the message or messages. `<cfexchangemail>` does not search subfolders. For the `get` and `move` actions, specifying a `<cffexchangefilter>` child tag with a `name="folder"` attribute is equivalent to setting this attribute and takes precedence over this attribute's value. If you omit this attribute, or for `get` and `move` actions, if you do not use the corresponding `cfexchangefilter` setting, Exchange looks in the top level of the Inbox.
`generateUniqueFilenames`	`getAttachments`	No	A Boolean value (default: `no`) specifying whether to automatically generate unique file names for multiple attachments with the same file name. If `yes` is specified, ColdFusion appends an incrementing number to the file name (before the extension) of conflicting attachments.
`mailUID`	`getMeetingInfo`	No	The case-sensitive UID of the mail message that contains the meeting request, response, or cancellation notification. Use this attribute if there are multiple messages about a single meeting.
`meetingUID`	`getMeetingInfo`	Yes	The case-sensitive UID of the meeting for which you received the notification.

Table 73.10 (continued)

ATTRIBUTE	ACTION	REQUIRED	DESCRIPTION
message	set	Yes	A structure containing the properties to set, and their values.
name	get getAttachments getMeetingInfo	Yes	A ColdFusion query variable name that contains the retrieved mail messages or information about the attachments or meeting that was retrieved.
uid	delete deleteAttachments getAttachments set	Yes	Case-sensitive Exchange UID value(s) that uniquely identifies event(s) on which actions are performed. Only the delete action accepts a comma-delimited list of UID values; all other actions accept a single UID value.

NOTE

If the file path value passed to the attachmentPath, folder, or the destinationFolder attribute, contains forward slashes (/), specify the folder name by using the _xF8FF_ escape character to prevent Exchange from interpreting the character as a path delimiter.

The delete attribute permanently deletes messages from the server; use the move action to move a message to the Deleted Items folder. You must specify one or more message UIDs in a comma-delimited list. ColdFusion will ignore any invalid UIDs and delete only messages specified with valid ones. It will throw an error if all the UIDs are invalid.

The deleteAttachments action removes the specified message's attachments. You must specify a single message UID; multiple UIDs are not allowed.

The get action retrieves information about existing messages. Use the name attribute to create a variable to contain the returned query. Optionally, use the <cfexchangefilter> child tag to filter the messages to retrieve.

TIP

Use the get action to retrieve the UID of items that you want to access with the delete, deleteAttachments, getAttributes, and modify actions.

The getAttachments action retrieves information about an existing message's attachments. You must specify a single message UID; multiple UIDs are not allowed. ColdFusion retrieves the attachment and returns a query to the variable specified in the name attribute. If you omit the attachmentPath attribute ColdFusion will retrieve only information about the attachment.

NOTE

For messages containing multiple attachments with the same name, the attachment information structure always lists the attachments with their original, duplicate name. The `generateUniqueFilenames` attribute affects only the physical file names on the disk.

The `getMeetingInfo` action retrieves meeting-specific information in messages about a meeting for which you have received a notification message, such as an invitation request or cancellation notice. This information is not directly reflected in the query returned by the `get` action.

Use the `meetingUID` attribute to specify an individual message. Use the `meetingUID` value returned in the `get` action's query object. If you receive multiple message notifications for a single meeting, you can use the `messageUID` attribute to specify an individual notification message to respond to. This action also returns a query object to the variable specified in the `name` attribute.

NOTE

See the ColdFusion 8 LiveDocs for a description of the `get`, `getAttachment`, and `getMessageInfo` returned query columns, at `http://livedocs.adobe.com/coldfusion/8/Tags_d-e_16.html`.

The `move` action moves messages between folders. You must provide the path for the destination folder. The default source folder is the mailbox root, but you can override this with the `folder` attribute. Using the `move` action to move messages to the `Deleted Items` folder is equivalent to a Microsoft Outlook user pressing the Delete key.

The `set` action modifies the read status, importance, and sensitivity message properties. You must specify a single contact UID; multiple UIDs are not allowed. Use the `message` attribute to specify a structure that defines the message properties to set. Table 73.11 lists valid property values.

Table 73.11 Message Property Values

PROPERTY	VALUES
`IsRead`	`yes, no`
`Importance`	`high, normal, low`
`Sensitivity`	`normal, company-confidential, personal, private`

`<cfexchangetask>`

Use `<cfexchangetask>` to create, delete, retrieve, and modify Exchange Server tasks and retrieve task attachments. A persistent or transient connection is required for this tag. Table 73.12 lists the `<cfexchangetask>` attributes.

Table 73.12 `<cfexchangetask>` Attributes

ATTRIBUTE	ACTION	REQUIRED	DESCRIPTION
`Action`	N/A	Yes	One of the following actions to perform: `create`: Create a task on the server. `delete`: Permanently delete tasks from the server. `deleteAttachments`: Delete a task's attachments. `get`: Retrieve one or more tasks using a filter specified with `<cfexchangefilter>`. `getAttachments`: Retrieve attachments for a specific task. `modify`: Modify an existing task.
`attachmentPath`	`getAttachments`	No	The path of the directory in which to save attachments. ColdFusion will create the directory if it does not exist. For relative paths, the directory root is the ColdFusion temporary directory, as returned by `getTempDirectory()`. Note that ColdFusion will not save any attachments if this attribute is omitted.
`connection`	All	No	The name of the Exchange Server connection specified in `<cfexchangeconnection>`. If omitted, you must create a connection by specifying the required `open` action `<cfexchangeconnection>` attributes in this tag.
`generateUniqueFilenames`	`getAttachments`	No	A Boolean value (default: `no`) specifying whether to automatically generate unique file names for multiple attachments with the same file name. If `yes` is specified, ColdFusion appends an incrementing number to the file name (before the extension) of conflicting attachments.
`name`	`get` `getAttachments`		A ColdFusion query variable name that contains the retrieved task records or information about the attachments that were retrieved.

Table 73.12 (continued)

ATTRIBUTE	ACTION	REQUIRED	DESCRIPTION
`result`	`create`	No	A variable name for the UID of the created task. Use this UID value in the `uid` attribute to specify that task for future actions on this task other than `create`.
`task`	`create` `modify`	Yes	A structure containing the task properties and their values to set or change.

`uid`	`delete`
	`deleteAttachments`
	`getAttachments`
	`modify`
		Yes	Case-sensitive Exchange UID value(s) that uniquely identifies task(s) on which actions are performed.
			Only the `delete` action accepts a comma-delimited list of UID values; all other actions accept a single UID value.

Use the `create` action to create a task. Use the `task` attribute to specify a structure that defines the task properties: for example, priority, status, and subject. Specify the `result` attribute to retrieve the UID of the created task. The following code accepts form values to create a simple task:

```
<cfscript>
  stTask.subject = FORM.subject;
  stTask.dueDate = FORM.dueDate;
</cfscript>
<cfexchangetask action="create" task="#stTask#"
   result="taskID" server="#session.server#"
   username="#SESSION.mailUser#" password="#SESSION.mailPasswd#"  />
<cfdump var="#taskID#" />
```

NOTE

The table of task properties can be found in the ColdFusion 8 LiveDocs at `http://livedocs.adobe.com/coldfusion/8/htmldocs/Tags_d-e_17.html`.

The `delete` action removes existing tasks from the server. You must specify one or more task UIDs in a comma-delimited list. ColdFusion will ignore any invalid UIDs and delete only tasks specified with valid ones. It will throw an error if all the UIDs are invalid.

The `deleteAttachments` action removes the specified existing task's attachments. You must specify a single task UID; multiple UIDs are not allowed.

The `get` action retrieves information about existing tasks. Use the `name` attribute to create a variable to contain the returned query. Optionally, use the `<cfexchangefilter>` child tag to filter the tasks to retrieve.

TIP

Use the `get` action to retrieve the UID of tasks that you want to access with the `delete`, `deleteAttachments`, `getAttributes`, `modify`, and `response` actions.

The `getAttachments` action retrieves information about an existing task's attachments. You must specify a single task UID; multiple UIDs are not allowed. Use the `name` attribute to create a variable to contain the returned query.

NOTE

See the ColdFusion 8 LiveDocs for a description of the `get` and `getAttachment` returned query columns, at `http://livedocs.adobe.com/coldfusion/8/Tags_d-e_17.html`.

The `modify` action modifies existing tasks. You must provide the task's UID and a task property structure. You can modify only one task at a time; multiple UIDs are not allowed. Populate the task structure only with the task properties you want to modify. ColdFusion will add any specified attachments to any existing attachments. You must use the `deleteAttachments` action to delete existing attachments.

Managing Exchange Server Connections

ColdFusion requires either a persistent or transient connection to the Exchange Server. These connections are made directly over either HTTP or HTTPS, or via a proxy server. ColdFusion connects to the mailbox of the login username by default, but you can also connect via Delegate Access.

Connection Requirements

The following conditions are required for a connection to an Exchange Server:

- Exchange Server, Exchange access, and WebDAV (Web-based Distributed Authoring and Versioning) configured in Microsoft IIS
- Outlook Web Access (OWA) enabled on the Exchange Server for all login users
- Valid SSL certificate for the Exchange Server in the JRE certificate store for an HTTPS connection

NOTE

ColdFusion relies on the JRE for SSL communication. It leverages the default JRE truststore for SSL certificate management and will allow (trust) SSL communications with any remote system whose certificate (or the certificate authority [CA] that created the certificate) is in the certificate truststore. For ColdFusion Server and Multiserver configurations, ColdFusion uses the JRE's `cacerts` file (`cf_root/runtime/jre/lib/security/cacerts` or `jrun_root/jre/lib/security/cacerts`) for remote computer certificates; for J2EE configurations, check your J2EE server's documentation for the location of the truststore.

You can change the JRE truststore by specifying the `javax.net.ssl.trustStore` system property as a JVM argument:

```
-javax.net.ssl.trustStore=<path_to_certificate_file>
```

For ColdFusion server configuration, you can set this property in the JVM Arguments text box in the ColdFusion Administrator's Server Settings > Java and JVM screen. For ColdFusion Multiserver configurations, you must set this property in the `java.args` section of the `jrun_root/bin/jvm.config` file. Consult your J2EE server documentations for ColdFusion J2EE configurations. Restart ColdFusion after the change is made.

Import certificates into the truststore using the Java `keytool` command, found in `jre_root/bin`. The basic syntax is:

```
keytool.exe -importcert -file <path_to_certificate_file> -keystore ..\jre\lib\
security\cacerts
```

You can provide a name for the imported certificate by specifying the `-alias` parameter. The `keytool` command will prompt you for the keystore password. The default password for the `cacerts` truststore is `changeit`.

To verify a successful import, use the `keytool` command with the `-list` argument:

```
keytool.exe -list -keystore ..\jre\lib\security\cacerts
```

This could be a relatively long list depending on the number of certificates in the keystore. Match your certificate fingerprint with the ones in the list. Using an alias for the import makes finding the certificate easier. If you provided an alias during the import, then specify the `-v` flag to the `list` command to force `keytool` to provide more verbose properties. Now find your alias in the list and verify that all the listed fields (for example, creation date, issuer, subject, and serial number) are complete and correct.

For more information about using the Java `keytool` command, visit `http://java.sun.com/javase/6/docs/technotes/tools/index.html#security` and select the correct `keytool` command page for your operating system (Solaris or Linux or Windows, for instance).

Persistent Connections

Persistent connections remain open until explicitly closed. This allows you to reuse a single connection for multiple tasks and can save resource overhead. When you use persistent connections, ColdFusion sets the `Keep-Alive` property for HTTP/S to `true` to keep the connection open beyond the current page request. Persistent connections should be manually closed; otherwise, ColdFusion will retain the connection until an inactivity timeout (typically 300 seconds) is reached, and then it will recover the connection resources.

TIP

Although a persistent connection lives beyond the current page request, subsequent page requests cannot reuse the connection. Create persistent connections in a shared scope (for example, application or session) to reuse them for multiple ColdFusion templates.

Use the `<cfexchangeconnection>` tag to create persistent connections. Specify the `open` action, a connection identifier, the Exchange server's IP address or host name, and a valid username and password. Specify the same connection identifier for `<cfexchangecalendar>`, `<cfexchangecontact>`, `<cfexchangemail>`, and `<cfexchangetask>` to reuse the connection. Use a second `<cfexchangeconnection>` with the same connection identifier and specify the `close` action to close the persistent connection. This code block shows how to use a persistent connection to retrieve a contact list:

```
<cfexchangeconnection connection="owsConn"
  action="open" server="#session.server#"
  username="#SESSION.mailUser#" password="#SESSION.mailPasswd#" />
<cfexchangecontact name="myContacts" action="get" connection="myConn" />
```

```
<cfdump var="#myContacts#">
<cfexchangeconnection connection="myConn" action="close" />
```

NOTE

You must use a `close` action with a matching connection identifier to close connections opened with the `open` action. Using a closing tag (`</cfexchangeconnection>`) has no effect.

NOTE

ColdFusion will throw an error if you call any Exchange tags with the connection attribute as children of `<cfexchangeconnection>`.

Transient Connections

Transient connections last for the duration of a tag's interaction with Exchange. Once the tag exits, the connection is closed. This feature is useful for executing single tasks in a ColdFusion template.

Create transient connections for `<cfexchangecalendar>`, `<cfexchangecontact>`, `<cfexchangemail>`, and `<cfexchangetask>` by specifying the necessary `<cfexchangeconnection>` `open` attributes—except the `connection` attribute—in the respective tags. Table 73.2 (earlier in this chapter) describes the `<cfexchangeconnection>` attributes. The following code sample uses a transient connection to retrieve a contact list:

```
<cfexchangecontact name="myContacts"
action="get" server="#session.server#"
username="#SESSION.mailUser#" password="#SESSION.mailPasswd#" />
<cfdump var="#myContacts#">
```

Delegate Account Access

Exchange Server users (called principals) can allow other users (delegates) to access their mailboxes and act on their behalf. This is called Delegate Access. Principals can grant reviewer (read-only), author (create and read), and editor (create, read, and modify) access to their calendars, contacts, inboxes, journals, notes, and tasks.

NOTE

Principals can grant access only to delegate accounts on the same Exchange Server. Delegate access must be granted on the Exchange Server prior to ColdFusion access.

ColdFusion can provide persistent or transient connection to the principal's calendar, contacts, inbox, and tasks. To access the principal's resources, specify the delegate's username and password in the `username` and `password` attributes, and the principal's mailbox name in the `mailboxName` attribute in one of ColdFusion's Exchange tags. For example, to give Nicole delegate access to Cynthia's contacts, use the following code:

```
<cfexchangecontact name="cynthiasContacts" action="get"
  connection="owsConn" mailboxname="cynthia" />
<cfdump var="#cynthiasContacts#">
```

Managing Exchange Server Items

ColdFusion can create, delete, retrieve, and modify Exchange Server events, contacts, and tasks with `<cfexchangecalendar>`, `<cfexchangecontact>`, and `<cfexchangetask>`, respectively. Exchange Server messages and their attachments can be read and deleted with `<cfexchangemail>`.

To manage the Exchange Server items, specify the appropriate action and connection information and a tag-specific structure containing the values to modify. The connection can be either persistent or transient. You specify Exchange Server UID values for each item being managed.

Retrieving Exchange Items and Attachments

Before you can access any Exchange items (events, contacts, messages, and tasks), you must retrieve the item's UID. The simplest method is to use the `get` action for the respective `<cfexchangecalendar>`, `<cfexchangecontact>`, `<cfexchangemail>`, and `<cfexchangetask>` tags. Specify the `name` attribute to provide a variable to hold the returned query object. Optionally, use `<cfexchangefilter>` to provide search properties to filter returned data. The general syntax for retrieving items is:

```
<cfexchange[calendar | contact | mail | task]
   action="get"
   name="variable name for result query"
   [connection information]
   <cfexchangefilter
      name="filter type"
      value"filter value>
    <cfexchangefilter
       name="data/time filter type"
       from="start date/time"
       to="end date/time">
</cfexchange[calendar | contact | mail | task]>
```

The following code will get all messages received today that have attachments:

```
<cfexchangeconnection action="open"
  connection="owsConn" server="#session.mailserver#"
  username="#session.mailuser#" password="#session.mailpasswd#" />
<cfexchangemail action="get" connection="owsConn" name="getMail2" >
  <cfexchangefilter name="timeReceived" from="#now()#" />
  <cfexchangefilter name="hasAttachment" value="true" />
</cfexchangemail>
<cfdump var="#getMail2#" />
<cfexchangeconnection action="close"
  connection="owsConn" />
```

To retrieve an item's attachments, you must first use the appropriate ColdFusion Exchange tag to retrieve the item's UID. Then reuse the ColdFusion Exchange tag specifying the following attributes:

- `action=getAttachments`
- `uid=`*`the UID of the retrieved item`*. The `getAttachments` action only accepts a single UID. If you are retrieving attachments for multiple items you must loop over the `getAttachments` action.

TIP

Each item type (event, contact, message, and task) has a different UID format.

- `name=a variable name to hold the returned query object`. This query object will contain the following columns: `attachmentFilename`, `attachmentFilePath`, `CID`, `isMessage`, `MIMEtype`, and `size`.

Specify the `attachmentPath` attribute to tell ColdFusion where to store the attachments; otherwise, ColdFusion simply retrieves the attachment information but not the physical file. ColdFusion will create the directory if it does not already exist. If an item has two or more attachments, use the `generateUniqueFilenames` attribute to resolve file name conflicts.

TIP

ColdFusion always lists attachments with their original name, so if a message has multiple attachments with the same name, you will see duplicates. The `generateUniqueFilenames` attribute affects only the physical file names on disk.

Let's retrieve the attachment information for the messages in the `getMail2` query. The following code loops over the `getMail2` query and returns a new query object for each UID returned by `getMail2`. Place this code after the `<cfdump>` tag and before the `<cfexchangeconnection action="close">` tag in the previous example.

```
<cfloop query="getMail2">
  <cfexchangemail action="getAttachments" name="getAttach" connection="owsConn" />
  <cfdump var="#getAttach#"><cfflush>
</cfloop>
```

Inline images in messages are retrieved as attachments. To display inline images in messages, do the following:

1. Get the message UID with the `<cfexchangemail>` `get` action.
2. Get the message attachments with the `<cfexchangemail>` tag `getattachments` action, specifying the UID of the mail message retrieved in the previous step. Also specify an `attachmentPath` attribute value that is under your Web root, so that you can access the saved files by using a URL.
3. Search through the `HTMLMessage` field text that you got in step 1 and find the image items by their content ID (CID) value.
4. Search the attachments query that you got in step 1. For each row with a CID column value that you got in step 3, get the corresponding `attachmentFilePath` column value.
5. Replace every `img` tag `src` attribute value with `attachmentFilePath`.
6. Display the resulting HTML.

Deleting Exchange Items

You can delete Exchange items by simply using the appropriate tag with the `delete` action and specifying the UID of the item to delete. All `delete` actions accept a comma-separated list of UIDs allowing deletion of multiple items with a single call. All attachments are deleted with the item. To delete attachments only, call the appropriate tag with the `deleteAttachments` action and the UID of the item whose attachments you want to delete. The following code will delete any all-day appointments from the past two weeks:

```
<cfexchangeconnection connection="owsConn"
  action="open" server="#session.mailserver#"
  username="#session.mailuser#" password="#session.mailpasswd#" />
<cfexchangecalendar name="oldAppts" action="get" connection="owsConn">
  <cfexchangefilter name="startDate"
    from="#dateAdd('ww', -2, now())#"  to="#now()#" />
  <cfexchangefilter name="allDayEvent" value="true" />
</cfexchangecalendar>
<cfif oldAppts.recordCount>
  <cfexchangecalendar action="delete"
     connection="owsConn" uid="#valueList(oldAppts.uid)#" />
</cfif>
<cfexchangeconnection connection="owsConn" action="close" />
```

Modifying Exchange Items

You can modify any Exchange calendar, contact, and task items that you can create with ColdFusion. You can set the `Importance`, `Sensitivity`, and `IsRead` flags for mail messages. You can also move messages to different Exchange folders.

NOTE

ColdFusion appends attachments to items with existing attachments; it does not replace them. To replace an attachment, first remove it with the `deleteAttachments` action; then add the new attachment with the `modify` action.

When using the `modify` action for `<cfexchangecalendar>`, `<cfexchangecontacts>`, and `<cfexchange-task>`, you must pass a structure containing the properties that you want to change and their new values. Specify only properties that you want changed; ColdFusion will not affect any properties not specified in the structure. The following code finds any contacts whose primary email address is an Adobe email address and sets their Company attributes to `Adobe Systems`:

```
<cfexchangeconnection action="open"
  connection="owsConn" server="#session.mailserver#"
  username="#session.mailuser#" password="#session.mailpasswd#" />
<cfexchangecontact name="getAdobeContacts" action="get" connection="owsConn" >
  <cfexchangefilter name="email1" value="@adobe">
</cfexchangecontact>
<cfscript>
  stContact.subject = "Adobe Systems";
</cfscript>
<cfloop query="getAdobeContacts">
  <cfexchangecontact action="modify" connection="owsConn"
    uid="#UID#" contact="#stContact#" />
</cfloop>
<cfexchangeconnection action="close" connection="owsConn" />
```

Use the `<cfexchangemail> set` action to modify a message's mail flags. Pass a structure of the flags you want to change to the `message` attribute. Use the `move` action to move messages from one folder to another. You must specify a new destination for the messages in the `destinationFolder` attribute. If your messages are not in the root `Inbox` folder, specify the source location in the `folder` attribute. This code block moves today's unread email to the `Junk` folder and marks it read.

```
<cfexchangeconnection action="open"
  connection="owsConn" server="#session.mailserver#"
  username="#session.mailuser#" password="#session.mailpasswd#">
<cfexchangemail action="get" connection="owsConn" name="getUnreadMail" >
  <cfexchangefilter name="timeReceived" from="#now()#" />
  <cfexchangefilter name="isRead" value="false" />
</cfexchangemail>
<cfset stMessage.isRead = true />
<cfloop query=="getUnreadMail">
  <cfexchangemail action="set" connection="owsConn"
     uid="#UID#" message="getUnreadMail" />
  <cfexchangemail action="move" connection="owsConn"
     uid="#UID#" destinationFolder="Junk" />
</cfloop>
<cfexchangeconnection action="close" connection="owsConn" />
```

Managing Meeting Notifications and Requests

Use `<cfexchangemail>` and `<cfexchangecalendar>` to manage meeting requests and notifications. Exchange sends meeting notices to your mailbox when someone:

- Sends you a meeting request
- Cancels a meeting on your calendar
- Responds to your meeting request and sets the `notify` flag `true`

Meeting requests do not appear on your calendar until you accept or tentatively accept them. The query object returned by a `<cfexchangemail>` `get` action provides the following meeting-related information: `meetingUID`, `messageType`, and `meetingResponse`. Use these fields to filter message items and to retrieve meeting messages.

The process is as follows:

1. Use a `<cfexchangemail>` tag with the `get` action and `<cfexchangefilter>` with a `name` attribute set to `messageType` and one of the following values: `MeetingUID`, `Meeting_Request`, `Meeting_Response`, or `Meeting_Cancel`.

   The returned query will populate the `meetingUID` field with the UIDs of matching meeting notifications.

2. Use the `<cfexchangemail>` tag with the `getMeetingInfo` action and pass the `meetingUID` value to the `meetingUID` attribute.

TIP

You can optionally specify the message UID value for the UID attribute to identify a specific message if the inbox contains multiple messages about a single meeting.

3. Code logic to use information in the returned query object: for example, to display only canceled meeting requests.
4. Use the `<cfexchangecalendar>` `respond` action to send a response to the meeting owner. Specify the following additional attributes:
   - Set `uid` attribute to the `meetingUID` value.
   - Set the `responseType` attribute to `accept`, `decline`, or `tentative`.
   - If you want to send response notification to the owner, set the `notify` attribute to `true`.

TIP

You can optionally use the `message` attribute to send the owner a message with your notification.

Here's a sample code snippet:

```
<cfexchangeconnection action="open"
  connection="owsConn" server="#session.mailserver#"
  username="#session.mailuser#" password="#session.mailpasswd#">
<cfexchangemail action="get" connection="owsConn" name="getRequests" >
  <cfexchangefilter name="messageType" from="Meeting_Request" />
</cfexchangemail>
<cfloop query="getRequests">
  <cfexchangemail action="getMeetingInfo" connection="owsConn"
     name="getMeeting" meetingUID="#UID#" />
</cfloop>
<cfdump var="#getMeeting#" />
<cfexchangeconnection action="close" connection="owsConn" />
```

CHAPTER 74

Integrating with .NET

IN THIS CHAPTER

Early in the year 2000, Bill Gates announced a new business strategy for Microsoft. Initially it was named Next Generation Windows Services (NGWS), and in the months following it was given the official title of .NET. The mission of the .NET platform as communicated by Microsoft was to provide for easier use of computers, meaning faster and simpler access to necessary applications, consistent communication, and improved security. These features would all use the most up-to-date Internet principles: XML (Extensible Markup Language) and the technology of ensuring confidentiality based on the P3P (Platform for Privacy Preferences Project) specification.

In this chapter, you'll learn how various .NET solutions can be designed and built to be easily integrated with ColdFusion 8.

NOTE

In our examples, we will be building all .NET solutions with the C# language. All examples in this chapter use Visual Studio .NET (VS.NET). For a free IDE, download one of Microsoft's free Visual Studio Express editions from `http://msdn.microsoft.com/vstudio/express/`.

.NET Fundamentals

At the programming level, .NET introduced an infrastructure that allows developers to build, deploy, and run applications and services that use .NET technologies. This includes the building of desktop and Web applications, business components, Web services, and more. At its core, the .NET Framework is made up of the Common Language Runtime (CLR) and the Framework Class Library (FCL). Microsoft has also developed various IDEs (integrated development environments) in support of architecting, building, and deploying applications built for the .NET platform.

The *Common Language Runtime (CLR)* is equivalent to the Java Virtual Machine (JVM). For those of you not familiar with either, the CLR is a run-time environment in which all .NET code executes. The CLR provides facilities for memory and exception management, debugging and profiling, and security.

The *Framework Class Library (FCL)* is how .NET exposes the Windows API. The FCL includes access to classes that allow for file I/O, database access, XML consumption and creation, the ability to exercise and build SOAP-based XML Web services, and run-time core functionality.

You can now integrate with .NET via ColdFusion in three ways: through a ColdFusion proxy (new to version 8), SOAP-based XML Web services, and a COM callable wrapper. This chapter focuses on ColdFusion to .NET via the new ColdFusion proxy support and ColdFusion and .NET interoperability via Web services, the two main and more current solutions associated with ColdFusion and Microsoft .NET integration. For information on COM callable wrapper-based integration, please visit MSDN (`http://msdn2.microsoft.com/en-us/library/f07c8z1c(VS.71).aspx`).

Accessing .NET Services

A new feature in ColdFusion 8 is support for connectivity to .NET assemblies or compiled `.dlls` (classes). This feature allows a developer to access .NET assemblies via Java proxies, ultimately exposing them as ColdFusion objects, and has been referred to as run-time unification. If you have used ColdFusion to access Microsoft's COM objects in past versions of ColdFusion and want to upgrade this infrastructure with .NET assemblies, then you will find the switchover easy. The engineers at Adobe continue to make ColdFusion integration with Microsoft solutions as seamless as possible.

ColdFusion supports two methods for connecting and retrieving information from .NET via the Java proxy. You can connect locally, with the ColdFusion 8 application server installed on the same machine as the .NET Framework, or remotely in a distributed configuration with .NET and ColdFusion running on separate machines. A typical infrastructure that would require a remote configuration is an installation of ColdFusion on a non-Windows platform such as Solaris or Red Hat. This machine would then connect to a Windows server via a remote call to the .NET side agent.

The connectivity between ColdFusion and .NET is maintained through a bridging technology known as JNBridgePro that allows the Java-based ColdFusion application server to connect seamlessly to .NET assemblies at run time. You can select the .NET-supported connectivity feature during installation if you are installing the full ColdFusion build on the same machine as the .NET framework. You use a separate standalone installer to use the .NET remote connection feature, i.e., if you are running ColdFusion on a Unix platform and are connecting remotely to a Windows machine hosting the .NET assemblies you wish to integrate with.

Whether you are installing the .NET connectivity support on a separate machine or on the same machine as the ColdFusion application server, after installation is complete, a service labeled ColdFusion 8 .NET Service is added to your services stack. This service provides all the administration and security features associated with configuring a registered .NET service on the Windows platform.

With the ColdFusion 8 .NET service installed, we'll look at a simple code example to see how easily the .NET Framework can be integrated into a ColdFusion application. Note that before starting any of these examples, the server on which you will be calling the .NET assemblies must have .NET version 2.0 installed. The examples use the `CFOBJECT` tag, although you can also use the `createObject` function in a similar way.

ColdFusion and .NET Local Integration Example

The first example uses one of the classes from the `System.Net` namespace. The `Dns` class enables basic domain name resolution. To call the `System.Net` namespace and instantiate the `Dns` class, the `CFOBJECT` tag is used. The `.net` and `dotNet` types were added in ColdFusion 8 to support the integration of .NET and ColdFusion with this tag.

The first set of examples uses a local version of the service to call the .NET Framework from ColdFusion.

Looking at Listing 74.1, we can see that with only two tags we can instantiate the `Dns` class and expose its public methods. The six key attributes added to the `CFOBJECT` tag to support .NET integration are `class`, `assembly`, `port`, `protocol`, `secure`, and `server`. These new attributes are detailed in the next section. Of the six new attributes, only `class` is required for instantiating a local .NET assembly.

Listing 74.1 `DnsMethods.cfm`—Instantiating a .NET Class

```
<!-- Instantiate the Dns class in System.Net.Dns Namespace -->
<cfobject type=".net"
    name="dns"
    protocol="tcp"
    class="System.Net.Dns"
    action="create"
    secure="no">

<!--- Investigate what the Dns class exposes --->
<cfdump var="#dns#">
```

We'll use `GetHostName()`, the second-to-last method in the dump output, for the next example. This method retrieves the host name of the computer (Listing 74.2). Run the `DnsGetHostName.cfm` file, and you should see the host name of your computer that is running ColdFusion.

Listing 74.2 `DnsGetHostName.cfm`—Exercise a .NET Method

```
<!-- Instantiate the Dns class in System.Net.Dns Namespace -->
<cfobject type=".net"
    protocol="tcp"
    name="dns"
    class="System.Net.Dns"
    action="create"
    secure="no">

<!--- Retrieve the host name --->
<cfdump var="#dns.GetHostName()#">
```

ColdFusion's new integration feature poses some concerns associated with data typing. If you have integrated with .NET via ColdFusion or Java in the past, you have likely experienced challenges in this area. ColdFusion does a good job of exposing the data or object type to be returned when calling a .NET class, although the more complex or proprietary the type, the greater the challenge consuming it will be. The ColdFusion development team at Adobe put impressive effort into automatic conversion of complex data types, as you will see later in this chapter when we discuss the automatic conversion of a .NET DataTable to a ColdFusion Query data type. Table 74.1 provides data type translation information for .NET, Java, and ColdFusion data types.

Table 74.1 .NET, Java, and ColdFusion Data Types

.NET TYPE	JAVA TYPE	COLDFUSION TYPE
`sbyte`	`byte`	`Integer`
`byte`	`short`	`Integer`
`short`	`short`	`Integer`
`ushort`	`int`	`Integer`
`int`	`int`	`Integer`
`uint`	`long`	`Number`
`char`	`char`	`Integer` or `String`
`long`	`long`	`Number`
`ulong`	`float`	`Number`
`float`	`float`	`Number`
`double`	`double`	`Number` Use the `PrecisionEvaluate()` function to access and display the full precision of a returned double value.
`bool`	`boolean`	`Boolean`
`enum`		No direct conversion; use dot notation to access enum elements—for example, `Person.LastName`.
`array`	`array`	`Array`
`string`	`string`	`String`
`System.Collection.Arraylist`	`java.util.ArrayList`	`Array` One-way .NET-to-ColdFusion conversion
`System.Collection.Hashtable`	`java.util.Hashtable`	`Structure` One-way .NET-to-ColdFusion conversion
`System.Data.DataTable`		`Query` One-way .NET-to-ColdFusion conversion
`System.DateTime`	`java.util.Date`	`Date/time`
`Decimal`	`java.math.Big`	`String`
`System.Decimal`	`Decimal`	`String`
`System.Object`		Strings are translated automatically, though other types require use of the `JavaCast()` function.

ColdFusion and .NET Remote Integration Example

This next example executes the same method as the first example but on a remote server. The six key attributes added to the `CFOBJECT` tag to support .NET integration are `class`, `assembly`, `port`, `protocol`, `secure`, and `server`. Table 74.2 describes these attributes.

NOTE

Make sure you have your server set up correctly before proceeding; here's an Adobe LiveDocs link to help you. See `http://livedocs.adobe.com/coldfusion/8/htmldocs/help.html?content=othertechnologies_10.html`.

Table 74.2 Attribute Changes for `<CFOBJECT>`

ATTRIBUTE	DESCRIPTION
`class`	This attribute specifies the .NET class name to be instantiated.
`assembly`	By default, this attribute points to `mscorlib.dll`, which is where the .NET core classes are housed. If the class that is to be instantiated requires libraries or assemblies outside the default `mscorelib.dll` library, you must specify a comma-delimited list of absolute paths if they are stored locally. If you are connecting remotely, you must identify the absolute path to the JAR files that represent the assembly. (This process is explained in detail later in this chapter.) Along with the default `mscorlib.dll`, if you have registered all supporting classes in the global assembly cache (GAC), you don't need to specify them in this `assembly` attribute either.
`port`	This attribute is optional. When specified, it must equal 6086, which is the attribute's only valid value because the .NET side agent listens on this port. This attribute and the value of 6086 are required only if the remote or side agent is used.
`protocol`	This attribute is optional. Its default value is `tcp`, which promotes binary data transfer over the TCP/IP protocol. Its other value, `http`, is slower, although it promotes the HTTP and SOAP communication protocol and may be necessary depending on the firewall configuration.
`secure`	If this attribute is true, it enables SSL communication between ColdFusion and the .NET side agent. Defaults to false.
`type`	This attribute is required, and there are two new types for .NET support. The values to designate .NET connectivity are `.net` and `dotNet`.

A separate configuration process is required when using ColdFusion to connect to a disparate Windows server hosting .NET. The process involves generating proxy JAR files. The generated JAR files allow for exposing the functionality built into the .NET assemblies (i.e., class names, methods, public properties).

To facilitate the creation of the Java proxy classes to be installed on the ColdFusion server, two applications are available: `jnbproxyGui.exe`, which is GUI based, and `jnbproxy.exe`, which is used from the command line. These programs are installed in the default `ColdFusion8DotNetService` root directory on the remote server along with detailed `jnbproxy.chm` help detailing the features of the GUI and command-line utilities.

The following steps describe how to create a Java proxy class using the GUI tool:

1. Open the root `ColdFusion8DotNetService` directory and execute the `jnbproxyGui.exe` application.
2. The first time you open the application, you must set the Java options.
   - Check the Start Java Automatically option.
   - Set the path to `java.exe` (for example, to `C:\ColdFusion8DotNetService\jre\bin\java.exe`).
   - Set the path to `jvm.dll` (for example, to `C:\ColdFusion8DotNetService\jre\bin\server\jvm.dll`).
   - Copy the `jnbcore.jar` file to a directory on the remote Windows server (for example, to `C:\ColdFusion8DotNetService\jre\lib`). Locate the file in your `cfroot/lib` folder if you're running ColdFusion in standalone mode, or in `cf_webapproot/WEB-INF/cfusion/lib` for a J2EE installation.
   - Copy the `bcel.jar` file to a directory on the remote Windows server and place it alongside the `jnbcore.jar` file.
   - Click OK to save your settings.

   Figure 74.1 shows sample settings.

Figure 74.1

JNBridgePro Java options.

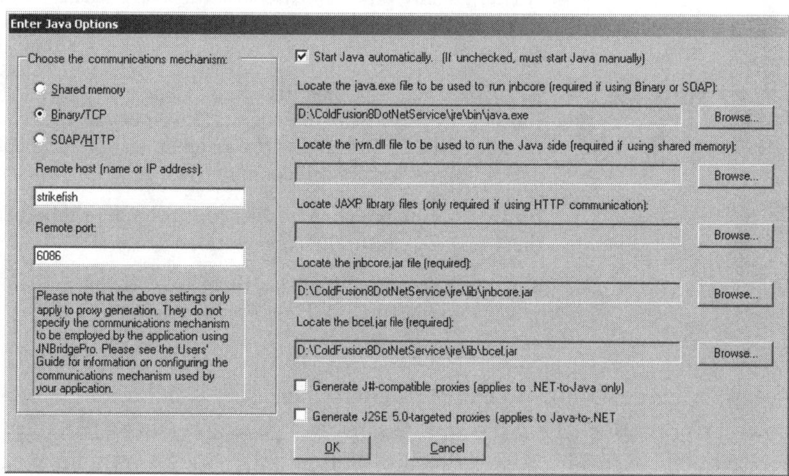

3. In the Launch JNBProxy dialog that appears, choose Create New Java > .NET Project and click OK.

   Now you're ready to set up and build the project.

4. From the Project menu, choose Edit Assembly List.

   You can add references to assemblies via the file path or the GAC. For this example, we're using Add from GAC.

5. Select Add from GAC. When the GAC browser screen appears, scroll to and select the System assembly (Figure 74.2).

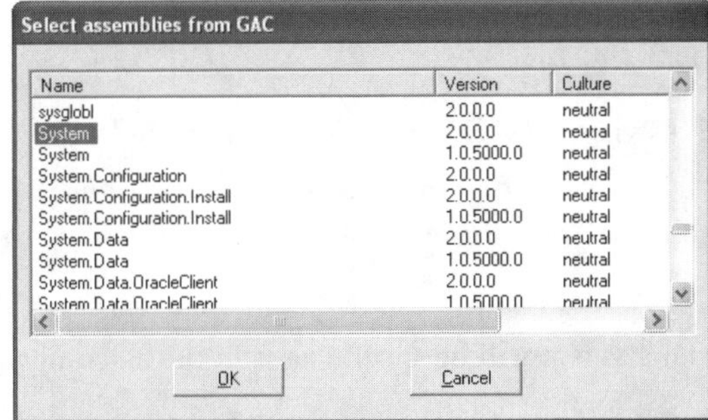

Figure 74.2
Global Assembly Cache browser panel.

   You will see the item registered in the Edit Assembly List panel.

6. Click OK.

7. From the Project menu, choose Add Classes from Assembly List.

8. In the Enter Class Name Here text box, enter the class: in this case, `System.Net.Dns` (Figure 74.3). Be sure to select include supporting class files for any assemblies where this option applies. Last, click Add to add the class.

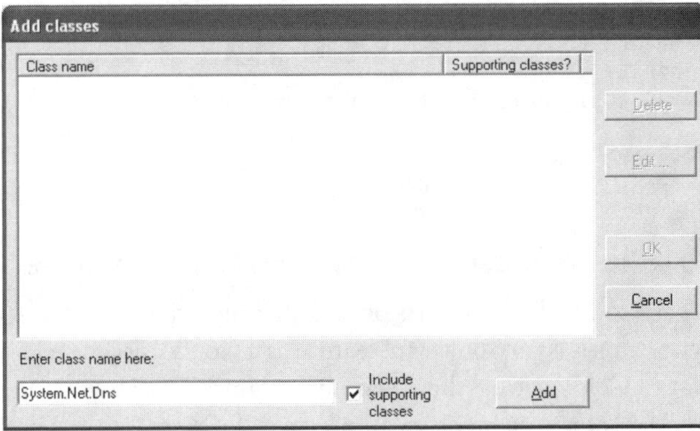

Figure 74.3
Add Classes window.

9. Click OK. Then, when you are prompted with a long operation notice, select Yes.

   The Environment panel will be populated with the class and supporting classes. Expand the `System.Net` item, and you will see that all the classes below it have been selected.

10. Click the Add button and make sure the all `System.Net` items are selected.

    You are ready to build your first proxy JAR file.

11. From the Project menu, choose Build, or click the Build icon.
12. Before you begin the build, specify a file name for the JAR file and make sure the ColdFusion 8 .NET service is stopped. For this example, name the file `FirstProject.jar`.
13. Save the `FirstProject.jar` file.

    You will see the status via the GUI as the file is constructed.

14. When the build is completed, copy the JAR file from the remote Windows server to the server running ColdFusion (for this example, the file was copied to a created directory at `C:\ColdFusion8\DotNetJars`).

    This path is important as you will be specifying it in the assembly attribute of the `CFOBJECT` tag.

15. Restart the ColdFusion 8 .NET service on the Windows server (if it is started, stop and restart it).

You are now ready to test. Listing 74.3 shows the code required to call the remote .NET assembly.

Listing 74.3 `DnsGetHostNameRemote.cfm`—Call a Remote Method

```
<!-- Instantiate the Dns class in System.Net.Dns Namespace -->
<cfobject type=".net"
    name="dns"
    class="System.Net.Dns"
    action="create"
    port="6086"
    secure="no"
    server="strikefish"
    assembly="C:\ColdFusion8\DotNetJars\FirstProject.jar">

<!--- Retrieve the host name --->
<cfdump var="#dns.GetHostName()#">
```

.NET `DataTable` to ColdFusion `Query` Conversion Example

As mentioned earlier, ColdFusion supports on-the-fly translation of a .NET `DataTable` to a ColdFusion `Query` data type. This is a very powerful feature as a ColdFusion `Query` is the most used complex data type, and prior to ColdFusion 8 there was no straightforward way to convert the proprietary data types. Listing 74.4 shows the mock creation of a .NET `DataTable`. The class name is `DtDemo`, and the method is `GetDataTable`. For this example, a class library project was created in Visual Studio 2005. This project was named `CFNETDemLib`, and it contains only one class, which is the `DtDemo` class.

Listing 74.5 demonstrates the call from ColdFusion to .NET that displays the contents of the created `DataTable` generated in the `DtDemo` class. When you run the `DisplayDataTable.cfm` code in your browser, you should see the output shown in Figure 74.4.

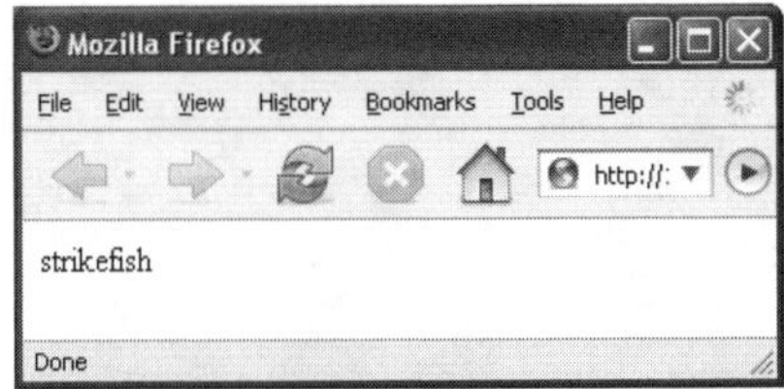

Figure 74.4
System.Dns.Net output.

Listing 74.4 `DtDemo.cs`—Create a .NET Data Table

```
using System;
using System.Collections.Generic;
using System.Data;
using System.Text;

namespace CFNETDemoLib
{
    public class DtDemo
    {
        public DataTable GetDataTable()
        {
  // Create a table specify some columns

      DataTable dTable = new DataTable("Authors");
      dTable.Columns.Add("firstName", System.Type.GetType("System.String"));
         dTable.Columns.Add("lastName", System.Type.GetType("System.String"));
         dTable.Columns.Add("age", System.Type.GetType("System.Int32"));

         // Create and add DataRow items to the table
         DataRow dRow1, dRow2, dRow3, dRow4;

        //Set dRow1 data
        dRow1 = dTable.NewRow();
        dRow1["firstName"] = "Ben";
        dRow1["lastName"] = "Forta";
        dRow1["age"] = 21;
        dTable.Rows.Add(dRow1);

        //Set dRow2 data
        dRow2 = dTable.NewRow();
        dRow2["firstName"] = "Ray";
        dRow2["lastName"] = "Camden";
        dRow2["age"] = 21;
        dTable.Rows.Add(dRow2);

        //Set dRow3 data
        dRow3 = dTable.NewRow();
        dRow3["firstName"] = "Robi";
        dRow3["lastName"] = "Sen";
        dRow3["age"] = 21;
        dTable.Rows.Add(dRow3);

        //Set dRow4 data
        dRow4 = dTable.NewRow();
        dRow4["firstName"] = "Jeff";
```

Listing 74.4 (continued)

```
            dRow4["lastName"] = "Bouley";
            dRow4["age"] = 21;
            able.Rows.Add(dRow4);

            //Return the DataTable
            return dTable;
            }
        }
    }
```

Listing 74.5 `DisplayDataTable.cfm`—Display Data Table

```
<!-- Instantiate the DtDemo class in CFNetDemoLib Namespace -->
<cfobject type=".net"
    protocol="tcp"
    name="dtDemo"
    class="CFNETDemoLib.DtDemo"
    assembly="C:\ColdFusion8DotNetService\CFNetDemo\CFNETDemoLib.dll"
    action="create"
    secure="no">

<!--- Retrieve the host name --->
<cfdump var="#dtDemo.GetDataTable()#">
```

.NET Web Service: Returning a Simple Type

Creating a Web service in Visual Studio .NET is relatively straightforward, as you will see by creating a new ASP.NET Web service project, shown in Figure 74.5. Once the creation process has been initialized, .NET creates all Web service projects under the `wwwroot` directory on the drive where you have IIS installed (Figures 74.6 and 74.7).

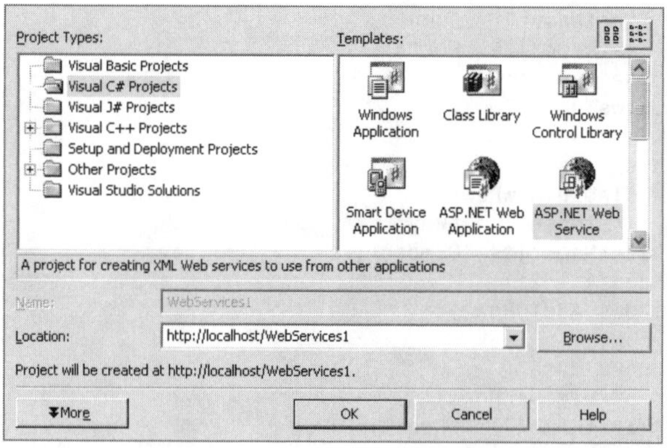

Figure 74.5

Building an ASP.NET Web Service with Visual C#.

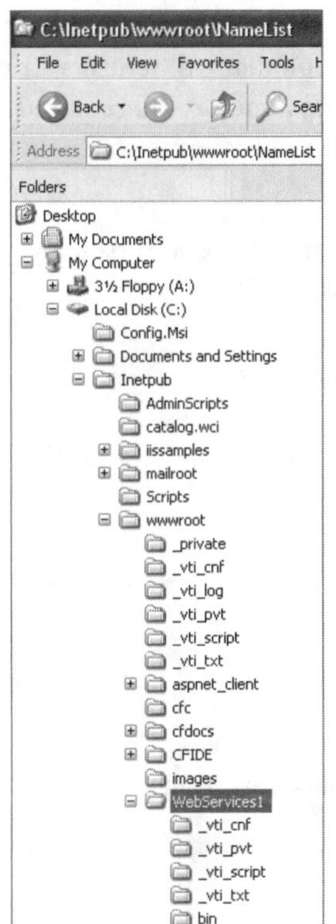

Figure 74.6

Creation of WebServices1 project under `wwwroot` directory.

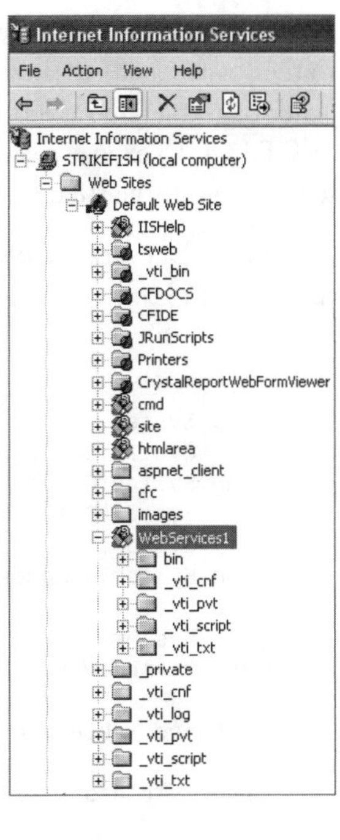

Figure 74.7

Creation of WebServices1 virtual directory in IIS.

Our first Web service example will return a simple data type of `string`. Table 74.3 shows the simple types natively supported between ColdFusion and .NET Web services through the common WSDL data type definitions.

Table 74.3 ColdFusion, WSDL, and .NET Data Types

COLDFUSION DATA TYPE	WSDL DATA TYPE	.NET DATA TYPE
`numeric`	`SOAP-ENC:double`	`Double`
`boolean`	`SOAP-ENC:boolean`	`Boolean`
`string`	`SOAP-ENC:string`	`String`
`array`	`SOAP-ENC:Array`	`primType[ ]`
`binary`	`xsd:base64Binary`	`Array of Byte objects`
`date`	`xsd:dateTime`	`DateTime`
`guid`	`SOAP-ENC:string`	`String`
`uuid`	`SOAP-ENC:string`	`String`

Notice that VS.NET creates an initial Web service skeleton; let's take a look at the code. We'll go to the [WebMethod] area of the code to create a method that will return a string containing none other than the famous Hello World. Notice how .NET imports all required libraries from the .NET FCL to expose the method as a Web service. See Listing 74.6 for the code generated along with the Hello World example.

Save the WebService1.asmx.cs file, and be sure to set it as the start page by right-clicking on it in the Solution Explorer window and choosing Set as Start Page.

Listing 74.6 WebService1.asmx.cs—Hello World Web Service

```
using System;
using System.Collections;
using System.ComponentModel;
using System.Data;
using System.Data.OleDb;
using System.Diagnostics;
using System.Web;
using System.Web.Services;
using System.Web.UI.WebControls;

namespace WebServices1
{
  public class WebService1 : System.Web.Services.WebService
  {
    //WebService1 class constructor
    public WebService1()
    {
      //CODEGEN: This call is required by the ASP.NET Web Services Designer
      InitializeComponent();
    }
    #region Component Designer generated code
      //Required by the Web Services Designer
      private IContainer components = null;
      /// <summary>
      /// Required method for Designer support - do not modify
      /// the contents of this method with the code editor.
      /// </summary>
      private void InitializeComponent()
      {
      }
      /// <summary>
      /// Clean up any resources being used.
      /// </summary>
      protected override void Dispose( bool disposing )
      {
        if(disposing && components != null)
        {
          components.Dispose();
        }
          base.Dispose(disposing);
      }
    #endregion
```

Listing 74.6 (continued)

```
        // Hello World example web service
      [WebMethod]
      public string HelloWorld()
      {
        return "Hello World";
      }
    }
  }
```

To compile the code in Visual Studio .NET, go to Build and select the proper build scenario. To build out all objects in the solution, select Build Solution or press Ctrl+Shift+B. Compile errors will be displayed in the output window.

The message "Build: 1 succeeded, 0 failed, 0 skipped" means you're ready to go and test your Web service. To do this, go to Debug and select Start. Internet Explorer will launch and display the `WebService1` class definition. The documentation provided through the .NET interface gives you the ability to test the `HelloWorld` method. Click it, and you'll see the test page. Click Invoke, and a browser window is displayed showing the XML generated by the operation. Figure 74.8 shows the screens and the expected results.

Figure 74.8

WebService1 class definition and test page with result.

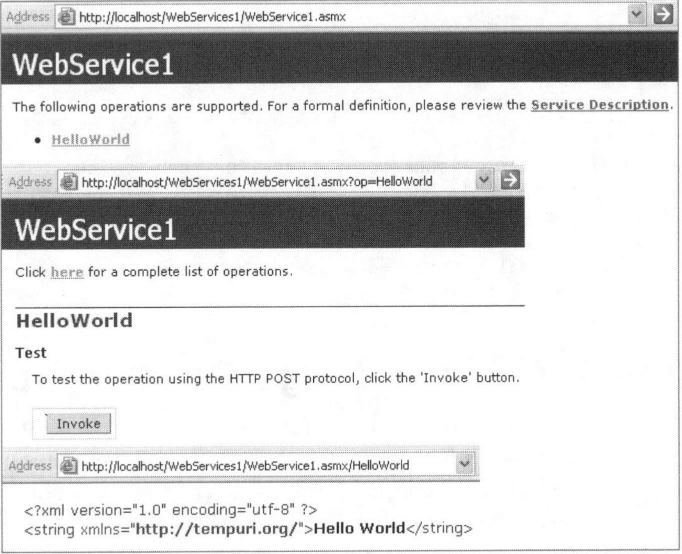

Notice that the default test scenario used here is exercised by an HTTP `POST`. This can prove problematic for applications that utilize an HTTP `GET` protocol to call the Web service. This issue is easily remedied by editing the `web.config` file associated with the .NET solution, so that it supports both protocols. This file is an XML-based text file that can contain standard XML document elements. It is located underneath the project tree when the project is created by default. Within the root element `<configuration>`, the `<system.web>` element supports configuring of Web services with the following:

```
<?xml version="1.0" encoding="utf-8" ?>
<configuration>

  <system.web>
    <webServices>
      <protocols>
        <add name="HttpGet"/>
        <add name="HttpPost"/>
      </protocols>
    </webServices>
```

ColdFusion and .NET Web Service Integration Example

Now let's call the Web service through ColdFusion. We'll be using the `<cfinvoke>` tag for our examples. Notice the code in Listing 74.7 that is required to connect to the .NET Web service. Browsing to the `HelloWorld.cfm` file displays the results of the call to the .NET Web service. A simple type of `string` with a value of `"Hello World"` is sent to the calling `<cfinvoke>` tag, and the `returnvariable` is displayed using `<cfdump>`.

Listing 74.7 `HelloWorld.cfm`—Call the ASP.NET Web Service

```
<cfsilent>
    <!--- Call the .NET web service with cfinvoke --->
    <cfinvoke
     webservice="http://localhost/WebServices1/WebService1.asmx?wsdl"
     method="HelloWorld"
     returnvariable="result" />
</cfsilent>
<!--- Display the value returned from the web service --->
<cfdump var="#result#" />
```

.NET Web Service: Returning a Complex Type

Passing simple types between .NET and ColdFusion is useful, but in most real-world situations complex types provide benefits that seasoned ColdFusion developers have become accustomed to—such as querying a database and displaying results with a minimal amount of code. Whether you're a seasoned ColdFusion developer or not, the next example will have you retrieving .NET `DataSet` objects into ColdFusion and sending ColdFusion queries to .NET.

In this first example of a complex-type scenario, we will be querying a Microsoft Access database and storing the result in an ADO.NET `DataSet`. A `DataSet` object in its most complex form stores a memory-resident representation of a relational database; that is, a collection of tables including queried data from various data stores. `DataSets` work very similarly to storing multiple ColdFusion queries inside of a `Structure`. Our example will not be enforcing any referential integrity within the `DataSet`. We will be using the `DataSet` object to store two result sets from two different SQL `SELECT` statements. The end result of this example will be a ColdFusion `Structure` containing multiple queries. We will achieve this by parsing the resulting XML from the .NET Web service and storing the data as such.

By analyzing the `NameService.asmx.cs` (Listing 74.8) code, we notice that there is one method defined: `GetNames`.

Listing 74.8 `NameService.asmx.cs`—ASP.NET Names Web Service

```
using System;
using System.Collections;
using System.ComponentModel;
using System.Data;
using System.Data.OleDb;
using System.Diagnostics;
using System.Web;
using System.Web.Services;
using System.Web.UI.WebControls;

namespace WebServices1
{
  public class NameService : System.Web.Services.WebService
  {
    private DataSet namesDataSet; //Declare the Dataset object
    //NameService class constructor
    public NameService()
    {
      //CODEGEN: This call is required by the ASP.NET Web Services Designer
      InitializeComponent();
    }
    #region Component Designer generated code
      //Required by the Web Services Designer
      private IContainer components = null;
      /// <summary>
      /// Required method for Designer support - do not modify
      /// the contents of this method with the code editor.
      /// </summary>
      private void InitializeComponent()
      {
      }
      /// <summary>
      /// Clean up any resources being used.
      /// </summary>
      protected override void Dispose( bool disposing )
      {
        if(disposing && components != null)
        {
          components.Dispose();
        }
        base.Dispose(disposing);
      }
    #endregion
    // The GetNames() example service returns a DataSet of names
    [WebMethod]
    public DataSet GetNames(string sFilter1, string sFilter2)
    {
      //Assign a SQL statement with wildcard filter to string variables
```

Listing 74.8 (continued)

```
        string sFilterWild1 = sFilter1 + "%'";
        string sFilterWild2 = sFilter2 + "%'";
        string sqlStr = "SELECT * FROM [names] "
                + "WHERE name LIKE '";
        string sqlStr1 = sqlStr + sFilterWild1;
        string sqlStr2 = sqlStr + sFilterWild2;
        //Create an OleDbConnection object
        OleDbConnection namesConn = new OleDbConnection(@"Provider="
                      + @"Microsoft.Jet.OLEDB.4.0; Data Source=C:\Inetpub\wwwroot\"
                      + @"WebServices1\Names.mdb;");
        //Create a DataSet object
        namesDataSet = new DataSet("TheDataSet");
        try
        {
          namesConn.Open();
          //Using the OleDbDataAdapter execute the query
          OleDbDataAdapter namesAdapter = new OleDbDataAdapter();
          //Define the command
          namesAdapter.SelectCommand = new OleDbCommand(sqlStr1,namesConn);
          //Add the Table 'names'to the dataset
          namesAdapter.Fill(namesDataSet,"TheDataSet");
          //Add second command result
          namesAdapter.SelectCommand = new OleDbCommand(sqlStr2,namesConn);
          namesAdapter.Fill(namesDataSet,"TheDataSet");
          namesAdapter.Dispose();
        }
        catch(Exception e)
        {
          Debug.WriteLine("Error in connecting! "+e.ToString(), "Error");
        }
        finally
        {
          //Close the OleDbConnection
          namesConn.Close() ;
          namesConn.Dispose();
        }
        return namesDataSet;
      }
    }
  }
```

The method `GetNames` accepts two string parameters, returning an object of type `DataSet`. This is clear-cut when analyzing the C# code. The waters muddy a bit when analyzing the WSDL that is generated from the service. Go to `http://localhost/WebServices1/NameService.asmx?wsdl` in the browser and analyze the resulting XML output. The key ingredient to look for in the WSDL XML is the `<wsdl:operation>` or `<operation>` element. This element defines the functions (methods) within the Web service. The `<wsdl:message>` or `<message>` element defines the input and output details. See Listing 74.9 for snippets of the WSDL generated for the `NameService.asmx`.

```
- <portType name="NameServiceHttpGet">
- <operation name="GetNames">
  <input message="s0:GetNamesHttpGetIn" />
  <output message="s0:GetNamesHttpGetOut" />
  </operation>
```

```
  </portType>

- <message name="GetNamesHttpGetIn">
  <part name="sFilter1" type="s:string" />
  <part name="sFilter2" type="s:string" />
  </message>
- <message name="GetNamesHttpGetOut">
  <part name="Body" element="s0:DataSet" />
  </message>
```

Listing 74.9 `NameService.asmx`—List of Methods

```
<!-- List of functions (methods) -->
<wsdl:portType name="NameServiceHttpGet">
        <wsdl:operation name="GetNames">
        <wsdl:input message="tns:GetNamesHttpGetIn" />
        <wsdl:output message="tns:GetNamesHttpGetOut" />
    </wsdl:operation>
</wsdl:portType>

<!-- List of input parameters -->
<wsdl:message name="GetNamesHttpGetIn">
    <wsdl:part name="sFilter1" type="s:string" />
    <wsdl:part name="sFilter2" type="s:string" />
</wsdl:message>

<!-- Output definition -->
<wsdl:message name="GetNamesHttpGetOut">
    <wsdl:part name="Body" element="tns:DataSet" />
</wsdl:message>
```

A ColdFusion user-defined function (UDF) was written to encapsulate the code required to consume a .NET `DataSet` returned from `NameService.asmx` (see Listing 74.10).

Listing 74.10 `NameDump.cfm`—Dataset Output from .NET Web Service

```
<cffunction name="convertDotNetDataset"
  returnType="struct">
  <cfargument name="dataset" required="true">
  <!--- Local Variables --->
  <cfset var result = structNew() />
  <cfset var aDataset = dataset.get_any() />
  <cfset var xSchema  = xmlParse(aDataset[1]) />
  <cfset var xTables = xSchema["xs:schema"]
    ["xs:element"]["xs:complexType"]["xs:choice"] />
  <cfset var xData  = xmlParse(aDataset[2]) />
  <cfset var xRows = xData["diffgr:diffgram"]
    ["TheDataSet"] />
  <cfset var tableName = "" />
  <cfset var thisRow = "" />
  <cfset var i = "" />
  <cfset var j = "" />

  <!--- Create Queries --->w
  <cfloop from="1" to="#arrayLen(xTables.xmlChildren)#" index="i">
    <cfset tableName = xTables.xmlChildren[i].xmlAttributes.name />
```

Listing 74.10 (CONTINUED)

```
    <cfset xColumns =
xTables.xmlChildren[i].xmlChildren[1].xmlChildren[1].xmlChildren/>
    <cfset result[tableName] = queryNew("") />
    <cfloop from="1" to="#arrayLen(xColumns)#" index="j">
      <cfset queryAddColumn(result[tableName], xColumns[j].xmlAttributes.name,
arrayNew(1)) />
    </cfloop>
  </cfloop>

  <!--- Populate Queries --->
  <cfloop from="1" to="#arrayLen(xRows.xmlChildren)#" index="i">
    <cfset thisRow = xRows.xmlChildren[i] />
    <cfset tableName = thisRow.xmlName />
    <cfset queryAddRow(result[tableName], 1) />
    <cfloop from="1" to="#arrayLen(thisRow.xmlChildren)#" index="j">
      <cfset querySetCell(result[tableName], thisRow.xmlChildren[j].xmlName,
thisRow.xmlChildren[j].xmlText, result[tableName].recordCount) />
    </cfloop>
  </cfloop>
  <cfreturn result>
</cffunction>

<!--- Create arguments for .NET Web Service(Web Method) --->
<cfset args = StructNew()>
<cfset args.sFilter1 = "j">
<cfset args.sFilter2 = "s">

<!--- Invoke the .NET Web Service(Web Method) --->
<cfinvoke webservice="http://localhost/WebServices1/NameService.asmx?wsdl"
          method="GetNames"
          argumentcollection="#args#"
          returnvariable="result">
<cfset aDataset = result.get_any() />
<cfset xSchema  = xmlParse(aDataset[1]) />
<cfset xData  = xmlParse(aDataset[2]) />
<!--- Convert result to CF queries --->
<cfset result = convertDotNetDataset(result) />

<!--- Display --->
<cfdump var="#xData#" /><cfabort />
<cfdump var="#result#" />
```

First let's focus on the code listed below the UDF. We initially need to define the two arguments to pass to `GetNames`. This is done by creating a `Structure` to hold the two arguments. Next, the `<cfinvoke>` tag is used to define the `webservice`, `method`, `argumentcollection`, and `returnvariable` associated with the Web service. A `<cfdump>` is used to display the result, containing the array of methods returned by the call to the Web service.

We must return the array of `MessageElement` objects by utilizing the `get_any()` method. Wrapping the `xmlParse` function around each array reference variable will expose the XML associated with the `Schema` and `DiffGram` data container. The `DiffGram` is a Microsoft proprietary format primarily used by the .NET Framework to serialize the contents of a `DataSet`.

Now that our references are in place, they are output in the example code to display their contents with <cfdump>. The results of the call to the UDF are also displayed. Figure 74.9 shows a snapshot of the collapsed structures and their descriptions.

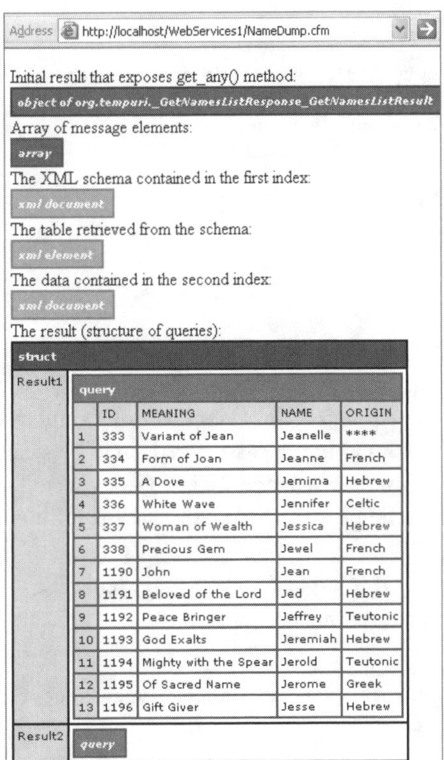

	ID	MEANING	NAME	ORIGIN
1	333	Variant of Jean	Jeanelle	****
2	334	Form of Joan	Jeanne	French
3	335	A Dove	Jemima	Hebrew
4	336	White Wave	Jennifer	Celtic
5	337	Woman of Wealth	Jessica	Hebrew
6	338	Precious Gem	Jewel	French
7	1190	John	Jean	French
8	1191	Beloved of the Lord	Jed	Hebrew
9	1192	Peace Bringer	Jeffrey	Teutonic
10	1193	God Exalts	Jeremiah	Hebrew
11	1194	Mighty with the Spear	Jerold	Teutonic
12	1195	Of Sacred Name	Jerome	Greek
13	1196	Gift Giver	Jesse	Hebrew

Figure 74.9
Dump of result returned from UDF.

The chicken came before the egg somewhat in this last scenario, and you are probably asking yourself how these references are used in the UDF to create a structure of queries. Notice how the <cffunction> `convertDotNetDataset` is used to parse the return from the call to the Web service described earlier. A `Structure` is created, along with the references to the resulting XML, and the query objects are created and populated with just a few lines of code. Observe the use of `xmlChildren` and `xmlAttributes` to reference the returned columns and related data through the use of a nested loop.

ColdFusion Web Service: Returning a Complex Type

Next we will return a ColdFusion query via a Web service, to a calling ASP.NET function. First let's create our CFC, which will contain the remote function (Listing 74.11).

Listing 74.11 `NameService.cfc`—ColdFusion Names Web Service

```
<cfcomponent>
  <cffunction access="remote"
   name="GetNames"
   output="false"
   returntype="query"
   displayname="GetNames"
   hint="This function accepts a string filter and returns a query.">
   <cfargument name="sFilter" type="string" required="true" />
   <cfquery name="result" datasource="names">
       SELECT *
       FROM [names]
       WHERE name LIKE '#sFilter#%'
   </cfquery>
   <cfreturn result>
  </cffunction>
</cfcomponent>
```

The query executes the same query as our .NET Web service did. Remember, a data source must be created in the ColdFusion Administrator to connect to the Access database. It will return a complex type of `QueryBean`. A `QueryBean` is an object that contains a one-dimensional array of column names, and a two-dimensional array containing the associated data. This can be seen in the WSDL output associated with the `GetNames` function (Listing 74.12). Go to `http://127.0.0.1:port/WebServices1/NameService.cfc?wsdl` in the browser and analyze the resulting XML output.

Listing 74.12 `NameServices.cfc`—WSDL Output from `NameServices.cfc`

```
<complexType name="ArrayOf_xsd_string">
  <complexContent>
   <restriction base="soapenc:Array">
     <attribute ref="soapenc:arrayType" wsdl:arrayType="xsd:string[]" />
   </restriction>
  </complexContent>
</complexType>
<complexType name="ArrayOfArrayOf_xsd_anyType">
  <complexContent>
    <restriction base="soapenc:Array">
      <attribute ref="soapenc:arrayType" wsdl:arrayType="xsd:anyType[][]" />
    </restriction>
  </complexContent>
</complexType>
<complexType name="QueryBean">
  <sequence>
    <element name="columnList" nillable="true" type="impl:ArrayOf_xsd_string" />
    <element name="data" nillable="true" type="impl:ArrayOfArrayOf_xsd_anyType" />
  </sequence>
</complexType>
```

Now that the CFC has been created, we'll access it in ASP.NET and bind the resulting object to a `DataGrid` for display purposes. In Listing 74.13, the code to retrieve the `QueryBean` object and data can be seen at the beginning of the `Page_Load` method.

Listing 74.13 `NameDump.aspx.cs`—`CFQUERY` Output from ColdFusion Web Service

```
using System;
using System.Collections;
using System.ComponentModel;
using System.Data;
using System.Drawing;
using System.Web;
using System.Web.SessionState;
using System.Web.UI;
using System.Web.UI.WebControls;
using System.Web.UI.HtmlControls;

namespace WebServices1
{
  public class NameDump : Page
  {
    protected DataGrid DataGrid1;
    private void Page_Load(object sender, EventArgs e)
    {
      //Create the string filter to pass to the web service
      string sFilter = "je";
      //Reference the ColdFusion web service
      GetNamesCFC.NameServiceService cfWs = new GetNamesCFC.NameServiceService();
      //Reference the QueryBean that ColdFusion returns from the web service
      GetNamesCFC.QueryBean qBean = cfWs.GetNames(sFilter);
      DataTable dTable = MakeTable(qBean.columnList);
      object oData = new object();
      DataRow row = null;
      int iCount = 0;

      //Add QueryBean data to the DataTable
      for (int i=0;i<=qBean.data.Length-1;i++)
      {
        oData = qBean.data[i];
        row = dTable.NewRow();
        foreach(object oLoopData in ((Array)(oData)))
        {
          row[iCount] = oLoopData;
          iCount = iCount + 1;
        }
        iCount = 0;
        dTable.Rows.Add(row);
      }
      DataGrid1.DataSource = dTable;
      DataBind();
    }

    private DataTable MakeTable(string[] sColumns)
    {
      //Make a table with all of the names from the array sColumns column
      //list contained in the QueryBean
      DataTable dTable = new DataTable("dTable");
      DataColumn dColumn;

      foreach(string columnName in sColumns)
      {
        dColumn = new DataColumn(columnName, Type.GetType("System.String"));
```

Listing 74.13 (CONTINUED)

```
            dTable.Columns.Add(dColumn);
          }
          return dTable;
        }
        #region Web Form Designer generated code
          override protected void OnInit(EventArgs e)
          {
            //
            // CODEGEN: This call is required by the ASP.NET Web Form Designer.
            //
            InitializeComponent();
            base.OnInit(e);
          }

          /// <summary>
          /// Required method for Designer support - do not modify
          /// the contents of this method with the code editor.
          /// </summary>
          private void InitializeComponent()
          {
            this.Load += new System.EventHandler(this.Page_Load);
          }
        #endregion
      }
    }
```

Before we can create the initial objects containing the `QueryBean` data, a Web Reference must be created. This is done by clicking the Project tab in the VS.NET window and then clicking Add Web Reference in the drop-down list. The Add Web Reference interface is then displayed; it has a text box for you to supply the URL to the CFC (`http://127.0.0.1:port/WebServices1/NameService.CFC?wsdl`). Click the Go button; when the connection is successful, the service's methods are displayed. Enter a Reference name to use in code, click Add Reference, and you're ready to include the call to the Web service in your code (Figure 74.10).

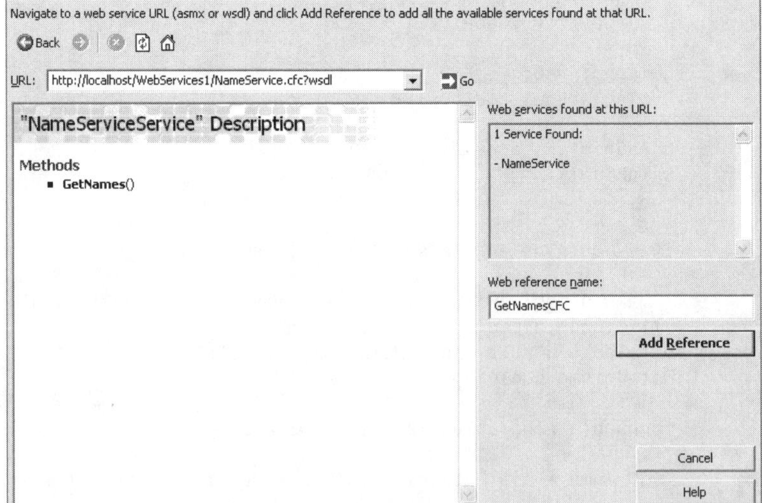

Figure 74.10

Add Web Reference window.

Looking over the code, you can see that the filter, the Web service reference, and the dynamically generated `DataTable` are created in the `Page_Load` method of the `NameDump.aspx` page. The `DataTable` is initially created by passing the `columnList` array to the `MakeTable` method. The returned `DataTable` is populated by looping over the `data` array associated with the `QueryBean`. Lastly, the `DataGrid` is bound to the `DataTable`. If you browse to `NameDump.aspx`, you will see the resulting output (Figure 74.11).

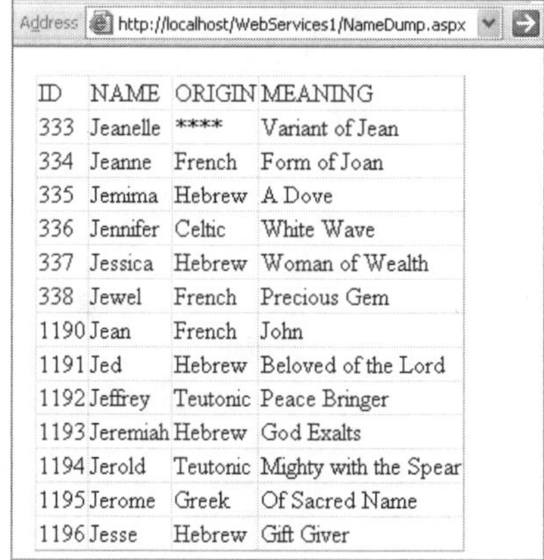

ID	NAME	ORIGIN	MEANING
333	Jeanelle	****	Variant of Jean
334	Jeanne	French	Form of Joan
335	Jemima	Hebrew	A Dove
336	Jennifer	Celtic	White Wave
337	Jessica	Hebrew	Woman of Wealth
338	Jewel	French	Precious Gem
1190	Jean	French	John
1191	Jed	Hebrew	Beloved of the Lord
1192	Jeffrey	Teutonic	Peace Bringer
1193	Jeremiah	Hebrew	God Exalts
1194	Jerold	Teutonic	Mighty with the Spear
1195	Jerome	Greek	Of Sacred Name
1196	Jesse	Hebrew	Gift Giver

Figure 74.11
Output from `NameDump.aspx`.

NOTE

It is important to understand that when retrieving any complex type from a Web service call, ColdFusion will expose `get` methods to reference them in code. These methods are exposed by using `<cfdump>` to expose the initial result returned from the Web service. You may have to take out a magnifying glass to examine the WSDL associated with the Web service, but this can prove to be quite entertaining, especially if you are a Sherlock Holmes or James Bond zealot.

Summing Up

The information in this chapter sets you well on your way to integrating .NET with ColdFusion. For references outside the context of this chapter regarding ColdFusion and .NET integration, go to `http://www.adobe.com/devnet` or `http://msdn.microsoft.com/netframework`.

CHAPTER 75

Extending ColdFusion with COM

IN THIS CHAPTER

One commonly overlooked feature of ColdFusion is its ability to interact with objects external to the ColdFusion Application Server. These objects can be third-party software packages such as Microsoft Office, or they can be custom objects created by the developer. Although external objects come in different flavors, such as COM and DCOM and CORBA, this chapter focuses on the implementation of COM in ColdFusion.

COM (Component Object Model) and DCOM (Distributed Component Object Model) are architecture specifications developed by Microsoft, used primarily on the Windows platform. COM enables applications to "talk" with one another through a set of interfaces such as methods and properties. DCOM, similarly, is for remote distribution of these same interfaces; for example, accessing an object remotely over a network. By developing COM objects that adhere to the COM specification, you can overcome some of the issues inherent in building any application:

- Extending functionality without damaging the application
- Removing, upgrading, and replacing features easily
- Integration of new applications with existing applications
- Building applications with more than one programming language

Understanding COM

In the context of a ColdFusion Application, ColdFusion 8 is the client, the object is the server, and the COM automation system is the liaison between the two. With a fundamental understanding of `<cfobject>` and the objects you are using, you can easily employ COM in a ColdFusion application. Following are some of the most basic benefits of using COM in your applications:

- Access to functionality otherwise unavailable to ColdFusion

- Use of built-in functionality of applications such as Microsoft Office and graphing and mapping applications
- Capability to perform complex operations that are better suited for the speed benefits of compiled objects, such as EXE files and DLL files

NOTE

Although third-party implementations of COM do exist on UNIX systems, ColdFusion's support for COM is limited to the Windows platform. In short, this chapter applies only to ColdFusion 8 for Windows.

Working with COM Objects in ColdFusion

There are two ways to work with COM objects in ColdFusion. Both accomplish the same result: returning an instance of the COM object that you want to work with. The method you choose is mainly a matter of personal preference. You can use either of the following interchangeably:

- The `<cfobject>` tag
- The `CreateObject()` function

To work with COM using `<cfscript>` syntax, you need to use the `CreateObject()` function; otherwise, the `<cfobject>` tag will probably feel more familiar to you and look more consistent with the rest of your CFML code. You could just as easily use the `CreateObject()` function within normal CFML code by using the `<cfset>` tag.

Using COM with `<cfobject>`

You can use the `<cfobject>` tag as you would any other ColdFusion tag, except that `<cfobject>` does not require a closing tag. Table 75.1 lists the attributes available to the `<cfobject>` tag, and their descriptions.

Table 75.1 `<cfobject>` Tag Syntax

ATTRIBUTE	DESCRIPTION
`action`	Required. Values are `CREATE` and `CONNECT`. Use `CREATE` to instantiate a COM object (typically a DLL) prior to invoking its methods and properties. Use `CONNECT` to connect to a COM object (typically an EXE) that is already running on the server, specified in the server attribute.
`class`	Required. The program identifier (`PROGID`) for the object you want to create or connect to. If the object resides on a remote server, you will use the server and class attributes, specifying the class identifier (`CLSID`) for the object. If a Java stub is used, use the `PROGID` of the COM object.
`name`	Required. An arbitrary value used to reference the object. This acts as the scope for all the object's operations in the code following the call to `<cfobject>`.
`type`	Optional. The type of object represented by the class attribute. Values are `COM`, `CORBA`, and `Java`. `COM` is the default and is the value discussed in this chapter. You will learn about `type="CORBA"` in Chapter 77, "Extending ColdFusion with CORBA," and `type="Java"` in Chapter 78, "Extending ColdFusion with Java."

Table 75.1 (CONTINUED)

ATTRIBUTE	DESCRIPTION
`context`	Optional. Possible values are `INPROC`, `LOCAL`, and `REMOTE`. `INPROC` is an in-process server object (typically a DLL) that is running in the same process space as the calling process, such as ColdFusion. `LOCAL` is an out-of-process server object (typically an EXE) that is running outside the process space, locally on the server. `REMOTE` is the same as `LOCAL`, except that the object resides on a remote server, specified in the server attribute.

`server`	Optional. It is required when `context="Remote"`. This represents the server hosting the object you want to instantiate. Enter a valid server name using Universal Naming Convention (UNC) or Domain Name Server (DNS) conventions, in one of the following forms:
	`server="\\lanserver"`
	`server="lanserver"`
	`server="http://www.servername.com"`
	`server="www.servername.com"`
	`server="127.0.0.1"`

Using COM with `CreateObject()`

An alternative way of using COM objects is through the `CreateObject()` function. For users more comfortable using scripting, this syntax might be preferable. If you are porting COM code from another scripting language such as ASP, you will find `CreateObject()` to be simpler and cleaner to implement. Table 75.2 lists the parameters available to the `CreateObjct()` function, in the order that they must be included, and their descriptions.

Table 75.2 `CreateObject()` Function Syntax

PARAMETER	DESCRIPTION
`type`	Required. The type of object represented by the `class` attribute. Values are `COM`, `CORBA`, `Java`, `component`, and `werbservice`.
`class`	Required. The program identifier (`ProgID`) for the object you want to create or connect to. If the object resides on a remote server, you will use the `server` and `class` attributes, specifying the class identifier (`CLSID`) for the object. If a Java stub is used, use the `ProgID` of the COM object.
`context`	Optional. Possible values are `INPROC`, `LOCAL`, and `REMOTE`. `INPROC` is an In-Process server object (typically a DLL) that is running in the same process space as the calling process, such as ColdFusion. `LOCAL` is an Out-of-Process server object (typically an EXE) that is running outside the process space, locally on the server. `remote` is the same as `LOCAL`, except that the object resides on a remote server, specified in the `server` attribute.

`server`	Optional. It is required when `context="Remote"`. This represents the server hosting the object you want to instantiate. Enter a valid server name using UNC or DNS conventions, in one of the following forms:
	`"\\lanserver"`
	`"lanserver"`
	`"http://www.servername.com"`
	`"www.servername.com"`
	`"127.0.0.1"`

When using `COM` as the value in the `type` attribute, `CreateObject()` takes four parameters, as follows (the third and fourth parameters are optional):

```
<cfscript>
objectName = CreateObject("COM","ProgID","InProc","Server" );
</cfscript>
```

➜ To learn more about `<cfscript>`, see Chapter 44, "ColdFusion Scripting," online.

Table 75.1 discusses the purpose of each of these parameters. At a minimum, you must specify the `TYPE` and `CLASS` of the object; optionally, you can also specify the `server` and `context` attributes.

The `objectName` variable shown in the preceding example represents the name you are assigning as the instance of that object. Use this variable to refer to the object later in your code:

```
<cfscript>
// Create the object instance
objectName = CreateObject("COM", "ProgID");
// Set a variable to a method's result
myVar = objectName.Method();
</cfscript>
```

The first step in any situation that requires COM is to connect to or create the object on the server. As you have already seen, the `<cfobject>` tag or the `CreateObject()` function handles this process:

```
<cfobject action="Create" class="Car.Builder"
          name="objCarBuilder" type="COM">
```

This code creates an instance of a fictitious `"Car Builder"` object on the server, at which point you may begin accessing its properties and methods. The examples in the next few sections will use an imaginary object to show COM's syntax and object hierarchies.

Setting and Retrieving Properties

A *property* is essentially a single attribute or *characteristic* of an object. To set or get a property, you must know which object you are using, as well as the properties that object exposes.

➜ See the documentation for your object to view the object hierarchies and supported properties in more depth.

If you have never used an object-oriented language, such as Java or C++, then the idea of properties might be new to you. To see how this works, you could use a car as an example. Following is a simple object "road map" for getting a car's exterior color:

```
extColor = objCarBuilder.Car.Body.Paint.Color
```

The variable `extColor` is set to the value held within the `Color` property. To get to the car's color property, you first have to drill down through the object's hierarchy until you have reached the object that contains the property. In this example, the `Paint` object contains the `Color` property and could possibly contain several other properties as well. The `Color` property is merely one possible property defined in the `Paint` object:

```
objCarBuilder.Car.Body.Paint.Color
objCarBuilder.Car.Body.Paint.Brand
objCarBuilder.Car.Body.Paint.Finish
```

As you can see, the theoretical `Paint` object contains not only the `Color` property but the `Brand` and `Finish` properties as well.

NOTE

For the discussion that follows, the term "nested attribute" is used to refer to any attribute that needs more than one dot (period character) after the actual COM object reference to identify the attribute. In this theoretical example, then, `Body`, `Paint`, `Color`, `Brand`, and `Finish` are all nested attributes.

Nested Attributes and Previous Versions of ColdFusion

In past versions of ColdFusion (ColdFusion version 5 or below), getting the `Color` property for the `Paint` object has required a little more work than in the first example. You would need to use several separate `<cfset>` lines, as shown here:

```
<cfset objCar = objCarBuilder.Car>
<cfset objBody = objCar.Body>
<cfset objPaint = objBody.Paint>
<cfset extColor = objPaint.Color>
```

Previous versions of ColdFusion did not have the capability to access the `Color` property directly from the `Paint` object. You would have to drill down each object level, one level at a time, by setting arbitrary variables for each level as shown above. This example uses the variables `objCar`, `objBody`, and `objPaint` to represent each object level. (You could use any valid variable name you wanted, but for consistency, it was best to use a name that described the object level it represented.)

To set the value of the `Color` property, you would do the following:

```
<cfset objCar = objCarBuilder.Car>
<cfset objBody = objCar.Body>
<cfset objPaint = objBody.Paint>
<cfset objPaint.Color = "red">
```

Nested Attributes and ColdFusion 8

ColdFusion 8 allows you to access nested attributes directly without having to drill down within the object hierarchy. Here is an example in ColdFusion 8:

```
<cfset extColor = objCarBuilder.Car.Body.Paint.Color>
```

Similarly, you can set a property's value using a single line:

```
<cfset objCarBuilder.Car.Body.Paint.Color = "Purple">
```

Occasionally, you might find that ColdFusion has trouble knowing how to work with nested objects when accessed in this manner. Such problems generally occur when one or more of the intermediary objects (in this example, the parts between `objCarBuilder` and `Color`) do not always return the same type of value. The problem usually manifests in an error message that reads "Method selection error" or something similar. If you have this problem when accessing nested properties, try the older, multistep syntax (several `<cfset>` tags, one for each nesting level).

Using Methods

The `Color` example in the previous section shows you how to fetch and set a property of an object. Like properties, objects also contain methods (functions) that perform specific tasks. Methods can take optional and required parameters, or they can be stand-alone routines. Either way, you invoke them in the same fashion.

NOTE

Some programming languages allow you to use a method without parentheses if it takes no parameters, as in `myObject.Close`. ColdFusion, however, requires that all methods end in parentheses, as in `myObject.Close()`, even if the object does not require them.

To invoke a method, you must first know which object hosts the method you want to use. The `Paint` object used earlier also contains a method called `getDefaultColor()`:

```
<cfset extColor = objPaint.getDefaultColor()>
```

If the default color for our car builder happens to be `"blue"`, then the `getDefaultColor()` method would set `extColor` to `"blue"`. In this context, the method specifically performs a single task, which is to contact the `Paint` object, ask what the default color is, and then return it to the `extColor` variable. This type of method is a one-way process. In other words, it returns a value and does not allow you to set the value.

To set the default color, the `Paint` object also has a method called `setDefaultColor()`. In this situation, the method accepts a string value representing a valid color name:

```
<cfset objPaint.setDefaultColor("red")>
```

This example may seem wrong to you. Unlike the `getDefaultColor()` operation, the `setDefaultColor()` expression does not use a variable before the invoked method. That is, when setting a one-way value with a method, you don't have to create a variable representing the operation. If you prefer, you can set a variable to the method call, but creating a variable in this context is unnecessary:

```
<cfset Temp = objPaint.setDefaultColor("red")>
```

The last type of method you will encounter accepts and returns values. Depending on the specific method, it might accept a single or multiple arguments, and it might return a single value or possibly a collection of values. To illustrate this, imagine that the `Paint` object has a method called `getColorShades()` that returns a collection of information based on the values it receives. The syntax for its arguments is as follows:

```
getColorShades("Color", intMaxRecords, boolReturnPrices)
```

This method takes three arguments: a string representing a color to compare and find similar colors for, an integer that sets the maximum number of records to return, and a Boolean value indicating whether to return pricing information.

The return value for this method is a collection of values that matches the criteria specified in the method's arguments. To see this, follow the next example:

```
<cfset objShades = objPaint.getColorShades("red", 10, True)>
```

NOTE

Some documentation may indicate a method argument is optional. With some objects, you must still supply the optional arguments even if they are not explicitly required. Without adequate documentation, this may be a matter of trial and error, so you will need to test to see which optional arguments throw an error when omitted.

The newly created object `objShades` now represents a collection of information returned from the method. To view the information, you have to use `<cfloop>`'s `collection` attribute:

```
<table>
<tr>
<td>Shade</td>
<td>Price</td>
</tr>
<cfloop collection="#objShades#" item="Shade">
<tr>
<td>#Shade.Name#</td>
<td>#Shade.Price#</td>
</tr>
</cfloop>
</table>
```

Collections returned from COM objects are arrays of structures. When looping through a COM collection, each item (`item="Shade"`) is a structure that has its own properties (`Shade.Name` and `Shade.Price`).

NOTE

With Visual Basic syntax, values sent to methods often consist of named values, such as `myObject.Open(vbOption)`. In ColdFusion, you must use the numerical equivalent of that named value, as in `myObject.Open(2)`, where the `(2)` represents the numerical equivalent of `vbOption`. More information on the numerical values is available in Microsoft Visual Studio or online at the MSDN Library site: `http://msdn.microsoft.com`.

ColdFusion Is Mostly Typeless; COM Is Mostly Not

Like any application accessing COM objects, ColdFusion must present data to the object in a format that is recognizable by that object's interfaces. An interface defines the format and type of data that an object can receive and send back to client, and in this case, the client is ColdFusion. Think of an interface as being a value sent or received from a function—some functions pass or fetch simple values, such as strings and numbers; however, others might use complex values such as arrays or structures. Without knowing an object's interfaces, you may accidentally send data to an object in a format that is incorrect for that particular interface, resulting in an error or inaccurate returned data.

To put this in perspective, recall that ColdFusion is a typeless environment, meaning that you do not explicitly set a variable's datatype. Because of this feature, it's up to you to make sure that the data sent to the object matches the object's requirements. On the other hand, the COM object may provide an interface to a method, for example, that expects an ambiguous value such as a variant (a datatype commonly used in Visual Basic). So how does ColdFusion know what datatype to send to the object? For objects, arrays, and strings, ColdFusion casts the values correctly. For integers, however, there is no guarantee that ColdFusion is sending the type expected by the object. If the object's method is expecting a datatype of `short`, ColdFusion may pass a datatype of `real`, due to the way ColdFusion internally represents numbers.

TIP

If you happen to be the developer creating the COM objects, it is easy to change the variable typing information. As a rule of thumb, always use strong variable typing when you know what the object is expecting.

Registering Objects

To begin using COM objects, make sure that the objects exist on the server or on a remote server to which your Web server has trusted access. If you have purchased a third-party software package, follow its instructions for installation and setup. In most cases, this will be enough to get you started, but sometimes you will be required to register an object manually on the server.

As noted earlier, objects come in two flavors, in-process (InProc) and out-of-process (Local). InProc object servers are typically DLL and OCX files; Local object servers are usually EXE files located on the server. The methods used to register each type of object differ slightly.

To register an InProc object server manually (DLL and OCX files), you use the `regsvr32.exe` file included with the Windows operating systems currently supported by ColdFusion. You can run the command through a standard command prompt (DOS) or by choosing Start, Run, and then typing in the command.

NOTE

OCX files are runtime ActiveX controls primarily used and scripted on the client side using JScript or VBScript. To use an OCX control, use the HTML `<embed>` or `<object>` tags. See the HTML reference included in Adobe Dreamweaver for more information. As a rule, do not use OCX files with `<cfobject>`.

Following is the usage for the `regsvr32.exe` file, with the parameters explained in Table 75.3:

```
regsvr32 [/u] [/s] [/n] [/i[:cmdline]] dllname
```

Table 75.3 `regsvr32.exe` Switches

SWITCH	DESCRIPTION
`/u`	Un-register the server
`/s`	Silent; display no message boxes
`/i`	Call `DllInstall`, passing it an optional `[cmdline]`; when used with `/u`, it calls a DLL uninstall
`/n`	Do not call `DllRegisterServer`; used with `/i`

Putting this to use, you call the actual DLL file name:

```
regsvr32 c:\path\servername.dll
```

The `servername.dll` represents the file you want to register, found in the `path` directory. The file does not have to be located on the `c:\` drive—you can specify any valid location to the object.

To register Local (Out-of-Process) object servers manually (EXE files), either you start them by double-clicking the executable file itself, or you can run a command line:

```
c:\path\servername.exe -register
```

Again, you specify the path to the executable file, and use the `-register` switch to register the object.

Upon issuing either registration command, you see a message saying that the object registered successfully. When all objects required for your application are registered, you are ready to put them to use.

NOTE

Some COM+ and DCOM objects on Windows 2000, XP, and 2003 systems require that you use the `clireg32.exe` program rather than `regsvr32.exe`. See the object's documentation for specific information regarding registration.

Viewing Objects with OLEView

Upon installing your object, you will need a way to see what methods, properties, and collections the object supports. Understanding this necessity, Microsoft created a program called the Object Viewer, more commonly known to developers as OLEView.

NOTE

OLEView is included with Microsoft Visual Studio. If you use Visual Basic, C#, Visual C++, or other tools in the suite, you may already have OLEView on your system. If you do not have it, you can download a copy from Microsoft's Web site at `http://download.microsoft.com/download/win2000platform/oleview/1.00.0.1/nt5/en-us/oleview_setup.exe`.

OLEView gathers information about all the installed COM objects on your system. From this information, you can retrieve the `ProgID`, `CLSID`, and other data for the object you are using. As a feature, OLEView groups and sorts objects based on each component category, such as Document Objects or Automation Objects. For example, you will find Microsoft Word Document and Excel worksheet are listed under the Document Objects category. This is handy if you have a general idea of what your object performs; otherwise, it can be time consuming to sift through the literally hundreds of objects listed.

NOTE

Versions of Microsoft Office before XP and 2000 place the Excel object in the Automation Objects category in OLEView.

The default OLEView screen consists of two panes: The left shows the objects and categories; the right displays object information (Figure 75.1).

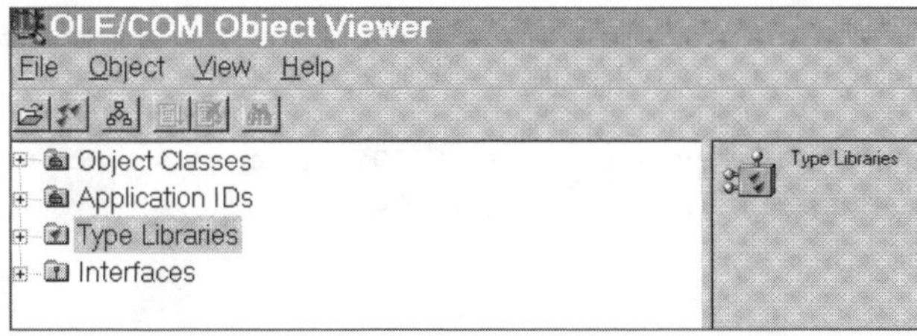

Figure 75.1

The OLEView program has two sections: the object categories and object information.

The first thing you'll need to gather is the object's `ProgID`. Think of the `ProgID` as a kind of map that tells the `<cfobject>` tag where to look for the object in the system Registry. For instance, the object information pane shows that the `ProgID` for the Microsoft Word Document object is `Word.Application.12` (Figure 75.2).

Microsoft Office Word 97 - 2003 Documen
Microsoft Office Word Document
Microsoft Office Word Macro-Enabled Do
Microsoft Office Word Macro-Enabled Ter

OfficeCompliant = 0
Printable
ProgID = Word.Document.12
TypeLib = {00020905-0000-0000-C000-000000000046}
Verb

Figure 75.2

Selecting the object from the categories on the left allows you to view the object's `ProgID` and other object information in the opposite pane.

The number at the end of the `ProgID`, if any, represents the object's version number; you do not need to specify this number when calling your object, as illustrated here:

```
<cfobject
type="COM"
action="CREATE"
class="Word.Application"
name="objWord">
```

TIP

While developing your application, keep OLEView open for easy access to your object's information.

At this point, the code illustrated previously simply creates the object in the server's memory. For the object to accomplish tasks, you need to understand its supported interfaces.

Drilling down a bit farther in OLEView's component category for the Microsoft Word object reveals something called the `IDispatch`. The `IDispatch` provides information for the object's properties and methods, as well as the arguments and return types. To view details about the interfaces, right-click `IDispatch` and choose the View option from the menu that appears (Figure 75.3).

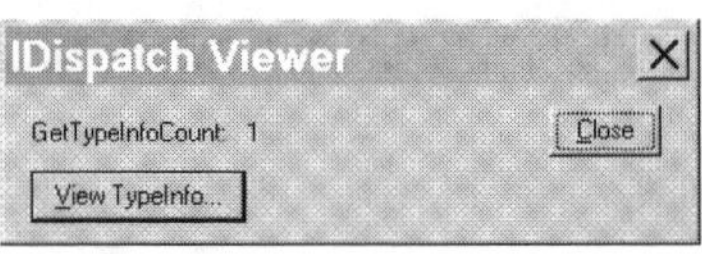

Figure 75.3

To view an object's interfaces, right-click that object's `IDispatch` and select the View option.

NOTE

If a component implements the `IDispatch` interface, it allows late binding.

A small window appears after opening the object's `IDispatch`. Clicking on the View TypeInfo button opens the object's ITypeInfo Viewer (Figure 75.4).

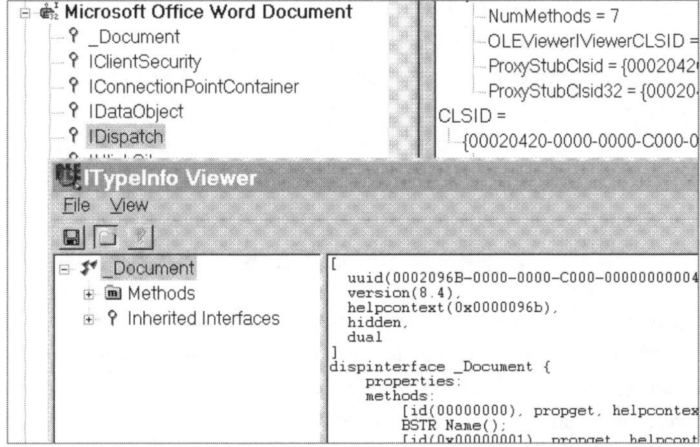

Figure 75.4

The ITypeInfo Viewer allows you to view an object's methods and supported interfaces.

Having an idea of what you are looking for in `IDispatch` saves you a great deal of time. Many objects provide literally hundreds of methods and properties—most of which are unsorted—so sifting through the `IDispatch` can be tedious. To get the best results with OLEView, know which method you want to reference and then use OLEView to see the arguments and return values for that method.

Using OLEView and the documentation provided with your software, you can easily reference the features of your objects. For instance, OLEView shows that the `Close()` method for the Microsoft Word object takes three optional input (`in`) arguments called `SaveChanges`, `OriginalFormat`, and `RouteDocument` (Figure 75.5). The `VARIANT` portion specifies the data type for that argument. Therefore, you can call the `Close()` method in your ColdFusion code as follows:

```
<cfset objWord.Close(1,1,0)>
```

You can view this same type of information for any method of any object.

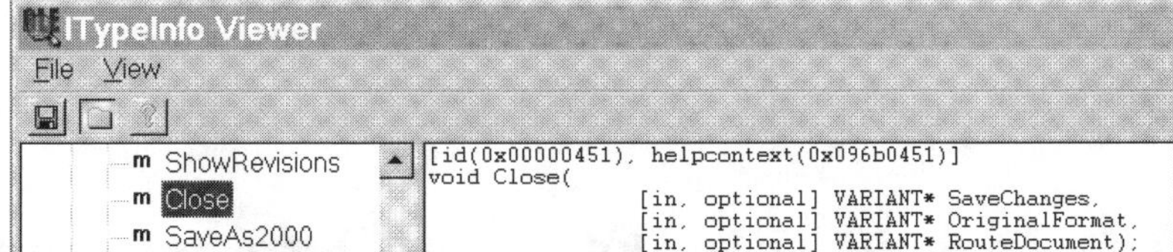

Figure 75.5

View a method's arguments and return values by selecting that method from the left pane.

Accessing Remote Objects

Overloading a Web server with applications will inevitably decrease performance as well as introduce security problems. Because of this, many development environments use a different server for hosting applications, separate from the Web/application server.

<cfobject> gives you the capability to specify a remote server via the server attribute. When you specify server, you must also provide the context attribute with a value of REMOTE. This tells ColdFusion to connect to the remote server for the object specified in the class attribute:

```
<cfobject
type="COM"
action="CREATE"
class="Word.Application"
name="objWord"
context="REMOTE"
server="http://www.forta.com/">
```

If you run this code as is, an error message might appear saying that the class is not registered. At first, an error like this may be confusing, especially knowing that object is indeed loaded on the remote server. To resolve this issue, you have to specify the object's class identifier (CLSID) of the remote server. For local objects, use the ProgID for the object. Remote objects, on the other hand, require that you specify the CLSID for the object, also found in OLEView (Figure 75.6).

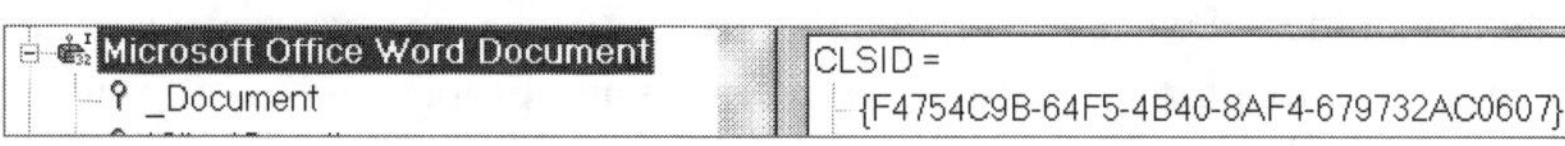

Figure 75.6

The CLSID for an object is in the same window as the object's ProgID.

To revise our example, we insert the CLSID in the class attribute:

```
<cfobject
type="COM"
action="CREATE"
class={00020400-0000-0000-C000-000000000046}
name="objWord"
context="REMOTE"
server="http://www.forta.com/">
```

Quotes around the class attribute are not required, and omitting them in this context is good form. For the server attribute, you can specify any one of the types previously listed in Table 75.1.

➜ To troubleshoot COM errors, see the section "Troubleshooting COM" later in this chapter.

New Techniques for Improving Performance and Reliability

As you know, the ColdFusion 8 application server is based on Java rather than on code compiled specifically for each platform. In general, that is an entirely good thing and brings all kinds of delightful benefits with it. With respect to COM integration, however, you could say that ColdFusion now sits one step farther away from Windows and thus one step farther away from COM.

Storing Objects in Shared Memory Scopes

Storing objects in shared memory scopes, such as the APPLICATION scope, is a safe practice that ultimately provides major performance gains when using the object repetitively. Your application can create and reuse a single object by all of the application's pages, thereby incurring the performance hit only once (until a server restart or scope timeout).

With ColdFusion 8, the recommendation is to use a shared variable scope to store a single instance of a COM object. In theory, you could use any of the shared memory scopes (APPLICATION, SERVER, or SESSION), but APPLICATION is the only scope that makes sense in practice. Listing 75.1 shows a reusable way to store COM objects in a shared scope. You should use this method for most COM objects.

Listing 75.1 SharedScope.cfm—Example of Loading a COM Object into Shared Scope

```
<cfif isObjectLoaded>
<!--- Shortcut variable for use in this page --->
<cfset xmlDom = APPLICATION.Microsoft.xmlDom>

</cfif>
</cflock>

<!--- If the object has not been loaded yet --->
<cfif not isObjectLoaded>
   <!--- We want this code to execute in one page request at a time. --->
   <!--- If another request is inside this block, wait here --->
   <cflock name="Microsoft.xmlDom" type="Exclusive" timeout="30">
   <!--- Has the object been loaded and placed into APPLICATION scope? --->
   <!--- We're doing this again here because ColdFusion may have waited --->
   <!--- for a while before this <cflock>, during which time the object --->
   <!--- may have been created and placed into the APPLICATION scope. --->
   <cfset isObjectLoaded = IsDefined("APPLICATION.Microsoft.xmlDom")>

   <!--- If it's already been loaded --->
   <cfif isObjectLoaded>
      <!--- Shortcut variable for use in this page --->
      <cfset xmlDom = APPLICATION.Microsoft.xmlDom>

      <!--- If the object has *still* not been loaded --->
   <cfelse>
      <!--- Create the reference to the object --->
      <cfobject action="CREATE"
                type="COM"
                class="Microsoft.xmlDom"
                name="APPLICATION.Microsoft.xmlDom">

      <!--- Shortcut variable for use in this page --->
      <cfset xmlDom = APPLICATION.Microsoft.xmlDom>

   </cfif>
   </cflock>
</cfif>
```

The first time Listing 75.1 executes, it creates an instance of the object and stores it as a persistent variable in the server's memory using the variable name APPLICATION.Microsoft.xmlDom. Subsequent requests simply reuse the APPLICATION.Microsoft.xmlDom object. That is, the <cfobject> tag executes only once for the lifetime of the application.

NOTE

The "lifetime of the application" means until ColdFusion restarts or until your application times out. You set the application timeout period on the Memory Variables page of the ColdFusion Administrator (located under Server Settings) or with the `applicationTimeout` attribute of the `<cfapplication>` tag.

NOTE

Microsoft recommends that you use a version dependent `ProgID` such as `Microsoft.XMLDOM.1.0` or `MSXML2.DOMDocument.5.0`. The example in Listing 75.1 uses the version independent `ProgID` for demonstration purposes – use the latest version your server has installed.

The first `<cflock>` block tests to see whether the COM object has already been instantiated and placed into the `APPLICATION` scope. If so, `isObjectLoaded` will be `True`. If not, `isObjectLoaded` will be `False`. If the object has already been loaded, we create a local variable called `xmlDom`, which the rest of the page request can use as a shortcut for `APPLICATION.Microsoft.xmlDom`. The `xmlDom` variable is a local variable that will die when the page request is complete, but `APPLICATION.Microsoft.xmlDom` will remain in the server's memory for the life of the application.

If the object has not already been loaded, the second `<cflock>` block executes, which is the code that actually creates the object instance via `<cfobject>`, storing it in the `APPLICATION` scope. Again, the local variable called `xmlDom` is an easier way to refer to the shared instance of the object. Place within this `<cflock>` block any additional code that needs executing only when the object is first instantiated.

Both portions of the code use `<cflock>` tags to make sure that simultaneous page requests do not create multiple instances of the new objects. The idea is that if an object instance is in the creation process with `<cfobject>`, then no other page request should do the same thing concurrently. The first block uses `type="ReadOnly"` instead of `type="Exclusive"`, which means that multiple page requests that are simply trying to reuse the shared COM object will not block each other. Blocking only occurs at runtime during the object creation process via `<cfobject>`.

NOTE

In this example, we use the `name` attribute of the `<cflock>` tag, rather than using the `scope` attribute. Using `scope` would block at the application or session level, which is most likely overkill in this situation. Using `name` allows you to lock with finer granularity; here, only the locks will block those operations that specifically relate to this particular COM object.

TIP

Another idea would be to create a ColdFusion Component (CFC) that stores a COM object in the `THIS` scope, and then store an instance of the CFC in the `APPLICATION` scope. See the later section "Using CFCs to Represent COM Objects" for a quick example of such a CFC.

Creating a Custom Tag to Make the Practice Easier

Although the Adobe-recommended approach demonstrated in Listing 75.1 makes a lot of sense and will serve you well, it is admittedly quite a bit of code to reproduce each time you want to use a COM object. You might want to create a custom tag or CFC to make it easier to use COM objects according to the recommendation.

The listings for this chapter (online) include one such custom tag. We call this one `<CF_UseComObject>`; it accepts the attributes shown in Table 75.4. You can adapt this custom tag to suit your needs, or just use it as a starting point. Alternatively, you could forego the custom tag approach and simply create a `<cfinclude>` template that includes the contents of Listing 75.1 (with the `class` and other attributes changed to reflect the object you are using, of course).

Table 75.4 `<CF_UseComObject>` Custom Tag Syntax

ATTRIBUTE	DESCRIPTION
`action`	Optional. You can specify `Connect` or `Create`, both of which work just like the `action` attribute of `<cfobject>`. You can also specify `ConnectOrCreate` (the default), which first attempts to connect to the program in memory, then creates a new object if the `Connect` is not successful.
`class`	Required. The `CLSID` or `ProgID` of the object you want to use. Corresponds to the `class` attribute of `<cfobject>`.
`localName`	Required. The variable name that you want to use to refer to the object in the remainder of the ColdFusion page. Same as the `name` attribute of `<cfobject>`.
`sharedName`	Required. The shared-scope variable name used to persist the object instance between page requests. It is expected that you will provide a variable name in the `APPLICATION` scope, although the `SERVER` and `SESSION` scopes are available as well.
`context`	Optional. `Local`, `Inproc`, or `Remote`, just like the `context` attribute of `<cfobject>`.
`server`	Optional. Used when `context="Remote"`, just like the `server` attribute of `<cfobject>`.
`lockTimeout`	Optional. The timeout, in seconds, that will be used in the two `<cflock>` blocks within the custom tag. If not specified, a default value of `30` seconds is used.
`lockName`	Optional. The lock name that will be used it the two `<cflock>` blocks within the custom tag. If not specified, the value you supply for `sharedName` is used for the lock name.

If there is any code that you want to execute only when the COM object is first instantiated and stored in the shared memory scope (such as initializing some kind of global properties), you can do so by placing the code between opening and closing `<CF_UseComObject>` tags, as shown in the accompanying online file `UseComObject.cfm`. The code will be executed only for the first successful execution of the tag and will be skipped for all subsequent executions (until the server is restarted or the application times out). If you do not want any special code to execute that first time, you can omit the closing `</CF_UseComObject>` tag.

`UseComObject.cfm` shows the code for the `<CF_UseComObject>` custom tag. Feel free to use it as is, or adapt it to suit your needs.

`SharedScope2.cfm` shows how you can use the custom tag in your own pages. This is a revision of Listing 75.1. The object is stored in a shared variable called `APPLICATION.Microsoft.xmlDom`, which persists for the lifetime of the application. You use the object locally as `xmlDom`, so the remainder of the example remains just as it appeared in Listing 75.1.

Creating Java Stubs for COM Objects

Certain COM objects will perform more quickly and reliably if you create something called a *Java stub* to represent the object. In particular, a COM object that has a large number of properties and methods is likely to perform better if you create a Java stub for it. If the object exposes *overloaded* methods (where the methods have several different forms, accepting different sets of parameters), then the object is even more likely to perform better as a Java stub. If you're having specific problems with an object, particularly error messages citing an inability for ColdFusion to determine the correct method to use (a method selection or similar error), you should consider creating a Java stub for the object.

A Java stub is a compiled Java class that contains wrapper functions for each of the COM object's methods and properties, respectively. The wrapper functions contain all the type information for method arguments, method return values, and properties. The functions speed things up because they eliminate the need for ColdFusion to determine the type information at run-time, making the conduit more efficient between the loosely typed CFML world and the tightly typed COM world.

Say you are using a COM object that exposes a method called `getUserByID()`, which accepts an integer (the user's ID number) and always returns a string (the user's name). Without the Java stub, ColdFusion will have to make sure the method actually exists, examine the method's list of arguments, examine the type of each argument, and examine the type of the return value each time the method is used. With the Java stub, the type information is already hard-coded into the wrapper function for the method, so the JVM (Java Virtual Machine) is able to take care of calling the correct method on ColdFusion's behalf. Essentially, creating a Java stub is a way of discovering and saving all of an object's methods and properties once, rather than having to do it repeatedly at run-time.

Creating the Java Stub

The actual process of creating a Java stub is somewhat involved. The Microsoft XML Parser object (MSXML) is an excellent example for explaining the steps required for creating a Java stub. Of course, to create a stub for some other object, simply adjust the various names and file locations accordingly.

In broad strokes, the creation of a Java stub involves these basic tasks:

- Generating the Java code for the stub classes
- Compiling the Java code into Java classes
- Packaging the classes into a Java Archive
- Configuring the ColdFusion server to use the stub

NOTE

Before you begin, download and install a copy of the Java JDK from `http://java.sun.com`. You must also make sure that the JDK's bin folder is included in the operating system's path environment variable. On Windows machines, that means opening a Command Prompt window and typing `PATH C:\Program Files\Java\jdk1.5.0_01\bin;%PATH%`, replacing the `C:\Program Files\Java\jdk1.5.0_01\bin` part with the actual installed location of the JDK.

To create the Java stub, follow these steps:

1. Decide on a Java *package name* for the COM object you want to use. The package name can be just about anything you choose, but Adobe recommends using a naming convention such as `com.companyname.object` in order to avoid potential naming conflicts. In this example, then, the package name will be `com.microsoft.msxml`.

2. Make a folder called `c:\JavaStub` on your server's drive. Name the folder anything you want and put it wherever you want; for this example, `c:\JavaStub` is the location used. If you place it somewhere else, you'll need to adjust the various paths throughout this section.

3. Within the `JavaStub` folder, create subfolders to reflect the package name for the object. In this example, the package name is `com.microsoft.msxml`, so create a folder called `c:\JavaStub\com\microsoft\msxml`. Refer to this as the *target folder*.

4. Launch the `com2java.exe` utility, which is located in the `C:\coldfusion8\jintegra\bin` folder. The J-Integra COM-to-Java tool appears (Figure 75.7).

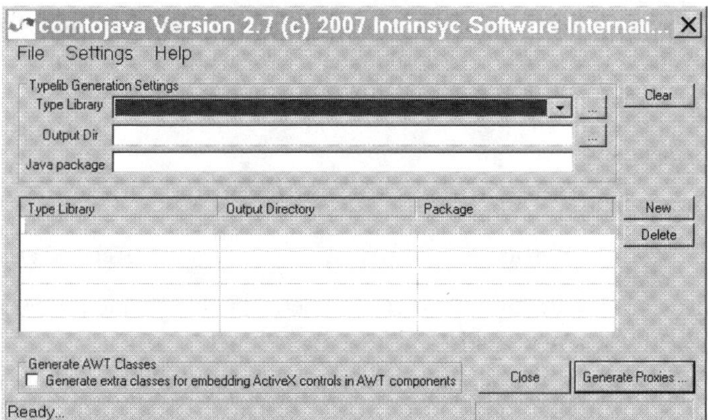

Figure 75.7

The COM-to-Java tool generates Java stub classes automatically.

5. Click the Select button and select the type library file for the COM object you are using. For this example, choose the `C:\WINDOWS\system32\msxml.dll` file. Most of the time you'll be using a `.dll` file, but it may also be an `.exe`, `.tlb`, or other file. In general, choose the main file that represents the installed COM object.

6. Click the Generate Proxies button and choose the target folder you created in Step 3 (Figure 75.8). At this point, the J-Integra tool will generate a series of `.java` files in the target folder.

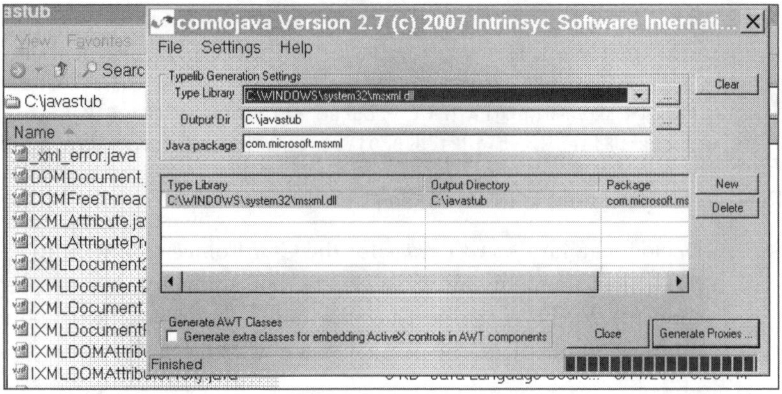

Figure 75.8

The tool places all generated Java code in the target folder you specify.

7. Use the `javac` utility from the JDK to compile the `.java` files into `.class` files. To do so, type the following in a command prompt (type it all on one line, adjusting any folder locations as appropriate):

```
javac -J-mx100m -J-ms100m c:\JavaStub\com\microsoft\msxml\*.java -classpath
c:\coldfusion8\lib\jintegra.jar
```

   At this point, a series of `.class` files should appear in the target folder.

8. Use the `jar` utility from the JDK to package the `.class` files into a Java Archive (`.jar`) file. To do so, make sure the current directory is `c:\JavaStub`, perhaps by typing the following on the command line (again, all on one line, and adjusting the paths as appropriate). Replace the `msxml.jar` part with a file name appropriate for the object you are working with (the name can be anything you want).

```
cd \JavaStub
```

   Now type:

```
jar -uvf c:\coldfusion8\lib\msxml.jar c:\JavaStub\com\microsoft\msxml\*.class
```

   Once you execute this command, the new `.jar` file should appear in the `c:\coldfusion8\lib` folder.

9. In the Java and JVM page of the ColdFusion Administrator (located under the Server Settings section), add the path for the `.jar` file (including the `.jar` extension) to the ColdFusion Class Path box and click the Save Settings button.

10. Open the `neo-comobjmap.xml` file in a text editor such as Notepad or Adobe Dreamweaver. The file is located in the `c:\coldfusion8\lib` folder.

11. Add an entry for the COM object to the `neo-comobjmap.xml` file. There are already a number of entries in the file; just add another entry like the existing ones. Supply the `ProgID` for the object in the `name` attribute, and provide the corresponding class name between the `<string>` tags.

12. After you save the `neo-comobjmap.xml` file, restart the ColdFusion 8 Application Server service.

NOTE

If you later install an updated version of the COM object that exposes slightly different methods and properties, you will need to go through this process again.

Using the Stub

Once you have completed the steps in the preceding section, ColdFusion should automatically use the new stub whenever you use the corresponding object via `<cfobject>` or `CreateObject()`.

If you are in doubt of whether the stub is accessible at run-time, you can test it: Stop the ColdFusion server, rename the `.jar` file temporarily, restart the server, and visit a page that uses the object. If you see a message reporting that the stub package does not exist, then you know ColdFusion is attempting to use the stub. Stop the server again, reinstate the `.jar` file's proper name, restart the server, and try again. If the `<cfobject>` or `CreateObject()` call now works correctly, the Java stub has been correctly created and configured. You can expect to see improved performance and stability from the object hereafter.

Using CFCs to Represent COM Objects

In the earlier section "Storing Objects in Shared Memory Scopes," you learned that Adobe recommends storing commonly used COM objects in a shared memory scope such as `APPLICATION` to improve the overall performance of your application. Depending on the situation, you may want to consider creating a ColdFusion Component (CFC) that uses `<cfobject>` or `CreateObject()` to instantiate the COM object. Then, store the instance in the `THIS` scope of the CFC. You can then store an instance of the CFC in the `APPLICATION` (or `SESSION` or `SERVER`) scope as needed.

Why would this be better than just storing the COM object directly in the shared scope? Depending on the object you're working with, you might be able to create methods for the CFC that expose the underlying functionality of the COM object in an easier-to-use, more ColdFusion-like manner. Thus, you kill two birds with one stone: storing the object in a shared scope, plus making the code in your application pages simpler and cleaner.

As an example, file `ExchangeCFC.cfc` creates a CFC called `ExchangeCFC`. As presented, `ExchangeCFC` exposes just one method, `SendMessage()`, but you could easily add others that expose other related Exchange concepts (such as appointments, calendars, and discussions).

NOTE

This particular CFC assumes that the username and password reside in a file called `ExchangeCFC.ini`, located in the same folder as the `.cfc` file. Such a practice is not secure if the `.cfc` is being kept somewhere within the Web server's document root. In fact, most developers would probably agree that usernames and passwords should not reside in unencrypted text files in the first place. This is not a fully formed example. It is meant to show how ColdFusion 8's support for COM objects and CFCs can be used together to simplify your code.

Within the CFC's constructor area (that is, outside the <cffunction> blocks), the COM object is instantiated and given the name of THIS.mapiSession. Because the object is being stored in the THIS scope, it will be maintained in the server's memory along with the CFC itself.

If you use the <cfinvoke> tag to invoke the SendMessage() method normally (using component="ExchangeCFC"), the underlying COM object is created, used, and then discarded at the end of the page request. However, if you decide to create an instance of the CFC via <cfobject> and store the instance in the APPLICATION scope, the COM object is maintained along with it. File ExchangeCFCdemo.cfm shows how you could create an instance of the CFC the first time you call a page (or application).

NOTE

The ExchangeCFCDemo.cfm file included with this chapter's listings uses these two code snippets in a simple demonstration page.

In short, you may find it advantageous to consider creating ColdFusion-style wrappers in the form of CFCs to represent COM objects that you plan to use often. This combines the practice of keeping COM objects in shared scopes with the higher-level concept of code abstraction.

➜ For more information about CFCs, see Chapter 27, "Creating Advanced ColdFusion Components," in *Adobe ColdFusion 8 Web Application Construction Kit, Volume 2: Application Development*.

Passing Complex Datatypes to COM Objects

You may sometime confront a challenge in your programming life where you need to pass complex datatypes such as structures or queries. The exact input and output options will vary based on the COM object being used. To see how ColdFusion can pass and return various datatypes, we can use the Scripting.Dictionary COM object, as shown here:

```
<!--- create the COM Object ---->
<CFOBJECT TYPE="COM" ACTION="create" CLASS="Scripting.Dictionary" NAME="COMDict"
server="\\localhost">
```

This code creates the COM object, and we then create a few complex datatypes such as a nested struct, a query, and a simple struct.

```
<CFQUERY DATASOURCE = "OWS" NAME="qryContacts">
 Select  *  from contacts
</CFQUERY>
<!---- create a complex variable ---->
<cfset stcInput = structnew()>
<cfset temp = StructInsert(stcInput ,"5", "1")>
<cfset temp = StructInsert(stcInput ,2, "2")>
<cfset stcInputnested = structnew()>
<cfset temp = StructInsert(stcInputnested  ,"Another key", "yes")>
<cfset temp = StructInsert(stcInput ,"substruct", stcInputnested)>

<!--- if the key does not exist then add it by passing the data type to the COM
object ---->
<cfif COMDict.Exists(5) neq true>
   <cfset temp = COMDict.Add(5, stcInput  )>
</cfif>
```

```
<cfif COMDict.Exists(99) neq true>
   <cfset temp = COMDict.Add(99, stcInputnested  )>
</cfif>
<cfif COMDict.Exists(66) neq true>
   <cfset temp = COMDict.Add(66, qryContacts  )>
</cfif>
```

After the datatypes have been created, we can then check to see if the item exists in the dictionary. If it does not, then we will add it (as in the preceding code). As shown in the following code, after the item has been added, we can call a method that returns an array of keys or an array of items. We can then loop through the key array and call the `Item` method of the dictionary to return the value of the specified key, or we can loop through the returned array of items that the `Items` method returns.

```
<!---- get the array of keys ---->
<cfset arrKeys =  COMDict.Keys() >
<!---- Loop throught the Keys and display it using the Item() method ---->
<cfloop from="1" to="#COMDict.Count()#"  index="curItem">
   <cfdump var="#COMDict.Item(arrKeys[curItem])#">
</cfloop>
<HR/>
<!---- get the array of Items ---->
<cfset arrItems="#COMDict.Items()#">
<!---- loop through the returned array displaying its contents---->
<cfloop from="1" to="#ArrayLen(arrItems)#"  index="curItem">
   <cfdump var="#arrItems[curItem]#">
</cfloop>
<!----
<cfdump var="#COMDict#">
<cfdump var="#arrKeys#">
<cfdump var="#arrItems#">---->
```

To determine what methods and properties are available after the COM is created, we can dump the COM object and the values returned from its methods.

Common Questions and Problems

The remainder of this chapter discusses several topics that are often the subject of questions and generally cause distress and confusion among developers using COM:

- Releasing COM objects
- Troubleshooting COM

Releasing COM Objects

ColdFusion 8 offers a built-in way to manually *kill* (or *release*) a COM object from server memory, using the `ReleaseComObject()` function. This function takes only one parameter, which is the name of the object you want to release:

```
<cfset ReleaseComObject(MyObject)>
```

Using `ReleaseComObject()` is not required for the object to work correctly. Nor is it needed to free up resources, since the Java garbage collection mechanism will eventually free up any tied resources created by the object. `ReleaseComObject()` is, however, very useful when you know you're finished using an object and want to regain those precious resources. It is recommended that you call the `ReleaseComObject()` only after you have called any native `Quit()` method (if it exists) within the object's own interface.

Troubleshooting COM

To troubleshoot COM errors, you have to understand the process in which the data sent to the object can affect the desired result.

After creating an object, ColdFusion sends a request to the OLE (Object Linking and Embedding) automation system. The automation system returns a code indicating whether the underlying operation succeeded. If it was unsuccessful, OLE returns an error code displayed to the user; otherwise, the operation runs smoothly. In most circumstances, ColdFusion is not throwing the error; rather, the automation system returns the error.

Determining whether you have received an automation error is easy to do because these errors contain a specific pattern:

```
0x800nnnnn error-description
```

In each error, you will see `0x800` followed by five numbers (`nnnnn`) and then a description (in most cases). These numbers represent the specific error number returned from the automation system, not ColdFusion.

Following are explanations of the most frequently encountered COM errors. Although you may encounter many others, these three errors are the ones most likely to surface when you're using COM for the first time:

- COM error 0x5. Access is denied.
- COM error 0x80040154. Class not registered.
- COM error 0x800401F3. Invalid class string.

COM Error 0x5 (Access Is Denied)

When you register an object on a Windows system, you must have login access to the same account the ColdFusion services use. By default, ColdFusion uses the `LocalSystem` account, which is the likely culprit responsible for the "Access is denied" error message.

One way to fix this problem is to assign administrative access to ColdFusion services. Start by opening your Services control panel in Windows NT, 2000, XP, or 2003 (found on the control panel on NT and 2000 and by choosing Control Panel > Administrative Tools in XP and 2003). Next, change the ColdFusion services' logon account from `LocalSystem` to `Administrator`.

On Windows 2000, XP, and 2003:

1. Double-click the ColdFusion 8 Application Server service to open its properties page.
2. On the properties page, click the Log On tab and then select the This Account radio button.
3. Click the Browse button to select the logon account, from which you choose Administrator.

On Windows NT:

1. Double-click the service to open its properties page.
2. In the Log On As box, select the This Account radio button.
3. Enter the account name (you can use the … button to browse the account list).
4. Enter the password twice.

NOTE

Remember that if the password to the account is ever changed, all services using that account as the logon must be updated, or they will fail at the next logon or reboot.

If the object requiring access is not a service, you can use OLEView to change the object's permission levels:

1. Open OLEView and locate the object for which you want to change permissions. In this example, the Word object is used.
2. Click the object heading in the left window to view that object's properties in the right window.
3. Click the Access Permissions tab.
4. Select the Use These Activation Permissions radio button.
5. Click the Modify button, which opens the Access Permissions dialog.
6. Select the Administrators group.

After you give administrative access to your ColdFusion services and object permissions, you should no longer receive an "Access is denied" message.

COM Error 0x80040154 (Class Not Registered)

A class can exist without being registered, which typically is what causes the "Class not registered" error message to appear. To register the object, refer to the earlier section "Registering Objects."

Another situation that can cause this error is including the version number in `ProgID`. Microsoft Access XP, for example, uses the following `ProgID`:

```
Access.Application.n
```

The `n` indicates the class version number, and removing it from the class in `<cfobject>` usually resolves this error issue.

You may also encounter this error when using the `Remote` context for the object. See the next error section for tips on troubleshooting this problem.

COM Error 0x800401F3 (Invalid Class String)

If you receive the "Invalid class string" error message, the problem is usually one of the following:

- Your `ProgID` or `CLSID` is misspelled. This problem is straightforward and easy to fix.
- The object you're trying to create is not registered on the server. Use OLEView to view the correct name for the class and to make sure that the object exists. To create an object, that object must be loaded on the server calling the object, or it must be on a remote server using the `context="Remote"` and `server` attributes of the `<cfobject>` tag.
- You are using the `Local` context name for the object in a `Remote` context invocation. This problem is a bit less obvious. When calling an object on a remote server, you do not use the `ProgID` for that object. The `ProgID` is the `InProc` or `Local` context name for the object. Therefore, to connect to an object in the `Remote` context, you need to use the `ClassID` (also called `CLSID`) for the object. This also requires that the `context` attribute of the `<cfobject>` tag be set to `Remote` and that you provide a valid server in the `server` attribute.

CHAPTER 76

Integrating with Microsoft Office

IN THIS CHAPTER

ColdFusion applications can integrate with Microsoft Office to provide advanced document functionality not available with traditional HTML output. Developers can take advantage of these features to provide users with editable documents, leverage features of the Office applications, import data from other applications, and produce specialized complex reports.

The ability to integrate ColdFusion with Microsoft Office products has been enhanced by Office's adoption of the Office Open XML (OOXML) format. Previously, developers had to manipulate a binary file; now we can navigate and control parts of an OOXML "file."

This chapter describes several techniques available to ColdFusion developers to work with Microsoft Office through OOXML:

- WordprocessingML
- SpreadsheetML
- Automation

Office Open XML

The new OOXML formats (`*.docx`, `*.xlsx`, `*.pptx` extensions) are actually Zip files that contain a number of XML documents (among other files) that provide content, formatting, data, structure, associations, relationships, and more. For example, in an OOXML Word document file (container), the part that stores the content of the document is the `document.xml` file. In an Excel container, worksheets are stored as individual files: `sheet1.xml`, `sheet2.xml`, and so on. PowerPoint maintains its slide content in a separate part of the document container.

The parts of a simple OOXML Word document are shown in Figure 76.1. This Word document contains only the text `Hello World`, but as you can see the file consists of a number of parts. You can open a `*.docx` file in a Zip program to view the document's parts.

Figure 76.1

A simple `.docx` container's listing of parts.

[Content_Types].xml		XML Document
.rels	_rels\	XML Document
app.xml	docProps\	XML Document
core.xml	docProps\	XML Document
document.xml	word\	XML Document
fontTable.xml	word\	XML Document
settings.xml	word\	XML Document
styles.xml	word\	XML Document
webSettings.xml	word\	XML Document
document.xml.rels	word_rels\	XML Document
theme1.xml	word\theme\	XML Document

NOTE

Office 2007 containers also may contain images, sounds, and other associated files and even nested OOXML containers.

As you can start to imagine, the need to run an Office desktop application on the server may be a thing of the past.

NOTE

Office Open XML formats are standardized by Ecma International, providing the specifications for the formats and infrastructure of the ZIP file. See `http://www.ecma-international.org/news/TC45_current_work/TC45-2006-50_final_draft.htm` for further information about the file formats.

ColdFusion applications can integrate with Microsoft Office 2007 file formats in a number of ways, as the parts of the container have defined purposes as well as consistent names and paths.

Creating a New OOXML Container

The fundamental process for creating a new container is as follows:

- Create and or manage the container parts by adding the content, formatting, formulas, relationships and associated files, and so on.
- Package the parts into a container (`CFZIP`).
- Store or forward the OOXML file.

NOTE

A new container's parts can be dynamically determined at run time, by building the container parts from existing files or even other storage facilities such as a database or Web service.

Accessing an Existing Container

To access an existing OOXML file, you use almost the same procedure:

- Open the container and navigate to the relevant files or file with `CFZIP`.

- Read the relevant parts of the file. This can be done in a number of ways, which we will discuss further.
- View or manipulate the data by adding, editing, or deleting the content, formatting, formulas, relationships and associated files, and so on.
- Package the parts back into a new or existing container with `CFZIP`.
- Store or forward the OOXML file.

NOTE

There are other ways to read, create, store, or deliver OOXML files. You can use .NET assemblies by calling them with the `cfobject` tag and processing them as described here.

Word OOXML Containers

Create a Word 2007 document and place the text `Hello world` in it. Make sure there is no formatting applied in this simple example.

Use Listing 76.1 to view the sample file's contents.

Listing 76.1 `76_1.cfm`—Viewing a Document's Contents

```
<CFZIP ACTION="Read"
   FILE="C:\Inetpub\wwwroot\ows\76\resources\word\Helloworld.docx"
   ENTRYPATH="word\document.xml"
   VARIABLE="strXMLtext">
<CFOUTPUT>   #strXMLtext#   </CFOUTPUT>
```

If you view the `#strXMLtext#` content, you will see that it is just XML. The format for this `.docx` file can be found at `http://www.ecma-international.org/publications/standards/Ecma-376.htm`.

The set of conventions (markup language, or ML) for an Office Open XML Word processing document is called the WordprocessingML.

It's easy to get started with the OOXML format. Here is a quick introduction to a Word file. Figure 76.2 shows the minimum required parts that a `.docx` container needs to be a valid Word 2007 file.

NOTE

See `http://msdn2.microsoft.com/en-us/library/ms771890.aspx` for the most basic of documents.

Figure 76.2

Skeleton `.docx` container's part listing.

.rels	_rels\	XML Document
[Content_Types].xml		XML Document
app.xml	docProps\	XML Document
core.xml	docProps\	XML Document
document.xml	word\	XML Document

The Word OOXML container uses the following folders:

- `_rels` folder: Defines the root relationships within the container. This folder is used to determine the schema of XML files in the container and identify the main document part. The folder is also relevant to Excel and PowerPoint files.
- `docProps` folder: Contains the parts of the applications properties. The folder is also present in Excel and PowerPoint containers.
- `word` folder: Contains the parts of the application's properties. This folder is specific to a Word document.

NOTE

Excel has an `xl` folder, and PowerPoint has a `ppt` folder.

The Word OOXML container uses the following files:

- `.rels`: Defines all the relationships between XML parts within a Word XML format document.
- `[Content_Types].xml`: Lists the types of parts that can be stored in a container.
- `app.xml`: Defines application-specific properties.
- `core.xml`: Defines file properties.
- `document.xml`: Stores the body, paragraph, rows, and text of the document.

The following XML provides a quick look at a bare-bones blank `document.xml` file. Notice the `t` attribute under the `<v>` element. This is where our document text is stored.

```
<?xml version="1.0" encoding="UTF-8" standalone="yes"?>
<w:document xmlns............>
<w:body>
   <w:p w:rsidR="00FD2236" w:rsidRDefault="00FD2236">
      <w:r>
         <w:t>   </w:t>
      </w:r>
   </w:p>
   <w:sectPr w:rsidR="00FD2236" w:rsidSect="00FD2236">
      <w:pgSz w:w="12240" w:h="15840"/>
      <w:pgMar w:top="1400" w:right="1400" w:bottom="1400" w:left="1400"
w:header="700" w:footer="700" w:gutter="0"/>
     <w:cols w:space="708"/>
      <w:docGrid w:linePitch="360"/>
   </w:sectPr>
</w:body>
</w:document>
```

NOTE

Notice the namespace `w:` and the reference `xmlns:w`. For more information, see `http://schemas.openxmlformats.org/wordprocessingml/2006/main`.

Creating a New Word OOXML File

To create a new Word document, follow this process:

- Assemble the container parts.
- Add content if required.
- Package container with `CFZIP`.

At this book's Web site, under this chapter, is an `OOXMLblankdocx.zip` file that we will use as a directory and file template to create new `.docx` files. Unzip the `OOXMLblankdocx.zip` file to your desired directory. It should reflect Figure 76.2. Once we have this directory available to use, we can create a new `*.docx` file without the use of an Office product. We can now use some code that will zip this directory structure into a `.docx` file. Listing 76.2 is the code snippet to do it.

Listing 76.2 `76_2.cfm`—Creating a New Word 2007 File

```
<CFSET UUIDTemp = CreateUUID()>
<CFFILE ACTION="Read"
   FILE="#Application.Word.strBlankTemplateDir#\word\document.xml"
   VARIABLE="strXMLtext">
<CFSET  XMLDoc=XMLParse("#strXMLtext#")>
<CFIF structkeyexists(XMLDoc.Document.body.p[1], "r")>
   <CFIF structkeyexists(XMLDoc.Document.body.p[1].r, "t") >
    <CFSET XMLDoc.Document.body.p[1].r[1].t[1].XMLText
                 = "This is my 1st paragraph"  >
   </CFIF>
</CFIF>
<CFSET  strNewXML = toString(XMLDoc)>
<CFFILE ACTION = "write"
   FILE="#Application.Word.strBlankTemplateDir#\word\document.xml"
   OUTPUT="#strNewXML#">
<CFZIP FILE="#Application.Word.strOutputDir#\createdocx_#UUIDTemp#.docx"
   STOREPATH="yes"
   RECURSE="true"
   OVERWRITE="yes"
   SOURCE="#Application.Word.strBlankTemplateDir#"  />
```

As you can see, this is a very simplified way to create one nonformatted paragraph within a `.docx` file that has at least one paragraph. We can further edit the code to loop through an array of paragraphs and add these to the `.docx` file (insert elements into `document.xml` using the XML object). Listing 76.3 shows the final listing, creating an array of text elements and then adding them as paragraphs to a blank Word OOXML file.

Listing 76.3 `76_3.cfm`—Adding Paragraphs to a Blank Word 2007 File

```
<CFSET UUIDTemp = CreateUUID()>
<CFFILE ACTION="Read"
FILE="#Application.physicalPath#\resources\word\docx\blank\word\document.xml"
   VARIABLE="strXMLtext">
<!---- read the document.xml file and parse it --->
<CFSET XMLDoc=XMLParse("#strXMLtext#")>
<CFQUERY DATASOURCE = "OWS" NAME="qryFilmRatings">
```

Listing 76.3 (continued)

```
Select MOVIETITLE, PITCHTEXT, RATINGID, SUMMARY
   from films
</CFQUERY>
<CFSET intAddParagraphCountr = ArrayLen(XMLDoc.Document.body.p)>
<CFLOOP QUERY="qryFilmRatings"   >
   <CFSET intAddParagraphCountr = intAddParagraphCountr+1>
   <CFSET temp = ArrayInsertAt(XMLDoc.Document.body.XMLChildren,
intAddParagraphCountr  , XMLElemNew(XMLDoc, "w:p"))>
<!--- add a new paragraph  and a new row to the inserted paragraph  ---->
    <CFSET temp =
ArrayAppend(XMLDoc.Document.body.p[intAddParagraphCountr].XMLChildren,
XMLElemNew(XMLDoc, "w:r"))>
    <CFSET temp =
ArrayAppend(XMLDoc.Document.body.p[intAddParagraphCountr].r.XMLChildren,
XMLElemNew(XMLDoc, "w:t"))>
    <CFSET  XMLDoc.Document.body.p[intAddParagraphCountr].r.t.XMLText =
"#MOVIETITLE#-#PITCHTEXT#  (#RATINGID#)">
</CFLOOP>
<CFSET strNewXML = toString(XMLDoc)   >
<CFFILE ACTION = "write"
   FILE="#Application.Word.strBlankTemplateDir#\word\document.xml"
   OUTPUT="#strNewXML#">
<CFZIP FILE="#Application.Word.strOutputDir#\createdocx_#UUIDTemp#.docx"
   STOREPATH="yes"   RECURSE="true"   OVERWRITE="yes"
   SOURCE="#Application.Word.strBlankTemplateDir#"   />
```

You should be able to now open and start to use the new `createdocx_XXXX.docx` file in Word 2007. Be careful; if you edit an OOXML document, it will add your edits in a different element.

```
<w:p w:rsidR="00FD2236" w:rsidRDefault="00FD2236" w:rsidP="00FD2236">
  <w:r>
  <w:t xml:space="preserve">Address</w:t>
  </w:r>
  </w:p>
```

The following XML is produced when the capital A was changed (revised) to a lowercase *a*:

```
<w:p w:rsidR="00FD2236" w:rsidRDefault="00FD2236" w:rsidP="00FD2236">
 <w:r w:rsidR="0016042A">
  <w:t>a</w:t>
 </w:r>
 <w:r>
  <w:t xml:space="preserve">ddress</w:t>
 </w:r>
</w:p>
```

`rsidR`is a revision identifier. It is a unique ID generated when an edit is made.

Viewing a Word OOXML File

Because of the revision identifier, the text can start to get lost within the SML. To view the raw text content of the `document.xml` file (without having document tracking, for instance), we can use the `XMLSearch` function as in Listing 76.4.

Listing 76.4 `76_4.cfm`—Viewing the Raw Text of a Word 2007 Document

```
<CFZIP ACTION="Read" FILE="#Application.Word.strOutputDir#\......docx"
   ENTRYPATH="word\document.xml"
   VARIABLE="strXMLtext">
<CFSET XMLDoc=XMLParse("#strXMLtext#")>
<CFSET xmlParagraphElements = XmlSearch(XMLDoc, "//*[local-
name()='document']/*[local-name()='body']/*[local-name()='p']")>
<CFSET xmlParagraphElements  = xmlParagraphElements  >
<CFLOOP FROM="1" TO="#ArrayLen(xmlParagraphElements)#"
   INDEX="intParaCountr">
   <CFSET xmlRowElements = XmlSearch(XMLParse(xmlParagraphElements[intParaCountr]),
"//*[local-name()='p']/*[local-name()='r']/*[local-name()='t']")>
   <CFLOOP FROM="1" TO="#ArrayLen(xmlRowElements)#"
      INDEX="intRowCountr">
   <CFOUTPUT>#xmlRowElements[intRowCountr].XMLText#</CFOUTPUT>
   </CFLOOP>
   <BR>
</CFLOOP>
```

Creating a Dynamic Word OOXML Document

You may be familiar with mail merging. In this example, we will create our own mail merge (dynamic) document by using a standard Word OOXML document.

These are the basic steps:

- Open a document template.
- Assign the part of the document to be dynamically populated.
- Save the document.

NOTE

If you save before you complete the document, you may have problems with the revision identification.

Create a document similar to Figure 76.3. Spell check it, ignoring all the checks and then save it; this will purge some of the spell check XML within the file `document.xml`.

This is the standard Word OOXML document that we will use as a server-side template. The dynamic content will be the placeholders marked with the # characters, and the blank line of the table will be used to dynamically iterate and place the relevant film information in its associated columns.

To create a new Word OOXML document from a template, follow these steps:

- Copy the template file with new name.
- Open `*.docx` with `CFZIP`.
- Read `word\document.xml`.
- Replace dynamic content with values.
- Close, store, view, and deliver the document.

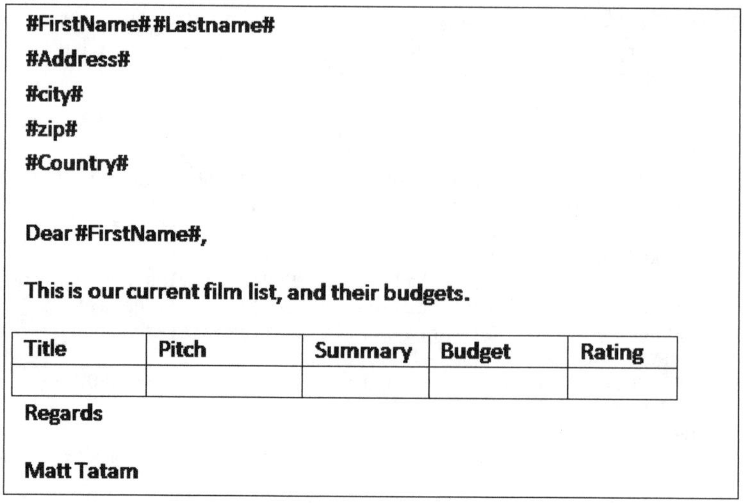

Figure 76.3

The standard Word OOXML document that we will use as a server-side template.

#FirstName# #Lastname#

#Address#

#city#

#zip#

#Country#

Dear #FirstName#,

This is our current film list, and their budgets.

Title	Pitch	Summary	Budget	Rating

Regards

Matt Tatam

Changing the purchaser is simple. All we need to do is replace the ## with dynamic variables (Listing 76.5).

Listing 76.5 `76_5.cfm`—Replacing Placeholders with Dynamic Content from a Query

```
<CFZIP ACTION="unzip"
   FILE="#Application.Word.strRootDir#\FilmBudgets.docx"
   DESTINATION="#Application.Word.strTempDir#\filmbudget"   OVERWRITE="yes">
<CFFILE ACTION = "read"
   FILE="#Application.Word.strTempDir#\filmbudget\word\document.xml"
   VARIABLE="strXMLText">
<CFQUERY DATASOURCE = "OWS" NAME="qryContacts">
   Select  *
   from contacts WHERE contactID = #intContactID#
</CFQUERY>
<CFOUTPUT QUERY="qryContacts"  >
   <CFSET  strXMLText=replaceNoCase(strXMLText,"##FirstName##","#FirstName#","All")>
   <CFSET  strXMLText=replaceNoCase(strXMLText,"##LastName##","#LastName#","All")>
   <CFSET  strXMLText=replaceNoCase(strXMLText,"##Address##","#Address#","All")>
   <CFSET  strXMLText=replaceNoCase(strXMLText,"##city##","#city#","All")>
   <CFSET strXMLText=replaceNoCase(strXMLText,"##zip##","#zip#","All")>
   <CFSET  strXMLText=replaceNoCase(strXMLText,"##country##","#country#","All")>
</CFOUTPUT>
```

Now we are presented with the issue of repeating the rows in the film table for every row of film details returned from the `films` database table. The following code represents a table row (Word Processing Markup Language) of the OOXML document in Figure 76.3:

```
<w:tr w:rsidR="00B507D2" w:rsidTr="00A718FF">
   <w:tc>
      <w:tcPr>
         <w:tcW w:w="1242" w:type="dxa" />
      </w:tcPr>
      <w:p w:rsidR="00B507D2" w:rsidRDefault="00B507D2" w:rsidP="00A718FF">
         <w:r>
```

```
            <w:t>#MovieTitle#</w:t>
         </w:r>
      </w:p>
   </w:tc>
   <w:tc>...........................................................................................</w:tc>
</w:tr>
```

NOTE

There must be at least one space in the table cell for it to contain `<w:t>`.

So all we need to do is copy this row of the document and dynamically populate it with data. To reference the first cell in the second row (`#MovieTitle#`), we can parse the text to XML and then navigate to the table cell using the code snippet in Listing 76.6.

Listing 76.6 `76_6.cfm`—Iterating the `qryfilms` Query to Create a Table Row and Populate Table Cells

```
<CFQUERY DATASOURCE = "OWS" NAME="qryFilms">
   Select MOVIETITLE, PITCHTEXT, SUMMARY, AMOUNTBUDGETED, RATINGID
   from films
</CFQUERY>
<CFSET intCellCountr = 1>
<CFSET curTotal = 0>
<CFSET XMLDoc = XMLParse(strXMLText)>
<CFSET XMLPart = Duplicate(XMLDoc.Document.body.tbl.tr[2]) >
<CFOUTPUT QUERY="qryFilms" MAXROWS=10 >
   <CFSET   curTotal = curTotal + AmountBudgeted>
   <CFSET  intCellCountr = intCellCountr  + 1>
   <CFSET temp = ArrayInsertAt(XMLDoc.Document.body.tbl.XMLChildren, INT(2
+intCellCountr),  XMLPart  ) >
   <CFSET   XMLDoc.Document.body.tbl.tr[intCellCountr].tc[1].p[1].r[1].t[1].XMLText
= "#MOVIETITLE#" >
   <CFSET    XMLDoc.Document.body.tbl.tr[intCellCountr].tc[2].p[1].r[1].t[1].XMLText
= "#PITCHTEXT#" >
   <CFSET    XMLDoc.Document.body.tbl.tr[intCellCountr].tc[3].p[1].r[1].t[1].XMLText
= "#SUMMARY#">
   <CFSET    XMLDoc.Document.body.tbl.tr[intCellCountr].tc[4].p[1].r[1].t[1].XMLText
= LScurrencyFormat(AMOUNTBUDGETED)>
   <CFSET    XMLDoc.Document.body.tbl.tr[intCellCountr].tc[5].p[1].r[1].t[1].XMLText
= "#RATINGID#">
</CFOUtPUT>
<CFSET  intCellCountr = intCellCountr  + 1>
<CFSET  XMLDoc.Document.body.tbl.tr[intCellCountr].tc[4].p[1].r[1].t[1].XMLText =
LScurrencyFormat(curTotal)>
 <CFFILE ACTION = "write"
   FILE="#Application.Word.strTempDir#\filmbudget\word\document.xml"
   OUTPUT="#toString(XMLDoc)#">
<CFZIP ACTION="zip"  STOREPATH="yes"
   FILE="#Application.Word.strOutputDir#\FILMbUDGET.docx"
   SOURCE="#Application.Word.strTempDir#\filmbudget"  >
```

As you can see, we have only scratched the surface. These examples deal with only the text content and not the formatting, clip art (*.`wmf`), charts (which use an embedded Excel OOXML container within the Word OOXML container), images, and so on that can also be associated with a Word

OOXML document. As you can see, there is now an easier interface for you to use with ColdFusion to manipulate a Microsoft Office Word document and its associated files.

The approach we took here was to predefine a document template and then replace and or replicate the data to create a dynamic Word document. We used this approach to see one of the methods we can use to interact with an OOXML file. Once you are familiar with the structure and relationships of the various containers, you will start to develop your own techniques to produce them.

Excel OOXML Containers

Most reporting solutions can provide data in Excel format, but these usually consist of static data and no formulas. With the new OOXML format, ColdFusion can manipulate an Excel spreadsheet and provide it with values as well as formulas.

The Excel OOXML container is similar to the Word container. It includes the `Content_Types`, `core` and `app` XML files as well as the `.rels` relationship file. In addition to these, a skeleton container requires a workbook and sheet1 XML document and the workbook's relationship file. It also has a predefined directory structure that stores these files. Figure 76.4 shows a sample file, `filmWorkbookxlsx`, which consists of four worksheets: Film, Expenses, Merchandise, and Merchandise Orders. These details are stored in the `worksheets.xml` file as a list of sheets and in the `apps.xml` file as a document summary. We will use the same data source as in the previous Word example; however, for instructional purposes we will take a different approach when creating an Excel OOXML container.

NOTE

We can also associate named styles with Excel workbooks, but that is beyond the scope of this chapter.

Figure 76.4

The `.xlsx` container's part listing.

workbook.xml.rels	xl_rels\	XML Document
workbook.xml	xl\	XML Document
theme1.xml	xl\theme\	XML Document
styles.xml	xl\	XML Document
sheet4.xml	xl\worksheets\	XML Document
sheet3.xml	xl\worksheets\	XML Document
sheet2.xml	xl\worksheets\	XML Document
sheet1.xml	xl\worksheets\	XML Document
sharedStrings.xml	xl\	XML Document
core.xml	docProps\	XML Document
app.xml	docProps\	XML Document
[Content_Types].xml		XML Document
.rels	_rels\	XML Document

The `workbook.xml` file is stored under the `xl` folder; it essentially stores the names and IDs for the worksheets that reside in the Excel container. Information about the worksheets and their contents is stored under the `xl\worksheets` folder. Every worksheet is a separate XML document. Within this individual file, the worksheet information and data is stored. The XML has a fundamental structure: there is a <row> element for every row and an element <c> for every cell. The associated attributes provide additional information about the type of information stored in the cell as well as the cell's reference. The cell's value and its related Excel function are stored under the `<c>` element as `<v>` and `<f>` respectively.

That's as simple as it gets; now we enter the underlying complexity of the relationships between worksheets and how they interrelate.

NOTE

The `calcChain.xml` file tells the container in what order the calculations are to be processed. If it doesn't exist, Excel will create it, so it will not be covered in this chapter.

As you can see, the container also has a `sharedStrings.xml` file, which stores a list of strings that are reusable throughout all worksheets (referenced in the `t=` attribute of the `<c>` element; its position is referenced in the `<v>` element in `sheets*.xml`). The basic hierarchy of a worksheet (`sheet*.xml`) is as follows:

```
<sheetData.......>
   <row r="2" >
      <c r="A2" t="s">
         <v>0</v>
         <f></f>
```

This example references the `sharedStrings.xml` file and tells us that the text in the first (index of 0) shared information `<si` element is the value for this cell.

Now that we have identified a few of the relationships within the Excel OOXML container, we will look at some code snippets to populate a four-sheet invoice workbook with the same data as in the previous Word example.

TIP

Dates are stored as the number of days since 1/1/1900, so `dateAdd ('d', *, '1/1/1900')` is needed to convert Excel date values.

With Excel, we have to start to think a bit more conceptually about how we need to accommodate the `sharedStrings.xml` file and it use within the workbook. We can either populate this file first with all our strings or append to it every time we encounter a new character string that has not been previously recorded. The approach we will take in this book is the latter.

Creating a Dynamic Excel OOXML Document

Unlike in the previous Word example, we will create and populate an OOXML container from the beginning. Most of the data will be dynamically added, but there will also be XML templates for the basic content that reside in a number of the container parts. These are the steps we will follow:

- Create the mandatory XML files necessary for a valid OOXML container.
- Create the required blank worksheets.
- Store these files in the predefined folders required.
- Zip the files in an `.xlsx` container.
- Add and save content to the cells within the specified worksheet.

NOTE

As you will see, the task of storing a string value in a cell is a little more complex, as we have to determine whether there is a string value in the `sharedString.xml` file and, if so, record its array position. Once we have the position, we need to identify it as a shared string by placing the attribute (`t`) of the `<c>` element and recording its value in the `<v>` element: `<c r="A2" t="s"><v>0</v>`.

In this example, to build a new Excel OOXML file we need a temporary directory to store the container's parts. Once we have created the basic container and its associated file structure, we will then zip these into a file with an `.xlsx` extension. Unlike the Word approach, this approach will use a CFC to assist in building and populating the container.

Building the OOXMLExcel Component

In this example, we will create a component that manipulates an OOXMLExcel container and a file that will retrieve data from data storage and pass it to the OOXMLExcel CFC.

We need to build the eight foundation files needed to create a primitive `.xlsx` file. These are `core.xml`, `app.xml`,`workbook.xml`, `workbookxml_rels`, `workbook`, `_rels`,`[Content_types].xml`, and `worksheetxx.xml`. The `core.xml`,`app.xml`, `_rels`, and `Content_types` files will be hard-coded in the CFC as the data in these files will not change throughout this chapter (for simplicity).

Our first step will be to create a blank workbook. To create a blank `.xlsx` container, we will create these eight files and then package them using `CZIP` into an `.xlsx` file. The `CreateBlank` function takes two parameters to produce a blank Excel 2007 spreadsheet. Its usage is as shown in Listing 76.7.

Listing 76.7 `76_7.cfm`—Calling the `CreateBlank` Method of the OOXMLExcel CFC

```
<CFINVOKE   COMPONENT="OOXMLExcel"
   METHOD="CreateBlank"
   STRTEMPDIRECTORY="c:\temp\test"
   STRXLSXFILENAME="c:\temp\blank.xlsx"
   RETURNVARIABLE="strFilename">
```

The main processing in this `CreateBlank` function is a call to the `write_worksheet` function. This function manipulates a worksheet and is the key to creating an OOXMLExcel container. When creating a new worksheet, we must store a reference to the worksheet in the `workbook.xml` file and then create a corresponding XML file in the `xl\worksheets` folder. The basic process for creating a blank container consists of creating the default six files and then creating an `xl\worksheets\sheet.xml` file and adding it to `workbook.xml`. The code for this function is available at this book's Web site in the `OOXMLExcel` component in this chapter's listings. The `workbook.xml` file must know about the sheets and map their names to the actual XML file name. The OOXML stores the sheets as `sheet(n).xml`, where `n` is a numeric value corresponding to the sheet order (`sheetId="n"`) in the workbook.

The `write workbook` function populates the `xl/workbook.xml` container part. It accepts the worksheet array, creating the required static elements, and then loops over all the worksheets, creating the sheet element and populating it with static and dynamic attributes and elements and their values. For this worksheet relationship to be easily created, we need to know how the worksheet names and positions in the workbook are stored (Listing 76.8).

Listing 76.8 `76_8.cfm`—Using `get_workbook` to Create an XML String Compliant with the OOXML Workbook Spec

```
<CFFUNCTION NAME="get_Workbook" OUTPUT="true" ACCESS="private" RETURNTYPE="XML" >
   <CFARGUMENT NAME="arrSheets" TYPE="array" REQUIRED="NO">
   <CFSET strReturn = '#variables.strXMLHeader8#'>
   <CFSET strReturn = '#strReturn#<workbook
xmlns="#variables.strSchemaSSML2006#/main"
xmlns:r="#variables.strSchemaOffDoc2006#/relationships">'>
   <CFSET strReturn = '#strReturn#<fileVersion appName="xl" lastEdited="4"
lowestEdited="4" rupBuild="4505"/>'>
   <CFSET strReturn = '#strReturn#<workbookPr defaultThemeVersion="124226"/>'>
   <CFSET strReturn = '#strReturn#<bookViews>'>
   <CFSET strReturn = '#strReturn#<workbookView xWindow="420" yWindow="810"
windowWidth="14835" windowHeight="6150"/>'>
   <CFSET strReturn = '#strReturn#</bookViews>'>
   <CFSET strReturn = '#strReturn#<sheets>'>
   <CFIF parameterexists(arguments.arrSheets)>
      <CFSET strSheets="">
      <CFLOOP FROM="1" TO="#ArrayLen(arrSheets)#" INDEX="intCountrSheet">
         <CFSET strSheets = '#strSheets#<sheet
name="#arrSheets[intCountrSheet].strWorkSheetName#" sheetId="#intCountrSheet#"
r:id="rId#intCountrSheet#"/>'>
      </CFLOOP>
   <CFELSE>
      <CFSET strSheets = '<sheet name="Sheet1" sheetId="1" r:id="rId1"/>'>
   </CFIF>
   <CFSET strReturn = '#strReturn##strSheets#'>
   <CFSET strReturn = '#strReturn#</sheets>'>
   <CFSET strReturn = '#strReturn#<calcPr calcId="124519"/>'>
   <CFSET strReturn = '#strReturn#</workbook>'>
   <CFSET strReturn = '#strReturn#'>
   <CFXML VARIABLE="XMLReturn">
      #strReturn#
   </CFXML>
   <CFRETURN XMLReturn>
</CFFUNCTION>
```

Creating a Worksheet as a Structure

To create the worksheet, we will call the `CreateWorksheet` function. This function accepts the worksheet name and the length of rows and columns required to hold its data (Listing 76.9).

Listing 76.9 `76_9.cfm`—Invoking the `CreateWorksheet` Method of the OOXMLExcel CFC

```
<CFOBJECT NAME="CFC_Excel" COMPONENT="OOXMLExcel">
<CFQUERY DATASOURCE = "OWS" NAME="qryFilmActors">
   SELECT  DISTINCT  ACTORS.NAMEFIRST, ACTORS.NAMELAST
   FROM    Films INNER JOIN FilmsActors ON films.FILMID =  Films.FilmID
           INNER JOIN  ACTORS ON FilmsActors.ACTORID = Actors.ActorID
   WHERE Films.filmID = #URL.FilmID#
</CFQUERY>
<CFQUERY DATASOURCE = "OWS" NAME="qryFilmDirectors">
   SELECT   Directors.*
   FROM    films INNER JOIN FilmsDirectors ON films.FILMID = FilmsDirectors.FILMID
           INNER JOIN Directors ON Directors.DirectorID = FilmsDirectors.DIRECTORID
```

Listing 76.9 (continued)

```
    WHERE Films.filmID = #URL.FilmID#
</CFQUERY>
<CFINVOKE   COMPONENT="#CFC_Excel#"
    METHOD="CreateWorkSheet"
    STRWORKSHEETNAME="Film"
    INTROWS= #int(qryFilmActors.Recordcount +9)#
    INTCOLUMNS = #int(qryFilmDirectors.Recordcount +1)#
    RETURNVARIABLE="stcWS1">
<CFSET temp= ArrayAppend(arrWS,stcWS1)>
```

Creation of a worksheet array consists of creating a worksheet and then adding it to an array. The approach we will take is to name and create a blank worksheet with the specific number of rows and columns and store it as a structure. In this example (Listing 76.10a), the `CreateWorkSheet` function returns a structure that has three keys: the worksheet name, an array of rows (with index and span values), and an array of columns that hold the column details (reference, value, function, and shared string association).

Listing 76.10a `76_10a.cfm`—`CreateWorksheet` Function in the OOXMLExcel CFC: First Section

```
<CFFUNCTION NAME="CreateWorkSheet" output="false" RETURNTYPE="STRUCT">
    <CFARGUMENT NAME="strWorkSheetName" TYPE="String" REQUIRED="YES">
    <CFARGUMENT NAME="intRows" TYPE="Numeric" REQUIRED="YES">
    <CFARGUMENT NAME="intColumns" TYPE="Numeric" REQUIRED="YES">
        <CFSET stcWS = Structnew()>
        <CFSET arrRows  = ArrayNew(1)>
        <CFSET arrCols  = ArrayNew(2)>
        <CFSET temp = StructInsert(stcWS ,
"strWorkSheetName","#arguments.strWorkSheetName#")>
        <CFLOOP FROM="1" TO="#int(arguments.intRows + 1)#" INDEX="intRowCountr">
            <CFSET arrRows[intRowCountr] = StructNew()>
            <CFSET temp = StructInsert(arrRows[intRowCountr] , "r","#intRowCountr#")>
            <CFSET temp = StructInsert(arrRows[intRowCountr] ,
"spans","#arguments.intRows#:#arguments.intColumns#")>
            <CFLOOP FROM="1" TO="#int(arguments.intColumns+1)#" INDEX="intColCountr">
                <CFSET arrCols[intRowCountr][intColCountr] = StructNew()>
                <CFSET temp = StructInsert(arrCols[intRowCountr][intColCountr] ,
"r","#getColumnLetter(intColCountr)##intRowCountr#")>
                <CFSET temp = StructInsert(arrCols[intRowCountr][intColCountr] ,
"s","")>
                <CFSET temp = StructInsert(arrCols[intRowCountr][intColCountr] ,
"t","")>
                <CFSET temp = StructInsert(arrCols[intRowCountr][intColCountr] ,
"v","")>
```

Here, `arrCols[intRowCountr][intColCountr].v` stores the value of the cell. At this point, we could manipulate the structure and start to place values within this key. However, because we will run into challenges if the values are nonnumeric, we will always create a blank `.xlsx` container and then populate it with data (Listing 76.10b).

Listing 76.10b `76_10b.cfm`—`CreateWorksheet` Function in the OOXMLExcel CFC: Second Section

```
                <CFSET temp = StructInsert(arrCols[intRowCountr][intColCountr] ,
"f","")>
```

Listing 76.10b (continued)

```
            </CFLOOP>
         </CFLOOP>
         <CFSET temp = StructInsert(stcWS , "arrColumns",arrCols)>
         <CFSET temp = StructInsert(stcWS , "arrRows",arrRows)>
      <CFRETURN stcWS>
   </CFFUNCTION>
```

We begin by creating a structure with a key called `strWorksheetname`. This key is used to populate data in the `workbook.xml` (`<workbook><sheets><sheet name =""> element`) file. Next, we create the row and column arrays by using two loops using the values provided in the rows and column parameters given to the function. In every row (the first `CFLOOP`), we create the two structure keys (which translate to attributes when we transform the structure into an `XMLobject`) that the row (`<r >`) element requires. We have a corresponding column array (the second `CFLOOP`) that builds the structure keys that are used to populate the attributes of the column element (`<c t= s=`) and the nested value (`<v>`) and function (`<f>`) elements. After the column array and row array are created within the `CFLOOP` tags, we insert them into the structure before returning the worksheet structure. This array is then passed to the following function.

So we now have a worksheet structure. Most workbooks may have a number of worksheets, so let's create an array of worksheet structures. Once we have our array of sheets (converted to XML), we can then create the container that will hold the individual sheets. `get_Sheet` converts this ColdFusion structure into an OOXML worksheet `XMLobject`.

The `get_Sheet` function returns an XML object. If it receives a sheet structure (created from the `createWorkSheet` function), it will loop through the rows (`arguments.stcSheet.arrRows`) and then loop through the columns (`arguments.stcSheet.arrColumns`) to produce a worksheet XML element conforming to the OOXML SpreadsheetML schema. After it has completed the rows associated with `sheetdata`, it will close the remaining XML tags to complete the XML object.

Once the container and worksheet has been created, we need to set the values of the cells. We are using this approach to allow us to see the shared string concept and the worksheet's interaction with the `sharedString.xml` file (Listing 76.11).

Listing 76.11 `76_11.cfm`—`get_sheet` Function of the OOXML CFC

```
<CFFUNCTION NAME="get_sheet" OUTPUT="true" ACCESS="private" RETURNTYPE="XML" >
   <CFARGUMENT NAME="stcSheet" TYPE="Struct" REQUIRED="NO">
      <CFSET strReturn = '#variables.strXMLHeader8#'>
      <CFSET strReturn = '#strReturn#<worksheet
xmlns="#variables.strSchemaSSML2006#/main"
xmlns:r="#variables.strSchemaOffDoc2006#/relationships">'>
      <CFIF parameterexists(arguments.stcSheet)>
         <CFSET strReturn = '#strReturn#<dimension
ref="#arguments.stcSheet.arrColumns[1][1].r#:#arguments.stcSheet.arrColumns[ArrayLen
(arguments.stcSheet.arrColumns)][ArrayLen(arguments.stcSheet.arrColumns[1])].r#"
/>'>
      <CFELSE>
         <CFSET strReturn = '#strReturn#<dimension ref="A1"/>'>
      </CFIF>
      <CFSET strReturn = '#strReturn#<sheetViews><sheetView tabSelected="1"
```

Listing 76.11 (CONTINUED)

```
workbookViewId="0"/></sheetViews><sheetFormatPr defaultRowHeight="15"/>'>'
      <CFSET strReturn = '#strReturn#<sheetData>'>
      <CFIF parameterexists(arguments.stcSheet)>
         <CFLOOP FROM="1" TO = "#ArrayLen(arguments.stcSheet.arrRows)#"
INDEX="intRowCountr">
            <CFSET strReturn = '#strReturn#<row r="#intRowCountr#"
spans="1:#ArrayLen(arguments.stcSheet.arrColumns[intRowCountr])#">'>
            <CFLOOP FROM="1" TO = "#ArrayLen(arguments.stcSheet.arrColumns[1])#"
INDEX="intColCountr">
               <CFSET strReturn = '#strReturn#<c
r="#arguments.stcSheet.arrColumns[intRowCountr][intColCountr].r#"'>
               <CFIF
len(trim(arguments.stcSheet.arrColumns[intRowCountr][intColCountr].s)) GT 0>
                  <CFSET strReturn = '#strReturn#
s="#arguments.stcSheet.arrColumns[intRowCountr][intColCountr].s#"'>
               </CFIF>
               <CFIF
len(trim(arguments.stcSheet.arrColumns[intRowCountr][intColCountr].t)) GT 0>
                  <CFSET strReturn = '#strReturn#
t="#arguments.stcSheet.arrColumns[intRowCountr][intColCountr].t#"'>
               </CFIF>
               <CFSET strReturn = '#strReturn#>'>
               <CFSET strReturn =
'#strReturn#<v>#arguments.stcSheet.arrColumns[intRowCountr][intColCountr].v#</v>'>
               <CFSET strReturn = '#strReturn#</c>'>
            </CFLOOP>
            <CFSET strReturn = '#strReturn#</row>'>
         </CFLOOP>
      <CFELSE>
         <CFSET strReturn = '#strReturn#<row r="1" spans="1:1"><c
r="A1"><v>0</v></c></row>'>
      </CFIF>
      <CFSET strReturn = '#strReturn#</sheetData>'>
      <CFSET strReturn = '#strReturn#<pageMargins left="0.7" right="0.7" top="0.75"
bottom="0.75" header="0.3" footer="0.3" />'>'
      <CFSET strReturn = '#strReturn#</worksheet>'>
      <CFXML VARIABLE="XMLReturn">
         #strReturn#
      </CFXML>
   <CFRETURN XMLReturn>
</CFFUNCTION>
```

After we create an array of worksheets, we call the `CreateNew` function of the `OOXMLExcel` component. The `createNew` function accepts the array of worksheets. It then creates the basic XML in all the required container parts and populates the workbook, worksheet, and shared strings XML files. After it creates and manages the files, it zips them into an `.xlsx` container using the `CFZIP` tag (Listing 76.12).

Listing 76.12 `76_12.cfm`—`CreateNew` Function of the OOXMLExcel CFC

```
<CFFUNCTION NAME="CreateNew" OUTPUT="true" ACCESS="public" RETURNTYPE="String">
   <CFARGUMENT NAME="strTempDirectory" Type="String" REQUIRED="Yes">
   <CFARGUMENT NAME="strXLSXFilename" Type="String" REQUIRED="Yes">
   <CFARGUMENT NAME="arrayWorksheets" Type="array" REQUIRED="Yes">
      <CFIF DirectoryExists(strTempDirectory)>
```

Listing 76.12 (continued)

```
            <CFSET temp = write_rels("#arguments.strTempDirectory#")>
            <CFSET temp =
outputToFile("#arguments.strTempDirectory#\[Content_types].xml",
toString(get_Content_Types(arrayWorksheets)))>
          <CFSET temp=write_workbook("#arguments.strTempDirectory#",
arguments.arrayWorksheets )>
          <CFSET temp =
write_workbookxml_rels("#arguments.strTempDirectory#",arguments.arrayWorksheets)>
          <CFSET temp = write_worksheet("#arguments.strTempDirectory#",
arguments.arrayWorksheets )>
          <CFSET
temp=write_app("#arguments.strTempDirectory#",arguments.arrayWorksheets)>
          <CFSET temp=write_core("#arguments.strTempDirectory#")>
          <CFSET temp=write_sharedStrings("#arguments.strTempDirectory#")>
          <CFSET temp =
createXLSXFile("#arguments.strTempDirectory#","#arguments.strXLSXFilename#")>
       </CFIF>
    <CFRETURN "#arguments.strXLSXFilename#">
</CFFUNCTION>
```

Now that we have the container created, it is time to populate the sheets with values. For `setWorkSheetCell` to function, it needs an existing container to manipulate. It then uses the `CFZIP` tag to read that container into a string variable that is then parsed to an XML object.

NOTE

We use integers for both rows and columns; however, Excel uses an alphabetical system to reference its columns. The function `getColumnLetter` is used to convert an integer value into the alphabetical character required by Excel.

The function can accept a single value associated with a single cell or it can accept an array of cells that it will populate. With either approach, the function will write the value and function to the XML file. This value may need to be manipulated before it is stored (`<v>` element) if it is not a numeric value. To do this, we need to be able to determine the data type; then, if required, the code will manipulate other container parts and evaluate the new shared string value before populating its (`<v>` element) data (`setWorkSheetCellValue`). The function is stored as text within the `<f>` element. After the cell or cells have been populated, a file is created in the `temp` directory structure and then is added back into the `.xlsx` container with the use of the `CFZIP` tag (Listing 76.13).

Listing 76.13 `76_13.cfm`—`setWorksheetCell` Function of the OOXMLExcel CFC

```
<CFFUNCTION NAME="setWorksheetCell" output="true" RETURNTYPE="Struct">
   <CFARGUMENT NAME="strXLSXFilename" TYPE="String" REQUIRED="YES">
   <CFARGUMENT NAME="strWorksheetName" TYPE="String" REQUIRED="YES">
   <CFARGUMENT NAME="intROW" TYPE="Numeric" REQUIRED="NO">
   <CFARGUMENT NAME="intCOLUMN" TYPE="Numeric" REQUIRED="NO">
   <CFARGUMENT NAME="strValue" TYPE="String" REQUIRED="NO">
   <CFARGUMENT NAME="strFunction" TYPE="String" REQUIRED="NO">
   <CFARGUMENT NAME="arrCells" TYPE="Array" REQUIRED="NO">
      <CFIF NOT DirectoryExists("#variables.strTempStorageDirectory#\xl")>
         <CFDIRECTORY ACTION="create" DIRECTORY=
"#variables.strTempStorageDirectory#\xl" >
      </CFIF>
```

Listing 76.13 (continued)

```
      <CFIF NOT
DirectoryExists("#variables.strTempStorageDirectory#\xl\worksheets")>
         <CFDIRECTORY ACTION=""create" DIRECTORY =
"#variables.strTempStorageDirectory#\xl\worksheets" >
      </CFIF>
      <CFINVOKE
         METHOD="getWorksheetXMLNumber"
         STRWORKSHEETNAME="#arguments.strWorksheetName#"
               STRXLSXFILENAME="#arguments.strXLSXFilename#"
         RETURNVARIABLE="strWorkSheetXMLFilename">
      <CFZIP ACTION="Read"
         FILE="#arguments.strXLSXFilename#"
               ENTRYPATH="xl\worksheets\#strWorkSheetXMLFilename#"
         VARIABLE="strXMLSheettext">
      <CFSET  XMLWorksheet=XMLParse("#strXMLSheettext#")>
      <CFIF parameterexists(arguments.intRow) AND
parameterexists(arguments.intCOLUMN) >
         <CFIF ArrayLen(XMLWorksheet.worksheet.sheetdata.XMLChildren) LT
arguments.intROW OR
ArrayLen(XMLWorksheet.worksheet.sheetdata.XMLChildren[arguments.intROW].XMLChildren)
LT arguments.intCOLUMN    >
            <CFTHROW MESSAGE="Cannot reference cell. Cell is out of worksheet
bounds">
         </CFIF>
         <CFIF  parameterexists(arguments.strValue)>
            <CFSET
XMLWorksheet.worksheet.sheetdata.XMLChildren[arguments.intROW].XMLChildren[arguments
.intCOLUMN] =
setworksheetCellValue(XMLWorksheet.worksheet.sheetdata.XMLChildren[arguments.intROW]
.XMLChildren[arguments.intCOLUMN],arguments.strvalue,arguments.strXLSXFilename)>
         </CFIF>
         <CFIF parameterexists(arguments.strFunction)>
            <CFSET
XMLWorksheet.worksheet.sheetdata.XMLChildren[arguments.intROW].XMLChildren[arguments
.intCOLUMN]=
setworksheetCellFunction(XMLWorksheet.worksheet.sheetdata.XMLChildren[arguments.intR
OW].XMLChildren[arguments.intCOLUMN],arguments.strFunction,arguments.strXLSXFilename
)>
         </CFIF>
      </CFIF>
      <CFIF parameterexists(arguments.arrCells)>
         <CFIF ArrayLen(XMLWorksheet.worksheet.sheetdata.XMLChildren) LT
intROWCountr>
         <CFELSE>
            <CFLOOP FROM="1" TO="#ArrayLen(arguments.arrCells)#"
INDEX="intROWCountr">
               <CFLOOP FROM="1" TO="#ArrayLen(arguments.arrCells[intROWCountr])#"
INDEX="intCOLUMNCountr">
                  <CFIF isStruct(arguments.arrCells[intROWCountr][intCOLUMNCountr])
AND structKeyexists(arguments.arrCells[intROWCountr][intCOLUMNCountr],"v")>
```

Listing 76.13 (continued)

```
                        <CFSET
XMLWorksheet.worksheet.sheetdata.XMLChildren[intROWCountr].XMLChildren[intCOLUMNCoun
tr] =
setworksheetCellValue(XMLWorksheet.worksheet.sheetdata.XMLChildren[intROWCountr].XML
Children[intCOLUMNCountr],arrCells[intROWCountr][intCOLUMNCountr].v,
arguments.strXLSXFilename)>
                     </CFIF>
                     <CFIF isStruct(arguments.arrCells[intROWCountr][intCOLUMNCountr])
AND  structKeyexists(arguments.arrCells[intROWCountr][intCOLUMNCountr],"f")>
                        <CFSET
XMLWorksheet.worksheet.sheetdata.XMLChildren[intROWCountr].XMLChildren[intCOLUMNCoun
tr]=setworksheetCellFunction(XMLWorksheet.worksheet.sheetdata.XMLChildren[intROWCoun
tr].XMLChildren[intCOLUMNCountr],arguments.arrCells[intROWCountr][intCOLUMNCountr].f,
#arguments.strXLSXFilename#)>
                     </CFIF>
                  </CFLOOP>
               </CFLOOP>
            </CFIF>
         </CFIF>
         <CFSET strWorksheet = replace(toString(XMLWorksheet), ' T=', ' t=','All')>
         <CFSET strWorksheet = replace(strWorksheet, ' S=', ' s=','All')>
         <CFFILE ACTION = "write"
FILE="#variables.strTempStorageDirectory#\xl\worksheets\#strWorkSheetXMLFilename#"
OUTPUT="#strWorksheet#">
         <CFZIP ACTION="zip"  STOREPATH="yes"
         FILE="#arguments.strXLSXFilename#"
         SOURCE="#variables.strTempStorageDirectory#\"  >
         <CFSET stcReturn =Structnew() >
   <CFRETURN stcReturn>
</CFFUNCTION>
```

If the value is not a number or a date, then we insert its value with the `setWorkSheet CellValue` function. This function returns the value of a cell that will be stored in the `sheet(n).xml` file's `<v>` element. In this example, we are assuming that if the value is not a date or number, then it will be a string. As discussed, strings are stored throughout the workbook as references to the `sharedStrings.xml` file. If the value is a number, it is returned unaltered. If it is a date, it will call the `getColumnDate` function and return its numeric value. If it is a string, we must be able to return an array reference to its string value in the `Sharedstrings.xml` file (Listing 76.14).

NOTE

As discussed, `getColumnDate` converts the date to the numeric value that Excel requires for a date value (days from 1/1/1900).

Listing 76.14 `76_14.cfm`—`setWorksheetCellValue` Function of the OOXMLExcel CFC

```
<CFFUNCTION NAME="setWorksheetCellValue" OUTPUT="true" RETURNTYPE="XML">
   <CFARGUMENT NAME="XMLCell" TYPE="XML" REQUIRED="YES">
   <CFARGUMENT NAME="strValue" TYPE="String" REQUIRED="YES">
   <CFARGUMENT NAME="strXLSXFilename" TYPE="String" REQUIRED="YES">
      <CFSET XMLCell = arguments.XMLCell>
         <CFIF IsNumeric(arguments.strValue)>
            <CFLOOP FROM="1" TO="#ArrayLen(XMLCell.XMLChildren)#"
INDEX="intChildCountr">
```

Listing 76.14 (continued)

```
                    <CFIF XMLCell.XMLChildren[intChildCountr].XMLName eq "v">
                       <CFSET XMLCell.XMLChildren[intChildCountr].XMLText =
"#arguments.strValue#" >
                    </CFIF>
                 </CFLOOP>
              <CFELSE>
                 <CFIF IsDate(arguments.strValue)>
                    <CFIF XMLCell.XMLName eq "v">
                       <CFSET XMLCell.XMLText =getColumnDate(arguments.strValue)>
                    </CFIF>
                 <CFELSE>
                    <CFINVOKE
                       METHOD="setSharedString"
                       STRVALUE = "#arguments.strValue#"
                             STRXLSXFILENAME="#arguments.strXLSXFilename#"
                                 RETURNVARIABLE="intSharedStringValue">
                    <CFLOOP FROM="1" TO="#ArrayLen(XMLCell.XMLChildren)#"
INDEX="intChildCountr">
                       <CFIF XMLCell.XMLChildren[intChildCountr].XMLName eq "v">
                          <CFSET XMLCell.XMLChildren[intChildCountr].XMLText
=intSharedStringValue   >
                       </CFIF>
                    </CFLOOP>
                    <CFSET XMLCell.XMLAttributes.t = "s" >
                    </CFIF>
                 </CFIF>
              <CFRETURN XMLCell>
</CFFUNCTION>
```

NOTE

The interchange of the way we manipulate the container's XML as a doc, struct, or text is for learning purposes, to demonstrate different approaches.

Excel uses a file to store shared strings. We will manage this within the `setSharedString` function. This function returns a reference to the string within the `sharedStrings.xml` file; if the string doesn't exist, we will append a new shared string and return its reference. As you can see in Listing 76.15, the function reads the contents of the `sharedStrings.xml` file and parses it to an XML object. In this example, we use ColdFusion's `XMLSearch` function to determine whether the string exists in the collection of string values. If it does, then the position of the string is returned to the code calling this function; otherwise, it duplicates an element, adds a value to the element, appends the new element to the collection, writes the file to a `temp` storage directory, and then adds the file with its folder location to the `.xlsx` container. Once it has completed the procedure of getting the reference, it returns the reference to the calling code.

NOTE

`getworkSheetXMLNumber` accepts the worksheet name and returns the number corresponding to the array position, which in turn translates to the name of the `sheet(n).xml` file that is stored in the `xl/worksheets/` location in the `.xlsx` container.

Listing 76.15 `76_15.cfm`—`setSharedString` Function of the OOXMLExcel CFC that Manages the Shared String OOXML Spec

```
<CFFUNCTION NAME="setSharedString" OUTPUT="false" ACCESS="private"
RETURNTYPE="Numeric" >
   <CFARGUMENT NAME="strXLSXFilename" TYPE="String" REQUIRED="YES">
   <CFARGUMENT NAME="strValue" REQUIRED="yes" TYPE="String"
      DISPLAYNAME="Value of Column"
      HINT=" Shared String array Value >">
      <CFSET intReturn = 0>
      <CFIF IsNumeric(arguments.strValue)>
         <CFSET intReturn = "#arguments.strValue#">
      <CFELSE>
               <CFZIP ACTION="Read"
                  FILE="#arguments.strXLSXFilename#"
                  ENTRYPATH="xl\sharedStrings.xml"
                  VARIABLE="strXMLSheettext">
               <CFSET  XMLDoc=XMLParse("#strXMLSheettext#")>
               <CFSET XMLEleSharedStrings = XmlSearch(XMLDoc, "/sst/si/t")>
         <CFIF ArrayLen(XMLEleSharedStrings) GT 0>
         <CFELSE>
            <CFSET XMLsiPart = Duplicate(XMLDoc.sst.si)>
            <CFSET intarrLen = ArrayLen(XMLDoc.sst.XMLChildren) >
            <CFSET intReturn =  intarrLen   >
            <CFSET temp = ArrayAppend(XMLDoc.sst.XMLChildren,
XmlElemNew(XMLDoc,"si"))>
            <CFSET temp = ArrayAppend(XMLDoc.sst.XMLChildren[intarrLen +
1].XMLChildren, XmlElemNew(XMLDoc,"t"))>
            <CFSET XMLDoc.sst.XMLChildren[intarrLen+1].XMLChildren[1].XMLText =
"#arguments.strValue#">
         </CFIF>
         <CFFILE ACTION = "write"
           FILE="#variables.strTempStorageDirectory#\xl\sharedStrings.xml"
           OUTPUT="#toString(XMLDoc)#">
         <CFZIP ACTION="zip"   STOREPATH="yes"
            FILE="#arguments.strXLSXFilename#"
                  SOURCE="#variables.strTempStorageDirectory#\"  >
      </CFIF>
   <CFRETURN intReturn>
</CFFUNCTION>
```

NOTE

For instructional purposes, this book demonstrates the use of structures as well as `XMLNewElement`. However, the result is the same, so which you use depends on your coding preferences.

Calling the OOXMLExcel Component

Define the queries for the Film worksheet (Figure 76.5) as `qryFilm`, `qryFilmDirectors`, and `qryFilmActors`.

Define the queries for the Merchandise(`qryMerchandise`), Expenses(`qryExpenses`), and MerchandiseOrders(`qryMerchandiseorders`) worksheets.

In this example, we then need to create an array of worksheets that we will pass to the `createnew` method of the OOXML component:

```
<CFSET arrWS = ArrayNew(1)>
```

To create a worksheet structure, we will call the `CreateWorkSheet` method, passing it the number of columns and rows that the worksheet will consist of as well as the name of the worksheet.

	A	B	C	D	E	F	G	H
1	Movie Title:	Charlie's Devils						
2	Summary:	It's a quiet peaceful day, no bad news, no bad guys, and no worries. But all that'						
3	Budget:	750000						
4	Expenses:	373500						
5	Merchandise Ordered:	361.479996						
6	Released:	23/12/2000						
7	Rating:	General						
8	Director:	George		Locust				
9	Actors:	Belinda		Foxile				
10		Carlease		Theron				
11		Dolly		Pardon				
12		Fabio						
13		Ferris		Beuller				
14		Halle		Beary				
15		Harry		Fjord				
16		Kevin		Space				
17		L.L.		P.J.				
18		Nick		Nutty				
19		Nicole		Kidmen				
20		Pam		Andrewson				
21		Patrik		Sway				
22		Robbie		Berry				
23		Sam		Gold				
24		Sean		Conway				
25		Sharon		Stoned				
26		Uno		Thorman				
27		William		Shitener				

Film / Expenses / Merchandise / MerchandiseOrders

Figure 76.5

The Film worksheet displays the film details.

To create the Film worksheet structure and then add it to the array, we use the code shown in Listing 76.16a.

Listing 76.16a `76_16a.cfm—filmworkbook.cfm` File Creating the Film Worksheet

```
<CFINVOKE COMPONENT="#CFC_Excel#"
   METHOD="CreateWorkSheet"
   STRWORKSHEETNAME="Film"
   INTROWS= #int(qryFilmActors.Recordcount +9)#
   INTCOLUMNS = #int(qryFilmDirectors.Recordcount +1)#
   RETURNVARIABLE="stcWS1">
<CFSET temp= ArrayAppend(arrWS,stcWS1)>
```

We will call the same method for the other three worksheets (Expenses, Merchandise, and Merchandise Orders), passing in the `STRWORKSHEETNAME`, `INTROWS`, and `INTCOLS` arguments, and append them to the workbook array. After we have our required array of worksheet structures, we then call the `createnew` method to create the new workbook. The `createnew` method accepts three arguments:

- `STRTEMPDIRECTORY`: Temporary directory and subdirectory that the XML files will be stored in before they are zipped
- `STRXLSXFILENAME`: The path and name of the `.xlsx` file that will be produced
- `ARRAYWORKSHEETS`: The array of worksheet structures that the `Createworksheet` method returns

We have created the `.xlsx` file; we can now set the cell values. To set the cell values in the Film worksheet, we will call the `setWorkSheetCell` method, passing it the following five arguments:

- `INTROW`: The row position of the cell value
- `INTCOLUMN`: The column position of the cell value
- `STRVALUE`: The actual value, whether it be string, numeric, or date
- `STRXLSXFILENAME`: The `.xlsx` path and file name of the container
- `STRWORKSHEETNAME`: The name of the worksheet

To populate the Director row of the file, we will loop through the directors, adding one per column on the same row (Listing 76.16b).

Listing 76.16b `76_16b.cfm`—`filmworkbook.cfm` File Setting a Cell Value (Directors) for the Film Worksheet

```
<CFSET intDirCellPosition=2>
<CFLOOP QUERY="qryFilmDirectors" >
   <CFINVOKE
      COMPONENT="#CFC_Excel#"
         METHOD="setWorksheetCell"
         INTROW= "8"
         INTCOLUMN=  "#intDirCellPosition#"
         STRVALUE= "#FIRSTNAME# #LASTNAME#"
         STRXLSXFILENAME="#strXLSXName#"
         STRWORKSHEETNAME="Film"
         RETURNVARIABLE="stcNewCell">
      <CFSET intDirCellPosition= intDirCellPosition + 1>
</CFLOOP>
```

We'll do the same for Actors, but this time we will add actor one per row (Listing 76.16c).

Listing 76.16c `76_16c.cfm`—`filmworkbook.cfm` File Setting a Cell Value (Actors) for the Film Worksheet

```
<CFSET intActorRowPosition=9>
<CFLOOP QUERY="qryFilmActors" >
   <CFINVOKE
      COMPONENT="#CFC_Excel#"
      METHOD="setWorksheetCell"
      INTROW= "#intActorRowPosition#"
      INTCOLUMN=  "2"
```

Listing 76.16c (continued)

```
        STRVALUE= "#NAMEFIRST# #NAMELAST#"
        STRXLSXFILENAME="#strXLSXName#"
        STRWORKSHEETNAME="Film"
        RETURNVARIABLE="stcNewCell">
    <CFSET intActorRowPosition= intActorRowPosition + 1>
</CFLOOP>
```

We have finished setting the values for the Film worksheet. We will take a different approach to create the Expenses worksheet (Figure 76.6), passing the `setWorkSheetCell` method an argument that is an array of cell structures (`ARRCELLS`).

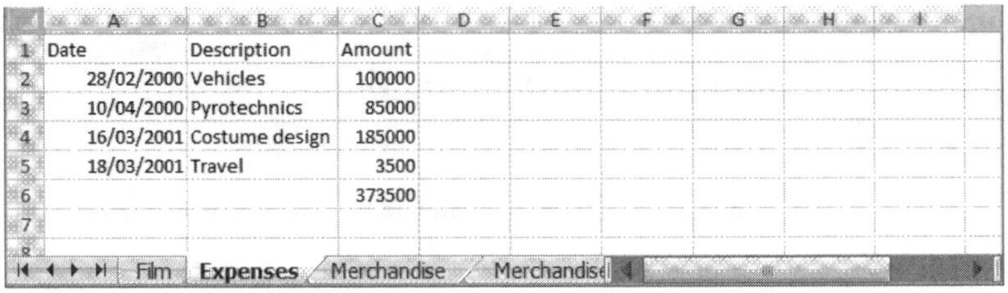

	A	B	C	D	E	F	G	H	I
1	Date	Description	Amount						
2	28/02/2000	Vehicles	100000						
3	10/04/2000	Pyrotechnics	85000						
4	16/03/2001	Costume design	185000						
5	18/03/2001	Travel	3500						
6			373500						
7									

Film | Expenses | Merchandise | Merchandise

Figure 76.6 The Expenses worksheet.

To create a two-dimensional array (rows of three columns) of cell structures, we will use the code shown in Listing 76.16.d.

Listing 76.16d `76_16d.cfm—filmworkbook.cfm` File Creating a 2D Array (Expenses) of Structures

```
<CFSET arrExpenses = ArrayNew(2)>
<!---- create a structure with a v key that corresponds with the  <v> element of an
OOXML Cell ---->
<CFSET stcCell = structnew()>
<CFSET temp = StructInsert(stcCell,"v","")>
<!---- Create the CELL headings of the three columns by duplicating the cell
structure and adding it to the 2D array of columns then setting the column header
text. ---->
<CFSET arrExpenses[intExpCountr][1]=Duplicate(stcCell)>
<CFSET arrExpenses[intExpCountr][1].v = "Date">
<CFSET arrExpenses[intExpCountr][2]=Duplicate(stcCell)>
<CFSET arrExpenses[intExpCountr][2].v = "Description">
<CFSET arrExpenses[intExpCountr][3]=Duplicate(stcCell)>
<CFSET arrExpenses[intExpCountr][3].v = "Amount">
```

With the headings of this worksheet set, we will loop through the `Expenses` query and add a row per expense (Listing 76.16e).

Listing 76.16e `76_16e.cfm—filmworkbook.cfm` File Populating the 2D Array (Expenses) of Structures from a Query

```
<CFLOOP QUERY="qryExpenses" >
   <CFSET intExpCountr = intExpCountr +1>
<!---- Duplicate the cell structure and add it to the 2D array of columns ---->
   <CFSET arrExpenses[intExpCountr][1]=Duplicate(stcCell)>
   <CFSET arrExpenses[intExpCountr][2]=Duplicate(stcCell)>
```

Listing 76.16e (continued)

```
    <CFSET arrExpenses[intExpCountr][3]=Duplicate(stcCell)>
<!---- then set the OOXML column values of date, description and expenseamount ----
>
    <CFSET arrExpenses[intExpCountr][1].v = "#qryExpenses.EXPENSEDATE#">
    <CFSET arrExpenses[intExpCountr][2].v = "#qryExpenses.DESCRIPTION#">
    <CFSET arrExpenses[intExpCountr][3].v = "#qryExpenses.EXPENSEAMOUNT#">
</CFLOOP>
```

To create a `SUM` function in Excel, we need the column set for an alphanumeric value. The method `getColumnLetter` returns the alphanumeric value when passed an integer (Listing 76.16f).

Listing 76.16f `76_16f.cfm`—`getColumnLetter` Call Converting a Number to an Alpha Character

```
<!---- Gets the Coulmn character for the third column (which is "c") ---->
<CFINVOKE
    COMPONENT="#CFC_Excel#"
    METHOD="getColumnLetter"
    INTCOLUMNNUMBER = "#int(3)#"
    RETURNVARIABLE="strColCell">
```

To set the cell directly below final expense amount (`arrExpenses[intExpCountr][3]`) as a `SUM` function, we will add a key of `f` to the cell structure (Listing 76.16g).

Listing 76.16g `76_16g.cfm`—`filmworkbook.cfm` File Creating a 2D Array (Expenses) of Structures that Include Excel `SUM`

```
<!---- Create the final row in the worksheet and set the third columns function
value to SUM( : ) ---->
    <CFSET intExpCountr = intExpCountr +1>
    <CFSET arrExpenses[intExpCountr][1] = structnew()>
    <CFSET arrExpenses[intExpCountr][2] = structnew()>
    <CFSET arrExpenses[intExpCountr][3] = structnew()>
    <CFSET temp =
structInsert(arrExpenses[intExpCountr][3],"f","sum(#strColCell#2:#strColCell##int(in
tExpCountr -1)#)")>
    <CFSET temp = structInsert(arrExpenses[intExpCountr][3],"v","0")>
```

We have created a two-dimensional array of cell structures. Now we will pass this array of cells to the `setWorksheetCell` function (Listing 76.16h).

Listing 76.16h `76_16h.cfm`—`filmworkbook.cfm` File Calling `setWorksheetCell` and Passing an Array

```
<CFINVOKE
    COMPONENT="#CFC_Excel#"
    METHOD="setWorksheetCell"
    STRXLSXFILENAME="#strXLSXName#"
    STRWORKSHEETNAME="Expenses"
    ARRCELLS="#arrExpenses#"
    RETURNVARIABLE="stcNewCell">
```

The Film worksheet requires a function to be populated that points to this value. Because the worksheet is dynamic—it gets its values from the query—we waited until we populated the Expenses worksheet before we linked the function to it. Once we have determined the location, we can then pass an individual cell in the Film worksheet (to the `setWorksheetCell` method) the function `"Expenses!#strColCell##int(intExpCountr)#")`, which references the expenses worksheet (Listing 76.16i).

Listing 76.16i `76_16i.cfm` —`filmworkbook.cfm` File Calling `setWorksheetCell` and Passing a Function Value

```
<CFINVOKE
   COMPONENT="#CFC_Excel#"
   METHOD="setWorksheetCell"
   STRXLSXFILENAME="#strXLSXName#"
   STRWORKSHEETNAME="Film"
   INTROW=4
   INTCOLUMN=2
   STRVALUE=0
   STRFUNCTION="Expenses!#strColCell##int(intExpCountr)#"
   RETURNVARIABLE="stcNewCell">
```

We will approach the other two worksheets (Figures 76.7 and 76.8) in a similar fashion, creating an array of cells and then calling the `setWorksheetCell` method.

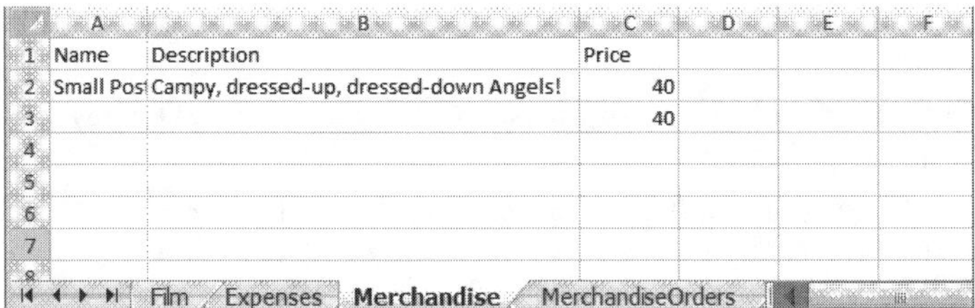

	A	B	C	D	E	F
1	Name	Description	Price			
2	Small Pos	Campy, dressed-up, dressed-down Angels!	40			
3			40			
4						
5						
6						
7						

Film / Expenses / **Merchandise** / MerchandiseOrders

Figure 76.7

The Merchandise worksheet.

The MerchandiseOrders worksheet (Figure 76.8) will sum the orders in the worksheet as well as add a function to the Film worksheet in the B5 cell.

	A	B	C	D	E	F	G	H	I
1	Name	Order Tot	State	Country	Ship Date	Ship Zip			
2	Ben	75	MI	USA	1/03/2001	48075			
3	Ben	108.98	MI	USA	3/03/2001	48075			
4	Jean	177.5		Belgium	1/03/2001	1234			
5		361.48							
6									
7									

Expenses / Merchandise / **MerchandiseOrders**

Figure 76.8

The MerchandiseOrders worksheet.

If you require more intelligent workbooks to be produced dynamically, ColdFusion provides a number of options to create and manipulate Excel documents. This has been a brief and limited introduction to OOXML and ColdFusion communication. Once you become familiar with the concept of the container and its parts, you can personalize your approach to suit your development style.

Automation

Automation is the process of launching another application and controlling it programmatically through a public interface. All Office applications support automation and provide a COM interface that is accessible from ColdFusion. However, when an Office application is launched through automation, the resources and effect are the same as when the application is launched by a logged-in user.

This behavior poses many problems for server-side integration, as with ColdFusion. The fact that there is no logged-in user can, in some circumstances, cause the Office application to lock up on launch, and lockups will occur at any point during use if an error message presents a modal dialog; the dialog will pop up and wait for a user to dismiss it. This behavior can pose a serious problem if someone isn't sitting at the server constantly. The same is true if the application runs into a feature that isn't installed and presents the "Install on first use" dialog.

Besides these serious problems, automation also presents concerns over scalability and security. The best recommendation regarding server-side automation of Microsoft Office applications comes directly from Microsoft:

Microsoft does not currently recommend, and does not support, Automation of Microsoft Office applications from any unattended, non-interactive client application or component (including ASP, DCOM, and NT Services), because Office may exhibit unstable behavior and/or deadlock when run in this environment.

`http://support.microsoft.com/default.aspx?scid=kb;en-us;257757`

Microsoft makes this recommendation regarding ASP, but it applies equally to ColdFusion, Java, and all other server-side programming technologies.

CHAPTER 77

Extending ColdFusion with CORBA

IN THIS CHAPTER

For both developers and companies, a common goal has been to reuse business logic for both internal and external applications. One major problem is that each organization standardizes and writes components on different platforms (such as Unix or NT) and in different development languages (such as Java, C++, or Ada). There needs to be a way for all of these component objects to communicate, appearing as a single application running on a single machine regardless of the language, host, or environment. One of the standards that has emerged to address this need is Common Object Request Broker Architecture (CORBA).

Introduction to CORBA

CORBA, basically a specification for building and using cross-platform distributed software objects, was created by the Object Management Group (OMG) in 1989. This allows a `PassengerManager` component written in Java, for instance, to be accessed by a C++ client, with the C++ client not knowing where the `PassengerManager` component is hosted or in what language it was written. The details on how this is possible will be discussed in this chapter. CORBA's mission, then, is somewhat similar conceptually to the mission of Web Services as discussed elsewhere in this book.

CORBA requires that all application logic be written in the form of objects, where its functionality can be described through an Interface Definition Language (IDL) definition. It is not required that the language the application logic is written in be object-oriented.

NOTE

IDL is discussed in the "OMG Interface Definition Language" section.

NOTE

CORBA principles were critical in the forming of the Enterprise JavaBeans standard as well as Java RMI.

As CORBA is a specification, it relies on various vendors and research organizations to provide implementations to host the CORBA objects. These are referred to as Object Request Brokers (ORB). The popular commercial ORBs available today are VisiBroker from Borland (`http://www.borland.com/visibroker`), Orbix from IONA (`http://www.orbix.com/products/orbix`), and e*ORB from PrismTech (`http://www.prismtechnologies.com`).

ColdFusion can communicate with CORBA through the `<cfobject>` tag or the `CreateObject()` function.

NOTE

Support for CORBA is currently only available in the Enterprise editions of ColdFusion.

Who Is the OMG?

The Object Management Group is an organization created in April 1989 by 11 companies (including Sun Microsystems, IBM, and American Airlines) with the purpose of "creating a component-based software marketplace by hastening the introduction of standardized object software." From the original 11 companies, the OMG has since grown to more than 800 members while still promoting its charter of providing a common framework for application development.

The OMG Web site is `http://www.omg.org` and contains the most up-to-date specification documentation on CORBA as well as information on the other standards that OMG supports.

How CORBA Works

Although this chapter doesn't cover how to write CORBA objects, you will learn some CORBA basics to help you understand the role that ColdFusion plays and how things work behind the scenes. There are several CORBA concepts and services that I have not covered due to the lack of relevance to the way ColdFusion uses CORBA.

The pieces of CORBA can be simplified into the following three parts: client, Object Request Broker, and object service. Basically, the client (ColdFusion in our case) makes a request for an object to the ORB. The ORB takes this request and invokes the method on the object through the object service. Return values from the method are passed back through the ORB to the client. An example might be of a `BankAccount` object that returns a balance based on the username passed in.

Object Request Broker

The ORB represents the cornerstone of the CORBA architecture. The function of the ORB is to provide communication between the client and the object service, which performs the work. The ORB is responsible for finding the requested object, passing parameters along, invoking the necessary object, and returning the results to the client. The ORB shields the location and the object implementation from the client. This shielding allows the client to transparently request and work with objects that are written in multiple languages and physically located throughout the network or even on the same machine. The client in essence views the entire system as one homogeneous environment, although in reality it may be diverse.

When a client requests an object from the ORB, the ORB returns to the client a reference to the object instance, which resides in the object service. This reference is known as the Interoperable Object Reference (IOR). The IOR contains the information necessary for the ORB to relocate the same object for subsequent requests.

NOTE

Another way to view this is as a client/server architecture. Think of the ORB as the communication mechanism between the client and object service.

Clients use the object references to make requests on the object. These object references can be obtained via directory services or by converting stringified IOR (`.ior`) files. Depending on how the object is requested, a new instance may be created in the object service. For example, if you are using an existing IOR (stringified `.ior` file) when requesting an object, a new object will not be created. However, if you use the Naming Service of the ORB to obtain an object, a new object would be created on the server. Using the Naming Service and existing (stringified) IOR files will be covered later in this section.

In any case, the ORB receives a request for an object and returns it. Notice that the ORB behaves the same by routing the request to the object service through the ORB "server" to the object server for both remote and local objects.

NOTE

Elaborating on the client/server parallel of the client and object service, you can think of each object as having a client interface and a server implementation.

Along with being responsible for locating and routing the request from the client to the corresponding component, the ORB is responsible for transferring data from the client to the server and passing the information back from the server to the client. For the data to be passed through the diverse environments, the data has to be converted into a standard format that can be passed through the network. The format, referred to as Over the Wire format, is done through the process called marshalling. The Over the Wire format is binary. The repackaging of the data into the native format is called unmarshalling.

NOTE

The terms marshalling and unmarshalling also are known as serialization and deserialization, respectively.

With the data being converted into a binary format, the ORB can pass the request onto another ORB server on the network if needed. This action is known as inter-ORB communication. The General Inter-ORB Protocol (GIOP) was created to allow the ORBs to communicate. However, because GIOP is a generalized protocol, it is not actually used. Instead, a protocol based on the GIOP, such as Internet Inter-ORB Protocol (IIOP), is used. IIOP is generally assigned to port 9100. Each ORB on the network is generally configured to listen to this port for requests from other systems. We can see at this point how it is possible for CORBA to allow objects to be hosted on remote machines running different operating systems.

NOTE

It is possible to create other protocols based on GIOP to use instead of IIOP. Be aware that stringified IOR (`.ior` files) are dependent on IIOP to work at all times.

Many ORB services can be used to locate and obtain an object reference. An ORB has an Interface Repository (IFR), which is in essence a database of all the objects, their interfaces, and their locations that the ORB knows about. If the ORB doesn't have knowledge of the object, then the client won't be able to gain access to it, even if it does exist somewhere on the network. The Naming Service is the only ORB service ColdFusion currently interfaces with. The Naming Service allows you to request an object reference through a literal name, such as `BankComponent` or `Adobe.Transactional.BankComponent`. This is similar to how COM components are generally accessed. After an object's location is determined, an object reference is created.

Another way to obtain an object reference is through its stringified IOR file. This file is basically an object reference encased in a file; the file consists of a string of hexadecimal numbers. An object reference just stores the location of the object in the network, not its interface definition. To work with the object, the object's interface needs to be stored in the ORB's IFR. Because the object's location is encased inside the `.ior` file, the connection performance is slightly better using `.ior` files than using the Naming Service. There is no difference between the two when invoking a method.

NOTE

Because the stringified IOR points to a previously created object instance, the success of the client connection through this `.ior` file depends on that object instance remaining.

Regardless of whether we used an `.ior` file or the Naming Service to obtain an object reference, the ORB uses its DII interface to dynamically build the method invocation on an object.

OMG Interface Definition Language

With the ORB being the cornerstone of the CORBA architecture, the Interface Definition Language is the mortar. The IDL is used for two main things: defining an object's interface and language mappings. The IDL is critical because it neutralizes the language-specific nature of the components and clients by providing a common way an object is viewed as well as the way data is passed.

An object's interface specifies the methods and properties that an object supports. An interface stores what is publicly available for the object, and is similar to `.h` files in C++ and interfaces in Java. The interface of an object is stored in the Interface Repository of the ORB and in an `.idl` file. From there, the clients can gain references and invoke methods.

In the "Object Request Broker" section earlier in the chapter we talked about how a request is made up of data being passed from the client and to the object on the remote server. The data was passed in On the Wire format (binary string). The ORB uses the IDL mapping to do its marshalling/unmarshalling of the data being used in the request.

OMG IDL is a declarative language, not a programming language; as such, it does not provide features such as control constructs, nor is it directly used to implement distributed applications. Instead, language mappings determine how OMG IDL features are mapped to the facilities of a given programming language. Language mappings force interfaces to be defined separately from object implementations. This allows objects to be constructed using different programming languages and yet still communicate with one another. Language-independent interfaces are important within large networks because not all programming languages are supported or available on all platforms. Several language mappings are currently available, such as ones for C, C++, Java, Smalltalk, and Ada. To see the complete list of the language mappings currently available, check the OMG and CORBA Web sites (`http://www.omg.org` and `http://www.corba.org`).

In Listing 77.1, we see a simplified IDL file for a conceptual `PassengerBoardingManager` object, living on an unknown host and developed using an unknown programming language. It defines a `Passenger`, a `Flight`, and a `Passport` structure, a `boardingAgentId` property, an enumeration named `seatType`, a type definition called `SeatPreferences` which is composed of a sequence of `seatType` items, and a single interface called `PassengerManager` which contains three methods and an exception called `PMException`. You'll notice that each of the methods raises a `PMException`. Since CORBA is by nature distributed, these exceptions become the means of capturing error information from our objects.

Listing 77.1 The Passenger Boarding Manager IDL File

```
module PassengerBoardingManager
{
   struct Passenger
   {
      string name;
      double ticketNumber;
      Passport passport;
      Flight flight;
   };

   struct Flight
   {
      string flightId;
      string airline;
      string origin;
      string destination;
   };

   struct Passport
   {
      string issuingCountry;
      string passportId;

   };

   string boardingAgentId;
   enum seatType {Window, Aisle, None};
   typedef sequence<seatType> SeatPreferences;

   interface PassengerManager
   {

      exception PMException
      {
```

Listing 77.1 (continued)

```
            string msg;
        };
        boolean validTicket( psngr Passenger )
            raises (PMException);
        boolean validBoardingPass( psngr Passenger, SeatPreferences )
            raises (PMException);
        boolean noFlyClear( psngr Passenger)
            raises (PMException);
    };
};
```

Configuring ColdFusion to Work with CORBA

Before you can work with CORBA objects in your ColdFusion pages, you'll first need to add the runtime libraries for your particular ORB to the ColdFusion classpath. The way in which this is accomplished will depend on whether you are using the J2EE configuration or not. If you are, you'll add the `jar` file to your application server classpath, using the method specific to the particular server.

In any case, in the ColdFusion Administrator navigate to Server Settings > Java and JVM. Assuming you are using a Borland VisiBroker product as your ORB infrastructure, you'll first enter the full path to your `vbjorb.jar` file in the ColdFusion Class Path text box. Second, if your JVM is 1.4 or newer, add `-Xbootclasspath/a:"C:/borland/bdp/lib/vbjorb.jar"` to the JVM Arguments text box, assuming the full path to your jar file `C:\Borland\bdp\lib\vbjorb.jar`.

Now that the `vbjorb.jar` file is in the classpath, you need to set up the Extensions > CORBA Connectors page in the ColdFusion Administrator.

Register a new CORBA connector with an ORB Name of `visibroker`, an ORB Class Name of `coldfusion.runtime.corba.VisibrokerConnector`, and an ORB Property File that points to the location of the `CFusion/lib/vbjorb.properties` file (the full location would be `c:\Cfusion8\lib\vbjorb.properties` in a typical Windows installation of ColdFusion 8). Leave the Classpath textbox empty, and submit your connector information. From the CORBA Connectors page select your newly registered connector. Finally, restart your ColdFusion server.

Working with CORBA in ColdFusion

The `<cfobject>` tag and the `CreateObject()` function are used by ColdFusion as the gateway to the CORBA world. These two mechanisms for working with CORBA are identical, and both will be used in the remaining examples. As discussed in earlier sections, the client needs to make a request to the ORB for an object reference before it can invoke an object method. The job of the `<cfobject>` tag and `CreateObject()` function is just that—get an object reference. The object reference stored in the ColdFusion variable returned from the `<cfobject>` tag is then used to invoke methods against the remote object.

NOTE

It is possible to store the object reference inside a persistent variable such as `application.PassengerManager`. It is important to note that this doesn't store the data about the object, just the object's IOR. Each request still needs to go through the ORB to be executed.

The following is the syntax of the `<cfobject>` tag and `CreateObject()` set to use CORBA. See Table 77.1 for a listing of all the attributes used by `<cfobject>` and `CreateObject()`:

```
<cfobject
action="Create"
type="CORBA"
context="context"
class="file or naming service"
name="myObject"
locale="">
```

and:

```
myObject = CreateObject( type, class, context, locale)
```

Table 77.1 Attributes for `<cfobject>` and `CreateObject()`

NAME	DESCRIPTION
`type`	Required. Specifies the object type to be accessed. May be `COM`, `Java`, or `CORBA`. This must be set to `CORBA` for ColdFusion to connect to the CORBA server. See Chapter 75, "Extending ColdFusion with COM," and Chapter 78, "Extending ColdFusion with Java," for COM and Java usage, respectively.
`context`	Required. Must be set to `IOR` or `NameService`. `IOR` causes ColdFusion to use the Interoperable Object Reference (IOR) stored in an `.ior` file to access the object reference. `NameService` causes ColdFusion to use the Naming Service of the ORB to get an object reference.
class	Required. Specifies different information, depending on the context specification. If `context` is `IOR`, this attribute specifies the name of a file that contains the stringified version of the IOR. ColdFusion must be able to read this file at all times; it should be local to the ColdFusion server or on the network in an open, accessible location.
`name`	Required. Specifies the name for the variable that will be created to hold the reference to the CORBA object. Your application uses this to reference the CORBA object's methods and attributes.
`locale`	Optional. If specified, this attribute must be the name of an ORB registered in the ORB Name field of the CORBA Connector screen in the ColdFusion Administrator.

For us to discuss an example of how this fits together, we'll need to know about one additional IDL module containing the `FlightManifestManager` module, which like the `PassengerBoardingManager` in Listing 77.1, defines a `Passenger`, a `Flight`, and a `Passport` structure, and a single interface.

There are no `seatTypes` or `SeatPreferences` items defined in this module, though. The interface looks like this:

```
interface FlightManifestManager {
exception FMException {
string msg;
};
boolean addPassengerToFlightManifest( psngr Passenger, fl Flight ) raises
(FMException);
};
```

Now we are ready to see how all of this pulls together in Listing 77.2, our conceptual airline passenger boarding application.

Listing 77.2 Working with CORBA Objects in Our ColdFusion Page

```
<!---
Filename: PassengerBoardingManagerApplication.cfm
Purpose:  Demonstrates use of CORBA objects in ColdFusion pages
--->

<!-- static HTML used to set the display -->
<html>
   <head>
      <title>CORBA Example</title>
   </head>
<body>

<table>
<tr>
<td colspan="2">Passenger Boarding Manager Application</td>
</tr>

<cftry>
   <!--- Check to see if there is already a reference
          to the remote object stored --->
   <cflock scope="APPLICATION"
           throwontimeout="Yes"
           timeout="10"
           type="ReadOnly">

   <cfif not IsDefined("APPLICATION.PassengerManager")>
      <cfset NewPMNeeded="1">
   <cfelse>
      <cfset NewPMNeeded="0">
      <cfset PassengerManager=APPLICATION.PassengerManager>
   </cfif>
</cflock>

<!--- If there is not a reference already stored then create
      a new reference and store it for re-use --->
<cfif NewPMNeeded>
   <cflock scope="APPLICATION"
           throwontimeout="Yes"
           timeout="10"
           type="EXCLUSIVE">
```

Listing 77.2 (continued)

```
        <cfobject action="Create"
                  type="CORBA"
                  name="APPLICATION.PassengerManager"
                  class="C:\corba\ior\PassengerManager.ior"
                  context="IOR"
                  locale="">
        <cfset PassengerManager=APPLICATION.PassengerManager>
     </cflock>
  </cfif>

  <!--- the "Flight" struct ---->
  <cfset fl=StructNew()>
  <cfset fl.flightId="cf2318">
  <cfset fl.airline="ColdFusionAirways">
  <cfset fl.origin="tmp">
  <cfset fl.destination="ord">

  <!--- the "Passport" struct ---->
  <cfset pass=StructNew()>
  <cfset pass.issuingCountry="US">
  <cfset pass.passportId="0425345346547698782356229874 56">

  <!--- the "Passenger" struct ---->
  <cfset psngr=StructNew()>
  <cfset psngr.name="Adam Smith">
  <cfset psngr.ticketNumber="8708963543">
  <cfset psngr.passport=pass>
  <cfset psngr.flight=fl>

  <!--- the SeatPreferences sequence
        needed by validateBoardingPass --->
  <cfset seatprefs=ArrayNew(1)>
  <cfset seatprefs[1]="1">
  <cfset seatprefs[2]="0">
  <cfset seatprefs[3]="2">

  <!--- output some basic passenger information --->
  <cfoutput>
  <tr>
  <td>Name:</td>
  <td>#psngr.name#</td>

  </tr>
  <tr>
  <td>Flight:</td>
  <td>#fl.flightId#</td>

  </tr>
  <tr> <td>Destination:</td>
  <td>#fl.destination#</td>
  </tr>
  </cfoutput>

  <!--- perform a series of validations on the passenger
        using the PassengerManager object via CORBA --->
```

Listing 77.2 (continued)

```
<cftry>
   <cfif PassengerManager.validTicket(psngr)
         AND PassengerManager.validBoardingPass(psngr)
         AND PassengerManager.noFlyClear(psngr)>
      <cfset passengerValidated="1")>
   </cfif>
   <!--- be sure to catch any exception
         thrown by the remote object --->
   <cfcatch TYPE="coldfusion.runtime.corba.CorbaUserException">
      <cfoutput>
      <tr>
      <td COLSPAN="2">
      Unable to verify information for #psngr.name#
      onboard flight #fl.flightId#. <br/>
      The passenger may <em>not</em> board the airplane!
      </td>
      </tr>
      </cfoutput>
      <cfset exceptionStructure=cfcatch.getContents()>
      <cftrace var="exceptionStructure"
               inline="No"
               type="Error"
               category="CORBA"
               abort="No">
   </cfcatch>
</cftry>

<!--- if the passenger validates,
      add to the manifest --->
<cfif passengerValidated>
   <!--- get an object reference to the FlightManifestMananger --->
   <cftry>
      <cfset FlightManifestManager=CreateObject("CORBA",
               "TSA/International/Manifest/FlightManifestManager",
               "NameService")>
      <!--- be sure to catch any exception thrown by
            the remote object --->
      <cfcatch type="Object">
         <cfoutput>
         <tr>
         <td COLSPAN="2">
         Unable to add #psngr.name# to the
         flight #fl.flightId# manifest. The system
         is unavailable at this time.<br/>
         The passenger may <EM>not</EM> board the airplane!
         </td>
         </tr>
         </cfoutput>
         <cfset exceptionStructure=cfcatch.getContents()>
         <cftrace VAR="exceptionStructure"
                  inline="No"
                  type="Error"
                  category="CORBA"
                  abort="No">
      </cfcatch>
```

Listing 77.2 (continued)

```
   </cftry>

   <!-- get an object reference to the FlightManifestMananger -->
   <cftry>
      <cfset addedToManifest=
        FlightManifestManager.addPassengerToFlightManifest(psngr,fl)>
      <cfif addedToManifest>
         <cfoutput>
         <tr>
         <td COLSPAN="2">Passenger may board now.</td>
         </tr>
         </cfoutput>
      <cfelse>
          <cfoutput>
          <tr>
          <td COLSPAN="2">
          Passenger may <em>not</em> not board the airplane!
          </td>
          </tr>
          </cfoutput>
       </cfif>
       <cfcatch TYPE="coldfusion.runtime.corba.CorbaUserException">
          <cfoutput>
          <tr>
          <td COLSPAN="2">
          Unable to add #psngr.name# to the
          flight #fl.flightId# manifest.<br/>
          The passenger may <em>not</em> board the airplane!
          </td>
          </tr>
          </cfoutput>
          <cfset exceptionStructure=cfcatch.getContents()>
          <cftrace var="exceptionStructure"
                   inline="No"
                   type="Error"
                   category="CORBA"
                   abort="No">
       </cfcatch>
   </cftry>

<!-- else if the passenger did not validate -->
<cfelse>
   <cfoutput>
      <tr>
      <td COLSPAN="2">
      #psngr.name# may <em>not</em> board flight
      #fl.flightId# to #fl.destination#.<br/>
      </td>
      </tr>
   </cfoutput>
</cfif>

<cfcatch type="Object">
   <cfoutput>
      <tr>
```

Listing 77.2 (continued)

```
            <td COLSPAN="2">
            The Passenger Boarding Manager is experiencing
            connectivity issues and is unavailable at this time.
            </td>
            </tr>
         </cfoutput>
         <cfset exceptionStructure="cfcatch.Detail">
         <cftrace var="exceptionStructure"
                  inline="No"
                  type="Error"
                  category="CORBA"
                  abort="No">

      </cfcatch>
   </cftry>

   <!-- close up the HTML tags -->
   </table>

   </body>
   </html>
```

The first thing that we do is drop in some generic HTML to handle creating and opening a table which will hold the results of the code processing. Next, we surround the entire CORBA interaction with a `<cftry>` block. We will cover exceptions in a moment. Following that we check to see whether a `PassengerManager` object reference is stored in the application scope. If it isn't, we grab a reference to the `PassengerManager` using an `.ior` file. By using the `APPLICATION` scope, we can persist and share the object connection throughout our many requests thereby eliminating the overhead of repeatedly establishing a connection to the same object. We could have alternatively used the session and server scopes to accomplish this:

```
<cfobject action="Create"
          type="CORBA"
          name="APPLICATION.PassengerManager"
          class="C:\corba\ior\PassengerManager.ior"
          context="IOR"
          locale="">
```

NOTE

ColdFusion doesn't support the IDL `module` type. Instead we dereference CORBA IDL interfaces as objects.

Next, using the `StructNew()` function, we create the structures we'll need to interact with the CORBA object methods before. Those are: `Flight`, `Passport`, and `Passenger`. Additionally, we create the `SeatPreferences` sequence, `seatprefs`. In Listing 77.1, the IDL for the `PassengerBoardingManager`, `seatType` is defined as an enumeration. ColdFusion considers an enumeration to be a zero-indexed integer. Hence, the Passenger's ordered seating preferences are: Aisle, Window, and None.

We use `<cfoutput>` to display some information from our structures inside a table, which will eventually display a result letting the boarding agent know whether or not to allow the passenger onboard the airplane. The code executes each of the three methods by the `PassengerManager` interface, passing in our `Passenger` structure. In this case, we do that by using a series of nested `<cfif>` tags because all of the methods return a Boolean value, and doing so makes clear some of the implied logic of our example application. If each of the methods returns `true`, the `passengerValidated` variable is set:

```
<cfif PassengerManager.validTicket(psngr)
      AND PassengerManager.validBoardingPass(psngr)
      AND PassengerManager.noFlyClear(psngr)>
   <cfset passengerValidated="1")>
</cfif>
```

In each of these method calls, we've passed the input parameter by value, not reference. CORBA `in` parameters are passed by value. Had these parameters been `out` or `inout` parameters of the method, CORBA would have expected a reference to the value. If you pass a variable by reference and the CORBA object modifies its value, the value also changes on your page.

We now check to see if the passenger's information validated. Assuming it did, we create a reference to another CORBA object using the `CreateObject()` function:

```
<cfset FlightManifestManager = CreateObject("CORBA",
"TSA/International/Manifest/FlightManifestManager", "NameService") >
```

Since we encountered no problems creating a reference to the remote object, we make a call to its `addPassengerToFlightManifest()` method, passing in our `Passenger` and `Flight` structures. Based on the Boolean return value, we output a friendly message letting the boarding agent know whether the passenger can proceed.

In addition to accessing the methods of an object, ColdFusion supports accessing a CORBA object's public properties. This is also done through dot notation. So the `boardingAgentId` property of the `PassengerManager` reference would be accessed as `PassengerManager.boardingAgentId`. Because I frequently use camel case (capitalizing the first letter of each word but placing no spaces between words) for many of my variables and method names, it is important to note that though ColdFusion is case-insensitive, CORBA is not. So when designing your CORBA objects, it is best to avoid method names which differ only in case. If an interface defines both `getMyResult()` and `getmyresult()`, you can never be certain which method ColdFusion will call!

Handling CORBA Exceptions

In Listing 77.2 we wrapped the entire code that deals with the CORBA interaction in a `<cftry>` block. Additionally, each time we accessed a CORBA object or created a new one, those too were wrapped in `<cftry>` blocks. Though it is always good development practice to include robust error handling, it is especially poignant here because CORBA relies on external resources which may or may not be available. By using error handling, we can capture and gracefully handle errors that occur while connecting to and using CORBA objects.

When an error occurs while connecting to or using a CORBA object, ColdFusion throws an error of type `Object`.

```
<cferror type="Exception"
         exception="object"
         template="../common/objexcept.cfm"
         mailto="admin@thiscompany.com">
```

When using the `<cftry>` block, additional error information may be provided by the CORBA mechanism; if so, it is available in a `<cfcatch>` block via the `cfcatch.getContents()` function as shown in Listing 77.2. The `getContents()` function returns a structure that contains formatted information about the exception as reported by the IDL.

You will notice that the `<cfcatch>` tags following operations where we created references to CORBA objects have a `type` attribute of `Object`. This is because ColdFusion raises an exception of type `Object` when there is an error creating a reference to a CORBA object. To ensure the capture of any exceptions raised by the remote object, we set the `type` attribute of other `<cfcatch>` tags to `coldfusion.runtime.corba.CorbaUserException`. Since it isn't desirable for the user to see a stack trace or exception information spewed onto the screen, we use the `<cfcatch>` block to output a friendly message for the user, and then dutifully write the contents of the exception to the log file.

In Listing 77.2, we extracted a meaningful set of data about the exception using `<cftrace>`. However, we could have also used `<cfdump var="#exceptionStructure#">`. Since the latter will write to the log each time it is called, it isn't a good option for a production application. Regardless of how we choose to utilize the error information, robust error handling is a requirement in distributed computing environments where network outages and bottlenecks can otherwise cause your ColdFusion applications to appear ill-behaved. A few well-placed `<cftry>` blocks provide the basis for both simple debugging during development and graceful handling of undesirable runtime results.

CHAPTER 78

Extending ColdFusion with Java

IN THIS CHAPTER

CFML is an exceedingly powerful language, but occasionally there are situations where it is not enough. Maybe you will find that you need to talk to a legacy system, interact with other applications more directly, create extremely high-performance code, or something else. All of these things can be done through Java and the J2EE platform.

This chapter introduces to you a variety of ways for interacting with various objects and services provided by the Java 2 platform from ColdFusion 8. You will learn to interact directly with nearly any class in any of the standard Java packages. Your pages can also interact with JavaBeans, Java servlets, JavaServer Pages (JSPs), JSP tag libraries, and more. Basically, anything you cannot do in ColdFusion can be accomplished in Java, and then you can easily integrate the two—often with little more than a basic understanding of Java and sometimes with just a few lines of CFML.

You do not necessarily need to understand Java to read this chapter, but we assume that you have some knowledge of Java. This chapter will not teach you Java.

NOTE

In addition to the integration methods discussed in this chapter, you have several other options for integrating with Java. These include CORBA, discussed in Chapter 77, "Extending ColdFusion with CORBA"; Java CFX tags (similar to CFML custom tags but written in Java), as discussed in Chapter 79, "Extending ColdFusion with CFX"; and Web Services, discussed in Chapter 68, "Creating and Consuming Web Services"; as well as the option of integrating with Java services, such as the Java Messaging Service (JMS,) via ColdFusion Gateways, discussed in Chapter 80, "Working with Gateways."

Using Java Class Objects

ColdFusion allows you to work with nearly any Java class. This means you can use the functionality provided by:

- The built-in classes provided in the Java 2, Standard Edition (J2SE) specification, including the members of such commonly used packages as `java.io`, `java.net`, and `java.lang`.

- The built-in classes provided in the Java 2, Enterprise Edition (J2EE) specification, including the members of `javax.ejb`, `javax.sql`, and `javax.security`.
- Other Java classes that you write yourself or obtain from a third party.

If you have already read Chapter 75, "Extending ColdFusion with COM," or Chapter 77, "Extending ColdFusion with CORBA," you are already familiar with the `<cfobject>` tag and the `CreateObject()` function. As you learned in those chapters, a call to `<cfobject>` or `CreateObject()` is always the first step when working with COM or CORBA objects. `<cfobject>` and `CreateObject()` both do the same thing: return an instance of the desired object. You then work with that instance in your ColdFusion code, generally by calling whatever methods (functions) the object provides.

Working with Java objects is not much different. First, you create an instance of the object with `<cfobject>` or `CreateObject()`. Then you call the object's methods (or work with its properties). In other words, the mechanics of dealing with any external object in ColdFusion are the same, regardless of whether the object has its roots in COM, CORBA, or Java.

Table 78.1 shows the syntax for the `<cfobject>` tag as it pertains to Java objects.

Table 78.1 `<cfobject>` Tag Syntax for Java Objects

ATTRIBUTE	DESCRIPTION
`ACTION`	Required, but the value must always be `Create`. There is no `Connect` action for Java objects as there is for COM objects (discussed in Chapter 75).
`TYPE`	Must be `Java` in order to connect to a Java object. The object can be an ordinary class or a Bean.
`CLASS`	The name of the Java class you want to use, including the appropriate package name. The class must be available somewhere in the class path shown in the Java and JVM page of the ColdFusion Administrator. Like most things in Java, the class name is case-sensitive, so make sure to get the name exactly right.
`NAME`	The variable name that you want to use for interacting with the new instance of the object.

The `CreateObject()` function can be used as an alternative to `<cfobject>`. Both do the same thing. Table 78.2 shows the `CreateObject()` syntax for working with Java objects.

Table 78.2 `CreateObject()` Syntax for Java Objects

ATTRIBUTE	DESCRIPTION
`type`	Must be `Java` in order to connect to a Java object. The object can be an ordinary class or a Bean.
`class`	The name of the Java class you want to use.

The fact that you can call arbitrary Java classes using the syntax shown in Tables 78.1 and 78.2 means that you have an enormous amount of flexibility when it comes to the number of tools at your disposal for creating applications with ColdFusion. If you find yourself in a situation where

ColdFusion doesn't provide a tag or function to fulfill a particular need, you can literally crack open a Java reference as a source of potential solutions. If you find that Java provides a class that does what you need, just instantiate the class with `<cfobject>` or `CreateObject()`, and then start calling whatever methods you need.

Instantiating Objects and Calling Methods

Let's look at a simple example of using the underlying Java platform to perform a useful function. Suppose you're building an application that requires users to log in to gain access to their account information, but your manager is worried about automated "brute force" attacks on the site. Your manager has called for a five-second time limit between login attempts. Since there is no ColdFusion "wait" tag, you need to figure out another way to design this requirement. This is a situation where you can call in the underlying Java foundations.

The Java API defines a `thread` class that has a method allowing you to make the currently executing thread "sleep" (temporarily cease execution) for a specified number of milliseconds. That method is perfect for what you need to do in this example. To call it, all you have to do is this:

```
<cfobject
 type="java"
 action="create"
 class="java.lang.Thread"
 name="thread">
```

And we can do the same thing using `CreateObject()`:

```
<cfset thread = CreateObject("java", "java.lang.Thread")>
```

Then to simply call the class and its method, you can do this:

```
<cfset thread.sleep(5000)>
```

A more complete test to see it working in action is demonstrated in Listing 78.1.

The `<cftimer>` tag is just there to make sure that the thread is taking a nap for the defined five seconds. So, as you can see, working with Java from ColdFusion 8 is amazingly simple!

Listing 78.1 `JavaObjectsleep.cfm`—Calling a Java Class's Methods

```
<cftimer label="I am a sleepy thread" type="outline">
       <cfset thread = CreateObject("java", "java.lang.Thread")>
       <!--- Stop processing for 5 seconds -
       Thread is sleeping<br>
       <cfflush>
       <cfset thread.sleep(5000)>
       Thread is awake again<br>
</cftimer>
```

NOTE

The Java language is case-sensitive, so the names of the methods you use must be capitalized correctly when they appear in ColdFusion code. In this case, that means `sleep` will work but `SLEEP` or `Sleep` will not. In contrast, because it is a CFML variable, the name of the `thread` variable is not case-sensitive, so you could type `thread.sleep()` or `Thread.sleep()`. This can get a bit confusing, so you should get in the habit of checking the case of the Java objects you're working with.

Listing 78.1 puts these lines into a simple ColdFusion template. When you view the page in a browser you should see something like the image in Figure 78.1.

Figure 78.1

An example of using a Java class to make a thread pause execution.

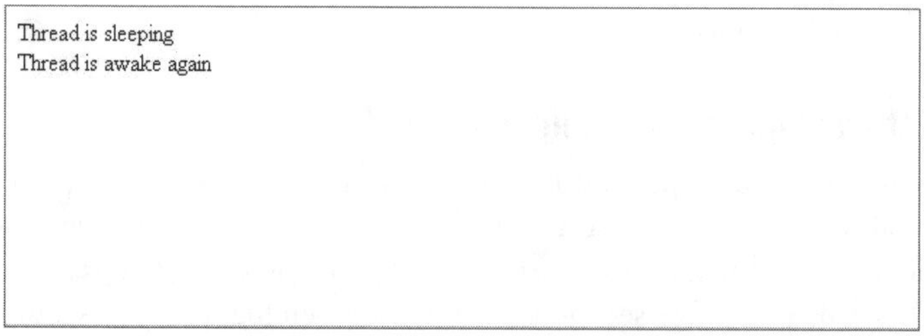

Thread is sleeping
Thread is awake again

By the way, ColdFusion 8 also allows you to call a method directly on the result of the `CreateObject()` function. Feel free to use syntax like the following if you're only going to call one method and thus have no need to hold on to the object instance itself:

```
<cfset NewStr = CreateObject("Java", "java.lang.Thread").sleep(5000)>
```

`<cfobject>` and `CreateObject()`: Separated at Birth?

In this chapter and the two that came before it, you've been learning about `<cfobject>` and `CreateObject()`, two syntaxes for doing the same thing: instantiating an object. Why are there two competing ways to create objects, anyway? Are they redundant?

The reason is this: At first, there was only the `<cfobject>` tag, which previously was only for working with COM objects. It was familiar and intuitive for CFML coders, but it didn't look familiar to people coming to ColdFusion from other COM-friendly environments such as Visual Basic and ASP. That's why the `CreateObject()` function was added a bit later on, to make things more familiar to those people (it looks and behaves much like ASP's method of the same name).

Later, with the introduction of user-defined functions (which could only be created in `<cfscript>` blocks at first), `CreateObject()` became more popular because it was the only way to interact with objects within script, and thus the only way to do so within a UDF. As of ColdFusion MX 6, you could create functions using the superior `<cffunction>` tag.

This has left `CreateObject()` looking more like a shortcut for `<cfobject>` than anything else. Neither syntax seems to have more of a *raison d'être* than the other. Many developers, though, find `CreateObject()` to be more intuitive when working with Java objects because there are only two arguments. For COM and CORBA objects, you may find `<cfobject>` to be more straightforward, since there are more options involved. Use whatever syntax you prefer.

Working with Constructors

Every Java class has at least one constructor. A *constructor* is a special method that initializes an object and places it in a valid state. In Java programming, you nearly always create a new instance of a class by calling the appropriate constructor in conjunction with Java's `new` keyword. In CFML, constructors are called automatically behind the scenes for you after you use `<cfobject>` or `CreateObject()`.

Here's how it works. When you create an object instance with `<cfobject>` or `CreateObject()`, ColdFusion gets ready to create an instance of the class (by checking for the class's existence) but doesn't go so far as to create the new instance. Instead, ColdFusion waits for you to actually use one of the object's methods (such as the `sleep()` method used in Listing 78.1). As soon as your code calls a method, ColdFusion creates the instance of the class by calling the class's *default constructor*, then calls the requested method on the new instance.

Java classes, though, often have more than one constructor. For instance, one constructor might not take any arguments, while another might allow the new instance to be initialized with some kind of value; another might allow the new instance to be initialized with two or three more specific values.

Consider a fictional Java class called `ChevyNova`. This class supports three different constructors. The first constructor doesn't take any arguments. The second one accepts the color, and another accepts the color plus the number of doors. In normal Java programming, these constructors might be called as follows:

```
ChevyNova myNova = new ChevyNova();
ChevyNova myRedNova = new ChevyNova("red");
ChevyNova myRedNovaHatchback = new ChevyNova("red", 5);
```

When you use this same object in a ColdFusion page, the default constructor (the first one, the one without any arguments) will always be called automatically the first time you actually use the object. Some classes won't be able to work the way you want them to if the default constructor is called; in this example, there might not be any other way to establish the car's color or number of doors.

How do you call one of the other constructors? ColdFusion allows you to call specific constructors through the ColdFusion function `init()`. The ColdFusion `init()` function calls the new function on the Java class constructor. You can use the `init()` function anytime after the `<cfobject>` or `CreateObject()` that creates the object variable, but before you actually use one of the object's methods. When you use `init()`, ColdFusion tries to find the appropriate constructor to use based on the number and data types of the arguments you pass to `init()`.

So, the ColdFusion equivalent of the earlier Chevy Nova snippet would be this:

```
<cfset myNova = CreateObject("Java", "ChevyNova")>
<cfset myRedNova = CreateObject("Java", "ChevyNova")>
<cfset myRedNova.init("red")>
<cfset myRedNovaHatchback = CreateObject("Java", "ChevyNova")>
<cfset myRedNovaHatchback.init("red", 5)>
```

Or, if you prefer using `<CFSCRIPT>` syntax, this:

```
<cfscript>
 myNova = CreateObject("Java", "ChevyNova");
 myRedNova = CreateObject("Java", "ChevyNova");
 myRedNova.init("red");
 myRedNovaHatchback = CreateObject("Java", "ChevyNova");
 myRedNovaHatchback.init("red", 5);
</cfscript>
```

In ColdFusion 8, you can create the new instance and call `init()` all at once, if you wish. It is not appreciably more efficient, but depending on your sensibilities it may seem cleaner or more intuitive. For instance, to call the three variations of the `ChevyNova` constructor, you could use lines like these:

```
<cfset myNova = CreateObject("Java", "ChevyNova")>
<cfset myRedNova = CreateObject("Java", "ChevyNova").init("red")>
<cfset myRedNovaHatchback = CreateObject("Java", "ChevyNova").init("red", 5)>
```

And here's the `<CFSCRIPT>` equivalent:

```
<cfscript>
 myNova = CreateObject("Java", "ChevyNova");
 myRedNova = CreateObject("Java", "ChevyNova").init("red");
 myRedNovaHatchback = CreateObject("Java", "ChevyNova").init("red", 5);
</cfscript>
```

There are two side effects of this `init()` mechanism:

- If a class does not have what ColdFusion calls a default constructor (that is, if there are no forms of the constructor that accept zero arguments), then you *must* use `init()` to specify the specific information with which to initialize the new instance.
- If the class actually exposes a normal method named `init()`, you won't be able to call it from ColdFusion. The method would have to be renamed before you could use it. If that's not under your control, one workaround would be to compile a quick subclass that exists only to expose the `init()` method under some other name.

Listing 78.2 shows how the `init()` method can be used with an actual Java class. This example uses the `StringTokenizer` class from the `java.util` package (part of the standard Java 2 API) to loop over a series of "tokens" in a string (Figure 78.1). The effect is very similar to a `<cfloop>` block that uses a `LIST` attribute.

Listing 78.2 `JavaObjectStringTokenizer.cfm`—Calling a Specific Constructor with `init()`

```
<!---
 Filename: JavaObjectStringTokenizer.cfm
 Author: Nate Weiss (NMW)
 Purpose: Demonstrates how to supply arguments to a class's constructor
--->

<html>
<head><title>String Tokenizer Example</title></head>
<body>

<!--- Create an instance of StringTokenizer --->
<cfset tokenizer = CreateObject("Java", "java.util.StringTokenizer")>

<!--- Pass information to the object's constructor --->
<cfset tokenizer.init("Sleater-Kinney rules!")>

<!--- Now the object's methods can be used as expected --->
<ol>
<cfloop condition="tokenizer.hasMoreElements()">
```

Listing 78.2 (continued)

```
    <cfoutput><li>#tokenizer.nextElement()#</li></cfoutput>
  </cfloop>
  </ol>

  </body>
  </html>
```

First, an instance of `StringTokenizer` called `tokenizer` is prepared, using the usual `CreateObject()` syntax. Then `init()` is used to supply a string to the constructor; it's at this moment that the new instance is actually created. If this were Java code, those two lines would be replaced with:

```
StringTokenizer tokenizer = new StringTokenizer("Sleater-Kinney rules!");
```

You can call constructors that accept several arguments by providing the corresponding number of arguments to `init()`. For instance, you could replace the `init()` line in Listing 78.2 with the following, which specifies the space and hyphen characters as token delimiters (basically the same as list delimiters in CFML). `Sleater` and `Kinney` would then be recognized as two separate words, rather than one:

```
<cfset tokenizer.init("Sleater-Kinney rules!", " -")>
```

In any case, once an object has been initialized properly, its methods can be called to get the desired behavior. In the case of `StringTokenizer`, there are only two available methods: `nextElement()`, which returns the next item in the sequence, and `hasMoreElements()`, which returns `true` until the last item has been returned. For details, consult a Java reference.

A Practical Example: Creating Histograms

In this example, we are going to look at how to create an image histogram. A histogram is a statistical graph that shows what proportion of cases fall into each of several or many specified categories. An image histogram is a histogram of an image by number of pixels (vertical axis) and by brightness value (horizontal axis). Image histograms are commonly used by digital artists to help them edit images, within software applications, and by technicians to detect image manipulation and fakery. Image histograms can also be used to make images searchable by ColdFusion. In this section, we are going to see how ColdFusion can take advantage of the Java Advanced Imaging library (to read more about the JAI library and API, see `http://java.sun.com/products/java-media/jai/forDevelopers/jaifaq.html`) that comes in ColdFusion 8. You will use Seth Duffy's `CFImageHistogram` to create your own image histograms from ColdFusion.

To get started. you need to download `CFImageHistogram` from Seth Duffy's Web site, at `http://www.leavethatthingalone.com/projects/cfhistogram/`. Unpack the zip file to a directory in your Web root (for this chapter, we will use `cfandjava` as the name of the directory, but you can use whatever you like). Then open `CFImageHistogram.cfc` in your editor. You should see something like Listing 78.3.

NOTE

Seth Duffy provided `CFImageHistogram` to the ColdFusion community as open source code under the Apache 2.0 license.

Listing 78.3 `imageHistogramCF8.cfc`—Using Java Functionality to Create Image Histograms

```
<!---
Project      : ColdFusion 8 Image Histogram
Version      : 0.1
URL          : http://leavethatthingalone.com/projects/cfhistogram/
Name         : imageHistogramCF8.cfc
Author       : Seth Duffey - sethduffey@gmail.com (send feedback, bugs, feature
requests, etc)
Purpose      : creates image histograms
--->

<cfcomponent output="false">

<!--- init --->
  <cffunction name="init" access="public" output="false" hint="I'm the constructor">
    <cfscript>
      //holder for image to get histogram from
      variables.inputImage = "";
      //create JAI object
      variables.JAI = createObject("Java","javax.media.jai.JAI");
      //input Image Is Planar Image (would be set from buffered image Buffered)
      variables.inputImageIsPlanarImage = false;
    </cfscript>
    <cfreturn this/>
  </cffunction>


<!--- ================================================================== --->
<!--- getHistogram --->
  <cffunction name="getHistogram" access="public" returntype="any" output="false"
hint="">
    <cfargument name="inputImage" required="no" type="string" default="" hint="I
return a histogram structure containing the histogram array and statistical values"
/>
    <cfscript>
      var histogram = "";
      //if input image is supplied then use it (otherwise image will come from set
buffered image)
      if(len(arguments.inputImage)) {
        createInputImage(arguments.inputImage);
      };
      histogram = createJAIHistogram();
      //return histogram
      return histogram;
    </cfscript>
  </cffunction>


<!--- ================================================================== --->
<!--- getColorHistogram --->
  <cffunction name="getColorHistogram" access="public" returntype="struct"
output="false" hint="I return a color histogram structure containing the histogram
array and statistical values">
    <cfargument name="inputImage" required="no" type="string" default=""
hint="Filename and path of image to create histogram of" />
    <cfscript>
      var histogram = "";
```

Listing 78.3 (continued)

```
      //if input image is supplied then use it (otherwise image will come from set
buffered image)
      if(len(arguments.inputImage)) {
        createInputImage(arguments.inputImage);
      };
      histogram = createJAIColorHistogram();
      //return histogram
      return histogram;
    </cfscript>
  </cffunction>

<!--- ========================================================================= --->
<!--- getHistogramImage --->
  <cffunction name="getHistogramImage" access="public" returntype="any"
output="false" hint="I create a color histogram PNG">
    <cfargument name="inputImage" required="yes" type="string" hint="Filename and
path of image to create histogram of" />
    <cfargument name="width" required="yes" default="256" type="numeric"
hint="height of png to create" />
    <cfargument name="height" required="yes" default="120" type="numeric"
hint="height of png to create" />

    <cfscript>
      //create color histgram
      var histogram = getHistogram(arguments.inputImage);
      //draw and return image
      return drawHistogram(histogram,arguments.width,arguments.height);
    </cfscript>
  </cffunction>

<!--- ========================================================================= --->
<!--- getColorHistogramImage --->
  <cffunction name="getColorHistogramImage" access="public" returntype="any"
output="false" hint="I create a color histogram PNG">
    <cfargument name="inputImage" required="yes" type="string" hint="Filename and
path of image to create histogram of" />
    <cfargument name="width" required="yes" default="256" type="numeric"
hint="height of png to create" />
    <cfargument name="height" required="yes" default="120" type="numeric"
hint="height of png to create" />

    <cfscript>
    //create color histgram
    var histogram = getColorHistogram(arguments.inputImage);
    //draw and return image
    return drawColorHistogram(histogram,arguments.width,arguments.height);
    </cfscript>
  </cffunction>

<!--- ========================================================================= --->
<!--- createInputImage --->
  <cffunction name="createInputImage" access="private" returntype="void"
output="false" hint="I create an image new">
    <cfargument name="inputImage" required="yes" type="string" default=""
hint="Filename and path of image to create histogram of" />
    <cfset variables.inputImage = imageNew(arguments.inputImage) />
```

Listing 78.3 (continued)

```
  </cffunction>


<!--- ====================================================================== --->
<!--- setBufferedImage --->
  <cffunction name="setBufferedImage" access="public" returntype="void"
output="false" hint="I set the the buffered image, i can be used if you want to set
a buffered image instead of specifying a image file name and path">
    <cfargument name="bufferedImage" required="yes" hint="Buffered image" />
    <cfset var pb = "" />
    <cfscript>
      pb = createObject("Java","java.awt.image.renderable.ParameterBlock").init();
      //add image source
      pb.add(arguments.bufferedImage);
      //create JAI PlanarImage
      variables.inputImage = variables.JAI.create("AWTImage", pb);
      //
      variables.inputImageIsPlanarImage = true;
    </cfscript>
  </cffunction>

<!--- ====================================================================== --->
<!--- createJAIHistogram --->
  <cffunction name="createJAIHistogram" access="private" returntype="struct"
output="false" hint="I create a histogram with JAI">
    <cfscript>
      var op = "";
      var bins = "";
      var i = 0;
      var histogram = "";
      var rgb = "";
      //create ParameterBlock
      var pb =
createObject("Java","java.awt.image.renderable.ParameterBlock").init();
      //create holder structure
      var histogramStruct = createHistogramHolderStruct();
      //add image source

      if (inputImageIsPlanarImage) {
        //already a planar image
        pb.addSource(variables.inputImage);
      } else {
        //need to convert
        pb.addSource(imageGetBufferedImage(variables.inputImage));
      }
      //RenderedOp
      op = variables.JAI.create("histogram", pb);
      //get histogram (javax.media.jai.Histogram)
      histogram = op.getProperty("histogram");
      //histogram bins - array[3][256]
      bins = histogram.getBins();
      //average colors into single array
      for(i=1;i LTE 256; i=i+1) {
        histogramStruct.histogram[i] = Round((bins[1][i] + bins[2][i] +
bins[3][i])/3);
      }
```

Listing 78.3 (continued)

```
        //get statistics
        rgb = getHistogramStatistics(histogramStruct.histogram);
        histogramStruct.mean = rgb.mean;
        histogramStruct.standarddeviation = rgb.standarddeviation;
        histogramStruct.min = rgb.min;
        histogramStruct.max = rgb.max;
        //return histogram structure
        return histogramStruct;
      </cfscript>
    </cffunction>

  <!--- ================================================================= --->
  <!--- createJAIColorHistogram --->
    <cffunction name="createJAIColorHistogram" access="private" returntype="struct"
  output="false" hint="I create a color histogram with JAI">
      <cfscript>
        var op = "";
        var bins = "";
        var meanArray = "";
        var sdArray = "";
        //create ParameterBlock
        var pb =
  createObject("Java","java.awt.image.renderable.ParameterBlock").init();
        //create holder struct for histogram
        var colorHistogram = structNew();
        //add image source
        if (inputImageIsPlanarImage) {
          //already a planar image
          pb.addSource(variables.inputImage);
        } else {
          //need to convert
          pb.addSource(imageGetBufferedImage(variables.inputImage));
        }
        //RenderedOp
        op = variables.JAI.create("histogram", pb);
        //get histogram (javax.media.jai.Histogram)
        histogram = op.getProperty("histogram");
        //histogram bins - array[3][256]
        bins = histogram.getBins();
        meanArray = histogram.getMean();
        sdArray = histogram.getStandardDeviation();
        //red
        colorHistogram.r.histogram = bins[1];
        colorHistogram.r.mean = meanArray[1];
        colorHistogram.r.standarddeviation = sdArray[1];
        colorHistogram.r.min = arrayMin(bins[1]);
        colorHistogram.r.max = arrayMax(bins[1]);
        //green
        colorHistogram.g.histogram = bins[2];
        colorHistogram.g.histogram = bins[2];
        colorHistogram.g.mean = meanArray[2];
        colorHistogram.g.standarddeviation = sdArray[2];
        colorHistogram.g.min = arrayMin(bins[2]);
        colorHistogram.g.max = arrayMax(bins[2]);
        //blue
        colorHistogram.b.histogram = bins[3];
```

Listing 78.3 (continued)

```
      colorHistogram.b.histogram = bins[3];
      colorHistogram.b.mean = meanArray[3];
      colorHistogram.b.standarddeviation = sdArray[3];
      colorHistogram.b.min = arrayMin(bins[3]);
      colorHistogram.b.max = arrayMax(bins[3]);
      //return histogram structure
      return colorHistogram;
    </cfscript>
  </cffunction>

<!--- ====================================================================== --->
<!--- drawHistogram --->
  <cffunction name="drawHistogram" access="private" returntype="any" output="false"
hint="I draw a histogram image">
    <cfargument name="histogram" required="yes" hint="histogram" />
    <cfargument name="width" required="yes" default="256" type="numeric" hint="width
of image to create" />
    <cfargument name="height" required="yes" default="120" type="numeric"
hint="height of image to create" />
    <cfscript>
      var ii = "";
      //create image
      var histImage = imageNew("",256,arguments.height,"argb");
      //set drawing color
      ImageSetDrawingColor(histImage,"black");
      //loop thru all bins in color
      for(ii=1;ii LTE 256; ii=ii+1) {
        //set max height based on the max size found in array
        lineHeight = arguments.height-
((arguments.histogram.histogram[ii]/arrayMax(arguments.histogram.histogram)) *
arguments.height);
        //draw line
        imageDrawLine(histImage,ii-1,arguments.height,ii-1,lineHeight);
      }
      //resize width if needed
      if(arguments.width != 256) {
        ImageSetAntialiasing(histImage,"on");
        ImageResize(histImage,arguments.width,arguments.height,"highestQuality");
      };
      //return image
      return histImage;
      </cfscript>
  </cffunction>

<!--- ====================================================================== --->
<!--- drawColorHistogram --->
  <cffunction name="drawColorHistogram" access="private" returntype="any"
output="false" hint="I draw a color histogram image">
    <cfargument name="histogram" required="yes" hint="histogram" />
    <cfargument name="width" required="yes" default="256" type="numeric" hint="width
of image to create" />
    <cfargument name="height" required="yes" default="120" type="numeric"
hint="height of image to create" />
    <cfscript>
      var i = "";
      var ii = "";
```

Listing 78.3 (continued)

```
        var color = "";
        //create image
        var histImage = imageNew("",256,arguments.height,"argb");
        //set drawing transpareceny
        ImageSetDrawingTransparency(histImage,66);
        //loop thru color bins r-g-b
        for(i=1;i LTE 3; i=i+1) {
          //set color based on bin
          if (i == 1) {//red
            ImageSetDrawingColor(histImage,"red");
            color = "r";
          } else if (i==2) {//green
            ImageSetDrawingColor(histImage,"green");
            color = "g";
          } else if (i==3) {//blue
            ImageSetDrawingColor(histImage,"blue");
            color = "b";
          }
          //loop thru all bins in color
          for(ii=1;ii LTE 256; ii=ii+1) {
            //set max height based on the max size found in array
            lineHeight = arguments.height-
((arguments.histogram[color].histogram[ii]/arrayMax(arguments.histogram[color].
histogram)) * arguments.height);
            //draw line
            imageDrawLine(histImage,ii-1,arguments.height,ii-1,lineHeight);
          }
        }
        //resize width if needed
        if(arguments.width != 256) {
          ImageSetAntialiasing(histImage,"on");
          ImageResize(histImage,arguments.width,arguments.height,"highestQuality");
        };
        //return image
        return histImage;
        </cfscript>
  </cffunction>

<!--- ==================================================================== --->
<!--- createHistogramHolderStruct --->
  <cffunction name="createHistogramHolderStruct" access="private"
returntype="struct" output="false" hint="I create a histogram array">
     <cfscript>
        var holderStruct = structNew();
        holderStruct.histogram = arrayNew(1);
        holderStruct.mean = "";
        holderStruct.standarddeviation = "";
        holderStruct.min = "";
        holderStruct.max = "";
        return holderStruct;
     </cfscript>
  </cffunction>

<!--- ==================================================================== --->
<!--- getHistogramStatistics --->
  <cffunction name="getHistogramStatistics" access="private" output="false">
```

Listing 78.3 (continued)

```
    <cfargument name="values" required="yes">
    <cfscript>
      var returnStruct = structNew();
      //var histArray = arguments.values;
      var NumValues = 0;
      var x = 0;
      var sumx = 0;
      var i=0;
      //min
      returnStruct.min = arrayMin(arguments.values);
      //max
      returnStruct.max = arrayMax(arguments.values);
      histLength = arrayLen(arguments.values);
      x = arrayAvg(arguments.values);
      for (i=1; i LTE histLength; i=i+1) {
        sumx = sumx + ((arguments.values[i] - x) * (arguments.values[i] - x));
      };
      //mean
      returnStruct.mean = x;
      //SD
      returnStruct.standarddeviation = sqr(sumx/histLength);
      return  returnStruct;
    </cfscript>
    </cffunction>

  </cfcomponent>
```

We will not go into depth about how this CFC works because we are assuming that you are familiar enough with Java to look up each class and method requested from the JAI library. One thing to note is how cleanly ColdFusion allows you to integrate with Java components and libraries using either standard CFML or CFSCRIPT.

Now let us use `CFIMAGE` to get a image from the Internet (or you can provide your own) and create a color image histogram of the image as in Listing 78.4.

Listing 78.4 `createhistogram.cfm`—Creating a Color Image Histogram

```
<cfset startTick = getTickCount() />

<!--- Read image --->
<cfimage action="read"
source="http://farm3.static.flickr.com/2411/2010794588_7fac3cde35.jpg?v=0"
name="image" />

  <cfoutput>Read image - #getTickCount() - startTick#ms<hr /></cfoutput>
<cfimage source="#image#" action="writeToBrowser"/>
<br />
<!--- create image histogram object --->
<cfset ih = createObject("component","imageHistogramCF8").init() />

  <cfoutput>Create imageHistogramCF8 object  - #getTickCount() - startTick#ms<hr
/></cfoutput>

<!--- get color histogram --->
<cfset hist = ih.getColorHistogram(image) />
```

Listing 78.4 (continued)

```
      <cfoutput>
          get color histogram  - #getTickCount() - startTick#ms<br />
          mean red: #hist.r.mean# -
          mean green: #hist.g.mean# -
          mean blue: #hist.b.mean#<br />
          <a href="example2.cfm">show histogram details</a>
          <hr />
      </cfoutput>


    <!--- get color histogram image --->
    <cfset hist = ih.getColorHistogramImage(image) />

      <cfoutput>
          get color histogram image  - #getTickCount() - startTick#ms<br />
          <cfimage action="writeToBrowser" source="#hist#">
          <hr />
      </cfoutput>

    <p> </p>
    <p> </p>
    <p> </p>
```

Listing 78.4 simply calls an image on Flikr, sows the image, and then uses `imageHistogramCF8.cfc` to generate a color image histogram. Assuming that you put your code in a directory called `cfandjava` under the Web root, you should see something like Figure 78.2 when you call `createHistogram.cfm` in your browser.

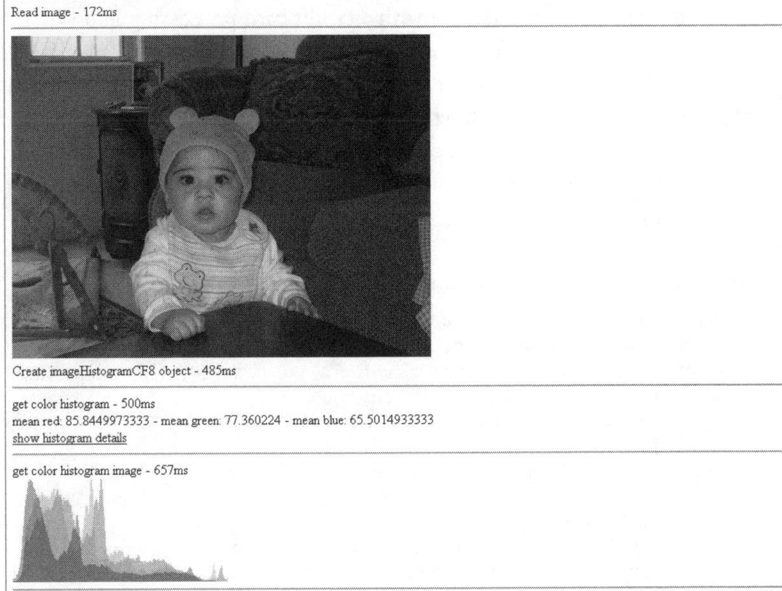

Figure 78.2

A color image histogram.

Now that you have seen how to work with classes and libraries that are already part of ColdFusion, you will see how to work with and use your own external Java classes.

Using External Java Classes

As stated earlier, you can call almost any Java class from ColdFusion 8. but sometimes you will need to make use of classes other than those in the Java SDK. Perhaps you want to work with Java code someone else in your organization has created, or with something you have found that will solve a specific problem. To do this, you do need to follow additional steps before you can use external Java classes in your application:

1. Install the class on your server. Typically, this means unpacking a `.class` or `.jar` file from a zip archive, or perhaps running some kind of installation program.
2. Make sure the class can be found in the class path shown in the Java and JVM page of the ColdFusion Administrator. Basically, this means placing the `.class` or `.jar` file into a folder that is already listed in the class path, or adding the file's location to the class path. (Remember that the ColdFusion Application Server service must be restarted if you change the class path.) An alternative is to copy your `.jar` file to `/coldfusion8/wwwroot/WEB-INF/lib`, or your `.class` files to `web_root/WEB-INF/classes`, and ColdFusion will automatically be able to access your Java objects.
3. Finally, use the class just as you would any other, using `<CFOBJECT>` or `CreateObject()`.

A Practical Example

Suppose you need to communicate with a credit card processing gateway that does not support requests via HTTP but rather expects straight TCP requests to a specific URL. Unfortunately, ColdFusion does not yet support the concept of a tag that allows you to work with a variety of network protocols, but Java has a host of networking classes. Let's also assume that you sit down and rapidly write a simple Java socket client that will take a string that represents a message you want to send to a server, an IP where you want to send the message, and a specific port. The code might look like Listing 78.5.

Listing 78.5 `SocketClient.java`—Simple Socket Client in Java

```
import java.io.BufferedReader;
import java.io.FileReader;
import java.io.IOException;
import java.io.InputStreamReader;
import java.io.PrintWriter;
import java.net.Socket;
import java.util.StringTokenizer;

/*Author: Robi Sen C
 * Description: Simple java client has two constructors
 * the first accepts a string and tries to connect to localhost
 * on port 1225.  the second accepts a string, a URL string, and an integer that
identifies the port
 * The client returns a string from the server.
```

Listing 78.5 (continued)

```
 *
 * Currently has several methods to read information from a file but these
 * methods are never called due to client requirement change.
 * To Do:  Add thread management for scalability.
 */


public class SocketClient {
  Socket sock;
  PrintWriter writer;
  BufferedReader reader;
  // the class reads from a file for connection data
  static String filename = "c:/client/connectiondata.txt";
  String URL = "";
  int Port = 0;
  /*
   *
   * int aSize = getFileSize(filename);
 String[] phrase = new String[aSize];
 phrase =  getFile(filename, phrase);
 accountsData = parseRecords(phrase);
   *
   */

String serverResponse = null;

public  SocketClient(String messageFromCF){
  setPort(9400);
  setURL("66.184.160.67");

  this.serverResponse = createClientSocket(messageFromCF);
} //close constructor


public SocketClient(String messageFromCF, String yourIP, int yourPort){
  setPort(yourPort);
  setURL(yourIP);
 // System.out.println("Port and Stuff " + yourPort + " " + yourIP + " More Stuff
");
 // System.out.println(getPort() + " " + getURL());
  this.serverResponse = createClientSocket(messageFromCF);
}

public String getServerResponse() {
  return this.serverResponse;
}// close

private void setupNetworking(String nURL, int nPort){
try {
  sock = new Socket(getURL(), getPort());
  InputStreamReader streamReader = new InputStreamReader(sock.getInputStream());
  reader = new BufferedReader(streamReader);
  writer = new PrintWriter(sock.getOutputStream());
  System.out.println("networking established");
  } catch (IOException ex) {
  ex.printStackTrace();
```

Listing 78.5 (continued)

```
      }

    } // close setupNetworking

    public String createClientSocket(String messagetosend ) {
      String message = null;

      StringBuffer results = new StringBuffer();
      setupNetworking(getURL(),getPort());

      try {
        writer.println(messagetosend);
        writer.flush();
          while((message = reader.readLine()) != null) {
          results.append(message);

          }// close while

          reader.close();
          writer.close();


       } catch (Exception ex) {ex.printStackTrace();}

       //System.out.println(results.toString());

       return results.toString();

      } // close createClientSocket


   //read file method


   public String getURL(){
       return URL;
     }

   public int getPort(){
       return Port;
     }

   public void setURL(String tempURL){

       URL = tempURL;

     }// close set URL

   public void setPort(int tempPort){
       Port = tempPort;

     } // close set port



    }// close class
```

Now that you have developed the class, you may want to test it to make sure that it does indeed send a message to an IP on a specific port. You can write a simple echo server that just listens on a specific port and echoes back (to standard output) whatever it was sent. That code might look like Listing 78.6.

Listing 78.6 `EchoServer.java`—Simple Echo Server in Java

```
import java.net.*;
import java.io.*;
// Listens for connection on port 1225,
// receives messages and echoes them back
public class EchoServer {
   public static void main(String args[]) throws Exception {
      ServerSocket server = new ServerSocket(1225);
      Socket socket = null;
         while(true) {
            socket = server.accept();
            BufferedReader br = new BufferedReader(
                     new InputStreamReader(socket.getInputStream()));
            PrintStream ps = new PrintStream(
                     socket.getOutputStream());
            ps.println(br.readLine()); // Echo input to output
            socket.close();
         }
   }
}
```

Now you need to call your Java socket client from ColdFusion, but before you can do that, you need to take the compiled class available in the class path as listed in the Java and JVM page of the ColdFusion Administrator. Either copy the file to a directory already listed in the class path or temporarily add the class's folder location to the class path. You will need to restart ColdFusion if you change the class path. Now that you have done that, you can generate the ColdFusion to call the class, which you can see in Listing 78.7.

Listing 78.7 `callSocketClient.cfm`—Using an External Java Class from ColdFusion

```
<cfobject type="Java" class="SocketClient" name="mySocketClient">
<cfset sendMessage=mySocketClient.init("test message", "127.0.0.1",1225)>
<cfset getResponse=mySocketClient.getServerResponse()>
<cfoutput>#getResponse#</cfoutput>
```

Once you have finished this class, you can either start your `EchoServer.java` at the command line or in your IDE (if it supports running Java like Eclipse) and then call `callSocketClient.cfm`. You should just see the simple message "Test Client," which is the message string you sent to the echo server and the Java object returned by the echo server that you captured by calling the `getResponse()` method.

As you can see, working with external Java objects is just like working with ColdFusion's underlying Java instance with the extra step of adding your external class to the class path. One point to note, though, is that when working with external Java classes, `.jar` files, tag libraries, and so on, you need to be careful because a number of class path issues may arise. Often external classes or `.jar` files have dependencies such as `log4j`, which are shared by ColdFusion. Your external classes' dependencies may also be newer or older than ColdFusion and cause conflicts, which can be frustrating to debug.

The only way to resolve this sort of issue is to make sure that you add your `.jar` file or class to the class before any other classes. To debug these sorts of issues when you are working with Java and ColdFusion, you can start your ColdFusion development server from the command line, which will allow you to see all classes loaded by ColdFusion; add `XX:+TraceClassLoading` to your `jvm.config` file, which will allow you to see the order of class files loaded to your JVM; or use Mark Mandel's JavaLoader tool, which is great for just this problem—see `http://www.compoundtheory.com/?action=javaloader.index`.

Managing Method-Selection Problems

CFML is an extremely loosely typed language. Variables are not declared with a specific data type; the type (date, number, string, and so on) is intuited at run time based on context, and conversions between types are handled automatically. And the data types that ColdFusion *does* have are drawn with broad strokes—there is just one data type for numbers, for instance, rather than separate data types for integers, floating-point numbers, real numbers, and so on. This general policy of type leniency is a big part of why ColdFusion is so easy (and fun!) to use and learn. As a ColdFusion developer, data types just are not on your mind very often.

In Java programming, however, data types and object types are absolutely critical, at the conceptual forefront of nearly any coding task. This is a big part of what gives Java its power and efficiency (at least *potential* efficiency, depending on how the JVM operates internally). This characteristic of Java also leads to a large number of overloaded methods. For instance, because integers and floating-point numbers are different, it's typical to find two different forms of a single method, one that accepts an `int` and one that accepts a `double`. In Java documentation, they might be listed like so:

```
void fillWithGasoline(int gallons)
void fillWithGasoline(double gallons)
```

If you want to call this method from a ColdFusion page, you might use code like the following, where `FORM.Gallons` is a number of some kind:

```
<cfset myNova.fillWithGasonline(FORM.Gallons)>
```

However, ColdFusion will not know which of the two forms of the method to call, possibly resulting in an exception message like "method selection error" or something similar. In such a situation, you need to give ColdFusion a hint by using the special `JavaCast()` function. `JavaCast()` takes just two arguments, as listed in Table 78.3.

Table 78.3 `JavaCast()` Function Syntax

ATTRIBUTE	DESCRIPTION
`type`	One of the following strings, which indicates how you want the value passed to Java: `int`, `long`, `double`, or `String`.
`value`	The value that you want to pass to Java. The value can be a variable, string, number, or any other CFML expression.

So, to call the `double` version of the `fillWithGasoline()` method, you would use:

```
<cfset myNova.fillWithGasonline(JavaCast("double", FORM.Gallons))>
```

NOTE

You can also use `JavaCast()` inside of an `init()` call to avoid similar ambiguities when calling an object's constructor. The type information you provide with `JavaCast()` can help ColdFusion know which of several constructors to use.

TIP

There is another important thing to note about working with Java methods. It is extremely common for Java methods to return a `null` value. In previous versions of ColdFusion, including 6.1, this will cause a ColdFusion exception. ColdFusion 8 has support for Java `null` values that are returned from Java methods, and ColdFusion 8 automatically converts the `null` value to an empty string (" "). Keep this in mind especially if you have worked with Java and ColdFusion prior to 8 and were accustomed to writing workaround code for this issue.

For some additional information on data type conversions, refer to the "Shared Variables and Data Types" and "Shared Variables and Multifaceted Values" sections later in this chapter.

Using JavaBeans

You can use JavaBeans in your ColdFusion pages in the same way that you use ordinary Java classes. For writing ColdFusion code, there is not much difference between a Bean and a normal class. You still use `<cfobject>` or `CreateObject()` to load the class, and then call its methods using `<cfset>` or other tags, as shown in the examples from the preceding section of this chapter.

The only difference is that any *properties* of the Bean can be accessed by name. JavaBean properties are the Bean's properly named `getter` and `setter` methods to store and retrieve the value of the property. So, if a Bean has a property called `modelYear` (which means nothing more than that `getModelYear()` and `setModelYear()` methods have been implemented within the Bean itself), then you could output the value of the property like so:

```
<cfset myNovaBean = CreateObject("java", "chevy.cars.NovaBean")>
...other lines of code...
<cfoutput>#myNovaBean.modelYear#</cfouptput>
```

When your code refers to the Bean's `modelYear` property as shown just above, you are implicitly calling the `getModelYear()` method behind the scenes. It's really just a more convenient, natural-looking syntax for calling the `getter` function. Similarly, to set the model year (assuming that the Bean allows such a thing) you could use a line such as the following:

```
<cfset myNovaBean.modelYear = 1986>
```

This causes ColdFusion to call the Bean's `setModelYear()` method behind the scenes. The following line would be functionally equivalent:

```
<cfset myNovaBean.setModelYear(1986)>
```

Again, there is no particular technical advantage in referring to the property name instead of explicitly calling the `getter` and `setter` methods. It just looks nicer to some developers. Use or ignore the option as you wish.

Using Tag Libraries

ColdFusion programmers have CFML custom tags. JavaServer Pages (JSP) programmers have something similar: JSP *custom tag libraries*, often called *taglibs* for short. As of ColdFusion 8, you should be able to use any taglib in your ColdFusion pages as well. So if you know that a solution for a particular task has already been created by some JSP developer as a tag library, you can just reuse it in your CFML pages rather than having to reinvent the proverbial wheel.

To work with a tag library, you follow these basic steps:

1. Find a taglib that looks interesting, then download or install it. The taglib will most likely come in the form of a `.jar` file, often with an accompanying `.tld` file.
2. Use the new `<cfimport>` tag to make the tag library available to your ColdFusion page. This is the CFML equivalent to the `<%@ taglib %>` directive that would normally be used to make the tag library available to a JSP page.
3. Use the tags provided by the tag library, using the same basic syntax as in a JSP page.

Finding Tag Libraries

Before you can start using tag libraries with ColdFusion, you first need to find and obtain the taglib that you want to use. You may already have one in mind, but if not, here are a few Web sites where you can look for interesting libraries:

- The Jakarta Tag Library project, at `jakarta.apache.org/taglibs`
- The JSPTags.com site, at `http://www.jsptags.com`
- The SourceForge site, at `http://sourceforge.net`
- The OpenSymphony site, at `http://www.opensymphony.com`

Installing the Tag Library

Whether you are using a tag library that you downloaded from a third party or a tag library that was developed in house, the library will most likely come to you as a Java Archive (`.jar`) file. There may or may not be an accompanying Tag Library Descriptor (`.tld`) file. Place the file or files in the `WEB-INF/lib` folder, which should be located within your Web server's (or virtual Web server's) document root folder.

NOTE

If there is no `WEB-INF/lib` folder, create it by first creating a folder called `WEB-INF`, then a subfolder called `lib`. Also, as far as ColdFusion is concerned, you can place the folder in other locations as well, but it's customary to place tag library files in `WEB-INF/lib`. The tag library may be expecting it internally.

In most cases, that's all you need to do to install the library. It's also possible that additional `.jar` files, `.property` files, or other files may need to exist in order for the tag library to work properly; the tag library's documentation should make all this clear to you.

NOTE

The installation instructions for many tag libraries discuss making a new entry for the library in the server's `WEB-INF/web.xml` file. Just ignore any discussion of altering the `web.xml` file.

NOTE

If you are using a commercial tag library, it may come with a formal installation program. In such a case, just run the installation, providing the installer with the location of the `WEB-INF/lib` folder if prompted. The installer probably expects you to be using the library with JSP pages rather than ColdFusion, so it's possible that you'll need to move the `.jar` and/or `.tld` files after installation.

Importing the Library with `<cfimport>`

Now that the tag library files have been placed into their correct location, you should be able to import the library with the `<cfimport>` tag, using the syntax described in Table 78.4.

Table 78.4 `<cfimport>` Tag Syntax for Importing Tag Libraries

ATTRIBUTE	DESCRIPTION
TAGLIB	The location of the tag library file(s). If the tag library came with a separate `.tld` file, provide that location. Otherwise, use the path to the `.jar` file. Assuming that you placed the files in the `WEB-INF/lib` folder, you would use `TAGLIB= "WEB-INF/lib/taglib.tld"` or `TAGLIB="WEB-INF/lib/taglib.jar"`, replacing the `taglib` part with the actual file names in question.
PREFIX	A prefix to use for referring to the tags in the tag library. For the remainder of the current ColdFusion page, you will be able to refer to the tags in the form `<prefix:tagname>`, where the `prefix` is the value you supply here.

TIP

You can provide any identifier you want as the `PREFIX`, as long as it is not a reserved word, but there will usually be a customary prefix for the tag library you're using (often the same prefix used in the documentation or examples that come with the library). I recommend that you use the customary prefix whenever possible.

NOTE

It's worth noting that the `<cfimport>` tag can be used in a few other ways as well, most importantly to import a set of CFML custom tags into their own namespace. This chapter is concerned only with using `<cfimport>` to import JSP tag libraries; please consult the ColdFusion documentation for information about using this tag with CFML custom tags.

Using the Tag Library's Tags

Once you've imported a tag library with `<cfimport>`, you can use the tags in the library using syntax that is very similar to the way the tags are used in JSP pages. Say you're using a fictional tag library that you have imported using the prefix `cars`, like so:

```
<cfimport
 taglib="/WEB-INF/lib/cars.tld"
 prefix="cars">
```

If this fictional library includes a tag called `displaycar`, you'd include it in your ColdFusion page like this:

```
<cars:displaycar />
```

Like custom tags, most JSP custom tags accept or require certain attributes. If the `displaycar` tag has attributes called `make` and `model`, you could call the tag with syntax similar to the following:

```
<cars:displaycar make="Ford" model="Mustang" />
```

Note the trailing slash before the end of the tag in these snippets. This is standard XML-style shorthand for an opening and closing tag. If you wish, you can write the opening and closing tags explicitly, like so:

```
<cars:displaycar make="Ford" model="Mustang"></cars:displaycar>
```

Some JSP tags will expect you to place some type of content between the opening and closing tags. Of course, the result will depend on the actual tag you're using, but the syntax is pretty much what you would expect:

```
<cars:displaycar make="Ford" model="Mustang">
 ...any content or nested JSP tags can appear here...
</cars:displaycar>
```

Using the Google Map Tag Library

For this example, we will take advantage of the ever-popular Google Maps via the Google Map Tag Library to rapidly create Google maps on our Web pages. First download the Google Maps Tag Library from `http://google-taglib.sourceforge.net/`; then unpack it and the `google.jar` file in your `lib` directory. Next, get a Google Maps API key from `http://www.google.com/apis/maps/index.html`.

You will also need to unpack the googlemaps.jar file (you can use WinZip) and get the `googlemaps.tld` file from it and place it in the same directory as the `.jar` file.

When you run the code in Listing 78.8, you should see in your browser a Google map as in Figure 78.3.

Figure 78.3
A simple Google map.

Listing 78.8 `googleMap.cfm`—Importing and Using a JSP Tag Library

```
<!-- simple demonstration of using the googlemaps tag lib -->

<cfimport taglib="/WEB-INF/lib/googlemaps.tld" prefix="googlemaps">
<googlemaps:map id="map" width="250" height="300" version="2" type="STREET"
zoom="15">
   <googlemaps:key domain="your domain" key="Yourkey"/>
   <googlemaps:point id="point1" address="74 Connors Lane" city="Elkton" state="MD"
zipcode="21921" country="US"/>
<googlemaps:marker id="marker1" point="point1"/>
</googlemaps:map>
```

As you can see, this listing uses several tags from an image tag library: `<googlemaps:map>`, `<googlemaps:key>`, `<googlemaps:point>`, and `<googlemaps:marker>`. The code is pretty self-explanatory, but essentially the Google Maps Tag Library API (which you can find at `http://www.lamatek.com/GoogleMaps/docs/`) provides JSP-type tags for the Google API (which you can find at `http://www.google.com/apis/maps/index.html`).

If you look closely at the tags we are using, you can see how similar the syntax and structure are to CFML. Many developers find that working with JSP tag libraries from CFML is very intuitive.

Explore the various open source Java tag libraries; you'll find an amazing number of excellent libraries to solve almost any problem. With the combination of ColdFusion 8 and the Java tag libraries, there is very little you cannot accomplish.

Creating Your Own JSP Tag Libraries

As you have learned in this section, JSP-style tag libraries can be used interchangeably in JSP pages and ColdFusion pages, using more or less the same syntax. If your shop uses both technologies, then you may want to consider creating some of your own tag libraries. That topic is beyond the scope of this book, but you can learn all about it in nearly any book or online reference about JavaServer Pages.

You might also consider installing a free developer version of Adobe JRun, which includes complete documentation on creating tag libraries.

Accessing the Underlying Servlet Context

With ColdFusion 8, each of your CFML pages is being converted to a Java servlet on-the-fly. It's natural that you should be able to access the various objects and methods exposed by the Java servlet API defined by Sun. In other words, if you feel like using the same methods and interfaces that Java developers use when writing servlets by hand, you are free to do so.

ColdFusion 8 uses the `GetPageContext()` function that gives you access to the underlying *page context*, which is a servlet term that refers to the current page request. The `GetPageContext()` function doesn't take any parameters; it just returns the current page context object. The returned object will be a descendent of the abstract `javax.servlet.jsp.PageContext` class, which just means that the object will have all the methods exposed by `PageContext`, plus any additional methods supplied by the J2EE server that is actually running ColdFusion.

Table 78.5 shows some of the interesting methods exposed by `PageContext`. A complete listing is beyond the scope of this book; the intention here is mainly to give you an idea of the kinds of methods available to you via the page context metaphor. Complete references for all the items listed in Table 78.5 (and much more) can be found in the Java 2 Enterprise Edition documentation, which was freely available from `http://java.sun.com` at the time of this writing.

Table 78.5 Some Interesting `PageContext` Methods

ATTRIBUTE	DESCRIPTION
`forward(relative_url)`	Similar conceptually to CFML's `<CFLOCATION>` tag, except that the redirection occurs on the server rather than on the client. You can use `forward()` to pass processing of the current page request to a JSP page running on the same server.
`include(relative_url)`	Similar conceptually to `<CFINCLUDE>` in CFML. You can use `include()` to include JSP pages running on the same server.
`getOut()`	Returns a `page writer` object that descends from `java.io.writer`. This object basically represents the page output stream; when you use `<cfoutput>` to generate dynamic output, the text eventually makes its way to this object's `print()` or similar methods.
`getRequest()`	Returns the underlying `PageRequest` object for the page, which in turn can be used to access all the methods exposed by the `HttpServletRequest` interface. In turn, the interface supports methods such as `isUserInRole()` and `getHeaders()`, which return data similar to that from CFML's own `isUserInRole()` and `getHttpRequestData()` methods. You might also want to check out the `isSecure()` and `getAuthType()` methods. The `getAttribute()` and `setAttribute()` methods are also of interest and will be discussed in the next section, "Integrating with Java Servlets and JSP Pages."
`getResponse()`	Returns the underlying `PageResponse` for the page, which exposes all methods of the `HttpServletResponse` interface. In turn, the interface supports methods such as `addCookie()` and `setHeader()`, which correspond to `<CFCOOKIE>` and `<CFHEADER>` in CFML.

NOTE

Page context functionality is probably most useful and interesting to developers who have worked with Java servlets or Java Server Pages (JSP). In general, most of the methods exposed by the page context have direct counterparts in CFML, so you might as well use the direct CFML representations of the functionality exposed by the page context and its members. That said, there may be special situations where the items in Table 78.5 will provide functionality that you can't get from CFML alone; we'll explore some of those situations throughout the remainder of this chapter.

The following quick example includes a JSP page. As will be discussed in the next section, the JSP page will be able to access the various CFML variables that may have been set in previous lines of ColdFusion code:

```
<cfset getPageContext().include("myPage.jsp")>
```

Or, to execute certain code only if a secure connection is being used between the browser and the server:

```
<cfif getPageContext().getRequest().isSecure()>
 ...
</cfif>
```

NOTE

There are other ways to implement the `<cfif>` test shown here, such as testing the value of `CGI.SERVER_PORT`. Using `isSecure()` might be considered preferable, however, especially since CGI variables tend to vary a bit among Web servers.

Integrating with Java Servlets and JSP Pages

ColdFusion 8 lets you use ColdFusion pages, JavaServer Pages (JSPs), and servlets together in a single application, or as a means to share certain Web pages among applications. This section explores exactly what you can and cannot do with respect to these technologies.

You can't freely mix the different types of code in the same code file, but you can do any of the following:

- Use the `getPageRequest().include()` method to include a JSP page or servlet midstream, within your ColdFusion page. You will be able to share variables among them.
- Use `getPageRequest().forward()` to pass responsibility for the page request to a JSP page or servlet. You can set certain variables in ColdFusion beforehand to make them visible to the JSP page or servlet. Again, `getPageRequest()` is new for ColdFusion 8, so this was not possible with earlier versions of the product.
- Use `<cfhttp>` to connect to a JSP page or servlet, perhaps including its output midstream. In general, the `include()` and `forward()` methods are more sophisticated, so I recommend that you use them instead of `<cfhttp>` unless you have a specific reason not to.
- Create client-driven links to JSP pages or servlets by specifying the appropriate URL in link `HREF` attributes, form `ACTION` attributes, and the like. Of course, you can pass whatever parameters you wish in the URL, and the pages may still be able to share application and session variables.

NOTE

ColdFusion 5 included `<cfservlet>` and `<cfservletparam>` tags for invoking servlets in ColdFusion pages. These tags have been removed (deprecated) from the CFML language. Don't use them when developing pages for ColdFusion MX or later.

Understanding Which Variables Can Be Shared

The following variables can be shared effortlessly among ColdFusion pages, JSP pages, and servlets:

- `REQUEST` variables, as long as you're using `forward()` or `include()` rather than `<cfhttp>` or client-driven linking

- APPLICATION variables
- SESSION variables, as long as the Use J2EE Session Variables option is enabled on the Memory Variables page of the ColdFusion Administrator

The following variables cannot be shared directly, but can be shared by copying their values into the REQUEST scope:

- Local CFML variables (that is, variables in the VARIABLES scope)
- CLIENT variables
- SERVER variables

Sharing REQUEST Variables

Sharing REQUEST variables among ColdFusion pages, JSP pages, and servlets is easy and straightforward. Here's how it works.

All servlets and JSP pages can access an instance of a class called ServletRequest. Within the body of a JSP or servlet, this ServletRequest instance is traditionally referred to as a variable called request. Among other things, the ServletRequest object allows developers to get and set *attributes* (basically variables) by name using methods called request.getAttribute() and request.setAttribute(). These methods are commonly used to share values between JSP pages and servlets. If a servlet sets a variable called age using request.setAttribute("age",31), then a JSP file participating in the same page request can read that value using request.getAttribute("age"), and vice versa. Simple enough.

So, what does this have to do with integrating with ColdFusion? Well, in ColdFusion 8, the REQUEST scope is really a set of JSP/servlet-style request attributes in disguise. Whenever you set a variable in the REQUEST scope, ColdFusion 8 is really using setAttribute() to set a variable in the J2EE request object, and when you use getAttribute(), you're really getting an attribute from the request object.

You can easily prove this to yourself in a ColdFusion page by setting an ordinary REQUEST variable called REQUEST.Age. You can now output the value of the variable using the getAttribute() method of the underlying J2EE response object. In ColdFusion, you get to the underlying response object using GetPageContext().getResponse(), as explained in Table 78.5. Putting all that together, the following snippet displays "Your age is 31," and then "Your age is 32."

```
<!--- Create request variable --->
<cfset REQUEST.Age = 31>
<!--- Output the request variable using underlying J2EE response object --->
<P>Your age is
<cfoutput>#GetPageContext().getRequest().getAttribute("age")#</cfoutput>
<!--- Change the value of the request variable --->
<cfset GetPageContext().getRequest().setAttribute("age", 32)>
<!--- Display the variable normally --->
<P>Your age is now
<cfoutput>#REQUEST.Age#</cfoutput>
```

If you have any experience with JSP or servlets, you can probably see where this is going. Assuming that it has been included in the same page request using `include()` or `forward()` as explained in Table 78.5, a JSP page could output the value of `REQUEST.Age` like so:

```
<%= request.getAttribute("age") %>
```

Similarly, a servlet could output the value using the following:

```
response.getWriter().print( request.getAttribute("age") );
```

Either a servlet or a JSP page could change the variable's value like this:

```
request.setAttribute("age", 32);
```

Shared Variables and Case-Sensitivity

ColdFusion's `REQUEST` scope is not case-sensitive, but J2EE request attributes are. ColdFusion resolves the difference by always setting attributes using lowercase attribute names. That's why `age` is used instead of `Age` in `getAttribute()` in that last code snippet.

Because ColdFusion isn't case-sensitive, this is all less of an issue when reading variables in your ColdFusion code. If you use `setAttribute()` to set a request variable in your JSP or servlet code, ColdFusion can get to the variable using `REQUEST.Age` or `REQUEST.age` or `REQUEST.AGE`, regardless of whether you used `Age` or `age` or some other capitalization in your `setAttribute()` call.

In the unlikely event that your JSP or servlet code is actually using `setAttribute()` to set two separate attributes called `age` and `Age`, the CFML `REQUEST` scope won't be able to discern between them; the one you would actually get at run time isn't defined. In such a situation, you can use `GetPageContext().getRequest().getAttribute()` in your ColdFusion code as a workaround.

TIP

Just to avoid confusion, you should consider using all lowercase variable names for any `REQUEST` variables that you intend to share with JSP pages or servlets. If you do so in your ColdFusion, JSP, and servlet code, you won't have any of these minor case-sensitivity issues to keep in mind.

Shared Variables and Data Types

In addition to being easy and forgiving in terms of case, ColdFusion is easy and forgiving when it comes to data types. Most simple CFML variables (strings and numbers) are stored internally as strings until you use them in some other context, in which case they are "automagically" parsed or converted to the appropriate type for you. This means that Java will receive most variables as strings unless you take specific steps otherwise.

For instance, when you create a variable like the following, it's stored internally as a string, even though there aren't any quotation marks around the right side of the statement:

```
<cfset REQUEST.Age = 31>
```

As such, `request.getAttribute("age")` will return a string in Java Land, which could be a problem if you are trying to refer to the value as an integer. For instance, the following will fail at run time because of a type mismatch between `java.lang.String` and `java.lang.Integer`:

```
Integer age = (Integer)request.getAttribute("age");
```

It's up to you whether you solve this issue on the ColdFusion side or Java side. In most cases, it probably makes the most conceptual sense to solve it on the ColdFusion side using `JavaCast()` whenever possible. The recommended way out of this particular dilemma, then, would be to cast the value as an `int` when you set the `REQUEST` variable, like so:

```
<cfset REQUEST.Age = JavaCast("int", 31)>
```

NOTE

I hope this won't confuse the issue, but if a value is already known to be a number on the ColdFusion side, it will be exposed to Java as a `Double`. For instance, if the `REQUEST.Age` variable were created as a result of a mathematical computation, or using `Val(31)` instead of just `31`, any Java code expecting the value to be a `java.lang.Double` would work fine without the need for an explicit `JavaCast()` in your ColdFusion code. To put it another way, `Val()` and `JavaCast("double")` are more or less synonymous in ColdFusion 8.

Shared Variables and Multifaceted Values

If you are using a multifaceted ColdFusion variable such as an array, you should be aware of how it will be received by Java. Table 78.6 summarizes the object types that will be received when Java's `getAttribute()` method is used to access a value in ColdFusion's `REQUEST` scope.

Table 78.6 How CFML Variables Are Exposed to Java

COLDFUSION TYPE	JAVA TYPE
`string`	`String`.
`date`	`java.util.Date`.
`number`	`java.lang.Double`, unless cast specifically as an `int` or `long` with `JavaCast()`.
`structure`	`coldfusion.runtime.struct`, which implements the `java.util.Map` interface, meaning that you can use it in the same basic way you use `java.util.Hashtable` objects. Nested structures within the structure will also be objects that implement `java.util.Map`.
`array`	`coldfusion.runtime.Array`, which is a subclass of `java.util.Vector`.
`query recordset`	`coldfusion.sql.QueryTable`, which implements the `java.sql.ResultSet` interface.

A Simple Example

The next few code listings show how easy it is to create ColdFusion pages that incorporate logic and output from existing JSP pages or servlets. Listing 78.9 is a ColdFusion page that uses

`GetPageContext().include()` to include output from a JSP page and then a servlet. The JSP page and servlet are both able to refer to the `REQUEST.Name` variable set by ColdFusion. The servlet also changes the value of the variable, and the change is reflected in ColdFusion and displayed at the bottom of the page (Figure 78.4).

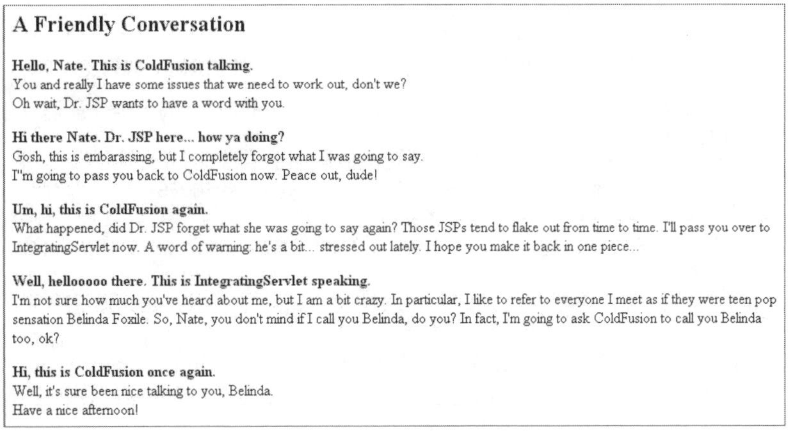

Figure 78.4
A ColdFusion page, JSP page, and servlet can all participate in the same page request.

A Friendly Conversation

Hello, Nate. This is ColdFusion talking.
You and really I have some issues that we need to work out, don't we?
Oh wait, Dr. JSP wants to have a word with you.

Hi there Nate. Dr. JSP here... how ya doing?
Gosh, this is embarassing, but I completely forgot what I was going to say.
I"m going to pass you back to ColdFusion now. Peace out, dude!

Um, hi, this is ColdFusion again.
What happened, did Dr. JSP forget what she was going to say again? Those JSPs tend to flake out from time to time. I'll pass you over to IntegratingServlet now. A word of warning: he's a bit... stressed out lately. I hope you make it back in one piece...

Well, hellooooo there. This is IntegratingServlet speaking.
I'm not sure how much you've heard about me, but I am a bit crazy. In particular, I like to refer to everyone I meet as if they were teen pop sensation Belinda Foxile. So, Nate, you don't mind if I call you Belinda, do you? In fact, I'm going to ask ColdFusion to call you Belinda too, ok?

Hi, this is ColdFusion once again.
Well, it's sure been nice talking to you, Belinda.
Have a nice afternoon!

Listing 78.9 `IntegratingCFML.cfm`—A ColdFusion Page that Includes a JSP Page and a Servlet Page

```
<!---
 Filename: IntegratingCFML.cfm
 Author: Nate Weiss (NMW)
 Purpose: Shows how ColdFusion pages, JSP pages, and Servlets can
 participate in the same page request
--->
<html>
<head><title>ColdFusion, JSP, and Servlet Integration</title></head>
<body>
<h2>A Friendly Conversation</h2>

<!--- Set a variable in the REQUEST scope. --->
<!--- This variable will be visible to any included JSP and Servlet pages --->
<cfset REQUEST.Name = "Nate">

<!--- Display a simple message, using normal ColdFusion syntax --->
<cfoutput>
 <b>Hello, #REQUEST.Name#. This is ColdFusion talking.</b><br>
 You and really I have some issues that we need to work out, don't we?<br>
 Oh wait, Dr. JSP wants to have a word with you.<br>
</cfoutput>

<!--- Include a JSP page --->
<cfset GetPageContext().include("IntegratingJSP.jsp")>

<!--- Another ColdFusion message --->
<cfoutput>
 <p><b>Um, hi, this is ColdFusion again.</b><br>
 What happened, did Dr. JSP forget what she was going to say again?
```

Listing 78.9 (continued)

```
 Those JSPs tend to flake out from time to time.
 I'll pass you over to IntegratingServlet now.
 A word of warning: he's a bit... stressed out lately.
 I hope you make it back in one piece...<br>
</cfoutput>

<!--- Include a Java Servlet --->
<cfset GetPageContext().include("/servlet/IntegratingServlet")>

<!--- Show that REQUEST variable can be changed by JSP pages or Servlets --->
<cfoutput>
 <p><b>Hi, this is ColdFusion once again.</b><br>
 Well, it's sure been nice talking to you, #REQUEST.Name#.<br>
 Have a nice afternoon!<br>
</cfoutput>

</body>
</html>
```

Listing 78.10 shows the code for the JSP page that is included by the ColdFusion page in Listing 78.9. Note that it is able to use standard JSP-style `request.getAttribute()` syntax to refer to the value that ColdFusion calls `REQUEST.Name`.

Listing 78.10 `IntegratingJSP.jsp`—JSP Page Included by Listing 78.9

```
<%--
 Filename: IntegratingJSP.jsp
 Author: Nate Weiss (NMW)
 Purpose: Demonstrates variable-sharing between environments
--%>


<%-- The REQUEST variable that was set in the ColdFusion page --%>
<%-- is available here as an attribute of the JSP "request" object --%>
<p>
<b>Hi there <%= request.getAttribute("name") %>.
Dr. JSP here... how ya doing?</b><br>
Gosh, this is embarrassing, but I completely forgot what I was going to say.<br>
I''m going to pass you back to ColdFusion now. Peace out, dude!<br>
```

NOTE

ColdFusion 8 can process JSP pages, so you're probably already all set to execute this part of the example. If you're not using ColdFusion 8's built-in Web server, it's possible that you'll need to add a mapping to your Web server software so it knows to pass requests for `.jsp` pages to ColdFusion. See your Web server documentation for details.

Listing 78.11 shows the Java code for the simple Java servlet that is included by the ColdFusion page from Listing 78.9. Again, the code is able to use standard servlet-style `getAttribute()` syntax to get the value of the `REQUEST.Name` variable known to ColdFusion. Similarly, it's able to use `setAttribute()` to change the value. The servlet could, of course, use `setAttribute()` to create entirely new variables, which would also become visible to ColdFusion in the `REQUEST` scope.

Listing 78.11 `IntegratingServlet.java`—Java Servlet Included by Listing 78.9

```
/*
 Filename: IntegratingServlet.java
 Author: Nate Weiss (NMW)
 Purpose: Demonstrates variable-sharing between environments
*/
import java.io.*;
import javax.servlet.*;
import javax.servlet.http.*;

public class IntegratingServlet extends HttpServlet {

 public void doGet(HttpServletRequest req, HttpServletResponse resp)
 throws IOException, ServletException {

 // Get reference to the servlet's PrintWriter. This object's print()
 // method is similar conceptually to <cfoutput> or WriteOutput() in CFML
 PrintWriter out = resp.getWriter();

out.print("<p><b>Well, hellooooo there.</b> ");
 out.print("<b>This is IntegratingServlet speaking.</b><br>");
 out.print("I'm not sure how much you've heard about me, but I am a bit");
 out.print(" crazy. In particular, I like to refer to everyone I meet");
 out.print(" as if they were teen pop sensation Belinda Foxile. So, ");
 out.print( req.getAttribute("name") );
 out.print(", you don't mind if I call you Belinda, do you? In fact, ");
 out.print(" I'm going to ask ColdFusion to call you Belinda too, ok?");
 // Change the value of the name attribute
 // (which corresponds to the REQUEST.name variable in ColdFusion)
 req.setAttribute("name", "Belinda");
 }
}
```

If you want to test out this servlet example, you need to use `javac` to compile the Java class into the corresponding `IntegratingServlet.class` file, and then place it into the appropriate location on your Web server. If you are using the stand-alone version of ColdFusion 8, that location is typically the `c:/coldfusion8/wwwroot/WEB-INF/classes` folder. If you're running ColdFusion under a different J2EE server, the location may be different. If you're using ColdFusion under IIS or some other non-J2EE server, then you may need to install a separate servlet host to see this example in action.

Integrating with EJBs

You can interact with Enterprise JavaBeans (EJBs) using ColdFusion 8. There is no specific tag or function built into ColdFusion for getting a reference to an EJB. Instead, you use a series of `<cfobject>` or `CreateObject()` to instantiate and work with the standard Java classes responsible for locating and maintaining EJBs, such as `javax.naming.Context` and `javax.naming.InitialContext`. The specific steps are very similar to the steps you would take when connecting to EJBs in normal Java code; you just use the CFML-style syntax to do so.

Once you have an instance of an EJB, you access its methods and properties just like any other Java class object or Bean. You will see a simple example of calling an EJB method in the next listing. For details about working with the methods and properties of a Java object, refer to the "Using Java Class Objects" section at the beginning of this chapter.

A Simple Example

Listing 78.12 shows how to instantiate and work with a sample EJB called `HelloBean`. This sample EJB exposes just one method, `getMessage()`, which always returns the same "Hello, World!" type of message. This page simply interacts with the appropriate JNDI objects to create an instance of the EJB called `myInstance`, and then calls `myInstance.getMessage()` to obtain and display the text of the sample message (Figure 78.5).

Figure 78.5

This page displays a message from the sample EJB called "HelloBean."

EJB Example Page

The following message was returned by the EJB:
Hello World from EJB

NOTE

This example assumes you are using Adobe JRun as the EJB host/container. If you are using some other J2EE server to host your EJBs, you will need to alter a few of the lines (most probably the ones that set the `INITIAL_CONTEXT_FACTORY` and `PROVIDER_URL`).

Listing 78.12 `EJBExample.cfm`—Instantiating and Working with an EJB

```
<!---
 Filename: EJBExample.cfm
 Author: Adobe (adapted from the ColdFusion 8 documentation)
 Purpose: Shows how to instantiate and use an Enterprise JavaBean (EJB)
--->

<!--- Create the Context object to get at the static fields. --->
<cfset ctx = CreateObject("Java", "javax.naming.Context")>

<!--- Create the Properties object and call an explicit constructor--->
<cfset props = CreateObject("Java", "java.util.Properties")>
<cfset props.init()>

<!--- Specify the properties These are required for a remote server only --->
<cfset props.put(ctx.INITIAL_CONTEXT_FACTORY, "jrun.naming.JRunContextFactory")>
<cfset props.put(ctx.PROVIDER_URL, "localhost:7808")>
<!---
  (You might add the following if security credentials need to be provided)
  <CFSET prop.put(ctx.SECURITY_PRINCIPAL, "admin")>
  <CFSET prop.put(ctx.SECURITY_CREDENTIALS, "admin")>
--->

<!--- Create the InitialContext --->
```

Listing 78.12 (continued)

```
<cfset initContext = CreateObject("Java", "javax.naming.InitialContext")>
<!--- Pass the properties to the InitialContext constructor. --->
<cfset initContext.init(props)>

<!--- Get reference to home object --->
<cfset home = initContext.lookup("HelloBean")>

<!--- Create new instance of entity bean --->
<cfset myInstance = home.create()>

<!--- Call a method in the entity bean --->
<cfset myMessage = myInstance.getMessage()>

<html>
<head><title>EJB Example</title></head>
<body>
<h2>EJB Example Page</h2>

<!--- Display the value returned by the method --->
<cfoutput>
  The following message was returned by the EJB:<br>
  <b>#myMessage#</b><br>
</cfoutput>

</body>
</html>

<!--- Close the context. --->
<cfset init
Context.close()>
```

Refer to the JRun documentation or an EJB reference or tutorial for more information on the way the `javax.naming.Context` and `javax.naming.InitialContext` are used in this listing. You will find that Listing 78.12 is a fairly straightforward port of the kind of EJB-instantiation code typically used by Java programmers.

NOTE

The sample `HelloBean` EJB is provided in a JAR file called `sample_hello_bean.jar` from Adobe included with this chapter's listings for your convenience. You will need to deploy the EJB before running the example. If you are using Adobe JRun 4, just copy the JAR to your server's deploy folder (perhaps `JRun4/servers/default`). For other J2EE servers, the specific steps for deploying an EJB will be different.

If you haven't used EJBs before and just want to see this example in action, download and install the free developer edition of JRun 4 from Adobe's site. Once JRun is installed and running, copy the `sample_hello_bean.jar` file (included with this chapter's listings) to the `servers/default` folder (that's `C:\JRun4\servers\default` in a typical Windows installation), which should automatically deploy the EJB. Assuming that JRun and ColdFusion 8 are now running on the same server and using the default HTTP ports, the example should work as presented here.

This example is adapted fairly directly from the ColdFusion documentation. We don't do this often in this book, but in this case it makes a lot of sense. There really aren't many different ways to slice this particular problem. We did take the liberty of changing the `<cfobject>` tags in the documentation's listing to `CreateObject()` function calls, because the code reads better and will be more familiar to Java coders in this form.

Making It Easier with a Custom Tag

Although the code in Listing 78.12 is a straightforward port of the Java code that you would typically use to deploy an EJB, it's not particularly simple or ColdFusion-like. This chapter includes code for a custom tag called `<CF_UseEJB>` that makes it easier to work with EJBs; this tag need merely be located and created in the typical fashion. You can use `<CF_UseEJB>` as is if you wish, or you can adapt the idea to suit your own needs. As presented here, the tag supports the four attributes listed in Table 78.7.

Table 78.7 `<CF_UseEJB>` Custom Tag Syntax

ATTRIBUTE	DESCRIPTION
`EJBName`	Required. The name of the EJB that you wish to work with, as it is known by the JNDI naming service.
`Variable`	Required. A variable name for the instantiated EJB object.
`InitialContextFactory`	Optional. The name of the appropriate initial context factory. As presented here, this attribute defaults to `jrun.naming.JRunContextFactory`, which means that the tag will automatically try to connect to JRun's naming implementation by default.
`ProviderURL`	Optional. The URL used to connect to the JNDI naming service. As presented here, this attribute defaults to `localhost:7808`, which means that you don't need to provide this attribute if JRun is installed on the same server as ColdFusion and is using the default port of 7808.
`SecurityPrincipal`	Optional. The *security principal* information (in most cases, some kind of username), if any, that is needed to connect to the naming service.
`SecurityCredentials`	Optional. The *security credentials* information (in most cases, some kind of password), if any, that is needed to connect to the naming service.

Listing 78.13 shows the code used to create the `<CF_UseEJB>` custom tag. Again, feel free to adapt this code to suit your needs, or to use it as a starting point for some other type of EJB-related abstraction. For instance, you might decide to redesign this code as a CFC rather than a custom tag.

Listing 78.13 `UseEJB.cfm`—A Custom Tag to Make It Easier to Work with EJBs

```
<!---
 Filename: UseEJB.cfm
 Author: Nate Weiss (NMW)
 Purpose: Creates a custom tag to ease the task of getting an EJB instance
--->

<cfsilent>
  <!--- Tag Attributes --->
  <cfparam name="ATTRIBUTES.EJBName" type="string">
  <cfparam name="ATTRIBUTES.Variable" type="variableName">
```

Listing 78.13 (continued)

```
<cfparam name="ATTRIBUTES.InitialContextFactory" type="string"
  default="jrun.naming.JRunContextFactory">
<cfparam name="ATTRIBUTES.ProviderURL" type="string"
  default="localhost:7808">

<!--- Create the Context object to get at the static fields --->
<cfset ctx = CreateObject("Java", "javax.naming.Context")>

<!--- Create the Properties object and call an explicit constructor --->
<cfset props = CreateObject("Java", "java.util.Properties")>

<!--- Specify the properties to pass to the initial context --->
<cfset props.put(ctx.INITIAL_CONTEXT_FACTORY, ATTRIBUTES.InitialContextFactory)>
<cfset props.put(ctx.PROVIDER_URL, ATTRIBUTES.ProviderURL)>
<!--- If a SecurityPrincipal attribute was provided --->
<cfif IsDefined("ATTRIBUTES.SecurityPrincipal")>
  <cfset prop.put(ctx.SECURITY_PRINCIPAL, "admin")>
</cfif>
<!--- If a SecurityCredentials attribute was provided --->
<cfif IsDefined("ATTRIBUTES.SecurityCredentials")>
  <cfset prop.put(ctx.SECURITY_CREDENTIALS, "admin")>
</cfif>

<!--- Create the InitialContext --->
<cfset initContext = CreateObject("Java", "javax.naming.InitialContext")>
<!--- Pass the properties to the InitialContext constructor. --->
<cfset initContext.init(props)>

<!--- Get reference to home object --->
<cfset home = initContext.lookup(ATTRIBUTES.EJBName)>

<!--- Create new instance of entity bean --->
<cfset instance = home.create()>

<!--- Return the completed instance --->
<cfset "CALLER.#ATTRIBUTES.Variable#" = instance>
</cfsilent>
```

Listing 78.14 shows how the new `<CF_EJB>` custom tag can be used in a ColdFusion page. Assuming that the EJB is being hosted by a JRun server running on the same physical machine as ColdFusion 8, and assuming that no security credentials (such as a username and password) need to be provided, the EJB can now be instantiated using just the `EJBName` and `Variable` attributes (add the other attributes from Table 78.7 as needed).

When visited with a browser, this page displays the same message as the first example in this section (see Figure 78.5).

Listing 78.14 `UseEJBDemo.cfm`—Using the `<CF_UseEJB>` Custom Tag

```
<!---
 Filename: UseEJBDemo.cfm
 Author: Nate Weiss (NMW)
 Purpose: Instantiates an EJB via <CF_UseEJB>
--->
```

Listing 78.14 (continued)

```
<!--- Create an instance of the HelloBean EJB --->
<CF_UseEJB
  EJBName="HelloBean"
  Variable="mySimple">

<html>
<head><title>EJB Example</title></head>
<body>
<h2>EJB Example Page</h2>

<!--- Display the value returned by the method --->
<cfoutput>
  The following message was returned by the EJB:<br>
  <b>#mySimple.getMessage()#</b><br>
</cfoutput>

</body>
</html>
```

Writing Java CFX Tags

There are several other ways to work with Java and ColdFusion that we have not discussed here. One is creating CFX tags with Java. As opposed to the Java topics you explored in this chapter, CFX tags are specific to ColdFusion and can't be reused in other environments. However, they are tightly integrated with ColdFusion, have direct access to CFML query objects, and can be used with earlier ColdFusion versions all the way back to ColdFusion 2.0. You'll learn all about CFX tags in Chapter 79, "Extending ColdFusion with CFX."

CHAPTER 79

Extending ColdFusion with CFX

IN THIS CHAPTER

As you have learned in previous chapters, you have the capability to write your own custom tags, user defined functions, and components—all using ColdFusion's native language, CFML. It's possible to extend ColdFusion's capabilities even farther with CFX tags. The main difference is that you don't use ColdFusion's markup language to create the tag; rather, you use an external programming language (Java or C++) to create the tags.

What Are CFX Tags?

You have already become familiar with CFML custom tags, which always start with `<cf_>`, the code for which appears in a similarly named `.cfm` file. In this chapter, you'll become familiar with tags that start with `<cfx_>`. These tags are compiled to a Dynamic Link Library (`.dll`) or a Java Class (`.class`) file. Table 79.1 describes the differences between `<cf_>` and `<cfx_>` tags.

Table 79.1 Quick Comparison: CFML Custom Tags Versus CFX Tags

CFML CUSTOM TAGS	CFX TAGS
Start with `cf_`.	Start with `cfx_`.
Written using normal ColdFusion tags and functions.	Written in C++ or Java.
Actual code is in a `.cfm` file.	Actual code is in a C++ `.dll` file or a Java `.class` file
Can only do things that CFML code can do.	Can do just about anything that the language (Java or C++) allows.
Don't need to be registered in ColdFusion Administrator.	Must be registered in the ColdFusion Administrator, in a step much like creating a data source or Verity collection.

When to Write (and Avoid Writing) a CFX Tag

Given the choice between creating a CFX tag or creating a CFML-based extension such as a custom tag, UDF, or CFC, it is generally best to consider one of the CFML-based alternatives first. Why? Mainly because CFML is so simple, and generally provides a rich enough feature set to get most tasks done with ease. Whenever possible, I recommend that you consider creating a CFML-based extension first.

That said, there are plenty of situations where creating a CFX tag makes lots of sense. In general, most CFX tags are created for one of the following reasons:

- To take advantage of a third-party C++ or Java API that makes something possible that isn't otherwise possible in ColdFusion. Perhaps the API knows how to connect to some kind of legacy mainframe database system, or knows how to create a special type of image file. In this situation, the CFX tag can be thought of as wrapper around the API.
- To take advantage of legacy code, open source code, or other snippets that have already been written in Java or C++. If you're working on a complex project, and you already have Java or C++ code available that can provide part of the functionality, it may make sense to just turn that code into a CFX tag, even if it would be possible to port the logic to CFML. If it's faster and easier for you and your project, go for it!
- To take advantage of faster processing. In general, your regular ColdFusion pages are compiled into Java classes that perform quite well. However, there will always be niche situations where you could write custom Java or C++ code that runs more efficiently.
- To circumvent method-selection problems or other errors when using Java classes (or Beans). Most Java classes can be used via `<cfobject>` or `CreateObject()` as discussed in Chapter 78, "Extending ColdFusion with Java." However, some Java methods and constructors are overloaded in such a way that ColdFusion can't determine which form to use at runtime, even if you use `JavaCast()`. In such a situation, you can create a CFX tag that acts as a sort of "poor man's proxy" between ColdFusion and the Java class.

Choosing Between C++ and Java

You can program a CFX tag in either Java or C++. Much of the time, the decision will have been made for you, because whatever third-party API or other existing code you are planning to use will force you to use one or the other.

The most obvious advantage to programming the CFX in Java is that it will be able to run on a ColdFusion server using any operating system (OS). Tags created with C++, however, will need to be recompiled for each OS you want to support. Of course, cross-platform support doesn't mean much if the nature of your project is such that the tag will be bound to one OS or the other anyway, so the importance of this advantage may or may not mean a whole lot to you. For instance, if you want the CFX tag to call native Windows APIs, then a C++ tag is the obvious choice; you'll probably only have to compile it once for any Win32 platform.

Another reason to use C++ is the fact that it is generally thought to be faster at extremely CPU-intensive tasks. However, recent advances in Java Virtual Machine technology have made Java code more likely than ever to perform nearly as well as comparable C++ code. Also, the ColdFusion server can invoke Java CFXs directly, but must go through an additional layer (the Java Native Interface, or JNI) when invoking a C++ tag. In my opinion, sheer performance issues should only guide you toward C++ in extreme situations.

All things considered, I recommend that you go with Java if you really have a choice between the two. The code will probably be faster, easier to write, and will almost certainly be easier to debug. Even if you don't anticipate using to use the tag on multiple platforms now, it will still be nice to know that your choice of Java keeps that option open for the future.

Introducing the CFX API

Regardless of the language you use to create a CFX tag, you need a way to pass information back and forth between the tag code and the ColdFusion page that is using the tag. You also need ways to safely throw exceptions (errors), create query objects, and include output in the current Web page. Adobe defines a set of objects and functions that provides all this functionality and more. The objects and functions are known collectively as the *CFX API.*

The following sections will introduce you to the various functions included in the CFX API, organized by subject. Within each section, the Java syntax will be shown in one table, followed by the C++ syntax in a second table. You will notice that the Java and C++ versions of the API are very similar. For the most part, there is a one-to-one relationship between the methods provided by both versions of the API. This is great because once you design a few tags in Java, you will be well on your way to understanding what's possible with C++, and vice versa.

Working with the Tag's Attributes

Like native ColdFusion tags or CFML custom tags, your CFX tags can accept any number of attributes. You can easily add code to your tag so that some of its attributes are required while others remain optional. The CFX API defines several functions that a tag can use to accept and validate attributes from the calling ColdFusion page. Table 79.2 shows the Java version of these functions, and Table 79.3 shows the C++ version.

Table 79.2 Java Methods for Working with Attributes

METHOD	DESCRIPTION
`request.attributeExists(name)`	Determines whether the specified attribute was actually passed to the CFX tag. Returns a Boolean value.
`request.getAttribute(name)`	Returns the value of the specified attribute, as it was passed to the CFX tag. Note that all attribute values are received by the CFX as String values.
`request.getAttributeList(name)`	Returns the names of all attributes that were actually passed to the CFX tag. The names are returned as an array of strings.

Table 79.3 C++ Methods for Working with Attributes

METHOD	DESCRIPTION
`pRequest->AttributeExists(lpszName)`	Determines whether the specified attribute was actually passed to the CFX tag. Returns a `BOOL`.
`pRequest->GetAttribute(lpszName)`	Returns the value of the specified attribute, as it was passed to the CFX tag. Note that all attribute values are received by the CFX as `LPCSTR` string values.
`pRequest->GetAttributeList()`	Returns the names of all attributes that were actually passed to the CFX tag. The names are returned as a `CFXStringSet`, which is similar to an array of strings.

Returning Variables and Text

Your CFX tag has the ability to include dynamically generated content in the ColdFusion page that is calling the tag. It can also return variables to the calling page. Table 79.4 shows the Java methods for these tasks, and Table 79.5 shows the C++ version.

Table 79.4 Java Methods for Returning Variables and Text

METHOD	DESCRIPTION
`request.setVariable(name, value)`	Returns a variable to ColdFusion with the specified name and value. Both name and value must be specified as strings.
`request.write(text)`	Includes text in the current page, just as if the text was generated by a `<cfoutput>` block. The text must be specified as a string.

Table 79.5 C++ Methods for Returning Variables and Text

METHOD	DESCRIPTION
`pRequest->SetVariable(name, value)`	Returns a variable to ColdFusion with the specified name and value. Both must be specified as `LPCSTR` compatible values.
`pRequest->Write(text)`	Includes text in the current page, just as if the text was generated by a `<cfoutput>` block. The text must be specified as a `LPCSTR` compatible value.

Working with Queries

Any CFX tag may return queries to the ColdFusion page that is calling the tag. The queries can then be used in ColdFusion code, just like the results of a `<cfquery>` or any other tag that returns a recordset. For instance, the queries can be used as the `query` parameter of a `<cfloop>` or `<cfoutput>` tag; they can even be re-queried or joined with other recordsets using in-memory-queries (where you set `dbtype="query"` in a separate `<cfquery>` tag; also known as "query-of-queries"). Table 79.6 shows the Java methods for working with queries, and Table 79.7 shows the C++ versions.

NOTE

Any CFX tag can return any number of queries to the calling template, but it can only access the data in one query that already exists in the calling template. To put it another way, multiple queries can be passed out from the CFX, but only one can be passed in.

Table 79.6 Java Methods for Working with Queries

METHOD	DESCRIPTION
`response.addQuery(name, columns)`	Creates a new query, which will be available in the calling ColdFusion page when the CFX tag finishes executing. Specify the name of the query as a string, and specify its columns as an array of strings.
`query.addRow()`	Adds a row to the query. You can then fill the individual cells (columns) of the new row using `setData()`. Returns the row number of the new row, as an `int`.
`query.setData(row, col, value)`	Places the value (which must be a string) into the query at the row and column position you specify. Rows and columns are both numbered beginning with 1. You can get the value for `col` using `getColumnIndex()`.
`request.getQuery()`	Retrieves the query (if any) that was passed to the CFX tag. Returns a Query object, or `null` if no `QUERY` attribute was provided.
`query.getColumnIndex(name)`	Returns the column index (position) of the column with the given name. You can then use the index to specify columns to `getData()` and `setData()`. Returns `-1` if the column doesn't exist.
`query.getColumns()`	Returns the names of the query's columns, as an array of strings.
`query.getData(row, col)`	Returns the value in the query at the given row and column position. The value is always returned as a string.
`query.getName()`	Returns the name of the query (as a string), as it is known in the calling ColdFusion page.
`query.getRowCount()`	Returns the number of rows in the query, as an `int`.

Table 79.7 C++ Methods for Working with Queries

METHOD	DESCRIPTION
`pRequest->AddQuery(name, columns)`	Creates a new query. Specify the name of the query as a `LPCSTR`, and columns as a `CCFXStringSet` (similar to an array of strings).
`pQuery->AddRow()`	Adds a row to the query.
`pQuery->SetData(row, col, value)`	Places the value (which must be a `LPCSTR`) into the query at the row and column position you specify.
`pRequest->GetQuery()`	Retrieves the query (if any) that was passed to the CFX tag. Returns a `CCFXQuery` object, or null if no `QUERY` attribute was provided to the tag.
`pQuery->GetColumns()`	Returns the names of the query's columns, as a `CFXStringSet`, which is similar conceptually to an array of strings. You can use any of the methods listed in Table 79.8 on the returned `CFXStringSet`. For instance, you can use `GetIndexForString()` to find the index position of a column by name; that index position could then be used in the `GetData()` or `SetData()` functions.
`pQuery->GetData(row, col)`	Returns the value in the query at the given row and column position. The value is always returned as a `LPCSTR`.
`pQuery->GetName()`	Returns the name of the query (as a `LPCSTR`), as it is known in the calling ColdFusion page.
`pQuery->GetRowCount()`	Returns the number of rows in the query, as an int.

To pass a query to a CFX tag, the name of the query must be specified as an attribute named `QUERY` (you don't get to determine the name of the attribute). So, if a `query="FilmsQuery"` attribute is supplied when the tag is called, then the `getQuery()` method will grab the query for use inside of the CFX tag. You can then use `getRecordCount()`, `getColumns()`, and `getData()` to refer to the data in the query.

Because standard C++ doesn't have a built-in notion of an ordered set of strings, the CFX API includes an additional class type called `CFXStringSet`, which is similar conceptually to an array of strings in Java. An object of this type is returned if you call the `GetAttributes()` method listed in Table 79.3 or the `GetColumns()` method from Table 79.7. Similarly, to create a new query object, you first create a new `CFXStringSet`, add column names to the string set using `AddString()`, then pass the string set to the `AddQuery()` method (also listed in Table 79.7). The methods supported by this class are listed in Table 79.8.

NOTE

This part of the CFX API is only included in the C++ version. There is no need for it in Java, which already includes the notion of a string set (the `String[]` type).

Table 79.8 C++ Methods for Working with String Sets

METHOD	DESCRIPTION
`stringset->AddString(string)`	Adds a `LPCSTR` value to the string set. Most commonly, this method is used to add column names to a string set that will later be passed to `pQuery->AddQuery()`. Returns the index position of the string that was just added.
`stringset->GetCount()`	Returns the number of strings in the string set, as an `int`. If you call this method on the result of the `GetAttributes()` method, you get the number of attributes passed to the tag. If you call it on the result of `GetColumns()`, you get the number of columns in the query.
`stringset->GetString(index)`	Returns the string (as a `LPCSTR`) at the index position you specify. The first string is at position 1, the second string is at position 2, and so on.
`stringset->GetIndexForString(string)`	Returns the index position of the string you specify. The search is not case sensitive. If the string is not in the set, the constant `CFX_STRING_NOT_FOUND` (defined as `-1` in `cfx.h`) is returned.

Working with Exceptions and Debugging

If anything goes wrong while your CFX tag is doing its work, you need a way to display a helpful error message in the ColdFusion page that is using the tag. To that end, the CFX API provides mechanisms for throwing exceptions that behave just like ColdFusion's own exceptions, and just like exceptions thrown by `<cfthrow>` tag in normal ColdFusion code. In addition, methods are provided that allow your tag to include debug messages that will be included in the current Web page when ColdFusion's debugging options are turned on. Table 79.9 shows the Java version of this part of the CFX API, and Table 79.10 shows the C++ version.

Table 79.9 Java Methods for Exceptions and Debugging

METHOD	DESCRIPTION
`throw new Exception(message)`	Creates an exception (error message), which will be displayed in ColdFusion just like any other error message. This is similar conceptually to the `<cfthrow>` tag in CFML. If it wishes, the calling template can use `<cftry>` and `<cfcatch>` to handle the exception gracefully. This isn't really part of the CFX API; it's standard Java syntax. I'm including it in this table for consistency's sake.
`request.debug()`	Determines whether the tag has been called with the debug attribute turned on. If so, you would presumably include some kind of debugging message in the current Web page with `writeDebug()`. For details, see the "Generating Debug Output" section later in this chapter.

Table 79.9 (continued)

METHOD	DESCRIPTION
`response.writeDebug(text)`	Includes a text message in the current Web page. Very similar to `response.write()`, except that the text is only included in the page if the tag has been called with a debug attribute.

Table 79.10 C++ Methods for Exceptions and Debugging

METHOD	DESCRIPTION
`pRequest->ThrowException (message, detail)`	Creates an exception (error message), similar to the `<cfthrow>` tag in CFML. The message and detail must be specified as `LPCSTR` compatible values.
`pRequest->Debug()`	Determines whether the tag has been called with the debug attribute turned on. If so, you would presumably include some kind of debugging message in the current Web page with `WriteDebug()`.
`pRequest->WriteDebug(text)`	Includes a text message in the current Web page. Very similar to `pRequest->Write()`, except that the text is only included in the page if the CFX is used with a debug attribute.

Writing CFX Tags with Java

Now that you've gotten an introduction to the methods available in the CFX API, you can get started creating CFX tags with Java or C++. Because I assume that more people will be writing tags in Java than C++ going forward, we'll start off with Java. If you plan to work with C++, just take a quick look through this section, then skip ahead to the "Writing CFX Tags with Visual C++" section, later in this chapter.

Getting Started

The process of creating a Java CFX tag can be broken down into the following steps:

1. Writing the Java code in a text editor or Java IDE
2. Compiling the Java code into the corresponding .class file
3. Registering the new CFX tag in the ColdFusion Administrator

In the next few pages, you'll learn how to perform each of these steps, producing a very simple CFX tag along the way. More complicated, fully featured examples will follow later in this chapter.

Writing the Java Code

The actual code for your CFX will be contained within an ordinary Java class file. Like any Java class, you can write the code in any text editor, such as the Windows Notepad, Adobe Dreamweaver, or the editor of your choice. Once the code is written, you can use the `javac` utility from the Java SDK to compile the class (discussed below, in the "Compiling the CFX Tag" section).

NOTE

Of course, you are also free to use a free or commercial Java Integrated Development Environment (IDE), which will be able to offer such niceties as automatic code completion, automatic compilation, and integrated help. One such IDE is Eclipse; another is Borland's JBuilder product.

This chapter's first example will be a simple CFX tag called `<CFX_HelloWorld>`. Listing 79.1 shows the Java source code for the tag.

Listing 79.1 `HelloWorld.java`—Creating the `<CFX_HelloWorld>` Tag with Java

```
import com.allaire.cfx.* ;
public class HelloWorld implements CustomTag {
public void processRequest( Request request, Response response )
throws Exception
{
// Make sure a NAME attribute is passed to the tag
if ( !request.attributeExists("NAME") ) {
throw new Exception("The NAME attribute is required!");
};

// Make sure an AGE attribute is passed as well
if ( !request.attributeExists("AGE") ) {
throw new Exception("The AGE attribute is required!");
};

// Respond by inserting a text message in the calling ColdFusion file
// The text will appear in place of the CFX tag in the final Web page
response.write("<P>Hello there " + request.getAttribute("NAME") + "!");
response.write("<BR>I hear you turned " + request.getAttribute("AGE"));
response.write(" sometime during the past year. Happy birthday!<BR>");
}

}
```

Even if you've never seen a line of Java code before, you can probably guess what this tag will do when it is used in a ColdFusion page. That's right, it will display a "Hello, World" type of message which contains the values of the `NAME` and `AGE` attributes that get passed to the tag.

For instance, the tag can be called as shown in the following code snippet. The resulting message will incorporate the words `Belinda` and `19`, just as you would expect.

```
<CFX_HelloWorld
NAME="Belinda"
AGE="19">
```

Of course, you can provide dynamic expressions to the tag's attributes, just like any native CFML tag. For instance, you could supply values from the SESSION and FORM scopes like so:

```
<CFX_HelloWorld
NAME="#SESSION.FirstName#
AGE="#FORM.Age#">
```

If a ColdFusion page tries to call the tag without supplying the NAME or AGE attributes, an exception will be thrown, resulting in a standard error message

Understanding the Java Code

Even though it's a very simple example, I'd like to spend a few moments going over a few key elements of the <CFX_HelloWorld> source code. For starters, take another look at the first few lines of the example (Listing 79.1); these are the lines that make it possible for ColdFusion to treat the class as a CFX tag.

Basically, every Java CFX tag needs to be a public class that implements the CustomTag interface in the com.allaire.cfx package. There isn't a whole lot to the CustomTag interface; you can think of it as a simple agreement which says that every custom tag must include a processRequest() function like the one shown in Listing 79.1. Each time the CFX tag is used in a ColdFusion page, the server will invoke the processRequest() method, passing information about the current page request to the request and response arguments. (The guts of the tag can then call the various methods exposed by request and response, as listed in the tables from the first part of this chapter.)

When you add these modest requirements up, it means that every Java CFX tag must include the following code skeleton, nearly verbatim. The only thing that will change from tag to tag is the name of the class (here, it's HelloWorld):

```
import com.allaire.cfx.* ;
public class HelloWorld implements CustomTag {
public void processRequest( Request request, Response response )
throws Exception
{
...CFX tag logic goes here...
}
}
```

The remainder of Listing 79.1 is simple. The request.attributeExists() method from Table 79.2 is used to make sure that the NAME and AGE attributes are passed to the tag each time it is used. If not, the standard Java throw statement is used to create an exception, which will bubble up to the ColdFusion server for display on the calling page.

Assuming the attributes have been provided, execution proceeds to the response.write() lines. As explained in Table 79.4, the response.write() method inserts any string into the current ColdFusion page, much like <cfoutput> or WriteOutput() in CFML (or response.getWriter().write() in a Java Servlet). In this case, the strings are a combination of static text and the actual values of the NAME and AGE attributes, available from the request.getAttribute() method (see Table 79.2).

That's it!

Compiling the CFX Tag

With the Java code written, the next step is to compile it into a Java class file. If you're using a dedicated Java IDE, you can probably just hit a Compile button on some kind of toolbar, but for this discussion I'll assume you need to compile the class manually using Sun's `javac` compiler.

If you don't have a copy of Sun's Java SDK (also known as the JDK) on your system, you will need to download one now. You can download the SDK at no charge from `http://java.sun.com`. Go ahead and run the installation program, making a mental note of the directory that the SDK gets installed into as you go.

NOTE

You can use any modern version of the SDK to compile your CFX tags, but for consistency's sake I would recommend using a version equal to (or later than) the version of the JRE that ColdFusion is using as its run-time engine

To compile your CFX, use `javac` on the command line to compile the `HelloWorld.java` file as shown below, adjusting the paths to the `cfx.jar` and `HelloWorld.java` files as appropriate for your system:

```
javac -classpath c:\Cfusion8\lib\cfx.jar HelloWorld.java
```

The `cfx.jar` file contains the `com.allaire.cfx` package, which defines the `Request` and `Response` interfaces referred to in the skeletal snippet shown in the previous section (and in Listing 79.1). The `cfx.jar` file is installed automatically to the ColdFusion lib folder when you install ColdFusion. The compiler needs to be able to find this file in order to be able to compile the class; typically, you provide the location using the `-classpath` switch as shown above. Consult the Java SDK documentation for the `javac` utility for details on the `-classpath` switch.

NOTE

Depending on how your system is configured, you may also need to provide a full path to the `javac` executable, which is located in the bin subfolder within the folder to which the Java SDK was installed.

After you compile the tag, a file named `HelloWorld.class` will appear in the same folder where the `HelloWorld.java` file is located. Copy this file to the `WEB-INF/`classes folder within ColdFusion's program root (typically `c:\coldfusion8\wwwroot\WEB-INF\`classes if you're using a Windows server).

NOTE

I'm having you place the class file in the `WEB-INF/classes` folder because that is recommended by Adobe as a good place for CFX class files during testing and development. Once you have finished developing the tag, you can place the class on your production servers in just about any location. The only caveat is that the class needs to be somewhere within the Class Path specified in the Java and JVM page of the ColdFusion Administrator.

NOTE

The ColdFusion documentation also refers to the `WEB-INF/classes` folder as a good place to put your class files during development. The documentation suggests that one of these folders (the `WEB-INF/classes` folder or the `coldfusion8/lib` folder) is meant to ease development by eliminating the need to restart ColdFusion after a Java CFX has been recompiled.

If you want, you can tell `javac` to place the class file directly in the lib folder as it is being compiled. As an example, I used the command shown below to compile the class. Of course, I typed this all on one line, but it's too long to print on one line in this book:

```
c:\jdk1.6\bin\javac c:\inetpub\wwwroot\79\HelloWorld.java -classpath
c:\coldfusion8\lib\cfx.jar -d c:\coldfusion8\wwwroot\WEB-INF\classes -verbose
```

This command assumes that the Java SDK was installed to the c:\jdk1.6 folder, that you are using the built-in Web server, that the `HelloWorld.java` file is stored with the other listings for this chapter (within the `ows` branch of the Web server document root), and that ColdFusion was installed to the default `c:\coldfusion8` location. Make whatever path adjustments are necessary for your system. You can leave off the `-verbose` switch if you want; it just causes `javac` to display some additional messages while it is compiling the class.

Registering the New Tag

Now that the class has been compiled and placed into ColdFusion's lib folder, the only thing left to do is to register the new tag in the ColdFusion Administrator. Follow these steps to register the tag:

1. Navigate to the CFX Tags page of the ColdFusion Administrator.
2. Press the Register Java CFX button. The Add/Edit Java CFX Tag page appears.
3. For the Tag Name field, enter the name of the tag, including the `CFX_` part but without the angle brackets (for this example, you will enter `CFX_HelloWorld`). The names of CFX tags are not case sensitive, so you don't need to get the capitalization exactly right. That said, it makes sense to use the same capitalization that you plan to use in your ColdFusion code.
4. For the Class Name field, enter the name of the class file, but without the .class extension. This part is case sensitive, so the capitalization you use here must match the capitalization of the class file (which, in turn, always matches the name of the class as specified in the Java code itself).
5. If you wish, enter a Description for the tag. The description comes in handy during development if several people on your team are creating different CFX tags.
6. Click the submit button to register the tag. The tag will now appear in the Registered CFX Tags list, indicating that it is ready for use in your ColdFusion pages.

Using the New Tag

Now that the `<CFX_HelloWorld>` tag has been written, compiled, and registered in the ColdFusion Administrator, it's ready to be used in your pages. Listing 79.2 shows the code for the simple test page.

Listing 79.2 `HelloWorldDemo.cfm`—Using the `<CFX_HelloWorld>` Tag

```
<!---
Filename: HelloWorldDemo.cfm
Author: Nate Weiss (NMW)
Purpose: Demonstrates how to use a CFX tag in a ColdFusion page
--->

<html>
<head>
<title>Using &lt;CFX_HelloWorld&gt;</title>
</head>
<body>

<!--- Invoke the Java CFX tag --->
<CFX_HelloWorld
NAME="Belinda"
AGE="19">

</body>
</html>
```

A Word on Exceptions

It's worth noting that the exceptions created by the `throw` statement in Listing 79.1 become true ColdFusion exceptions that behave just like exceptions thrown by native CFML tags, or by the `<cfthrow>` tag. The look and feel of the error messages can be customized with the `<cferror>` tag.

You can even catch exceptions thrown by a CFX and handle them intelligently, using `<cftry>` and `<cfcatch>`, like so:

```
<cftry>
<CFX_HelloWorld
NAME="#SESSION.FirstName#"
AGE="#FORM.Age#">

<cfcatch type="Any">
...error handling code goes here...
</cfcatch>
</cftry>
```

Returning Query Objects

Now that you've seen how to create a simple CFX tag with Java, it's time to move on to something a bit more complicated and useful. Our next project will be a CFX tag called `<CFX_DatabaseMetaData>`, which can be used to inspect the structure of a database on the fly. To use the tag in a ColdFusion page, you will specify the type of information you want (a list of tables, columns, indexes, or the like), and the tag will return a query object filled with items like column names, table names, data types, and so on.

Table 79.11 shows the syntax that will be supported by the completed tag.

Table 79.11 `<CFX_DatabaseMetaData>` Tag Syntax

ATTRIBUTE	DESCRIPTION
`action`	Required. A string indicating the type of information you are interested in, such as `GetTables` or `GetColumns`. You can provide any of the actions listed in Table 79.12.
`driver`	Required. The name of the JDBC driver to use. For ODBC databases, you can use Sun's ODBC Bridge driver, as in `driver="sun.jdbc.odbc.JdbcOdbcDriver."`
`connect`	Required. Whatever connection information the driver needs to connect to the database. In the case of ODBC data sources, you can use a string in the form `jdbc:odbc:dsn_name`, as in `connect="jdbc:odbc:ows"` for the Orange Whip Studios example database.
`username`	Required. The username for the data source (may be case sensitive).
`password`	Required. The password for the data source (may be case sensitive).
`name`	Required. Like the name attribute for `<cfquery>`, a name for the query object that the tag returns. The returned query will contain different columns depending on the action you choose, as listed in Table 79.12.
`dbcatalog`	Optional. The catalog name that you want to get information about. With most database systems, the catalog name is the name or name of the database. If you don't specify a catalog name, all information is returned (for all available catalogs or databases). Can be used for all actions except `GetCatalogs` and `GetSchemas`.
`dbschema`	Optional. The name of the database schema. Not all database systems have the notion of a schema; for Access databases, specifying this attribute will generate an error. For SQLServer databases, the schema is often `dbo`. Can be used for all actions except `GetCatalogs` and `GetSchemas`.
`dbtablename`	Optional. The name of the table you want to get information about. Omit or leave blank for all tables. Can be used for `GetColumns`, `GetTables`, `GetViews`, `GetIndexInfo`, and `GetPrimaryKeys`.
`dbcolumnname`	Optional. The name of the column you want information about. Omit or leave blank for all columns. Can be used for `GetColumns` and `GetProcedureColumns`.
`dbprocedurename`	Optional. The name of the stored procedure you want information about; omit or leave blank for all procedures. Can be used for `GetProcedures` or `GetProcedureColumns`.

Table 79.12 shows the various actions you can specify for the tag's `action` attribute. The query object returned by the tag will contain different information based on which action you choose, as shown in this table.

Table 79.12 Information Returned by `<CFX_DatabaseMetaData>` Actions

ACTION	DESCRIPTION	COLUMNS RETURNED
`GetTables`	A listing of tables in the database. The returned query includes these columns: By default, all tables are returned; you can filter the list using the DBCATALOG, DBSCHEMA, or DBTABLENAME attributes.	TABLE_CAT, TABLE_NAME, TABLE_SCHEM, and TABLE_TYPE
`GetViews`	Same as `GetTables`, except for views.	TABLE_CAT, TABLE_NAME, TABLE_SCHEM, and TABLE_TYPE
`GetColumns`	A listing of columns. All columns in the entire database will be returned unless you specify a DBTABLENAME (or DBSCHEMA or DBCATALOG).	COLUMN_NAME, COLUMN_SIZE, IS_NULLABLE, SQL_DATA_TYPE, TABLE_CAT, TABLE_NAME, TABLE_SCHEM, and TYPE_NAME
`GetCatalogs`	A listing of catalogs (databases).	TABLE_CAT
`GetSchemas`	A listing of schemas.	TABLE_SCHEM
`GetProcedures`	A listing of all stored procedures in the database.	PROCEDURE_NAME
`GetProcedureColumns`	A listing of columns returned by stored procedures. Also includes information about the procedure's input and output parameters.	PROCEDURE_NAME, COLUMN_NAME, COLUMN_TYPE
`GetPrimaryKeys`	A description of primary keys.	TABLE_NAME, COLUMN_NAME, KEY_SEQ
`GetIndexInfo`	A description of the indexes in the database.	ASC_OR_DESC, COLUMN_NAME, TABLE_NAME, INDEX_NAME, NON_UNIQUE, TYPE

NOTE

You can get more specific information about the columns returned by each action by looking through the Java SDK documentation for the `java.sql.DatabaseMetaData` interface.

Writing the Java Code

The `<CFX_DatabaseMetaData>` tag will use a number of classes and methods from the `java.sql` package, which are standard, built-in classes supported by the Java 2 SDK and JRE. It's not possible for me to explain everything about these classes in these pages, but here is a quick introduction to the most important classes used in the next example listing:

- `java.sql.DriverManager`. This static class is used to obtain connections to data sources. Its most important method is `getConnection()`, which connects to a database based on a set of connection arguments (the name and location of the database and so on). Before the `getConnection()` method is called, it is traditional to load a database driver using `Class.forName()` (see the Java SDK documentation for details).

- `java.sql.Connection`. This class is returned by `getConnection()` and represents an active connection to a database. In this example, we will be most interested in its `getMetaData()` method, which returns a `DatabaseMetaData` object (discussed next).
- `java.sql.DatabaseMetaData`. This is the class that the CFX tag is most interested in using. The various actions supported by the tag (see Table 79.12) map directly to many of this class's methods, such as `getTables()` and `getColumns()`. These methods all return `ResultSet` objects containing the requested information.
- `java.sql.ResultSet`. This class is the Java equivalent to a ColdFusion query recordset. Within the CFX tag, the `ResultSet` object returned by `DatabaseMetaData` is converted to a ColdFusion query using the methods outlined in Table 79.6.
- `java.sql.ResultSetMetaData`. This class is conceptually similar to `DatabaseMetaData` in that it returns metadata (column names, data types, and so on), but is smaller in scope and only returns metadata about a particular `ResultSet`, rather than the database as a whole. This CFX tag uses this class to get the names of the columns in the `ResultSet` returned by `DatabaseMetaData`.

Listing 79.3 shows how these objects can be used together to create the `<CFX_DatabaseMetaData>` tag. This is a relatively long listing, but it you look at it part by part you'll see that the code is really quite simple and straightforward. To a large extent, you will find examples in the Java SDK documentation that contain lines quite similar to many of the lines in this listing.

Listing 79.3 `DatabaseMetaData.java`—Using Functionality from the `java.sql` Package in a CFX Tag

```
import com.allaire.cfx.* ; import java.sql.* ;
public class DatabaseMetaData implements CustomTag
{ // Constant string for error messages final String msgError = "Error occurred in a
<CFX_DATABASEMETADATA> tag. ";
// This gets called each time the tag is used in a ColdFusion page
public void processRequest( Request request, Response response )
throws Exception
{
// Obtain the values for the tag's attributes, and throw exceptions
// if any of the required attributes have not been provided.
String strAction = getTagAttr("ACTION", request);
String userName = getTagAttr("USERNAME", request);
String password = getTagAttr("PASSWORD", request);
String driver = getTagAttr("DRIVER", request);
String connect = getTagAttr("CONNECT", request);
String strQueryName = getTagAttr("NAME", request);
// These are optional attributes
String DBCatalog = getTagAttr("DBCATALOG", request, null);
String DBSchema = getTagAttr("DBSCHEMA", request, null);
String DBTableName = getTagAttr("DBTABLENAME", request, "%");
String DBColumnName = getTagAttr("DBCOLUMNNAME", request, "%");
String DBProcedureName = getTagAttr("DBPROCEDURENAME", request, "%");
```

Listing 79.3 (continued)

```
// For the DBTableName attribute, consider an empty string to mean null
//if (DBTableName.equals("")) DBTableName = null;

// Load the specified database driver
Class.forName(driver).newInstance();

// Attempt to connect to the data source
Connection conn = DriverManager.getConnection(connect, userName, password);

// Get the metadata object from the database connection
java.sql.DatabaseMetaData dbmd = conn.getMetaData();

// This ResultSet will be returned to ColdFusion as a query object ResultSet rs =
null;
// Handle ACTION="GetTables" (user wants a list of tables)
if ( strAction.equalsIgnoreCase("GetTables") ) {
String[] types = {"TABLE"};
rs = dbmd.getTables(DBCatalog, DBSchema, DBTableName, types);

// Handle ACTION="GetViews" (user wants a list of views)
} else if ( strAction.equalsIgnoreCase("GetViews") ) {
String[] types = {"VIEW"};
rs = dbmd.getTables(DBCatalog, DBSchema, DBTableName, types);

// Handle ACTION="GetColumns" (user wants a list of columns)
} else if ( strAction.equalsIgnoreCase("GetColumns") ) {
rs = dbmd.getColumns(DBCatalog, DBSchema, DBTableName, DBColumnName);

// Handle ACTION="GetCatalogs" (user wants a list of catalogs)
} else if ( strAction.equalsIgnoreCase("GetCatalogs") ) {
rs = dbmd.getCatalogs();

// Handle ACTION="GetSchemas" (user wants a list of schemas)
} else if ( strAction.equalsIgnoreCase("GetSchemas") ) {
rs = dbmd.getSchemas();

// Handle ACTION="GetProcedures" (a list of stored procedures)
} else if ( strAction.equalsIgnoreCase("GetProcedures") ) {
rs = dbmd.getProcedures(DBCatalog, DBSchema, DBProcedureName);

// Handle ACTION="GetProcedureColumns" (list of stored procedure columns) } else if
( strAction.equalsIgnoreCase("GetProcedureColumns") ) { rs =
dbmd.getProcedureColumns(DBCatalog, DBSchema, DBProcedureName, DBColumnName);
// Handle ACTION="GetPrimaryKeys"
} else if ( strAction.equalsIgnoreCase("GetPrimaryKeys") ) {
rs = dbmd.getPrimaryKeys(DBCatalog, DBSchema, DBTableName);

// Handle ACTION="GetIndexInfo"
} else if ( strAction.equalsIgnoreCase("GetIndexInfo") ) {
rs = dbmd.getIndexInfo(DBCatalog, DBSchema, DBTableName, false, false);

// Throw an error if the ACTION attribute was not recognized
} else {
throw new Exception("Unknown ACTION attribute!");
}
```

Listing 79.3 (continued)

```
// The rs ResultSet now contains the metadata info about tables/columns
// Return it to the calling ColdFusion page as a query
returnAsQuery(rs, strQueryName, response);
}

// Helper function that accepts any java.sql.ResultSet // and returns it to
ColdFusion as a CFML query object private void returnAsQuery(ResultSet rs, String
name, Response response) throws Exception { // Get metadata about the ResultSet (so
we can find out its column names) ResultSetMetaData rsmd = rs.getMetaData();
// Create an array of strings to hold the ResultSet's column names
String[] arColumns = new String[rsmd.getColumnCount()];

// Fill the array with this ResultSet's column names
for (int col = 1; col <= rsmd.getColumnCount(); col++ ) {
arColumns[col-1] = rsmd.getColumnName(col);
};

// Create a new com.allaire.Query object
Query q = response.addQuery(name, arColumns);

// For each row of the ResultSet...
while ( rs.next() ) {
// Add a row to the CFML query
int row = q.addRow();

// For each column of the ResultSet...
for (int col = 1; col <= rsmd.getColumnCount(); col++) {
// Copy the data at this row/column from ResultSet to Query
// (an error will be thrown if the data can't be read as a string)
q.setData(row, col, rs.getString(col));
};
};

}

// Helper function that returns the value of an attribute
// An exception is thrown if the attribute was not provided
private String getTagAttr(String name, Request request)
throws Exception
{
if ( request.attributeExists(name) ) {
return request.getAttribute(name);
} else {
throw new Exception(msgError + "The "+name+" attribute is required.");
};
}

// Helper function that returns the value of an attribute
// If the attribute is not provided, it defaults to def.
private String getTagAttr(String name, Request request, String def)
throws Exception
{
return request.attributeExists(name) ? request.getAttribute(name) : def;
}

}
```

Just by scanning over this example listing with your eye, you can divide this tag into three conceptual parts:

- The `processRequest()` handler method, which is executed by ColdFusion whenever the CFX tag is used in a ColdFusion page. This portion of the code does the work of connecting to the database and retrieving the requested information as a `java.sql.ResultSet` object.
- The `returnAsQuery()` function, which accepts any Java-style `ResultSet` object and makes it available to the calling page as a ColdFusion-style query object. You can cut and paste this code into other CFX tags that need to return `ResultSet` objects as CFML queries.
- The two forms of the `getTagAttr()` function, which wraps around the `attributeExists()` and `getAttribute()` methods from the CFX API that were used previously in Listing 79.1. The first form requires that the attribute be passed to the tag, and the second form makes an attribute be considered optional by using a default value when it is not provided. Again, you can cut and paste these functions into your own CFX tags if you find them convenient.

Within `processRequest()`, the first portion calls `getTagAttr()` repeatedly to establish the required and optional attributes for the tag. If any required attributes are missing, an error message will be shown; optional attributes will be assigned default value when not provided. The next few lines load the JDBC driver class specified in the tag's `driver` attribute with `Class.forName()`, then connect to the data source by supplying the `connect`, `username`, and `password` attributes to `getConnection()`, then create an object called `dbmd` to represent the data source's metadata structure.

Next, a series of `if` and `else if` tests are used to call the appropriate `DatabaseMetaData` method depending on the `action` attribute that the tag is being called with. No matter which method ends up being called (`getTables()`, `getColumns()`, or the like), the result is always a `ResultSet` object called `rs`. The `returnAsQuery()` function is then called to return the data in the `ResultSet` to the calling ColdFusion page.

The main task of `returnAsQuery()` is to create the new CFML query object with the `addQuery()` method. That method requires the new query's column names to be specified as an array of strings, so a few lines of code are required first to obtain the recordset's column names using `getMetaData()`, `getColumnCount()`, and `getColumnName()` (all described in the Java SDK documentation). Once the query has been created, it is a relatively simple task to loop through the `ResultSet`, adding rows to the CFML query and filling it with data from the `ResultSet` along the way. See Table 79.6, earlier in this chapter, for details about the `addQuery()`, `addRow()`, and `setData()` methods used in this portion of the listing.

NOTE

Please consult the Java SDK documentation for more information on the classes and methods used in this listing (except for the ones specific to CFX development; those are detailed in the tables at the beginning of this chapter). Most of them are in the `java.sql` package.

Using the New Tag in ColdFusion

To use the new `<CFX_DatabaseMetaData>` tag in a ColdFusion page, you need to use `javac` to compile Listing 79.1, then register the resulting `DatabaseMetaData.class` file with the ColdFusion Administrator. These steps are described in the "Getting Started" section earlier in this chapter.

You can then use the tag in any CFML page, such as the simple example shown in Listing 79.4. This listing creates a page that allows the user to select from the tables in the `ows.mdb` database file using a drop-down list. When the user selects a table, the names, types, and widths for each of the table's columns are displayed.

CAUTION

Be careful if you place pages such as this on a public Web server. This example won't allow you to view the structure of any table that is not in the `ows` sample database, but code similar to this may make it possible for people to gain unwanted access to the structure of your databases. The tag is not a security risk in and of itself, but you should use it carefully so that your users don't see more than you want them to see.

Listing 79.4 `DatabaseMetaDataDemo.cfm`—Using `<CFX_DatabaseMetaData>` in a ColdFusion Page

```
<!---Filename: DatabaseMetaDataDemo.cfm Author: Nate Weiss (NMW) Purpose: Uses
<CFX_DatabaseMetaData> to display column names and data types --->
<!--- The database table to display information about --->
<cfparam name="FORM.TableName"
type="string"
default="">

<html>
<head>
<title>Database Metadata</title>
</head>

<body>
<h2>Database Metadata</h2>

<!--
Get infomration about the tables in the database
--->
<CFX_DatabaseMetaData

ACTION="GetTables"
USERNAME="Admin"
PASSWORD=""
DRIVER="sun.jdbc.odbc.JdbcOdbcDriver"
CONNECT="jdbc:odbc:ows"
NAME="TablesQuery">

<!--
Provide drop-down list of tables
--->
<cfform action="DatabaseMetaDataDemo.cfm"

method="POST">
<p>
Select Table:
```

Listing 79.4 (continued)

```
<cfselect name="TableName"

query="TablesQuery" value="TABLE_NAME" selected="#FORM.TableName#"
onChange="this.form.submit()"/>
</cfform>
<!--
If a table name has been selected
--->
<cfif FORM.TableName NEQ "">

<cfoutput>
<h3>Columns in Table #TableName#</h3>
</cfoutput>

<!--
Get information about the selected table's columns
--->
<CFX_DatabaseMetaData action="GetColumns"

username="Admin"
password=""
driver="sun.jdbc.odbc.JdbcOdbcDriver"
connect="jdbc:odbc:ows"
dbtablename="#TableName#"
name="FilmsMetaData">

<!--
Display information returned by the CFX tag
--->

<cfoutput query="FilmsMetaData">
<p>
<strong>Column: #COLUMN_NAME#</strong>
<br>
Data Type: #TYPE_NAME#<br>
<cfif TYPE_NAME contains "char">

Maximum Length: #COLUMN_SIZE#<br>
</cfif>
</cfoutput>
</cfif>

</body>
</html>
```

Writing CFX Tags with Visual C++

The first part of this chapter introduced you to the various methods that make up the CFX API. The second part showed you how to work with the methods in Java code.

NOTE

The exact step-by-step instructions will vary based on the version of Visual Studio or Visual C++ you are using.

NOTE

Technically, you can use the CFX API for C++ to create CFX tags in other languages and development environments. For instance, it is possible to create CFX tags using Borland's Delphi product; you can find information about this on the Web. That said, Java and C++ are the only languages that the API is officially designed for.

Getting Started

The next few pages will walk you through the process of creating a new tag with the C++ version of the CFX API. The basic steps are similar to the steps you follow when creating a tag with Java:

1. Writing the C++ code in Visual C++.
2. Compiling the C++ code into the corresponding `.dll` file.
3. Registering the new CFX tag in the ColdFusion Administrator.

Installing the Tag Wizard and Libraries

The best way to start a new CFX tag is with the ColdFusion Tag Wizard, which is a simple tool that plugs into the New Project dialog in Visual C++. The wizard is not distributed with ColdFusion, but is freely available from the Adobe Web site. It is also included with this chapter's listings for your convenience.

To install the CFX Tag Wizard, follow these steps:

1. If Visual C++ is currently running, close it.
2. Copy the cfxwiz_vc50.awx file to Visual Studio's Template folder.
3. Copy the `cfx.h` file from the `Cfusion8\cfx\include` folder to the Visual C++ Include folder.
4. Locate the `CreateRegistryKey.reg` file (included with this chapter's listings) and double-click on it. If you get a confirmation message, click OK to accept the change to the Registry. After a moment, you should receive a message saying the information was imported successfully.
5. Start Visual C++. The ColdFusion Tag Wizard should appear if you choose File, New, then select the Projects tab.

Starting a New CFX Tag Project

Now that the ColdFusion Tag Wizard has been installed, you can use it to quickly create skeleton code for a new CFX tag. Just follow these steps:

1. Launch Visual Studio or Visual C++.
2. Choose File, New.... The New dialog appears.
3. Select the Projects tab, then select the Cold Fusion Tag Wizard.

4. Enter a name for your new project in the Project name field. I recommend using the name of the CFX tag. For this example, use `CFX_ComputeStandardDeviation` as the project name.
5. Leave the Create new workspace and Win32 options checked.
6. Click OK. The ColdFusion Tag Wizard appears.
7. Enter the name of your CFX tag, including the `CFX_` part. If you wish, you may also enter a description.
8. Unless you have a specific reason for not doing so, leave the As A Statically Linked Library option checked.
9. Click the Finish button to create your new project.

You should now have a new project workspace that includes a number of new files. For the most part, you need only concern yourself with the `ProcessTagRequest()` function, which is implemented in the `Request.cpp` file generated by the Wizard. You can get to this function easily by clicking on the `ProcessTagRequest` item in the `ClassView` tree.

Listing 79.5 shows the code generated by the ColdFusion Tag Wizard. In the next section, this code will be modified to create a CFX tag that actually does something useful.

Listing 79.5 Code Generated Automatically by the Tag Wizard

```
///////////////////////////////////////////////////////////////////////
//
// CFX_COMPUTESTANDARDDEVIATION - Cold Fusion custom tag
//
// Copyright 2002. All Rights Reserved.
//

#include "stdafx.h" // Standard MFC libraries
#include "cfx.h" // CFX Custom Tag API

void ProcessTagRequest( CCFXRequest* pRequest )
{
try
{
// Retrieve attributes passed to the tag
// For example:
// LPCSTR lpszColor = pRequest->GetAttribute("COLOR") ;
// Write output back to the user here...
pRequest->Write( "Hello from CFX_COMPUTESTANDARDDEVIATION!" ) ;

// Output optional debug info
if ( pRequest->Debug() )
{
pRequest->WriteDebug( "Debug info..." ) ;
}
}

// Catch Cold Fusion exceptions & re-raise them
```

Listing 79.5 (CONTINUED)

```
catch( CCFXException* e )
{
pRequest->ReThrowException( e ) ;
}

// Catch ALL other exceptions and throw them as
// Cold Fusion exceptions (DO NOT REMOVE! --
// this prevents the server from crashing in
// case of an unexpected exception)
catch( ... )
{
pRequest->ThrowException(
"Error occurred in tag CFX_COMPUTESTANDARDDEVIATION",
"Unexpected error occurred while processing tag." ) ;
}

}
```

Writing the C++ Code

At this point, you could compile and register the new tag using the steps described in the next section. If you do so, the code generated by the Wizard will simply display a "Hello, World" type of message when the tag is actually used in a ColdFusion page. Of course, to actually give your new tag its functionality, you need to remove the line that outputs the "Hello, World" message and add your own C++ code that accomplishes whatever task you want the tag to perform.

The code example we'll be discussing in this chapter creates a CFX tag called `<CFX_Compute StandardDeviation>`. The tag accepts a query recordset and computes the *standard deviation* of the numbers in one of the query's columns. Tools like Excel provide built-in functions for computing standard deviations and other common statistical tasks, but CFML does not. The problem can be solved fairly easily with C++, so it makes for a good CFX tag example.

NOTE

If you're not familiar with what a standard deviation is, it's a statistical measure commonly used for analyzing data. Basically, the standard deviation can be thought of as a way of describing the similarity of a set of numbers. You're no doubt already familiar the concept of a mathematical average (also called the mean), right? Well, the standard deviation measures how much the individual numbers tend to deviate from the average. A set of numbers that fluctuates wildly from number to number will have a higher standard deviation; numbers that fluctuate less will have a lower standard deviation. If all the numbers are the same (which is another way of saying that they all conform exactly to the average), the standard deviation is zero. In any case, the standard deviation (and the related concept of variance) forms the foundation of many strategies for analyzing trends in data, so this CFX tag can put you on the path of creating pages that perform relatively sophisticated data analysis.

NOTE

The tag computes the population standard deviation, which means that it is most appropriate for analyzing a complete set of data. You could easily alter it to compute the sample standard deviation instead, which would make it more appropriate for analyzing a random subset of the data.

The attributes for the new tag are listed in Table 79.13. If you want to see how this tag is used in a ColdFusion page, skip ahead to Listing 79.7.

Table 79.13 `<CFX_ComputeStandardDeviation>` Tag Syntax

ATTRIBUTE	DESCRIPTION
`query`	The name of a query, such as the result of a `<cfquery>` tag, that contains numbers for which to compute the standard deviation.
`column`	The column of the query that contains the numbers for which to compute the standard deviation.
`variable`	A variable name; the tag will return the computed standard deviation (a single number) in the variable you specify here.

Listing 79.6 shows the C++ source code used to create the `<CFX_ComputeStandardDeviation>` tag. The code is quite simple. About half of it is concerned only with the actual mathematical computations, which have little to do with the CFX API itself. The remainder (mostly at the top and bottom of the listing) are straightforward CFX calls that use the methods described in the first section of this chapter to exchange information with the ColdFusion page using the tag.

Listing 79.6 `Request.cpp`—C++ Source Code for the `<CFX_ComputeStandardDeviation>` Tag

```
////////////////////////////////////////////////////////////////////// // //
CFX_COMPUTESTANDARDDEVIATION - Cold Fusion custom tag // // Copyright 2002. All
Rights Reserved. //
#include "stdafx.h" // Standard MFC libraries
#include "cfx.h" // CFX Custom Tag API
#include "math.h"

void ProcessTagRequest( CCFXRequest* pRequest )
{
try
{
/* BEGIN ATTRIBUTE VALIDATION */

// Make sure a VARIABLE attribute was actually passed to the tag
if ( pRequest->AttributeExists("VARIABLE")==FALSE ) {
pRequest->ThrowException(
"Error in CFX_ComputeStandardDeviation Tag",
"No VARIABLE attribute specified.");
}

// Retrieve value of VARIABLE attribute
LPCSTR lpszVariable = pRequest->GetAttribute("VARIABLE") ;

// Make sure a VARIABLE attribute was actually passed to the tag
if ( pRequest->AttributeExists("COLUMN")==FALSE ) {
pRequest->ThrowException(
"Error in CFX_ComputeStandardDeviation Tag",
"No COLUMN attribute specified.");
}
```

Listing 79.6 (continued)

```
// Retrieve value of VARIABLE attribute
LPCSTR lpszColumn = pRequest->GetAttribute("COLUMN") ;

// Retrieve the query specified in the tag's QUERY attribute
CCFXQuery* pQuery = pRequest->GetQuery();

// Make sure a query was actually passed to the tag
if ( pQuery == NULL ) {
pRequest->ThrowException(
"Error in CFX_ComputeStandardDeviation Tag",
"No QUERY provided.");
}

// Find the index position of the column named in the COLUMN attribute
int colIndex = pQuery->GetColumns()->GetIndexForString( lpszColumn );

// If the column specified in COLUMN attribute does not exist in query
if ( colIndex == CFX_STRING_NOT_FOUND ) {
pRequest->ThrowException(
"Error in CFX_ComputeStandardDeviation Tag",
"The COLUMN attribute does not match up to a column in the query.");
}

/* FINISHED WITH ATTRIBUTE VALIDATION */

// Local variables
double dTotal = 0;
double dMean = 0;
double dStdDev = 0;
double dSumSq = 0;
double dVariance = 0;
int iValueCount = 0;

// Compute the total of all the numbers in the data set for ( int Row = 1; Row <=
pQuery->GetRowCount(); Row++) {
// Get the value (as a string) from the query
LPCSTR thisVal = pQuery->GetData(Row, colIndex);

// Assuming the value is not an empty string
if ( strlen(thisVal) > 0) {

// Add this value to the total
dTotal += atof(thisVal);

// Increment the counter of non-null values
iValueCount++;

// Include optional debug messages for skipped rows
} else if ( pRequest->Debug() ) {
char buffer[50];
sprintf(buffer, "Skipping row %i because value is empty/NULL.", Row);
pRequest->WriteDebug(buffer);

}
}
```

Listing 79.6 (CONTINUED)

```
// The rest of the computations will be dividing by iValueCount, // so check it to
protect ourselves against a divide-by-zero situation if ( iValueCount > 0 ) {
// Compute the mean (average) of the numbers
dMean = dTotal / iValueCount;

// Begin calculating the variance
for ( Row = 1; Row <= pQuery->GetRowCount(); Row++) {
// Get the value (as a string) from the query
LPCSTR thisVal = pQuery->GetData(Row, colIndex);
// Assuming the value is not an empty string
if ( strlen(thisVal) > 0) {
dSumSq += pow( dMean - atof(thisVal), 2);
}
}
// Finish computing the variance
dVariance = dSumSq / iValueCount;

// The standard deviation is the square root of the variance dStdDev =
sqrt(dVariance); }
// Convert the standard deviation to a string,
// then return it to the calling ColdFusion page
char result[20];
gcvt(dStdDev, 10, result);
pRequest->SetVariable( lpszVariable, result);
}

// Catch Cold Fusion exceptions & re-raise them
catch( CCFXException* e )
{
pRequest->ReThrowException( e ) ;
}

// Catch ALL other exceptions and throw them as
// Cold Fusion exceptions (DO NOT REMOVE! --
// this prevents the server from crashing in

// case of an unexpected exception)
catch( ... )
{
pRequest->ThrowException(
"Error occurred in tag CFX_COMPUTESTANDARDDEVIATION",
"Unexpected error occurred while processing tag." ) ;
}

}
```

As you can see, the basic skeleton of the `ProcessTagRequest()` function has not been changed from the code generated by the Tag Wizard (Listing 79.5). An additional `#include` directive for the standard `math.h` library has been added at the top of the listing; all the other changes are within the body of the `try` block within the `ProcessTagRequest()` function. The `ProcessTagRequest()` function serves the same purpose as the `processRequest()` method in the Java interface; basically, ColdFusion will call this function each time the CFX tag is actually used in a ColdFusion page. Think of this function as being similar conceptually to the ubiquitous `main()` function that would appear in a stand-alone C++ program.

NOTE

Actually, you can change the name of the `ProcessTagRequest()` function if you wish, as long as you specify the same name in the Procedure field when you register the tag with the ColdFusion Administrator (discussed in the next section). You can even create several custom tags in a single C++ file (and thus in one compiled `.dll` file), simply by including several functions that have the same basic form as `ProcessTagRequest()` (including the `try` and `catch` blocks as shown in Listing 79.5). However, the customary thing is to leave the name of the function alone and simply create each custom tag as a separate C++ project. I recommend that you do the same unless there is some specific reason why you really want them all compiled into the same DLL.

At the top of `ProcessTagRequest()`, the `AttributeExists()` and `GetAttribute()` methods are used to make sure that the appropriate attributes have been passed to the tag (refer back to Table 79.13). If an attribute is missing, the `ThrowException()` method is used to throw a ColdFusion-style exception, which in turn displays an error message in the calling page (unless the exception is caught with `<cftry>` and `<cfcatch>`).

NOTE

Please refer to the "A Word on Exceptions" section, earlier in this chapter, for a few additional notes on throwing exceptions from CFX tags.

Some of the attribute validation code at the top of this listing involves making sure that a valid ColdFusion query has been passed to the tag. As explained near Table 79.7 (near the beginning of this chapter), the only way to pass a query to a CFX tag is to provide a `query` attribute to the tag; the query is then accessible to the tag via the `pRequest->GetQuery()` method, as shown in Listing 79.6. Once `GetQuery()` has been used to get a reference to the query, the `GetRowCount()`, `GetData()`, and other methods listed in Table 79.7 can be used to retrieve or modify the data in the query. For instance, this tag uses `pQuery->GetColumns()->GetIndexForString()` to verify that the column name specified in the `COLUMN` attribute of the tag actually exists in the query that was passed to the tag. It also uses `pQuery->GetRowCount()` to make sure that the query includes at least one row.

NOTE

Queries cannot be passed using any attribute name other than `query`; therefore, only one query can be passed to any given CFX tag. In contrast, CFX tags are free to return as many queries as they wish, simply by calling `pRequest->AddQuery()` multiple times (using a different query name each time).

Once the tag's attributes have been reasonably validated, execution continues to the next portion of the code (beginning with the series of `double` declarations). After defining a few local variables, this portion of the code uses two `for` loops to perform the necessary mathematical calculations. Each of the loops iterates from 1 to the number of rows in the query; within the loops, the value of the `Row` variable indicates the row currently being processed. The first thing each of these loops does is to populate a string variable called `thisVal` with the current value of the column specified in the tag's `COLUMN` attribute. It's worth noting that values retrieved from queries are always retrieved as strings; if you want to work with values as numbers, you need to use `atof()` or some similar function to convert the string to the desired numeric data type.

Speaking of which, the first loop uses an `if` test to make sure that the length of the current row's value is not zero (that is, to make sure that the value is not an empty string). If it is, that probably means that a `NULL` is occupying that row of the query. ColdFusion represents null values as empty strings whenever such a value is accessed as string; since `GetData()` always accesses all data as strings, you will always get an empty string for any null value in a query.

If the value is not an empty string, the tag adds the current numeric value to the `dTotal` variable and increments the `iValueCount` variable by one. When the first `for` loop is complete, `dTotal` will hold the total (sum) of all numbers in the data set, and `iValueCount` will hold the number of data points included in the total (that is, the number of rows that were not skipped because of suspected null values).

If, on the other hand, a particular value is determined to be an empty string, the code checks to see if the tag has been called with a `DEBUG` attribute. If so, it uses `pRequest->WriteDebug()` to display a debugging message whenever an empty string is found in the data set. See the "Generating Debug Output" section, later in this chapter, to see what the debugging messages look like.

In any case, as long as at least one valid data point was found in the query, the next line of code computes the mathematical average (mean) of the data points by dividing the `dTotal` by `iValueCount`. The average is stored in the variable called `dMean` (which is not meant to imply that it's demeaning to be average). Another `for` loop is used to iterate over the set of numbers again, this time subtracting each value from the mean and squaring the result. After this loop finishes, the average of these results is computed by dividing by the number of data points; this is called the *variance*. The square root of the variance is then computed with the standard `sqrt()` function; this is the standard deviation.

The tag has now completed its work, so the only thing left to do is to return the standard deviation to the calling ColdFusion page using `pRequest->SetVariable()`. Since `SetVariable()` only accepts string values, the standard deviation must first be converted to a string using the standard `gcvt()` function.

NOTE

The `atof()` function returns 0 if it encounters a string that can't be parsed into a number. It doesn't generate an error. This means that this CFX tag will treat anything other than a number as a 0, which will affect the tag's computations. In other words, the tag is smart enough to skip over null values, but it is not smart enough to skip over other non-numeric data points. This should not be a problem because a column would not typically include both numbers and strings.

Compiling Your New CFX Tag

To compile the tag, simply choose the Build option from the Build menu in Visual C++, or use the Build toolbar button. Assuming there are no syntax or other problems with the code, the compiler should be able to compile the tag in a few seconds. The result will be a Dynamic Link Library (`.dll`) file, located in either the `project\Debug` or `project\Release` subfolder of Visual Studio's My Projects folder (where the *project* part is most likely the name of your CFX tag).

It's worth noting that you will be building a Debug version of the DLL by default. I recommend switching to the Win32 Release configuration before compiling the tag. You may use the default Win32 Debug configuration if you wish during testing, but you will probably be doing most of your debugging via `pRequest->WriteDebug()` rather than conventional debugging methods, so the Win32 Debug build is unlikely to do you much good in terms of actual debugging. To switch to the Win32 Release configuration, choose Build, Set Active Configuration from the Visual C++ menu.

NOTE

Either type of build should perform the same way in your ColdFusion pages, but the debug version will be larger and cannot be deployed to ColdFusion servers that don't contain Microsoft's debugging symbols. In general, the debugging symbols are only installed on machines that have Visual C++ installed on them, which means that debug builds of CFX tags will probably only work on the ColdFusion server installed on your local machine (if any).

Registering the New Tag

Once the tag has been compiled, you need to register it in the ColdFusion Administrator. The registration process is simple and very similar to the process for Java CFX tags. Just follow these steps:

1. Open the ColdFusion Administrator and navigate to the CFX Tags page.
2. Click the Register C++ CFX button. The Add/Edit C++ CFX Tag page appears.
3. In the Tag Name field, enter the name of the tag, including the `CFX_` part. This does not have to be the same as the tag name you used while creating the C++ code, but I recommend that you keep them consistent to keep from getting confused. The tag name is not case sensitive.
4. In the Server Library field, provide the location of the `.dll` file that represents the compiled version of your CFX tag. If you are registering the tag on a ColdFusion server installed on the same machine that you compiled the tag on, you can just specify the DLL's current location within Visual Studio's directory tree. That way, whenever you rebuild the tag, the server will automatically be looking at the newly built version. If the server is not on your local development machine, you will need to copy the DLL to the server's local drive first (you can place the DLL in whatever location you wish).
5. Leave the Procedure field set to `ProcessTagRequest` unless you changed the name of the `ProcessTagRequest()` function produced by the ColdFusion Tag Wizard when you created your project's workspace.
6. Leave the Keep Library Loaded unless your DLL will occupy a large amount of space in the server's memory and will be used infrequently. Another reason to uncheck this box is if your DLL is not thread safe. See the section "Using CFX Tags Safely: Locking and Thread Safety" later in this chapter for details.
7. If you wish, fill in the optional Description field.
8. Press OK to register the tag. It will now appear in the list of registered tags in the CFX Tags page, and is ready for use in your ColdFusion pages.

Using the New Tag

Listing 79.7 shows how the new `<CFX_ComputeStandardDeviation>` tag can be used in a ColdFusion page. First, data from the Films table is retrieved using an ordinary `SELECT` query. Then the CFX tag is called, specifying the `RatingID` column of the query as the column for which to compute the standard deviation. After the tag executes, the computed standard deviation will be available to

ColdFusion in the `FilmsStdDev` variable. Similar steps are used to compute the standard deviation of the prices in the Merchandise table.

Listing 79.7 `ComputeStandardDeviationDemo.cfm`—Computing the Standard Deviation

```
<!---Filename: ComputeStandardDeviationDemo.cfm Author: Nate Weiss (NMW) Purpose:
Computes standard deviations
--->
<!--
Retrieve film information from database
--->
<cfquery datasource="ows"

name="GetFilms">
SELECT * FROM Films
</cfquery>

<!--
Compute the standard deviation of the ratings for each film
--->
<CFX_ComputeStandardDeviation query="GetFilms"

column="RatingID" variable="FilmsStdDev">
<!--
Retrieve merchandise information from database
--->
<cfquery datasource="ows"

name="GetMerch">
SELECT * FROM Merchandise
</cfquery>

<!--
Insert empty row to prove tag is smart enough to skip NULL values
--->
<cfset QueryAddRow(GetMerch)>

<!--
Compute the standard deviation of the merchandise prices
--->
<CFX_ComputeStandardDeviation query="GetMerch"

column="MerchPrice" variable="MerchStdDev">
<html>
<head>
<title>Orange Whip Statistics</title>
</head>

<body>
<h2>Orange Whip Statistics</h2>

<!--
Display the standard deviation
--->
<cfoutput>
```

Listing 79.7 (continued)

```
<p>
Standard deviation of the films' ratings:
<strong>#NumberFormat(FilmsStdDev, "0.00")#</strong>
<br>

<p>
Standard deviation of the merchandise prices:
<strong>#NumberFormat(MerchStdDev, "0.00")#</strong>
<br>

<p>
<emp>(numbers rounded to two decimal points)</emp>
<br>


</cfoutput>
</body>
</html>
```

Because the merchandise prices vary greatly (there are only about a dozen data points in the sample database, but the prices range from $7.50 to $950.00), we will expect to see a relatively high standard deviation. Conversely, since the film ratings vary only slightly (many of the rating values are exactly the same from film to film, and the total range is only from 1 to 6), we will expect to see a low standard deviation. Happily, the page generated by Listing 79.7 is consistent with these expectations.

Other C++ Examples

Other examples of CFX tags created with C++ can be found in the ColdFusion8\cfx\examples folder that gets installed automatically with ColdFusion. The examples include a `<CFX_Directory List>` tag that operates similarly to the built-in `<cfdirectory>` tag, and a `<cfx_nt_userdb>` tag that allows you to add and remove users from a Windows domain or workgroup.

Generating Debug Output

If your CFX tag encounters any problems during its execution, or if you need help figuring out why your tag isn't doing what you expect it to, you can have your tag include debug messages in the calling template. Debug messages can include whatever text you want; usually you use them to display some kind of diagnostic information that indicates whether the tag was able to connect to some kind of data source, was denied access to some kind of file, or encountered some other type of unexpected condition.

In the `<CFX_ComputeStandardDeviation>` example, the tag is expecting to find only numbers in the query column passed to the tag. It knows to skip over null values, and generally does so silently. But since it's avoiding a potential problem, you might want to be able to see which values are being skipped over. The code in Listing 79.6 uses the following lines to output debug messages:

```
if ( pRequest->Debug() )
{ char buffer[50];
  sprintf(buffer, "Skipping row %i because value is empty/NULL.", Row);
 pRequest->WriteDebug(buffer);
}
```

The `pRequest->Debug()` method always returns `FALSE` unless the tag is being called in debug mode, so these lines are usually skipped and thus add almost no overhead to normal tag execution. To call a CFX tag in debug mode, add a `debug` flag (attribute) to the CFX tag when you use it, like so:

```
<!--- Compute the standard deviation of the merchandise prices --->
<CFX_ComputeStandardDeviation
query="GetMerch"
column="MerchPrice"
variable="MerchStdDev"
debug>
```

Whenever a tag is called with the `debug` flag, the `pRequest->Debug()` method (or the `request.debug()` method if you're using Java) always returns `TRUE`, and the `WriteDebug()` method includes the specified text along with the tag name when the page is visited with a browser. You can use this simple but effective debugging facility whenever you want to include special messages for developers but not for the rest of the world.

NOTE

`Debug` behaves like a flag rather than a Boolean (`Yes` or `No`) attribute, so the only thing that matters is whether it is present. The value after the =sign is ignored, so `debug="Yes"` and `debug="No"` both result in debug messages being shown. You must remove the `debug` flag altogether to stop the messages.

NOTE

The `debug` functionality is unfortunately not integrated with the Debugging Settings page of the ColdFusion Administrator, so the settings on that page have no bearing on whether debug messages from CFX tags are shown. In particular, debug messages from CFX tags are not restricted by the Debugging IP Addresses list in the Administrator.

NOTE

The CFX API for Java also includes an additional set of classes for debugging Java CFX tags. You can use the classes to test CFX tags without actually supplying them with run-time attributes in ColdFusion pages. If you find this idea interesting, consult the "ColdFusion Java CFX Reference" section of the CFML Reference that ships with ColdFusion.

Returning Structures from CFX Tags

As you probably already know, ColdFusion supports a feature referred to in the documentation as Smart Structs. The idea behind the Smart Structs feature is to make it easier to construct complex data structures in CFML code. Basically, if you use `<cfset>` or some other mechanism to create a variable, and the variable name contains dots or square brackets such that the new variable would be nested within a structure of structures, ColdFusion will automatically create any intermediary structures necessary to allow the `<cfset>` to execute without errors.

To illustrate, consider the following line:

```
<CFSET OrangeWhip.Actresses.HotList.July = "Belinda Foxile">
```

This line will execute successfully even if the `OrangeWhip` structure does not exist yet. The same goes for the `Actresses` or `HotList` parts.

CFX Tags Are Smart, Too

So what does this have to do with CFX tags? It turns out that the CFX interface uses the same internal functions within the ColdFusion server to set variables. So, if you supply a variable name that contains dots to `response.setVariable()` (in Java) or `Request->SetVariable()` (in C++), ColdFusion will automatically create the intermediary structures needed to set the variable with the name you specify.

For instance, the code listings for this chapter include a file called `Request2.cpp`, which contains the source code for a new CFX tag called `<CFX_ComputeStatistics>`. This listing is very similar to the `<CFX_ComputeStandardDeviation>` tag created earlier in this chapter and takes the same attributes. The difference is that instead of returning a single number, it returns a structure with five keys (values), named `StandardDeviation`, `Variance`, `Mean`, `Sum`, and `Count` (the number of non-null data points).

Aside from the name of the tag, the code is exactly the same as Listing 79.6 except that these lines:

```
// Convert the standard deviation to a string,
// then return it to the calling ColdFusion page
char result[20];
gcvt(dStdDev, 10, result);
pRequest->SetVariable( lpszVariable, result);
```

have been replaced with the following lines:

```
// Return statistics to the calling ColdFusion page
char result[20];
gcvt(dStdDev, 10, result);
pRequest->SetVariable(lpszVariable + ".StandardDeviation", result);
gcvt(dVariance, 10, result);
pRequest->SetVariable(lpszVariable + ".Variance", result);
gcvt(dMean, 10, result);
pRequest->SetVariable(lpszVariable + ".Mean", result);
gcvt(dTotal, 10, result);
pRequest->SetVariable(lpszVariable + ".Sum", result);
gcvt(iValueCount, 10, result);
pRequest->SetVariable(lpszVariable + ".Count", result);
```

NOTE

Because it is a bit long and because all the other lines are the same, I am not including the `<CFX_ComputeStatistics>` source code as a separate printed listing here. However, the Request2.cpp file is included with this chapter's listings, and the Windows-compiled version of the finished tag (`CFX_ComputeStatistics.dll`) is included as well.

Listing 79.8 shows how the new <CFX_ComputeStatistics> tag can be used in a ColdFusion page. The resulting Web page shows the number of data points, the average, the statistical variance, and the standard deviation for each set of data. Note that either dots or square brackets can be used to refer to the members of the returned structure, just like any other CFML structure.

Listing 79.8 `ComputeStatisticsDemo.cfm`—Using Structures Returned by a CFX Tag

```
<!---
Filename: ComputeStatisticsDemo.cfm
Author: Nate Weiss (NMW)
Purpose: Computes standard deviations
--->

<!--
Retrieve film information from database
--->
<cfquery datasource="ows"

name="GetFilms">
SELECT * FROM Films
</cfquery>

<!--
Compute statistics for the ratings of each film
--->
<CFX_ComputeStatistics query="GetFilms"

column="RatingID" variable="FilmsStats">
<!--
Retrieve merchandise information from database
--->
<cfquery datasource="ows"

name="GetMerch">
SELECT * FROM Merchandise
</cfquery>

<!--
Insert empty row to prove tag is smart enough to skip NULL values
--->
<cfset QueryAddRow(GetMerch)>

<!--
Compute statistics for the merchandise prices
--->
<CFX_ComputeStatistics query="GetMerch"

column="MerchPrice" variable="MerchStats">
<html>
<head>
<title>Orange Whip Statistics</title>
</head>

<body>
<h2>Orange Whip Statistics</h2>
```

Listing 79.8 (continued)

```
<!--- Display the statistics --->
<cfoutput> <!--- First for films ---> <h3>Statistics for the film ratings</h3>
Number of data points: <strong>#NumberFormat(FilmsStats["Count"], "0")#</strong>
<br> Average (Mean): <strong>#NumberFormat(FilmsStats["Mean"], ",0.00")#</strong>
<br> Variance: <strong>#NumberFormat(FilmsStats.Variance, ",0.00")#</strong> <br>
Standard Deviation: <strong>#NumberFormat(FilmsStats.StandardDeviation,
",0.00")#</strong> <br>
<!--- Then for merchandise --->
<h3>Statistics for the merchandise prices</h3>
Number of data points:
<strong>#NumberFormat(MerchStats["Count"], "0")#</strong>
<br>
Average:
<strong>#NumberFormat(MerchStats["Mean"], ",0.00")#</strong>
<br>
Variance:
<strong>#NumberFormat(MerchStats.Variance, ",0.00")#</strong>

<br>
Standard Deviation:
<strong>#NumberFormat(MerchStats.StandardDeviation, ",0.00")#</strong>
<br>

</cfoutput>
</body>
</html>
```

An Important Warning

If this all sounds too good to be true, it is—kind of. This whole strategy will fail if there is there is already a variable called `FilmsStats` in the calling ColdFusion page and that variable is anything other than a structure. In such a case, ColdFusion will crash if a C++ CFX attempts to reference the variable as a structure. With a Java CFX, the program won't crash, but the tag will still throw an error. To protect yourself against such a possibility, you could use a line like one of the following, just before calling the CFX tag each time.

This line simply deletes the `FilmsStats` variable if it exists already (if it doesn't exist, nothing happens, so this line does no harm):

```
<cfset StructDelete(VARIABLES, "FilmsStats")>
```

Alternatively, this line creates a new, empty `FilmsStats` structure (regardless of whether it already exists):

```
<cfset FilmsStats = StructNew()>
```

Either line of code, used immediately before the CFX tag, will guard against any potential problems if the CFX tag tries to add nested structures to an existing variable that is not itself a structure. Whew, that was close!

Using CFX Tags Safely: Locking and Thread Safety

Because the ColdFusion server responds to page requests in a multithreaded fashion (meaning that it can process more than one page request at the same time), it is possible that two instances of a CFX tag may execute on the same server at the same time. If the CFX tag is not thread-safe in terms of how it deals with memory or how it works logically, problems might arise unless you take steps to avoid them. Like other concurrency issues, such problems are likely to show up only under load, making it appear that the tag (or ColdFusion itself) does not scale well, when in fact the problem could be avoided by making sure the tag does not execute in more than one page request at once.

Understanding Thread Safety

A full discussion of what it means for a compiled program to be thread-safe is well beyond the scope of what can be explained in this chapter. For purposes of this discussion, it will have to suffice that *thread-safe* basically means that the tag has been coded in such a way that it can run in several threads at the same time without any possibility of the various threads being able to create, change, edit— or, in some instances, merely access-a shared resource (where *shared resource* means any shared variable, memory, file, or the like).

Generally speaking, a CFX tag is probably thread-safe if it does not use any global variables (that is, if none of the variables are declared outside of the `processRequest()` function in Java or the `ProcessTagRequest()` function in C++) and also does not access any external or third-party APIs that themselves are not thread-safe.

NOTE

If you're not familiar with what a thread is, don't worry about it too much right now. In the context of ColdFusion, a thread is basically the same thing conceptually as a page request from a user (because each simultaneous page request is processed by a different worker thread within the server).

Locking CFX Tags with `<cflock>`

You can still use CFX tags even if you know they aren't thread-safe. Just wrap the `<cflock>` tag around every use of the tag, using `type="Exclusive"` and a `name` attribute equal to the name of the CFX tag (or some other name, as long as it is always the same for every single use of the tag). For instance, if you knew (or suspected) that the `<CFX_ComputeStatistics>` tag was not thread-safe, you would use code similar to the following:

```
<cflock type="Exclusive"
name="CFX_ComputeStatistics"
timeout="10">
<!--- Compute statistics for the ratings of each film -->
<CFX_ComputeStatistics query="GetFilms"
column="RatingID"
variable="FilmsStats">
</cflock>
```

If the CFX Tag Works with Files

If the guts of the CFX tag are thread-safe, but you are asking the tag to do something like create or manipulate a file on the server's drive, then you might want to lock access to the file, rather than to the tag itself. The `<cflock>` tags would still surround the CFX tag in your ColdFusion code, but you would most likely use the complete file name as the `NAME` of the lock, rather than the tag. If the tag is merely reading the file, you could use `type="ReadOnly"`; if the tag might be creating or changing the file, you would have to use `type="Exclusive"`.

You would also want to surround other portions of your CFML code that access the same file—regardless of whether they involve CFX tags—with `<cflock>` tags. The `<cflock>` tags should have the same `name` as the ones around the CFX tag itself, and should use `type="Exclusive"` for creation or modifications and `type="ReadOnly"` if merely reading the file.

Keeping the Page Itself in Mind

It's worth noting that just because a tag is thread-safe internally, that doesn't automatically mean that a ColdFusion page's *use* of the tag is thread-safe. For instance, if you were supplying `APPLICATION` or `SESSION` variables to the various attributes of a CFX tag, or if you were asking the CFX tag to set variables in the `APPLICATION` or `SESSION` scope, then it is theoretically possible for a logical "race condition" problem to occur if one page request changes those variables at the same time, perhaps resulting in some kind of data loss or logical data corruption. If the nature of your application is such that this could be a problem (and only you can determine that), you should continue to lock.

NOTE

As you probably already know, the need for locking dramatically decreased as of ColdFusion. That doesn't change the fact that any access to shared resources in CFML pages–whether dealing with CFX tags or not–must be locked if the nature of the application logic (that means your stuff, not ColdFusion's internals) is such that problems could arise if multiple threads execute the code at the same time. For more details on this topic, see Chapter 19, "Introducing the Web Application Framework," in *Adobe ColdFusion 8 Web Application Construction Kit, Volume 1: Getting Started.*

Using CFX Tags with Previous Versions of ColdFusion

CFX tags are not something that can only be used with current versions of ColdFusion. The CFX API was actually the means of extending the server introduced first in the product's history, predating CFML custom tags, user-defined functions, and CFCs.

CFX tags written with C++ can be used with any version of the product after (drum roll, please) ColdFusion 2.0.

CFX tags written with Java can be used with ColdFusion 4.5 or later without any additional software. You can use Java CFX tags with version 4.0 using the `<CFX_J>` add-on package, which was freely available from Adobe's Web site as of this writing.

Of course, the exception to this rule is the newfound ability for CFX tags to return structures to ColdFusion pages (which was first introduced in ColdFusion MX). See the "Returning Structures from CFX Tags" section earlier in this chapter for details.

CHAPTER 80

Working with Gateways

IN THIS CHAPTER

ColdFusion MX 7 introduced some exciting new features into the ColdFusion developer's repertoire, including the ColdFusion event gateway. Event gateways are to application server environments what the `CFQUERY` tag was to database interaction. As you will see, the event gateway technology transforms ColdFusion 8 from just another Web application server to an enterprise services platform, allowing ColdFusion 8 applications to work with just about any other application and/or platform over any well-defined protocol including SMS, RMI, MQ, JSM, AMS, TCP, and UDP. If you have ever worked with message-oriented middleware, much of the paradigm behind event gateways will be obvious to you. On the other hand, if you've not, the ColdFusion event gateway operates like MOM.

Event gateways also allow ColdFusion applications to perform in new and nontrivial ways. You, the developer, can move away from an HTTP-based request/response development approach to event-based frameworks that respond to events created by such things as a folder change or a phone call.

Before you begin this chapter, take a breath and clear your mind. Try to forget what you know about traditional Web development. Read this chapter with an open mind, knowing that there is no possible way a single chapter can cover everything that event gateways can do. The only limit now to ColdFusion 8 is your imagination. Okay, let's begin.

What Is an Event Gateway?

ColdFusion 8 gateways are Java classes that implement an application programming interface (API) provided with the ColdFusion 8 application server. Figure 80.1 shows a high-level diagram of the event gateway communications. Event gateways communicate with the ColdFusion *event gateway services* through `CFEvent` objects, which we will define later in this chapter. The event gateway service system puts `CFEvent` objects, if necessary, in a queue and then passes them to the ColdFusion run-time engine for processing as input to ColdFusion Components (`Listener` CFCs). The `Listener` CFC might return output to the event gateway services subsystem and then back to the event gateway.

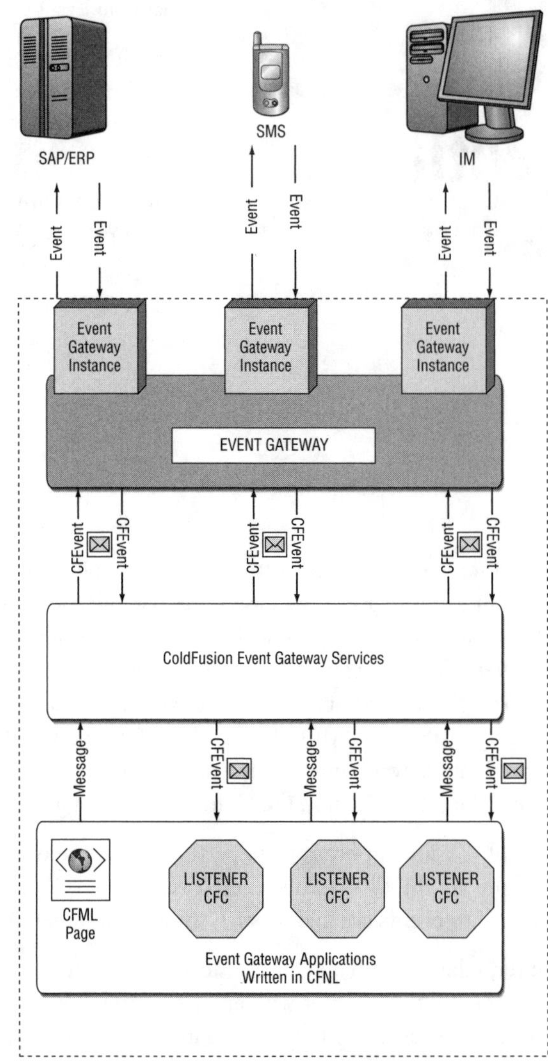

Figure 80.1
ColdFusion event gateway communications.

You create gateway instances from a gateway type. Instances correspond to individual copies of a gateway that are running. Gateway instances are Java objects that are started/stopped through the ColdFusion Administrator. Each gateway instance specifies a CFC to handle incoming messages. You can have more than one instance of an event gateway type, and each instance will have its own configuration. For example, you can have multiple instances of a given gateway type, each with a different login, phone number, buddy name, directories to watch, and so forth.

Simply put, ColdFusion's event gateway exposes the power of J2EE's underlying messaging technology. This allows you to use ColdFusion in a way different from the traditional HTTP-based request/response model. Web application have grown more sophisticated and moved from isolated information-retrieval applications to mission-critical applications that not only expose some applications to users but tie together older processing systems, databases, enterprise resource-planning systems, and so on. As this evolution progressed, developers frequently had to kludge special and proprietary connections to other applications. ColdFusion developers often found it hard to connect to legacy applications, ERP systems, package applications, and other commercial off-the-shelf applications—usually by using a variety of other languages and proprietary integrations tools.

This difficult task was compounded by previous ColdFusion versions sometimes having difficulty scaling. Requests to these applications often hold open a connection and/or thread while ColdFusion connects to another application, retrieves that information, and creates a response, even though no user or application is waiting for a response. For example, a scheduled task that fires off a batch process sending thousands of emails to subscribers could tie up ColdFusion threads for an hour until the process is finished. With ColdFusion event gateways, you can fire an event from a ColdFusion page or CFC and run that batch process in the background, while keeping your ColdFusion threads free to handle Web requests.

Events in ColdFusion are asynchronous requests, which means that a request can occur but the actual requested action can occur at another time; this is different from traditional HTTP requests, which either are fulfilled or timed out. ColdFusion events can reside in a queue where each event is fulfilled when the server has capacity and resources to handle it. This is especially useful for applications in which a transaction or process does not need to happen at the time a user requests it, such as notifying a system that an order has been placed. Asynchronous messaging has many other uses as well.

Categories of Event Gateways

Event gateway systems essentially fall into two categories:

Initiators are ColdFusion 8 applications that generate an event message from a CFC or CFML application page and send the message using an event gateway instance. An example of an initiator would be an application that checks a POP 3 server for new messages and, if new messages are there, sends an SMS notification that forwards the information to your cell phone. This is done by using the `sendGatewayMessage` function to send outgoing messages like these SMS text messages through an event gateway.

Responders are ColdFusion 8 applications that receive an event message from some external source through the listening event gateway instance. The event gateway service then routes the event to a listener CFC that you configure when you create an event instance. Depending on the method triggered by the event, the CFC can return a response. An example could be an IM Help Desk application. Let's say you want to give users the ability to IM your company and get help on technical problems. You could set up an IM event gateway and instance, and have a listener CFC that waits for IMs and then routes them to the first available technical support person or, if no one is free, sends a message asking the customer to wait. The customer is then put into a queue and later connected to the first available technical-support person.

A responder listener CFC listens for an event from a given gateway instance and processes the event structure passed to it, to return a response. The event structure contains the message, along with some detail about its origin. If you dumped the `CFEvent` message, it might look something like Figure 80.2.

Figure 80.2

Detail of a `CFEvent` message.

CFCMETHOD	onAdd	
CFCPATH	C:\Inetpub\wwwroot\gatewaychapter\DirectoryWatcher.cfc	
DATA	FILENAME	C:\Inetpub\wwwroot\gatewaychapter\gallery\aimage.jpg
	LASTMODIFIED	{ts '2007-11-01 17:16:27'}
	TYPE	ADD
GATEWAYID	PotoAlbum	
GATEWAYIDTYPE	FileWatcher	
ORIGINATORID	[empty string]	

Creating a Simple Gateway Application

In this section, we are going to use ColdFusion gateways to create a simple batch process that takes images in a directory and converts them all to thumbnails. With `CFIMAGE`, you can easily accomplish this, but you would most likely not want to make a user who is uploading lots of images at once wait for each image to be processed in a synchronous HTTP request because not only would that most likely cause the user to wait for all the images to be processed, but it would also tie up Web proxy threads that could be used to respond to other HTTP sessions.

For this example, the `DirectoryWatcher` event gateway (supplied with ColdFusion 8) will create a simple responder application. The `DirectoryWatcher` gateway sends events to a listener CFC when a file is created, deleted, or modified in a directory you tell the gateway to watch. It runs checks the directory at an interval specified in a configuration file that you edit, and when the interval has passed, checks for changes since last time. If it finds any changes, `DirectoryWatcher` sends a message to a listener CFC, which can perform the unzipping and creation of thumbnails.

First you need to configure the gateway configuration file, found in:

```
coldfusion_root\gateway\config\directory-watcher.cfg
```

For this example we'll assume that your ColdFusion root is on drive C, so a literal example of the file path would look like this:

```
C:\CFusion8\gateway\config\directory-watcher.cfg
```

Open this file and edit the very first attribute, `directory`, and have it point to where you will FTP your zipped files. For this example, the directory is called `gallery` and the path is as follows:

```
directory=C:/Inetpub/wwwroot/gatewaychapter/gallery
```

Table 80.1 lists a number of other configuration file attributes you can set. After you've edited the directory path, save the file.

NOTE

For the `directory` gateway configuration file, you want to use the forward slash (`/`) rather than the normal backslash (`\`).

Table 80.1 Gateway Configuration File Attributes

VALUE	REQUIRED OR OPTIONAL	DESCRIPTION
`directory`	Required	Path to the directory to watch.
`recurse`	Optional	Whether to check subdirectories. The default value is `No`.
`extensions`	Optional	Comma-delimited list of extensions to watch. The event gateway logs only changed files that have these extensions. An asterisk (`*`) indicates all files; this is the default.
`interval`	Optional	Number of milliseconds between the event gateway's checks on the directory. The default value is 60 seconds.
`addFunction`	Optional	Name of the function to call when a file is added. The default value is `onAdd`.
`changeFunction`	Optional	Name of the function to call when a file is changed. The default value is `onChange`.
`deleteFunction`	Optional	Name of the function to call when a file is deleted. The default value is `onDelete`.

NOTE

Not all event gateways will have a configuration file, and each configuration file will be unique to that specific gateway.

Next, we'll create a CFC that listens for events from the gateway. For this example, we'll only use the `onAdd` method supplied by the `DirectoryWatcher` gateway. What we want our CFC to do is listen for an event from the directory watcher, saying that files have been added to the `gallery` directory. Then the CFC will use the `CFIMAGE` tag to create the thumbnails. For this example, create a directory `gatewaychapter` under your Web root and create another directory under `gatewaychapter` called `gallery`. You will place `DirectoryWatcher.cfc` defined in Listing 80.1 in the `gatewaychapter` directory.

Listing 80.1 `DirectoryWatcher.cfc`—Simple CFC that Creates Thumbnails of New Images

```
<cfcomponent>

  <cffunction name="onAdd" output="no">
    <cfargument name="CFEvent" type="struct">
    <!--- get event data --->
    <cfset data=CFEvent.data>
    <!--- watcher will ignore outgoing messages --->
    <!--- Location of images --->
    <cfset GalleryFolder = ExpandPath("gallery")>
    <!--- Get list of images --->
     <cftry>
       <cfdirectory  action="list"
                     name="GetImages"
                     directory="#GalleryFolder#"
                     filter="*.jpg">
```

Listing 80.1 (continued)

```
          <!--- Loop over images --->
          <cfloop query="GetImages">
          <!--- Proposed location of thumbnail --->
          <cfset ThumbPath = ExpandPath("gallery/thumbs/#Name#")>
          <!--- If the thumbnail does not exist --->
          <cfif not FileExists(ThumbPath)>
            <!--- Invoke our image-resizing function --->
            <cfimage action="resize"
                     height = "25%"
                     source="#GalleryFolder#/#Name#"
                     width="25%"
                     destination="#ThumbPath#"
                     overwrite="true" />
          </cfif>
          <cfscript>
            logMessage = structNew();
            logMessage.message = "watch";
            logMessage.message = "a file was #data.type# and the name was
#data.filename#";
          </cfscript>
        </cfloop>
        <!--- log a message --->
        <cfcatch type="Any">
        <cfscript>
           logMessage = structNew();
           logMessage.message = "watch";
           logMessage.message = "An exception, #CFCATCH.TYPE#, was thrown in
DirectoryWatcher.CFC, the error message is #cfcatch.message#";
        </cfscript>
        </cfcatch>
      </cftry>
    </cffunction>

</cfcomponent>
```

Most of the code here is pretty straightforward. The first is that the listener CFC expects a struct called `CFEvent`, which is a Java object that is mapped to a ColdFusion struct. The `CFEvent` object contains a variety of information, including a `GatewayID`, `OriginatorId`, `GatewayType`, `CFCPath`, `CFCMethod`, `CFCTimeout`, and `Data`. Figure 80.2 shows an example of what the `CFEvent` message might look like in our example. Table 80.2 describes each node in the structure.

Table 80.2 `CFEvent` Information

FIELD	DESCRIPTION
`GatewayID`	The event gateway that sent the event or will handle the outgoing message. The value is the ID of an event gateway instance configured on the ColdFusion Administrator Gateways page. If the application calls the `SendGatewayMessage` function to respond to the event gateway, it uses this ID as the function's first parameter.
`OriginatorID`	The originator of the message. The value depends on the protocol or event gateway type. Some event gateways might require this value in response messages to identify the destination of the response. Identifies the sender of the message.

Table 80.2 (CONTINUED)

FIELD	DESCRIPTION
`Data`	A structure containing the event data, including the message. Contents depend on the event gateway type. This field corresponds to the `SendGatewayMessage` function's second parameter.
`GatewayType`	The type of event gateway, such as SMS. This field can be used by an application that can process messages from multiple event gateway types. This value is the gateway type name specified by the event gateway class. It is not necessarily the same as the gateway type name in the ColdFusion Administrator.
`CFCPath`	The location of the listener CFC. The listener CFC does not need to use this field.
`CFCMethod`	The listener method that ColdFusion invokes to process the event. The listener CFC does not need to use this field.
`CFCTimeout`	The timeout, in seconds, for the listener CFC to process the event request. The listener CFC does not need to use this field.

In Listing 80.1, the `CFEvent` message is used only to log the `DirectoryWatcher` method that was used, `data.type`, as well as the file and file path, `data.filename`. In a more complex application, you may want your CFC to take actions based on specific information from the `CFEvent` message.

Now to get our code to actually work, we need to do two other things. The first is to go into the ColdFusion Administrator and create a mapping for the `DirectoryWatcher` CFC; otherwise, the event gateway will not know where to look. The second thing we need to do is create an instance of the event gateway.

Creating an Event Gateway Instance

Before you can use the example in Listing 80.1, you must create an instance of the event gateway.

First go to the ColdFusion Administrator and select Event Gateways > Gateway Instances. You will see something like Figure 80.3.

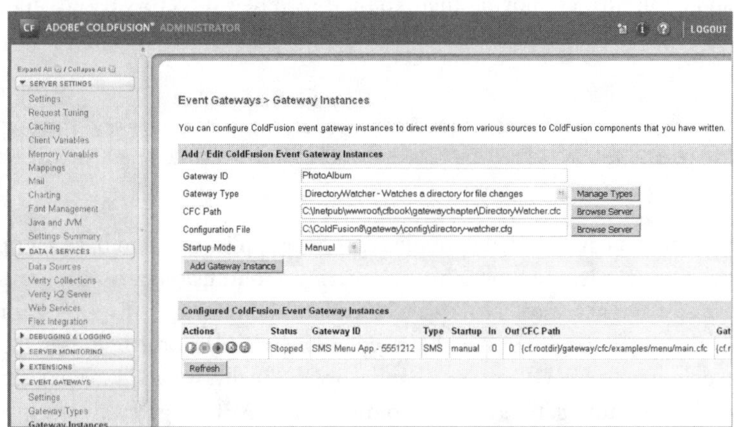

Figure 80.3

The Event Gateways > Gateway Instances configuration screen in the ColdFusion Administrator.

You should now see a form with a number of fields including Gateway ID, Gateway Type, CFC Path etc. To create the gateway follow these steps:

- The first field is the Gateway ID, which can be anything; for our example, let's just use `PhotoAlbum`.
- The next field is Gateway Type, which is a drop-down list of all the registered gateways. For this example, we select `DirectoryWatcher`, which watches a directory for file changes.
- The next field is CFC Path, which is the CFC path to our listener `DirectoryWatcher.cfc`. After that you need to add the path to the `directory-watcher.cfg`.
- Finally, select the Startup Mode drop-down list to choose whether you want the event instance to be started automatically, manually, or disabled on startup of ColdFusion. Choose Automatic and then click Add Gateway Instance.

You should now see your gateway instance in the Configured ColdFusion Event Gateway Instances area of the page. Be sure to click the green button to start your event gateway instance. Now your event gateway instance is running and ready to respond to events.

You can make as many instances as you want of a specific gateway, so you could create several `DirectoryWatcher` instances in order to watch many directories (although it would probably be better to just change the `DirectoryWatcher` class to support multiple directories). For each event gateway for which you want to create applications, you must have at least one instance actually running if you want to use it.

Now that you have the `DirectoryWatcher` instance running, you can test the example by copying some images into the `gallery` folder. Then navigate to your ColdFusion logs directory; you should see a new log created, `watcher.log`, which is our listener CFC's log. If you have set your `directory-watcher.cfg` to 60 seconds, you may have to wait, but eventually you'll see the `watcher.log` update. Look there, and you'll see that it has recorded the action, add, and the file and file path of the images you added to the directory. Examine the thumbnails directory under `gallery` to see the thumbnails that have been created. At this point it is easy to add code to support things like unzipping zip files of images, moving them to their own new directory based on the zip file names, and then creating the thumbnails—or any other cool functionality you like.

NOTE

If you change or delete a file in the watched directory you'll see an error in the `gateway.log` file and the `cfexception` log file. This is because we did not define these methods in our CFC. You can easily do this and just add these methods and have them do nothing, or log the change to a file, etc.

At this point you have created a simple responder application and have set up an event gateway instance. You have learned something about how ColdFusion event gateways work—but there is a lot more to event gateways. Now we will explore them further, discussing initiator applications, some of the particular differences between coding CFML for gateways and other applications, and how to debug your CFML gateway applications. Finally, we will look at a simple example of creating your own custom gateway using ColdFusion 8's API for gateways using Java.

Creating an Initiator Application Using the ColdFusion Gateway

So far, you've seen how to create a responder application that listens for events from an event gateway instance and takes some sort of action. Now we'll study an application called an *initiator application* that sends a message to an event gateway. This example uses the ColdFusion Gateway to asynchronously log messages to a file via a simple CFC.

Logging may seem trivial, especially since you can just use `CFLOG`, but CFML pages that use `CFLOG` to write large amounts of data to a log file can seriously degrade an application's performance, as well as tie up threads that could be better used serving your application's Web users. In addition, you might have an application like a B2B that needs to log large amounts of information, such as every type of transaction between partners for legal reasons. Thus you might want to decouple logging into its own subsystem, not only for performance but for good design. Using the ColdFusion Gateway allows you to create applications that call CFCs asynchronously, which is perfect for this example. Okay; let's look at some code (Listing 80.2).

Listing 80.2 `DataLogger.cfc`—Simple CFC that Logs Incoming ColdFusion Events

```
<cfcomponent>
    <cffunction name="onIncomingMessage" output="no">
    <cfargument name="CFEvent" type="struct" required="yes">
    <cfif not IsDefined("CFEvent.Data.file")><cfset
CFEvent.Data.file="defaultEventLog"></cfif>
    <cfif not IsDefined("CFEvent.Data.type")><cfset CFEvent.Data.type="info"></cfif>
    <cflog text="#CFEvent.Data.message#"
        file="#CFEvent.Data.file#"
        type="#CFEvent.Data.type#"
        thread="yes"
        date="yes"
        time="yes"
        application="yes">
    </cffunction>
</cfcomponent>
```

As you can see, this is a very simple CFC that accepts a `CFEvent` message and logs information from it. After you save this file to a directory, create an event gateway instance in the Event Gateways page of the Administrator, as described earlier in this chapter. For this example, give the instance a Gateway ID of `DataLogger` and point it to this CFC. Then leave the Configuration File field blank, create the instance, and start it running.

Now we can take our previous code and, instead of using `CFLOG` directly for logging information, send a message to the event gateway that will call the `DataLogger.cfc` to log the event. We do this using `SendGatewayMessage` with `"GatewayID"` and a struct with an event message. Let us look at Listing 80.3.

Listing 80.3 `DirectoryWatcher.cfc`—Addition of Asynchronous Logging Requests

```
<cfcomponent>

  <cffunction name="onAdd" output="no">
    <cfargument name="CFEvent" type="struct">
    <!--- get event data --->
    <cfset data=CFEvent.data>
    <!--- watcher will ignore outgoing messages --->
    <!--- Location of images --->
    <cfset GalleryFolder = ExpandPath("gallery")>
    <!--- Get list of images --->
     <cftry>
      <cfdirectory  action="list"
                    name="GetImages"
                    directory="#GalleryFolder#"
                    filter="*.jpg">
      <!--- Loop over images --->
      <cfloop query="GetImages">
      <!--- Proposed location of thumbnail --->
      <cfset ThumbPath = ExpandPath("gallery/thumbs/#Name#")>
      <!--- If the thumbnail does not exist --->
      <cfif not FileExists(ThumbPath)>
        <!--- Invoke our image-resizing function --->
        <cfimage action="resize"
                 height = "25%"
                 source="#GalleryFolder#/#Name#"
                 width="25%"
                 destination="#ThumbPath#"
                 overwrite="true" />
      </cfif>
      <cfscript>
        logMessage = structNew();
        logMessage.message = "watch";
        logMessage.message = "a file was #data.type# and the name was
#data.filename#";
      </cfscript>
      <cfset logAppInfo = SendGatewayMessage("DataLogger", logMessage)>
     </cfloop>
     <!--- log a message --->
     <cfcatch type="Any">
     <cfscript>
        logMessage = structNew();
        logMessage.message = "watch";
        logMessage.message = "A exception, #CFCATCH.TYPE#, was thrown in
DirectoryWatcher.CFC, the error message is #cfcatch.message#";
     </cfscript>
     </cfcatch>
   </cftry>
 </cffunction>
 </cfcomponent>
```

We have just added some simple code in a `CFSCRIPT` block and then used the `SendGatewayMessage()` function, which takes two required attributes. The first is the Gateway ID and the second is data, a structure that conforms to the specific gateway type. In this case, the gateway expects the event to contain a message node as well as an optional file node.

As you can see, creating an initiator application is simple enough, and in this case we have a listener that both responds to an event from a gateway and fires an event to a gateway.

In Chapter 81, "Integrating with SMS and IM," you'll make extensive use of the `SendGatewayMessage()` function.

Debugging CFML Applications for Event Gateways

When you need to develop ColdFusion applications that use event gateways, you need to be particularly careful—CFCs that are responding to events work differently than when they are responding to a normal page request. If an event gateway triggers a CFC and that CFC throws an error, the event gateway continues to function without pause and does not display any sort of debugging information back to you. For this reason, you will need to follow some different development paradigms—especially with regard to debugging, so that you can make sure your CFCs and event gateways are functioning as expected. In this section we'll examine some techniques you can and should use to help you debug and write better code.

The first technique is to make extensive use of `CFTRY`, `CFCATCH`, and `CFLOG`. Keep in mind that CFCs called by the event gateway will fail, but the event gateway will continue processing requests without returning anything to you. Catching any exceptions in your CFML and dumping them to a specific file will allow you to much more easily debug your applications.

You can also use `CFDUMP` in your application code and write the output of `CFDUMP` to a file. An easy way to do this is to use `CFSAVECONTENT` to wrap things like `CFDUMP`, loop over stack traces and so forth, and then put the `CFSAVECONTENT` variable in the `text=""` attribute of the `cflog` file.

TIP

> Using these techniques in Listings 80.2 and 80.3 to log and trap error information from your gateway applications is an excellent way to add debugging/logging to your event gateway applications.

Something else you can do is to put debugging and tracking variables in your `Application` scope. Then you can dump the contents of the scope and see any information about what you are tracking.

Another major debugging approach that should always be part of any development—but especially with CFCs and CFML applications that use gateways—is creating unit tests. You can easily do this by creating simple CFML pages that use the `SendGateWayMessage` function to simulate a message from a CFC to the event gateway. We will discuss this shortly, as well as how to call those pages.

Finally, consider running the ColdFusion 8 server from the command line. If you do this, you can use Java `System.out.println` to dump error message information to your DOS or command shell. This technique is really useful when working with Java objects from ColdFusion 8. Simply add into your code something like this:

```
<cfscript>
  sys = createObject("java", "java.lang.System");
  sys.out.println("Debugging message goes here");
</cfscript>
```

Creating Your Own Custom Gateways

Although ColdFusion 8 comes with a number of useful gateways, what happens when you want to connect to something that's not covered by one of the gateways provided? What if you want to connect to your MQ Series server, or SAP via the BAPI messaging interface? The answer is to create your own gateway. Writing ColdFusion 8 gateways is a fairly straightforward task, but gateways are developed completely in Java and you'll need to have a solid understanding of Java to write your own event gateways.

ColdFusion Event Gateway Architecture

Event gateways listen for events and pass them to ColdFusion for handling by an application's listener CFC. The gateway does this by implementing the `ColdFusion.eventgateway.Gateway` interface and by using the ColdFusion `gatewayServices` class.

Let's take a more detailed look at the overall architecture of the ColdFusion Gateway. In Figure 80.4 you can follow the path of a simple event through the system. Consider an incoming Instant Messaging event. The event gateway has a listener thread that will receive the message and call the Gateway Services `addEvent` method to send ColdFusion a `CFEvent` HashMap, which will be converted into a ColdFusion structure.

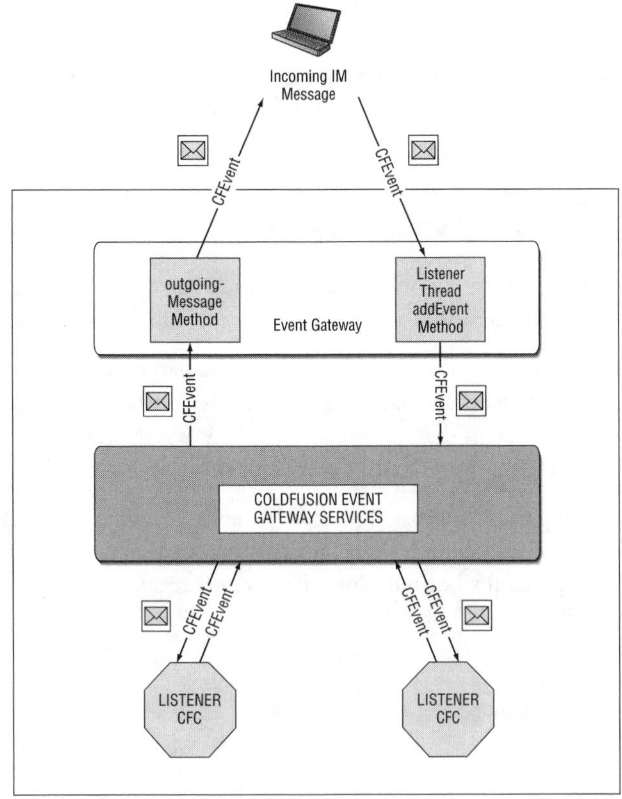

Figure 80.4

The flow of an event through a gateway application.

Now let's say your ColdFusion event application sends an event pack to the same IM source from a CFC. The event from the CFC would be passed to the ColdFusion event gateway via the event gateway's `outgoingMessage` method, which creates a `CFEvent` object with the appropriate destination and payload information.

The following sections introduce each of the major elements in constructing an event gateway.

Event Gateway Elements

There are six basic elements that are used to create and configure a ColdFusion Gateway: the Gateway interface, the `GatewayServices` class, the `CFEvent` class, the `GatewayHelper` class, the Gateway configuration class, and the Gateway development tools.

NOTE

The classes for the ColdFusion Gateway are in the `cfusion.jar`. Make sure when you compile your Java event gateways that you add the `cfusion.jar` to your class path as well as any other `.jar` files you plan to use. The `cfusion.jar` file can usually be found in the `C:\coldfusion8\lib` directory.

Gateway Interface

All ColdFusion event gateways have to implement the `ColdFusion.eventservice.Gateway` interface. Table 80.3 gives a list of the Gateway interface's methods. You can also find this information in a handy Javadoc at `cf_root/gateway/docs/api/index.html`.

Table 80.3 Methods of the ColdFusion Gateway Interface

DATA TYPE	METHOD	DESCRIPTION
void	`setGatewayID(String id)`	Sets the ID that uniquely defines the gateway instance.
void	`setCFCListeners(String[]listeners)`	Sets an array of CFC listeners.
`GatewayHelper`	`getHelper()`	Returns a gateway helper class (if there is one) so that a CFC can invoke gateway-specific functions that might be useful to the CFML developer.
String	`getGatewayID()`	Returns the gateway ID.
int	`getStatus()`	Gets the event gateway status, which can be either `STARTING`, `RUNNING`, `STOPPING`, `STOPPED`, `FAILED`.
void	`start()`	Starts the event gateway. ColdFusion calls this method on startup.
void	`stop()`	This method stops the event gateway and kills any threads and cleans up any resources it was using.

Table 80.3 (continued)

DATA TYPE	METHOD	DESCRIPTION
void	`restart()`	Restarts a running event gateway.
String	`outgoingMessage (CFEvent cfmesg)`	Sends a message from the gateway to a resource.

Gateway Services Class

To interact with the ColdFusion event gateway services, you used the Gateway class `ColdFusion.eventgateway.GatewayServices`. Table 80.4 lists the methods that the `GatewayServices` class implements. Like the Gateway interface, `GatewayServices` is summarized in the gateway Javadoc.

Table 80.4 Methods of the `GatewayServices` Class

DATA TYPE	METHOD	DESCRIPTION
`GatewayServices`	`getGatewayServices()`	Returns a `GatewayServices` object.
`int`	`getQueueSize()`	Returns the current size of the gateway event queue.
`int`	`getMaxQueueSize()`	Returns the maximum size of the gateway event queue.
`Logger`	`getLogger()`	Gets the default event logging object.
`Logger`	`getLogger(String logfile)`	Gets a custom event logging object.
`boolean`	`addEvent(CFEvent msg)`	Adds an event to the ColdFusion event service processing queue for delivery to a listener CFC.

`CFEvent` Class

As you have seen earlier in the chapter, the `CFEvent` object is the container for the message passed to CFCs from gateways. Your gateway does this by using the `GatewayServices.addEvent` method to send an instance of the `CFEvent` object. Gateways receive `CFEvents` when ColdFusion calls a gateway's `outgoingMessage` method.

The `CFEvent` class uses `java.util.Hashtable` to create a HashMap that models your message. That HashMap converts the contents into case-insensitive information for consumption by ColdFusion (which is caseless). Table 80.5 relates the methods for the `CFEvent` class.

Table 80.5 Methods of the `CFEvent` Class

DATA TYPE	METHOD	DESCRIPTION
CFEvent	`String gatewayID)`	`CFEvent` constructor that expects a string, which is the `gatewayID`.
void	`setGatewayType(String type)`	Sets the type of event gateway, such as IM, SMS, or EMail.
void	`setData(Map data)`	Adds the gateway-specific data, including any message contents, as a Java Map to the `CFEvent` object.
void	`setOriginatorID(String id)`	Sets the originator of an incoming message.
void	`setCFCPath(String path)`	Specifies the listener CFC that will process this event.
void	`setCFCMethod(String method)`	Sets the name of the CFC method that should process an incoming message.
void	`setCFCTimeout(String seconds)`	Sets the timeout, in seconds, during which the listener CFC must process the event request before ColdFusion gateway services terminates the request and logs an error in the `application.log` file.
String	`getGatewayType()`	Identifies the type of the gateway from which this message originated.
Map	`getData()`	Gets the message contents and other gateway-specific information.
String	`getOriginatorID()`	Identifies the originator of an incoming message.
String	`getCFCPath()`	Gets the path to the listener CFC that processes this message.
String	`getCFCMethod()`	Gets the name of the CFC method that processes the message.
String	`getGatewayID()`	Identifies the event gateway instance, as specified in the ColdFusion Administrator.

Gateway Helper Class

The `GatewayHelper` class provides an interface (Marker class) that can be used to mark a helper class that can be returned by a gateway. ColdFusion developers creating CFCs can use the functions `Gateway.getHelper()` and `getGatewayHelper` to invoke gateway-specific utility functions such as retrieving an IM phone book.

This class is returned by the CFML function `getGatewayCFCHelper(gatewayID)`. CFCs cannot get a direct reference to the Gateway object in order to protect the gateway's key operations, such as start, stop, and restart. Look in `cf_root\gateway\src\examples\socket\SocketGatewat.java` to see an example of how to implement a `GatewayHelper`.

Gateway Configuration Files

Depending on what your gateway will do, creating a configuration file can be very useful. The example in Listing 80.4, which we'll examine shortly, connects to a POP3 server to see if there are new messages on the mail server. Instead of hard-coding the host name, login, and password for the mail account, we'll use a configuration file to store this information. To do this, you'll want to use the `java.util.Properties` to create a properties file using `name=value` pairs.

NOTE

The Sun Javadoc for the Properties class can be found here:
`http://java.sun.com/j2se/1.4.2/docs/api/java/util/Properties.html`.

Gateway Development Tools

ColdFusion ships with several useful tools to help you in developing your ColdFusion custom gateways. The first of these is a generic abstract gateway class from which you can derive your gateway class.

Another useful tool is the `EmptyGateway` class found in `cf_root\gateway\src\examples\EmptyGateway.java`. You can use this Java class as a template for building your own custom classes. Before reading the next section on the POP3 Custom Gateway, it's recommended that you review this class, as well as compare it to some of the example classes provided in the examples directory which can be usually found in your `cf_root\gateway\src\examples`.

If you are an Apache ANT user, look into the `build.xml` file found at `cf_root\gateway\src\build.xml`. This useful tool lets you build all the examples in the examples directory and contains the paths to all the `.jar` files needed by these examples. If you are an Eclipse user, right-click `gateway/src/build.xml` and click Run to compile the examples.

All the CFCs to create gateway instances to deploy and test the examples are found in `cf_root\gateway\cfc`. Also, the configuration file for any of the examples can be found in `cf_root\gateway\config`. You can use these configuration files as samples for making your own. The ColdFusion 8 documentation has even more comprehensive information on the gateway classes and tools available to you.

A POP3 Custom Gateway

You've read about the architecture and classes that make up the event gateway, so let's go ahead and walk through making our own custom gateway. In this example, you're going to make a simple gateway that connects to a POP3 server and, if there are new emails on the POP server for a specific account defined in a configuration file, the gateway will send an event to a listener CFC with the number of new emails.

To work through this example, you'll need to have the `J2EE.jar`, to make use of the `javax.mail` classes, and the `cfusion.jar` in your classpath. If you are using Ant you can modify the `build.xml` file that can usally be found at `cf_root\gateway\src\` and use that. When you do compile the example, you'll want to compile the code and then deploy it as `POP3Gateway.jar` along with the `J2EE.jar`. Now let's look at Listing 80.4.

Listing 80.4 `POP3Gateway.java`—Check for New Email and Create an Event

```
import coldfusion.eventgateway.CFEvent;
import coldfusion.eventgateway.Gateway;
import coldfusion.eventgateway.GatewayServices;
import coldfusion.server.ServiceRuntimeException;
import coldfusion.eventgateway.Logger;

import java.io.File;
import java.io.FileInputStream;
import java.io.IOException;
import java.util.ArrayList;
import java.util.Hashtable;
import java.util.Properties;
import javax.mail.*;
import javax.mail.internet.*;

public class POP3Gateway implements Gateway
{

    private GatewayServices gatewayService = null;
    private String gatewayID = "";
    private String[] listeners = null;
    private String config = null;
    private Thread listenerThread = null;
    private boolean shutdown = false;
    private int status = STOPPED;

    private String hostname = null;
  private String username = null;
  private String password = null;

    private long pollingInterval = 60000;
  private long listenerThreadWait = 10000;

  private Logger logger = null;

    public POP3Gateway(String gatewayID, String config)
    {
        this.gatewayID = gatewayID;
        this.config = config;
        this.gatewayService = GatewayServices.getGatewayServices();
    this.logger = gatewayService.getLogger("pop3");
    this.loadPropertiesFromFile();
    this.logger.info("POP3Gateway(" + gatewayID + "," + config + ").constructor:
complete");
```

Listing 80.4 (continued)

```
    }

    public String outgoingMessage(coldfusion.eventgateway.CFEvent cfmsg)
  {
    return "We have no outgoing messages from this gateway.";
  }

  public void setCFCListeners(String[] listeners)
    {
        this.listeners = listeners;
    }

    public coldfusion.eventgateway.GatewayHelper getHelper()
    {
        return null;
    }

    public void setGatewayID(String id)
    {
        gatewayID = id;
    }

    public String getGatewayID()
    {
        return gatewayID;
    }

    public void start()
    {
    this.logger.info("POP3Gateway.start():enter");
        this.status = STARTING;

        // Start up listener thread
        Runnable r = new Runnable()
        {
            public void run()
            {
                pollForNewMessages();
            }
        };
        this.listenerThread = new Thread(r);
        this.shutdown = false;
        this.listenerThread.start();

        this.status = RUNNING;
    this.logger.info("POP3Gateway.start():exit");
    }

    public void stop()
    {
    this.logger.info("POP3Gateway.stop():enter");
        this.status = STOPPING;

        this.shutdown = true;
        try
```

Listing 80.4 (continued)

```
        {
            listenerThread.interrupt();
            listenerThread.join(this.listenerThreadWait);
        }
        catch (InterruptedException e)
        {
            // ignore
        }
        this.status = STOPPED;
    this.logger.info("POP3Gateway.stop():exit");
    }

  public void restart()
    {
        stop();
        loadPropertiesFromFile();
        start();
    }

    public int getStatus()
    {
        return status;
    }

    private void loadPropertiesFromFile() throws ServiceRuntimeException
    {

    this.logger.info("POP3Gateway.loadPropertiesFromFile():enter");

        Properties properties = new Properties();

        try
        {
            FileInputStream propsFile = new FileInputStream(config);
            properties.load(propsFile);
            propsFile.close();
        }
        catch (IOException e)
        {
            String error = "POP3Gateway (" + gatewayID + ") Unable to load
configuration file";
            throw new ServiceRuntimeException(error, e);
        }

        this.hostname = properties.getProperty("hostname");
    this.username = properties.getProperty("username");
    this.password = properties.getProperty("password");

    this.logger.info("POP3Gateway.loadPropertiesFromFile():exit");
    }

    private void pollForNewMessages()
    {
    this.logger.info("POP3Gateway.pollForNewMessages():enter");
        int lastMessageCount = 0;
```

Listing 80.4 (continued)

```
        Store store = null;
        Folder folder = null;

        try
        {
          Properties properties = new Properties();
          Session session = Session.getDefaultInstance(properties, null);
           store = session.getStore("pop3");
          store.connect(hostname, username, password);
        }
        catch (javax.mail.MessagingException e)
        {
          throw new ServiceRuntimeException(e.getMessage());
        }

        while (!shutdown)
        {
          this.logger.info("POP3Gateway.pollForNewMessages():testing for mail");
          int newMessageCount = 0;
          try
          {
            folder = store.getFolder("INBOX");
            folder.open(Folder.READ_ONLY);
            newMessageCount = folder.getMessageCount();
            folder.close(false);
          }
          catch (javax.mail.MessagingException e)
          {
            throw new ServiceRuntimeException(e.getMessage());
          }
          this.logger.info("POP3Gateway.pollForNewMessages():new message count=" +
    newMessageCount);

          if (lastMessageCount != newMessageCount)
          {
            this.logger.info("POP3Gateway.pollForNewMessages(): lastMessageCount==" +
    lastMessageCount + "; newMessageCount==" + newMessageCount);
            this.sendMessageCountToCF(newMessageCount-lastMessageCount);
          }

          lastMessageCount = newMessageCount;

          try
          {
            Thread.sleep(this.pollingInterval);
          }
          catch (InterruptedException e)
          {
            //  ignore
          }
        }

        try
        {
          folder.close(false);
```

Listing 80.4 (continued)

```
        }
        catch (Exception e)
        {}

        this.logger.info("POP3Gateway.pollForNewMessages():exit");
    }

        private void sendMessageCountToCF(int newMessageCount)
        {
        this.logger.info("POP3Gateway.sendMessageCountToCF(" + newMessageCount +
"):enter");
            CFEvent cfEvent = new CFEvent(gatewayID);
            cfEvent.setCfcMethod("newMailCount");

            Hashtable returnedData = new Hashtable();
            returnedData.put("NEWMAILCOUNT", Integer.toString(newMessageCount));
            cfEvent.setData(returnedData);

            cfEvent.setGatewayType("POP3Gateway");
            cfEvent.setOriginatorID("POP3Gateway");

            // Send to each listener
            for (int i = 0; i < listeners.length; i++)
            {
                // Set CFC path
                cfEvent.setCfcPath(listeners[i]);

                // send it to the event service
                gatewayService.addEvent(cfEvent);
            }
        this.logger.info("POP3Gateway.sendMessageCountToCF(" + newMessageCount +
"):exit");
        }
}
```

Compare this fairly straightforward code to the `ExampleGateway.java`, and you can see that more or less all we added is the `pollForNewMessages()`, the setting of various variables, and the creation of the event that passes `NewMessageCount`. All the gateway does is check the POP3 server every 60 seconds and, if there is mail flagged as new, sends an event to the associated listener CFC. Another thing you might notice is the usage of the Gateway `logger` class. Developing custom gateways can be difficult in that you often have to run the gateway on ColdFusion before you can tell if there are any problems ColdFusion will not return much in the way of debugging information so it's a good idea to use the `logger` class to output information to aid in the development of your code.

Now that we have developed the code for our gateway, let's deploy this new gateway type via the ColdFusion Administrator.

Deploying a Custom Event Gateway

Deploying an event gateway is about as easy as creating a new gateway instance. First you need to compile the POP3Gateway and place it in a `.jar` file; then make sure you place the `.jar` file in the cf_root\gateway\lib. For this example, you also need to make sure the J2EE.jar and the POP3Gateway.jar are in this directory.

NOTE

On J2EE configurations, you want to put your .jars in cf_root\WEB-INF\cfusion\gateway\.

When you're sure that your .jar files are in the right place, go to the ColdFusion Administrator and click on Event Gateway and then on Gateway Types.

The first field is the event Type Name. Enter POP3Gateway. The Description field should show a description of the event type in the Event Gateways > Gateway Instances creation screen, so for this example, use Test of Gateway using POP3. Then enter the .jar name in the Java Class field—POP3Gateway in this example. For Startup Timeout, leave the default of 30 seconds. Leave the Stop on Startup Timeout option checked. Your finished page should look something like Figure 80.5.

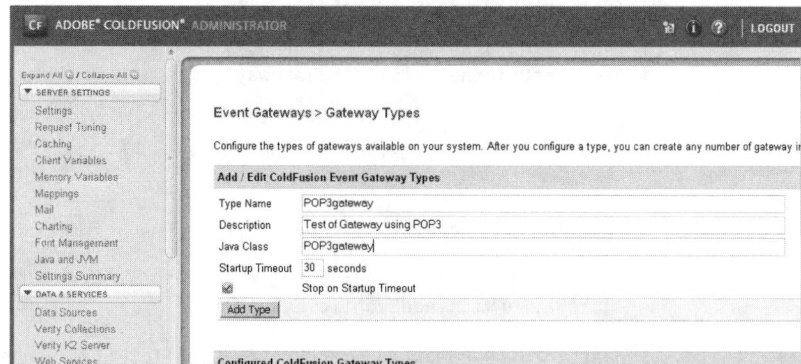

Figure 80.5

The POP3Gateway event type before it has been deployed in the ColdFusion Administrator.

Now click on Add Type to deploy your new event gateway type. You'll see the POP3Gateway event type now under Configured ColdFusion Gateway Types.

With the gateway deployed, you can test it by using Listing 80.5, creating a config file, and setting up a new event instance.

Listing 80.5 POP3Gateway.CFC—Simple CFC to Log Messages from the POP3 Gateway

```
<cfcomponent>
      <cffunction name="newMailCount" output="no">
       <cfargument name="CFEvent" type="struct" required="yes">
       <cfset data = CFEvent.data>

         <!--- NEWMAILCOUNT --->
            <cflog file="pop3gateway" text="you have #data.NewMailCount#">
      </cffunction>
</cfcomponent>
```

For this example, you can create a configuration file called `pop3gateway.cfg` and add your POP3 server's host name, your email login, and your email password like this:

```
hostname=mail.robisen.com
login=robisen
password=gloreibel2!
```

Save these files in an appropriate location, and then make a new event instance in the ColdFusion Administrator. When you test this gateway, you should add a new log file and record whether you have any new emails in your POP account. You could make this example more interesting by forwarding the message about the number of new emails to your IM or SMS account. To make the Java gateway example more interesting, let it provide more information or allow you to send email or do anything else that POP3 allows you to do. Although `CFMAIL` and `CFPOP` offer a lot of functionality, creating your own POP gateway lets you add greater functionality and work with your POP accounts asynchronously.

ColdFusion gateways are the most exciting and powerful feature to be added to ColdFusion since the original `CFQUERY` tag. With ColdFusion gateways, you can connect to almost anything and develop a whole new type of ColdFusion application. In Chapter 81, you will explore ColdFusion gateways even more, focusing on SMS and IM applications.

CHAPTER 81

Integrating with SMS and IM

IN THIS CHAPTER

This chapter will expand on your knowledge of gateways and introduce you to two specific gateways, the SMS and IM gateways. While these gateways behave in a very similar manner to other ColdFusion gateways, they do have some particularly interesting features that can help you build incredible and sophisticated messaging applications.

For instance, let us take the humble helpdesk every company has. They are there to help you out with computer problems. Typically every helpdesk is busy and every user thinks that his or her problem is the most important and should be fixed first.

Many helpdesks have a ticketing system that allows users to log an issue and track the status of the issue. The normal helpdesk workflow looks something like this: User logs issue, helpdesk agent receives issue, agent fixes issue, agent returns to desk, agent receives new issue. Unless the staff is a little more demanding. In that case they will log the issue and immediately walk around to the helpdesk area to find that they are all out and assume (incorrectly) that they are on an extended lunch break.

What if we could extend the reach of our helpdesk and allow helpdesk agents to "see" the state of the helpdesk from the intranet, grab new tasks from their cell phones, close tickets from an IM client, and never have to go back to their desk between tasks? Now your Web application has broken out of the browser and is available anywhere.

Over the course of this chapter we will build a very simple helpdesk application that does exactly this. This chapter assumes that you have an understanding of how gateways behave and that you have read Chapter 80, "Working with Gateways."

Understanding IM

Instant messaging, or IM as it is more commonly called, is something that many users of the Internet take for granted. It is the simple ability to send a message instantly to another user. Like SMS it does not sound like much but there is a lot going on behind the scenes.

The first challenge facing someone developing an IM-based application is the concept that the event gateway itself is, in effect, an IM client. The server will log on to the IM network in the same way that any other user will log on. It will appear in your IM list as a user and to all outward respects, it is a normal user.

The second challenge is how to build an application that makes sense to a user who is coming in from an IM client and to have that user interact with the rest of the application in a meaningful way.

The other challenge in the IM space is "Whose IM client are we going to support?" Personally I have IM accounts with MSN, Yahoo!, AOL, and Jabber. Why so many? Well, this all has to do with standards, as with almost everything on the Internet today. There are a multitude of de facto standards that evolved before we really knew what we were doing and everyone had their own idea about which IM client was their favorite. This led to a series of different protocols and different clients and now it seems that you need an account on every different IM network just to talk to everyone you know. Luckily there is a solution; the IETF (the Internet Engineering Task Force) has ratified an open standard, the Extensible Messaging and Presence protocol (XMPP), which will allow for a degree of interoperability and a wider range of supported clients in the future.

➜ For more information on XMPP head to `http://www.xmpp.org`.

Out of the box ColdFusion only has native support for two IM protocols, XMPP and Lotus SameTime. Some have mentioned that this appears to be a bit limiting but as with all of the gateways, you can always create your own and at the time of this writing there are various third-party organizations that are in the process of doing just this. In particular, Zion Software has a product called JBuddy that lets you connect to other messaging networks, such as AOL's AIM network. They are currently working on a version, called JBuddyCF, that will plug into ColdFusion to provide similar access natively in ColdFusion.

As XMPP begins to evolve there will be a huge selection of XMPP clients and server gateways that will broaden the horizon of the gateways in ColdFusion today.

NOTE

To make life easier, this chapter will focus on XMPP but exactly the same principles apply to Lotus SameTime.

Understanding Presence

One of the key differences to note between and SMS application and an IM application is Presence. What does this mean? With IM, you can tell if someone is connected to the network, or not, so before you send a user a message you can check to see if that user is there to receive it.

At first this does not seem to be much but if you think of how we use IM today, this could radically change how ColdFusion applications interact with users. Let's take a simple helpdesk application as an example. In a traditional system a user would log a support ticket and the application would email the helpdesk staff group as a whole. alerting them to the fact that there was a new ticket that needed to be addressed. Everyone in the support team would get that email, even if they weren't in the office to deal with it.

In a presence-aware application, sending out a blanket email as above would be a last resort. The application could query an IM server to determine which support engineers where online at present and IM them directly with a link to the support ticket so that it could be assigned almost instantly. If there were no support staff online, then the system could fall back to its existing email system (or maybe send an SMS message to the support engineer on call) and send an alert email.

Creating a Development Environment

Unlike the SMS gateway emulator in ColdFusion, when you are working with IM testing you need to connect your application to an IM server.

NOTE

While writing this we used the Jive Messenger XMPP server (`http://www.jivesoftware.org/`) as our test server so we could totally control the environment. This is a relatively simple XMPP-compliant IM server to install and configure and is available for Windows and Unix platforms.

XMPP Clients

To test your new system you will need to use an XMPP client to connect to the Labber network. There are a huge selection of clients out there; head to `http://www.jabber.org/software/clients.shtml` and just select one. For testing we used PSI (`http://psi.affinix.com/`) on a Mac and Trillian Pro (`http://www.trillian.cc/`) on a PC.

To complete our helpdesk application you will need to have installed an IM server (Jive in this case) and to have an IM client connected to your IM server.

Once you have your IM server installed, open up your IM client and create a new IM user. One of the neat benefits of XMPP is that users can create their own user accounts from within their IM client. You will need to create a user in the form of `username@yourJiveServerName`.

Once you have created your own user account, it helps to make your ColdFusion server's IM account in the same manner. Go ahead and repeat this process, creating an account for `coldfusion-server@yourJiveServerName` with a password of `WACK`. We will be using this account shortly so log out for the time being.

Defining IM Gateways

Defining your IM gateway is fairly straightforward. You will need your CFC and a gateway configuration file that will tell the gateway how to connect to the IM server itself. Just to get things started, let's create a stub CFC that will contain all of our methods. When compared to other gateways, the IM gateway has quite a few default methods.

- `onIncomingMessage`: This is your normal gateway method. It catches every incoming IM message and allows you to process it and respond to it. You might want to make sure that you always respond in some way to an incoming message; otherwise, your virtual IM user will appear to be ignoring your users.

- `onAddBuddyRequest`: This method is called when another user attempts to add your virtual IM user to their buddy list. Once they have added you to their list they can then see the presence state of your application. This can be very powerful especially in our helpdesk scenario as this could say if the helpdesk is manned and if it is busy or not at one glance to a buddy list.
- `onAddBuddyResponse`: When your gateway adds other users to its own buddy list, the responses to these requests will be handled here. Also if a user asks to be removed from your buddy list, you will need to handle it here as well.
- `onBuddyStatus`: Once you have other IM users on your list, their status will be relayed to you every time it changes and captured in this method. You will need to capture and store this status information if you wish to use it in your application.

Listing 81.1 is an example of what your IM Gateway CFC should look like.

Listing 81.1 `xmpp_stub.cfc`—Empty XMPP Gateway CFC

```
<cfcomponent>
   <cffunction name="onIncomingMessage" hint="Standard message from IM users">
      <cfargument name="CFEvent" type="struct" required="YES">
   </cffunction>

   <cffunction name="onAddBuddyRequest" hint="Requests from others to add the
gateway ID to their buddy list.">
      <cfargument name="CFEvent" type="struct" required="YES">
   </cffunction>

   <cffunction name="onAddBuddyResponse" hint="Responses from others to requests
from your gateway to add them to your buddy lists. Also used by
buddies to ask to be removed from your list.">
      <cfargument name="CFEvent" type="struct" required="YES">
   </cffunction>

   <cffunction name="onBuddyStatus" hint="Presence status messages from other
users.">
      <cfargument name="CFEvent" type="struct" required="YES">
   </cffunction>

   <cffunction name="onIMServerMessage" hint="Error and status messages from the
IM server.">
      <cfargument name="CFEvent" type="struct" required="YES">
   </cffunction>
</cfcomponent>
```

Even though our application may not use all of these events, it is good practice to code them all so that it is very clear to other users what is going on and what is not. You do not have to use the default names for any of these methods; you can replace them with your own names. This is done in the individual gateway configuration files.

To build our application, we will need to create our own gateway CFC. Take a copy of this file from the book's Web site and call it `im.cfc`.

The Gateway Configuration File

One very simple thing that you will need to get prepared before you begin creating your gateway instance is the configuration file for your IM client.

There are two example configuration files in your ColdFusion installation: one for XMPP and one for Lotus SameTime. They are found in the `cf_root\WEB-INF\cfusion\gateway\config` directory on J2EE configurations, and in the `cf_root\gateway\config` directory on standard server configurations.

To make life easier, here is the default setting that you will need for a standard XMPP connection. If you used different settings when you created your ColdFusion user, here is where you tell ColdFusion your settings. You will need to save this as `helpdesk.cfg` as we will need it when we create our gateway instance:

```
userid=coldfusionserver@yourJiveServerNamw
password=CFMX7
resourceName=ColdFusion
serverip=yourJiveServerName
serverport=5222
```

TIP

Before you go too much further, make sure that you can log in as this user using a normal IM client–it one of the most annoying things to get everything written only to find that your user does not exist. To do this, just add your server's IM account into your IM client as another user, and then you can send messages to yourself.

This file is also used to define optionally configurable items, including security settings and additional events. This can be really handy if you have one CFC controlling both XMPP and SameTime interactions.

Creating the Gateway Instance

Inside the ColdFusion Administrator you will need to go to the Event Gateway Instances property page and add a new gateway instance. For this application, we called our gateway `Helpdesk`, we called our gateway CFC `im.cfc`, and we called our configuration file `helpdesk.cfg`, as shown in Figure 81.1.

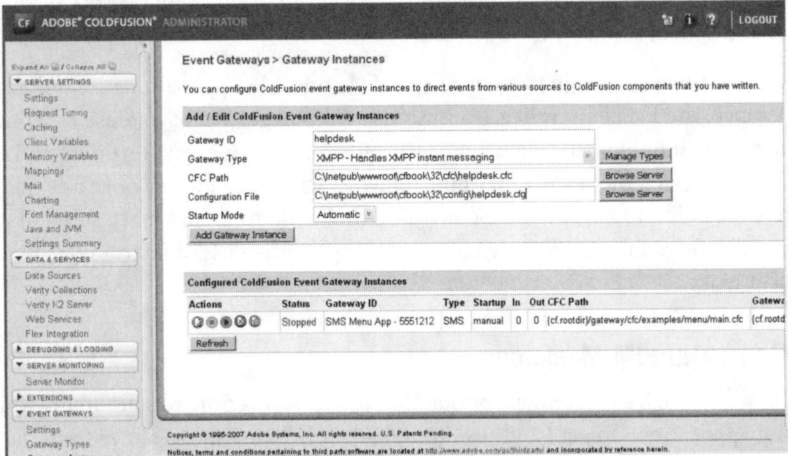

Figure 81.1

The configuration page for our gateway.

There are two key details in creating your new instance: the CFC that will handle all of your requests and the configuration file itself. Make sure you get these both right and you will be set.

TIP

At this point it would be wise to test your new gateway. Jump into the ColdFusion Administrator and make sure that it starts.

Creating Your First IM Application

Now that you have your gateway set up, it would be great to test it and make sure that it works. To do so we will use a simple "Hello World" application.

NOTE

Throughout this chapter we will be building an IM and SMS client for a helpdesk application. This application is already created and can be downloaded. For this application we will need a few additional bits and pieces. In the code for this chapter (found at the accompanying Web site) you will find a Microsoft Access database and the MySQL scripts needed to generate this database. You will need to set up this database inside ColdFusion. We used the data source name "helpdesk" in our code.

Quickly modify the `onIncomingMessage` function in your `im.cfc` to look like Listing 81.2.

Listing 81.2 `im.cfc`—Modify the `onIncomingMessage` Function

```
<cffunction name="onIncomingMessage">
        <cfargument name="CFEvent" type="struct" required="YES">
        <!--- Generate and return the message.--->
        <cfscript>
        msg = structNew();
        msg.command = "submit";
        msg.buddyID = arguments.CFEvent.data.SENDER;
        msg.message = Trim(arguments.CFEvent.data.MESSAGE);

        return msg;
        </cfscript>
</cffunction>
```

This is a little more advanced than your average "Hello World" application. It will echo any message it receives back to the person who sent it. Now we know that the system works and we can have a conversation with ourselves!

It does, however, begin to show us why IM and SMS applications are quite hard to write. In essence, the IM client is like a very simple Web page. We have presented our users with the ability to type in anything and click Send, as in a form with only one text field and a Submit button. We have not given them any other guidelines on what the gateway does or explained how to use it. We are going to have to accept anything they send to us and make sense of it and then respond intelligently. Taking a text string and turning it into a list of instructions for the server is not as easy as it looks.

Generating IM Messages

Now that we have a conduit for our IM messages, it is time to start adding this new functionality into our application. To get ColdFusion to send an IM message to a user from our existing application, it is almost as easy as coding a `<cfmail>` tag. By now you should be familiar with the `SendGatewayMessage()` function:

```
<cfscript>
msg = StructNew();
msg.command = "Submit"; msg.message = "Hi there from the all new ColdFusion 8!";
msg.buddyID = "LucasSherwood@jabber.com";
SendGatewayMessage("helpdesk", msg);
</cfscript>
```

In this code, there is one new argument being passed to our gateway, the `BuddyID` and our message is sent.

Now we can send and receive messages, we can move on to more complicated issues and get our ColdFusion application to mimic a real-world user on an IM network.

There are two key things that we need to do to get our application IM ready. We need to make sure people can add our virtual helpdesk to their buddy list and so make sure that we can track the status of all of our helpdesk agents and assign them to tasks when we know that they are free.

Making New Friends

As our users begin to use our application, we would like them to be able to add the virtual helpdesk to their list of users. As we are building an internal application we are going to be very open and allow anyone to add the helpdesk to their buddy list. If you wanted to restrict this, you should place some logic in here to either ignore the request and queue it for manual approval or to decline it.

As before, you will need to modify your `onAddBuddyRequest` function in your `im.cfc` file, as seen in Listing 81.3.

Listing 81.3 Adding an `onBuddyRequest` Method

```
<cffunction name="onAddBuddyRequest" hint="Requests from others to add the
            gateway ID to their buddy list.">
        <cfargument name="CFEvent" type="struct" required="YES">

        <!--- Return the action decision. --->
        <cfset retValue = structNew()>
        <cfset retValue.command = "accept">
        <cfset retValue.BuddyID = CFEvent.DATA.SENDER>
        <cfset retValue.Reason = "Because we are nice!">
        <cfreturn retValue>
</cffunction>
```

User Status Management

Inside our gateway CFC you may have noticed a method called `onBuddyStatus()`. This is called when one of the members of our buddy list change their status. We will cache this information in the application scope, so that we can use this in the rest of our application. If we add the following code into our onBuddyStatus function we will have the status of all of our buddies available to the rest of the application:

```
<cffunction name="onBuddyStatus" hint="Presence status messages from other users.">
  <cfargument name="CFEvent" type="struct" required="YES">
  <cflock scope="APPLICATION" timeout="10" type="EXCLUSIVE">
    <cfscript>
    // Create the status structures if they don't exist.
    if (NOT StructKeyExists(APPLICATION, "buddyStatus")) {
    APPLICATION.buddyStatus=StructNew();
    }
    if (NOT StructKeyExists(APPLICATION.buddyStatus, CFEvent.Data.BUDDYNAME)) {

APPLICATION.buddyStatus[#CFEvent.Data.BUDDYNAME#]=StructNew();
  }
  // Save the buddy status and timestamp.
  APPLICATION.buddyStatus[#CFEvent.Data.BUDDYNAME#].status =
CFEvent.Data.BUDDYTATUS;
    APPLICATION.buddyStatus[#CFEvent.Data.BUDDYNAME#].timeStamp =
CFEvent.Data.TIMESTAMP;

</cfscript>
  </cflock>
</cffunction>
```

You will notice that we have put a <cflock> around this code. This is just in case multiple users change their status at exactly the same time. We don't want to overwrite one change with the other.

The IM Gateway Helper

As with all gateways, there is a helper class that carries out additional tasks that are specific to that gateway type. In the case of IM gateways there are four main areas of responsibility that our helper takes care of.

Buddy List Management

One of the first things we want our application to do when it starts up is to check the status of our helpdesk staff. Typically all of our helpdesk staff will already be buddies in our application but it never hurts to check.

Now our application is starting to grow, it is time to build an Application.cfc file into our application. If you haven't already got one, create an Application.cfc file in your test directory. In our Application.cfc (Listing 81.4), we will add some code that checks our list of users against the buddy list of the IM Gateway and requests authorization to add those users who are not buddies to the list when our application starts using the onApplicationStart() function. To do this we need the addBuddy() helper function.

NOTE

Your application will not automatically see changes in the status of any user on the IM network unless you add them to your buddy list.

Listing 81.4 `Application.cfc`

```
<cffunction name="onApplicationStart" returnType="boolean">
<!--- go and get the list of buddies from the Gateway --->
<cfscript>
        helper = getGatewayHelper("Helpdesk");
        aBuddyList = helper.getBuddyList();
</cfscript>

<!--- go and get the list of all users who can access this system from the DB --->
<cfquery datasource="helpdesk" name="qGetUsers">
SELECT userid,imid,name
FROM helpdeskstaff
<cfif ArrayLen(aBuddyList) gt 0>
        WHERE IMID not in(#ListQualify(ArraytoList(aBuddyList),"'")#)
</cfif>
</cfquery>
<!--- loop over this query and generate buddy list requests --->
<cfloop query="qGetUsers">
        <cfset rc =helper.addBuddy(qGetUsers.IMID,qGetUsers.Name,"Helpdesk Staff")>
</cfloop>
<cfreturn true />
</cffunction>
```

The next step is to check the online status of all of our helpdesk staff. To do this we will need to poll their status one by one using the `getBuddyInfo()` helper function. This will also need to go into our `onApplicationStart` function in our `Application.cfc` file:

```
<cfscript>
// go and get the buddy list again as it now may have new users in it
aBuddyList = helper.getBuddyList();
for(i=1;i lte arrayLen(aBuddyList);i=i+1) {
  // store this status in an application var so the rest of the application has
access to it
  // Create the status structures if they don't exist.
  if (NOT StructKeyExists(APPLICATION, "buddyStatus")) {
  APPLICATION.buddyStatus=StructNew();
  }
  if (NOT StructKeyExists(APPLICATION.buddyStatus, aBuddyList[i])) {
    APPLICATION.buddyStatus[#aBuddyList[i]#]=StructNew();
  }

  //get the status for this buddy
  status = helper.getBuddyInfo(aBuddyList[i]);
  //find the node in the array that contains the data that we need
  for(j=1;j lte arrayLen(status);j=j+1) {
    if(status[j].BuddyListType eq "BUDDY_LIST")
    {
      // save the status data
      APPLICATION.buddyStatus[#aBuddyList[i]#].status = status[j].BUDDYSTATUS;
      APPLICATION.buddyStatus[#aBuddyList[i]#].timeStamp =
status[j].BUDDYSTATUSTIME;
    }
  }
}
</cfscript>
```

In our application we abstracted this functionality into its own function in the `Application.cfc` file so that we can reuse it elsewhere if needed. We now know enough information that we can go and build an application that takes helpdesk requests and IMs them to an available support staff member. This is done in `index.cfm`.

Gateway Status Management

It would be nice to add some more functionality to our application so that the users in our organization could see at a glance if their helpdesk staff where busy or not, but to protect our helpdesk staff, we are not going to publish their IM details directly. Instead, we are going to integrate their status into that of our gateway. The virtual helpdesk should reflect whether the agents are busy or free.

The gateway helper has a method, `setStatus()`, that we will be using to very simply show our busy/free status.

We will loop over the application scope cache of our agents' status and use this to set the gateway's presence status to reflect our helpdesk team.

In your `im.cfc` modify the `onBuddyStatus()` function to include the following code:

```
<cfloop collection="#Application.BuddyStatus#" item="key">
        <cfif NOT StructKeyExists(stStatus, APPLICATION.buddyStatus[key].Status)>
                <cfset stStatus[APPLICATION.buddyStatus[key].Status] = structNew()>
        </cfif>
        <cfset stStatus[APPLICATION.buddyStatus[key].Status][key] = true>
</cfloop>
<!--- now work out what status to put us in --->
<cfif structKeyExists(stStatus,"ONLINE")>
        <cfset newstatus = "ONLINE">
<cfelseif structKeyExists(stStatus,"AWAY")>
        <cfset newstatus = "AWAY">
<cfelse>
        <cfset newstatus = "NA">
</cfif>
<cfset helper = getGatewayHelper("Helpdesk")>
<cfset ret=helper.setStatus(newstatus, "")>
```

As the status of our gateway should be updated whenever a member of our helpdesk team changes their status, it will go into the `onBuddyStatus()` event of our gateway. An advancement of this would be to make it an application-level function so that it also could be called when the application starts to set our initial status.

NOTE

Depending on your IM gateway type you will have different options for the status of your gateway. Be sure to check the docs to make sure that the status you select is supported.

TIP

You can always use the `setStatus()` helper method to add a custom away message to your status to help convey additional information to the users of our application.

Another nice thing we could do for our normal Web-based users would be to tell them the status of the helpdesk when they submit their issue. In our application our users log issues via a plain old Flash form on your regular intranet (this is in `index.cfm`) and to keep things simple, we will leave it that way. However, it would be great to advertise the status of our helpdesk staff on this page so that users who do not have an IM client are in the loop.

This could not be easier; our gateway helper can do this for us. You may want to use a `<cfswitch>` statement to present this information to the user a little better.

On our issue logging page, `index.cfm`, we have the following code to show our users the status of our helpdesk when they log issues:

```
<cfset helper = getGatewayHelper("Helpdesk")>
<cfset helpDeskStatus=helper. getStatusAsString ()>
<cfoutput>the helpdesk is currently #helpDeskStatus#.</cfoutput>
```

There are several other Gateway Status helpers, such as `isOnline()`, that you many want to look at using elsewhere in your application. Have a look at the ColdFusion docs for more details.

Permission Management

Once your application is up and running you may want to start controlling who can see the status of our virtual helpdesk and who cannot. The IM server itself maintains two lists of users, the permit list and the deny list. These two lists on their own do not control how the IM server will respond; they are just lists. In addition to filling either of these lists, we must tell the IM server to change its default behavior.

By default, the server is set to permit all users to view our status and to disregard the permit and deny list. We can change this using the `setPermitMode()` helper. There are three modes we can set the gateway to: `PERMIT_ALL`, `PERMIT_SOME`, and `DENY_SOME`. The combinations here are straightforward. If `permit_some` is used, the permit list is used to specify which users can see the status of the gateway; if the `deny_some` condition is set, then all users on the deny list will be unable to see the status of our gateway.

In the case of our application we will not be using these. For more details of the specifics of these methods, please refer to the ColdFusion docs.

Gateway Configuration

Beyond the normal helper methods, there are a few that provide statistics on the gateway itself:

- `GetName()`: This returns the username of the IM user.
- `GetProtocolName()`: This returns the IM protocol (JABBER for XMPP, or SAMETIME).
- `GetNickName()`: This returns the Display Name of the gateway (the nickname).
- `setNickName()`: This sets the nickname of the gateway.

- `numberOfMessagesSent()`: This returns the number of messages received by the gateway since it was started.
- `numberOfMessagesReceived()`: This returns the number of messages received by the gateway since it was started.

While the last two don't explicitly have a use in our application, you may want to build a nice little stats logger to show you just how much usage your IM helpdesk is getting.

Creating Interactive Applications

Once you have the basics of an application, you will want to allow users to have conversations with the gateway itself. While these conversations may not resemble those of a normal human user, they can be programmed to provide a very high level of access to information over a small connection if the application is able to recognize a few simple commands.

In the case of our application it would be great if helpdesk staff could IM in and mark a task as complete and request the next task to be assigned to them. We can create a limited vocabulary of words that the gateway will understand and share this with our users; then we can get the application to communicate to our helpdesk operatives quite easily.

TIP

You might want to build a simple form that calls your `onIncomingEvent` method directly as apposed to using an IM client to test your application. That way you will get the debug output when things go wrong.

We have opted for a very small selection of words that our gateway will understand. It will understand Accept, Assign, Reject, Deny, Complete, Close, and Details. For many of the functions, we have also allowed the user to just enter the first letter of the command and we will understand it.

When building the request/response logic, you will want to make sure that you locate any and all of the backend data-gathering code elsewhere. In this example we told our gateway CFC to extend another CFC, our helpdesk CFC, so it would have access to all of the underlying database access code. In our application (Listing 81.5), they provide access to the issues database.

Listing 81.5 `im.cfc`—Interactive IM Gateway CFC

```
<cfcomponent extends="helpdesk">

<cffunction name="onIncomingMessage">
  <cfargument name="CFEvent" type="struct" required="YES">
  <!--- Generate and return the message.--->
  <cfset message = trim(arguments.CFEvent.data.MESSAGE)>
  <cfset keyword = listFirst(message," ")>
  <cfset msg = "">
  <cfscript>
    switch (keyword) {
    case "accept":
          staffDetails = getStaffDetails(imid=arguments.CFEvent.data.SENDER);
          taskID = assignTask(staffDetails.userid);
          msg = staffDetails.name & " thankyou for accepting this task.
```

Listing 81.5 (continued)

```
                The task ID is " & taskID;
          break;
    case "A":
    case "Assign":
          staffDetails =getStaffDetails(imid=arguments.CFEvent.data.SENDER);
          taskID = assignTask(staffDetails.userid);
          if(len(taskID) eq 0) {
            msg = "there are no unassigned tasks at this time";
          } else {
            msg = "You have been assigned a new task.";
          }
          break;
    case "R":
    case "reject":
    case "deny":
          msg = "This task has been rejected, it will be returned to the queue."
                & chr(13);;
          msg = msg & "You can always mark yourself as 'Away' and the helpdesk
                system will not automatically alert you to new tasks";
          break;
    case "C":
    case "Complete":
    case "Close":
          // work out who this user is and get their current list of tasks
          staffDetails =getStaffDetails(imid=arguments.CFEvent.data.SENDER);
          aDetails = getTaskDetails(staffDetails.userid);
          switch(arrayLen(aDetails)) {
          case 0:
               msg = "You do not have any tasks currently active" & chr(13);
               break;
          case 1:
               closeIssue(aDetails[1].id);
               msg = "You have marked your currently active task as complete."
                     & aDetails[1].id& chr(13);
               break;
          default:
               // this user has more than one case
               //check for a number after the keyword if present,
               //close that case
               if(listLen(message,' ') gt 1
                  and isNumeric(ListGetAt(message,2,' '))) {
                 thisTask =ListGetAt(message,2,' ');
                 closeIssue(aDetails[thisTask].id);
                 msg = "You have closed task " & thisTask & ".";
               } else {
                 msg = "You have more than one task open at present.
                        Please confirm which task you wish to close." & chr(13);
                 for(i =1;i lte arrayLen(aDetails);i=i+1) {
                   msg = msg & i & ". " & aDetails[i].Subject & chr(13);
                 }
               }
           }
           break;
```

Listing 81.5 (CONTINUED)

```
        case "D":
        case "Details":
             staffDetails =getStaffDetails(imid=arguments.CFEvent.data.SENDER);
             aDetails = getTaskDetails(staffDetails.userid);
             if(listLen(message,' ') gt 1 and
                isNumeric(ListGetAt(message,2,' '))) {
               // this user has asked for a task
               thisTask = ListGetAt(message,2,' ');
               msg = "Details for task " & thisTask &chr(13);
               msg = msg & "Subject: " & aDetails[thisTask].Subject & chr(13);
               msg = msg & aDetails[thisTask].body & chr(13);
               msg = msg & "Requested by: " & aDetails[thisTask].loggedby & chr(13);
             } else {
               // work out how many cases this user has and send details
               switch (arrayLen(aDetails)) {
               case 0:
                    msg = "You currently have no cases assigned to you.
                           Do you wish to be assigned a new support case?
                           (Assign?)";
                    break;
               case 1:
                    msg = "Subject: " & aDetails[1].Subject & chr(13);
                    msg = msg & aDetails[1].body & chr(13);
                    msg = msg & "Requested by: " & aDetails[1].loggedby & chr(13);
                    break;
               default:
                    msg = "You have " & arrayLen(aDetails)
                          & " currently assigned to you." & chr(13);
                    msg = msg & "To have the details of one issue use
                          the command 'D xx' where xx is the number in front
                          of the subject" & chr(13);
                          for(i =1;i lte arrayLen(aDetails);i=i+1) {
                            msg = msg & i & ". " & aDetails[i].Subject & chr(13);
                 }
               }
             }
             break;
        default:
             if(len(keyword) neq 0) msg = "Your keyword '" &
                keyword & "' was not recognized." & chr(13) & chr(13);
             msg = msg & "Help" & chr(13);
             msg = msg & "The following keywords are accepted by this system" & chr(13);
             msg = msg & "Details - lists the details of your
                          current task. You can append a task id to this
                          command if you want the details of a single task." & chr(13);
             msg = msg & "Help - Displays this page" & chr(13);
        }
    </cfscript>

      <!--- return the message --->
      <cfscript>
        retrunVal = structNew();
        retrunVal.command = "submit";
        retrunVal.buddyID = arguments.CFEvent.data.SENDER;
        retrunVal.message = msg;
```

Listing 81.5 (continued)

```
      return retrunVal;
    </cfscript>
  </cffunction>

</cfcomponent>
```

As you can see, a lot of code goes into working out what the user actually wants and this is not the most intelligent system out there. If you want to see just how smart an automated IM system (often called an IM Robot or bot for short) is, using your AOL chat client, chat to ZolaOnAol. She is a completely code-driven IM interface, only in Java, not ColdFusion.

➔ For more details visit `http://aimtoday.aol.com/features/main_redesign.adp?fid=zola`.

Understanding SMS

SMS (Short Message Service) is the ability to send and receive short messages or "texts" between cell phones. When you put it like this, it doesn't sound like such a big deal, but in the 10-odd years since the first SMS message was sent, these small text messages have rapidly grown to be a huge part of the mobile market. In Europe alone, there are in excess of two billion text messages sent every month.

Where does ColdFusion fit in here? At the moment, creating an SMS-based application takes a specialized application server and a ton of custom programming. In the same manner that ColdFusion has been making it simple to create dynamic Web pages for the last 10 years, it is now easy to create SMS-based applications in ColdFusion.

What kinds of applications can be built with this new interface to ColdFusion? Well, the possibilities are almost endless. A few that jump to mind include: voting for your favorite character on the latest round of reality TV shows, getting your new password for a Web application, or even monitoring the health of your ColdFusion server. This could be as important to your Web applications as `<cfmail>` is today.

The gateway in ColdFusion does some amazing things for you when it comes to IM—it is able to keep track of sessions for you. Even though there is not a Web browser as such, it is very helpful to be able to apply the same concepts we use for our Web development to a series of text messages, thus allowing us to take our existing applications and convert them to SMS applications without much code refactoring.

Second, the SMS gateway is also able to authenticate the phone itself, so you know which user is using your application. This does not mean that you don't need to implement some kind of user authentication or verification at some point. I would still like to know that if I lose my phone someone can't just pick it up and find out my bank balance.

The GSM (Global System for Mobile Communications) standard provides for encrypted traffic between the SMSC (Short Message Service Center) and the cell phone. This gives us a secure environment without having to program in security.

Lastly, as your application will be leaving the confines of the Internet, you will need a way to get your SMS messages from your ColdFusion server out onto the cell phone network. Nowadays this is not that hard, but it does take some planning. Many people think that they need to have their own SMS gateway and related infrastructure to get this kind of application up and running, and at one time you did. Recently a new protocol called SMPP (Short Message Peer to Peer) allows you to send an SMS message over a TCP/IP network to an SMS gateway server (SMSC), thus saving you the hassle of having your own. You will need an account with a provider that will support SMPP 3.4 over TCP/IP, but we will cover that later on.

NOTE

The ColdFusion SMS event gateway conforms to the SMPP 3.4 specification, which you can download from the SMS Forum at `http://www.smsforum.net/`.

TIP

You will also want to make sure that your connection to your SMSC provider is encrypted or protected in some way as the SMPP protocol does not have inherent support for encrypted communication. Most providers will insist on some sort of VPN connection around your connection to their SMPP.

ColdFusion contains an SMS test server that simulates an SMSC. It will listen on port 7901 for SMPP connection requests from any SMS resource. In our case this will be our SMS gateway. There is also an SMS client simulator, a limited function cell phone. It can connect to the SMS test server and exchange messages with it. This is very handy for testing your application prior to deploying it on the Internet.

Testing Your SMS Applications

When you are developing your SMS application you do not want to be running up a huge phone bill every time you need to test a new piece of code. To help with this, there is an SMS gateway and a cell phone emulator built into ColdFusion. While this is good, don't forget that nothing beats testing in the real world.

TIP

Don't forget to go into the ColdFusion Administrator and actually start the SMS test server or none of your gateways will start. It does not actually automatically restart if you restart your ColdFusion server.

By default the ColdFusion server is set up with a phone number of 555-1212. It will make life easy if you reuse the example configuration file for testing of your application, but it does have one downside: you will need to be sure that only one gateway is using this number at once. If you want to have two SMS gateways running, you will need to assign them each different configuration files and different phone numbers.

Getting Your Messages Out

The last step in deploying your SMS application is to change your SMS gateway from the test server that you have been using for development to a real gateway that sends real messages to real phones.

The first step is to set up an account with a provider of SMPP access to the SMS network. This can be done either with your telecom provider directly or an SMS service provider. There are two main things to think about when you go shopping for an SMSC provider. The first decision you will need to make is if your application will be push only and send only SMS messages or if it will be a two-way application and will allow users to SMS in requests to your application.

The main effect here is price; a push-style gateway is very cheap and easy to set up and can be done almost instantly. A two-way application requires some more setup as you will need your own phone number or short code for your users to send their messages to.

A good place to start looking for an SMS provider is with the telecom company that provides your existing phone line or cell phone infrastructure. This is primarily due to differential pricing. In some parts of the world it is cheaper to send text messages to other users on the same network as opposed to going across to another carrier's network.

This is really only an introduction and just enough to get you going. If you wish to learn more about the inner workings of SMPP, point your browser to `http://smsforum.net` for full details of the SMPP specification. Figure 81.2 shows the path of your SMS traffic between your ColdFusion gateways and various mobile devices.

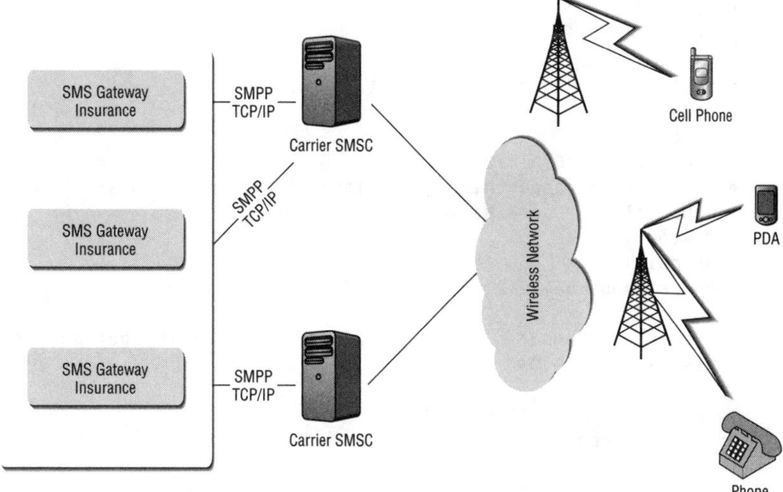

Figure 81.2
The path of your SMS traffic.

Defining SMS Gateways

Like our IM application, before you can actually use it or even begin testing it, you will need a configuration file and a stub CFC and you will have to create a gateway instance (Listing 81.6). The SMS gateway is fairly straightforward in that it has only one method that needs to be exposed, the `onIncomingMessage()` method that listens for inbound SMS messages.

Listing 81.6 `sms_stub.cfc`—Empty SMS Gateway CFC

```
<cfcomponent>
   <cffunction name="onIncomingMessage" hint="Standard message from SMS users">
      <cfargument name="CFEvent" type="struct" required="YES">
   </cffunction>
</cfcomponent>
```

To keep things relatively simple we will be using the inbuilt test SMS server, so go and grab the default configuration file from your ColdFusion installation. It is found in the `cf_root\WEB-INF\cfusion\gateway\config` directory on J2EE configurations, and in the `cf_root\gateway\config` directory on standard server configurations.

Unlike the IM configuration file there are a lot of different settings that you will need for your configuration file, the most basic of which are the connection details to the SMSC server. These are the basic settings but you will want to copy the default settings from within your ColdFusion installation as there are many options that you can tweak if needed. You will find the default configuration file in the `cf_root\WEB-INF\cfusion\gateway\config` directory on J2EE configurations, and in the `cf_root\gateway\config` directory on standard server configurations. Here's an example:

```
# SMSC server details
ip-address=127.0.0.1
port=7901
system-id=cf
password=cf

# Source address for this client
source-ton=1
source-npi=1
source-address=5551212
# The address range this smpp client will serve
# Generally the same as your source address
addr-ton=1
addr-npi=1
address-range=5551212

#this is the number of messages per second that the gateway is permitted to send.
message-rate=100.0

# network communication mode
mode= synchronous

# network retry settings
network-retry=no
transient-retry=no
```

Unlike the IM gateway configuration file, many of these settings are foreign to many ColdFusion developers. The first group of settings, the SMSC server details, are fairly straightforward; they are just the IP address, the port and the username and password that will be supplied by your SMSC provider.

The second group refers to the source phone details that your gateway will be sending messages as and the range of addresses that this SMPP client can serve.

Lastly there are the actual connection settings, including the number of messages this gateway will support per second, and the retry settings on message failure. The most important setting in this section is the communication mode. The default is synchronous communication mode; in this mode the gateway will wait for a response from the SMSC with the message ID of the message so you can track delivery reports. If the gateway is set to use asynchronous mode, the ColdFusion gateway will not wait for a response from the SMSC and thus can send messages faster. However, you will lose the ability to track receipt of messages.

TIP

Be sure to include the rest of the default settings in your SMS configuration file or your gateway may not start.

Now we are going to extend our helpdesk application to use SMS to communicate with the various helpdesk staff. We are going to call our gateway instance "Helpdesk," and create a gateway instance called "Helpdesk—5551212." We have added the phone number that the gateway uses to the end of the instance name to make it nice and easy to identify which gateway uses which phone number. When you create your gateway, rename the stub CFC to `sms.cfc` so it is clear that this is the file actually in use.

Generating SMS Messages

Once you have defined your gateway, it is time to write your first SMS application and start sending some text messages. For the time being, let's put this in a test file:

```
<cfscript>
        msg = structNew();
        msg.command = "submit";
        msg.destAddress = "5551234";
        msg.shortMessage = "Hi from ColdFusion!";
        ret = sendGatewayMessage("Helpdesk - 5551212", msg);
</cfscript>
```

It is nice to note that this will work and send out our text message even though we have not written any code inside our gateway CFC yet.

One of the benefits of the SMS gateway over the IM gateway is the ability to send the same message to multiple people. There is an additional submit command, called `submitMulti`, which will allow you to create a message that will go to multiple users:

```
<cfscript>
        destAddress = ArrayNew(1);
        ArrayAppend(destAddress,"+44 7880 333555");
        ArrayAppend(destAddress,"+49 173 666 5555");
        ArrayAppend(destAddress,"+1 248 777 5555");

        msg = structNew();
        msg.command = "submitMulti";
        msg.destAddresses = destAddress;
        msg.shortMessage = "Hi from ColdFusion!";
        ret = sendGatewayMessage("Helpdesk - 5551212", msg);
</cfscript>
```

NOTE

The gateway will only accept the destination addresses as an array, so you will need to convert any database queries to an array.

Responding to SMS Messages

Sending messages is one thing; responding to them is a different matter. As with the IM gateway, our SMS gateway is always listening for incoming messages to answer. Modify your gateway CFC (`sms.cfc`) as below:

```
<cffunction name="onIncomingMessage">
        <cfargument name="CFEvent" type="struct" required="YES">
        <!--- Generate and return the message.--->
        <cfscript>
        msg = structNew();
        msg.command = "submit";
        msg.destAddress = arguments.CFEvent.originatorID;
        msg.shortMessage = Trim(arguments.CFEvent.data.message);

        return msg;
        </cfscript>
</cffunction>
```

While this is quite similar to the IM gateway `onIncomingMessage()` function, you will notice that there is a very different set of properties exposed to you—in particular the `originatorID`, or the phone number from which the message was generated.

Ensuring Delivery of Your Messages

Now that you have sent your message, it would be nice to make sure that your user has received it. This can be done with the SMS protocol, but it does require a little more work.

First you will need to make sure that your gateway is configured for synchronous message delivery and that when you call the `SendGatewayMessage()` function you capture the `messageID` as it comes back and store it for future reference. Typically this would be in a database somewhere.

Next when you submit your message to the gateway you will need to include a `RegisteredDelivery` field in the message request. This takes one of three options:

- **0**: This is the default; do not return any status information.
- **1**: Return a receipt if the message is not delivered before the time out (Validity Period).
- **2**: Return a receipt if the message is delivered or fails.

The second two options instruct the SMSC to return a message back to our gateway reporting on the status of the message. You will need to recode your `onIncomingMessage()` method of the gateway CFC to look for these messages and separate them from regular incoming messages.

This message is returned in the following format:

```
"id:IIIIIIIII sub:SSS dlvrd:DDD submit date:YYMMDDhhmm done date:YYMMDDhhmm
stat:DDDDDDD err:E Text: ..."
```

Now that you have the status of the message, you can query your `messageID` database table and make an intelligent decision about what should be done with this message—whether we choose to resend this message or maybe escalate it to another user.

Sessions and SMS

As with standard ColdFusion, the first time an SMS user sends a message to our gateway ColdFusion generates a session for that user. As the users' interaction with the server is much more limited than it would be if they were using a browser, this session becomes much more important. It allows us to store and track information about their past interactions with the gateway.

For example, in our helpdesk application, if agents asked for a new case to be assigned to them and then asked for the details of their cases, it would be fairly safe to assume that they only really want the details of their latest opened case to be sent to their phone, not the details of every single case. This allows us to reduce the number of keystrokes that users may be required to send to the gateway to get the details that they need. There is nothing fancy that you need to add to your application beyond the normal session code that you would add in a normal ColdFusion application.

Extending Your Application Even Further

By now you will have noticed that both the IM and SMS interfaces are very similar in their approach to sending and receiving messages. They share an almost identical message send and receive structure; the only real difference is the source/destination address. Thus it should be relatively straightforward to build a gateway CFC that handles both IM and SMS messages. In fact, it is only the `onIncomingMessage()` method that you will need to modify to get this to work. Let's see what is needed to get this to work.

For starters, let's reproduce our simple "echo" method.

In this example we do not cater to any unknown gateways but we could have quite easily put a default case in our application. The next evolution of this would be to take the incoming message and pass it off to another part of the application that would work out the appropriate response to the incoming message.

Modify the `onIncomingMessage()` function of your `sms.cfc` to include the following code:

```
<cffunction name="onIncomingMessage">
        <cfargument name="CFEvent" type="struct" required="YES">
        <!--- Generate and return the message.--->
        <cfset incomingMessage = Trim(arguments.CFEvent.data.message)>

        <cfscript>
        msg = structNew();
        msg.command = "submit";
        newmsgText = incomingMessage;

        if(arguments.CFEvent.GatewayType eq 'SMS') {
                msg.destAddress = arguments.CFEvent.originatorID;
                msg.shortMessage = newmsgText;
```

```
        }
        elseif(arguments.CFEvent.GatewayType eq 'XMPP') {
               msg.buddyID = arguments.CFEvent.data.SENDER;
               msg.message = newmsgText;
        }
        msg.command = "submit";
        return msg;
        </cfscript>
</cffunction>
```

If we were to extend this a step further, it is not hard to see how we could take our IM application and twist it into an SMS and IM application without too much refactoring. In fact the entire switch statement block that we created earlier in our IM application would just get dropped in above the `<cfscript>` tag.

The next set is to put our SMS application live and actually start sending text messages to real cell phones and not just our test phone. To do this you will need to get a real SMPP account for your gateway to connect to. You can of course talk to your telecom provider and see if they can let you access their SMSC server. Most of the major cell phone carriers provide SMPP accounts directly (AT&T, BT, France Telecom, etc.) for access to a specific carrier's cell customers. The one limitation here is that these accounts may not give you access to any cell phone; they may only give you access to that carrier's cell phone users.

For access to cross-carrier cell phone subscribers, you'll need an SMPP account with a "Connection Aggregator." This is a company that will provide you with a single, simple SMPP account, and then they will take responsibility for routing messages to and from the individual cell phone networks.

This is much more of an issue in the North American market where cross wireless network interoperability is much more of an issue. For our North America readers, here is a short list of a few connection aggregations:

- SimpleWire: `http://www.simplewire.com/services/smpp/`
- World Text: `http://www.world-text.com/index.php`
- Hay Systems Ltd: `http://www.hslsms.com/apply-1.html`

The other thing you may want to look into at the same time as you set up your SMSC account is to get a short code for your gateway instead of a long phone number. A short code is a small, easy-to-remember number, like 55481, that users can send messages to instead of +44 7881 803 170. It is plain to see that one is much easier to remember than the other. In the United States, short codes are managed by the Common Short Code Administration (CSCA) and can be found at `http://www.usshortcodes.com/`.

Index

B

D

K

L

M

N

O

P

Q

R

S